CHINESE RECIPES 500

CHINESE RECIPES 500

Fabulous dishes from China and classic influential recipes from the surrounding region, including Korea, Indonesia, Hong Kong, Singapore, Thailand, Vietnam and Japan

Superb aromatic, spicy and exotic recipes made simple – from soups and appetizers to fish, meat, rice, noodles and desserts – all shown in more than 500 beautiful photographs

Contributing Editor: Jenni Fleetwood

HH
HERMES HOUSE

This edition is published by Hermes House, an imprint of Anness Publishing Ltd, Hermes House, 88–89 Blackfriars Road, London SE1 8HA tel. 020 7401 2077; fax 020 7633 9499

www.hermeshouse.com; www.annesspublishing.com

Publisher: Joanna Lorenz
Editorial Director: Helen Sudell
Project Editor: Catherine Stuart
Copy-editor: Jenni Fleetwood
Design: SMI and Diane Pullen
Production Controller: Don Campaniello

A CIP catalogue record for this book is available from the British Library.

Main image on front cover: Fruity Duck Chop Suey, page 144

Notes

Bracketed terms are intended for American readers.

For all recipes, quantities are given in both metric and imperial measures and, where appropriate, in standard cups and spoons. Follow one set, but not a mixture, because they are not interchangeable. Standard spoon and cup measures are level. 1 tsp = 5ml, 1 tbsp = 15ml, 1 cup = 250ml/8fl oz. Australian standard tablespoons are 20ml. Australian readers should use 3 tsp in place of 1 tbsp for measuring small quantities of gelatine, flour, salt etc. American pints are 16fl oz/2 cups. American readers should use 20fl oz/2.5 cups in place of 1 pint when measuring liquids.

Electric oven temperatures in this book are for conventional ovens. When using a fan oven, the temperature will probably need to be reduced by about 10–20°C/20–40°F. Since ovens vary, you should check your manufacturer's instruction book for guidance.

The nutritional analysis given for each recipe is calculated per portion (i.e. serving or item), unless otherwise stated. If the recipe gives a range, such as Serves 4–6, then the nutritional analysis will be for the smaller portion size, i.e. 6 servings. Measurements for sodium do not include salt added to taste. Medium (US large) eggs are used unless otherwise stated.

Important: pregnant women, the elderly, the ill and very young children should avoid recipes using raw or lightly cooked eggs.

Contents

Introduction

If you've ever been impressed by the range of dishes on offer at a Chinese restaurant, you'll be overwhelmed by what this book has to offer – over 500 quick and easy recipes for every

occasion, from simple snacks to stylish desserts. Many of the dishes will be familiar, including classics like Chinese Crab and Sweetcorn Soup, Crispy Shanghai Spring Rolls, Salt and Pepper Prawns, Peking Duck and Sweet and Sour Pork. Others are less well known, but the superb full colour photographs of the finished dishes will tempt you try such specialities as Parchment-wrapped Prawns, Steamed Scallops with Ginger, and Chilli Beef and Butternut.

China is a vast country with several distinctly different cuisines. From the south comes Cantonese cooking, characterized by subtle yet sophisticated sauces and restrained use of spices. Sweet and sour dishes come from this region, and snack foods, including dim sum pastries and dumplings, are a speciality. You can create your own dim sum party with a number of dishes from the Appetizer and Light Bites chapters of this book, including treats such as Rice Balls with Four Fillings, Chicken and Vegetable Bundles, Crispy Pork Balls and Five-spice Steamed Rolls.

In the east, dishes tend to be sweeter. This applies to meat and poultry as well as the grain-based foods for which the area is well known. By contrast, Sichuan cooking is hot and spicy. Liberal use of chillies, Sichuan peppercorns, garlic and onions make for dishes like Kung Po Chicken, which pack a pleasurable punch. Striking contrasts in flavours are also a feature and can be experienced in Hot and Sour Prawn Soup and Pork Soup with Cloud Ears – edible funghi with a delightful shape. In the north, where winters are wild and cold, ribsticking stews are favoured, as are dishes like Mongolian Firepot and Braised Pork Belly with Beans.

Chinese cooks enjoy experimenting with new flavours and textures, and will happily adapt, and adopt, recipes from neighbouring lands like Thailand, Vietnam, India, Korea, and even Japan. These countries, in turn, have embraced traditional Chinese dishes, with the inevitable result that it is sometimes difficult to determine just who staked the original claim.

In all its many guises, Chinese food remains immensely popular throughout the world, with the result that once-scarce ingredients are now commonplace. Fresh root ginger is to be found in every supermarket and even lemon grass and galangal are widely available. You can now obtain fresh shiitake, oyster and even enokitake mushrooms – or grow them yourself, using kits that produce a fine crop on garden logs or even recycled books. Sauces are a staple of Chinese cooking, and many supermarkets now stock several kinds of soy sauce, including shoyu and kecap manis, as well as black and yellow bean sauces, oyster and mushroom, hoi-sin and plum. Noodles and spring roll wrappers are also on sale everywhere, so finding what you need to make the dishes in this exciting collection should never prove a problem. If you do lack a key ingredient, however, don't instantly reach for your car keys. You may well have a suitable substitute in your refrigerator or pantry. Many recipes include suggestions for variations, and you will doubtless come up with even more, some of which may prove to be successful surprises.

The biggest challenge could be in choosing just what to make first. It might be Egg Knot Soup, delicate and pretty, or a hearty bowl of Chinese Leaf Soup with Meatballs. Perhaps you fancy a light snack, like some Prawn Fritters or Rice Vermicelli and Salad Rolls. Vegetarians are exceptionally well catered for, with such delights as Tofu and Broccoli with Fried Shallots, Aubergine and Sweet Potato Stew and Stir-fried Water Spinach providing a welcome change from more prosaic choices. If fish is what is fancied, try Trout with Tamarind, Steamed Sea Bass with Ginger or Mackerel with Black Beans. With more than 60 recipes for poultry, and half as much again for meat, not to mention noodle and rice dishes, salads, sides and superb sweets, you could cook something different every night for over a year without any trouble at all.

Cellophane Noodle Soup

The noodles used in this soup go by various names: glass, cellophane, bean thread or transparent.

Ingredients

4 large dried shiitake mushrooms
15g/½oz dried lily buds
½ cucumber, coarsely chopped
2 garlic cloves, halved
90g/3½oz white cabbage, coarsely chopped
1.2 litres/2 pints/5 cups boiling water
115g/4oz cellophane noodles
30ml/2 tbsp soy sauce
15ml/1 tbsp palm sugar (jaggery) or light muscovado (brown) sugar
90g/3½oz block silken tofu, diced
fresh coriander (cilantro) leaves, to garnish

Serves 4

1 Soak the shiitake mushrooms in warm water for 30 minutes. In a separate bowl, soak the dried lily buds in warm water, also for 30 minutes.

2 Meanwhile, put the cucumber, garlic and cabbage in a food processor and process to a smooth paste. Scrape the mixture into a large pan and add the measured boiling water.

3 Bring to the boil. Reduce the heat and cook for 2 minutes, stirring occasionally. Strain this stock into another pan, return to a low heat and bring to simmering point.

4 Drain the lily buds, rinse under cold running water, then drain again. Cut off any hard ends. Add the lily buds to the stock with the noodles, soy sauce and sugar and cook for 5 minutes more.

5 Strain the mushroom soaking liquid into the soup. Discard the mushroom stems, then slice the caps. Divide them and the tofu among four bowls. Pour the soup over, garnish and serve.

Cook's Tip

Tough and brittle, it is better not to try to break or chop cellophane noodles before adding to a hot stock, soup or stew.

Sour Noodle Soup

The sour notes in this classic soup emanate from the tamarind and salted soya beans.

Ingredients

vegetable oil, for deep-frying
225g/8oz firm tofu, rinsed, drained and cut into cubes
60ml/4 tbsp dried prawns (shrimp), soaked until rehydrated
5ml/1 tsp shrimp paste
4 garlic cloves, chopped
4–6 dried red chillies, soaked to soften, drained, seeded and the pulp scraped out
90g/3½oz/¾ cup roasted peanuts, ground
50g/2oz salted soya beans
2 lemon grass stalks, trimmed, halved and bruised
30ml/2 tbsp sugar
15–30ml/1–2 tbsp tamarind paste
150g/5oz dried rice vermicelli, soaked in hot water until pliable
a handful of beansprouts, rinsed and drained
4 quail's eggs, hard-boiled, shelled and halved
2 spring onions (scallions), sliced
salt and ground black pepper
fresh coriander (cilantro) leaves, finely chopped, to garnish

Serves 4

1 In a wok, heat enough vegetable oil for deep-frying. Drop in the tofu and deep-fry until golden. Drain on kitchen paper. Grind the soaked dried prawns with the shrimp paste, garlic and chilli pulp to form a paste.

2 Heat 30ml/2 tbsp vegetable oil in a wok and fry the paste for 1 minute. Add the peanuts, soya beans and lemon grass. Fry for another minute and stir in the sugar and tamarind paste, followed by 900ml/1½ pints/3¾ cups water. Mix well, bring to the boil, then simmer gently for 10 minutes. Season with salt and pepper.

3 Drain the noodles and heat through in the broth. Divide among individual bowls, sprinkle over the beansprouts and add the tofu, quail's eggs and spring onions. Garnish with the coriander and serve.

cellophane noodle Energy 148kcal/618kJ; Protein 4.1g; Carbohydrate 29.7g, of which sugars 5.7g; Fat 1.1g, of which saturates 0.1g; Cholesterol 0mg; Calcium 139mg; Fibre 0.7g; Sodium 546mg.
sour noodle Energy 477kcal/1993kJ; Protein 27.5g; Carbohydrate 44.8g, of which sugars 10.7g; Fat 21.2g, of which saturates 3.6g; Cholesterol 71mg; Calcium 376mg; Fibre 2.9g; Sodium 83mg.

Miso Broth with Mushrooms

Shiitake mushrooms give this soup superb flavour.

Ingredients
1.2 litres/2 pints/5 cups boiling water
3 tbsp light miso paste
3 fresh shiitake mushrooms, sliced
115g/4 oz tofu diced
1 spring onion (scallion), green part only, sliced

Serves 4

1 Mix the boiling water and miso in a pan. Add the mushrooms and simmer for 5 minutes. Divide the tofu among four warmed soup bowls, ladle in the soup, scatter with sliced spring onions and serve.

Miso Broth with Tofu

This nutritious soup is standard breakfast fare, and the tofu adds great texture.

Ingredients
5 baby leeks
15g/½oz fresh coriander (cilantro), including the stalks
3 thin slices fresh root ginger
2 star anise
1 small dried red chilli
1.2 litres/2 pints/5 cups dashi stock or vegetable stock
225g/8oz pak choi (bok choy), thickly cubed
200g/7oz firm tofu, cubed
60ml/4 tbsp red miso
30–45ml/2–3 tbsp shoyu

Serves 4

1 Cut the tops off the leeks and slice the rest finely. Place the tops in a large pan. Chop the coriander leaves and set aside. Add the coriander stalks, ginger, star anise and chilli to the pan. Pour in the dashi or vegetable stock. Bring to the boil, then simmer for 10 minutes. Strain, return to the pan and reheat.

2 Add the sliced leeks to the pan with the pak choi and tofu. Cook for 2 minutes, then mix 45ml/3 tbsp of the miso with a little of the hot soup and stir it into the mixture. Stir in the chopped coriander, cook for a further minute, and serve.

Miso Broth with Noodles

This delicate, fragrant soup is flavoured with just a hint of chilli.

Ingredients
45ml/3 tbsp mugi miso
200g/7oz/scant 2 cups udon, soba or Chinese noodles
30ml/2 tbsp sake or dry sherry
15ml/1 tbsp rice or wine vinegar
45ml/3 tbsp soy sauce
115g/4oz asparagus tips or mangetouts (snow peas), sliced
50g/2oz/scant 1 cup shiitake mushrooms, stalks removed and thinly sliced
1 carrot, sliced into julienne strips
3 spring onions (scallions), thinly sliced diagonally
salt and ground black pepper
5ml/1 tsp dried chilli flakes, to serve

Serves 4

1 Bring 1 litre/1¾ pints/4 cups water to the boil in a pan. Pour 150ml/¼ pint/⅔ cup of the boiling water over the miso and stir until dissolved, then set aside.

2 Meanwhile, bring another large pan of lightly salted water to the boil, add the noodles and cook according to the packet instructions until just tender.

3 Drain the noodles in a colander. Rinse under cold running water, then drain again.

4 Add the sake or sherry, rice or wine vinegar and soy sauce to the pan of boiling water. Boil gently for 3 minutes or until the alcohol has evaporated, then reduce the heat and stir in the miso mixture.

5 Add the asparagus or mangetouts, mushrooms, carrot and spring onions, and simmer for about 2 minutes until the vegetables are just tender. Season to taste.

6 Divide the noodles among four warm bowls and pour the soup over the top. Serve, sprinkled with the chilli flakes.

miso broth w. mushrooms Energy 25kcal/103kJ; Protein 2.4g; Carbohydrate 2.6g, of which sugars 2.4g; Fat 0.6g, of which saturates 0.1g; Cholesterol 0mg; Calcium 107mg; Fibre 1.6g; Sodium 882mg.
miso broth w. tofu Energy 71kcal/297kJ; Protein 7.2g; Carbohydrate 4.2g, of which sugars 3.5g; Fat 2.9g, of which saturates 0.4g; Cholesterol 0mg; Calcium 372mg; Fibre 2.6g; Sodium 884mg.
miso broth w. noodles Energy 230kcal/973kJ; Protein 7.7g; Carbohydrate 42.6g, of which sugars 5.1g; Fat 3.5g, of which saturates 0.1g; Cholesterol 0mg; Calcium 34mg; Fibre 2.9g; Sodium 809mg.

Red Onion & Vermicelli Laksa

Sliced red onions mimic flour noodles in this soup.

Ingredients

150g/5oz/2½ cups dried shiitake mushrooms
1.2 litres/2 pints/5 cups boiling vegetable stock
30ml/2 tbsp tamarind paste
250ml/8fl oz/1 cup hot water
6 large dried red chillies, stems removed and seeded
2 lemon grass stalks, finely sliced
5ml/1 tsp ground turmeric
15ml/1 tbsp grated fresh galangal
1 onion, chopped
5ml/1 tsp dried shrimp paste
30ml/2 tbsp oil
10ml/2 tsp palm sugar (jaggery)
175g/6oz rice vermicelli
1 red onion, very finely sliced
1 small cucumber, seeded and cut into strips
handful of fresh mint leaves, to garnish

Serves 6

1 Place the mushrooms in a bowl and pour in enough boiling stock to cover them, then leave to soak for 30 minutes. Put the tamarind paste into a bowl and pour in the hot water. Mash, then strain and reserve the liquid, discarding the pulp.

2 Soak the chillies in hot water to cover for 5 minutes, then drain, reserving the liquid. Place in a food processor and blend with the lemon grass, turmeric, galangal, onion and shrimp paste, adding a little soaking water to form a paste.

3 Heat the oil in a large, heavy pan and cook the paste over a low heat for 4–5 minutes. Add the tamarind liquid and bring to the boil, then simmer for 5 minutes. Remove from the heat.

4 Drain the mushrooms and reserve the stock. Discard the stems, then halve or quarter the mushrooms, if large. Add the mushrooms to the pan with their soaking liquid, the remaining stock and the sugar. Simmer for 25–30 minutes or until tender.

5 Put the rice vermicelli into a large bowl and cover with boiling water, then leave to soak for 4 minutes until softened. Drain well, then divide among six bowls. Top with onion and cucumber, then ladle in the boiling shiitake soup. Add a small bunch of mint leaves to each bowl and serve.

Noodle Soup with Tofu

This light and refreshing soup is an excellent pick-me-up. The aromatic, spicy broth is simmered first, and then the tofu, beansprouts and noodles are added.

Ingredients

150g/5oz dried thick rice noodles
1 litre/1¾ pints/4 cups vegetable stock
1 fresh red chilli, seeded and thinly sliced
15ml/1 tbsp light soy sauce
juice of ½ lemon
10ml/2 tsp sugar
5ml/1 tsp finely sliced garlic
5ml/1 tsp finely chopped fresh root ginger
200g/7oz firm tofu
90g/3½oz/scant 1 cup beansprouts
50g/2oz/½ cup peanuts
15ml/1 tbsp chopped fresh coriander (cilantro)
spring onion (scallion) slivers and red chilli slivers, to garnish

Serves 4

1 Spread out the noodles in a shallow dish and pour over boiling water to cover. Soak according to the packet instructions until they are just tender. Drain, rinse and set aside.

2 Meanwhile, place the stock, red chilli, soy sauce, lemon juice, sugar, garlic and ginger in a wok over high heat. Bring to the boil, cover, reduce to low heat and simmer the mixture gently for 10–12 minutes.

3 Cut the tofu into cubes. Add it to the wok with the drained noodles and the beansprouts. Cook the mixture gently for 2–3 minutes.

4 Roast the peanuts in a dry non-stick wok, then chop them. Stir the coriander into the soup. Serve in warm bowls with peanuts, spring onions and chilli on top.

Cook's Tip

It is important to use vegetable stock with plenty of flavour for this simple soup.

red onion & vermicelli Energy 161kcal/671kJ; Protein 4.1g; Carbohydrate 26.6g, of which sugars 2.7g; Fat 4.3g, of which saturates 0.6g; Cholesterol 4mg; Calcium 32mg; Fibre 0.2g; Sodium 41mg.
noodle soup w. tofu Energy 261kcal/1092kJ; Protein 10g; Carbohydrate 36.4g, of which sugars 4.3g; Fat 8g, of which saturates 1.4g; Cholesterol 0mg; Calcium 275mg; Fibre 1.2g; Sodium 97mg.

Tom Yam Gung

One of the most refreshing and healthy soups, this fragrant dish would make an ideal light lunch or supper.

Ingredeints

30ml/2 tbsp groundnut oil
300g/11oz firm tofu, diced
1.2 litres/2 pints/5 cups good vegetable stock
15ml/1 tbsp chilli jam
grated rind of 1 kaffir lime
1 shallot, finely sliced
1 garlic clove, finely chopped
2 kaffir lime leaves, shredded
3 fresh red chillies, seeded and shredded
1 lemon grass stalk, finely chopped
6 shiitake mushrooms, thinly sliced
4 spring onions (scallions), shredded
45ml/3 tbsp fish sauce
45ml/3 tbsp lime juice
5ml/1 tsp sugar
45ml/3 tbsp chopped fresh coriander (cilantro)
salt and ground black pepper

Serves 4

1 Heat the oil in a wok and fry the tofu for 4–5 minutes until golden, turning occasionally. Use a slotted spoon to remove it and set aside. Tip the oil from the wok into a large, heavy pan.

2 Add the stock, chilli jam, kaffir lime rind, shallot, garlic, lime leaves, two-thirds of the chillies and the lemon grass to the pan. Bring to the boil, reduce the heat and simmer for 20 minutes.

3 Strain the stock into a clean pan. Stir in the remaining chilli, the shiitake mushrooms, spring onions, fish sauce, lime juice and sugar. Simmer for 3 minutes.

4 Add the fried tofu and heat through for 1 minute. Mix in the chopped coriander and season with salt and pepper to taste. Serve at once in warmed bowls.

Cook's Tip

Fresh kaffir limes and leaves are available from South-east Asian stores. If you cannot find them, use freeze dried leaves, which are widely available, or ordinary lime rind.

Hot & Sour Soup

This spicy, warming soup really whets the appetite and is the perfect introduction to a simple Chinese meal.

Ingredients

10g/¼oz dried cloud ear (wood ear) mushrooms
8 fresh shiitake mushrooms
900ml/1½ pints/3¾ cups vegetable stock
75g/3oz firm tofu, cubed
50g/2oz/½ cup shredded, drained, canned bamboo shoots
15ml/1 tbsp caster (superfine) sugar
45ml/3 tbsp rice vinegar
15ml/1 tbsp light soy sauce
1.5ml/¼ tsp chilli oil
2.5ml/½ tsp salt
large pinch of ground white pepper
15ml/1 tbsp cornflour (cornstarch)
15ml/1 tbsp cold water
1 egg white
5ml/1 tsp sesame oil
2 spring onions (scallions), cut into fine rings

Serves 4

1 Soak the dried cloud ears in hot water for 20 minutes or until soft. Drain, trim off and discard the hard base from each cloud ear and then chop the fungus roughly.

2 Remove and discard the stems from the shiitake mushrooms. Cut the caps into thin strips.

3 Place the stock, mushrooms, tofu, bamboo shoots and cloud ear mushrooms in a large pan. Bring the stock to the boil, lower the heat and simmer for about 5 minutes.

4 Stir in the sugar, vinegar, soy sauce, chilli oil, salt and pepper. Mix the cornflour to a paste with the water. Add to the soup, stirring constantly until it thickens slightly.

5 Lightly beat the egg white, then pour it slowly into the soup in a steady stream, stirring constantly until it forms threads. Add the sesame oil, ladle into heated bowls and garnish with spring onion rings.

tom yam gung Energy 122kcal/506kJ; Protein 7.1g; Carbohydrate 3.6g, of which sugars 2.9g; Fat 8.9g, of which saturates 1.5g; Cholesterol 0mg; Calcium 395mg; Fibre 0.7g; Sodium 273mg.
hot & sour soup Energy 102kcal/429kJ; Protein 7.3g; Carbohydrate 7.3g, of which sugars 0.3g; Fat 5.1g, of which saturates 1g; Cholesterol 44mg; Calcium 135mg; Fibre 0g; Sodium 208mg.

Spicy Tomato & Egg Drop Soup

Served on its own with chunks of crusty bread, or accompanied by jasmine or ginger rice, this is a tasty dish for a light supper.

Ingredients
30ml/2 tbsp vegetable oil
3 shallots, finely sliced
2 garlic cloves, finely chopped
2 fresh red chillies, seeded and finely sliced
25g/1oz galangal, shredded
8 large, ripe tomatoes, skinned, seeded and finely chopped
15ml/1 tbsp sugar
30ml/2 tbsp fish sauce
4 lime leaves
900ml/1½ pints/3¾ cups chicken stock
15ml/1 tbsp wine vinegar
4 eggs
sea salt and ground black pepper

For the garnish
chilli oil, for drizzling
1 small bunch fresh coriander (cilantro), finely chopped
1 small bunch fresh mint leaves, finely chopped

Serves 4

1 Heat the oil in a wok or heavy pan. Stir in the shallots, garlic, chillies and galangal and cook until golden and fragrant. Add the tomatoes with the sugar, fish sauce and lime leaves. Stir until it resembles a sauce. Pour in the stock and bring to the boil. Reduce the heat and simmer for 30 minutes. Season.

2 Just before serving, bring a wide pan of water to the boil. Add the vinegar and half a teaspoon of salt. Break the eggs into individual cups or small bowls.

3 Stir the water rapidly to create a swirl and drop an egg into the centre of the swirl. Follow immediately with the others, or poach two at a time, and keep the water boiling to throw the whites up over the yolks. Turn off the heat, cover the pan and leave to poach until firm enough to lift. Poached eggs are traditional, but you could use lightly fried egg instead.

4 Using a slotted spoon, lift the eggs out of the water and slip them into the hot soup. Drizzle a little chilli oil over the eggs, sprinkle with the coriander and mint, and serve.

Egg Flower Soup

This simple, healthy soup is flavoured with fresh root ginger and Chinese five-spice powder. It is quick and delicious and can be made at the last minute.

Ingredients
1.2 litres/2 pints/5 cups fresh chicken or vegetable stock
10ml/2 tsp peeled, fresh root ginger, grated
10ml/2 tsp light soy sauce
5ml/1 tsp sesame oil
5ml/1 tsp Chinese five-spice powder
15–30ml/1–2 tbsp cornflour (cornstarch)
2 eggs
salt and ground black pepper
1 spring onion (scallion), very finely sliced and 15ml/1 tbsp roughly chopped coriander (cilantro) to garnish

Serves 4

1 Put the chicken or vegetable stock into a large pan with the ginger, soy sauce, oil and five-spice powder. Bring to the boil and allow to simmer gently for about 10 minutes.

2 Blend the cornflour in a measuring jug with 60–75ml/4–5 tbsp water and stir into the stock. Cook, stirring constantly, until slightly thickened. Season to taste with salt and pepper.

3 In a jug (pitcher), beat the eggs with 30ml/2 tbsp cold water until the mixture becomes frothy.

4 Bring the soup back just to the boil and drizzle in the egg mixture, stirring vigorously with chopsticks. Serve at once in warmed individual serving bowls sprinkled with the sliced spring onions and chopped coriander or parsley.

Cook's Tip
This soup is a good way of using up leftover egg yolks or whites, which have been stored in the freezer and then thawed. When adding the egg to the soup, use a jug with a fine spout to form a very thin drizzle.

tomato & egg drop Energy 181kcal/756kJ; Protein 8g; Carbohydrate 12.3g, of which sugars 11.5g; Fat 11.7g, of which saturates 2.4g; Cholesterol 190mg; Calcium 52mg; Fibre 2.3g; Sodium 284mg.
egg flower soup Energy 58kcal/244kJ; Protein 3.3g; Carbohydrate 3.8g, of which sugars 0.3g; Fat 3.6g, of which saturates 0.9g; Cholesterol 95mg; Calcium 16mg; Fibre 0g; Sodium 304mg.

Omelette Soup

A very satisfying soup that is quick and easy to prepare. It is versatile, too, in that you can vary the vegetables according to what is available in the season.

Ingredients

1 egg
15ml/1 tbsp groundnut (peanut) oil
900ml/1½ pints/3¾ cups well-flavoured vegetable stock
2 large carrots, finely diced
4 outer leaves Savoy cabbage or pak choi (bok choy), shredded
30ml/2 tbsp soy sauce
2.5ml/½ tsp sugar
2.5ml/½ tsp ground black pepper
fresh coriander (cilantro) leaves, to garnish

Serves 4

1 Put the egg in a bowl and beat lightly with a fork. Heat the oil in a small frying pan until it is hot, but not smoking. Pour in the egg and swirl the pan so that it coats the base evenly. Cook over a medium heat until the omelette has set and the underside is golden.

2 Slide the omelette out of the pan and roll it up like a pancake. Slice into 5mm/¼in rounds and set aside for the garnish.

3 Put the stock into a large pan. Add the carrots and cabbage or pak choi and bring to the boil. Reduce the heat and simmer for 5 minutes, then add the soy sauce, sugar and pepper to season.

4 Stir well, then pour into warmed bowls. Lay a few omelette rounds on the surface of each portion and complete the garnish with the coriander leaves.

Variation
Use thinly sliced green beans or mangetouts (snow peas) instead of savoy cabbage. Simmer for just 2 minutes.

Egg Knot Soup

Omelettes are often used to add protein to light Oriental soups like this one.

Ingredients

1 spring onion (scallion), thinly shredded
800ml/1⅓ pints/3½ cups well-flavoured stock or instant dashi
5ml/1 tsp soy sauce
dash of sake or dry white wine
pinch of salt

For the prawn balls

200g/7oz/generous 1 cup raw large prawns (shrimp), shelled and deveined
65g/2½ oz cod fillet, skinned
5ml/1 tsp egg white
5ml/1 tsp sake or dry white wine, plus a dash extra
22.5ml/4½ tsp cornflour (cornstarch)
2–3 drops soy sauce
pinch of salt

For the omelette

1 egg, beaten
dash of mirin
pinch of salt
oil, for cooking

Serves 4

1 To make the prawn balls, place the prawns, cod, egg white, sake or dry white wine, cornflour, soy sauce and a pinch of salt in a food processor and process to a thick, sticky paste. Shape the mixture into 4 balls, place in a steaming basket and steam over a pan of vigorously boiling water for about 10 minutes.

2 To make the garnish, soak the spring onion in iced water for about 5 minutes, until the shreds curl, then drain.

3 To make the omelette, mix the egg with the mirin and salt. Heat a little oil in a frying pan and pour in the egg mixture, coating the pan evenly. When the omelette has set, turn it over and cook for 30 seconds. Leave to cool.

4 Cut the omelette into strips and tie each in a knot. Heat the stock or dashi, then add the soy sauce, sake or wine and salt. Divide the prawn balls and egg-knots among four bowls and add the soup. Garnish with the spring onion.

omelette soup Energy 64kcal/264kJ; Protein 2.3g; Carbohydrate 4.3g, of which sugars 4.1g; Fat 4.3g, of which saturates 0.7g; Cholesterol 48mg; Calcium 27mg; Fibre 1.1g; Sodium 560mg.
egg knot soup Energy 98kcal/412kJ; Protein 13.6g; Carbohydrate 7.1g, of which sugars 0.2g; Fat 1.9g, of which saturates 0.5g; Cholesterol 153mg; Calcium 51mg; Fibre 0.1g; Sodium 218mg.

Pumpkin & Coconut Soup

The natural sweetness of the pumpkin is balanced by chillies, shrimp paste and dried shrimp in this colourful soup. The cooked shellfish adds further colour and a decent amount of bite, making this dish a real delight to the senses.

Ingredients

2 garlic cloves, crushed
4 shallots, finely chopped
2.5ml/½ tsp shrimp paste
1 lemon grass stalk, chopped
2 fresh green chillies, seeded
15ml/1 tbsp dried shrimp soaked for 10 minutes in warm water
600ml/1 pint/2½ cups chicken stock
450g/1lb pumpkin, peeled, seeded and diced
600ml/1 pint/2½ cups coconut cream
30ml/2 tbsp fish sauce
5ml/1 tsp sugar
115g/4oz small cooked shelled prawns (shrimp)
salt and ground black pepper

To garnish

2 fresh red chillies, seeded and thinly sliced
10–12 fresh basil leaves

Serves 4–6

1 Put the garlic, shallots, shrimp paste, lemon grass, green chillies and salt to taste in a mortar. Drain the dried shrimp, discarding the soaking liquid, and add them to the mortar, then use a pestle to grind the mixture into a paste. Alternatively, place all the ingredients in a food processor and process until you have a paste.

2 Bring the chicken stock to the boil in a large pan. Add the ground paste and stir well to dissolve. Add the pumpkin chunks and simmer for 10–15 minutes, or until tender.

3 Stir in the coconut cream, then bring the soup back to simmering point. Do not let it boil. Add the fish sauce, sugar and ground black pepper to taste.

4 Add the prawns and cook for a further 2–3 minutes, until they are heated through. Serve in warm soup bowls, garnished with chillies and basil leaves.

Spicy Squash Soup

This highly flavoured soup comes from northern Thailand but similar recipes are found in southern China. It is quite hearty, something of a cross between a soup and a stew.

Ingredients

1 butternut squash, about 300g/11oz
1 litre/1¾ pints/4 cups vegetable stock
90g/3½oz/scant 1 cup green beans, cut into 2.5cm/1in pieces
45g/1¾oz dried banana flower (optional)
15ml/1 tbsp fish sauce
225g/8oz raw prawns (shrimp)
small bunch fresh basil
cooked rice, to serve

For the chilli paste

115g/4oz shallots, sliced
10 drained bottled green peppercorns
1 small fresh green chilli, seeded and finely chopped
2.5ml/½ tsp shrimp paste

Serves 4

1 Peel the butternut squash and cut it in half. Scoop out the seeds with a teaspoon and discard, then cut the flesh into neat cubes. Set aside.

2 Make the chilli paste by pounding the shallots, peppercorns, chilli and shrimp paste together using a mortar and pestle or puréeing them in a spice blender.

3 Heat the stock gently in a large pan, then stir in the chilli paste. Add the squash, beans and banana flower, if using. Bring to the boil and cook for 15 minutes.

4 Add the fish sauce, prawns and basil. Bring to simmering point, then simmer for 3 minutes. Serve in warmed bowls, accompanied by rice.

Variation
Use pumpkin instead of butternut squash, or try acorn squash instead.

pumpkin & coconut soup Energy 73kcal/310kJ; Protein 6.5g; Carbohydrate 10.4g, of which sugars 9.8g; Fat 0.9g, of which saturates 0.4g; Cholesterol 56mg; Calcium 102mg; Fibre 1.3g; Sodium 399mg.
spicy squash soup Energy 68kcal/287kJ; Protein 11.2g; Carbohydrate 4.7g, of which sugars 3.4g; Fat 0.7g, of which saturates 0.2g; Cholesterol 110mg; Calcium 82mg; Fibre 1.7g; Sodium 108mg.

Clear Vegetable Soup

In China and Central Asia, this type of clear soup is usually made in large quantities, then stored as appropriate and reheated for consumption over a number of days. If you would like to do the same, double or treble the quantities listed below. Chill leftover soup rapidly and always reheat thoroughly before serving.

Ingredients

30ml/2tbsp groundnut (peanut) oil
15ml/1 tbsp magic paste (see Cook's Tip)
100g/3½oz Savoy cabbage or Chinese leaves (Chinese cabbage), finely shredded
100g/3½oz mooli (daikon), finely diced
1 medium cauliflower, coarsely chopped
4 celery sticks, coarsely chopped
1.2 litres/2 pints/5 cups vegetable stock
130g/4½oz fried tofu, cut into 2.5cm/1in cubes
5ml/1 tsp palm sugar (jaggery) or light muscovado (brown) sugar
45ml/3 tbsp light soy sauce

Serves 4

1 Heat the groundnut oil in a large, heavy pan or wok. Add the magic paste and cook over a low heat, stirring frequently, until it gives off its aroma. Add the shredded Savoy cabbage or Chinese leaves, mooli, cauliflower and celery.

2 Pour in the vegetable stock, increase the heat to medium and bring to the boil, stirring occasionally. Gently stir in the tofu cubes.

3 Add the sugar and soy sauce. Reduce the heat and simmer for 15 minutes, until the vegetables are cooked and tender. Taste and add a little more soy sauce if needed. Serve hot.

Cook's Tip
Magic paste is a mixture of crushed garlic, white pepper and coriander (cilantro). Look for it at Thai markets.

Bean & Beansprout Soup

This popular soup is based on beans, but any seasonal vegetables can be added or substituted.

Ingredients

225g/8oz green beans
1.2 litres/2 pints/5 cups lightly salted water
1 garlic clove, roughly chopped
2 macadamia nuts or 4 almonds, finely chopped
1cm/½ in cube shrimp paste
10–15ml/2–3 tsp coriander seeds, dry fried
30ml/2 tbsp vegetable oil
1 onion, finely sliced
400ml/14fl oz can coconut milk
2 bay leaves
225g/8oz/1 cup beansprouts
8 thin lemon wedges
30ml/2 tbsp lemon juice
salt and ground black pepper

Serves 8

1 Trim the beans, then cut them into small pieces. Bring the water to the boil, add the beans and cook for 3–4 minutes. Drain, reserving the cooking water. Set the beans aside.

2 Finely grind the chopped garlic, macadamia nuts or almonds, shrimp paste and the coriander seeds to a paste using a pestle and mortar or in a food processor.

3 Heat the oil in a wok, and fry the onion until transparent. Remove with a slotted spoon. Add the nut paste to the wok and fry it for 2 minutes without allowing it to brown.

4 Pour in the reserved vegetable water. Spoon off 45–60ml/3–4 tbsp of the cream from the top of the coconut milk and set it aside. Add the remaining coconut milk to the wok, bring to the boil and add the bay leaves. Cook for 15–20 minutes.

5 Reserve a few beans, onions and beansprouts for garnish; stir the rest into the soup. Add the lemon wedges, reserved coconut cream, lemon juice and seasoning; stir well. Pour into soup bowls and serve, garnished with the reserved vegetables.

clear vegetable soup Energy 205kcal/851kJ; Protein 13.8g; Carbohydrate 8.6g, of which sugars 7.5g; Fat 13g, of which saturates 1.3g; Cholesterol 0mg; Calcium 579mg; Fibre 3.4g; Sodium 845mg.
bean & beansprout soup Energy 73kcal/304kJ; Protein 2.3g; Carbohydrate 5.7g, of which sugars 4.2g; Fat 4.8g, of which saturates 0.6g; Cholesterol 0mg; Calcium 40mg; Fibre 1.3g; Sodium 57mg.

Hot & Sour Prawn Soup

This is a classic seafood soup, combining sour, salty, spicy and hot flavours. Variations on the theme are enjoyed throughout Asia.

Ingredients

450g/1lb raw king prawns (jumbo shrimp), thawed if frozen
1 litre/1¾ pints/4 cups chicken stock or water
3 lemon grass stalks, root trimmed
10 kaffir lime leaves, torn in half
225g/8oz can straw mushrooms
45ml/3 tbsp fish sauce
60ml/4 tbsp lime juice
30ml/2 tbsp chopped spring onion (scallion)
15ml/1 tbsp fresh coriander (cilantro) leaves
4 fresh red chillies, seeded and thinly sliced
salt and ground black pepper

Serves 4–6

1 Shell the prawns, putting the shells in a colander. Devein the prawns and set them aside on a plate.

2 Rinse the shells under cold water, then put in a large pan with the stock or water. Bring to the boil.

3 Bruise the lemon grass stalks and add them to the stock with half the kaffir lime leaves. Simmer gently for 5–6 minutes, until the stock is fragrant.

4 Strain the stock, return it to the clean pan and reheat. Add the drained mushrooms and the prawns, then cook until the prawns turn pink.

5 Stir in the fish sauce, lime juice, chopped spring onion, fresh coriander, chillies and the remaining kaffir lime leaves. Taste and adjust the seasoning if necessary. The soup should be sour, salty, spicy and hot.

Cook's tip
Be sure to buy uncooked prawns (shrimp) in the shell.

Coconut & Seafood Soup

The marriage of flavours works beautifully in this soup, which is easy to make.

Ingredients

600ml/1 pint/2½ cups fish stock
5 thin slices fresh root ginger
2 lemon grass stalks, chopped
3 kaffir lime leaves, shredded
bunch garlic chives, about 25g/1oz
small bunch fresh coriander (cilantro), about 15g/½oz
15ml/1 tbsp vegetable oil
4 shallots, chopped
400ml/14fl oz can coconut milk
30–45ml/2–3 tbsp fish sauce
45–60ml/3–4 tbsp green curry paste
450g/1lb raw large prawns (shrimp), peeled and deveined
450g/1lb prepared squid
a little fresh lime juice (optional)
salt and ground black pepper
60ml/4 tbsp crisp fried shallot slices, to serve

Serves 4

1 Pour the fish stock into a large pan and add the slices of ginger, the lemon grass and half the shredded lime leaves.

2 Reserve a few garlic chives for the garnish, then chop the remainder. Add half the chopped garlic chives to the pan. Strip the coriander leaves from the stalks and set the leaves aside. Add the stalks to the pan. Bring to the boil, reduce the heat to low and cover the pan, then simmer gently for 20 minutes. Strain the stock into a bowl.

3 Rinse and dry the pan. Add the oil and shallots. Cook for 5–10 minutes, until the shallots begin to brown.

4 Stir in the strained stock, coconut milk, the remaining kaffir lime leaves and 30ml/2 tbsp of the fish sauce. Heat gently until simmering and cook over a low heat for 5–10 minutes.

5 Stir in the curry paste and prawns, then cook for 3 minutes. Add the squid and cook for a further 2 minutes. Add the lime juice, if using, and season, adding more fish sauce to taste. Stir in the remaining chives and the reserved coriander leaves. Serve in bowls sprinkled with fried shallots and chives.

hot & sour prawn soup Energy 96kcal/404kJ; Protein 20.9g; Carbohydrate 0.8g, of which sugars 0.5g; Fat 1g, of which saturates 0.2g; Cholesterol 219mg; Calcium 94mg; Fibre 0.7g; Sodium 217mg.
coconut & seafood soup Energy 205kcal/871kJ; Protein 37.7g; Carbohydrate 7.5g, of which sugars 5.8g; Fat 3g, of which saturates 0.8g; Cholesterol 473mg; Calcium 144mg; Fibre 0.4g; Sodium 449mg.

Prawn & Pineapple Broth

This simple dish is often served as an appetite enhancer because of its hot and sour flavour. It is also popular as a tasty accompaniment to plain rice or noodles. In some restaurants, the broth is presented in a hollowed-out pineapple, which has been halved lengthways.

Ingredients

30ml/2 tbsp vegetable oil
15–30ml/1–2 tbsp tamarind paste
15ml/1 tbsp sugar
450g/1lb fresh prawns (shrimp), peeled and deveined
4 thick fresh pineapple slices, cored and cut into bitesize chunks
salt and ground black pepper
fresh coriander (cilantro) and mint leaves, to garnish
steamed rice or plain noodles, to serve (optional)

For the spice paste

4 shallots, chopped
4 red chillies, chopped
25g/1oz fresh root ginger, peeled and chopped
1 lemon grass stalk, trimmed and chopped
5ml/1 tsp shrimp paste

Serves 4

1 Make the spice paste. Using a mortar and pestle or a food processor, grind the shallots, chillies, ginger and lemon grass to a paste. Add the shrimp paste and mix well.

2 Heat the oil in a wok or heavy pan. Stir in the spice paste and fry until fragrant. Stir in the tamarind paste and the sugar, then pour in 1.2 litres/2 pints/5 cups water. Mix well and bring to the boil. Reduce the heat and simmer for 10 minutes. Season the broth with salt and pepper.

3 Add the prawns and pineapple to the broth and simmer for 4–5 minutes, or until the prawns are cooked. Using a slotted spoon, lift the prawns and pineapple out of the broth and divide them among four warmed bowls. Ladle over some of the broth and garnish with coriander and mint leaves. The remaining broth can be served separately as a drink, or spooned over steamed rice or plain noodles, if you want to transform this into a slightly more substantial dish.

Wonton, Pak Choi & Prawn Soup

A well-flavoured chicken stock is a must for this classic Chinese snack, which is popular on fast-food stalls in towns and cities throughout southern China.

Ingredients

200g/7oz minced (ground) pork
200g/7oz cooked, peeled prawns (shrimp), thawed if frozen
10ml/2 tsp rice wine or dry sherry
10ml/2 tsp light soy sauce
5ml/1 tsp sesame oil
24 thin wonton wrappers
1.2 litres/2 pints/5 cups chicken stock
12 tiger prawns (jumbo shrimp), shelled, with tails still on
350g/12oz pak choi (bok choy), coarsely shredded (about 6 cups)
salt and ground black pepper
4 spring onions (scallions), sliced and 1cm/½in piece fresh root ginger, finely shredded, to garnish

Serves 4

1 Put the pork, prawns, rice wine or sherry, soy sauce and sesame oil in a large bowl. Add plenty of seasoning and toss the ingredients, until well mixed.

2 Put about 10ml/2 tsp of pork mixture in the centre of each wonton wrapper. Bring up the sides of the wrapper and pinch them together to seal the filling in a small bundle.

3 Bring a large pan of water to the boil. Add the wontons and cook for 3 minutes, then drain well and set aside.

4 Pour the stock into a large pan and bring to the boil. Season to taste. Add the tiger prawns and cook for 2–3 minutes, until just tender. Add the wontons and pak choi, then cook for a further 1–2 minutes. Ladle the soup into bowls and garnish with spring onions and ginger.

Cook's Tip
Use a classic "spider" or large slotted spoon to lower the wontons into the hot oil.

prawn/pineapple Energy 192kcal/808kJ; Protein 20.4g; Carbohydrate 14.2g, of which sugars 13.9g; Fat 6.4g, of which saturates 0.8g; Cholesterol 219mg; Calcium 111mg; Fibre 1.3g; Sodium 216mg.
wonton/pak choi/prawn Energy 208kcal/874kJ; Protein 26.8g; Carbohydrate 11.8g, of which sugars 2.2g; Fat 6.2g, of which saturates 2g; Cholesterol 179mg; Calcium 234mg; Fibre 2.4g; Sodium 655mg.

Crab & Asparagus Soup

Generally, jars of asparagus preserved in brine are used for this recipe, or fresh asparagus that has been steamed until tender.

Ingredients

15ml/1 tbsp vegetable oil
2 shallots, finely chopped
2 garlic cloves, finely chopped
15ml/1 tbsp rice flour or cornflour (cornstarch)
225g/8oz/1⅓ cups cooked crab meat, chopped
450g/1lb preserved asparagus, finely chopped, or 450g/1lb fresh asparagus, trimmed and steamed
salt and ground black pepper
basil and coriander (cilantro) leaves, to garnish
fish sauce, to serve

For the stock

1 meaty chicken carcass
25g/1oz dried shrimp, soaked in water for 30 minutes, rinsed and drained
2 onions, peeled and quartered
2 garlic cloves, crushed
15ml/1 tbsp fish sauce
6 black peppercorns
sea salt

Serves 4

1 To make the stock, put the chicken carcass into a large pan. Add all the other stock ingredients, except the salt, and pour in 2 litres/3½ pints/8 cups water. Bring to the boil, boil for a few minutes, skim off any foam, then reduce the heat and simmer with the lid on for 1½–2 hours. Remove the lid and simmer for a further 30 minutes to reduce the stock. Skim off any fat, season, then strain the stock and measure out 1.5 litres/2½ pints/6¾ cups.

2 Heat the oil in a deep pan or wok. Stir in the shallots and garlic, until they begin to colour. Remove from the heat, stir in the flour, and then pour in the stock. Put the pan back over the heat and bring to the boil, stirring constantly, until smooth.

3 Add the crab meat and asparagus, reduce the heat and leave to simmer for 15–20 minutes. Season to taste with salt and pepper, then ladle the soup into bowls, garnish with fresh basil and coriander leaves, and serve with a splash of fish sauce.

Chinese Crab & Sweetcorn Soup

There's no denying the delightful combination of shellfish and corn in this universal favourite, but dressing fresh crab does increase the preparation time somewhat. Using frozen white crab meat will work just as well.

Ingredients

600ml/1 pint/2½ cups fish or chicken stock
2.5cm/1in piece fresh root ginger, peeled and very finely sliced
400g/14oz can creamed sweetcorn
150g/5oz cooked white crab meat
15ml/1 tbsp arrowroot or cornflour (cornstarch)
15ml/1 tbsp rice wine or dry sherry
15–30ml/1–2 tbsp light soy sauce
1 egg white
salt and ground white pepper
shredded spring onions (scallions), to garnish

Serves 4

1 Put the stock and ginger in a large pan and bring to the boil. Reduce the heat a little while you stir in the creamed sweetcorn, then bring the mixture back to the boil.

2 Switch off the heat and add the crab meat to the pan. Put the arrowroot or cornflour in a cup and stir in the rice wine or sherry to make a smooth paste; stir this into the soup. Cook over a low heat for about 3 minutes until the soup has thickened and is slightly glutinous in consistency. Add light soy sauce, salt and white pepper to taste.

3 In a bowl, whisk the egg white to a stiff foam. Gradually fold it into the soup. Ladle the soup into heated bowls, garnish each portion with spring onions and serve.

Cook's Tip

This soup is sometimes made with whole kernel corn, but creamed corn gives a better texture. If you can't find it in a can, use thawed frozen creamed sweetcorn instead; the result will be just as good.

crab & asparagus soup Energy 158kcal/652kJ; Protein 9.8g; Carbohydrate 7.6g, of which sugars 4g; Fat 9.9g, of which saturates 5.6g; Cholesterol 38mg; Calcium 87mg; Fibre 3.2g; Sodium 147mg.
crab & sweetcorn soup Energy 201kcal/852kJ; Protein 11.3g; Carbohydrate 33.8g, of which sugars 9.9g; Fat 3.2g, of which saturates 0.5g; Cholesterol 27mg; Calcium 17mg; Fibre 1.4g; Sodium 695mg.

Crab & Chilli Soup

Prepared fresh crab is perfect for creating an exotic soup in minutes.

Ingredients

45ml/3 tbsp olive oil
1 red onion, finely chopped
2 fresh red chillies, seeded and finely chopped
1 garlic clove, finely chopped
450g/1lb fresh white crab meat
30ml/2 tbsp chopped fresh parsley
30ml/2 tbsp chopped fresh coriander (cilantro)
juice of 2 lemons
1 lemon grass stalk
1 litre/1¾ pints/4 cups good fish or chicken stock
15ml/1 tbsp fish sauce
150g/5oz vermicelli or angel hair pasta, broken into 5–7.5cm/2–3in lengths
salt and ground black pepper

For the coriander relish

50g/2oz/1 cup fresh coriander (cilantro) leaves
1 fresh green chilli, seeded and chopped
15ml/1 tbsp sunflower oil
25ml/1½ tbsp lemon juice
2.5ml/½ tsp ground roasted cumin seeds

Serves 4

1 Heat the oil in a pan and cook the onion, chillies and garlic. Cook until the onion is very soft. Transfer to a bowl. Stir in the crab meat, parsley, coriander and lemon juice. Set aside.

2 Bruise the lemon grass with a pestle. Pour the stock and fish sauce into a pan. Add the lemon grass and bring to the boil, then add the pasta. Simmer, uncovered, for 3–4 minutes or according to the packet instructions, until just tender.

3 Meanwhile, make the relish. Place the fresh coriander, chilli, oil, lemon juice and cumin in a food processor or blender and process to form a coarse paste. Season to taste.

4 Remove and discard the lemon grass from the soup. Stir the chilli and crab mixture into the soup and season it well. Bring to the boil, reduce the heat and simmer for 2 minutes. Ladle the soup into four deep, warmed bowls and put a spoonful of the relish in the centre of each. Serve at once.

Snapper & Tamarind Soup

Tamarind gives this light, fragrant noodle soup a slightly sour taste.

Ingredients

2 litres/3½ pints/8 cups water
1kg/2¼lb red snapper (or other red fish such as mullet)
1 onion, sliced
50g/2oz tamarind pods
15ml/1 tbsp fish sauce
15ml/1 tbsp sugar
30ml/2 tbsp vegetable oil
2 garlic cloves, finely chopped
2 lemon grass stalks, very finely chopped
4 ripe tomatoes, peeled and coarsely chopped
30ml/2 tbsp yellow bean paste
225g/8oz rice vermicelli, soaked in warm water until soft
115g/4oz/½ cup beansprouts
8–10 fresh basil or mint sprigs
25g/1oz/¼ cup roasted peanuts, ground
salt and ground black pepper

Serves 4

1 Bring the water to the boil in a pan. Lower the heat and add the fish and onion, with 2.5ml/½ tsp salt. Simmer gently until the fish is cooked through.

2 Remove the fish from the stock; set aside. Add the tamarind, fish sauce and sugar to the stock. Cook for 5 minutes, then strain the stock into a large bowl. Carefully remove all of the bones from the fish, keeping the flesh in big pieces.

3 Heat the oil in a large frying pan. Add the garlic and lemon grass and cook for a few seconds. Stir in the tomatoes and bean paste. Cook gently for 5–7 minutes, until the tomatoes are soft. Add the stock, bring back to a simmer and adjust the seasoning. Stir to mix.

4 Drain the vermicelli and divide among individual serving bowls. Add the beansprouts, fish and basil or mint, and sprinkle the ground peanuts on top. Top up each bowl with the hot soup.

Cook's Tip

Use about 1 tbsp prepared tamarind paste instead of the pods.

crab & chilli soup Energy 228kcal/951kJ; Protein 23.6g; Carbohydrate 5.4g, of which sugars 5g; Fat 12.6g, of which saturates 3.7g; Cholesterol 90mg; Calcium 199mg; Fibre 1.1g; Sodium 767mg.
snapper & tamarind Energy 495kcal/2079kJ; Protein 43.1g; Carbohydrate 55.5g, of which sugars 9.1g; Fat 11.4g, of which saturates 1.9g; Cholesterol 65mg; Calcium 108mg; Fibre 2.4g; Sodium 165mg.

Monkfish Broth

Lemon grass, chillies and galangal are among the flavourings used in this fragrant soup.

Ingredients

1 litre/1¾ pints/4 cups fish or light chicken stock
4 lemon grass stalks
3 limes
2 small fresh hot red chillies, seeded and thinly sliced
2cm/¾in piece fresh galangal, peeled and thinly sliced
6 coriander (cilantro) stalks, with leaves
2 kaffir lime leaves, coarsely chopped (optional)
350g/12oz monkfish fillet, skinned and cut into 2.5cm/1in pieces
15ml/1 tbsp rice vinegar
45ml/3 tbsp fish sauce
30ml/2 tbsp chopped coriander (cilantro) leaves, to garnish

Serves 2–3

1 Pour the stock into a pan and bring it to the boil. Meanwhile, slice the bulb end of each lemon grass stalk diagonally into pieces about 3mm/⅛ in thick. Peel off four wide strips of lime rind with a potato peeler, taking care to avoid the white pith underneath which would make the soup bitter. Squeeze the limes and reserve the juice.

2 Add the sliced lemon grass, lime rind, chillies, galangal and coriander stalks to the stock, with the kaffir lime leaves, if using. Simmer for 1–2 minutes.

3 Add the monkfish, rice vinegar and fish sauce, with half the reserved lime juice. Simmer for about 3 minutes, until the fish is just cooked. Lift out and discard the coriander stalks, taste the broth and add more lime juice if necessary; the soup should taste quite sour. Sprinkle with the coriander leaves and serve.

Variations
Prawns (shrimp), scallops, squid, sole or flounder can be substituted for the monkfish. If you use kaffir lime leaves, you will need the juice of only 2 limes.

Red Monkfish Soup

This light and creamy coconut soup provides a base for a colourful fusion of red-curried monkfish and rice noodles.

Ingredients

175g/6oz flat rice noodles
30ml/2 tbsp vegetable oil
2 garlic cloves, chopped
15ml/1 tbsp red curry paste
450g/1lb monkfish tail, cut into bitesize pieces
300ml/½ pint/1¼ cups coconut cream
750ml/1¼ pints/3 cups hot chicken stock
45ml/3 tbsp fish sauce
15ml/1 tbsp palm sugar (jaggery)
60ml/4 tbsp roasted peanuts, roughly chopped
4 spring onions (scallions), shredded lengthways
50g/2oz/½ cup beansprouts
large handful of fresh Thai basil leaves
salt and ground black pepper
1 fresh red chilli, seeded and cut lengthways into slivers, to garnish

Serves 4

1 Soak the noodles in a bowl of boiling water for 10 minutes, or according to the packet instructions. Drain.

2 Heat the oil in a wok or pan over a high heat. Add the garlic and cook for 2 minutes. Stir in the curry paste and cook for 1 minute, until fragrant.

3 Add the monkfish and stir-fry over a high heat for 4–5 minutes, until just tender. Pour in the coconut cream and stock.

4 Stir in the fish sauce and sugar, and bring just to the boil. Add the drained noodles and cook for 1–2 minutes, until tender.

5 Stir in half the peanuts, half the spring onions, half the beansprouts, the basil and seasoning. Ladle the soup into deep individual soup bowls and sprinkle over the remaining peanuts. Garnish with the remaining spring onions, beansprouts and the slivers of red chilli.

monkfish broth Energy 92kcal/394kJ; Protein 19.8g; Carbohydrate 1.8g, of which sugars 1.6g; Fat 0.8g, of which saturates 0.1g; Cholesterol 16mg; Calcium 50mg; Fibre 0.8g; Sodium 1096mg.
red monkfish soup Energy 379kcal/1589kJ; Protein 25.5g; Carbohydrate 41.2g, of which sugars 4.7g; Fat 12g, of which saturates 2g; Cholesterol 18mg; Calcium 49mg; Fibre 0.9g; Sodium 111mg.

Smoked Mackerel & Tomato Soup

All the ingredients for this unusual soup are cooked in a single pan, so it is not only quick and easy to prepare, but requires little clearing up afterwards. Smoked mackerel gives the soup a robust flavour, but it is tempered by the citrus tones provided by the lemon grass and tamarind.

Ingredients

200g/7oz smoked mackerel fillets
4 tomatoes
1 litre/1¾ pints/4 cups vegetable stock
1 lemon grass stalk, finely chopped
5cm/2in piece fresh galangal or root ginger, finely diced or sliced
4 shallots, finely chopped
2 garlic cloves, finely chopped
2.5ml/½ tsp dried chilli flakes
15ml/1 tbsp fish sauce
5ml/1 tsp palm sugar (jaggery) or light muscovado (brown) sugar
45ml/3 tbsp thick tamarind juice, made by mixing tamarind paste with warm water
small bunch fresh chives or spring onions (scallions), to garnish

Serves 4

1 Prepare the smoked mackerel fillets. Remove and discard the skin, if necessary, then chop the flesh into large pieces. Carefully remove any stray bones with your fingers or by using a pair of sterilized tweezers.

2 Cut the tomatoes in half, squeeze out and discard most of the seeds, then finely dice the flesh with a sharp knife. Place in bowls and set aside.

3 Pour the stock into a large pan and add the lemon grass, galangal or ginger, shallots and garlic. Bring to the boil, reduce the heat and simmer for 15 minutes.

4 Add the fish, tomatoes, chilli flakes, fish sauce, sugar and tamarind juice. Simmer for around 4–5 minutes, until the fish and tomatoes are heated through. Ladle into individual soup bowls, garnish with the chives or spring onions and serve.

Chinese Fish Ball Soup

This light Chinese soup can be found in coffee shops and at the tze char stalls, where the food is ordered from the menu and cooked on the spot. Often eaten as a snack or light lunch, the soup is garnished with spring onions and fresh chillies, and the Malays often add an extra drizzle of chilli sauce or chilli sambal.

Ingredients

For the fish balls

450g/1lb fresh fish fillets (such as haddock, cod, whiting or bream), boned and flaked
15–30ml/1–2 tbsp rice flour
salt and ground black pepper

For the soup

1.5 litres/2½ pints/6 cups fish or chicken stock
15–30ml/1–2 tbsp light soy sauce
4–6 mustard green leaves, chopped
90g/3½oz mung bean thread noodles, soaked in hot water until soft

For the garnish

2 spring onions (scallions), trimmed and finely sliced
1 fresh red or green chilli, seeded and finely sliced
fresh coriander (cilantro) leaves, finely chopped

Serves 4–6

1 To make the fish balls, grind the flaked flesh to a paste, using a mortar and pestle or food processor. Season with salt and pepper and stir in 60ml/4 tbsp water. Add enough rice flour to form a paste. Take small portions of fish paste into your hands and squeeze them to mould into balls.

2 Meanwhile, bring the stock to the boil in a deep pan and season to taste with soy sauce. Drop in the fish balls and simmer for 5 minutes. Add the shredded mustard greens and cook for 1 minute.

3 Divide the noodles among four to six bowls. Using a slotted spoon, add the fish balls and greens to the noodles, then ladle over the hot stock. Garnish with the spring onions and chilli and sprinkle the chopped coriander over the top.

mackerel/tomato soup Energy 226kcal/940kJ; Protein 11.2g; Carbohydrate 10.2g, of which sugars 8.5g; Fat 15.9g, of which saturates 3.3g; Cholesterol 53mg; Calcium 39mg; Fibre 2.1g; Sodium 653mg.
chinese fish ball soup Energy 127kcal/533kJ; Protein 14.9g; Carbohydrate 14.8g, of which sugars 0.5g; Fat 0.6g, of which saturates 0.1g; Cholesterol 35mg; Calcium 17mg; Fibre 0.2g; Sodium 408mg.

Chicken Soup with Crab Cakes

This tasty noodle soup can be a meal in itself.

Ingredients

small bunch of coriander (cilantro), with roots on
1.2–1.4kg/2½–3lb chicken
8 garlic cloves, sliced
2 star anise
2 carrots, chopped
2 celery sticks, chopped
1 onion, chopped
30ml/2 tbsp soy sauce
150g/5oz egg noodles
30ml/2 tbsp vegetable oil
60ml/4 tbsp fish sauce
1.5ml/¼ tsp chilli powder
150g/5oz/2½ cups beansprouts
2 spring onions (scallions), sliced
salt and ground black pepper

For the crab cakes

5ml/1 tsp red curry paste
5ml/1 tsp cornflour (cornstarch)
5ml/1 tsp fish sauce
1 small egg yolk
15ml/1 tbsp chopped fresh coriander (cilantro)
175g/6oz white crab meat
50g/2oz/1 cup fresh white breadcrumbs
30ml/2 tbsp vegetable oil

Serves 6

1 Cut the roots off the coriander stems and place in a heavy pan. Strip the stems and set the leaves aside. Add the chicken to the pan with half the garlic, the star anise, carrots, celery, onion and soy sauce. Add water to cover, bring to the boil, cover and simmer for 1 hour, or until the chicken is cooked.

2 Make the crab cakes by combining all the ingredients except the oil in a bowl and dividing into 12 small patties. Cook the noodles according to the packet instructions. Drain and set aside. Fry the remaining garlic until golden, then drain.

3 Lift the chicken out of the stock, pull off the skin, and tear the meat into large strips. Strain the stock and pour 1.2 litres/2 pints/5 cups into a large pan. Stir in the fish sauce, chilli powder and seasoning. Bring to simmering point.

4 Fry the crab cakes in hot oil for 2–3 minutes on each side. Divide the noodles, fried garlic, beansprouts, spring onions and chicken among soup bowls. Arrange two of the crab cakes on each, ladle in the chicken broth and garnish with the coriander.

Chicken & Crab Noodle Soup

The chicken makes a delicious stock for this light noodle soup.

Ingredients

2 chicken legs, skinned
1.75 litres/3 pints/7½ cups cold water
large bunch of spring onions (scallions)
2.5cm/1in piece fresh root ginger, sliced
5ml/1 tsp black peppercorns
2 garlic cloves, halved
75g/3oz rice noodles
115g/4oz fresh white crab meat
30ml/2 tbsp light soy sauce
salt and ground black pepper
coriander (cilantro) leaves, to garnish

For the omelettes

4 eggs
30ml/2 tbsp chopped fresh coriander (cilantro) leaves
15ml/1 tbsp extra virgin olive oil

Serves 6

1 Put the chicken and water in a pan. Bring to the boil, reduce the heat and cook gently for 20 minutes. Skim the surface occasionally. Slice half the spring onions and add to the pan with the ginger, peppercorns, garlic and salt to taste. Cover and simmer for 1½ hours.

2 Meanwhile, soak the noodles according to the packet instructions. Drain and refresh under cold water. Shred the remaining spring onions and set aside.

3 To make the omelettes, beat the eggs with the coriander and seasoning. Heat a little of the olive oil in a small frying pan and use the mixture to make three omelettes. Roll up the omelettes tightly one at a time and slice thinly.

4 Remove the chicken from the stock and leave to cool. Strain the stock into a clean pan. Remove and finely shred the chicken meat.

5 Bring the stock to the boil. Add the noodles, chicken, spring onions and crab meat, then simmer for 1–2 minutes. Stir in the soy sauce and season. Ladle the soup into bowls and top each with sliced omelette and coriander leaves.

chicken w. crab cakes Energy 250kcal/1049kJ; Protein 10.9g; Carbohydrate 28.8g, of which sugars 3.5g; Fat 10.9g, of which saturates 1.8g; Cholesterol 62mg; Calcium 74mg; Fibre 1.9g; Sodium 638mg.
chicken/crab noodle soup Energy 159kcal/664kJ; Protein 13.5g; Carbohydrate 10.6g, of which sugars 0.4g; Fat 6.9g, of which saturates 1.7g; Cholesterol 157mg; Calcium 46mg; Fibre 0g; Sodium 526mg.

Chicken & Tiger Prawn Laksa

Laksa is a spicy noodle soup enriched with coconut milk.

Ingredients

6 dried red chillies, seeded
225g/8oz vermicelli, broken
15ml/1 tbsp shrimp paste
10 shallots, chopped
3 garlic cloves
1 lemon grass stalk, roughly chopped
25g/1oz/¼ cup macadamia nuts
grated rind and juice of 1 lime
60ml/4 tbsp groundnut (peanut) oil
2.5ml/½ tsp ground turmeric
5ml/1 tsp ground coriander
1.5 litres/2½ pints/6 cups fish or chicken stock
450g/1lb raw tiger prawns (jumbo shrimps), shelled and deveined
450g/1lb skinless, boneless chicken breast portions, cut into long thin strips
2 x 400g/14oz cans coconut milk
115g/4oz/1 cup beansprouts
½ cucumber, cut into strips
small bunch of spring onions (scallions), shredded, plus extra to garnish
salt and ground black pepper
1 lime, cut into wedges, to serve

Serves 6

1 Soak the chillies in hot water for 45 minutes. Cook the vermicelli according to the packet instructions. Drain; set aside. Drain the chillies and put them in a food processor or blender with the shrimp paste, shallots, garlic, lemon grass, nuts, lime rind and juice. Process to form a thick paste.

2 Heat 45ml/3 tbsp of the oil in a large, heavy pan. Add the spice paste and cook for 1–2 minutes, stirring. Add the turmeric and coriander and cook for 2 minutes more. Stir in the stock; simmer for 25 minutes, then strain and set aside.

3 Heat the remaining oil in the clean pan and fry the prawns until pink. Remove and set aside. Add the chicken and fry for 4–5 minutes, until just cooked.

4 Pour in the stock and coconut milk. Reheat gently. Add the vermicelli and prawns; and heat for 2 minutes. Stir in the beansprouts, cucumber and spring onions, spoon into bowls, garnish with spring onions and serve with lime wedges.

Steamboat

This dish is named after the utensil in which it is cooked – a type of fondue with a funnel and a moat.

Ingredients

8 Chinese dried mushrooms, soaked in warm water
1.5 litres/2½ pints/6¼ cups well-flavoured chicken stock
10ml/2 tsp rice wine
10ml/2 tsp sesame oil
225g/8oz each lean pork and rump (round) steak, thinly sliced
1 skinless boneless chicken breast portion, thickly sliced
2 chicken livers, trimmed and sliced
225g/8oz raw prawns (shrimp), peeled
450g/1lb white fish fillets, skinned and cubed
200g/7oz fish balls (from Asian food stores)
115g/4oz fried tofu, each piece halved
leafy green vegetables, such as lettuce, Chinese leaves, spinach leaves and watercress, cut into 15cm/6in lengths
225g/8oz Chinese rice vermicelli
8 eggs
½ bunch spring onions (scallions), chopped
salt and ground white pepper
soy sauce, chilli sauce, plum sauce and hot mustard, to serve

Serves 8

1 Drain the mushrooms, reserving the soaking liquid in a large pan. Cut off and discard the stems; slice the caps finely. Add the stock to the pan, with the rice wine and sesame oil. Bring to the boil, season, then reduce to a simmer.

2 Put the meat, seafood, fish balls, tofu, green vegetables and mushrooms in bowls on the table with the sauces. Soak the vermicelli in hot water for 5 minutes, drain and place in eight soup bowls. Crack an egg for each diner in a small bowl; place on a side table.

3 Add the spring onions to the stock, bring to the boil and fuel the steamboat. Pour the stock into the moat. Each guest cooks the foods of his choice in the hot stock, using chopsticks or fondue forks. When all the ingredients have been cooked, pour the stock into the bowls of noodles. Slide an egg into each bowl and stir so that the egg cooks and forms threads, then serve.

chicken/prawn laksa Energy 414kcal/1734kJ; Protein 36.4g; Carbohydrate 38.9g, of which sugars 8.8g; Fat 12.6g, of which saturates 1.9g; Cholesterol 199mg; Calcium 129mg; Fibre 1.1g; Sodium 352mg.
steamboat Energy 243kcal/1020kJ; Protein 35g; Carbohydrate 4.1g, of which sugars 0.8g; Fat 9.7g, of which saturates 2.6g; Cholesterol 299mg; Calcium 168mg; Fibre 0.4g; Sodium 304mg.

Chicken Soup with Crispy Shallots

This Thai-inspired soup is topped with crisp shallots.

Ingredients

40g/1½oz/3 tbsp butter
1 onion, finely chopped
2 garlic cloves, chopped
2.5cm/1in piece fresh root ginger, finely chopped
10ml/2 tsp green curry paste
2.5ml/½ tsp turmeric
400ml/14fl oz can coconut milk
475ml/16fl oz/2 cups chicken stock
2 lime leaves, shredded
1 lemon grass stalk, finely chopped
8 skinless, boneless chicken thighs
350g/12oz spinach, chopped
10ml/2 tsp fish sauce
30ml/2 tbsp lime juice
30ml/2 tbsp vegetable oil
salt and ground black pepper
2 shallots, thinly sliced
handful of Thai basil leaves, to garnish

Serves 6

1 Melt the butter in a large, heavy pan. Add the onion, garlic and ginger, then cook for 4–5 minutes, until softened. Stir in the curry paste and turmeric, and cook for a further 2–3 minutes, stirring continuously.

2 Pour in two-thirds of the coconut milk; cook for 5 minutes. Add the stock, lime leaves, lemon grass and chicken. Heat until simmering; cook for 15 minutes or until the chicken is tender.

3 Remove the chicken thighs with a draining spoon and set them aside to cool. Add the spinach to the pan and cook for 3–4 minutes. Stir in the remaining coconut milk and seasoning, then process the soup in a food processor or blender until almost smooth. Return the soup to the rinsed-out pan. Cut the chicken thighs into bitesize pieces and stir these into the soup with the fish sauce and lime juice.

4 Reheat the soup gently until hot, but do not let it boil. Meanwhile, heat the oil in a frying pan and cook the shallots for 6–8 minutes, until crisp and golden, stirring occasionally. Drain on kitchen paper. Ladle the soup into bowls, then top with the basil leaves and fried shallots, and serve.

Chinese Chicken & Chilli Soup

Ginger and lemon grass add an aromatic note to this tasty, refreshing soup, which can be served as a light lunch or appetizer. The soft vermicelli rice noodles are the perfect foil to the crunch of the cooked vegetables, and soak up the flavoursome liquid of this soup wonderfully well.

Ingredients

150g/5oz skinless boneless chicken breasts, cut into strips
2.5cm/1in piece fresh root ginger, finely chopped
5cm/2in piece lemon grass stalk, finely chopped
1 fresh red chilli, seeded and thinly sliced
8 baby corn cobs, halved lengthways
1 large carrot, cut into thin sticks
1 litre/1¾ pints/4 cups hot chicken stock
4 spring onions (scallions), thinly sliced
12 small shiitake mushrooms, sliced
115g/4oz/1 cup vermicelli rice noodles
30ml/2 tbsp soy sauce
salt and ground black pepper

Serves 4

1 Place the chicken strips, chopped ginger, chopped lemon grass and sliced chilli in a Chinese sand pot. Add the halved baby corn and the carrot sticks. Pour over the hot chicken stock and cover the pot.

2 Place the Chinese sand pot in an unheated oven. Set the temperature to 200°C/400°F/Gas 6 and cook the soup for 30–40 minutes, or until the stock is simmering and the chicken and vegetables are tender.

3 Add the spring onions and mushrooms, cover and return the pot to the oven for 10 minutes. Meanwhile place the noodles in a large bowl and cover with boiling water – soak for the required time, following the packet instructions.

4 Drain the noodles and divide among four warmed serving bowls. Stir the soy sauce into the soup and season with salt and pepper. Divide the soup among the bowls and serve.

chicken soup w. shallots Energy 198kcal/827kJ; Protein 16.5g; Carbohydrate 6.5g, of which sugars 5.5g; Fat 12g, of which saturates 4.6g; Cholesterol 84mg; Calcium 157mg; Fibre 2.3g; Sodium 266mg.
chicken & chilli soup Energy 165kcal/693kJ; Protein 13.3g; Carbohydrate 26g, of which sugars 3.1g; Fat 0.9g, of which saturates 0.2g; Cholesterol 26mg; Calcium 23mg; Fibre 1.4g; Sodium 852mg.

Chicken & Ginger Soup

This aromatic soup is rich with coconut milk and intensely flavoured with galangal, lemon grass and kaffir lime leaves.

Ingredients

4 lemon grass stalks, roots trimmed
2 x 400ml/14fl oz cans coconut milk
475ml/16fl oz/2 cups chicken stock
2.5cm/1in piece root ginger, peeled and thinly sliced
10 black peppercorns, crushed
10 kaffir lime leaves, torn
300g/11oz skinless boneless chicken breast portions, cut into thin strips
115g/4oz/1 cup button (white) mushrooms
50g/2oz/½ cup baby corn cobs, quartered lengthways
60ml/4 tbsp lime juice
45ml/3 tbsp fish sauce
chopped fresh red chillies, spring onions (scallions) and fresh coriander (cilantro) leaves, to garnish

Serves 4–6

1 Cut off the lower 5cm/2in from each lemon grass stalk and chop it finely. Bruise the remaining pieces of stalk. Bring the coconut milk and chicken stock to the boil in a large pan. Add all the lemon grass, the ginger, peppercorns and half the lime leaves, lower the heat and simmer gently for 10 minutes. Strain into a clean pan.

2 Return the soup to the heat, then add the chicken, mushrooms and corn. Simmer for 5–7 minutes or until the chicken is cooked.

3 Stir in the lime juice and fish sauce, then add the remaining lime leaves. Serve hot, garnished with chillies, spring onions and coriander.

Cook's Tip
Store root ginger in the freezer. It thaws rapidly or can be shaved or grated while frozen.

Chicken Rice Soup

Light and refreshing, this soup is the perfect choice for a hot day. In the great tradition of chicken soup recipes, it also acts as a wonderful pick-me-up when you are feeling low or a little tired.

Ingredients

2 lemon grass stalks, trimmed, cut into 3 pieces, and lightly bruised
15ml/1 tbsp fish sauce
90g/3½ oz/½ cup short grain rice, rinsed
ground black pepper
sea salt
chopped coriander (cilantro) and 1 fresh green or red chilli, seeded and cut into thin strips, to garnish
1 lime, cut in wedges, to serve

For the stock

1 small chicken, about 900g/2lb
1 onion, quartered
2 garlic cloves, crushed
25g/1oz fresh root ginger, sliced
2 lemon grass stalks, cut in half lengthways and bruised
2 dried red chillies
30ml/2 tbsp fish sauce

Serves 4

1 Put the chicken into a deep pan. Add all the other stock ingredients and pour in 2 litres/3½ pints/8 cups water. Bring to the boil for a few minutes, then reduce the heat and simmer gently with the lid on for 2 hours.

2 Skim off any fat from the stock, strain and reserve. Remove the skin from the chicken and shred the meat with your fingers, or chop roughly using a sharp knife. Set aside.

3 Pour the stock back into the deep pan and bring to the boil. Reduce the heat and stir in the lemon grass stalks and fish sauce. Stir in the rice and simmer, uncovered, for about 40 minutes. Add the shredded chicken and season with the black pepper and sea salt to taste.

4 Ladle the piping hot soup into warmed individual bowls, garnish with chopped coriander and the thin strips of chilli. Put the lime wedges into a separate bowl and serve for squeezing over the soup if desired.

chicken & ginger soup Energy 87kcal/371kJ; Protein 13.1g; Carbohydrate 6.8g, of which sugars 6.7g; Fat 1.1g, of which saturates 0.4g; Cholesterol 35mg; Calcium 42mg; Fibre 0.3g; Sodium 620mg.
chicken rice soup Energy 147kcal/615kJ; Protein 12.8g; Carbohydrate 19.8g, of which sugars 1.4g; Fat 1.7g, of which saturates 0.4g; Cholesterol 53mg; Calcium 37mg; Fibre 0.8g; Sodium 317mg.

Spicy Chicken Soup

This fragrant soup is particularly popular in Singapore. Originally from Java, various versions are served at soup and noodle stalls specializing in Indonesian and Malay food.

Ingredients

1 small chicken, about 900g/2lb
2 lemon grass stalks, bruised
25g/1oz fresh root ginger, peeled and sliced
2 fresh kaffir lime leaves
1 dried red chilli
30ml/2 tbsp vegetable oil
50g/2oz mung bean thread noodles, soaked until pliable
3 hard-boiled eggs, peeled and halved
115g/4oz/½ cup beansprouts
a small bunch of fresh coriander (cilantro), roughly chopped, to garnish
2 limes, quartered, chilli oil and soy sauce, to serve

For the rempah

8 shallots, chopped
8 garlic cloves, chopped
6 candlenuts or macadamia nuts
50g/2oz galangal, chopped
2 lemon grass stalks, chopped
4 fresh kaffir lime leaves
15ml/1 tbsp ground coriander
10ml/2 tsp ground turmeric
15ml/1 tbsp vegetable oil

Serves 6

1 Using a mortar and pestle or a food processor, grind all the rempah ingredients to a paste. Set aside.

2 Put the chicken, lemon grass, ginger, lime leaves and chilli into a deep pan and pour in enough water to just cover. Bring to the boil, then cover and simmer for about 1 hour, until the chicken is tender. Remove the chicken, take off and discard the skin and tear the meat into shreds. Strain the stock.

3 In a wok or heavy pan, heat the oil. Stir in the rempah and cook for 1–2 minutes, until fragrant. Pour in the stock and stir well. Season to taste with salt and pepper.

4 Divide the noodles among six bowls. Add the hard-boiled eggs, beansprouts and shredded chicken. Ladle the steaming broth into each bowl and garnish with coriander. Serve immediately with the lime wedges, chilli oil and soy sauce.

Corn & Chicken Soup

Using a combination of chicken, creamed corn and whole kernels gives this classic Chinese soup a lovely texture. It tastes delicious, is suitably warming on a cold day and, above all, easy to make if you are in a hurry or have friends for lunch.

Ingredients

1 skinless chicken breast fillet, about 115g/4oz, cubed
10ml/2 tsp light soy sauce
15ml/1 tbsp Chinese rice wine
5ml/1 tsp cornflour (cornstarch)
60ml/4 tbsp cold water
5ml/1 tsp sesame oil
15ml/1 tbsp vegetable oil
5ml/1 tsp grated fresh root ginger
1 litre/1¾ pints/4 cups chicken stock
425g/15oz can creamed corn
225g/8oz can whole kernel corn
2 eggs, beaten
salt and ground black pepper
2–3 spring onions (scallions), green parts only, cut into tiny rounds, to garnish

Serves 4–6

1 Mince (grind) the chicken in a food processor, taking care not to overprocess. Transfer the chicken to a bowl and stir in the soy sauce, rice wine, cornflour, water, sesame oil and seasoning. Cover with clear film (plastic wrap) and leave for about 15 minutes so the chicken absorb the flavours.

2 Heat a wok over medium heat. Add the vegetable oil and swirl it around. Add the ginger and stir-fry for a few seconds. Pour in the stock with the creamed corn and corn kernels. Bring to just below boiling point.

3 Spoon about 90ml/6 tbsp of the hot liquid into the chicken mixture until it forms a smooth paste and stir. Return to the wok. Slowly bring to the boil, stirring constantly, then simmer for 2–3 minutes or until the chicken is cooked.

4 Pour the beaten eggs into the soup in a slow steady stream, using a fork or chopsticks to stir the top of the soup in a figure-of-eight pattern. The egg will set in lacy shreds. Serve immediately with the spring onions on top.

spicy chicken soup Energy 411kcal/1708kJ; Protein 30g; Carbohydrate 7.1g, of which sugars 0.8g; Fat 29.3g, of which saturates 7.6g; Cholesterol 215mg; Calcium 39mg; Fibre 0.7g; Sodium 148mg.
corn & chicken soup Energy 196kcal/831kJ; Protein 10g; Carbohydrate 29.9g, of which sugars 10.7g; Fat 4.7g, of which saturates 1g; Cholesterol 77mg; Calcium 17mg; Fibre 1.6g; Sodium 447mg.

Duck & Preserved Lime Soup

This rich soup originates in the Chiu Chow region of southern China. This recipe can be made with chicken stock and leftover duck meat from a roasted duck, or by roasting a duck, slicing off the breast portion and thigh meat for the soup.

Ingredients

1 lean duck, about 1.5kg/3lb 5oz
2 preserved limes
25g/1oz root ginger, thinly sliced
sea salt and ground black pepper

For the garnish

vegetable oil, for frying
25g/1oz fresh root ginger, thinly sliced into strips
2 garlic cloves, thinly sliced into strips
2 spring onions (scallions), finely sliced

Serves 4–6

1 Place the duck in a large pan with enough water to cover. Season with salt and pepper and bring the water to the boil. Reduce the heat, cover the pot, and simmer for 1½ hours.

2 Add the preserved limes and ginger. Continue to simmer for another hour, skimming off the fat from time to time, until the liquid has reduced a little and the duck is so tender that it almost falls off the bone.

3 Meanwhile heat some vegetable oil in a wok. Stir in the ginger and garlic strips and fry until gold and crispy. Drain them well on kitchen paper and set aside for garnishing.

4 Remove the duck from the broth and shred the meat into individual bowls. Check the broth for seasoning, then ladle it over the duck in the bowls. Sprinkle the spring onions with the fried ginger and garlic over the top and serve.

Cook's Tip
Preserved limes have a distinct bitter flavour. Look for them in Asian markets.

Duck & Nut Soup with Jujubes

This rich soup is delicious. Packed with nuts and sweetened with jujubes (dried Chinese red dates), it resembles neither a soup nor a stew, but something in between. Served on its own, or with rice and pickles, it is a meal in itself.

Ingredients

30–45ml/2–3 tbsp vegetable oil
4 duck legs, split into thighs and drumsticks
juice of 1 coconut
60ml/4 tbsp fish sauce
4 lemon grass stalks, bruised
12 chestnuts, peeled
90g/3½oz unsalted cashew nuts, roasted
90g/3½oz unsalted almonds, roasted
90g/3½oz unsalted peanuts, roasted
12 jujubes
sea salt and ground black pepper
1 bunch fresh basil leaves, to garnish

Serves 4

1 Heat the oil in a wok or heavy pan. Brown the duck legs in the oil and drain on kitchen paper.

2 Bring 2 litres/3½ pints/7¾ cups water to the boil. Reduce the heat and add the coconut juice, fish sauce, lemon grass and duck legs. Cover the pan and simmer over a gentle heat for 2–3 hours. Skim off any fat.

3 Add the nuts and jujubes and cook for 40 minutes, until the chestnuts are soft and the duck is very tender. Skim off any fat, season to taste and sprinkle with basil leaves to serve.

Variation
Replace the jujubes with dates if you cannot find them.

Cook's Tip
To extract the coconut juice, pierce the eyes on top and turn the coconut upside down over a bowl.

duck & lime soup Energy 124kcal/520kJ; Protein 19.8g; Carbohydrate 0.3g, of which sugars 0.3g; Fat 6.5g, of which saturates 1.3g; Cholesterol 110mg; Calcium 19mg; Fibre 0g; Sodium 110mg.
duck & nut w. jujubes Energy 604kcal/2512kJ; Protein 43.8g; Carbohydrate 8.9g, of which sugars 3.6g; Fat 44g, of which saturates 9.2g; Cholesterol 165mg; Calcium 49mg; Fibre 3.1g; Sodium 231mg.

Pork & Lotus Root Broth

In this clear broth, which is served as an appetizer, the thin, round slices of fresh lotus root look like delicate flowers floating in water.

Ingredients

450g/1lb fresh lotus root, peeled and thinly sliced
ground black pepper
1 fresh red chilli, seeded and finely sliced, and 1 small bunch basil leaves, to garnish

For the stock

450g/1lb pork ribs
1 onion, quartered
2 carrots, cut into chunks
25g/1oz dried squid or dried shrimp, soaked in water for 30 minutes, rinsed and drained
15ml/1 tbsp fish sauce
15ml/1 tbsp soy sauce
6 black peppercorns
sea salt

Serves 4–6

1 Put the ribs into a pan and cover with 1.5 litres/2½ pints/6¼ cups water. Bring to the boil, skim, and add the other ingredients. Reduce the heat, cover, and simmer for 2 hours.

2 Take off the lid and simmer for a further 30 minutes to reduce the stock. Strain the stock and shred the meat off the pork ribs.

3 Pour the stock back into the pan and bring it to the boil. Reduce the heat and add the lotus root. Partially cover the pan and simmer gently for 30–40 minutes, until the lotus root is tender.

4 Stir in the shredded meat and season the broth with salt and pepper. Ladle the soup into bowls and garnish with the chilli and basil leaves.

Cook's Tip

The lotus, an edible water lily, has been grown in China for centuries and is prized for its delicate flavour.

Pork & Prawn Soup

The secret of this soup is its richly flavoured stock.

Ingredients

225g/8oz pork fillet (tenderloin)
225g/8oz rice vermicelli, soaked in lukewarm water for 20 minutes
20 prawns (shrimp), shelled and deveined
115g/4oz/½ cup beansprouts
2 spring onions (scallions), sliced
2 fresh red chillies, seeded and finely sliced
1 garlic clove, finely sliced
chopped basil and coriander (cilantro) leaves
1 lime, cut into quarters, and fish sauce, to serve

For the stock

25g/1oz dried squid
675g/1½lb pork ribs
1 onion, peeled and quartered
2 carrots, cut into chunks
15ml/1 tbsp fish sauce
15ml/1 tbsp soy sauce
6 black peppercorns
salt

Serves 4

1 Make the stock, soak the squid in water for 30 minutes, rinse and drain. Put the ribs in a large pan with 2.5 litres/4½ pints/10 cups water. Boil, skim, and add the dried squid and remaining stock ingredients. Cover, simmer for 1 hour, then skim, remove the lid and continue to simmer for a further 1½ hours.

2 Strain the stock into a deep pan and bring to the boil. Add the pork and simmer for 25 minutes. Lift out the pork and slice it thinly. Keep the stock simmering over a low heat.

3 Drain the rice sticks and cook them in boiling water for 5 minutes until tender. Drain and divide among four bowls.

4 Cook the prawns in the stock for 1 minute, lift them out and add to the bowls with the pork slices. Ladle over the hot stock and sprinkle with beansprouts, spring onions, chillies, garlic and herbs.

5 Serve each bowl of soup with a wedge of lime to squeeze over it and fish sauce to splash on top.

pork & lotus root broth Energy 181kcal/756kJ; Protein 23.8g; Carbohydrate 4g, of which sugars 3.1g; Fat 7.8g, of which saturates 2.7g; Cholesterol 74mg; Calcium 65mg; Fibre 1.4g; Sodium 269mg.
pork & prawn soup Energy 234kcal/981kJ; Protein 26.2g; Carbohydrate 24.8g, of which sugars 1.6g; Fat 3.3g, of which saturates 1g; Cholesterol 137mg; Calcium 84mg; Fibre 1.1g; Sodium 681mg.

Sweet-and-Sour Pork Soup

This very quick, sharp and tangy soup is perfect for an impromptu supper. It can also be made with shredded chicken breast.

Ingredients

900g/2lb pork fillet (tenderloin), trimmed
1 unripe papaya, halved, seeded, peeled and shredded
3 shallots, chopped
5ml/1 tsp crushed black peppercorns
5 garlic cloves, chopped
15ml/1 tbsp shrimp paste
30ml/2 tbsp vegetable oil
1.5 litres/2½ pints/6 cups chicken stock
2.5cm/1in piece fresh root ginger, grated
120ml/4fl oz/½ cup tamarind water
15ml/1 tbsp honey
juice of 1 lime
4 spring onions (scallions), sliced
salt and ground black pepper
2 small fresh red chillies, seeded and sliced, to garnish

Serves 6–8

1 Cut the pork into very fine strips, 5cm/2in in length. Mix with the papaya and set aside. Process the shallots, crushed black peppercorns, garlic and shrimp paste together in a food processor or blender to form a paste.

2 Heat the oil in a heavy pan and fry the shallot paste for 1–2 minutes. Add the stock and bring to the boil. Reduce the heat. Add the pork and papaya, ginger and tamarind water. Simmer for 7–8 minutes, until the pork is tender.

3 Stir in the honey, lime juice, most of the chillies and spring onions. Season to taste. Ladle the soup into bowls and serve at once, garnished with the remaining chillies and onions.

Cook's Tip
Unripe papayas are often served in salads in Asia and are also cooked as a vegetable.

Pork Bone Tea

This aromatic, peppery broth is a favourite at late-night hawker stalls.

Ingredients

500g/1¼lb meaty pork ribs, trimmed and cut into 5cm/2in lengths
225g/8oz pork loin
8 garlic cloves, unpeeled and bruised
2 cinnamon sticks
5 star anise
120ml/4fl oz/½ cup light soy sauce
50ml/2fl oz/¼ cup dark soy sauce
15ml/1 tbsp sugar
salt and ground black pepper
steamed rice, to serve

For the dipping sauce
120ml/4fl oz/½ cup light soy sauce
2 fresh red chillies, seeded and finely chopped

For the spice bag
6 cloves
15ml/1 tbsp dried orange peel
5ml/1 tsp black peppercorns
5ml/1 tsp coriander seeds
5ml/1 tsp fennel seeds

Serves 4–6

1 To make the dipping sauce, stir the soy sauce and chillies together in a small bowl and set aside. To make the spice bag, lay a piece of muslin (cheesecloth) flat and place all the spices in the centre. Gather up the edges and tie together.

2 Put the pork ribs and loin into a deep pan. Add the garlic, cinnamon sticks, star anise and spice bag. Pour in 2.5 litres/4½ pints/10 cups water and bring to the boil.

3 Skim off any fat from the surface, then stir in the soy sauces and sugar. Reduce the heat and simmer, partially covered, for about 2 hours, until the pork is almost falling off the bones. Season to taste with salt and lots of black pepper.

4 Remove the loin from the broth and cut it into bitesize pieces. Divide the meat and ribs among four to six bowls and ladle the steaming broth over the top. Serve with the soy and chilli sauce, as a dip for the pieces of pork, and steamed rice.

sweet & sour pork Energy 229kcal/963kJ; Protein 32.8g; Carbohydrate 11.1g, of which sugars 10.9g; Fat 6.2g, of which saturates 2.1g; Cholesterol 95mg; Calcium 37mg; Fibre 2.3g; Sodium 111mg.
pork bone tea Energy 49kcal/206kJ; Protein 8.1g; Carbohydrate 0.8g, of which sugars 0.8g; Fat 1.5g, of which saturates 0.5g; Cholesterol 24mg; Calcium 3mg; Fibre 0g; Sodium 145mg.

Pork & Sichuan Pickle Soup

Noodle soup can taste a bit bland, but not when Sichuan hot pickle is one of the ingredients. This tasty soup makes a great winter warmer.

Ingredients

1 litre/1¾ pints/4 cups chicken stock
350g/12oz egg noodles
15ml/1 tbsp dried shrimp, soaked in water
30ml/2 tbsp vegetable oil
225g/8oz lean pork, such as fillet (tenderloin), finely shredded
15ml/1 tbsp yellow bean paste
15ml/1 tbsp soy sauce
115g/4oz Sichuan hot pickle, rinsed, drained and shredded
pinch of sugar
salt and ground black pepper
2 spring onions (scallions), finely sliced, to garnish

Serves 4

1 Bring the stock to the boil in a large pan. Add the noodles and cook until almost tender. Drain the dried shrimp, rinse them under cold water, drain again and add to the stock. Lower the heat and simmer for a further 2 minutes. Keep hot.

2 Heat the oil in a frying pan or wok. Add the pork and stir-fry over a high heat for about 3 minutes.

3 Add the bean paste and soy sauce to the pork and stir-fry the mixture for 1 minute more. Add the hot pickle with a pinch of sugar. Stir-fry for 1 minute more.

4 Divide the noodles and soup among individual serving bowls. Spoon the pork mixture on top, then sprinkle with the spring onions and serve immediately.

Cook's Tip
Sichuan hot pickle, also known as Szechuan (or Sichuan) preserved vegetables, is a pickle made from the stems of mustard cabbage, which are dried in the sun and then pickled in brine with chillies and spices.

Broth with Stuffed Cabbage Leaves

The Chinese have a tradition of cooking dumplings or stuffed vegetables in a clear broth.

Ingredients

10 Chinese leaves (Chinese cabbage) halved, main ribs removed
4 spring onions (scallions), green tops left whole, white part finely chopped
5–6 dried cloud ear (wood ear) mushrooms, soaked in hot water for 15 minutes
115g/4oz minced (ground) pork
115g/4oz prawns (shrimp), shelled, deveined and chopped
1 fresh chilli, seeded and chopped
30ml/2 tbsp fish sauce
15ml/1 tbsp soy sauce
4cm/1½in fresh root ginger, peeled and very finely sliced
chopped fresh coriander (cilantro), to garnish

For the stock

1 meaty chicken carcass
2 onions, peeled and quartered
4 garlic cloves, crushed
4cm/1½in fresh root ginger, chopped
30ml/2 tbsp fish sauce
30ml/2 tbsp soy sauce
6 black peppercorns
a few sprigs of fresh thyme
sea salt

Serves 4

1 To make the chicken stock, put the chicken carcass into a deep pan with all the other stock ingredients except the salt. Add 2 litres/3½ pints/8 cups of water. Bring to the boil. Skim, then cover and simmer for 1½–2 hours. Remove the lid and simmer for 30 minutes more. Skim, season, then strain. Measure 1.5 litres/2½ pints/6 cups into a clean pan.

2 Blanch the cabbage leaves in boiling water for 2 minutes, lift out and refresh under cold water. Blanch the spring onion tops and refresh. Tear each piece into 5 strips. Drain the cloud ears, squeeze dry, trim, chop and mix with the pork, prawns, spring onion whites, chilli, fish sauce and soy sauce. Divide the mixture among the cabbage leaves, fold in the bottom edges and sides, roll up and tie with the spring onion green.

3 Heat the stock, stir in the ginger and add the cabbage bundles. Cook very gently for 20 minutes. Garnish with coriander.

pork & sichuan pickle soup Energy 218kcal/911kJ; Protein 24.5g; Carbohydrate 7.8g, of which sugars 0.9g; Fat 9.7g, of which saturates 3g; Cholesterol 74mg; Calcium 90mg; Fibre 0.8g; Sodium 454mg.
broth w. stuffed leaves Energy 80kcal/334kJ; Protein 12.7g; Carbohydrate 3.9g, of which sugars 3.7g; Fat 1.5g, of which saturates 0.5g; Cholesterol 74mg; Calcium 68mg; Fibre 1.4g; Sodium 891mg.

Pork Soup with Cloud Ears

One of China's most popular soups, this is famed for its clever balance of flavours. The "hot" comes from the pepper, the "sour" from the vinegar.

Ingredients

4–6 Chinese dried mushrooms
2–3 small pieces of cloud ear (wood ear) mushrooms
115g/4oz pork fillet (tenderloin), cut into fine strips
45ml/3 tbsp cornflour (cornstarch)
150ml/¼ pint/⅔ cup water
15–30ml/1–2 tbsp sunflower oil
1 small onion, finely chopped
1.5 litres/2½ pints/6 cups good quality beef or chicken stock
150g/5oz fresh firm tofu, diced
60ml/4 tbsp rice vinegar
15ml/1 tbsp light soy sauce
1 egg, beaten
5 ml/1 tsp sesame oil
salt and ground black pepper
2–3 spring onions (scallions), shredded, to garnish

Serves 6

1 Place the dried mushrooms in a bowl, with the pieces of cloud ear. Add sufficient warm water to cover and leave to soak for about 30 minutes.

2 Drain the mushrooms, reserving the soaking water. Cut off and discard the mushroom stems and slice the caps finely. Trim away any tough stem from the wood ears, then chop them.

3 Lightly dust the strips of pork with some of the cornflour; mix the remaining cornflour to a paste with the water.

4 Heat the oil in a wok and fry the onion until soft. Increase the heat and fry the pork until it changes colour. Add the stock, mushrooms, soaking water and cloud ears. Bring to the boil, then simmer for 15 minutes. Stir in the cornflour paste to thicken. Add the tofu, vinegar, soy sauce, and salt and pepper.

5 Bring the soup to just below boiling point, then drizzle in the beaten egg so that it forms threads. Stir in the sesame oil and serve at once, garnished with spring onion shreds.

Pork Broth with Winter Melon

This soup uses two traditional South-east Asian ingredients – winter melon to absorb the flavours and tiger lilies to lift the broth with a floral scent. When choosing tiger lilies make sure they are light golden in colour. If you can't find winter melon, you could make the soup using another winter squash.

Ingredients

350g/12oz winter melon
25g/1oz light golden tiger lilies, soaked in hot water for 20 minutes
salt and ground black pepper
1 small bunch each coriander (cilantro) and mint, stalks removed, leaves chopped, to garnish

For the stock

25g/1oz dried shrimp, soaked in water for 15 minutes
500g/1¼lb pork ribs
1 onion, peeled and quartered
175g/6oz carrots, peeled and cut into chunks
15ml/1 tbsp fish sauce
15ml/1 tbsp soy sauce
4 black peppercorns

Serves 4

1 To make the stock, drain and rinse the dried shrimp. Put the pork ribs in a large pan and cover with 2 litres/3½ pints/8 cups water. Bring the water to the boil, skim off any fat, and add the dried shrimp and the remaining stock ingredients. Cover and simmer for 1½ hours, then skim again. Continue simmering, uncovered, for a further 30 minutes. Strain and check the seasoning. You should have about 1.5 litres/2½ pints/6 cups.

2 Halve the winter melon lengthways and remove the seeds and inner membrane. Finely slice the flesh into half-moons. Squeeze the soaked tiger lilies dry and tie them in a knot.

3 Bring the stock to the boil in a deep pan or wok. Reduce the heat and add the winter melon and tiger lilies. Simmer for 15–20 minutes, or until the melon is tender. Season to taste with salt and pepper, and serve in heated bowls, with the herbs on the top.

pork soup w. cloud ears Energy 109kcal/458kJ; Protein 7.8g; Carbohydrate 8.3g, of which sugars 1g; Fat 5.3g, of which saturates 1g; Cholesterol 44mg; Calcium 141mg; Fibre 0.4g; Sodium 210mg.
pork broth w. winter melon Energy 25kcal/103kJ; Protein 1.6g; Carbohydrate 2.6g, of which sugars 1.9g; Fat 0.9g, of which saturates 0.1g; Cholesterol 0mg; Calcium 55mg; Fibre 1.5g; Sodium 616mg.

Beef Noodle Soup

Nutritious and filling, this makes an intensely satisfying meal at any time of day.

Ingredients

500g/1¼lb dried noodles, soaked in water for 20 minutes
1 onion, halved and finely sliced
6–8 spring onions (scallions), cut into long pieces
2–3 fresh red chillies, seeded and finely sliced
115g/4oz/½ cup beansprouts
1 large bunch each fresh coriander (cilantro) and mint, stalks removed, leaves chopped, to garnish
2 limes, cut in wedges, and hoisin sauce and fish sauce, to serve

For the stock

1.5kg/3lb 5oz oxtail, trimmed of fat and cut into thick pieces
1kg/2¼lb beef shank or brisket
2 large onions
2 carrots
7.5cm/3in fresh root ginger, cut into chunks
6 cloves
2 cinnamon sticks
6 star anise
5ml/1 tsp black peppercorns
30ml/2 tbsp soy sauce
45–60ml/3–4 tbsp fish sauce
salt

Serves 6

1 To make the stock, put the oxtail into a large, deep pan and cover with water. Bring it to the boil and cook for 10 minutes. Drain the oxtail, rinsing off any scum, and return it to the clean pan with the other stock ingredients, apart from the fish sauce. Cover with 3 litres/5¼ pints/12 cups water. Boil, then simmer for 2–3 hours with the lid on, and 1 hour without it. Skim, then strain 2 litres/3½ pints/8 cups stock into another pan.

2 Cut the cooked meat into thin pieces; discard the bones. Bring the stock to the boil, stir in the fish sauce, season to taste, and keep simmering until ready to use.

3 Cook the noodles in boiling water until tender, then drain and divide among six wide soup bowls. Top each serving with beef, onion, spring onions, chillies and beansprouts. Ladle the hot stock over the top, sprinkle with fresh herbs and serve with the lime wedges to squeeze over and the sauces to pass around.

Chinese Leaf Soup with Meatballs

This wonderfully fragrant combination makes for a hearty, warming soup.

Ingredients

10 dried shiitake mushrooms
90g/3½oz bean thread noodles
675g/1½lb minced (ground) beef
10ml/2 tsp finely grated garlic
10ml/2 tsp finely grated fresh root ginger
1 fresh red chilli, seeded and chopped
6 spring onions (scallions), sliced
1 egg white
15ml/1 tbsp cornflour (cornstarch)
15ml/1 tbsp Chinese rice wine
30ml/2 tbsp sunflower oil
1.5 litres/2½ pints/6 cups beef or chicken stock
50ml/2fl oz/¼ cup light soy sauce
5ml/1 tsp sugar
150g/5oz enokitake mushrooms, trimmed
200g/7oz Chinese leaves (Chinese cabbage) very thinly sliced
salt and ground black pepper

Serves 4

1 Place the dried mushrooms in a medium bowl and pour over 250ml/8fl oz/1 cup boiling water. Leave to soak for 30 minutes and then squeeze dry, reserving the liquid. Remove and discard the mushroom stems; thickly slice the caps and set aside.

2 Put the noodles in a large bowl and pour over boiling water to cover. Soak for 3–4 minutes, then drain, rinse and set aside.

3 Place the beef, garlic, ginger, chilli, spring onions, egg white, cornflour, rice wine and seasoning in a food processor. Process to combine well. Divide the mixture into 30 portions, then shape each one into a ball. Heat the stock.

4 Heat a wok and add the oil. Fry the meatballs, in batches, for 2–3 minutes on each side. Remove with a slotted spoon and drain on kitchen paper. Add the meatballs to the simmering beef stock with the soy sauce, sugar, shiitake mushrooms and reserved soaking liquid. Cook gently for 20–25 minutes.

5 Add the noodles, enokitake mushrooms and cabbage and cook gently for 4–5 minutes. Serve in wide bowls.

beef noodle soup Energy 180kcal/748kJ; Protein 10.8g; Carbohydrate 4.8g, of which sugars 4.1g; Fat 4.2g, of which saturates 1.6g; Cholesterol 24mg; Calcium 35mg; Fibre 1g; Sodium 219mg.
chinese leaf w. meatballs Energy 102kcal/424kJ; Protein 5.4g; Carbohydrate 5.8g, of which sugars 3g; Fat 6.5g, of which saturates 1.9g; Cholesterol 13mg; Calcium 39mg; Fibre 0.9g; Sodium 308mg.

Beef Broth with Water Spinach

Water spinach is a popular vegetable throughout Vietnam. When cooked, the stems remain crunchy while the leaves soften, lending a delightful contrast of texture to the dish. Served as an appetizer, this is a light soup with tender bites of beef and sour notes of lemon juice.

Ingredients

30ml/2 tbsp fish sauce
5ml/1 tsp sugar
175g/6oz beef fillet, finely sliced across the grain into 2.5cm/1in strips
1.2 litres/2 pints/5 cups beef or chicken stock
175g/6oz water spinach, trimmed, rinsed, leaves and stalks separated
juice of 1 lemon
ground black pepper
1 fresh red or green chilli, seeded and finely sliced, to garnish

Serves 4–6

1 In a bowl, stir the fish sauce with the sugar until it has dissolved. Toss in the beef strips and leave to marinate for 30 minutes. Pour the stock into a pan and bring it to the boil. Reduce the heat and add the water spinach. Stir in the lemon juice and season with pepper.

2 Place the meat strips in individual soup bowls and ladle the hot broth over the top. Garnish with chillies and serve.

Cook's Tip

It is important to marinate the beef strips so that they take on the flavourings. If you have time to prepare them in advance, they can be left to marinate overnight.

Variation

You can sprinkle coriander (cilantro) and mint or fried garlic and ginger over the top if you prefer.

Paper-thin Sliced Beef Soup

This dish is great for sharing with friends, as the cooking is done at the table.

Ingredients

600g/1 ⅓lb rump (round) steak
2 thin leeks, cut into thin strips
4 spring onions (scallions), quartered
8 shiitake mushrooms caps
175g/6oz/2 cups oyster mushrooms, base part removed, torn into small pieces
½ head Chinese leaves (Chinese cabbage), cut into squares
300g/11oz shungiku, halved
275g/10oz firm tofu, halved and cut crossways in slices
10 x 6cm/4 x 2½in dashi-konbu, wiped with a damp cloth

For the lime sauce

1 lime
20ml/4 tsp mirin
60ml/4 tbsp rice vinegar
120ml/4fl oz/½ cup shoyu
4 x 6cm/1½ x 2½in dashi-konbu
5g/⅛oz kezuri-bushi

For the pink daikon

1 piece mooli (daikon), 6cm/2½in in length, peeled
1 dried chilli, seeded and sliced

Serves 4

1 To make the lime sauce, squeeze the lime and make up the juice to 120ml/4fl oz/½ cup with water. Pour into a bowl and add the mirin, rice vinegar, shoyu, dashi-konbu and kezuri-bushi. Cover and leave to stand overnight.

2 Make the pink mooli. Pierce the mooli in several places and insert the chilli strips. Leave for 20 minutes, then grate, squeeze out the liquid and divide among four small bowls.

3 Slice the meat thinly. Arrange meat, vegetables and tofu on platters. Fill a casserole three-quarters full of water and add the dashi-konbu. Boil, then transfer to a table burner. Strain the citrus sauce and add 45ml/3 tbsp to each bowl of daikon.

4 Remove the konbu from the stock. Add some tofu and vegetables to the pot. Each guest cooks a slice of beef in the stock, then dips it in sauce. Tofu and vegetables are removed and dipped in the same way, and more are added to the pot.

beef broth w. water spinach Energy 61kcal/254kJ; Protein 7.4g; Carbohydrate 1.2g, of which sugars 1.1g; Fat 3g, of which saturates 1.1g; Cholesterol 17mg; Calcium 51mg; Fibre 0.6g; Sodium 60mg.
thin sliced beef soup Energy 290kcal/1216kJ; Protein 42.2g; Carbohydrate 8.3g, of which sugars 7.4g; Fat 9.9g, of which saturates 3.1g; Cholesterol 89mg; Calcium 425mg; Fibre 3.9g; Sodium 1000mg.

Tomato & Beef Soup

Another wholesome and much-loved classic, the tomatoes and spring onions give this light beef broth a superb flavour. It is quick and easy to make, and ideal as an appetizer or light lunch on a warm day. Use fresh rather than canned tomatoes to achieve the best flavour.

Ingredients

75g/3oz rump (round) steak
900ml/1½ pints/3¾ cups beef stock
30ml/2 tbsp tomato purée (paste)
6 tomatoes, halved, seeded and chopped
10ml/2 tsp caster (superfine) sugar
15ml/1 tbsp cornflour (cornstarch)
15ml/1 tbsp cold water
1 egg white
2.5ml/½ tsp sesame oil
salt and ground black pepper
2 spring onions (scallions), finely shredded

Serves 4

1 Cut the beef into thin strips and place in a pan. Pour over boiling water to cover. Cook for 2 minutes, then drain thoroughly and set aside.

2 Bring the stock to the boil in a clean pan. Stir in the tomato purée, then the tomatoes and sugar.

3 Add the beef strips, allow the stock to boil again, then lower the heat and simmer for 2 minutes.

4 Mix the cornflour to a paste with the water. Add the mixture to the soup, stirring constantly until it thickens slightly. Lightly beat the egg white in a cup.

5 Pour the egg white into the soup, stirring. When the egg white changes colour, season, stir and pour the soup into heated soup bowls. Drizzle with sesame oil, sprinkle with spring onions and serve.

Beef & Ginger Soup

This fragrant soup is often eaten for breakfast.

Ingredients

1 onion
1.5kg/3–3½lb beef shank with bones
2.5cm/1in fresh root ginger
1 star anise
1 bay leaf
2 whole cloves
2.5ml/½ tsp fennel seeds
1 piece of cinnamon stick
3 litres/5 pints/12 cups water
fish sauce, to taste
juice of 1 lime
150g/5oz fillet (tenderloin) steak
450g/1lb fresh flat rice noodles
salt and ground black pepper

For the accompaniments

1 small red onion, sliced into rings
115g/4oz/½ cup beansprouts
2 fresh red chillies, seeded and sliced
2 spring onions (scallions), sliced
coriander (cilantro) leaves
lime wedges

Serves 4–6

1 Cut the onion in half. Grill (broil) under a high heat, cut side up, until the exposed sides are caramelized. Set aside.

2 Cut the meat into large chunks and then place with the bones in a large pan. Add the caramelized onion with the ginger, star anise, bay leaf, cloves, fennel seeds and cinnamon.

3 Add the water, bring to the boil, then simmer gently for 2–3 hours, skimming off the fat and scum occasionally.

4 Remove the meat from the stock and cut into small pieces, discarding the bones. Strain the stock and return to the pan together with the meat. Bring back to the boil and season with the fish sauce and lime juice.

5 Slice the fillet steak very thinly and then chill until required. Place the accompaniments in separate bowls.

6 Cook the noodles in boiling water until just tender. Drain and divide among soup bowls. Top with steak, pour the hot stock over and serve, offering the accompaniments separately so that each person may garnish their soup as they like.

tomato & beef soup Energy 79kcal/337kJ; Protein 6.2g; Carbohydrate 11.1g, of which sugars 7.6g; Fat 1.5g, of which saturates 0.5g; Cholesterol 11mg; Calcium 16mg; Fibre 1.5g; Sodium 58mg.
beef & ginger soup Energy 532kcal/2222kJ; Protein 36.7g; Carbohydrate 63.6g, of which sugars 1.6g; Fat 13.4g, of which saturates 5.4g; Cholesterol 82mg; Calcium 26mg; Fibre 0.6g; Sodium 102mg.

Beef & Aubergine Soup

A wonderful Khmer dish, this soup is sweet and spicy.

Ingredients

4 dried New Mexico chillies
15ml/1 tbsp vegetable oil
75ml/5 tbsp kroeung
2–3 fresh red chillies
75ml/5 tbsp tamarind extract
15–30ml/1–2 tbsp fish sauce
30ml/2 tbsp palm sugar (jaggery)
12 Thai aubergines (eggplants), cut into bitesize chunks
1 bunch watercress, trimmed and chopped
1 handful fresh curry leaves
sea salt and ground black pepper

For the stock

1kg/2¼lb beef shanks or brisket
2 large onions, quartered
2–3 carrots, cut into chunks
90g/3½oz fresh root ginger, sliced
2 cinnamon sticks
4 star anise
5ml/1 tsp black peppercorns
30ml/2 tbsp soy sauce
45–60ml/3–4 tbsp fish sauce

Serves 6

1 To make the stock, mix all the ingredients, apart from the soy sauce and fish sauce, in a large pan. Cover with 3 litres/5 pints/12 cups water and bring to the boil. Simmer, covered, for 2–3 hours.

2 Meanwhile, soak the New Mexico chillies in water for 30 minutes. Split them open, remove the seeds and scrape out the pulp. Stir the sauces into the stock and simmer, uncovered, until it has reduced to about 2 litres/3½ pints/8 cups. Skim, strain into a bowl and set aside. Tear the meat into thin strips and put half of it aside for the soup. Save the rest for another dish.

3 Heat the oil in a wok. Stir in the kroeung and chilli pulp with the whole chillies. Stir until the mixture sizzles. Add the tamarind extract, fish sauce, sugar and reserved stock. Stir well and bring to the boil. Add the reserved beef, aubergines and watercress. Continue cooking for 20 minutes.

4 Dry-fry the curry leaves until they begin to crackle. Season the soup, stir in half the curry leaves and serve in heated bowls, with the remaining leaves on top.

Spicy Beef & Mushroom Soup

Ginger gives this satisfying soup a delightful tang.

Ingredients

10g/¼oz dried porcini mushrooms
6 spring onions (scallions)
115g/4oz carrots
350g/12oz lean rump (round) steak
about 30ml/2 tbsp oil
1 garlic clove, crushed
2.5cm/1in fresh root ginger, grated
1.2 litres/2 pints/5 cups beef stock
45ml/3 tbsp light soy sauce
60ml/4 tbsp sake or dry sherry
75g/3oz dried thin egg noodles
75g/3oz spinach, shredded
salt and ground black pepper

Serves 4

1 Break up the dried porcini, place them in a bowl and pour over 150ml/¼ pint/⅔ cup boiling water. Cover and leave the mushrooms to soak for 15 minutes.

2 Cut the spring onions and carrots into fine 5cm/2in-long strips. Trim any fat off the meat and slice into thin strips.

3 Heat the oil in a large pan and cook the beef in batches until browned. Remove and drain on kitchen paper. Add the garlic, ginger, spring onions and carrots to the pan and stir-fry for 3 minutes.

4 Add the beef stock, the mushrooms and their soaking liquid, the soy sauce, sherry and plenty of seasoning. Bring to the boil, reduce the heat and simmer, covered, for 10 minutes.

5 Break up the noodles slightly and add to the pan, with the spinach. Simmer gently for 5 minutes, or until the beef is tender. Adjust the seasoning before serving in warmed bowls.

Cook's Tip
Chilling the beef briefly in the freezer will make it much easier to slice into thin strips.

beef & aubergine Energy 303kcal/1276kJ; Protein 36.7g; Carbohydrate 16.5g, of which sugars 14.5g; Fat 10.6g, of which saturates 4.2g; Cholesterol 90mg; Calcium 35mg; Fibre 2.4g; Sodium 303mg.
spicy beef & mushroom Energy 315kcal/1316kJ; Protein 23.4g; Carbohydrate 17.4g, of which sugars 4g; Fat 15.5g, of which saturates 4.5g; Cholesterol 56mg; Calcium 57mg; Fibre 1.9g; Sodium 713mg.

Mongolian Firepot

This mode of cooking was introduced to China by 13th-century invaders. Guests cook the assembled ingredients at the table, dipping the meats in sauces.

Ingredients
900g/2lb boned leg of lamb
225g/8oz lamb's liver, trimmed
900ml/1½ pints/3¾ cups hot lamb stock
900ml/1½ pints/3¾ cups hot chicken stock
1cm/½in piece fresh root ginger, peeled and thinly sliced
45ml/3 tbsp rice wine
½ head Chinese leaves (Chinese cabbage), shredded
115g/4oz cellophane noodles
salt and ground black pepper

For the dipping sauce
50ml/2fl oz/¼ cup red wine vinegar
7.5ml/½ tbsp dark soy sauce
1cm/½in piece fresh root ginger, peeled and finely shredded
1 spring onion (scallion), shredded

To serve
tomato sauce, sweet chilli sauce, mustard oil and sesame oil
dry-fried coriander seeds, crushed

Serves 6–8

1 When buying the lamb, ask your butcher to slice it thinly on a slicing machine. Place the liver in the freezer; slice it thinly too.

2 Mix both types of stock in a large pan. Add the ginger and rice wine, with salt and pepper to taste. Heat to simmering point; simmer for 15 minutes.

3 Arrange the meats and greens on platters. Soak the noodles, following the instructions on the packet.

4 Mix the dipping sauce ingredients in a small bowl. Place the other accompaniments in separate small dishes.

5 Fill the moat of the hotpot with the simmering stock. Each guest cooks a portion of meat in the hot stock, then dips it in sauce and coats it in seeds.

6 When the meat has been eaten, add the vegetables and drained noodles. Cook for a minute or two, then serve as soup.

Sukiyaki

You will need a special cast-iron sukiyaki pan and burner or a similar table top cooker for this dish.

Ingredients
1kg/2¼lb beef topside (pot roast), thinly sliced
lard (or white cooking fat), for cooking
4 leeks, sliced diagonally into 1cm/½in pieces
8 shiitake mushrooms, stems removed
300g/11oz shirataki noodles, boiled for 2 minutes, drained and halved
2 pieces fried tofu, cubed
4 fresh eggs, to serve

For the sukiyaki stock
100ml/3½fl oz/scant ½ cup mirin (sweet rice wine)
45ml/3 tbsp sugar
105ml/7 tbsp soy sauce

For the seasoning mix
200ml/7fl oz/scant 1 cup dashi
100ml/3½fl oz/scant ½ cup sake
15ml/1 tbsp soy sauce

Serves 4

1 Make the sukiyaki stock. Mix the mirin, sugar and soy sauce in a pan, bring to the boil, then set aside. To make the seasoning mix, heat the dashi, sake and soy sauce in a pan. As soon as it boils, set aside.

2 Fan out the beef slices on a large serving plate. Put the lard for cooking on the same plate. Arrange all the remaining ingredients, except the eggs, on one or more large plates.

3 Stand the portable cooker on a suitably heavy mat. Melt the lard or white cooking fat, add three or four slices of beef and some leeks, then pour in the sukiyaki stock. Gradually add the remaining ingredients, except the eggs.

4 Place each egg in a ramekin and beat lightly. When the beef and vegetables are cooked, diners help themselves and dip the food in the raw egg before eating.

5 When the stock has thickened, stir in the seasoning mix and carry on cooking until all the ingredients have been eaten.

mongolian firepot Energy 144kcal/606kJ; Protein 12.3g; Carbohydrate 12g, of which sugars 1.2g; Fat 5.1g, of which saturates 1.1g; Cholesterol 128mg; Calcium 193mg; Fibre 0.9g; Sodium 49mg.
sukiyaki Energy 868kcal/3633kJ; Protein 71.5g; Carbohydrate 51.7g, of which sugars 11.1g; Fat 43.2g, of which saturates 13.1g; Cholesterol 662mg; Calcium 605mg; Fibre 6.5g; Sodium 1695mg.

Rice Porridge

Originating in China, this dish has now spread through much of Asia and is loved for its comforting blandness. It is invariably served, though, with a few strongly flavoured accompaniments.

Ingredients

900ml/1 ½ pints/3¾ cups vegetable stock
200g/7oz/1¾ cups cooked rice
225g/8oz minced (ground) pork
15ml/1 tbsp fish sauce
2 heads pickled garlic, finely chopped
1 celery stick, finely diced
salt and ground black pepper

To garnish

30ml/2 tbsp groundnut (peanut) oil
4 garlic cloves, thinly sliced
4 small red shallots, finely sliced

Serves 2

1 Make the garnishes by heating the groundnut oil in a frying pan and cooking the garlic and shallots over a low heat until brown. Drain well on kitchen paper and reserve for the soup.

2 Pour the stock into a large pan. Bring to the boil and add the rice. Season the minced pork. Add it by taking small teaspoons and tapping the spoon on the side of the pan so that the meat falls into the soup in small lumps.

3 Stir in the fish sauce and pickled garlic and simmer for about 10 minutes, until the pork is cooked. Stir in the celery.

4 Serve the rice porridge in individual warmed bowls. Sprinkle the prepared garlic and shallots on top and season with plenty of ground pepper.

Cook's Tip
Pickled garlic has a distinctive flavour and is available from Asian food stores.

Congee with Chinese Sausage

Congee – soft rice – is comfort food. Gentle on the stomach, it is frequently eaten for breakfast or served to convalescents. Throughout the East, people will frequently have just a cup of tea on rising; later they will settle down to a bowl of congee.

Ingredients

115g/4oz/generous ½ cup long-grain rice
25g/1oz/3 tbsp glutinous rice
1.2 litres/2 pints/5 cups water
about 2.5ml/½ tsp salt
5ml/1 tsp sesame oil
thin slice of fresh root ginger, peeled and bruised
2 Chinese sausages
1 egg, lightly beaten (optional)
2.5ml/½ tsp light soy sauce
roasted peanuts, chopped, and thin shreds of spring onion (scallion), to garnish

Serves 2–3

1 Wash both rices thoroughly. Drain and place in a large pan. Add the water, bring to the boil and immediately reduce to the lowest heat, using a heat diffuser if you have one.

2 Cook gently for 1¼–1½ hours, stirring from time to time. If the congee thickens too much, stir in a little boiling water. It should have the consistency of creamy pouring porridge.

3 About 15 minutes before serving, add salt to taste and the sesame oil, together with the piece of ginger.

4 Steam the Chinese sausages for about 10 minutes, then slice and stir into the congee. Cook for 5 minutes.

5 Just before serving, remove the ginger and stir in the lightly beaten egg, if using. Serve hot, garnished with the peanuts and spring onions and topped with a drizzle of soy sauce.

Variation
If you prefer, use roast duck instead of Chinese sausages. Congee is also popular with tea eggs.

rice porridge Energy 152kcal/636kJ; Protein 15.2g; Carbohydrate 17g, of which sugars 1.8g; Fat 2.5g, of which saturates 0.3g; Cholesterol 34mg; Calcium 12mg; Fibre 0g; Sodium 45mg.
congee w. chinese sausage Energy 301kcal/1254kJ; Protein 7.2g; Carbohydrate 40.4g, of which sugars 0.8g; Fat 12g, of which saturates 4.2g; Cholesterol 16mg; Calcium 23mg; Fibre 0.2g; Sodium 610mg.

Corn Fritters

These crunchy corn fritters are very easy to prepare.

Ingredients
3 corn cobs
1 garlic clove, crushed
small bunch fresh coriander (cilantro), chopped
1 small fresh red or green chilli, seeded and finely chopped
1 spring onion (scallion), chopped
15ml/1 tbsp soy sauce
75g/3oz/¾ cup rice flour or plain (all-purpose) flour
2 eggs, lightly beaten
60ml/4 tbsp water
oil, for shallow frying
salt and ground black pepper
sweet chilli sauce, to serve

Makes 12

1 Slice the kernels from the cobs into a large bowl. Add the garlic, chopped coriander, red or green chilli, spring onion, soy sauce, flour, beaten eggs and water; mix well and season.

2 Heat the oil in a large frying pan. Add spoonfuls of the corn mixture, gently spreading each one with the back of the spoon to make a roundish fritter. Cook for 1–2 minutes on each side. Drain and serve hot with sweet chilli sauce.

Crab & Water Chestnut Wontons

Serve these mouthwatering parcels as part of a dim sum selection.

Ingredients
50g/2oz/⅓ cup drained, canned water chestnuts
115g/4oz/generous ½ cup fresh white crab meat
12 wonton wrappers
salt and ground black pepper

Serves 4

1 Finely chop the water chestnuts, mix them with the crab meat and season. Fill the wonton wrappers, spring-roll fashion.

2 Steam the filled wontons for 5–8 minutes and serve.

Prawn Fritters

These are a favourite snack or appetizer. Unusually, they are first shallow fried, then deep fried. They are best eaten fresh from the pan, dipped in the piquant sauce.

Ingredients
16 raw prawns (shrimp) in the shell
225g/8oz/2 cups plain (all-purpose) flour
5ml/1 tsp baking powder
2.5ml/½ tsp salt
1 egg, beaten
1 small sweet potato
1 garlic clove, crushed
115g/4oz/½ cup beansprouts, soaked in cold water and well drained
vegetable oil, for shallow and deep frying
4 spring onions (scallions), chopped

For the dipping sauce
1 garlic clove, sliced
45ml/3 tbsp rice vinegar
15–30ml/1–2 tbsp water
salt, to taste
6–8 small fresh red chillies

Serves 2–4

1 Mix together all the ingredients for the dipping sauce and divide between two small bowls.

2 Put the whole prawns in a pan with water to cover. Bring to the boil, then simmer for 4–5 minutes or until the prawns are pink and tender. Lift the prawns from the pan with a slotted spoon. Discard the heads and the body shell, but leave the tails on. Strain and reserve the cooking liquid. Allow to cool.

3 Sift the flour, baking powder and salt into a bowl. Add the beaten egg and about 300ml/½ pint/1¼ cups of the prawn stock to make a batter that has the consistency of double (heavy) cream.

4 Peel and grate the sweet potato using the large holes on a grater, and add it to the batter, then stir in the crushed garlic and the drained beansprouts.

5 Pour enough oil for shallow frying into a large frying pan. It should be about 5mm/¼in deep. Pour more oil into a wok for deep frying. Heat the oil in the frying pan. Taking a generous spoonful of the batter, drop it carefully into the frying pan so that it forms a fritter, about the size of a large drop scone.

6 Make more fritters in the same way. As soon as the fritters have set, top each one with a single prawn and a few chopped spring onions. Continue to cook over a medium heat for 1 minute, then remove with a fish slice or metal spatula.

7 Heat the oil in the wok to 190°C/375°F and deep fry the prawn fritters in batches until they are crisp and golden brown. Drain the fritters on kitchen paper and then arrange on a serving plate or platter. Offer a bowl of the sauce for dipping.

Variation
Use cooked tiger prawns if you prefer. In this case, make the batter using fish stock or chicken stock.

corn fritters Energy 49kcal/208kJ; Protein 2.3g; Carbohydrate 7.5g, of which sugars 0.6g; Fat 1.3g, of which saturates 0.3g; Cholesterol 32mg; Calcium 21mg; Fibre 0.6g; Sodium 102mg.
crab & water chestnut Energy 88kcal/374kJ; Protein 7g; Carbohydrate 14.7g, of which sugars 0.4g; Fat 0.5g, of which saturates 0.1g; Cholesterol 21mg; Calcium 66mg; Fibre 0.7g; Sodium 166mg.
prawn fritters Energy 711kcal/2996kJ; Protein 34g; Carbohydrate 101g, of which sugars 6.4g; Fat 21.9g, of which saturates 3.2g; Cholesterol 290mg; Calcium 282mg; Fibre 5.9g; Sodium 253mg.

Bacon-rolled Enokitake Mushrooms

The Japanese name for this dish is Obimaki enoki: an obi (belt or sash) is made from bacon and wrapped around enokitake mushrooms before they are cooked. The strong, smoky flavour of the bacon complements the subtle flavour of the mushrooms.

Ingredients

450g/1lb fresh enokitake mushrooms
6 rindless smoked streaky (fatty) bacon rashers (strips)
4 lemon wedges, to serve

Serves 4

1 Cut off the root part of each enokitake cluster 2cm/¾in from the end. Do not separate the stems. Cut the bacon rashers in half lengthways.

2 Divide the enokitake into 12 equal bunches. Take one bunch, then place the middle of the enokitake near the edge of one bacon rasher, with 2.5–4cm/1–1½in of enokitake protruding at each end.

3 Carefully roll up the bunch of enokitake in the bacon. Tuck any straying short stems into the bacon and slide the bacon slightly upwards at each roll to cover about 4cm/1½in of the enokitake. Secure the end of the bacon roll with a cocktail stick (toothpick). Repeat using the remaining enokitake and bacon to make 11 more rolls.

4 Preheat the grill (broiler) to a high temperature. Place the enokitake rolls on an oiled wire rack. Grill (broil) both sides until the bacon is crisp and the enokitake start to char. This takes about 10–13 minutes.

5 Remove the enokitake rolls and place on a board. Using a fork and knife, chop each roll in half in the middle of the bacon belt. Arrange the top part of the enokitake roll standing upright, the bottom part lying down next to it. Add a wedge of lemon to each portion and serve.

Mini Phoenix Rolls

These filled omelette parcels are legendary.

Ingredients

2 large eggs, plus 1 egg white
75ml/5 tbsp cold water
5ml/1 tsp vegetable oil
175g/6oz lean pork, diced
75g/3oz/½ cup drained, canned water chestnuts
5cm/2in piece fresh root ginger, grated
4 dried Chinese mushrooms, soaked in hot water until soft
15ml/1 tbsp dry sherry
1.5ml/¼ tsp salt
large pinch of ground white pepper
30ml/2 tbsp rice vinegar
2.5ml/½ tsp sugar
fresh coriander (cilantro) or flat leaf parsley, to garnish

Serves 4

1 Lightly beat the 2 whole eggs with 45ml/3 tbsp of the water. Use the mixture to make 4 omelettes.

2 Mix the pork and water chestnuts in a food processor. Add 5ml/1 tsp of the ginger. Drain the mushrooms, chop the caps roughly and add these to the mixture. Process until smooth.

3 Scrape the pork paste into a bowl. Stir in the egg white, sherry, remaining water, salt and pepper. Mix thoroughly, cover the bowl and leave in cool place for about 15 minutes.

4 Divide the pork mixture among the omelettes and roll them up. Steam over a high heat for 15 minutes.

5 Make a dipping sauce by mixing the remaining ginger with the rice vinegar and sugar in a small dish. Lift the rolls out of the steamer, then cut them diagonally in 1cm/½in slices. Arrange them on a plate, garnish with the coriander or flat leaf parsley leaves and serve with the sauce.

Cook's Tip

These rolls can be prepared a day in advance and steamed just before serving.

bacon-rolled enokitake Energy 84kcal/348kJ; Protein 6g; Carbohydrate 0.5g, of which sugars 0.2g; Fat 6.5g, of which saturates 2.2g; Cholesterol 16mg; Calcium 8mg; Fibre 1.3g; Sodium 321mg.
mini pheonix rolls Energy 110kcal/460kJ; Protein 13.8g; Carbohydrate 0.8g, of which sugars 0.5g; Fat 5.4g, of which saturates 1.5g; Cholesterol 123mg; Calcium 22mg; Fibre 0.3g; Sodium 82mg.

Coriander Omelette Parcels

Stir-fried vegetables in black bean sauce make a great omelette filling.

Ingredients

130g/4½oz broccoli, cut into small florets
30ml/2 tbsp groundnut (peanut) oil
1cm/½in piece fresh root ginger, finely grated
1 large garlic clove, crushed
2 fresh red chillies, seeded and finely sliced
4 spring onions (scallions), sliced diagonally
175g/6oz/3 cups pak choi (bok choy), shredded
50g/2oz/2 cups fresh coriander (cilantro) leaves, plus extra to garnish
100g/4oz/½ cup beansprouts
45ml/3 tbsp black bean sauce
4 eggs
salt and ground black pepper

Serves 4

1 Blanch the broccoli in boiling salted water for 2 minutes, drain, then refresh under cold running water.

2 Meanwhile, heat 15ml/1 tbsp of the oil in a frying pan or wok. Add the ginger, garlic and half the chilli and stir-fry for 1 minute. Add the spring onions, broccoli and pak choi, and stir-fry for 2 minutes more.

3 Chop three-quarters of the coriander and add to the frying pan or wok. Add the beansprouts and stir-fry for 1 minute, then add the black bean sauce and heat through for 1 minute more. Remove the pan from the heat and keep warm.

4 Mix the eggs lightly with a fork and season well. Heat a little of the remaining oil in a small frying pan and add a quarter of the beaten egg. Swirl the egg until it covers the base of the pan, then scatter over a quarter of the reserved coriander leaves. Cook until set, then turn out on to a plate and keep warm while you make three more omelettes, adding more oil, when necessary.

5 Spoon the vegetable stir-fry on to the omelettes and roll up. Cut in half crossways and serve garnished with coriander leaves and the remaining chilli.

Rice Omelette Rolls

Rice omelettes make a great supper dish and are popular with children, who usually top them with a liberal helping of tomato ketchup.

Ingredients

1 skinless, boneless chicken thigh, about 115g/4oz, cubed
40ml/8 tsp butter
1 small onion, chopped
½ carrot, diced
2 shiitake mushrooms, stems removed and chopped
15ml/1 tbsp finely chopped fresh parsley
225g/8oz/2 cups cooked long grain white rice
30ml/2 tbsp tomato ketchup
6 eggs, lightly beaten
60ml/4 tbsp milk
5ml/1 tsp salt, plus extra to season
freshly ground black pepper
tomato ketchup, to serve

Serves 4

1 Season the chicken with salt and pepper. Melt 10ml/2 tsp butter in a frying pan. Fry the onion for 1 minute, then add the chicken and fry until the cubes are cooked. Add the carrot and mushrooms, stir-fry over a medium heat until soft, then add the parsley. Set this mixture aside.

2 Wipe the frying pan, then add a further 10ml/2 tsp butter and stir in the rice. Mix in the fried ingredients, ketchup and pepper. Stir well, adding salt to taste, if necessary. Keep the mixture warm. Beat the eggs with the milk in a bowl. Stir in the measured salt and add pepper to taste.

3 Melt 5ml/1 tsp of the remaining butter in an omelette pan. Pour in a quarter of the egg mixture and stir it briefly with a fork, then allow it to set for 1 minute. Top with a quarter of the rice mixture.

4 Fold the omelette over the rice and slide it to the edge of the pan to shape it into a curve. Slide it on to a warmed plate, cover with kitchen paper and press neatly into a rectangular shape. Keep hot while cooking three more omelettes from the remaining ingredients. Serve immediately, with tomato ketchup.

omelette parcels Energy 148kcal/614kJ; Protein 10.4g; Carbohydrate 6.2g, of which sugars 5.4g; Fat 9.3g, of which saturates 2.2g; Cholesterol 190mg; Calcium 152mg; Fibre 3g; Sodium 323mg.
rice omelette rolls Energy 322kcal/1347kJ; Protein 18.1g; Carbohydrate 22.8g, of which sugars 4.9g; Fat 18.5g, of which saturates 8.1g; Cholesterol 337mg; Calcium 80mg; Fibre 1.1g; Sodium 325mg.

Stuffed Omelettes

A chilli filling makes an interesting contrast to the delicate flavour of the egg.

Ingredients

30ml/2 tbsp groundnut (peanut) oil
2 garlic cloves, finely chopped
1 small onion, finely chopped
225g/8oz minced (ground) pork
30ml/2 tbsp fish sauce
5ml/1 tsp sugar
2 tomatoes, peeled and chopped
15ml/1 tbsp chopped fresh coriander (cilantro)
ground black pepper
fresh coriander (cilantro) sprigs and sliced fresh red chillies, to garnish

For the omelettes

5 eggs
15ml/1 tbsp fish sauce
30ml/2 tbsp groundnut (peanut) oil

Serves 4

1 Heat the oil in a wok and fry the garlic and onion for 3–4 minutes, until soft. Add the pork and cook for about 8 minutes, stirring frequently, until lightly browned.

2 Stir in the fish sauce, sugar and tomatoes, season to taste with pepper and simmer until slightly thickened. Mix in the fresh coriander. Remove from the heat and cover to keep warm while you make the omelettes.

3 Beat the eggs and fish sauce together lightly with a fork. Heat 15ml/1 tbsp of the oil in an omelette pan over a medium heat. When the oil is hot, but not smoking, add half the egg mixture and immediately tilt the pan to spread the egg into a thin, even layer. Cook over a medium heat until the omelette is just set and the underside is golden.

4 Spoon half the filling into the centre of the omelette. Fold into a neat square parcel by bringing the opposite sides of the omelette towards each other. Slide the parcel on to a serving dish, folded side down. Make another omelette parcel in the same way. Garnish with the coriander sprigs and chillies. Cut each omelette in half to serve.

Egg Foo Yung

Hearty and full of flavour, this can be cooked either as one large omelette or as individual omelettes. Either way, it is a clever way of using up leftover roast pork.

Ingredients

6 dried Chinese mushrooms soaked for 20 minutes in warm water
50g/2oz/¼ cup beansprouts
6 drained canned water chestnuts, finely chopped
50g/2oz baby spinach leaves, washed
45ml/3 tbsp vegetable oil
50g/2oz lean roast pork, cut into strips
3 eggs
2.5ml/½ tsp sugar
5ml/1 tsp rice wine or dry sherry
salt and ground black pepper
fresh coriander (cilantro) sprigs, to garnish

Serves 4

1 Drain the mushrooms. Cut off and discard the stems; slice the caps finely and mix with the beansprouts, water chestnuts and spinach leaves.

2 Heat 15ml/1 tbsp oil in a large heavy frying pan. Add the pork and vegetables and toss over the heat for 1 minute.

3 Beat the eggs in a bowl. Add the strips of roast pork and the vegetables and mix well.

4 Wipe the frying pan and heat the remaining oil. Pour in the egg mixture and tilt the pan so that it covers the base. When the omelette has set on the underside, sprinkle the top with salt, pepper and sugar.

5 Invert a plate over the pan, turn both the pan and the plate over, and slide the omelette back into the pan to cook on the other side.

6 Cut the omelette into wedges, drizzle with rice wine or dry sherry and serve immediately, garnished with the sprigs of coriander.

stuffed omelettes Energy 305kcal/1267kJ; Protein 19.2g; Carbohydrate 4.8g, of which sugars 4.5g; Fat 23.6g, of which saturates 5.7g; Cholesterol 275mg; Calcium 48mg; Fibre 0.7g; Sodium 130mg.
egg foo yung Energy 153kcal/634kJ; Protein 8.1g; Carbohydrate 0.7g, of which sugars 0.5g; Fat 13.1g, of which saturates 2.3g; Cholesterol 151mg; Calcium 46mg; Fibre 0.5g; Sodium 80mg.

Oyster Omelette

Often devoured as a late-night treat, oyster omelette is a favourite hawker stall snack in the streets of Singapore. Almost decadent in its rich use of oysters, this is a tasty and satisfying dish, inspired by the Chinese.

Ingredients

30ml/2 tbsp vegetable oil
2 garlic cloves, finely chopped
1 fresh red or green chilli, finely chopped
8 large fresh oysters, shelled and rinsed
15ml/1 tbsp light soy sauce
15ml/1 tbsp Chinese rice wine
4 eggs, lightly beaten with 30ml/2 tbsp milk
8 small fresh oysters, shelled and rinsed
chilli oil
salt and ground black pepper
fresh coriander (cilantro) leaves, finely chopped, to garnish

Serves 2

1 Heat the oil in a heavy frying pan. Stir in the garlic and chilli until they become fragrant.

2 Add the large oysters and cook for 1 minute, then stir in the soy sauce and rice wine. Season to taste with salt and black pepper.

3 Pour in the beaten egg mixture and, using a wooden spatula, pull it back from the edge of the pan until it begins to set.

4 Reduce the heat. Sprinkle the small oysters over the top of the egg and drizzle with chilli oil. Cover the pan and leave to steam for 5–10 minutes until firm.

5 Sprinkle the omelette with chopped coriander, cut it into wedges and serve it from the pan.

Variation
Clams can be used instead if oysters. Remove them from the shells and rinse them before adding them to the omelette.

Steamed Eggs with Shrimp Paste

Throughout China – and elsewhere in Asia – variations on this type of steamed omelette are cooked as a snack and may be eaten at any time of the day. As a finishing touch, cut the omelette into strips and splash it with chilli oil. Alternatively, serve it with a spicy dipping sauce.

Ingredients

5 eggs
115g/4oz small, fresh prawns (shrimp), shelled and deveined
a handful of beansprouts
2 spring onions (scallions), trimmed and finely sliced
10ml/2 tsp shrimp paste
1 bunch coriander (cilantro), chopped
15ml/1 tbsp vegetable oil
chilli oil, for drizzling
sea salt and ground black pepper
fresh coriander (cilantro) leaves, to garnish
dipping sauce, to serve

Serves 2–4

1 Beat the eggs in a bowl. Stir in the prawns, beansprouts, spring onions, shrimp paste and coriander. Season well.

2 Fill a pan one-third full with water and bring to the boil. Lightly oil a shallow, heatproof dish and place on top of the pan. Pour in the egg mixture and steam for 5–10 minutes, until the eggs are firm.

3 Cut the steamed omelette into strips and place these on a plate. Drizzle a little chilli oil over the strips and garnish with coriander leaves.

4 Serve the omelette strips with a dipping sauce, preferably one that is chilli based or has a pungent flavour. Shrimp sauce or chilli sauce are good options.

Variation
If you prefer not to steam the omelette, fry it in a non-stick pan.

oyster omelette Energy 370kcal/1543kJ; Protein 32.2g; Carbohydrate 6.1g, of which sugars 1.3g; Fat 24.6g, of which saturates 4.9g; Cholesterol 481mg; Calcium 322mg; Fibre 0g; Sodium 1573mg.
eggs w. shrimp paste Energy 146kcal/606kJ; Protein 13.5g; Carbohydrate 0.9g, of which sugars 0.6g; Fat 10g, of which saturates 2.3g; Cholesterol 294mg; Calcium 64mg; Fibre 0.4g; Sodium 144mg.

Hard-boiled Eggs in Red Sauce

A perennially popular snack, this spicy egg dish originally came from Indonesia. Served wrapped in a banana leaf, the Malays often eat it with plain steamed rice, sliced chillies, onion and coriander – ideal for a quick, tasty snack or light lunch.

Ingredients

vegetable oil, for deep-frying
8 eggs, hard-boiled and shelled
1 lemon grass stalk, trimmed, quartered and crushed
2 large tomatoes, skinned, seeded and chopped to a pulp
5–10ml/1–2 tsp sugar
30ml/2 tbsp dark soy sauce
juice of 1 lime
fresh coriander (cilantro) and mint leaves, coarsely chopped, to garnish

For the rempah

4–6 fresh red chillies, seeded and chopped
4 shallots, chopped
2 garlic cloves, chopped
2.5ml/½ tsp shrimp paste

Serves 4

1 Using a mortar and pestle or food processor, grind the ingredients for the rempah to form a smooth puree. Set aside.

2 Heat enough oil for deep-frying in a wok or heavy pan and deep-fry the whole boiled eggs until golden brown. Lift them out and drain.

3 Reserve 15ml/1 tbsp of the oil and discard the rest. Heat the oil in the wok or heavy pan and stir in the rempah until it becomes fragrant. Add the lemon grass, followed by the tomatoes and sugar. Cook for 2–3 minutes, until it forms a thick paste. Reduce the heat and stir in the soy sauce and lime juice.

4 Add 30ml/2 tbsp water to thin the sauce. Toss in the eggs, making sure they are thoroughly coated, and serve hot, garnished with chopped coriander and mint leaves.

Variation
For a fusion twist, serve these with a cucumber raita.

Son-in-law Eggs

The fascinating name for this dish comes from a story about a prospective bridegroom who very much wanted to impress his future mother-in-law and devised a new recipe based on the only dish he knew how to make – boiled eggs.

Ingredients

30ml/2 tbsp vegetable oil
6 shallots, thinly sliced
6 garlic cloves, thinly sliced
6 fresh red chillies, sliced
oil, for deep-frying
6 hard-boiled eggs, shelled
salad leaves, to serve
sprigs of fresh coriander (cilantro), to garnish

For the sauce

75g/3oz/6 tbsp palm sugar (jaggery) or muscovado (brown) sugar
75ml/5 tbsp fish sauce
90ml/6 tbsp tamarind juice

Serves 4–6

1 To make the sauce, put the sugar, fish sauce and tamarind juice in a pan. Bring to the boil, stirring until the sugar dissolves, lower the heat and simmer for 5 minutes. Taste and add more sugar, fish sauce or tamarind juice, if needed. Transfer the sauce to a bowl and set it aside.

2 Heat the vegetable oil in a frying pan and cook the shallots, garlic and chillies for 5 minutes. Transfer to a bowl.

3 Heat the oil in a deep-fryer or wok to 190°C/375°F or until a cube of bread, added to the oil, browns in about 45 seconds. Deep-fry the eggs in the hot oil for 3–5 minutes, until golden brown. Remove and drain well on kitchen paper. Cut the eggs in quarters and arrange them on a bed of leaves. Drizzle with the sauce and sprinkle over the shallot mixture. Garnish with coriander sprigs and serve immediately.

Cook's Tip
The level of heat varies, depending on which type of chillies are used and whether you include the seeds.

eggs in red sauce Energy 266kcal/1104kJ; Protein 15.6g; Carbohydrate 7.1g, of which sugars 6.7g; Fat 19.9g, of which saturates 4.2g; Cholesterol 387mg; Calcium 99mg; Fibre 1g; Sodium 739mg.
son-in-law eggs Energy 180kcal/752kJ; Protein 7.3g; Carbohydrate 18g, of which sugars 17.1g; Fat 9.4g, of which saturates 2g; Cholesterol 190mg; Calcium 50mg; Fibre 0.5g; Sodium 666mg.

Rice Cakes with Coconut

These rice cakes take time to prepare but are very easy to make.

Ingredients
150g/5oz/scant 1 cup jasmine rice
400ml/14fl oz/1⅔ cups boiling water

For the dip
1 garlic clove, coarsely chopped
small bunch fresh coriander (cilantro), coarsely chopped
90g/3½oz cooked prawns (shrimp), peeled and deveined
250ml/8fl oz/1 cup coconut milk
15ml/1 tbsp fish sauce
15ml/1 tbsp light soy sauce
15ml/1 tbsp tamarind juice, made by mixing tamarind pulp with warm water
5ml/1 tsp palm sugar (jaggery) or light muscovado (brown) sugar
30ml/2 tbsp roasted peanuts, coarsely chopped
1 fresh red chilli, seeded and chopped

Serves 4–6

1 Rinse the rice in a sieve (strainer) under running cold water until the water runs clear, then place the rice in a large, heavy pan and pour over the measured boiling water. Stir, bring back to the boil, then simmer, uncovered, for 15 minutes, by which time almost all the water should have been absorbed.

2 Reduce the heat to the lowest possible setting – use a heat diffuser if you have one. Cook the rice for a further 2 hours, by which time it should be crisp and stuck to the base of the pan. Continue to cook for a further 5–10 minutes, until the sides of the rice cake begin to come away from the edges of the pan.

3 Preheat the oven to 180°C/350°F/Gas 4. Remove the rice cake carefully and place it on a baking sheet. Bake the rice cake for 20 minutes, until it is crisp, then leave it to cool.

4 Meanwhile, make the dip. Place all the ingredients in a food processor and process to a smooth paste. Tip into a wide serving bowl. Serve the rice cake with the dip. It can either be left whole for guests to break, or sliced or broken into pieces by the cook.

Rice Balls with Four Fillings

Japanese rice is ideal for making rice balls as it is easily moulded.

Ingredients
3 umeboshi, stoned (pitted)
45ml/3 tbsp sesame seeds, toasted
2.5ml/½ tsp mirin (sweet rice wine)
50g/2oz salmon fillet, skinned
50g/2oz smoked mackerel fillet
2 nori sheets, each cut into 8 strips
6 pitted black olives, chopped
fine salt
Japanese pickles, to serve

For the rice
450g/1lb/2¼ cups Japanese short grain rice, rinsed
550ml/18fl oz/2½ cups water

Serves 4

1 Put the rice in a heavy pan. Pour in the water and leave for 30 minutes. Cover tightly and bring to the boil, then simmer for 12 minutes. When you hear a crackling noise, remove from the heat and leave to stand, covered, for 15 minutes.

2 Toss the rice to aerate it. Leave to cool for 30 minutes. Mash the umeboshi and mix to a paste with 15ml/1 tbsp of the sesame seeds and the mirin. Break the salmon and mackerel into loose, chunky flakes.

3 Rinse a cup and shake off excess water. Scoop 30 ml/2 tbsp warm rice into the cup. Make a well in the centre and put in a quarter of the salmon. Cover with rice, pressing down well. Wet your hands and rub them with salt. Turn the rice in the cup out into one hand and squeeze to make a densely packed ball.

4 Wrap the rice ball with a nori strip. Make three more balls with salmon, four with mackerel and four with umeboshi paste.

5 Scoop about 45ml/ 3 tbsp rice into the cup. Mix in a quarter of the olives and mould into four balls. Coat with sesame seeds, but do not wrap with nori. Serve with pickles.

rice cakes w. coconut Energy 152kcal/638kJ; Protein 6.2g; Carbohydrate 25.7g, of which sugars 5.3g; Fat 2.8g, of which saturates 0.5g; Cholesterol 29mg; Calcium 50mg; Fibre 0.7g; Sodium 255mg.
rice balls w. fillings Energy 548kcal/2288kJ; Protein 15.4g; Carbohydrate 90.8g, of which sugars 1g; Fat 13g, of which saturates 2.1g; Cholesterol 19mg; Calcium 108mg; Fibre 1.3g; Sodium 243mg.

Parchment-wrapped Prawns

These succulent pink prawns coated in a fragrant spice paste make the perfect dish for informal entertaining. Serve the prawns in their paper parcels and allow your guests to unwrap them at the table and enjoy the aroma of exotic spices as the parcel is opened, and the contents are revealed.

Ingredients

2 lemon grass stalks, very finely chopped
5ml/1 tsp galangal, very finely chopped
4 garlic cloves, finely chopped
finely grated rind and juice of 1 lime
4 spring onions (scallions), chopped
10ml/2 tsp palm sugar (jaggery)
15ml/1 tbsp soy sauce
5ml/1 tsp fish sauce
5ml/1 tsp chilli oil
45ml/3 tbsp chopped fresh coriander (cilantro) leaves
30ml/2 tbsp chopped fresh Thai basil leaves
1kg/2¼lb raw tiger prawns (jumbo shrimp), heads and shells removed; tails left on
basil leaves and lime wedges, to garnish

Serves 4

1 Place the lemon grass, galangal, garlic, lime rind and juice and spring onions in a food processor or blender. Blend in short bursts until the mixture forms a coarse paste.

2 Transfer the paste to a large bowl and stir in the palm sugar, soy sauce, fish sauce, chilli oil and chopped herbs. Add the prawns to the paste and toss to coat evenly. Cover and marinate in the refrigerator for 30 minutes–1 hour.

3 Cut out eight 20cm/8in squares of baking parchment. Place one-eighth of the prawn mixture in the centre of each one, then fold over the edges and twist together to make a neat sealed parcel.

4 Place the parcels in a large bamboo steamer, cover and steam over a wok of simmering water for 10 minutes, or until the prawns are just cooked through. Serve immediately, garnished with basil leaves and lime wedges.

Grilled Prawns with Lemon Grass

In every market in Vietnam and Cambodia, there is bound to be someone cooking up citrus-scented snacks. The fragrant scent of lemon grass is hard to resist, but check what's cooking first, because the Vietnamese also like to cook frogs' legs and snails this way. The use of aromatic lemon grass for grilling, stir-frying or steaming shellfish is one of the classic features of Indo-Chinese cooking.

Ingredients

16 king prawns (jumbo shrimp), cleaned, with shells intact
120ml/4fl oz/½ cup fish sauce
30ml/2 tbsp sugar
15ml/1 tbsp vegetable or sesame oil
3 lemon grass stalks, trimmed and finely chopped

Serves 4

1 Using a small sharp knife, carefully slice open each king prawn shell along the back and pull out the black vein, using the point of the knife. Try to keep the rest of the shell intact. Place the deveined prawns in a shallow dish and set aside.

2 Put the fish sauce in a small bowl with the sugar, and beat together until the sugar has dissolved completely. Add the oil and lemon grass and mix well.

3 Pour the marinade over the prawns, using your fingers to rub it all over the prawns and inside the shells too. Cover the dish with clear film (plastic wrap) and chill for at least 4 hours.

4 Cook the prawns on a barbecue or under a conventional grill (broiler) for 2–3 minutes each side. Serve with little bowls of water for rinsing sticky fingers.

Cook's Tip

Big, juicy king prawns (jumbo shrimp) are best for this recipe, but smaller ones work equally well if king prawns are not available in your local shops.

wrapped prawns Energy 169kcal/713kJ; Protein 35.4g; Carbohydrate 2.4g, of which sugars 2.4g; Fat 2g, of which saturates 0.3g; Cholesterol 390mg; Calcium 163mg; Fibre 0.2g; Sodium 381mg.
prawns w. lemongrass Energy 97kcal/409kJ; Protein 9.2g; Carbohydrate 8.8g, of which sugars 8.7g; Fat 3.1g, of which saturates 0.4g; Cholesterol 98mg; Calcium 46mg; Fibre 0g; Sodium 897mg.

Soft Shell Crabs with Chilli

If fresh soft-shell crabs are unavailable, you can buy frozen ones in Asian supermarkets. Allow two small crabs per serving, or one if they are large. Adjust the quantity of chilli according to your taste.

Ingredients

8 small soft-shell crabs, thawed if frozen
50g/2oz/½ cup plain (all-purpose) flour
60ml/4 tbsp vegetable oil
2 large fresh red chillies, or 1 green and 1 red, seeded and thinly sliced
4 spring onions (scallions) or a small bunch of garlic chives, chopped
coarse sea salt and ground black pepper

To serve

shredded lettuce, mooli (daikon) and carrot
light soy sauce

Serves 4

1 Pat the crabs dry with kitchen paper. Season the flour with pepper and coat the crabs lightly with the mixture.

2 Heat the oil in a shallow pan until very hot, then put in the crabs. Fry for 2–3 minutes on each side, until the crabs are golden brown but still juicy in the middle. Drain the cooked crabs on kitchen paper and keep hot.

3 Add the sliced chillies and spring onions or garlic chives to the oil remaining in the pan and cook gently for about 2 minutes. Sprinkle over a generous pinch of salt, then spread the mixture on to the crabs.

4 Mix the shredded lettuce, mooli and carrot together. Arrange on plates, top each portion with two crabs and serve, with light soy sauce for dipping.

Cook's Tip

Don't overcrowd the pan when cooking the crabs. Rather cook them in two or three batches.

Steamed Crab Dim Sum

These delectable Chinese-style dumplings have a wonderfully sticky texture and make a perfect appetizer. You can make them in advance, and steam them just before serving.

Ingredients

150g/5oz fresh white crab meat
115g/4oz/½ cup lean minced (ground) pork
30ml/2 tbsp chopped Chinese chives
15ml/1 tbsp finely chopped red (bell) pepper
30ml/2 tbsp sweet chilli sauce
30ml/2 tbsp hoisin sauce
24 fresh dumpling wrappers (available from Asian stores)
Chinese chives, to garnish
chilli oil and soy sauce, to serve

Serves 4

1 Place the crab meat, pork and chopped chives in a bowl. Add the red pepper, sweet chilli and hoisin sauces and mix well to combine.

2 Working with 2–3 wrappers at a time, put a small spoonful of the crab meat and pork mixture into the centre of each wrapper. Brush the edges of each wrapper with water and fold over to form a half-moon shape. Press and pleat the edges to seal, and tap the base of each dumpling to flatten.

3 Cover with a clean, damp cloth and make the remaining dumplings in the same way. Arrange the dumplings on one or more lightly oiled plates and fit inside one or more tiers of a bamboo steamer.

4 Cover the steamer and place over simmering water (making sure the water does not touch the steamer). Steam for 8–10 minutes, or until the dumplings are cooked through and become slightly translucent.

5 Make a dipping sauce by mixing equal amounts of chilli oil and soy sauce in a bowl.

6 Divide the dumplings among four plates. Garnish with Chinese chives and serve immediately with the sauce.

soft shell crabs w. chilli Energy 306kcal/1280kJ; Protein 37.6g; Carbohydrate 10g, of which sugars 0.5g; Fat 13g, of which saturates 1.5g; Cholesterol 144mg; Calcium 262mg; Fibre 0.5g; Sodium 1101mg.
steamed crab dim sum Energy 146kcal/617kJ; Protein 15.3g; Carbohydrate 14.8g, of which sugars 5.2g; Fat 3.3g, of which saturates 0.7g; Cholesterol 45mg; Calcium 35mg; Fibre 0.5g; Sodium 961mg.

Mussels in Black Bean Sauce

Large green-shelled mussels are perfect for this delicious dish, although smaller ones will work just as well. Buy the cooked mussels on the half shell, and take care not to overcook them, or they will become tough and rubbery.

Ingredients

15ml/1 tbsp vegetable oil
2.5cm/1in piece fresh root ginger, finely chopped
2 garlic cloves, finely chopped
1 fresh red chilli, seeded and chopped
15ml/1 tbsp black bean sauce
15ml/1 tbsp sake or dry sherry
5ml/1 tsp caster (superfine) sugar
5ml/1 tsp sesame oil
10ml/2 tsp dark soy sauce
20 cooked (New Zealand) green-shelled mussels
2 spring onions (scallions), 1 shredded and 1 cut into fine rings

Serves 4

1 Heat the vegetable oil in a small frying pan until very hot. Fry the ginger, garlic and chilli with the black bean sauce for a few seconds, then add the sake or sherry and caster sugar and cook for 30 seconds more.

2 Remove the sauce from the heat and stir in the sesame oil and soy sauce. Mix thoroughly, using a pair of chopsticks or a wooden spoon.

3 Place a trivet in the base of a heavy pan, then pour in boiling water to a depth of 5cm/2in. Place the mussels on a heatproof plate that will fit over the trivet. Spoon over the sauce.

4 Sprinkle the spring onions over the mussels, cover the plate tightly with foil and place it on the trivet in the pan.

5 Steam the mussels over a high heat for about 10 minutes or until the mussels have heated through.

6 Lift the plate carefully out of the pan and serve immediately.

Stir-fried Clams with Orange

Zesty orange juice combined with pungent garlic and shallots make surprisingly good partners for the sweet-tasting shellfish. Fresh, plump clams will release plenty of juices while they are cooking, so serve this tangy dish with a spoon, or with some crusty bread so you can mop up all the delicious sauce. You could also serve this with rice or noodles.

Ingredients

1kg/2¼lb fresh clams
15ml/1 tbsp sunflower oil
30ml/2 tbsp finely chopped garlic
4 shallots, finely chopped
105ml/7 tbsp vegetable or fish stock
finely grated rind and juice of 1 orange
a large handful of roughly chopped flat leaf parsley
salt and ground black pepper

Serves 4

1 Wash and scrub the clams under cold running water. Check carefully and discard any that are open and do not close when tapped lightly with a knife or on the worktop.

2 Heat a wok over a high heat and add the sunflower oil. When hot, add the garlic, shallots and clams and stir-fry the mixture for 4–5 minutes.

3 Add the stock and orange rind and juice to the wok and season well. Cover and cook for 3–4 minutes, or until all the clams have opened. (Discard any unopened clams.)

4 Stir the chopped flat leaf parsley into the clams, then remove from the heat and serve immediately.

Cook's Tip

To avoid the risk of food poisoning, it is essential that the clams are live before cooking. Tap any open clams with the back of a knife. Any that do not close are dead and so must be discarded; and any that remain closed after cooking should also be thrown away immediately.

mussels in black bean Energy 218kcal/921kJ; Protein 27.2g; Carbohydrate 5.1g, of which sugars 2.5g; Fat 8.6g, of which saturates 1.2g; Cholesterol 60mg; Calcium 305mg; Fibre 0.5g; Sodium 852mg.
clams w. orange Energy 142kcal/596kJ; Protein 21.4g; Carbohydrate 5.9g, of which sugars 1.6g; Fat 3.8g, of which saturates 0.6g; Cholesterol 84mg; Calcium 121mg; Fibre 1.2g; Sodium 1506mg.

Grilled Stingray Wings with Chilli

Chargrilled stingray is a very popular street snack in Singapore. The grill stalls selling grilled chicken wings and satay often serve grilled stingray wings on a banana leaf with a generous dollop of chilli sambal. The cooked fish is eaten with fingers, or chopsticks, by tearing off pieces and dipping them in the sambal. If you can't find stingray wings, you could substitute a flat fish, such as plaice or flounder.

Ingredients

4 medium-sized stingray wings, about 200g/7oz, rinsed and patted dry
salt
4 banana leaves, about 30cm/12in square
2 fresh limes, halved

For the chilli sambal

6–8 fresh red chillies, seeded and chopped
4 garlic cloves, chopped
5ml/1 tsp shrimp paste
15ml/1 tbsp tomato purée (paste)
15ml/1 tbsp palm sugar (jaggery)
juice of 2 limes
30ml/2 tbsp vegetable or groundnut (peanut) oil

Serves 4

1 First make the chilli sambal. Using a mortar and pestle or food processor, grind the chillies with the garlic to form a paste. Beat in the shrimp paste, tomato purée and sugar. Add the lime juice and bind with the oil.

2 Prepare a charcoal grill. Rub each stingray wing with a little of the chilli sambal and place them on the rack. Cook for about 3–4 minutes on each side, until tender. Sprinkle with salt and serve on banana leaves with the remaining chilli sambal and the lime halves.

Cook's Tip
Banana leaves are available in Chinese and Asian markets, but you could also use lettuce leaves.

Fish Cakes in Banana Leaves

The oily flesh of mackerel is ideal for these spicy cakes.

Ingredients

4 shallots, chopped
1 lemon grass stalk, trimmed and chopped
25g/1oz galangal, chopped
4 macadamia nuts, roasted
4 dried red chillies, soaked in warm water until soft, squeezed dry and seeded
5ml/1 tsp shrimp paste
5–10ml/1–2 tsp ground turmeric
250ml/8fl oz/1 cup coconut cream
15ml/1 tbsp dark soy sauce
10ml/2 tsp palm sugar (jaggery)
450g/1lb fresh mackerel, cleaned, skinned and flaked
4–6 kaffir lime leaves, finely shredded
2 eggs, lightly beaten
salt and ground black pepper
12 banana leaves, cut into pieces about 20cm/8in square
2 limes, quartered lengthways, and chilli or peanut sambal, to serve

Serves 4–6

1 Using a food processor, grind the shallots, lemon grass, galangal, nuts and chillies to a paste. Blend in the shrimp paste, turmeric, coconut cream, soy sauce and sugar.

2 Put the flaked mackerel and lime leaves in a bowl. Pour in the spiced coconut cream and the beaten eggs. Season with salt and pepper. Mix to coat the fish.

3 Lay a square of banana leaf on a flat surface. Place 30ml/2 tbsp of the fish mixture just off centre and fold the sides of the leaf over the top, leaving room for expansion. Secure the package with a cocktail stick (toothpick) threaded through each end. Repeat with the rest of the mixture. Place on a baking sheet.

4 Preheat the oven to 200°C/400°F/Gas 6. Bake the fish cakes for 30 minutes.

5 Serve in the banana leaves with the lime quarters for squeezing and the sambal for dipping.

stingray winges w. chilli Energy 195kcal/823kJ; Protein 30.4g; Carbohydrate 4.5g, of which sugars 4.5g; Fat 6.3g, of which saturates 0.7g; Cholesterol 0mg; Calcium 83mg; Fibre 0.1g; Sodium 249mg.
fish cakes in leaves Energy 235kcal/977kJ; Protein 16.7g; Carbohydrate 6.2g, of which sugars 5.9g; Fat 16.1g, of which saturates 3.4g; Cholesterol 104mg; Calcium 44mg; Fibre 0.3g; Sodium 332mg.

Rolled Sardines with Plum Paste

This Japanese dish celebrates the harvest, when the sardine season peaks.

Ingredients

8 sardines, cleaned and filleted
5ml/1 tsp salt
4 umeboshi, about 30g/1¼oz total weight (choose the soft type)
5ml/1 tsp sake
5ml/1 tsp toasted sesame seeds
16 shiso leaves, cut in half lengthways
1 lime, thinly sliced, the centre hollowed out to make rings, to garnish

Serves 4

1 Carefully cut the sardine fillets in half lengthways and place them side by side in a large, shallow container. Sprinkle with salt.

2 Remove the stones (pits) from the umeboshi and put the fruit in a small mixing bowl with the sake and toasted sesame seeds. Mash to form a smooth paste.

3 Wipe the sardine fillets with kitchen paper. With a butter knife, spread some umeboshi paste thinly on to one of the sardine fillets, then press some shiso leaves on top. Roll up the sardine starting from the tail and pierce with a wooden cocktail stick (toothpick). Repeat to make 16 rolled sardines.

4 Preheat the grill (broiler) to high. Lay a sheet of foil on a baking tray, and arrange the sardine rolls on this, spaced well apart. Grill (broil) for 4–6 minutes on each side, turning once.

5 Lay a few lime rings on four individual plates and arrange the rolled sardines alongside. Serve hot.

Cook's Tip

Sardines deteriorate very quickly and must be bought and eaten on the same day. Be careful when buying: the eyes and gills should not be too pink. If the fish "melts" like cheese when grilled (broiled), throw it away.

Eel Wrapped in Bacon

Firm-fleshed and rich in flavour, eel is delicious grilled, braised, or stir-fried. This is best served with a dipping sauce, a crunchy salad, and jasmine rice.

Ingredients

2 lemon grass stalks, trimmed and chopped
25g/1oz fresh root ginger, peeled and chopped
2 garlic cloves, chopped
2 shallots, chopped
15ml/1 tbsp palm sugar (jaggery)
15ml/1 tbsp vegetable oil
30ml/2 tbsp fish sauce
1.2kg/2½lb fresh eel, skinned and cut into 2.5cm/1in pieces
12 slices streaky (fatty) bacon
ground black pepper
a small bunch of fresh coriander (cilantro) leaves, to garnish
chilli sambal for dipping

Serves 4–6

1 Using a mortar and pestle, pound the lemon grass, ginger, garlic and shallots with the sugar to form a paste. Add the oil and fish sauce, mix well and season with black pepper. Put the eel pieces in a dish and smear them thoroughly in this paste. Cover and place in the refrigerator for 2–3 hours to marinate.

2 Wrap each piece of marinated eel in a strip of bacon, including as much of the marinade as possible.

3 To cook the eel parcels, you can use a conventional grill (broiler), a well-oiled griddle pan, or a barbecue. If grilling over charcoal, you can skewer the eel parcels; otherwise, spread them over the grill or griddle pan. Cook the eel parcels until nice and crispy, roughly 2–3 minutes on each side. Serve with fresh coriander leaves and chilli sambal for dipping.

Cook's Tip

When buying fresh eel, it's worth asking the fishmonger to gut it, cut off the head, bone it, skin it and slice it for you – it makes life a lot easier!

sardines in plum paste Energy 177kcal/740kJ; Protein 20.9g; Carbohydrate 0.7g, of which sugars 0.7g; Fat 9.9g, of which saturates 2.8g; Cholesterol 0mg; Calcium 94mg; Fibre 0.2g; Sodium 121mg.
eel in bacon Energy 460kcal/1911kJ; Protein 39.3g; Carbohydrate 0.8g, of which sugars 0.6g; Fat 33.3g, of which saturates 9.1g; Cholesterol 324mg; Calcium 43mg; Fibre 0.1g; Sodium 651mg.

Scented Chicken Wraps

For sheer sophistication, these leaf-wrapped chicken bites take a lot of beating. They are surprisingly easy to make and can be deep-fried in minutes in the wok.

Ingredients

400g/14oz skinless chicken thighs, boned
45ml/3 tbsp soy sauce
30ml/2 tbsp finely grated garlic
15ml/1 tbsp cumin
15ml/1 tbsp ground coriander
15ml/1 tbsp golden caster (superfine) sugar
5ml/1 tsp finely grated fresh root ginger
1 fresh bird's eye chilli
30ml/2 tbsp oyster sauce
15ml/1 tbsp fish sauce
1 bunch of pandanus leaves, to wrap
vegetable oil, for deep-frying
sweet chilli sauce or chilli sambal, to serve

Serves 4

1 Using a cleaver or sharp knife, cut the chicken into bitesize pieces and place in a large mixing bowl.

2 Place the soy sauce, garlic, cumin, coriander, sugar, ginger, chilli, oyster sauce and fish sauce in a blender and process until smooth. Pour over the chicken, cover and leave to marinate in the refrigerator for 6-8 hours.

3 When ready to cook, drain the chicken from the marinade and wrap each piece in a pandanus leaf (you will need to cut the leaves to size) and secure with a cocktail stick (toothpick).

4 Fill a wok one-third full of oil and heat to 180°C/350°F or until a cube of bread, dropped into the oil, browns in 45 seconds. Carefully add the chicken parcels, 3–4 at a time, and deep-fry for 3–4 minutes, or until cooked through. Drain on kitchen paper and serve with the chilli sauce or sambal. (Do not eat the leaves!)

Cook's Tip
Pandanus leaves are usually available from Asian supermarkets.

Chicken & Vegetable Bundles

Leeks form the wrappers for these enchanting little vegetable bundles. They taste good on their own, but even better with the soy and sesame oil dip.

Ingredients

4 skinless, boneless chicken thighs
5ml/1 tsp cornflour (cornstarch)
10ml/2 tsp dry sherry
30ml/2 tbsp light soy sauce
2.5ml/½ tsp salt
large pinch of ground white pepper
4 fresh shiitake mushrooms
1 small carrot
1 small courgette (zucchini)
50g/2oz/½ cup sliced, drained, canned bamboo shoots
1 leek, trimmed
1.5ml/¼ tsp sesame oil

Serves 4

1 Remove any fat from the chicken thighs before cutting each thigh lengthways into eight strips. Place the strips in a bowl. Add the cornflour, sherry and half the soy sauce to the chicken in the bowl. Stir in the salt and pepper and mix well. Cover with clear film (plastic wrap) and leave in a cool place to marinate for 10 minutes.

2 Remove and discard the mushroom stems, then cut each mushroom cap in half (or in slices if very large). Cut the carrot and courgette into eight batons, each about 5cm/2in long, then mix the mushroom halves and bamboo shoots together.

3 Bring a small pan of water to the boil. Add the leek and blanch until soft. Drain thoroughly, then slit the leek down its length. Separate each layer to give eight long strips.

4 Divide the marinated chicken into eight portions. Do the same with the vegetables. Wrap each strip of leek around a portion of chicken and vegetables to make eight neat bundles. Prepare a steamer.

5 Steam the chicken and vegetable bundles over a high heat for 12–15 minutes or until the filling is cooked. Serve with a sauce made by mixing the remaining soy sauce with the sesame oil.

scented chicken wraps Energy 159kcal/669kJ; Protein 24.5g; Carbohydrate 6.8g, of which sugars 6.6g; Fat 3.9g, of which saturates 0.6g; Cholesterol 70mg; Calcium 10mg; Fibre 0.1g; Sodium 1055mg.
chicken/veg. bundles Energy 450kcal/1891kJ; Protein 46.9g; Carbohydrate 36.2g, of which sugars 16.4g; Fat 14g, of which saturates 2.3g; Cholesterol 105mg; Calcium 131mg; Fibre 10.8g; Sodium 901mg.

Drunken Chicken

As the chicken is marinated for several days, it is important to use a very fresh bird from a reputable supplier.

Ingredients

1 chicken, about 1.4kg/3lb
1cm/½in piece of fresh root ginger, peeled and thinly sliced
2 spring onions (scallions), trimmed
1.75 litres/3 pints/7½ cups water
15ml/1 tbsp salt
300ml/½ pint/1¼ cups dry sherry
spring onions (scallions), shredded, and fresh herbs, to garnish

Serves 4–6

1 Rinse and dry the chicken inside and out. Place the ginger and spring onions in the body cavity. Put the chicken in a large pan or flameproof casserole and just cover with water. Bring to the boil, skim and cook for 15 minutes.

2 Turn off the heat, cover the pan or casserole tightly and leave the chicken in the cooking liquid for 3–4 hours, by which time it will be cooked. Drain well. Pour 300ml/½ pint/1¼ cups of the stock into a jug (pitcher). Freeze the remaining stock.

3 Remove the skin from the chicken, joint it neatly. Divide each leg into a drumstick and thigh. Make two more portions from the wings and some of the breast. Finally cut away the remainder of the breast pieces (still on the bone) and divide each breast into two even portions.

4 Arrange the chicken portions in a shallow dish. Rub salt into the chicken and cover with clear film (plastic wrap). Leave in a cool place for several hours or overnight in the refrigerator.

5 Later, lift off any fat from the stock. Mix the sherry and stock and pour over the chicken. Cover again and marinate in the refrigerator for 2 or 3 days, turning occasionally.

6 To serve, cut the chicken in chunky pieces and arrange on a platter garnished with spring onion shreds and herbs.

Duck Egg Nests

These attractive parcels are usually made using a conical dispenser, but a thin funnel also works well.

Ingredients

4 coriander (cilantro) roots
2 garlic cloves
10 white peppercorns
pinch of salt
45ml/3 tbsp oil
1 small onion, finely chopped
115g/4oz minced (ground) pork
75g/3oz shelled prawns (shrimp), chopped
50g/2oz/½ cup roasted peanuts, ground
5ml/1 tsp palm sugar (jaggery)
fish sauce, to taste
6 duck eggs
coriander (cilantro) leaves
spring onion (scallion) tassels and sliced red chillies, to garnish

Makes about 12–15

1 Using a mortar and pestle, grind the coriander roots, garlic, white peppercorns and salt into a paste.

2 Heat 30ml/2 tbsp of the oil, add the paste and fry until fragrant. Add the onion and cook until softened. Add the pork and prawns and continue to stir-fry until the meat is cooked.

3 Add the peanuts, palm sugar, salt and fish sauce, to taste. Stir the mixture and continue to cook until it becomes a little sticky. Remove from the heat. Transfer the mixture to a small bowl and set aside.

4 Beat the duck eggs in a bowl. Grease a non-stick frying pan with the remaining oil and heat. Using a small hole funnel or squeezy bottle, trail the eggs across the pan to make a net pattern, about 13cm/5in in diameter.

5 When the net is set, carefully remove it from the pan, and repeat until all the eggs have been used up.

6 To assemble, lay a few coriander leaves on each nest and top with a spoonful of the filling. Turn in the edges to make neat square shapes. Repeat with the rest of the nests. Arrange on a serving dish, garnish and serve.

drunken chicken Energy 608kcal/2553kJ; Protein 35.4g; Carbohydrate 52.7g, of which sugars 29g; Fat 17.6g, of which saturates 1.9g; Cholesterol 82mg; Calcium 107mg; Fibre 3.7g; Sodium 97mg.
duck egg nests Energy 90kcal/376kJ; Protein 6.1g; Carbohydrate 1.1g, of which sugars 0.8g; Fat 6.9g, of which saturates 1.4g; Cholesterol 151mg; Calcium 23mg; Fibre 0.3g; Sodium 43mg.

Crispy Pork Balls

These crispy balls make a delicious party food.

Ingredients

4 slices of white bread, crusts removed
5ml/1 tsp olive oil
225g/8oz skinless, boneless pork meat, roughly chopped
50g/2oz/⅓ cup drained, canned water chestnuts
2 fresh red chillies, seeded and roughly chopped
1 egg white
10g/¼oz/¼ cup fresh coriander (cilantro) leaves
5ml/1 tsp cornflour (cornstarch)
2.5ml/½ tsp salt
1.5ml/¼ tsp ground white pepper
30ml/2 tbsp light soy sauce
5ml/1 tsp caster (superfine) sugar
30ml/2 tbsp rice vinegar
2.5ml/½ tsp chilli oil
shredded red chillies and fresh coriander (cilantro) sprigs

Serves 4–6

1 Preheat the oven to 120°C/250°F/Gas ½. Brush the bread slices with olive oil and cut them into 5mm/¼in cubes. Spread over a baking sheet and bake for 15 minutes until dry and crisp.

2 Meanwhile, mix together the pork meat, water chestnuts and chillies in a food processor. Process to a coarse paste.

3 Add the egg white, coriander, cornflour, salt, pepper and half the soy sauce. Process for 30 seconds. Scrape into a bowl, cover and set aside.

4 Remove the toasted bread cubes from the oven and set them aside. Raise the oven temperature to 200°C/400°F/Gas 6. Shape the pork mixture into 12 balls.

5 Crush the toasted bread cubes and coat the pork balls in the crumbs. Place on a baking sheet and bake for about 20 minutes or until the pork filling is cooked.

6 In a small bowl, mix the remaining soy sauce with the caster sugar, rice vinegar and chilli oil. Serve the sauce with the pork balls, garnished with shredded chillies and coriander sprigs.

Pork-stuffed Green Peppers

Small, thin-skinned peppers are best for this traditional Chinese dish.

Ingredients

225g/8oz minced (ground) pork
4–6 drained canned water chestnuts, finely chopped
2 spring onions (scallions), finely chopped
2.5ml/½ tsp finely chopped fresh root ginger
15ml/1 tbsp light soy sauce
15ml/1 tbsp Chinese rice wine or dry sherry
3–4 green (bell) peppers
15ml/1 tbsp cornflour (cornstarch)
oil for deep-frying

For the sauce

30ml/2 tbsp light soy sauce
5ml/1 tsp soft light brown sugar
1–2 fresh red chillies, finely chopped
75ml/5 tbsp ham stock or water

Serves 4

1 Mix the minced pork, chopped water chestnuts, spring onions and ginger. Add the soy sauce and wine or sherry and work them into the pork mixture so that they are evenly distributed.

2 Cut the peppers in half lengthways and remove the cores and seeds. If the peppers are large, halve them again to make quarters. Stuff the peppers with the pork mixture, pressing it down firmly. Sprinkle a little cornflour over the filled peppers.

3 Heat the oil for deep-frying in a wok, or use a deep-fryer. Using a spider or a large slotted spoon, carefully add the stuffed peppers, meat-side down, and fry them for 2–3 minutes. If you have cut the peppers into quarters, you will probably need to do this in batches. Lift out and drain on kitchen paper.

4 Let the oil cool slightly, then pour most of it into a separate pan and set aside. Heat the oil remaining in the wok and add the peppers, this time placing them meat-side up. Add the sauce ingredients, shivering the wok so they do not stick to the bottom, and braise the peppers for 2–3 minutes. Lift them on to a serving dish, meat-side up, pour the sauce over and serve.

crispy pork balls Energy 161kcal/676kJ; Protein 12.9g; Carbohydrate 15g, of which sugars 7.1g; Fat 5.9g, of which saturates 1.3g; Cholesterol 55mg; Calcium 19mg; Fibre 0.4g; Sodium 446mg.
pork-stuffed peppers Energy 198kcal/825kJ; Protein 12.5g; Carbohydrate 4.7g, of which sugars 4.3g; Fat 14.2g, of which saturates 3.1g; Cholesterol 37mg; Calcium 26mg; Fibre 2.3g; Sodium 942mg.

Lion's Head Meat Balls

These larger-than-usual pork balls are first fried, then simmered in stock. They are often served with a fringe of greens such as pak choi to represent the lion's mane.

Ingredients
450g/1lb lean pork, minced (ground) finely with a little fat
4–6 drained canned water chestnuts, finely chopped
5ml/1 tsp finely chopped fresh root ginger
1 small onion, finely chopped
30ml/2 tbsp dark soy sauce
beaten egg, to bind
30ml/2 tbsp cornflour (cornstarch), seasoned with salt and ground black pepper
30ml/2 tbsp groundnut (peanut) oil
300ml/½ pint/1¼ cups chicken stock
2.5ml/½ tsp sugar
115g/4oz pak choi (bok choy), stalks trimmed and the leaves rinsed
salt and ground black pepper

Serves 2–3

1 Mix the pork, water chestnuts, ginger and onion with 15ml/1 tbsp of the soy sauce in a bowl. Add salt and pepper to taste, stir in enough beaten egg to bind, then form into 8 or 9 balls. Toss a little of the cornflour into the bowl and make a paste with the remaining cornflour and water.

2 Heat the oil in a large frying pan and brown the meat balls all over. Using a slotted spoon, transfer the meat balls to a wok or deep frying pan.

3 Add the stock, sugar and the remaining soy sauce to the oil that is left in the pan. Heat gently, stirring to incorporate the sediment on the bottom of the pan. Pour over the meat balls, cover and simmer for 20–25 minutes.

4 Increase the heat and add the pak choi. Continue to cook for 2–3 minutes or until the leaves are just wilted.

5 Lift out the greens and arrange on a serving platter. Top with the meat balls and keep hot. Stir the cornflour paste into the sauce. Bring to the boil, stirring, until it thickens. Pour over the meat balls and serve immediately.

Dry-cooked Pork Strips

This very simple dish is quick and light on a hot day. Pork, chicken, prawns and squid can all be cooked this way. With the lettuce and herbs, the pork strips make a very flavoursome snack, but you can also serve them with a dipping sauce.

Ingredients
15ml/1 tbsp groundnut (peanut) oil
30ml/2 tbsp fish sauce
30ml/2 tbsp soy sauce
5ml/1 tsp sugar
225g/8oz pork fillet (tenderloin), cut into thin, bitesize strips
8 lettuce leaves
shreds of spring onion (scallion)
chilli oil, for drizzling
fresh coriander (cilantro) leaves
a handful of fresh mint leaves

Serves 2–4

1 In a wok or heavy pan, heat the oil, fish sauce and soy sauce with the sugar. Add the pork and stir-fry over a medium heat, until all the liquid has evaporated. Cook the pork until it turns brown, almost caramelized, but not burnt.

2 For a light snack, serve the dry-cooked pork strips with a few salad leaves and add a few shreds of spring onion (scallion).

3 For wraps, drop a few strips onto large lettuce leaves, drizzle a little chilli oil over the top, add a few coriander and mint leaves, wrap them up and serve immediately. These make good finger food.

Cook's Tip
"Dry-cooking" usually refers to the large-scale reduction of the liquid content during cooking, rather than an absence of liquid.

Variation
Try serving the pork strips on basil leaves or flat leaf parsley, sprinkled with sliced red onion.

lion's head meat balls Energy 326kcal/1363kJ; Protein 35.2g; Carbohydrate 13.1g, of which sugars 3.3g; Fat 15g, of which saturates 3.4g; Cholesterol 139mg; Calcium 91mg; Fibre 1.1g; Sodium 893mg.
dry-cooked pork strips Energy 104kcal/435kJ; Protein 12.5g; Carbohydrate 2.1g, of which sugars 2g; Fat 5.1g, of which saturates 1.2g; Cholesterol 35mg; Calcium 13mg; Fibre 0.2g; Sodium 574mg.

Roasted Coconut Cashew Nuts

Serve these wok-fried hot and sweet cashew nuts in paper or cellophane cones at parties. Not only do they look enticing and taste terrific, but the cones help to keep your guests' clothes and hands clean and can simply be crumpled up and thrown away afterwards.

Ingredients

15ml/1 tbsp groundnut (peanut) oil
30ml/2 tbsp clear honey
250g/9oz/2 cups cashew nuts
115g/4oz/1⅓ cups desiccated (dry unsweetened) coconut
2 small fresh red chillies, seeded and finely chopped
salt and ground black pepper

Serves 6–8

1 Heat the oil in a wok or large frying pan and then stir in the honey. After a few seconds add the nuts and coconut and stir-fry until both are golden brown.

2 Add the chillies, with salt and pepper to taste. Toss until all the ingredients are well mixed. Serve warm or cooled in paper cones or on saucers.

Cook's Tip
When preparing chillies, it is a good idea to wear rubber gloves to avoid getting capsaicin on your hands. This chemical, which is concentrated in chilli seeds and pith, is a strong irritant and will cause a burning sensation if it comes into contact with delicate skin. If you don't wear gloves, wash your hands with soap after handling chillies.

Variations
Whole almonds also work well if you cannot get hold of any cashews, but for the a more economical snack, simply roast whole unsalted peanuts using the method described here.

Fried Dried Anchovies with Peanuts

The Malays and Peranakans love fried dried anchovies. Generally, they are served as a snack with bread or as an accompaniment to coconut rice. The Malays also enjoy them with rice porridge, for breakfast.

Ingredients

4 shallots, chopped
2 garlic cloves, chopped
4 dried red chillies, soaked in warm water until soft, seeded and chopped
30ml/2 tbsp tamarind pulp, soaked in 150ml/¼ pint/⅔ cup water until soft
vegetable oil, for deep-frying
115g/4oz/1 cup peanuts
200g/7oz dried anchovies, heads removed, washed and drained
30ml/2 tbsp sugar
bread or rice, to serve

Serves 4

1 Using a mortar and pestle or food processor, grind the shallots, garlic and chillies to a coarse paste.

2 Squeeze the tamarind pulp to help soften it in the water and press it through a sieve (strainer). Measure out 120ml/4floz/½ cup of the tamarind water.

3 Heat enough oil for deep-frying in a wok. Lower the heat and deep-fry the peanuts in a wire basket, until they colour. Drain them well on kitchen paper. Add the anchovies to the oil and deep-fry until brown and crisp. Drain the anchovies on kitchen paper.

4 Pour out most of the oil from the wok, reserving 30ml/2 tbsp. Stir in the spice paste and fry. Add the sugar, anchovies and peanuts. Gradually stir in the tamarind water, so the mixture remains dry. Serve hot or cold with bread or rice.

Cook's Tip
Fresh chillies can be used instead of dried. Remove the skins by placing them under a hot grill (broiler) until the skins blacken and can be pulled off. Discard the seeds.

roasted cashew nuts Energy 301kcal/1247kJ; Protein 7.2g; Carbohydrate 9.7g, of which sugars 5.5g; Fat 26.2g, of which saturates 11.1g; Cholesterol 0mg; Calcium 14mg; Fibre 3g; Sodium 95mg.
anchovies w. peanuts Energy 338kcal/1400kJ; Protein 17g; Carbohydrate 4.8g, of which sugars 2.6g; Fat 28g, of which saturates 4.4g; Cholesterol 24mg; Calcium 134mg; Fibre 2g; Sodium 1475mg.

Spiced Noodle Pancakes

The delicate rice noodles puff up in the hot oil to give a fabulous crunchy bite that melts in the mouth. For maximum enjoyment, serve the golden pancakes as soon as they are cooked and savour the subtle blend of spices and wonderfully crisp texture.

Ingredients

150g/5oz dried thin rice noodles
1 fresh red chilli, finely diced
10ml/2 tsp garlic salt
5ml/1 tsp ground ginger
¼ small red onion, very finely diced
5ml/1 tsp finely chopped lemon grass
5ml/1 tsp ground cumin
5ml/1 tsp ground coriander
large pinch of ground turmeric
salt
vegetable oil, for frying
sweet chilli sauce, for dipping

Serves 4

1 Roughly break up the noodles and place in a large bowl. Pour over enough boiling water to cover, and soak for 4–5 minutes. Drain and rinse under cold water. Dry on kitchen paper.

2 Transfer the noodles to a bowl and add the chilli, garlic salt, ground ginger, red onion, lemon grass, ground cumin, coriander and turmeric. Toss well to mix, and season with salt.

3 Heat 5–6cm/2–2½in oil in a wok. Working in batches, drop tablespoons of the noodle mixture into the oil. Flatten using the back of a skimmer and cook for 1–2 minutes on each side until crisp and golden. Lift out from the wok.

4 Drain the noodle pancakes on kitchen paper and carefully transfer to a plate or deep bowl. Serve immediately with the chilli sauce for dipping.

Cook's Tip
For deep-frying, choose very thin rice noodles. These can be cooked dry, but here are soaked and seasoned first.

Coconut Chips

Coconut chips are a tasty nibble to serve with drinks. The chips can be sliced ahead of time and frozen (without salt), on open trays. When frozen, simply shake into plastic boxes. You can then take out as many as you wish for the party.

Ingredients

1 fresh coconut
salt

Serves 8

1 Preheat the oven to 160°C/325°F/Gas 3. First drain the coconut juice, either by piercing one of the coconut eyes with a sharp instrument or by breaking it carefully.

2 Lay the coconut on a board and hit the centre sharply with a hammer. The shell should break cleanly in two.

3 Having opened the coconut, use a broad-bladed knife to ease the flesh away from the hard outer shell. Taste a piece of the flesh just to make sure it is fresh. Peel away the brown skin with a potato peeler, if you like.

4 Slice the coconut flesh into wafer-thin shavings, using a food processor, mandoline or sharp knife. Sprinkle the shavings evenly all over one or two baking sheets and sprinkle with salt. Bake for about 25–30 minutes or until crisp, turning them from time to time. Cool and serve. Any leftovers can be stored in airtight containers.

Cook's Tip
This is the kind of recipe where the slicing blade on a food processor comes into its own. It is worth preparing two or three coconuts at a time, and freezing, surplus chips. The chips can be cooked from frozen, but will need to be spread out well on the baking sheets, before being salted. Allow a little longer for frozen chips to cook.

noodle pancakes Energy 248kcal/1031kJ; Protein 2.4g; Carbohydrate 32.7g, of which sugars 0.9g; Fat 11.5g, of which saturates 1.3g; Cholesterol 0mg; Calcium 32mg; Fibre 1.1g; Sodium 22mg.
coconut chips Energy 41kcal/178kJ; Protein 0.6g; Carbohydrate 9.2g, of which sugars 9.2g; Fat 0.6g, of which saturates 0.4g; Cholesterol 0mg; Calcium 54mg; Fibre 0g; Sodium 206mg.

Deep-fried Tofu Balls

There are many variations of these tasty tofu balls.

Ingredients

2 x 300g/11oz packets firm tofu
½ small carrot, diced
6 green beans, chopped
2 large (US extra large) eggs
30ml/2 tbsp sake
10ml/2 tsp mirin (sweet rice wine)
5ml/1 tsp salt
10ml/2 tsp soy sauce
pinch of caster (superfine) sugar
vegetable oil, for deep-frying

For the lime sauce

45ml/3 tbsp soy sauce
juice of ½ lime
5ml/1 tsp rice vinegar

To garnish

300g/11oz mooli (daikon), peeled
2 dried red chillies, halved and seeded
4 chives, finely chopped

Makes 16

1 Drain the tofu and wrap it in kitchen paper. Set a large plate with a weight, on top and leave for 2 hours, or until it loses most of its liquid. Make the lime sauce by mixing all the ingredients in a bowl.

2 Cut the mooli for the garnish into 4cm/1½in thick slices. Make 3–4 holes in each slice with a skewer and insert chilli pieces into the holes. Leave for 15 minutes, then grate the mooli finely. Cook the carrot and beans for 1 minute in boiling water, then drain well.

3 In a food processor, process the tofu, eggs, sake, mirin, salt, soy sauce and sugar until smooth. Transfer to a bowl and mix in the carrot and beans. Oil your hands and shape the mixture into 16 little balls.

4 Deep-fry the tofu balls in oil until they are crisp and golden. Drain on kitchen paper.

5 Arrange on a serving plate and sprinkle with chives. Put 30ml/2 tbsp grated mooli in each of four small bowls. Mix the lime sauce ingredients in a serving bowl. Serve the balls with the lime sauce to be mixed with grated mooli by each guest.

Curried Sweet Potato Balls

These sweet potato balls, with roots in Chinese and South-east Asian cooking, are delicious dipped in a fiery red chilli sauce, fried black chilli sauce or hot peanut dipping sauce. Simple to make they are ideal for serving as a nibble with a drink.

Ingredients

450g/1lb sweet potatoes or taro root, boiled or baked, and peeled
30ml/2 tbsp sugar
15ml/1 tbsp Indian curry powder or spice blend of your choice
25g/1oz fresh root ginger, peeled and grated
150g/5oz/1¼ cups glutinous rice flour or plain (all-purpose) flour
salt
sesame seeds or poppy seeds
vegetable oil, for deep-frying
dipping sauce, to serve

Serves 4

1 In a bowl, mash the cooked sweet potatoes or taro root. Beat in the sugar, curry powder and ginger. Add the rice flour (sift it if you are using plain flour) and salt, and work into a stiff dough – add more flour if necessary.

2 Pull off lumps of the dough and mould them into small balls – you should be able to make roughly 24 balls. Roll the balls on a bed of sesame seeds or poppy seeds until they are completely coated.

3 Heat enough oil for deep-frying in a wok. Fry the sweet potato balls in batches, until golden. Drain on kitchen paper. Serve the balls with wooden skewers to make it easier to dip them into a dipping sauce of your choice.

Variation

Also known as "dasheen", taro root is a starchy tuber cultivated in many parts of Asia. If you opt to use it instead of the sweet potato in this recipe, you may need to add more sugar as it has a much nuttier taste when cooked.

deep-fried tofu balls Energy 40kcal/164kJ; Protein 3.9g; Carbohydrate 1.1g, of which sugars 0.9g; Fat 2.2g, of which saturates 0.4g; Cholesterol 24mg; Calcium 187mg; Fibre 0.3g; Sodium 380mg.
sweet potato balls Energy 354kcal/1495kJ; Protein 4.9g; Carbohydrate 61g, of which sugars 14.8g; Fat 11.8g, of which saturates 1.5g; Cholesterol 0mg; Calcium 84mg; Fibre 3.9g; Sodium 47mg.

Fried Prawn Balls

When the moon waxes in September, the Japanese celebrate the arrival of autumn by making an offering to the moon. The dishes offered, such as tiny rice dumplings, sweet chestnuts and these Shinjyo, should all be round in shape.

Ingredients

150g/5oz raw prawns (shrimp), peeled
75ml/5 tbsp freshly made dashi (kombu and bonito stock) or instant dashi
1 large (US extra large) egg white, well beaten
30ml/2 tbsp sake
15ml/1 tbsp cornflour (cornstarch)
1.5ml/¼ tsp salt
vegetable oil, for deep-frying

To serve

25ml/1½ tbsp ground sea salt
2.5ml/½ tsp sansho
½ lemon, cut into 4 wedges

Makes about 14

1 Mix the prawns, dashi stock, beaten egg white, sake, cornflour and salt in a food processor or blender, and process until smooth. Scrape from the mixture into a small mixing bowl.

2 In a wok or small pan, heat the vegetable oil to 175°C/347°F.

3 Take two dessertspoons and wet them with a little vegetable oil. Scoop about 30ml/2 tbsp prawn-ball paste into the spoons and form a small ball. Carefully plunge the ball into the hot oil and deep-fry until lightly browned. Drain on a wire rack. Repeat this process, one at a time, until all the prawn-ball paste is used.

4 Mix the salt and sansho on a small plate. Serve the fried prawn balls on a large serving platter or on four serving plates. Garnish with lemon wedges and serve hot with the sansho salt.

Cook's Tip

Sansho is ground spice made from the dried pod of the prickly ash. Serve the sansho and salt in separate mounds if you like.

Tempeh Cakes with Dipping Sauce

These tasty little rissoles go very well with the light dipping sauce that accompanies them.

Ingredients

1 lemon grass stalk, outer leaves removed and inside finely chopped
2 garlic cloves, chopped
2 spring onions (scallions), finely chopped
2 shallots, finely chopped
2 fresh red chillies, seeded and finely chopped
2.5cm/1in piece fresh root ginger, finely chopped
60ml/4 tbsp chopped fresh coriander (cilantro), plus extra to garnish
250g/9oz/2¼ cups tempeh, thawed if frozen, sliced
15ml/1 tbsp fresh lime juice
5ml/1 tsp sugar
45ml/3 tbsp plain (all-purpose) flour
1 large (US extra large) egg, lightly beaten
salt and ground black pepper
vegetable oil, for frying

For the dipping sauce

45ml/3 tbsp mirin
45ml/3 tbsp white wine vinegar
2 spring onions (scallions), thinly sliced
15ml/1 tbsp sugar
2 fresh red chillies, seeded and finely chopped
30ml/2 tbsp chopped fresh coriander (cilantro)
large pinch of salt

Makes 8

1 Make the dipping sauce. Mix together the mirin, vinegar, spring onions, sugar, chillies, coriander and salt in a small bowl. Cover with clear film (plastic wrap) and set aside.

2 Place the lemon grass, garlic, spring onions, shallots, chillies, ginger and coriander in a food processor or blender, then process to a coarse paste. Add the tempeh, lime juice and sugar and process until combined. Add the flour and egg, with salt and pepper to taste. Process to a coarse, sticky paste.

3 Scrape the paste into a bowl. Take one-eighth of the mixture at a time and form it into rounds with your hands.

4 Fry the tempeh cakes in a wok for 5–6 minutes, turning once, until golden. Drain, then serve with the sauce.

fried prawn balls Energy 41kcal/170kJ; Protein 2.1g; Carbohydrate 1g, of which sugars 0g; Fat 3.2g, of which saturates 0.4g; Cholesterol 21mg; Calcium 9mg; Fibre 0g; Sodium 446mg.
tempeh cakes w. sauce Energy 79kcal/332kJ; Protein 4.5g; Carbohydrate 9.1g, of which sugars 4.3g; Fat 2.3g, of which saturates 0.4g; Cholesterol 26mg; Calcium 192mg; Fibre 0.8g; Sodium 15mg.

Clear Rice Paper Rolls

Pretty as a picture, these transparent rollls allow the filling to be glimpsed through the wrap.

Ingredients

50g/2oz fine rice vermicelli
225g/8oz/1 cup beansprouts, rinsed and drained
8 crisp lettuce leaves, halved
fresh mint and coriander (cilantro) leaves
225g/8oz tender cooked pork, sliced in strips
175g/6oz peeled cooked prawns (shrimp), thawed if frozen
16 large rice-paper roll wrappers
ground black pepper
black bean sauce, to serve

Serves 8

1 Soak the vermicelli in warm water until softened. Drain, then snip into short lengths. Heat a pan of boiling water for 1 minute, drain, rinse and drain again. Tip into a serving bowl. Put the beansprouts in a dish and arrange the lettuce and herb leaves on a platter. Put the prawns and port in separate bowls.

2 Soften the rice papers in water as described on the packet, then place two on each plate. Each guest places a piece of lettuce on one end of a wrapper, tops it with noodles, beansprouts and herbs and adds some strips of pork.

3 The wrapper is rolled one turn and then a few prawns are placed on the open part and the roll is completed and dipped in sauce. The second roll is prepared the same way.

Variation

A simpler version of this recipe uses flavoured minced (ground) pork to fill these rice paper rolls. Begin by heating 15ml/1 tbsp oil in a frying pan, then fry 350g/12oz/1½ cups minced pork for 5–6 minutes, until browned all over. Season well, stir in 30ml/1 tbsp oyster sauce and leave to cool. Use the mixture to fill 8 softened rice-paper wrappers, using the technique described in the recipe above. Serve with chilli sauce for dipping.

Crunchy Summer Rolls

These delightful rice paper rolls filled with crunchy raw summer vegetables and fresh herbs are light and refreshing, either as a snack or an appetizer to a meal.

Ingredients

12 rice-paper roll wrappers
1 lettuce, leaves separated and ribs removed
2–3 carrots, cut into julienne strips
1 small cucumber, peeled, halved lengthways and seeded, and cut into julienne strips
3 spring onions (scallions), trimmed and cut into julienne strips
225g/8oz/1 cup beansprouts
1 bunch fresh mint leaves
1 bunch coriander (cilantro) leaves
dipping sauce, to serve

Serves 4

1 Pour some lukewarm water into a shallow dish. Soak the rice papers, 2–3 at a time, for about 5 minutes until they are pliable. Place the soaked papers on a clean dish towel and cover with a second dish towel to keep them moist.

2 Work with one paper at a time. Place a lettuce leaf towards the edge nearest to you, leaving about 2.5cm/1in to fold over. Place a mixture of the vegetables on top, followed by some mint and coriander leaves.

3 Fold the edge nearest to you over the filling, tuck in the sides, and roll tightly to the edge on the far side. Place the filled roll on a plate and cover with clear film (plastic wrap), so it doesn't dry out. Repeat with the remaining rice papers and vegetables. Serve with a dipping sauce of your choice. If you are making these summer rolls ahead of time, keep them in the refrigerator, under a damp dish towel, so that they remain moist.

Cook's Tip

Rice paper wrappers can be bought in Chinese and South-east Asian markets. You can also add pre-cooked shredded pork or prawn to summer rolls.

clear rice paper rolls Energy 127kcal/534kJ; Protein 11.6g; Carbohydrate 16.5g, of which sugars 1g; Fat 1.5g, of which saturates 0.4g; Cholesterol 58mg; Calcium 36mg; Fibre 0.9g; Sodium 62mg.
crunchy summer rolls Energy 106kcal/445kJ; Protein 3.5g; Carbohydrate 21.2g, of which sugars 4.7g; Fat 0.7g, of which saturates 0.2g; Cholesterol 0mg; Calcium 44mg; Fibre 2.2g; Sodium 15mg.

Rice Vermicelli & Salad Rolls

Here, a hearty noodle salad is wrapped in rice sheets.

Ingredients

50g/2oz rice vermicelli, soaked in warm water until soft
1 large carrot, shredded
15ml/1 tbsp sugar
15–30ml/1–2 tbsp fish sauce
8 x 20cm/8in rice-paper roll wrappers
8 large lettuce leaves
350g/12oz roast pork, sliced
115g/4oz/½ cup beansprouts
handful of mint leaves
8 cooked king prawns (jumbo shrimp), peeled, deveined and halved
½ cucumber, cut into fine strips
coriander (cilantro) leaves, to garnish

Makes 8 rolls

1 Drain the noodles. Cook in a pan of boiling water for about 2–3 minutes until tender. Drain, rinse under cold running water, drain well. Tip into a bowl. Add the carrot and season with the sugar and fish sauce.

2 Assemble the rolls, one at a time. Dip a rice sheet in a bowl of warm water, then lay it flat on a surface. Place 1 lettuce leaf, 1–2 scoops of the noodle mixture, a few slices of pork, some of the beansprouts and several mint leaves on the rice sheet.

3 Start rolling up the rice sheet into a cylinder. When half the sheet has been rolled up, fold both sides of the sheet towards the centre and lay two pieces of prawn along the crease.

4 Add a few of strips of cucumber and some of the coriander leaves. Continue to roll up the sheet to make a tight packet.

Cook's Tip

Make a spicy dip by combining some chopped garlic and chilli with 5ml/1tsp tomato purée (paste) and bringing to the boil in 120ml/4fl oz/½ cup water. Stir in 15ml/1 tbsp peanut butter, 30ml/2 tbsp hoisin sauce, a pinch of sugar the juice of a lime. Simmer for 3–4 minutes, add 50g/2oz ground peanuts, and cool.

Popiah

This Nonya creation is a great do-it-yourself dish.

Ingredients

45ml/3 tbsp vegetable oil
225g/8oz firm tofu, rinsed, drained and diced
4 garlic cloves, finely chopped
4 rashers (strips) streaky (fatty) bacon, finely sliced
45ml/3 tbsp fermented soya beans, mashed
450g/1lb fresh prawns (shrimp), peeled and deveined
225g/8oz jicama (sweet turnip), peeled and shredded
450g/1lb bamboo shoots, rinsed and grated
15ml/1 tbsp dark soy sauce
10ml/2 tsp sugar
4–6 fresh red chillies, seeded and pounded
6–8 garlic cloves, crushed
kecap manis
12 cos or romaine lettuce leaves
1 small cucumber, peeled, seeded and finely shredded
225g/8oz/1 cup beansprouts
2 Chinese sausages, fried and sliced
225g/8oz cooked prawns (shrimp), peeled
225g/8oz cooked crab meat
1 omelette, sliced into thin ribbons
fresh coriander (cilantro) leaves, roughly chopped
12 popiah wraps or Mexican corn tortillas

Serves 4–6

1 Heat the oil in a wok or heavy pan. Fry the tofu until golden brown. Remove from the oil and pat dry on kitchen paper.

2 Fry the garlic and bacon in the oil until they begin to colour. Stir in the fermented soya beans and fresh prawns. Add the jicama, bamboo shoots, soy sauce and sugar. Fry over a high heat to reduce the liquid. Toss in the fried tofu and cook the mixture gently until almost dry. Transfer to a serving dish.

3 Put the remaining ingredients in separate bowls on the table. Place the wraps on a serving plate. To serve, let everyone help themselves to a wrap. Smear the wrap with the chilli and garlic pastes, followed by the kecap manis, a lettuce leaf, a layer of cucumber and beansprouts, and a spoonful of the cooked filling. Add Chinese sausage, prawns and crab meat. Place a few strips of omelette on top with a sprinkling of coriander, then fold the edge of the wrap over the filling, tuck in the ends and roll it up.

rice vermicelli & salad Energy 202kcal/843kJ; Protein 15.4g; Carbohydrate 18.4g, of which sugars 2.7g; Fat 7.3g, of which saturates 1.6g; Cholesterol 52mg; Calcium 27mg; Fibre 1.1g; Sodium 66mg.
popiah Energy 457kcal/1916kJ; Protein 32.3g; Carbohydrate 39.3g, of which sugars 5.8g; Fat 20.1g, of which saturates 4.9g; Cholesterol 213mg; Calcium 396mg; Fibre 4.5g; Sodium 989mg.

Crab Spring Rolls

Chilli and grated ginger add heat to these little treats.

Ingredients

15ml/1 tbsp groundnut (peanut) oil
5ml/1 tsp sesame oil
1 garlic clove, crushed
1 fresh red chilli, seeded and finely sliced
450g/1lb fresh stir-fry vegetables, such as beansprouts and shredded carrots, peppers and mangetouts (snow peas)
30ml/2 tbsp chopped coriander (cilantro)
2.5cm/1in piece of fresh root ginger, grated
15ml/1 tbsp dry sherry
15ml/1 tbsp soy sauce
350g/12oz fresh dressed crab meat (brown and white meat)
12 spring roll wrappers
1 small egg, beaten
oil, for deep-frying
salt and ground black pepper
lime wedges and fresh coriander, to garnish
sweet-sour dipping sauce, to serve

Serves 4–6

1 Heat the groundnut and sesame oils in a clean, preheated wok. When hot, stir-fry the crushed garlic and chilli for 1 minute. Add the vegetables, coriander and ginger and stir-fry for 1 minute more. Drizzle over the rice wine or dry sherry and soy sauce. Allow the mixture to bubble up for 1 minute.

2 Using a slotted spoon, transfer the vegetables to a bowl. Set aside until cool, then stir in the crab meat and season with salt and pepper.

3 Soften the spring roll wrappers, following the directions on the packet. Place some of the filling on a wrapper, fold over the front edge and the sides and roll up neatly, sealing the edges with a little beaten egg. Repeat with the remaining wrappers and filling.

4 Heat the oil for deep-frying in the wok and fry the spring rolls in batches, turning several times, until brown and crisp. Remove with a slotted spoon, drain on kitchen paper and keep hot while frying the remainder. Garnished with lime wedges and coriander and serve with a dipping sauce.

Crackling Rice Paper Fish Rolls

The wrappers hold their shape during cooking, yet dissolve in your mouth when eaten.

Ingredients

12 rice paper sheets, each about 20 x 10cm/8 x 4in
45ml/3 tbsp flour mixed to a paste with 45ml/3 tbsp water
vegetable oil, for deep-frying
fresh herbs, to garnish

For the filling

24 young asparagus spears, trimmed
225g/8oz raw prawns (shrimp), peeled and deveined
25ml/1½ tbsp olive oil
6 spring onions (scallions), finely chopped
1 garlic clove, crushed
2cm/¾in piece of fresh root ginger, grated
30ml/2 tbsp chopped fresh coriander (cilantro)
5ml/1 tsp five-spice powder
5ml/1 tsp finely grated lime or lemon rind
salt and ground black pepper

Makes 12

1 Make the filling. Bring a pan of lightly salted water to the boil; cook the asparagus for 3–4 minutes until tender. Drain, refresh under cold water and drain again. Cut the prawns into thirds.

2 Heat half of the oil in a small frying pan or wok and stir-fry the spring onions and garlic over a low heat for 2–3 minutes until soft. Transfer to a bowl and set aside.

3 Heat the remaining oil in the pan and stir-fry the prawns until they start to go pink. Add to the spring onion mixture with the remaining ingredients. Stir to mix.

4 To make each roll, brush a sheet of rice paper liberally with water and lay it on a clean surface. Place two asparagus spears and a spoonful of the prawn mixture just off centre. Fold in the sides and roll up to make a fat cigar. Seal the ends with a little of the flour paste.

5 Heat the oil in a deep-fryer and fry the rolls in batches until pale golden. Drain well, garnish with herbs and serve.

crab spring rolls Energy 203kcal/844kJ; Protein 15g; Carbohydrate 13.9g, of which sugars 1.9g; Fat 9.3g, of which saturates 1.3g; Cholesterol 74mg; Calcium 94mg; Fibre 1.6g; Sodium 515mg.
crackling rice paper fish rolls Energy 105kcal/438kJ; Protein 5g; Carbohydrate 8.8g, of which sugars 0.7g; Fat 5.6g, of which saturates 0.7g; Cholesterol 37mg; Calcium 36mg; Fibre 0.8g; Sodium 38mg.

Fiery Tuna Spring Rolls

This modern take on the classic spring roll is substantial enough to serve as a main meal.

Ingredients

1 large chunk of very fresh thick tuna steak
45ml/3 tbsp light soy sauce
30ml/2 tbsp wasabi
16 mangetouts (snow peas), trimmed
8 spring roll wrappers
sunflower oil, for deep-frying
soft noodles and stir-fried Asian greens, to serve
soy sauce and sweet chilli sauce, for dipping

Serves 4

1 Place the tuna on a board. Using a sharp knife cut it into eight slices, each measuring about 12 x 2.5cm/4½ x 1in.

2 Place the tuna in a large, non-metallic dish in a single layer. Mix together the soy sauce and the wasabi and spoon evenly over the fish. Cover and marinate for 10–15 minutes.

3 Meanwhile, blanch the mangetouts in boiling water for about 1 minute, drain and refresh under cold water. Drain and pat dry with kitchen paper.

4 Place a spring roll wrapper on a clean work surface and place a piece of tuna on top, in the centre.

5 Top the tuna with two mangetouts and fold over the sides and roll up. Brush the edges of the wrappers to seal.

6 Repeat with the remaining tuna, mangetouts and wrappers.

7 Fill a large wok one-third full with oil and heat to 180°C/350°F or until a cube of bread browns in 45 seconds. Working in batches, deep-fry the rolls for 1–2 minutes, until crisp and golden.

8 Drain the rolls on kitchen paper and serve immediately with soft noodles and Asian greens. Serve the spring rolls with side dishes of soy sauce and sweet chilli sauce for dipping.

Crispy Shanghai Spring Rolls

Crunchy on the outside, succulent in the centre, these are irresistible.

Ingredients

12 spring roll wrappers
30ml/2 tbsp plain (all-purpose) flour mixed to a paste with water
sunflower oil, for deep-frying

For the filling

6 Chinese dried mushrooms, soaked for 30 minutes in warm water
150g/5oz fresh firm tofu
30ml/2 tbsp sunflower oil
225g/8oz minced (ground) pork
225g/8oz peeled cooked prawns (shrimp), roughly chopped
2.5ml/½ tsp cornflour (cornstarch), mixed to a paste with 15ml/1 tbsp soy sauce
75g/3oz each shredded bamboo shoot or grated carrot, sliced water chestnuts and beansprouts
6 spring onions (scallions) or 1 young leek, finely chopped
a little sesame oil

Makes 12

1 Make the filling. Drain the mushrooms. Cut off and discard the stems and slice the caps finely. Slice the tofu.

2 Heat the oil in a wok and stir-fry the pork for 2–3 minutes or until the colour changes. Add the prawns, cornflour paste and bamboo shoot or carrot. Stir in the water chestnuts.

3 Increase the heat, add the beansprouts and spring onions or leek and toss for 1 minute. Stir in the mushrooms and tofu. Season, then stir in the sesame oil. Cool quickly on a platter.

4 Separate the spring roll wrappers. Place a wrapper on the work surface with one corner nearest you. Spoon some of the filling near the centre of the wrapper and fold the nearest corner over the filling. Smear a little of the flour paste on the free sides, turn the sides to the middle and roll up. Repeat this procedure with the remaining wrappers and filling.

5 Deep-fry the spring rolls in batches until they are crisp and golden. Drain and serve at once with a dipping sauce.

fiery tuna spring rolls Energy 171kcal/717kJ; Protein 14.1g; Carbohydrate 11.4g, of which sugars 1.7g; Fat 8g, of which saturates 1.3g; Cholesterol 14mg; Calcium 36mg; Fibre 0.8g; Sodium 825mg.
crispy shaghai spring rolls Energy 38kcal/161kJ; Protein 1.1g; Carbohydrate 6.6g, of which sugars 0.6g; Fat 1g, of which saturates 0.1g; Cholesterol 0mg; Calcium 15mg; Fibre 0.5g; Sodium 88mg.

Lettuce Parcels

Known as Sang Choy in Hong Kong, this is a popular "assemble-it-yourself" treat.

Ingredients

2 chicken breast fillets
4 Chinese dried mushrooms, soaked for 30 minutes in warm water to cover
30ml/2 tbsp vegetable oil
2 garlic cloves, crushed
6 drained canned water chestnuts, thinly sliced
30ml/2 tbsp light soy sauce
5ml/1 tsp Sichuan peppercorns, dry fried and crushed
4 spring onions (scallions), finely chopped
5ml/1 tsp sesame oil
vegetable oil, for deep-frying
50g/2oz cellophane noodles
salt and ground black pepper
1 crisp lettuce and 60ml/4 tbsp hoisin sauce, to serve

Serves 6

1 Remove the skin from the chicken fillets, pat dry and set aside. Chop the chicken into thin strips. Drain the soaked mushrooms. Cut off and discard the mushroom stems; slice the caps finely and set aside.

2 Heat the oil in a wok or large frying pan. Add the garlic, then add the chicken. Stir-fry until the pieces are cooked through.

3 Add the sliced mushrooms, water chestnuts, soy sauce and peppercorns. Toss for 2–3 minutes, then season, if needed. Stir in half of the spring onions, then the sesame oil. Remove from the heat and set aside.

4 Cut the chicken skin into strips, deep fry in hot oil until very crisp and drain on kitchen paper. Deep fry the noodles until crisp. Drain on kitchen paper.

5 Crush the noodles and put in a serving dish. Top with the chicken skin, chicken mixture and the remaining spring onions. Arrange the lettuce leaves on a platter. Toss the chicken and noodles to mix. Invite guests to take a lettuce leaf, spread the inside with hoisin sauce and add a spoonful of filling, turning in the sides of the leaf and rolling it into a parcel before eating it.

Cabbage & Noodle Parcels

The noodles and mushrooms give an Oriental flavour to the cabbage rolls.

Ingredients

4 dried Chinese mushrooms, soaked in hot water until soft
50g/2oz cellophane noodles, soaked in hot water until soft
450g/1lb minced (ground) pork
2 garlic cloves, finely chopped
8 spring onions (scallions)
30ml/2 tbsp fish sauce
12 large outer green cabbage leaves

For the sauce

15ml/1 tbsp vegetable oil
1 small onion, finely chopped
2 garlic cloves, crushed
400g/14oz can chopped plum tomatoes
pinch of sugar
salt and ground black pepper

Serves 6

1 Drain the mushrooms, discard the stems and chop the caps. Put them in a bowl. Next, drain the noodles and cut them into short lengths. Add to the bowl with the pork and garlic. Chop two of the spring onions and add to the bowl. Season with the fish sauce and pepper.

2 Blanch the cabbage leaves a few at a time in a pan of boiling, lightly salted water for about 1 minute. Remove the leaves from the pan with a spoon and refresh under cold water. Drain the leaves and dry them well on kitchen paper. Blanch the remaining six spring onions in the same fashion. Drain well.

3 Fill one of the cabbage leaves with a generous spoonful of the pork and noodle filling. Roll up the leaf to enclose the filling, then tuck in the sides and continue rolling to make a tight parcel. Make more parcels in the same way.

4 Split each spring onion lengthways and use to tie the cabbage parcels together.

5 To make the sauce, fry the onion and garlic in the oil in a large pan until soft. Add the tomatoes, season with salt, pepper and a pinch of sugar, then bring to simmering point. Add the cabbage parcels. Cover and simmer for 20–25 minutes. Serve.

lettuce parcels Energy 237kcal/984kJ; Protein 15.3g; Carbohydrate 7.6g, of which sugars 1.1g; Fat 16.1g, of which saturates 2g; Cholesterol 41mg; Calcium 24mg; Fibre 0.6g; Sodium 41mg.
cabbage & noodle parcels Energy 159kcal/670kJ; Protein 18g; Carbohydrate 9.8g, of which sugars 3.4g; Fat 5.6g, of which saturates 1.4g; Cholesterol 47mg; Calcium 20mg; Fibre 1.3g; Sodium 238mg.

Egg Rolls

The title of this recipe could lead to some confusion, especially in the United States, where egg rolls are the same as spring rolls. These egg rolls, however, are wedges of a rolled Thai-style flavoured omelette. They are frequently served as finger food at parties.

Ingredients

3 eggs, beaten
15ml/1 tbsp soy sauce
1 bunch garlic chives, thinly sliced
1–2 small fresh red or green chillies, seeded and finely chopped
small bunch fresh coriander (cilantro), chopped
pinch of sugar
salt and ground black pepper
15ml/1 tbsp groundnut (peanut) oil

For the dipping sauce

60ml/4 tbsp light soy sauce
fresh lime juice, to taste

Serves 2

1 Make the dipping sauce. Pour the soy sauce into a bowl. Add a generous squeeze of lime juice. Taste and add more lime juice if needed. Set the sauce aside.

2 Mix the eggs, soy sauce, chives, chillies and coriander. Add the sugar and season to taste. Heat the oil in a large frying pan, pour in the egg mixture and swirl the pan to cover the base and make an omelette.

3 Cook for 1–2 minutes, until the omelette is just firm and the underside is golden. Slide it out on to a plate and roll up as though it were a pancake. Leave to cool completely.

4 When the omelette is cool, slice it diagonally in 1cm/½in pieces. Arrange the slices on a serving platter and serve with the bowl of dipping sauce.

Cook's Tip

Wear gloves while preparing chillies or cut them up with a knife and fork. Wash your hands afterwards in warm, soapy water.

Five-spice Steamed Rolls

A great favourite at the hawker stalls in Singapore, these deep-fried steamed rolls are delicious with a dipping sauce.

Ingredients

225g/8oz minced (ground) pork
150g/5oz fresh prawns (shrimp), peeled and finely chopped
115g/4oz water chestnuts, finely chopped
15ml/1 tbsp light soy sauce
15ml/1 tbsp dark soy sauce
15ml/1 tbsp sour plum sauce
7.5ml/1½ tsp sesame oil
10ml/2 tsp Chinese five-spice powder
5ml/1 tsp glutinous rice flour or cornflour (cornstarch)
1 egg, lightly beaten
4 fresh tofu sheets or rice-paper roll wrappers, 18–20cm/7–8in square, soaked in warm water
vegetable oil, for deep-frying
chilli oil, for drizzling
soy sauce mixed with chopped chillies, to serve

Serves 4

1 Put the minced pork, chopped prawns and water chestnuts in a bowl. Add the soy sauces, sour plum sauce and sesame oil and mix well. Stir in the five-spice powder, glutinous rice flour or cornflour, and egg. Mix well.

2 Lay the tofu sheets on a flat surface and divide the minced pork mixture between them, placing spoonfuls towards the edge nearest you. Pull the nearest edge up over the filling, tuck in the sides and roll into a log, just like a spring roll. Moisten the last edge with a little water to seal the roll.

3 Fill a wok one-third of the way up with water and place a bamboo steamer into it. Heat the water and place the tofu rolls in the steamer. Cover and steam for 15 minutes. Remove the steamed rolls with tongs and place them on a clean dishtowel.

4 Heat enough oil for deep-frying in a wok. Fry the steamed rolls in batches until crisp and golden. Drain them on kitchen paper and serve whole or sliced into portions. Drizzle with chilli oil and serve with a bowl of soy sauce mixed with chopped chillies for dipping.

egg rolls Energy 305kcal/1269kJ; Protein 19.2g; Carbohydrate 4.9g, of which sugars 4.5g; Fat 23.6g, of which saturates 5.7g; Cholesterol 275mg; Calcium 48mg; Fibre 0.7g; Sodium 130mg.
five-spiced rolls Energy 278kcal/1157kJ; Protein 20.4g; Carbohydrate 10.8g, of which sugars 1.8g; Fat 17g, of which saturates 3.7g; Cholesterol 158mg; Calcium 61mg; Fibre 0.6g; Sodium 740mg.

Prawn Toasts with Sesame Seeds

This healthy version of the ever-popular appetizer has lost none of its classic crunch and taste. Serve it as a snack, too. It is great for getting a party off to a good start.

Ingredients

6 slices medium-cut white bread, crusts removed
225g/8oz raw tiger prawns (jumbo shrimp), peeled and deveined
50g/2oz/⅓ cup drained, canned water chestnuts
1 egg white
5ml/1 tsp sesame oil
2.5ml/½ tsp salt
2 spring onions (scallions), finely chopped
10ml/2 tsp dry sherry
15ml/1 tbsp sesame seeds, toasted (see Cook's Tip)
shredded spring onion (scallion), to garnish

Serves 4–6

1 Preheat the oven to 120°C/250°F/Gas ½. Cut each slice of bread into four triangles. Spread out on a baking sheet and bake for 25 minutes or until crisp.

2 Meanwhile, put the prawns in a food processor with the water chestnuts, egg white, sesame oil and salt. Process the mixture, using the pulse facility, until a coarse purée is formed.

3 Scrape the mixture into a bowl, stir in the chopped spring onions and sherry and set aside for 10 minutes at room temperature to allow the flavours to blend.

4 Remove the toast from the oven and raise the temperature to 200°C/400°F/Gas 6. Spread the prawn mixture on the toast, sprinkle with the sesame seeds and bake for 12 minutes. Garnish the prawn toasts with spring onion and serve hot or warm.

Cook's Tip
To toast sesame seeds, put them in a dry frying pan and place over a medium heat until the seeds change colour. Shake the pan constantly so the seeds brown evenly and do not burn.

Firecrackers

It's easy to see how these snacks got their name. They whiz round the wok like rockets, and when you take a bite, they explode with flavour.

Ingredients

16 large, raw king prawns (jumbo shrimp), heads and shells removed but tails left on
5ml/1 tsp red curry paste
15ml/1 tbsp fish sauce
16 small wonton wrappers, about 8cm/3¼in square, thawed if frozen
16 fine egg noodles, soaked in water until soft
oil, for deep-frying

Makes 16

1 Place the prawns on their sides and cut two slits through the underbelly of each, one about 1cm/½in from the head end and the other about 1cm/½in from the first cut, cutting across the prawn. This will prevent the prawns from curling when cooked.

2 Mix the curry paste with the fish sauce in a shallow dish. Add the prawns and turn them in the mixture until they are well coated. Cover and leave to marinate for 10 minutes.

3 Place a wonton wrapper on the work surface at an angle so that it forms a diamond shape, then fold the top corner over so that the point is in the centre. Place a prawn, slits down, on the wrapper, with the tail projecting from the folded end, then fold the bottom corner over the other end of the prawn.

4 Fold each side of the wrapper over in turn to make a tightly folded roll. Tie a noodle in a bow around the roll and set it aside. Repeat with the remaining prawns and wrappers.

5 Heat the oil in a wok to 190°C/375°F or until a cube of bread, added to the oil, browns in 40 seconds. Fry the prawns, a few at a time, for 5–8 minutes, until golden brown and cooked through. Drain well on kitchen paper and keep hot while you cook the remaining batches.

toasts w. seeds Energy 392kcal/1635kJ; Protein 19.1g; Carbohydrate 21.1g, of which sugars 1.2g; Fat 25.9g, of which saturates 3.4g; Cholesterol 110mg; Calcium 270mg; Fibre 2.7g; Sodium 558mg.
firecrackers Energy 71kcal/298kJ; Protein 3.2g; Carbohydrate 7.1g, of which sugars 0.2g; Fat 3.5g, of which saturates 0.5g; Cholesterol 25mg; Calcium 20mg; Fibre 0.3g; Sodium 30mg.

Chilli Prawn Skewers

Choose very fresh prawns for this recipe.

Ingredients
16 giant raw prawns (shrimp), shelled with the tail section left intact
1 lime, cut into 8 wedges
60ml/4 tbsp sweet chilli sauce, for dipping

Serves 4

1 Using eight soaked bamboo skewers, thread each with a prawn, then a lime wedge, then another prawn. Brush the sweet chilli sauce over. Grill (broil) until cooked through. Serve immediately with more chilli sauce for dipping.

Tamarind Prawns

The flavour of tamarind is perfect with the prawns.

Ingredients
500g/1¼lb fresh, large prawns (shrimp)
45ml/3 tbsp tamarind pulp
30ml/2 tbsp kecap manis
15ml/1 tbsp sugar
ground black pepper
fresh coriander (cilantro) leaves and 2–4 fresh green chillies, seeded and quartered lengthways, to garnish

Serves 2–4

1 Devein the prawns. Remove the feelers and legs. Rinse well, pat dry and, using a sharp knife, make an incision along the curve of the tail.

2 Mix the tamarind pulp with 250ml/8fl oz/1 cup warm water. Soak until soft, squeezing it with your fingers to help soften it. Strain into a bowl and add the kecap manis, sugar and pepper. Pour over the prawns, cover and marinate for 1 hour.

3 Grill (broil) the prawns for 3 minutes on each side until cooked through, brushing frequently with the marinade as they cook. Serve immediately, garnished with coriander and chillies.

Shrimp Paste on Sugar Cane Sticks

To appreciate the full impact of this classic dish, eat it by itself.

Ingredients
50g/2oz pork fat
7.5ml/1½ tsp vegetable oil
1 onion, finely chopped
2 garlic cloves, crushed
1 egg
15ml/1 tbsp fish sauce
15ml/1 tbsp raw cane or soft dark brown sugar
15ml/1 tbsp cornflour (cornstarch)
350g/12oz raw prawns (shrimp), peeled and deveined
a piece of fresh sugar cane, about 20cm/8in long
salt and ground black pepper

Serves 4

1 Place the pork fat in a large pan of boiling water and boil for 2–3 minutes. Drain well and chop using a sharp knife. Set aside.

2 Heat the oil in a heavy pan and stir in the onion and garlic. Just as they begin to colour, remove from the heat and transfer them to a bowl. Beat in the egg, fish sauce and sugar, until the sugar has dissolved. Season with a little salt and plenty of black pepper, and then stir in the cornflour.

3 Add the pork fat and prawns to the mixture, and mix well. Grind in a mortar using a pestle.

4 Divide the paste into eight portions. Using a strong knife or cleaver, cut the sugar cane in half and then cut each half into quarters lengthways. Take a piece of sugar cane in your hand and mould a portion of the paste around it, pressing it gently so the edges are sealed. Place the coated sticks on an oiled tray, while you make the remaining skewers in the same way.

5 For the best flavour, cook the shrimp paste skewers over a barbecue for 5–6 minutes, turning them frequently until they are nicely browned all over.

6 Alternatively, cook the skewers under a conventional grill (broiler). Serve immediately, while still hot.

chilli prawn skewers Energy 59kcal/247kJ; Protein 11.3g; Carbohydrate 2.6g, of which sugars 2.5g; Fat 0.4g, of which saturates 0.1g; Cholesterol 122mg; Calcium 61mg; Fibre 0.1g; Sodium 242mg.
tamarind prawns Energy 92kcal/387kJ; Protein 14.2g; Carbohydrate 6.1g, of which sugars 6g; Fat 1.3g, of which saturates 0.3g; Cholesterol 48mg; Calcium 121mg; Fibre 0.8g; Sodium 1627mg.
shrimp/sugar cane Energy 256kcal/1066kJ; Protein 17.5g; Carbohydrate 12g, of which sugars 4.8g; Fat 15.7g, of which saturates 5.7g; Cholesterol 239mg; Calcium 85mg; Fibre 0.2g; Sodium 192mg.

Scallops with Ginger Relish

Buy scallops in their shells to ensure their freshness; your fishmonger will open them for you if you find this difficult. The shells make excellent serving dishes.

Ingredients

8 king or queen scallops
4 whole star anise
30ml/2 tbsp vegetable oil
salt and ground white pepper
fresh coriander (cilantro) sprigs and whole star anise, to garnish

For the relish

½ cucumber, peeled
salt, for sprinkling
5cm/2in piece fresh root ginger, peeled and sliced into strips
10ml/2 tsp caster (superfine) sugar
45ml/3 tbsp rice wine vinegar
10ml/2 tsp syrup from a jar of preserved stem ginger
5ml/1 tsp sesame seeds, for sprinkling

Serves 4

1 To make the relish, halve the cucumber lengthways, remove the seeds, then slice the cucumber into a colander and sprinkle liberally with salt. Set aside to drain for 30 minutes.

2 To prepare the scallops, cut each into 2–3 slices and place the scallop with the corals in a bowl. Coarsely grind the star anise using a mortar and pestle and add it with the seasoning. Cover the bowl and marinate the scallops in the refrigerator for about 1 hour.

3 Rinse the cucumber under cold water, then drain and pat dry with kitchen paper. Place in a bowl with the ginger, sugar, rice wine vinegar and syrup. Mix well, then cover with clear film (plastic wrap) and chill until the relish is needed.

4 Heat a wok and add the oil. When the oil is very hot, add the scallop slices and stir-fry them for 2–3 minutes. Place the cooked scallops on kitchen paper to drain off any excess oil.

5 Garnish the scallops with sprigs of coriander and whole star anise, and serve with the cucumber relish, sprinkled lightly with sesame seeds.

Shiitake & Scallop Bundles

A wok does double duty for making these delicate mushroom and seafood treats, first for steaming and then for deep frying.

Ingredients

4 scallops
8 large fresh shiitake mushrooms
225g/8oz long yam, unpeeled
20ml/4 tsp miso
50g/2oz/1 cup fresh breadcrumbs
cornflour (cornstarch), for dusting
2 eggs, beaten
vegetable oil, for deep-frying
salt
4 lemon wedges, to serve

Serves 4

1 Slice the scallops in two horizontally, then sprinkle with salt. Remove the stalks from the shiitake and discard them. Cut shallow slits on the top of the shiitake to form a "hash" symbol. Sprinkle with a little salt.

2 Heat a steamer and steam the long yam for 10–15 minutes, or until soft. Test with a skewer. Leave to cool, then remove the skin. Mash the flesh in a bowl, add the miso and mix well. Take the breadcrumbs into your hands and break them down finely. Mix half into the mashed long yam, keeping the rest on a small plate.

3 Fill the underneath of the shiitake caps with a scoop of mashed long yam. Smooth down with the flat edge of a knife and dust the mash with cornflour. Add a little mash to a slice of scallop and place on top.

4 Spread another 5ml/1 tsp mashed long yam on to the scallop and shape to completely cover. Make sure all the ingredients are clinging together. Repeat to make eight little mounds.

5 Place the beaten eggs in a shallow container. Dust the shiitake and scallop mounds with cornflour, then dip into the egg. Handle with care as the mash and scallop are quite soft. Coat well with the remaining breadcrumbs and deep-fry in hot oil until golden. Drain well on kitchen paper. Serve hot on individual plates with a wedge of lemon.

scallops w. ginger relish Energy 130kcal/542kJ; Protein 12.1g; Carbohydrate 4.9g, of which sugars 3.2g; Fat 7g, of which saturates 1g; Cholesterol 24mg; Calcium 31mg; Fibre 0.3g; Sodium 92mg.
shiitake bundles Energy 812kcal/3396kJ; Protein 45.8g; Carbohydrate 54g, of which sugars 12.6g; Fat 47.8g, of which saturates 7.5g; Cholesterol 428mg; Calcium 279mg; Fibre 7g; Sodium 741mg.

Crispy Salt & Pepper Squid

These delicious morsels of squid look stunning and are perfect served with drinks, or as an appetizer. The crisp, golden coating contrasts beautifully with the succulent squid inside. Serve them piping hot straight from the wok.

Ingredients

750g/1lb 10oz fresh squid, cleaned
juice of 4–5 lemons
15ml/1 tbsp ground black pepper
15ml/1 tbsp sea salt
10ml/2 tsp caster (superfine) sugar
115g/4oz/1 cup cornflour (cornstarch)
3 egg whites, lightly beaten
vegetable oil, for deep-frying
chilli sauce or sweet-and-sour sauce, for dipping
skewers or toothpicks, to serve

Serves 4

1 Cut the squid into large bitesize pieces and score a diamond pattern on each piece, using a sharp knife or a cleaver.

2 Trim the tentacles. Place in a large mixing bowl and pour over the lemon juice. Cover and marinate for 10–15 minutes. Drain well and pat dry.

3 In a separate bowl mix together the pepper, salt, sugar and cornflour. Dip the squid pieces in the egg whites and then toss lightly in the seasoned flour, shaking off any excess.

4 Fill a wok one-third full of oil and heat to 180°C/350°F or until a cube of bread, dropped into the oil, browns in 40 seconds. Working in batches, deep-fry the squid for 1 minute. Drain the crispy pieces on kitchen paper and serve immediately, threaded on to skewers, with chilli or sweet-and-sour sauce for dipping.

Cook's Tip
Keep egg whites in a sealed plastic tub in the freezer, ready to thaw for use in dishes such as this.

Sweet & Sour Deep-fried Squid

This is an example of a dish where the Western influence comes into play – with tomato ketchup and Worcestershire sauce used alongside more traditional ingredients.

Ingredients

900g/2lb fresh young, tender squid
vegetable oil, for deep-frying

For the marinade

60ml/4 tbsp light soy sauce
15ml/1 tbsp sugar

For the dipping sauce

30ml/2 tbsp tomato ketchup
15ml/1 tbsp Worcestershire sauce
15ml/1 tbsp light soy sauce
15ml/1 tbsp vegetable/sesame oil
sugar or honey, to sweeten
chilli oil, to taste

Serves 4

1 First prepare the squid. Hold the body in one hand and pull off the head with the other. Sever the tentacles and discard the rest. Remove the backbone and clean the body sac inside and out. Pat dry using kitchen paper and cut into rings.

2 In a bowl, mix the soy sauce with the sugar until it dissolves. Toss in the squid rings and tentacles and marinate for 1 hour.

3 Meanwhile prepare the sauce. Mix together the tomato ketchup, Worcestershire sauce, soy sauce and oil. Sweeten with sugar or honey to taste and a little chilli oil to give the sauce a bit of bite. Set aside.

4 Heat enough oil for deep-frying in a wok or heavy pan. Thoroughly drain the squid of any marinade, pat with kitchen paper to avoid spitting, and fry until golden and crispy. Pat dry on kitchen paper and serve immediately with the dipping sauce.

Cook's Tip
To avoid the spitting fat, lightly coat the squid in flour before deep-frying. Alternatively, fry in a deep-fat fryer with a lid or use a spatterproof cover on the wok or pan.

salt & pepper squid Energy 346kcal/1462kJ; Protein 31.2g; Carbohydrate 31.3g, of which sugars 2.6g; Fat 11.6g, of which saturates 1.8g; Cholesterol 422mg; Calcium 32mg; Fibre 0g; Sodium 1741mg.
sweet & sour squid Energy 315kcal/1320kJ; Protein 35.2g; Carbohydrate 4.5g, of which sugars 1.7g; Fat 17.6g, of which saturates 2.5g; Cholesterol 506mg; Calcium 39mg; Fibre 0g; Sodium 1361mg.

Crisp-fried Crab Claws

Crab claws are readily available from the freezer cabinet of many Asian stores and supermarkets. Thaw them thoroughly and dry on kitchen paper before coating them.

Ingredients

50g/2oz/⅓ cup rice flour
15ml/1 tbsp cornflour (cornstarch)
2.5ml/½ tsp sugar
1 egg
60ml/4 tbsp cold water
1 lemon grass stalk
2 garlic cloves, finely chopped
15ml/1 tbsp chopped fresh coriander (cilantro)
1–2 fresh red chillies, seeded and finely chopped
5ml/1 tsp fish sauce
vegetable oil, for deep-frying
12 half-shelled crab claws, thawed if frozen
ground black pepper

For the chilli vinegar dip

45ml/3 tbsp sugar
120ml/4fl oz/½ cup water
120ml/4fl oz/½ cup red wine vinegar
15ml/1 tbsp fish sauce
2–4 fresh red chillies, seeded and chopped

Serves 4

1 First make the chilli vinegar dip. Mix the sugar and water in a pan. Heat gently, stirring until the sugar has dissolved, then bring to the boil. Lower the heat and simmer for 5–7 minutes. Stir in the red wine vinegar, fish sauce and chopped chillies, pour into a serving bowl and set aside.

2 Combine the rice flour, cornflour and sugar in a bowl. Beat the egg with the cold water, then stir the egg and water mixture into the flour mixture and beat well until it forms a light batter without any lumps.

3 Cut off the lower 5cm/2in of the lemon grass stalk and chop it finely. Add the lemon grass to the batter, with the garlic, coriander, red chillies and fish sauce. Stir in pepper to taste.

4 Heat the oil in a wok or deep-fryer to 190°C/375°F or until a cube of bread browns in 40 seconds. Dip the crab claws into the batter, then fry, in batches, until golden. Serve with the dip.

Crab & Tofu Dumplings

These little crab and ginger-flavoured dumplings are usually served as a side dish.

Ingredients

115g/4oz frozen white crab meat, thawed
115g/4oz tofu
1 egg yolk
30ml/2 tbsp rice flour or wheat flour
30ml/2 tbsp finely chopped spring onion (scallion), green part only
2cm/¾in fresh root ginger, grated
10ml/2 tsp light soy sauce
salt
vegetable oil, for deep-frying
50g/2oz mooli (daikon), very finely grated, to serve

For the dipping sauce

120ml/4fl oz/½ cup vegetable stock
15ml/1 tbsp sugar
45ml/3 tbsp dark soy sauce

Serves 4–6

1 Squeeze as much moisture out of the crab meat as you can. Press the tofu through a fine strainer with the back of a tablespoon. Combine the tofu and crab meat in a bowl.

2 Add the egg yolk, rice or wheat flour, spring onion, ginger and soy sauce and season to taste with salt. Mix thoroughly with a metal spoon to form a light paste.

3 To make the dipping sauce, combine the vegetable stock, sugar and soy sauce in a serving bowl.

4 Line a baking sheet with kitchen paper. Heat the vegetable oil in a wok or frying pan to 190°C/375°F. Meanwhile, shape the crab and tofu mixture into thumb-sized pieces. Fry in batches of three at a time for 1–2 minutes. Drain on the kitchen paper and serve with the sauce and mooli.

Cook's Tip
Grate the mooli before serving and press it in a sieve or strainer to remove excess liquid.

crips-fried crab claws Energy 224kcal/933kJ; Protein 10.1g; Carbohydrate 16.9g, of which sugars 0g; Fat 12.9g, of which saturates 1.7g; Cholesterol 78mg; Calcium 62mg; Fibre 0.3g; Sodium 256mg.
crab & tofu dumplings Energy 74kcal/310kJ; Protein 6.3g; Carbohydrate 7.8g, of which sugars 3.6g; Fat 2g, of which saturates 0.4g; Cholesterol 47mg; Calcium 132mg; Fibre 0.3g; Sodium 762mg.

Asparagus with Crab Meat Sauce

The subtle flavour of fresh asparagus is enhanced by the equally delicate taste of the crab meat in this classic dish, which is relatively low in saturated fat.

Ingredients

450g/1lb asparagus spears, trimmed
4 thin slices of peeled fresh root ginger
15ml/1 tbsp vegetable oil
2 garlic cloves, finely chopped
115g/4oz/⅔ cup fresh or thawed frozen white crab meat
5ml/1 tsp sake or dry sherry
150ml/¼ pint/⅔ cup semi-skimmed (low-fat) milk
15ml/1 tbsp cornflour (cornstarch)
45ml/3 tbsp cold water
salt and ground white pepper
1 spring onion (scallion), thinly shredded, to garnish

Serves 4

1 Bring a large pan of lightly salted water to the boil. Poach the asparagus for about 5 minutes until just crisp-tender. Drain well and keep hot in a shallow serving dish.

2 Bruise the slices of ginger with a rolling pin. Heat the oil in a non-stick frying pan or wok. Add the ginger and garlic for 1 minute and cook to release their flavour, then lift them out with a slotted spoon and discard them.

3 Add the crab meat to the flavoured oil and toss to mix. Drizzle over the sake or sherry, then pour in the milk. Cook, stirring often, for 2 minutes.

4 Meanwhile, put the cornflour in a small bowl with the water and mix to a smooth paste.

5 Add the cornflour paste to the pan, stirring constantly, then cook the mixture, continuing to stir, until it forms a thick and creamy sauce.

6 Season to taste with salt and pepper, spoon over the asparagus, garnish with shreds of spring onion and serve.

Singapore Chilli Crab

Perhaps Singapore's signature dish could be chilli crab. An all-time favourite at hawker stalls and coffee shops, steaming woks of crab deep-frying are a common sight. The crabs are placed in the middle of the table with a bowl for the discarded pieces of shell, and small bowls of water for cleaning your fingers. Crack the shells, then dip the meat into the cooking sauce. Mop up the spicy sauce with lots of crusty bread.

Ingredients

vegetable oil, for deep-frying
4 fresh crabs, about 250g/9oz each, cleaned
30ml/2 tbsp sesame oil
30–45ml/2–3 tbsp chilli sauce
45ml/3 tbsp tomato ketchup
15ml/1 tbsp soy sauce
15ml/1 tbsp sugar
250ml/8fl oz/1 cup chicken stock
2 eggs, beaten
salt and ground black pepper
finely sliced spring onions (scallions), and chopped coriander (cilantro) leaves, to garnish

For the spice paste

4 garlic cloves, chopped
25g/1oz fresh root ginger, chopped
4 fresh red chillies, seeded and chopped

Serves 4

1 Using a mortar and pestle or food processor, grind the ingredients for the spice paste and set aside.

2 Deep-fry the crabs in hot oil until the shells turn bright red. Remove from the oil and drain.

3 Heat the sesame oil in a wok and stir in the spice paste. Fry until fragrant and stir in the chilli sauce, ketchup, soy sauce and sugar. Toss in the fried crab and coat well. Pour in the chicken stock, bring to the boil, then simmer for 5 minutes. Season.

4 Pour in the eggs, stirring gently, to let them set in the sauce. Serve immediately, garnished with spring onions and coriander.

asparagus w. crab Energy 121kcal/507kJ; Protein 10.4g; Carbohydrate 7.5g, of which sugars 3.9g; Fat 5.6g, of which saturates 1.1g; Cholesterol 23mg; Calcium 84mg; Fibre 1.9g; Sodium 126mg.
singapore chilli crab Energy 276kcal/1144kJ; Protein 12.1g; Carbohydrate 8.6g, of which sugars 8.1g; Fat 21.7g, of which saturates 3.1g; Cholesterol 126mg; Calcium 23mg; Fibre 0.3g; Sodium 674mg

Fish Cakes with Cucumber Relish

These wonderful small fish cakes are a very familiar and popular appetizer in Asia.

Ingredients

8 kaffir lime leaves
300g/11oz cod fillet, cut into chunks
30ml/2 tbsp red curry paste
1 egg
30ml/2 tbsp fish sauce
5ml/1 tsp sugar
30ml/2 tbsp cornflour (cornstarch)
15ml/1 tbsp chopped fresh coriander (cilantro)
50g/2oz/½ cup green beans, thinly sliced
vegetable oil, for deep-frying

For the cucumber relish

60ml/4 tbsp rice vinegar
50g/2oz/¼ cup sugar
60ml/4 tbsp water
1 head pickled garlic
1cm/½in piece fresh root ginger, peeled
1 cucumber, cut into thin batons
4 shallots, thinly sliced

Makes about 12

1 Make the cucumber relish. Heat the vinegar, sugar and water in a small pan until the sugar has completely dissolved. Remove the pan from the heat and leave to cool.

2 Separate the pickled garlic into cloves. Chop the cloves finely, along with the ginger, and place in a bowl. Add the cucumber batons and shallots, pour over the vinegar mixture and mix lightly. Cover and set aside.

3 Reserve five kaffir lime leaves for the garnish and thinly slice the remainder. Put the chunks of fish, curry paste and egg in a food processor and process to a smooth paste. Transfer the mixture to a bowl and stir in the fish sauce, sugar, cornflour, sliced kaffir lime leaves, coriander and green beans. Mix well, then shape the mixture into about 12 5mm/¼in thick cakes, each measuring about 5cm/2in in diameter.

4 Deep fry the fish cakes in batches in hot oil for about 4–5 minutes, until evenly brown. Lift out the fish cakes and drain. Garnish with the lime leaves and serve with the relish.

Crab Cakes with Wasabi

There's more than a hint of heat in these crab cakes, thanks to wasabi, a powerful Japanese condiment, and root ginger. The dipping sauce doubles the dramatic impact.

Ingredients

4 spring onions (scallions)
450g/1lb fresh dressed crab meat (brown and white meat)
2.5cm/1in piece fresh root ginger, grated
30ml/2 tbsp chopped fresh coriander (cilantro)
30ml/2 tbsp mayonnaise
2.5–5ml/½–1 tsp wasabi paste
15ml/1 tbsp sesame oil
50–115g/2–4oz/1–2 cups fresh white breadcrumbs
30ml/2 tbsp vegetable oil, for frying
salt and ground black pepper

For the dipping sauce

5ml/1 tsp wasabi paste
90ml/6 tbsp soy sauce

Serves 6

1 Make the dipping sauce. Mix the wasabi and soy sauce in a small bowl. Set aside.

2 Chop the spring onions. Mix the crab meat, spring onions, ginger, coriander, mayonnaise, wasabi paste and sesame oil in a bowl. Season and stir in enough breadcrumbs to make a mixture that is firm enough to form patties. Chill the mixture for 30 minutes.

3 Form the crab mixture into 12 cakes. Heat the oil in a non-stick frying pan and fry the crab cakes for about 3–4 minutes on each side, until browned. Serve with the sauce.

Cook's Tips

- *Fresh crab meat will have the best flavour, but if it is not available, use frozen or canned crab meat.*
- *Wasabi is often described as horseradish mustard, although this Japanese paste is unrelated to either condiment. It is very hot, so use with caution.*

fishcakes w. relish Energy 83kcal/346kJ; Protein 5.5g; Carbohydrate 5.8g, of which sugars 5.6g; Fat 4.4g, of which saturates 0.6g; Cholesterol 27mg; Calcium 15mg; Fibre 0.3g; Sodium 111mg.
crab cakes w. wasabi Energy 190kcal/795kJ; Protein 16.2g; Carbohydrate 7.1g, of which sugars 0.6g; Fat 11g, of which saturates 1.4g; Cholesterol 55mg; Calcium 35mg; Fibre 0.3g; Sodium 388mg.

Thai Fish Cakes with Egg

These tangy little fish cakes, with a kick of Eastern spice, make a great brunch.

Ingredients
225g/8oz smoked haddock
225g/8oz fresh cod or haddock
1 small fresh red chilli, seeded and finely chopped
2 garlic cloves, chopped
1 lemon grass stalk, chopped
2 large spring onions (scallions), finely chopped
30ml/2 tbsp fish sauce
60ml/4 tbsp thick coconut milk
2 large eggs, lightly beaten
15ml/1 tbsp chopped fresh coriander (cilantro)
15ml/1 tbsp cornflour (cornstarch), plus more for moulding
oil, for frying
soy sauce, rice vinegar and/or fish sauce, for dipping

Makes about 20

1 Remove the skin and any bones from the fish. Set the white fish aside and place the smoked fish in a bowl of cold water. Leave to soak for 10 minutes. Drain and dry well on kitchen paper. Chop the smoked and fresh fish roughly and place in a food processor.

2 Add the chilli, garlic, lemon grass, spring onions, fish sauce and coconut milk, and process until the fish is well blended with the spices. Add the eggs and coriander, and blend for a further few seconds. Scrape into a bowl, cover and chill for 1 hour.

3 To make the fish cakes, coat your hands with cornflour and shape large teaspoonfuls of fish mixture into neat balls, lightly coating each with the cornflour.

4 Heat 5–7.5cm/2–3in oil in a medium pan until it is hot enough to turn a crust of bread golden in about 1 minute. Fry the fish balls, 5–6 at a time, turning them carefully with a slotted spoon for 2–3 minutes, until they turn golden all over. Remove them with a slotted spoon and drain on kitchen paper. Keep the cooked fish cakes warm in a low oven until you have finished frying them all. Serve immediately with one or more of the dipping sauces.

Salmon & Ginger Fish Cakes

These light fish cakes are scented with the exotic flavours of sesame, lime and ginger. They make a tempting appetizer served simply with a wedge of lime for squeezing over, but are also perfect for a light lunch or supper, served with a crunchy, refreshing salad.

Ingredients
500g/1¼lb salmon fillet, skinned and boned
45ml/3 tbsp dried breadcrumbs
30ml/2 tbsp mayonnaise
30ml/2 tbsp sesame seeds
30ml/2 tbsp light soy sauce
finely grated rind of 2 limes
10ml/2 tsp finely grated fresh root ginger
4 spring onions (scallions), finely sliced
vegetable oil, for frying
salt and ground black pepper
spring onions (scallions), to garnish
lime wedges, to serve

Makes 25

1 Finely chop the salmon and place in a bowl. Add the breadcrumbs, mayonnaise, sesame seeds, soy sauce, lime rind, ginger and spring onions and use your fingers to mix well.

2 With wet hands, divide the mixture into 25 portions and shape each into a small round cake. Place the cakes on a baking sheet lined with baking parchment, cover and chill for at least two hours. They can be left overnight.

3 When you are ready to cook the fish cakes, heat about 5cm/2in vegetable oil in a wok and fry the fish cakes in batches, over a medium heat, for 2–3 minutes on each side.

4 Drain the fish cakes well on kitchen paper and serve warm or at room temperature, garnished with spring onion slivers and plenty of lime wedges for squeezing over.

Cook's Tip
When chopping the salmon, look out for stray bones and pick these out with tweezers.

thai fish cakes w. egg Energy 60kcal/250kJ; Protein 6.2g; Carbohydrate 0.9g, of which sugars 0.2g; Fat 3.5g, of which saturates 0.5g; Cholesterol 29mg; Calcium 15mg; Fibre 0.1g; Sodium 152mg.
salmon/ginger fish cakes Energy 83kcal/343kJ; Protein 4.6g; Carbohydrate 1.6g, of which sugars 0.2g; Fat 6.5g, of which saturates 0.9g; Cholesterol 11mg; Calcium 16mg; Fibre 0.2g; Sodium 117mg.

Chicken Teriyaki

A simple bowl of boiled rice is the ideal accompaniment to this subtle Japanese chicken dish.

Ingredients

450g/1lb boneless chicken breast portions, skinned
orange segments and mustard and cress (fine curled cress), to garnish

For the marinade

5ml/1 tsp sugar
15ml/1 tbsp sake
15 ml/1 tbsp dry sherry
30ml/2 tbsp dark soy sauce
grated rind of 1 orange

Serves 4

1 Place the chicken on a board and slice into long, thin strips using a cleaver or sharp knife.

2 Mix together the sugar, sake, dry sherry, soy sauce and grated orange rind in a bowl.

3 Place the chicken in a separate bowl, pour over the marinade and set aside to marinate for 15 minutes.

4 Add the chicken and the marinade to a preheated wok and stir-fry for 4–5 minutes, until the chicken is fully cooked. Serve garnished with orange segments and mustard and cress.

Cook's Tip

Chicken Teriyaki makes a good sandwich filling. Let it cool in the marinade so that it remains moist and succulent. Watercress goes well with the chicken, as would a little pickled ginger.

Variation

This Japanese classic has gained exceptional popularity in the United States, where it is served at food outlets nationwide. Some recipes add fresh ginger, and a tablespoon or honey or maple syrup instead of the sugar to sweeten the marinade.

Grilled Chicken Balls on Skewers

These little morsels make a great low-fat snack.

Ingredients

300g/11oz skinless chicken, minced (ground)
2 eggs
2.5ml/½ tsp salt
10ml/2 tsp plain (all-purpose) flour
10ml/2 tsp cornflour (cornstarch)
90ml/6 tbsp dried breadcrumbs
2.5cm/1in piece ginger, grated

For the yakitori sauce

60ml/4 tbsp sake
75ml/5 tbsp shoyu
15ml/1 tbsp mirin
15ml/1 tbsp sugar
2.5ml/½ tsp cornflour (cornstarch) blended with 5ml/1 tsp water

Serves 4

1 Soak eight bamboo skewers for about 30 minutes in water. Put all the ingredients for the chicken balls, except the ginger, in a food processor and process to blend well.

2 Shape the mixture into a small ball about half the size of a golf ball. Make a further 30–32 balls in the same way.

3 Squeeze the juice from the grated ginger into a small mixing bowl. Discard the pulp. Preheat the grill (broiler).

4 Add the ginger juice to a small pan of boiling water. Add the chicken balls, and boil for about 7 minutes, or until the colour of the meat changes and the balls float to the surface. Scoop the balls out using a slotted spoon and drain on kitchen paper.

5 In a small pan, mix all the ingredients for the yakitori sauce, except the cornflour liquid. Bring to the boil, then simmer until the sauce has reduced slightly. Add the cornflour liquid and stir until thickened. Transfer to a small bowl.

6 Drain the skewers and thread 3–4 balls on each. Grill (broil) for a few minutes, turning frequently until they brown. Brush with sauce and return to the heat. Repeat twice, then serve.

chicken teriyaki Energy 149kcal/630kJ; Protein 27.4g; Carbohydrate 3.8g, of which sugars 3.8g; Fat 1.3g, of which saturates 0.3g; Cholesterol 79mg; Calcium 21mg; Fibre 0.5g; Sodium 70mg.
chicken balls Energy 332kcal/1398kJ; Protein 30.4g; Carbohydrate 29g, of which sugars 7.4g; Fat 9.7g, of which saturates 2.6g; Cholesterol 339mg; Calcium 84mg; Fibre 0.6g; Sodium 325mg.

Spicy Chicken Wings

Whole chickens or just the wings and drumsticks, marinated in spicy or tangy pastes and then grilled (broiled) over charcoal or fried in a wok, are a common sight in the food stalls of Malaysia and Singapore. Spicy wings and drumsticks are very popular as a quick snack, and are often served on their own with a few sprigs of coriander and slices of chilli to munch on.

Ingredients

12 chicken wings
fresh coriander (cilantro) leaves, roughly chopped, and 2–3 fresh green chillies, seeded and quartered lengthways, to garnish

For the spice paste

4 shallots, chopped
4 garlic cloves, chopped
25g/1oz fresh root ginger, chopped
8 fresh red chillies, seeded and chopped
1 lemon grass stalk, trimmed and chopped
30ml/2 tbsp sesame oil
15ml/1 tbsp tomato purée (paste)
10ml/2 tsp sugar
juice of 2 limes
salt and ground black pepper

Serves 4

1 First make the spice paste. Using a mortar and pestle or food processor, grind the shallots, garlic, ginger, chillies and lemon grass to a paste. Bind with the oil and stir in the tomato purée, sugar and lime juice. Season with salt and pepper. Rub the spice paste into the chicken wings, place in a bowl, cover and leave to marinate for 2 hours.

2 Heat a grill (broiler) or prepare the barbecue. Lift the wings out of the marinade and place them on a rack. Cook them for about 5 minutes each side until cooked through, brushing with marinade while they cook. Serve immediately, garnished with coriander and chillies.

Lamb Saté

These spicy lamb skewers are traditionally served with dainty diamond-shaped pieces of compressed rice.

Ingredients

1kg/2¼lb leg of lamb, boned
3 garlic cloves, crushed
15–30ml/1–2 tbsp chilli sambal or 5–10ml/1–2 tsp chilli powder
90ml/6 tbsp dark soy sauce
juice of 1 lemon
salt and ground black pepper
groundnut (peanut) or sunflower oil, for brushing

For the sauce

6 garlic cloves, crushed
15ml/1 tbsp chilli sambal or 2–3 fresh chillies, seeded and ground to a paste
90ml/6 tbsp dark soy sauce
25ml/1½ tbsp lemon juice
30ml/2 tbsp boiling water

For the sauce

thinly sliced onion
cucumber wedges

Makes 25–30 skewers

1 Cut the lamb into neat 1cm/½in cubes. Remove any pieces of gristle, but do not trim off any of the fat because this keeps the meat moist during cooking and enhances the flavour. Spread out the lamb cubes in a single layer in a shallow bowl.

2 Put the garlic, chilli sambal or chilli powder, soy sauce and lemon juice in a mortar. Add salt and pepper and grind to a paste. Alternatively, process the mixture using a food processor. Pour over the lamb and mix to coat. Cover and leave in a cool place for at least 1 hour. Soak wooden or bamboo skewers in water to prevent them from scorching during cooking.

3 Prepare the sauce. Put the garlic into a bowl. Add the chilli sambal or fresh chillies, soy sauce, lemon juice and boiling water. Stir well.

4 Preheat the grill (broiler). Thread the meat on to the skewers. and brush with oil and grill (broil), turning often. Brush the saté with a little of the sauce and serve hot, with the onion and cucumber wedges. Offer the sauce separately.

chicken wings Energy 350kcal/1455kJ; Protein 30.7g; Carbohydrate 2.6g, of which sugars 2.6g; Fat 24.1g, of which saturates 5.9g; Cholesterol 134mg; Calcium 11mg; Fibre 0.1g; Sodium 99mg.
lamb saté Energy 994kcal/4157kJ; Protein 104.1g; Carbohydrate 18.5g, of which sugars 9.4g; Fat 56.6g, of which saturates 26.1g; Cholesterol 380mg; Calcium 74mg; Fibre 3.7g; Sodium 2572mg.

Spicy Pork Spareribs

These make a great appetizer – if slightly messy – to an informal meal.

Ingredients

675–900g/1½–2lb meaty pork spareribs
5ml/1 tsp Sichuan peppercorns
30ml/2 tbsp coarse sea salt
2.5ml/½ tsp Chinese five-spice powder
25ml/1½ tbsp cornflour (cornstarch)
groundnut (peanut) oil, for deep-frying
coriander (cilantro) sprigs, to garnish

For the marinade

30ml/2 tbsp light soy sauce
5ml/1 tsp caster (superfine) sugar
15ml/1 tbsp dry sherry
ground black pepper

Serves 4

1 Using a sharp, heavy cleaver, chop the spareribs into pieces about 5cm/2in long. Place them in a shallow dish and set aside.

2 Heat a wok to medium heat. Add the Sichuan peppercorns and salt and dry-fry for about 3 minutes, stirring until the mixture colours slightly. Remove from the heat and stir in the five-spice powder. Cool, then grind to a fine powder.

3 Sprinkle 5ml/1 tsp of the spice powder over the spareribs and rub in well with your hands. Add all the marinade ingredients and toss the ribs to coat thoroughly. Cover and leave in the refrigerator to marinate for about 2 hours.

4 Pour off any excess marinade from the spareribs. Sprinkle the ribs with the cornflour and mix to coat evenly.

5 Deep fry the spareribs in batches for 3 minutes until golden. Remove and set aside. When all the batches have been cooked, reheat the oil and deep-fry the ribs for a second time for 1–2 minutes, until crisp and thoroughly cooked. Drain on kitchen paper. Transfer the ribs to a warm serving platter and sprinkle over 5–7.5ml/1–1½ tsp of the remaining spice powder. Garnish with coriander sprigs and serve immediately.

Pork Saté with Pineapple Sauce

Children love these lightly spiced kebabs.

Ingredients

500g/1¼lb pork fillet (tenderloin), cubed
salt and ground black pepper

For the marinade

4 shallots, chopped
4 garlic cloves, chopped
5ml/1 tsp ground coriander
5ml/1 tsp ground cumin
2.5ml/½ tsp ground turmeric
30ml/2 tbsp dark soy sauce
30ml/2 tbsp sesame oil
fresh coriander (cilantro) leaves, roughly chopped, to garnish

For the sauce

4 shallots, chopped
2 garlic cloves, chopped
4 dried red chillies, soaked in warm water until soft, seeded and chopped
1 lemon grass stalk, chopped
25g/1oz fresh root ginger, chopped
30ml/2 tbsp sesame oil
200ml/7fl oz/scant 1 cup coconut milk
10ml/2 tsp tamarind paste
10ml/2 tsp palm sugar
1 fresh pineapple, peeled, cored and cut into slices

Serves 4

1 To make the marinade, using a mortar and pestle, grind the shallots and garlic to a paste. Stir in the spices, soy sauce and oil. Rub the marinade into the meat. Cover and set aside for 2 hours at cool room temperature.

2 Meanwhile, prepare the sauce. Pound the shallots, garlic, chillies, lemon grass and ginger to form a paste. Heat the oil in a heavy pan and cook the paste for 2–3 minutes, then stir in the coconut milk, tamarind paste and sugar. Bring to the boil, then simmer for 5 minutes. Season and leave to cool.

3 Using a mortar and pestle, crush three pineapple slices; beat them into the sauce. Soak eight bamboo skewers in cold water. Prepare a barbecue. Drain the skewers and thread them with the marinated meat. Cook over the coals with the remaining slices of pineapple alongside. Char the pineapple slices and chop them into chunks. Grill the meat until just cooked, about 2–3 minutes each side, and serve immediately with the pineapple chunks and the sauce.

spicy pork spareribs Energy 424kcal/1763kJ; Protein 32.2g; Carbohydrate 2.6g, of which sugars 1.3g; Fat 31.4g, of which saturates 9.8g; Cholesterol 111mg; Calcium 33mg; Fibre 0g; Sodium 345mg.
pork saté Energy 306kcal/1286kJ; Protein 28.4g; Carbohydrate 20.3g, of which sugars 19g; Fat 12.9g, of which saturates 2.9g; Cholesterol 79mg; Calcium 48mg; Fibre 2.3g; Sodium 98mg.

Steamed Pork Balls

Bitesize balls of steamed pork and mushrooms rolled in jasmine rice make a fabulous snack.

Ingredients
30ml/2 tbsp vegetable oil
200g/7oz/scant 3 cups finely chopped shiitake mushrooms
400g/14oz lean minced (ground) pork
4 spring onions (scallions), chopped
2 garlic cloves, crushed
15ml/1 tbsp fish sauce
15ml/1 tbsp soy sauce
15ml/1 tsp grated root ginger
60ml/4 tbsp finely chopped coriander (cilantro)
1 egg, lightly beaten
salt and ground black pepper
200g/7oz/1 cup cooked jasmine rice

For the dipping sauce
120ml/4fl oz/½ cup sweet chilli sauce
105ml/7 tbsp soy sauce
15ml/1 tbsp Chinese rice wine
5–10ml/1–2 tsp chilli oil

Serves 4

1 Heat the oil in a wok, then stir-fry the mushrooms for 2–3 minutes. Transfer to a food processor with the pork, spring onions, garlic, fish sauce, soy sauce, ginger, coriander and beaten egg. Process for 30–40 seconds. Scrape the mixture into a bowl, cover and chill for 3–4 hours or overnight.

2 Place the jasmine rice in a bowl. With wet hands, divide the mushroom mixture into 20 portions and roll each one into a firm ball. Roll each ball in the rice then arrange the balls, spaced apart, in two baking parchment-lined tiers of a bamboo steamer.

3 Cover the steamer and place over a wok of simmering water. Steam for 1 hour 15 minutes.

4 Meanwhile, combine all the dipping sauce ingredients in a small bowl.

5 When the pork balls are fully cooked, remove them from the steamer and serve them warm with the spicy dipping sauce.

Pork on Lemon Grass Sticks

This simple recipe makes a substantial snack, and the lemon grass sticks not only add a subtle flavour but also make a good talking point.

Ingredients
300g/11oz finely minced (ground) pork
4 garlic cloves, crushed
4 fresh coriander (cilantro) roots, finely chopped
2.5ml/½ tsp sugar
15ml/1 tbsp soy sauce or kecap manis
salt and ground black pepper
8 x 10cm/4in lengths of lemon grass stalk
sweet chilli sauce or chilli sambal, to serve

Serves 4

1 Place the minced pork, crushed garlic, chopped coriander root, sugar and soy sauce or kecap manis in a large bowl. Season with salt and pepper to taste and mix well.

2 Divide into eight portions and mould each one into a ball. It may help to dampen your hands before shaping the mixture to prevent it from sticking.

3 Stick a length of lemon grass halfway into each ball, then press the meat mixture around the lemon grass to make a shape like a chicken leg.

4 Cook the pork sticks under a hot grill (broiler) for 3–4 minutes on each side, until golden and cooked through. Serve with the chilli sauce or sambal for dipping.

Variations
- *Slimmer versions of these pork sticks are perfect for parties. The mixture will be enough for 12 lemon grass sticks if you use it sparingly.*
- *Sweet and sour sauce can be used instead of sweet chilli sauce, or try a peach chutney for a fusion flavour.*

pork balls Energy 322kcal/1353kJ; Protein 25.8g; Carbohydrate 29.9g, of which sugars 14.3g; Fat 11.8g, of which saturates 2.7g; Cholesterol 111mg; Calcium 39mg; Fibre 0.8g; Sodium 893mg.
pork on lemon grass Energy 132kcal/552kJ; Protein 14.7g; Carbohydrate 2g, of which sugars 1.6g; Fat 7.3g, of which saturates 2.7g; Cholesterol 50mg; Calcium 10mg; Fibre 0.2g; Sodium 317mg.

Bacon-wrapped Beef on Skewers

In northern Vietnam, beef often features on the street menu. Grilled, stir-fried, or sitting majestically in a steaming bowl of pho, beef is used with pride. In Cambodia and southern Vietnam, snacks like this one would normally be made with pork or chicken.

Ingredients

225g/8oz beef fillet (tenderloin) or rump (round) steak, cut across the grain into 12 strips
12 thin strips of streaky (fatty) bacon
ground black pepper
chilli sambal, for dipping

For the marinade

15ml/1 tbsp groundnut (peanut) oil
30ml/2 tbsp fish sauce
30ml/2 tbsp soy sauce
4–6 garlic cloves, crushed
10ml/2 tsp sugar

Serves 4

1 To make the marinade, mix all the ingredients in a large bowl until the sugar dissolves. Season generously with black pepper. Add the beef strips, stir to coat them in the marinade, and set aside for about an hour.

2 Preheat a griddle pan over a high heat. Roll up each strip of beef and wrap it in a slice of bacon. Thread the rolls on to the skewers, so that you have three on each one.

3 Cook the bacon-wrapped rolls on the hot griddle for 4–5 minutes, turning once, until the bacon is golden and crispy. Serve immediately, with a bowl of chilli sambal for dipping.

Cook's Tip

These tasty skewers can also be cooked under a preheated grill (broiler), or over hot coals on the barbecue. Simply cook for 6–8 minutes, turning every couple of minutes so that the bacon is browned by not burned. Serve them as an appetizer ahead of the main course – they are light enough to whet the appetite without spoiling anticipation of the rest of the meal.

Beef Saté

The spicy peanut paste, saté, is a great favourite in South-east Asia and is used for grilling and stir-frying meats and seafood.

Ingredients

500g/1¼lb beef sirloin, cut in bitesize pieces
15ml/1 tbsp groundnut (peanut) oil
1 bunch rocket (arugula) leaves

For the saté

60ml/4 tbsp groundnut (peanut) or vegetable oil
5 garlic cloves, crushed
5 dried Serrano chillies, seeded and ground
10ml/2 tsp curry powder
50g/2oz/⅓ cup roasted peanuts, finely ground

Serves 4–6

1 To make the saté, heat the oil in a wok or heavy pan and stir in the garlic until it begins to colour. Add the chillies, curry powder and peanuts and stir over a gentle heat until the mixture forms a paste. Remove from the heat and leave to cool.

2 Put the beef into a large bowl. Beat the groundnut oil into the saté and add the mixture to the pieces of beef. Mix well, so that the beef is evenly coated, and put aside to marinate for 30–40 minutes.

3 Soak four to six wooden skewers in water for 30 minutes. Prepare a barbecue. Thread the meat on to the skewers and cook for 2–3 minutes on each side. Serve the meat with the rocket leaves for wrapping.

Variations

This is a great barbecue dish that works just as well with pork tenderloin, chicken breast, prawns or shrimp. Jars of saté are now available in many stores but they taste nothing like the homemade paste, which you can pep up with as much garlic and chilli as you like. The beef is also delicious served with a salad, rice wrappers and a light dipping sauce.

bacon-wrapped beef Energy 282kcal/1172kJ; Protein 21.7g; Carbohydrate 1.1g, of which sugars 1.1g; Fat 21.3g, of which saturates 7.1g; Cholesterol 69mg; Calcium 7mg; Fibre 0g; Sodium 745mg.
beef saté Energy 289kcal/1199kJ; Protein 22.3g; Carbohydrate 2.5g, of which sugars 0.9g; Fat 21.1g, of which saturates 5g; Cholesterol 48mg; Calcium 52mg; Fibre 1.4g; Sodium 85mg.

Beef Fondue

The stock for this dish is flavoured with onion, soy sauce, fish sauce and warm spices.

Ingredients

30ml/2 tbsp sesame oil
1 garlic clove, crushed
2 shallots, finely chopped
2.5cm/1in fresh root ginger, peeled and finely sliced
1 lemon grass stalk, cut into several pieces and bruised
30ml/2 tbsp sugar
250ml/8½fl oz/1 cup white rice vinegar
300ml/½ pint/1¼ cups beef stock
700g/1lb 10oz beef fillet (tenderloin), thinly sliced into rectangular strips
salt and ground black pepper
chopped or sliced salad vegetables, herbs and rice wrappers, to serve

For the dipping sauce

15ml/1 tbsp white rice vinegar
juice of 1 lime
5ml/1 tsp sugar
1 garlic clove, peeled and chopped
2 fresh red chillies, seeded and chopped
12 canned anchovy fillets, drained
2 slices of pineapple, cored and chopped

Serves 4–6

1 To make the dipping sauce, in a bowl, mix the vinegar and lime juice with the sugar, until the sugar dissolves. Using a mortar and pestle, pound the garlic, chillies and anchovy fillets to a paste, then add the pineapple and pound it to a pulp. Stir in the vinegar and lime juice mixture, and set aside.

2 When ready to eat, heat 15ml/1 tbsp of the sesame oil in a heavy pan, wok or fondue pot. Quickly stir-fry the garlic, shallots, ginger and lemon grass until fragrant and golden, then add the sugar, vinegar, beef stock and the remaining sesame oil. Bring to the boil, stirring and season with salt and pepper.

4 Transfer the pan or fondue pot to a lighted burner at the table. Lay the beef strips on a large serving dish. Using chopsticks or fondue forks, each person cooks their own meat in the broth and dips it into the sauce. Serve with salad vegetables, chopped herbs and rice wrappers.

Chilli & Honey-cured Beef

When it comes to ingredients, Asian cooks will dry almost anything – fish, chillies, mushrooms, snake, mangoes, pigs' ears and beef are just some of them. Some dried goods are destined for stews, soups and medicinal purposes, whereas others are just for chewing on.

Ingredients

450g/1lb beef sirloin
2 lemon grass stalks, trimmed and chopped
2 garlic cloves, chopped
2 dried Serrano chillies, seeded and chopped
30–45ml/2–3 tbsp honey
15ml/1 tbsp fish sauce
30ml/2 tbsp soy sauce
rice wrappers, fresh herbs and dipping sauce, to serve (optional)

Serves 4

1 Trim the beef and cut it across the grain into thin, rectangular slices, then set aside.

2 Using a mortar and pestle, grind the chopped lemon grass, garlic and chillies to a paste. Stir in the honey, fish sauce and soy sauce. Put the beef into a bowl, add the paste and rub it into the meat. Spread out the meat on a wire rack and place it in the refrigerator, uncovered, for 2 days, or until dry and hard.

3 Cook the dried beef on the barbecue or under a conventional grill (broiler), and serve it as a snack on its own or with rice wrappers, fresh herbs and a dipping sauce.

Variation

This recipe also works well with venison. Cut the meat into thin strips and dry exactly as above. The resulting dish will give you a South-east Asian version of the famous biltong, a dish with Dutch roots created by South Africa's European pioneers. Biltong is often likened to beef jerky, but it is more likely to use game meats, including venison and ostrich.

beef fondue Energy 293kcal/1225kJ; Protein 28.9g; Carbohydrate 10.4g, of which sugars 10.1g; Fat 15.4g, of which saturates 5.1g; Cholesterol 72mg; Calcium 42mg; Fibre 0.5g; Sodium 333mg.
chilli & honey-cured beef Energy 158kcal/659kJ; Protein 17.3g; Carbohydrate 6.7g, of which sugars 6.6g; Fat 7g, of which saturates 2.9g; Cholesterol 43mg; Calcium 6mg; Fibre 0.1g; Sodium 405mg.

Fried Garlic Tofu

A simple and inexpensive recipe that can be quickly and easily prepared to make a tasty and nutritious midweek family supper. In summer, serve with mixed salad leaves or steamed greens and minted new potatoes and, in winter, serve with baked potatoes.

Ingredients

500g/1¼lb firm tofu
50g/2oz/¼ cup butter
2 garlic cloves, thinly sliced
200g/7oz enokitake or other mushrooms
45ml/3 tbsp soy sauce
30ml/2 tbsp sake or lemon juice

Serves 4

1 Wrap the tofu in kitchen paper, place a weighted plate on top and leave for up to 1 hour to drain off excess water.

2 Slice the tofu to make 16 slices using a sharp knife.

3 Melt one-third of the butter in a frying pan. Add the garlic and cook over a medium heat, stirring, until golden, but do not allow it to burn. Remove the garlic from the pan.

4 Melt half the remaining butter to the pan, add the mushrooms and cook for 3–4 minutes, until golden and softened, then remove the mushrooms from the pan.

5 Place the tofu in the pan with the remaining butter and cook over a medium heat. Turn over and cook the other side until golden and the tofu is warmed through.

6 Return the garlic to the pan, add the soy sauce and sake or lemon juice and simmer for 1 minute. Transfer to warm serving plates and serve immediately with the mushrooms.

Cook's Tip
Enoki mushrooms are slender and extremely delicate, with long thin stems and tiny white caps. They have a sweet, almost fruity flavour.

Stir-fried Crispy Tofu

The asparagus grown in the part of Asia where this recipe originated tends to have slender stalks. Look for it in Thai markets or substitute the thin asparagus popularly known as sprue.

Ingredients

250g/9oz fried tofu cubes
30ml/2 tbsp groundnut (peanut) oil
15ml/1 tbsp green curry paste
30ml/2 tbsp light soy sauce
2 kaffir lime leaves, rolled into cylinders and thinly sliced
30ml/2 tbsp sugar
150ml/¼ pint/⅔ cup vegetable stock
250g/9oz Asian asparagus, trimmed and sliced into 5cm/2in lengths
30ml/2 tbsp roasted peanuts, finely chopped

Serves 2

1 Preheat the grill (broiler) to medium. Place the tofu cubes in a grill pan and grill (broil) for 2–3 minutes, then turn them over and continue to cook until they are crisp and golden brown all over. Watch them carefully; they must not be allowed to burn.

2 Heat the oil in a wok or heavy frying pan. Add the green curry paste and cook over a medium heat, stirring constantly, for 1–2 minutes, until it gives off its aroma.

3 Stir the soy sauce, lime leaves, sugar and vegetable stock into the wok or pan and mix well. Bring to the boil, then reduce the heat to low so that the mixture is just simmering.

4 Add the asparagus and simmer gently for 5 minutes. Meanwhile, chop each piece of tofu into four, then add to the pan with the peanuts.

5 Toss to coat all the ingredients in the sauce, then spoon into a warmed dish and serve immediately.

Variation
Substitute slim carrot sticks or broccoli florets for the asparagus.

fried garlic tofu Energy 196kcal/810kJ; Protein 11.5g; Carbohydrate 2.1g, of which sugars 1.4g; Fat 15.8g, of which saturates 7.2g; Cholesterol 27mg; Calcium 645mg; Fibre 0.6g; Sodium 884mg.
crispy tofu Energy 287kcal/1195kJ; Protein 14.3g; Carbohydrate 20.3g, of which sugars 19.5g; Fat 17g, of which saturates 2.1g; Cholesterol 0mg; Calcium 682mg; Fibre 2.1g; Sodium 1075mg.

Spiced Tofu Stir-fry

Any cooked vegetable could be added to this tasty stir-fry but it is always a good idea to try to achieve a contrast in colours and textures to make the dish more interesting.

Ingredients

10ml/2 tsp ground cumin
15ml/1 tbsp paprika
5ml/1 tsp ground ginger
good pinch of cayenne pepper
15ml/1 tbsp caster (superfine) sugar
275g/10oz firm tofu
60ml/4 tbsp olive oil
2 garlic cloves, crushed
1 bunch of spring onions (scallions), sliced
1 red (bell) pepper, seeded and sliced
1 yellow (bell) pepper, seeded and sliced
225g/8oz/generous 3 cups brown-cap (cremini) mushrooms, halved or quartered
1 large courgette (zucchini), sliced
115g/4oz fine green beans, halved
50g/2oz/⅔ cup pine nuts
15ml/1 tbsp lime juice
15ml/1 tbsp maple syrup
salt and ground black pepper

Serves 4

1 Mix together the ground cumin, paprika, ginger, cayenne and sugar in a bowl and season with plenty of salt and pepper. Cut the tofu into cubes with a sharp knife and gently toss the cubes in the spice mixture to coat.

2 Heat half the olive oil in a wok or large, heavy frying pan. Add the tofu cubes and cook over a high heat for 3–4 minutes, turning carefully from time to time. Remove with a slotted spoon and set aside. Wipe out the wok or pan.

3 Add the remaining oil to the wok or pan and cook the garlic and spring onions for 3 minutes. Add the remaining vegetables and cook over a medium heat for 6 minutes, or until they are beginning to soften and turn golden. Season well.

4 Return the tofu cubes to the wok or frying pan and add the pine nuts, lime juice and maple syrup. Heat through gently, stirring, then transfer to warm serving bowls and serve.

Thai Vegetable Curry with Lemon Grass Rice

Fragrant jasmine rice, subtly flavoured with lemongrass and cardamom, is the perfect accompaniment to this richly spiced vegetable curry. Don't be put off by the long list of ingredients, this curry is very simple to make.

Ingredients

10ml/2 tsp vegetable oil
400ml/14fl oz/1⅔ cups coconut milk
300ml/½ pint/1¼ cups vegetable stock
225g/8oz new potatoes, halved or quartered, if large
130g/4½oz baby corn cobs
5ml/1 tsp golden caster (superfine) sugar
185g/6½oz broccoli florets
1 red (bell) pepper, seeded and sliced lengthways
115g/4oz spinach, tough stalks removed and shredded
30ml/2 tbsp chopped fresh coriander (cilantro)
salt and ground black pepper

For the spice paste

1 red chilli, seeded and chopped
3 green chillies, seeded and chopped
1 lemongrass stalk, outer leaves removed and lower 5cm/2in finely chopped
2 shallots, chopped
finely grated rind of 1 lime
2 garlic cloves, chopped
5ml/1 tsp ground coriander
2.5ml/½ tsp ground cumin
1cm/½in fresh galangal, finely chopped or 2.5ml/½ tsp dried (optional)
30ml/2 tbsp chopped fresh coriander (cilantro)
15ml/1 tbsp chopped fresh coriander (cilantro) roots and stems (optional)

For the rice

225g/8oz/generous 1 cup jasmine rice, rinsed
1 lemon grass stalk, outer leaves removed and cut into 3 pieces
6 cardamom pods, bruised

Serves 4

1 Make the spice paste. Place all the ingredients in a food processor or blender and blend to a coarse paste.

2 Heat the oil in a large heavy pan and fry the spice paste for 1–2 minutes, stirring constantly. Add the coconut milk and stock, and bring to the boil.

3 Reduce the heat, add the potatoes and simmer for about 15 minutes. Add the baby corn and seasoning, then cook for 2 minutes. Stir in the sugar, broccoli and red pepper, and cook for 2 minutes more until the vegetables are tender. Stir in the shredded spinach and half the fresh coriander. Cook for 2 minutes.

4 Meanwhile, prepare the rice. Tip the rinsed rice into a large pan and add the lemon grass and cardamom pods. Pour over 475ml/16fl oz/2 cups water.

5 Bring to the boil, then reduce the heat, cover, and cook for 10–15 minutes until the water is absorbed and the rice is tender and slightly sticky. Season with salt, leave to stand for 10 minutes, then fluff up the rice with a fork.

6 Remove the spices and serve the rice with the curry, sprinkled with the remaining fresh coriander.

spiced tofu stir-fry Energy 294kcal/1218kJ; Protein 10.3g; Carbohydrate 11.4g, of which sugars 10.4g; Fat 23.4g, of which saturates 2.4g; Cholesterol 0mg; Calcium 383mg; Fibre 3.3g; Sodium 11mg.
Thai vegetable curry Energy 300kcal/1256kJ; Protein 3.2g; Carbohydrate 35.1g, of which sugars 14.3g; Fat 3g, of which saturates 0.8g; Cholesterol 0mg; Calcium 72mg; Fibre 5.9g; Sodium 123mg.

Tofu with Lemon Grass & Basil

In parts of Asia, aromatic pepper leaves are used as the herb element in this dish but, because these can be difficult to track down, you can use basil leaves instead. For the best results, leave the tofu to marinate for the full hour. This very tasty dish is a wonderful way to cook tofu.

Ingredients

3 lemon grass stalks, finely chopped
45ml/3 tbsp soy sauce
2 fresh red Serrano chillies, seeded and finely chopped
2 garlic cloves, crushed
5ml/1 tsp ground turmeric
10ml/2 tsp sugar
300g/11oz tofu, rinsed, drained, patted dry and cut into bitesize cubes
30ml/2 tbsp groundnut (peanut) oil
45ml/3 tbsp roasted peanuts, chopped
1 bunch fresh basil, stalks removed
salt

Serves 3–4

1 In a bowl, mix together the lemon grass, soy sauce, chillies, garlic, turmeric and sugar until the sugar has dissolved. Add a little salt to taste and add the tofu, making sure it is well coated. Leave to marinate for 1 hour.

2 Heat a wok or heavy pan. Pour in the oil, add the marinated tofu, and cook, stirring frequently, until it is golden brown on all sides. Add the peanuts and most of the basil leaves and stir-fry quickly so that the basil becomes aromatic without wilting.

3 Divide the tofu among individual serving dishes, sprinkle the remaining basil leaves over the top and serve hot or at room temperature.

Variation

Lime, coriander (cilantro) or curry leaves would work well in this simple stir-fry.

Crisp-fried Tofu in Tomato Sauce

This is a light, tasty tofu-based dish. Soy sauce is used here, but fish sauce can be substituted for those who eat fish. You can use a combination of vegetable and peanut oils if you want the nutty taste without fear of burning.

Ingredients

vegetable or groundnut (peanut) oil, for deep-frying
450g/1lb firm tofu, rinsed and cut into bitesize cubes
4 shallots, finely sliced
1 fresh red chilli, seeded and chopped
25g/1oz fresh root ginger, peeled and finely chopped
4 garlic cloves, finely chopped
6 large ripe tomatoes, peeled, seeded and finely chopped
15–30ml/1–2 tbsp light soy sauce
10ml/2 tsp sugar
mint leaves and strips of fresh red chilli, to garnish
ground black pepper

Serves 4

1 Heat enough oil for deep-frying in a wok or heavy pan. Fry the tofu, in batches, until crisp and golden. Remove with a slotted spoon and drain on kitchen paper.

2 Reserve 30ml/2 tbsp oil in the wok. Add the shallots, chilli, ginger and garlic and stir-fry until fragrant. Stir in the tomatoes, soy sauce and sugar. Reduce the heat and simmer the mixture for 10–15 minutes until it resembles a sauce. Stir in 105ml/7 tbsp water and bring to the boil.

3 Season with a little pepper and return the tofu to the pan. Mix well and simmer gently for 2–3 minutes to heat through. Spoon into heated bowls, garnish with mint leaves and chilli strips and serve immediately.

Cook's Tip

This recipe is delicious as a side dish or as a main dish with noodles or rice. It is nutritious too, thanks to the tofu, which is an excellent vegetable protein, free from cholesterol.

tofu w. lemon grass Energy 115kcal/480kJ; Protein 7.4g; Carbohydrate 4.5g, of which sugars 3.9g; Fat 7.6g, of which saturates 1g; Cholesterol 0mg; Calcium 388mg; Fibre 0.2g; Sodium 804mg.
tofu in tomato sauce Energy 234kcal/974kJ; Protein 11g; Carbohydrate 11.1g, of which sugars 10.1g; Fat 16.5g, of which saturates 2g; Cholesterol 0mg; Calcium 619mg; Fibre 2.7g; Sodium 25mg.

Snake Beans with Tofu

Another name for snake beans is yard-long beans. This is something of an exaggeration but they do grow to lengths of 35cm/14in and more. Look for them in Asian stores and markets, but if you can't find any, substitute other green beans, such as French beans or runner beans. Mangetouts (snow peas) or sugarsnaps also work well in this dish.

Ingredients

500g/1¼lb snake beans, thinly sliced
200g/7oz silken tofu, cut into cubes
2 shallots, thinly sliced
200ml/7fl oz/scant 1 cup coconut milk
115g/4oz/1 cup roasted peanuts, chopped
juice of 1 lime
10ml/2 tsp palm sugar (jaggery) or muscovado (brown) sugar
60ml/4 tbsp soy sauce
5ml/1 tsp dried chilli flakes

Serves 4

1 Bring a pan of lightly salted water to the boil. Add the beans and blanch them for 30 seconds.

2 Drain the beans immediately, then refresh under cold water and drain again, shaking well to remove as much water as possible. Place in a serving bowl and set aside.

3 Put the tofu and shallots in a pan with the coconut milk. Heat gently, stirring, until the tofu begins to crumble.

4 Add the peanuts, lime juice, sugar, soy sauce and chilli flakes. Heat, stirring, until the sugar has dissolved. Pour the sauce over the beans, toss to combine and serve immediately.

Variations
The sauce also works very well with podded broad (fava) beans. Alternatively, stir in sliced yellow or red (bell) pepper.

Peanut & Tofu Cutlets

These delicious patties make a filling and satisfying midweek meal served with lightly steamed green vegetables or a crisp salad, and a tangy salsa or ketchup.

Ingredients

90g/3½oz/½ cup brown rice
15ml/1 tbsp vegetable oil
1 onion, finely chopped
1 garlic clove, crushed
200g/7oz/1¾ cups peanuts
small bunch of fresh coriander (cilantro), chopped
250g/9oz firm tofu, drained and crumbled
30ml/2 tbsp soy sauce
30ml/2 tbsp olive oil, for frying

Serves 4

1 Cook the rice according to the instructions on the packet until tender, then drain. Heat the vegetable oil in a large, heavy frying pan and cook the onion and garlic over a low heat, stirring occasionally until softened and golden.

2 Meanwhile, spread out the peanuts on a baking sheet and toast under the grill (broiler) for a few minutes, until browned. Place the peanuts, onion, garlic, rice, coriander, tofu and soy sauce in a blender or food processor and process until the mixture comes together in a thick paste.

3 Divide the paste into eight equal-size mounds and form each mound into a cutlet shape or square.

4 Heat the olive oil for shallow frying in a large, heavy frying pan. Add the cutlets, in two batches if necessary, and cook for 5–10 minutes on each side, until golden and heated through. Remove from the pan and drain well. Serve immediately.

Variations
The herbs and nuts can be varied. Try:
- *Walnuts with rosemary or sage*
- *Cashew nuts with coriander (cilantro) or parsley*
- *Hazelnuts with parsley, thyme or sage.*

snake beans w. tofu Energy 167kcal/697kJ; Protein 9.9g; Carbohydrate 12.9g, of which sugars 9.3g; Fat 10g, of which saturates 1g; Cholesterol 7mg; Calcium 327mg; Fibre 3.4g; Sodium 191mg.
peanut/tofu cutlets Energy 495kcal/2059kJ; Protein 20.2g; Carbohydrate 27.1g, of which sugars 5.3g; Fat 34.7g, of which saturates 5.9g; Cholesterol 0mg; Calcium 381mg; Fibre 4.4g; Sodium 543mg.

Tofu with Four Mushrooms

Four different kinds of mushrooms combine beautifully with tofu in this sophisticated and substantial recipe.

Ingredients

350g/12oz firm tofu
2.5ml/½ tsp sesame oil
10ml/2 tsp light soy sauce
15ml/1 tbsp vegetable oil
2 garlic cloves, finely chopped
2.5ml/½ tsp grated fresh root ginger
115g/4oz/scant 2 cups fresh shiitake mushrooms, stalks removed
175g/6oz/scant 2 cups fresh oyster mushrooms
115g/4oz/scant 2 cups canned straw mushrooms, drained
115g/4oz/scant 2 cups button (white) mushrooms, halved
15ml/1 tbsp dry sherry
15ml/1 tbsp dark soy sauce
90ml/6 tbsp vegetable stock
5ml/1 tsp cornflour (cornstarch)
15ml/1 tbsp cold water
ground white pepper
salt
2 shredded spring onions (scallions), to garnish

Serves 4

1 Put the tofu in a dish. Sprinkle with the sesame oil, light soy sauce and a large pinch of pepper. Marinate for 10 minutes, then drain and cut into 2.5 × 1cm/1 × ½in pieces.

2 Heat the vegetable oil in a large non-stick frying pan or wok. Add the garlic and ginger and stir-fry for a few seconds. Add all the mushrooms and stir-fry for a further 2 minutes.

3 Stir in the dry sherry, dark soy sauce and stock. Season to taste. Lower the heat and simmer gently for 4 minutes.

4 Place the cornflour in a bowl with the water. Mix to make a smooth paste. Stir the cornflour mixture into the pan or wok and cook, stirring constantly to prevent lumps, until thickened.

5 Carefully add the pieces of tofu, toss gently to coat thoroughly in the sauce and simmer for 2 minutes.

6 Sprinkle the shredded spring onions over the top of the mixture to garnish and serve immediately.

Simmered Tofu with Vegetables

Quick and easy, this is perfect for a family supper.

Ingredients

4 dried shiitake mushrooms
450g/1lb mooli (daikon)
350g/12oz firm tofu
115g/4oz/¾ cup green beans,
5ml/1 tsp long-grain rice
115g/4oz carrot, sliced
300g/11oz baby potatoes, unpeeled
750ml/1¼ pints/3 cups vegetable stock
30ml/2 tbsp sugar
75ml/5 tbsp shoyu
45ml/3 tbsp sake
15ml/1 tbsp mirin

Serves 4

1 Put the dried shiitake in a bowl. Add 250ml/8fl oz/1 cup water and soak for 2 hours. Drain, discarding the liquid. Remove and discard the stems.

2 Peel the mooli and slice it into 1cm/½in discs. Put the slices in cold water to prevent them from discolouring.

3 Drain and rinse the tofu, then pat dry with kitchen paper. Cut the tofu into pieces of about 2.5 × 5cm/1 × 2in.

4 Bring a pan of water to the boil. Blanch the beans for 2 minutes. Drain, cool under running water and drain again.

5 Put the daikon slices in the clean pan. Pour in water to cover and add the rice. Bring to the boil, then reduce the heat and simmer for 15 minutes. Drain off the liquid and the rice.

6 Add the drained mushrooms, carrot and potatoes to the daikon in the pan. Pour in the vegetable stock, boil, skim, then add the sugar, shoyu and sake. Shake the pan gently to mix the ingredients thoroughly.

7 Cover with a circle of baking parchment and a tight-fitting lid and simmer for 30 minutes or until the sauce has reduced by half. Add the tofu and green beans. Warm through for 2 minutes, then add the mirin. Taste the sauce and adjust with shoyu if required. Serve immediately in warmed bowls.

tofu w. four mushrooms Energy 118kcal/491kJ; Protein 9.3g; Carbohydrate 2.9g, of which sugars 1.1g; Fat 7.4g, of which saturates 0.9g; Cholesterol 0mg; Calcium 456mg; Fibre 1.2g; Sodium 455mg.
tofu w. vegetables Energy 142kcal/597kJ; Protein 4.2g; Carbohydrate 27.6g, of which sugars 15.1g; Fat 0.9g, of which saturates 0.3g; Cholesterol 0mg; Calcium 92mg; Fibre 3.3g; Sodium 1406mg.

Tofu with Peppers & Pinenuts

Variations on stuffed peppers appear the world over, but this is a good alternative to the more usual meat- or rice-based recipes. The use of garlic or herb olive oil enhances the flavour, while the pine nuts create a crunchy topping a that contrasts nicely with the filling.

Ingredients
4 red (bell) peppers
1 orange (bell) pepper, seeded and coarsely chopped
1 yellow (bell) pepper, seeded and coarsely chopped
60ml/4 tbsp garlic olive oil
250g/9oz firm tofu
50g/2oz/½ cup pine nuts

Serves 4

1 Preheat the oven to 220°C/425°F/Gas 7. Cut the red peppers in half, leaving the stalks intact, and discard the seeds. Place the red pepper halves on a baking sheet and fill with the chopped orange and yellow peppers. Drizzle with half the garlic or herb olive oil and bake for 25 minutes, until the edges of the peppers are beginning to char.

2 Meanwhile, unpack the tofu blocks and discard the liquid, then wrap the tofu in layers of kitchen paper. Put a large plate on top as a weight and leave for 30 minutes to allow the excess liquid to be absorbed by the paper.

3 Cut the tofu into small, even cubes using a sharp knife.

4 Remove the peppers from the oven, but leave the oven on. Tuck the tofu cubes in among the chopped orange and yellow peppers. Sprinkle evenly with the pine nuts and drizzle with the remaining garlic oil. Bake for a further 15 minutes, or until well browned. Serve warm or at room temperature.

Cook's Tip
Once you have opened a packet of tofu, any that is unused should be rinsed and put in a bowl with fresh water to cover. Change the water every day and use the tofu within 5 days.

Tofu & Broccoli with Fried Shallots

This meltingly tender tofu flavoured with spices and served with broccoli makes a perfect lunch. To give the recipe that little bit extra, deep-fry some crispy shallots to serve on the side, if you like.

Ingredients
500g/1¼lb block of firm tofu, drained
45ml/3 tbsp kecap manis
30ml/2 tbsp sweet chilli sauce
45ml/3 tbsp soy sauce
5ml/1 tsp sesame oil
5ml/1 tsp finely grated fresh root ginger
400g/14oz tenderstem broccoli, halved lengthways
45ml/3 tbsp roughly chopped coriander (cilantro), and 30ml/2 tbsp toasted sesame seeds, to garnish

Serves 4

1 Make the crispy shallots. Add the shallot rings to a wok one-third full of hot oil, then lower the heat and stir constantly until crisp. Lift out and spread on kitchen paper to drain.

2 Cut the tofu into 4 triangular pieces: slice the block in half widthways, then diagonally. Place in a heatproof dish.

3 In a small bowl, combine the kecap manis, chilli sauce, soy sauce, sesame oil and ginger, then pour over the tofu. Leave the tofu to marinate for at least 30 minutes, turning occasionally.

4 Place the broccoli on a heatproof plate and place on a trivet or steamer rack in the wok. Cover and steam for 4–5 minutes, until just tender. Remove and keep warm.

5 Place the dish of tofu on the trivet or steamer rack in the wok, cover and steam for 4–5 minutes. Divide the broccoli among four warmed serving plates and top each one with a triangle of tofu.

6 Spoon the remaining juices over the tofu and broccoli, then sprinkle with the coriander and toasted sesame seeds. Serve immediately with steamed white rice or noodles.

tofu w. peppers Energy 311kcal/1287kJ; Protein 9.3g; Carbohydrate 17g, of which sugars 15.9g; Fat 23.2g, of which saturates 2.7g; Cholesterol 0mg; Calcium 340mg; Fibre 4.2g; Sodium 13mg.
tofu/broccoli w. shallots Energy 202kcal/840kJ; Protein 16.5g; Carbohydrate 6.9g, of which sugars 5.6g; Fat 12.1g, of which saturates 1.7g; Cholesterol 0mg; Calcium 750mg; Fibre 3.5g; Sodium 938mg.

Herb & Chilli Aubergines

Plump and juicy aubergines taste sensational steamed until tender and then tossed in a fragrant mint and coriander dressing with crunchy water chestnuts.

Ingredients

500g/1¼lb firm baby aubergines (eggplants)
30ml/2 tbsp vegetable oil
6 garlic cloves, very finely chopped
15ml/1 tbsp fresh root ginger, very finely chopped
8 spring onions (scallions), cut diagonally into 2.5cm/1in lengths
2 fresh red chillies, seeded and thinly sliced
45ml/3 tbsp light soy sauce
15ml/1 tbsp Chinese rice wine
15ml/1 tbsp golden caster (superfine) sugar
a large handful of mint leaves
30–45ml/2–3 tbsp roughly chopped coriander (cilantro) leaves
8 drained canned water chestnuts
50g/2oz/½ cup roasted peanuts, roughly chopped
steamed egg noodles or rice, to serve

Serves 4

1 Cut the aubergines in half lengthways and place them on a heatproof plate. Fit a steamer rack in a wok and add 5cm/2in of water. Bring the water to the boil, lower the plate on to the rack and reduce the heat to low.

2 Cover the plate and steam the aubergines for 25–30 minutes, until they are cooked through. Remove the plate from on top of the steamer and set the aubergines aside to cool.

3 Heat the oil in a clean, dry wok and place over medium heat. When hot, add the garlic, ginger, spring onions and chillies and stir-fry for 2–3 minutes. Remove from the heat and stir in the soy sauce, rice wine and sugar.

4 Add the mint leaves, chopped coriander, water chestnuts and peanuts to the cooled aubergine and toss.

5 Pour the garlic-ginger mixture evenly over the vegetables, toss gently and serve with steamed egg noodles or rice.

Vegetable Stew with Roasted Tomato & Garlic Sauce

This lightly spiced stew makes a perfect match for rice, enriched with a little butter or olive oil. Add some chopped fresh coriander and a handful each of raisins and toasted pine nuts to the rice to make it extra special.

Ingredients

45ml/3 tbsp olive oil
250g/9oz shallots
1 large onion, chopped
2 garlic cloves, chopped
5ml/1 tsp cumin seeds
5ml/1 tsp ground coriander seeds
5ml/1 tsp paprika
5cm/2in piece cinnamon stick
2 fresh bay leaves
300–450ml/½–¾ pint/1¼–scant 2 cups good vegetable stock
good pinch of saffron threads
450g/1lb carrots, thickly sliced
2 green (bell) peppers, seeded and thickly sliced
115g/4oz ready-to-eat dried apricots, halved if large
5–7.5ml/1–1½ tsp ground toasted cumin seeds
450g/1lb squash, peeled, seeded and cut into chunks
pinch of sugar, to taste
25g/1oz/2 tbsp butter (optional)
salt and ground black pepper
45ml/3 tbsp fresh coriander (cilantro) leaves, to garnish

For the roasted tomato and garlic sauce

1kg/2¼lb tomatoes, halved
5ml/1 tsp sugar
45ml/3 tbsp olive oil
1–2 fresh red chillies, seeded and chopped
2–3 garlic cloves, chopped
5ml/1 tsp fresh thyme leaves

Serves 6

1 Preheat the oven to 180°C/350°F/Gas 4. For the sauce, place the tomatoes, cut sides uppermost, in a roasting pan. Season well with salt and pepper and sprinkle the sugar over the top, then drizzle with the olive oil. Roast for 30 minutes.

2 Sprinkle the chillies, garlic and thyme over the tomatoes, stir to mix and roast for another 30–45 minutes, until the tomatoes are collapsed but still a little juicy. Cool, then process in a food processor to make a thick sauce. Sieve to remove the seeds.

3 Heat 30ml/2 tbsp of the oil in a large pan or deep frying pan and cook the shallots until browned all over. Remove from the pan and set aside. Add the chopped onion to the pan and cook over a low heat for 5–7 minutes, until softened. Stir in the garlic and cumin seeds and cook for a further 3–4 minutes.

4 Add the ground coriander seeds, paprika, cinnamon stick and bay leaves. Cook, stirring constantly, for another 2 minutes, then mix in the vegetable stock, saffron, carrots and green peppers. Season well, cover and simmer gently for 10 minutes.

5 Stir in the apricots, 5ml/1 tsp of the ground toasted cumin, the browned shallots and the squash. Stir in the tomato sauce. Cover the pan and cook for a further 5 minutes. Uncover and continue to cook, stirring occasionally, for 10–15 minutes.

6 Adjust the seasoning, adding a little more cumin and a pinch of sugar to taste. Remove and discard the cinnamon stick. Stir in the butter, if using, and serve sprinkled with coriander leaves.

herb & chilli aubergines Energy 177kcal/739kJ; Protein 6.2g; Carbohydrate 12.1g, of which sugars 9g; Fat 12g, of which saturates 1.9g; Cholesterol 0mg; Calcium 46mg; Fibre 4.4g; Sodium 823mg.
vegetable stew Energy 133kcal/552kJ; Protein 5.7g; Carbohydrate 10.5g, of which sugars 7.1g; Fat 8g, of which saturates 0g; Cholesterol 0mg; Calcium 94mg; Fibre 4.3g; Sodium 32mg.

Aubergine & Sweet Potato Stew

This is a particularly good combination of flavours.

Ingredients

60ml/4 tbsp vegetable oil
400g/14oz baby aubergines (eggplants), halved
225g/8oz Thai red shallots or other small shallots or pickling onions
5ml/1 tsp fennel seeds, lightly crushed
4–5 garlic cloves, thinly sliced
25ml/1½ tbsp finely chopped fresh root ginger
475ml/16fl oz/2 cups vegetable stock
2 lemon grass stalks, outer layers discarded, finely chopped
15g/½oz/⅔ cup fresh coriander (cilantro), stalks and leaves chopped separately
3 kaffir lime leaves, lightly bruised
2–3 small fresh red chillies
60ml/4 tbsp green curry paste
675g/1½lb sweet potatoes, cut in chunks
400ml/14fl oz/1⅔ cups coconut milk
2.5–5ml/½–1 tsp light brown sugar
250g/9oz/3½ cups mushrooms, thickly sliced
juice of 1 lime, to taste
salt and ground black pepper
basil leaves, to garnish

Serves 6

1 Heat half the oil in a wide pan and cook the aubergines until lightly browned on all sides. Remove from the pan; set aside.

2 Slice four shallots. Cook the whole shallots in the oil remaining in the pan, until lightly browned. Add to the aubergines. Add more oil to the pan and cook the sliced shallots, fennel seeds, garlic and ginger over a low heat for 5 minutes.

3 Add the stock, lemon grass, chopped coriander stalks, lime leaves and chillies. Simmer for 5 minutes, the stir in half the curry paste and the sweet potatoes. Simmer for 10 minutes, add the aubergines and shallots and cook for 5 minutes more.

4 Stir in the coconut milk and sugar. Season, then stir in the mushrooms and simmer until the vegetables are cooked. Stir in more curry paste and lime juice to taste, followed by the chopped coriander leaves. Sprinkle basil leaves over the stew and serve with rice in warm bowls.

Crisp Deep-fried Vegetables

Stir-fried, steamed or deep-fried vegetables served with a dipping sauce are common fare throughout Asia, and often appear among the delightful "no-name" dishes popular in Thai tourist fare.

Ingredients

6 eggs
1 long aubergine (eggplant), peeled, halved lengthways and sliced into half moons
1 long sweet potato, peeled and sliced into rounds
1 small butternut squash, peeled, seeded, halved lengthways and cut into half moons
salt and ground black pepper
vegetable oil, for deep-frying
chilli sambal or hot chilli sauce for dipping

Serves 4–6

1 Beat the eggs in a wide bowl. Season with salt and pepper. Toss the vegetables in the egg to coat thoroughly.

2 Heat enough oil for deep-frying in a large wok. Cook the vegetables in small batches, making sure there is plenty of egg coating each piece.

3 When they turn golden, lift them out of the oil with a slotted spoon and drain on kitchen paper.

4 Keep the vegetables hot while successive batches are being fried. Serve warm with chilli sambal, hot chilli sauce or a dipping sauce of your choice.

Cook's Tips

- *To encourage the beaten egg coating to adhere to the pieces of aubergine (eggplant) sweet potatoes and butternut squash, toss them in flour or cornflour (cornstarch) first.*
- *Courgettes (zucchini), angled loofah, taro root or pumpkin could also be used.*

aubergine/sweet potato Energy 228kcal/960kJ; Protein 4.3g; Carbohydrate 34g, of which sugars 13.4g; Fat 9.3g, of which saturates 1.2g; Cholesterol 0mg; Calcium 130mg; Fibre 7.2g; Sodium 159mg.
deep-fried vegetables Energy 280kcal/1164kJ; Protein 8.3g; Carbohydrate 11.9g, of which sugars 5.7g; Fat 22.7g, of which saturates 3.7g; Cholesterol 190mg; Calcium 90mg; Fibre 3.5g; Sodium 84mg.

Mushrooms with Garlic Chilli Sauce

Succulent spiced mushrooms taste great when cooked over coals.

Ingredients

12 large field (portabello), chestnut or oyster mushrooms
4 garlic cloves, roughly chopped
6 coriander (cilantro) roots, roughly chopped
15ml/1 tbsp sugar
30ml/2 tbsp light soy sauce
ground black pepper

For the dipping sauce

15ml/1 tbsp sugar
90ml/6 tbsp rice vinegar
5ml/1 tsp salt
1 garlic clove, crushed
1 small fresh red chilli, seeded and finely chopped

Serves 4

1 If using wooden skewers, soak eight of them in cold water for at least 30 minutes to prevent them from burning when exposed to direct heat.

2 Make the dipping sauce by heating the sugar, rice vinegar and salt in a small pan, stirring occasionally until the sugar and salt have dissolved.

3 Add the garlic and chilli to the mixture, pour into a serving dish and keep warm.

4 In a mortar pound or blend the garlic and coriander roots. Scrape the mixture into a bowl and mix with the sugar, soy sauce and a little pepper.

5 Trim and wipe the mushrooms and cut them in half. Thread three mushroom halves on to each skewer. Lay the filled skewers side by side in a shallow dish.

6 Brush the soy sauce mixture over the mushrooms and leave to marinate for 15 minutes.

7 Cook on a barbecue or under a hot the grill (broiler) for 2–3 minutes on each side. Serve with the dipping sauce.

Mushrooms with Loofah Squash

Winter gourds, such as pumpkins, bitter melons, loofah squash and a variety of other squash that come under the kabocha umbrella, are popular ingredients for soups and braised vegetable dishes. Any of these vegetables can be used for this side dish, but loofah squash – also known as ridged gourd – is easy to work with and is available in most Asian markets. It resembles a long courgette, usually lighter in colour and with ridges from one end to the other.

Ingredients

750g/1lb 10oz loofah squash, peeled
30ml/2 tbsp groundnut (peanut) or sesame oil
2 shallots, halved and sliced
2 garlic cloves, finely chopped
115g/4oz/1½ cups button (white) mushrooms, quartered
15ml/1 tbsp mushroom sauce
10ml/2 tsp soy sauce
4 spring onions (scallions), cut into 2cm/¾in pieces
fresh coriander (cilantro) leaves and thin strips of spring onion (scallion), to garnish

Serves 4

1 Using a sharp knife, cut the loofah squash diagonally into 2cm/¾in-thick pieces and set aside.

2 Heat the oil in a large wok or heavy pan. Stir in the halved shallots and garlic, stir-fry until they begin to colour and turn golden, then add the mushrooms.

3 Add the mushroom and soy sauces, and the squash. Reduce the heat, cover and cook gently for a few minutes until the squash is tender. Just before serving, stir in the spring onion pieces and allow to warm through. Spoon into warmed serving bowls and garnish with the coriander and spring onion strips.

Cook's Tip

Choose a mushroom sauce suitable for vegetarians. Some contain anchovies, so check the label. Mushroom seasoning is usually a safe bet.

mushrooms w. chilli sauce Energy 51kcal/215kJ; Protein 2.5g; Carbohydrate 9.7g, of which sugars 8.7g; Fat 0.5g, of which saturates 0.1g; Cholesterol 0mg; Calcium 12mg; Fibre 1.3g; Sodium 1031mg.
mushrooms w. luffa squash Energy 89kcal/371kJ; Protein 2.3g; Carbohydrate 6.7g, of which sugars 5.2g; Fat 6.1g, of which saturates 0.9g; Cholesterol 0mg; Calcium 65mg; Fibre 2.6g; Sodium 221mg.

Stir-fried Water Spinach

In the countryside, this dish is a favourite with roadside vendors. Water spinach is an excellent source of Vitamin A, which helps to promote healthy bones, skin, hair and also aids vision. Serve this aromatic dish as part of a vegetarian meal, or as a side dish to accompany main meat or fish courses.

Ingredients
30ml/2 tbsp groundnut (peanut) oil
2 garlic cloves, finely chopped
2 fresh red or green chillies, seeded and finely chopped
500g/1¼lb fresh water spinach
45ml/3 tbsp chilli sauce
salt and ground black pepper

Serves 3–4

1 Heat a wok or large pan and add the oil. Stir in the garlic and chillies and stir-fry for 1 minute, then add the water spinach and toss around the pan.

2 Once the water spinach leaves begin to wilt, add the chilli sauce, making sure it coats the spinach. Season to taste with salt and pepper and serve immediately.

Variations

• *Although water spinach is traditionally favoured in this recipe, you coud substitute it for any type of green, leafy vegetaable, particularly ordinary spinach. The latter – a relative in common name only – has a slightly tougher texture, however, and leaves should be blanched in boiling water prior to stir-frying with the other ingredients. Thoroughly wash the spinach and trim off the stems, then immerse the leaves in boiling water for about 15 seconds until softened slightly.*

• *Some non-leafy vegetables also work well as the principal component. Cauliflower and, when in season, asparagus, can be stir-fried in the same way. With the cauliflower, simply cut off the heads, divide into florets and add directly to the pan with the garlic and chillies. The asparagus will require blanching. Trim off the woody tips and stand the heads in a small jug (pitcher) of boiling water for 3–4 minutes. Slice and add to the pan.*

Okra & Coconut Stir-fry

Stir-fried okra spiced with mustard, cumin and red chillies and sprinkled with freshly grated coconut makes a great quick supper. It is the perfect way to enjoy these succulent pods, with the sweetness of the coconut complementing the warm spices.

Ingredients
600g/1lb 6oz okra
60ml/4 tbsp sunflower oil
1 onion, finely chopped
15ml/1 tbsp mustard seeds
15ml/1 tbsp cumin seeds
2–3 dried red chillies
10–12 curry leaves
2.5ml/½ tsp ground turmeric
90g/3½oz freshly grated coconut
salt and ground black pepper
poppadums, rice or naan, to serve

Serves 4

1 With a sharp knife, cut each of the okra pods diagonally into 1cm/½in lengths. Set aside. Heat a wok and add the sunflower oil.

2 When the oil is hot add the chopped onion and stir-fry over a medium heat for about 5 minutes until softened.

3 Add the mustard seeds, cumin seeds, chillies and curry leaves to the onions and stir-fry over a high heat for about 2 minutes.

4 Add the okra and turmeric to the wok and continue to stir-fry over a high heat for 3–4 minutes.

5 Remove the wok from the heat, sprinkle over the coconut and season well with salt and ground black pepper. Serve immediately with poppadums, steamed rice or naan bread.

Cook's Tip

Fresh okra is widely available from many supermarkets and Asian stores. Choose fresh, firm, green specimens and avoid any pods that are limp or turning brown.

stir-fried water spinach Energy 92kcal/379kJ; Protein 3.8g; Carbohydrate 4.6g, of which sugars 4g; Fat 6.5g, of which saturates 0.8g; Cholesterol 0mg; Calcium 214mg; Fibre 2.8g; Sodium 297mg.
okra/coconut stir fry Energy 191kcal/790kJ; Protein 5.1g; Carbohydrate 6.2g, of which sugars 5.1g; Fat 16.5g, of which saturates 5.1g; Cholesterol 0mg; Calcium 249mg; Fibre 7.1g; Sodium 15mg.

Glazed Pumpkin

Pumpkins, butternut squash and winter melons can all be cooked in this way. Variations of this sweet, mellow dish are often served as an accompaniment to rice or a spicy curry.

Ingredients

200ml/7fl oz/scant 1 cup coconut milk
15ml/1 tbsp fish sauce
30ml/2 tbsp palm sugar (jaggery)
30ml/2 tbsp groundnut (peanut) oil
4 garlic cloves, finely chopped
25g/1oz fresh root ginger, peeled and finely shredded
675g/1½lb pumpkin flesh, cubed
ground black pepper
a handful of curry or basil leaves, to garnish
chilli oil, for drizzling
fried onion rings, to garnish
plain or coconut rice, to serve

Serves 4

1 In a bowl, beat the coconut milk and the fish sauce with the sugar, until it has dissolved. Set aside.

2 Heat the oil in a wok or heavy pan and stir in the garlic and ginger. Stir-fry until they begin to colour, then stir in the pumpkin cubes, mixing well.

3 Pour in the coconut milk and mix well. Reduce the heat, cover and simmer for about 20 minutes, until the pumpkin is tender and the sauce has reduced. Season with pepper and garnish with curry or basil leaves and fried onion rings. Serve hot with plain or coconut rice, drizzled with a little chilli oil.

Cook's Tip

For a quick coconut rice, rinse 350g/12oz/1¾ cups Thai fragrant rice and put in a pan with 400ml/14 fl oz/1¾ cups coconut milk, 2.5ml/½ tsp ground coriander, a cinnamon stick, a bruised lemon grass stalk and a bay leaf. Add salt to taste. Bring to the boil, cover and simmer for 8–10 minutes, or until the liquid has been absorbed. Fork through lightly, remove the solid spices and serve.

Sweet Pumpkin & Peanut Curry

A hearty, soothing curry perfect for autumn or winter evenings. Its cheerful colour alone will raise the spirits – and the combination of pumpkin and peanuts tastes great.

Ingredients

30ml/2 tbsp vegetable oil
4 garlic cloves, crushed
4 shallots, finely chopped
30ml/2 tbsp yellow curry paste
600ml/1 pint/2½ cups vegetable stock
2 kaffir lime leaves, torn
15ml/1 tbsp chopped fresh galangal
450g/1lb pumpkin, peeled, seeded and diced
225g/8oz sweet potatoes, diced
90g/3½oz/scant 1 cup unsalted, roasted peanuts, chopped
300ml/½ pint/1¼ cups coconut milk
90g/3½oz/1½ cups chestnut mushrooms, sliced
30ml/2 tbsp soy sauce
50g/2oz/⅓ cup pumpkin seeds, toasted, and fresh green chilli flowers, to garnish

Serves 4

1 Heat the oil in a wok. Add the garlic and shallots and cook over a medium heat, stirring occasionally, for 10 minutes, until softened and golden. Do not let them burn.

2 Add the yellow curry paste and stir-fry over medium heat for 30 seconds, until fragrant, then add the stock, lime leaves, galangal, pumpkin and sweet potatoes. Bring to the boil, stirring frequently, then simmer gently for 15 minutes.

3 Add the peanuts, coconut milk and mushrooms. Stir in the soy sauce and simmer for 5 minutes more. Spoon into bowls, garnish with the pumpkin seeds and chillies and serve.

Cook's Tip

The well-drained vegetables from any of these curries would make a very tasty filling for a pastry or pie. This may not be a Thai tradition, but it is a good example of fusion food.

glazed pumpkin Energy 114kcal/477kJ; Protein 1.5g; Carbohydrate 14.3g, of which sugars 13.4g; Fat 6g, of which saturates 0.9g; Cholesterol 0mg; Calcium 68mg; Fibre 1.7g; Sodium 323mg.
pumpkin & peanut Energy 306kcal/1279kJ; Protein 9.6g; Carbohydrate 24.5g, of which sugars 11.4g; Fat 19.6g, of which saturates 3.3g; Cholesterol 0mg; Calcium 160mg; Fibre 6.4g; Sodium 409mg.

Corn & Cashew Nut Curry

This is a substantial curry, thanks largely to the potatoes and corn kernels, which makes it a great winter dish. It is deliciously aromatic, but, as the spices are added in relatively small amounts, the resulting flavour is fairly mild.

Ingredients

30ml/2 tbsp vegetable oil
4 shallots, chopped
90g/3½oz/scant 1 cup cashew nuts
5ml/1 tsp red curry paste
400g/14oz potatoes, peeled and cut into chunks
1 lemon grass stalk, finely chopped
200g/7oz can chopped tomatoes
600ml/1 pint/2½ cups boiling water
200g/7oz/generous 1 cup drained canned whole kernel corn
4 celery sticks, sliced
2 kaffir lime leaves, central rib removed, rolled into cylinders and thinly sliced
15ml/1 tbsp tomato ketchup
15ml/1 tbsp light soy sauce
5ml/1 tsp palm sugar (jaggery) or light muscovado (brown) sugar
4 spring onions (scallions), thinly sliced
small bunch fresh basil, chopped

Serves 4

1 Heat the oil in a wok. Add the shallots and stir-fry over a medium heat for 2–3 minutes, until softened. Add the cashew nuts and stir-fry for a few minutes until they are golden.

2 Stir in the red curry paste. Stir-fry for 1 minute, then add the potatoes, lemon grass, tomatoes and boiling water.

3 Bring back to the boil, then reduce the heat to low, cover and simmer gently for 15–20 minutes, or until the potatoes are tender when tested with the tip of a knife.

4 Stir the corn, celery, lime leaves, ketchup, soy sauce, sugar and spring onions into the wok. Simmer for a further 5 minutes, until heated through, then spoon into warmed serving bowls. Sprinkle with the sliced spring onions and basil and serve.

Jungle Curry

This fiery, flavoursome vegetarian curry is almost dominated by the chilli. Its many variations make it a favourite with Buddhist monks who value the way it adds variety to their vegetarian diet. Often sold from countryside stalls, jungle curry can be served with plain rice or noodles, or chunks of crusty bread. It can be eaten for breakfast or enjoyed as a pick-me-up at any time of day.

Ingredients

30ml/2 tbsp vegetable oil
2 onions, roughly chopped
2 lemon grass stalks, roughly chopped and bruised
4 fresh green chillies, seeded and finely sliced
4cm/1½in galangal or fresh root ginger, peeled and chopped
3 carrots, peeled, halved lengthways and sliced
115g/4oz long beans
grated rind of 1 lime
15ml/3 tsp soy sauce or 10ml/2 tbsp soy sauce and 5ml/1 tsp vegetarian fish sauce
15ml/1 tbsp rice vinegar
5ml/1 tsp black peppercorns, crushed
15ml/1 tbsp sugar
10ml/2 tsp ground turmeric
115g/4oz canned bamboo shoots
75g/3oz spinach, steamed and roughly chopped
150ml/¼ pint/⅔ cup coconut milk
chopped fresh coriander (cilantro) and mint leaves, to garnish

Serves 4

1 Heat a wok or heavy pan and add the oil. Once hot, stir in the onions, lemon grass, chillies and galangal or ginger. Add the carrots and beans with the lime rind and stir-fry for 1–2 minutes.

2 Stir in the soy sauce and rice vinegar or soy sauce, rice vinegar and vegetarian fish sauce. Add the crushed peppercorns, sugar and turmeric, then stir in the bamboo shoots and the chopped spinach.

3 Stir in the coconut milk and simmer for about 10 minutes, until the vegetables are tender. Garnish with coriander and mint.

corn & cashew nut Energy 298kcal/1245kJ; Protein 8.8g; Carbohydrate 27.6g, of which sugars 8.9g; Fat 17.7g, of which saturates 3.1g; Cholesterol 0mg; Calcium 33mg; Fibre 3.5g; Sodium 981mg.
jungle curry Energy 119kcal/496kJ; Protein 3.8g; Carbohydrate 18.6g, of which sugars 15.3g; Fat 3.8g, of which saturates 0.5g; Cholesterol 0mg; Calcium 125mg; Fibre 4.3g; Sodium 60mg.

Yellow Vegetable Curry

This hot and spicy curry made with coconut milk has a creamy richness that contrasts wonderfully with the heat of chilli and the bite of lightly cooked vegetables.

Ingredients

30ml/2 tbsp sunflower oil
30–45ml/2–3 tbsp yellow curry paste (see Cook's Tip)
200ml/7fl oz/scant 1 cup coconut cream
300ml/½ pint/1¼ cups coconut milk
150ml/¼ pint/⅔ cup vegetable stock
200g/7oz snake beans, cut into 2cm/¾in lengths
200g/7oz baby corn
4 baby courgettes (zucchini), sliced
1 small aubergine (eggplant), cubed or sliced
10ml/2 tsp palm sugar (jaggery)
fresh coriander (cilantro) leaves, to garnish
noodles or rice, to serve

Serves 4

1 Heat a large wok over a medium heat and add the oil. When hot add the curry paste and stir-fry for 1–2 minutes. Add the coconut cream and cook gently for 8–10 minutes, or until the mixture starts to separate.

2 Add the coconut milk, stock and vegetables and cook gently for 8–10 minutes, until the vegetables are just tender. Stir in the palm sugar, garnish with coriander leaves and serve with noodles or rice.

Cook's Tip

To make the curry paste, mix 10ml/2 tsp each hot chilli powder, ground coriander and ground cumin in a sturdy food processor, preferably one with an attachment for processing smaller quantities. Add 5ml/1 tsp ground turmeric, 15ml/1 tbsp chopped fresh galangal, 10ml/2 tsp crushed garlic, 30ml/2 tbsp finely chopped lemon grass, 4 finely chopped red shallots and 5ml/1 tsp chopped lime rind. Add 30ml/2 tbsp cold water and blend to a smooth paste. Add a little more water is necessary.

Vegetable Forest Curry

This is a thin, soupy curry with lots of fresh green vegetables and robust flavours. In the forested regions of Thailand, where it originated, it would be made using edible wild leaves and roots. Serve it with rice or noodles for a simple lunch or supper.

Ingredients

600ml/1 pint/2½ cups water
5ml/1 tsp red curry paste
5cm/2in piece fresh galangal or fresh root ginger
90g/3½oz/scant 1 cup green beans
2 kaffir lime leaves, torn
8 baby corn cobs, halved widthways
2 heads Chinese broccoli, chopped
90g/3½oz/scant ½ cup beansprouts
15ml/1 tbsp drained bottled green peppercorns, crushed
10ml/2 tsp sugar
5ml/1 tsp salt

Serves 2

1 Heat the water in a large pan. Add the red curry paste and stir until it has dissolved completely. Bring to the boil.

2 Meanwhile, using a sharp knife, peel and finely chop the fresh galangal or root ginger.

3 Add the galangal or ginger, green beans, lime leaves, baby corn cobs, broccoli and beansprouts to the pan. Stir in the crushed peppercorns, sugar and salt. Bring back to the boil, then reduce the heat to low and simmer for 2 minutes. Serve immediately.

Cook's Tips

- *To prepare the Chinese broccoli, trim the outer leaves and woody stalks, then wash thoroughly before chopping.*
- *Chinese broccoli has more in common with purple sprouting broccoli than the plump, tight heads of Calabrese – the variety of brassica often sold universally as "broccoli". The Chinese version has long, slender stems, loose leaves and – unlike the purple sprouting – tiny white or yellow flowers in the centre.*

yellow vegetable curry Energy 126kcal/528kJ; Protein 4.7g; Carbohydrate 12.7g, of which sugars 11.9g; Fat 6.7g, of which saturates 1.1g; Cholesterol 5mg; Calcium 90mg; Fibre 2.5g; Sodium 752mg.
veg. forest curry Energy 154kcal/643kJ; Protein 14.9g; Carbohydrate 14.1g, of which sugars 11.8g; Fat 4.5g, of which saturates 0.8g; Cholesterol 0mg; Calcium 173mg; Fibre 9.1g; Sodium 678mg.

Vegetable & Coconut Milk Curry

Fragrant jasmine rice is the perfect accompaniment for this spicy and flavoursome vegetable curry.

Ingredients

10ml/2 tsp vegetable oil
400ml/14fl oz/1⅔ cups coconut milk
300ml/½ pint/1¼ cups vegetable stock
225g/8oz new potatoes, halved
8 baby corn cobs
5ml/1 tsp sugar
185g/6½oz/1¼ cups broccoli florets
1 red (bell) pepper, seeded and sliced lengthways
115g/4oz spinach, tough stalks removed, leaves shredded
30ml/2 tbsp chopped fresh coriander (cilantro)
salt and ground black pepper
cooked fragrant jasmine rice, to serve

For the spice paste

1 fresh red chilli, seeded and chopped
3 fresh green chillies, seeded and chopped
1 lemon grass stalk, outer leaves removed and lower 5cm/2in finely chopped
2 shallots, chopped
finely grated rind of 1 lime
2 garlic cloves, chopped
5ml/1 tsp ground coriander
2.5ml/½ tsp ground cumin
1cm/½in piece fresh galangal, finely chopped, or 2.5ml/½ tsp dried galangal (optional)
30ml/2 tbsp chopped fresh coriander

Serves 4

1 Make the spice paste. Place all the ingredients in a food processor and process to a coarse paste. Heat the oil in a large, heavy pan. Add the paste and stir-fry for 1–2 minutes. Pour in the coconut milk and stock. Boil, then add the potatoes and simmer for about 15 minutes, until almost tender.

2 Add the baby corn to the potatoes, season with salt and pepper to taste, then cook for 2 minutes. Stir in the sugar, broccoli and red pepper, and cook for 2 minutes more, until the vegetables are tender.

3 Stir in the shredded spinach and half the fresh coriander. Cook for 2 minutes, then spoon into a serving dish and garnish with the remaining fresh coriander. Serve with the jasmine rice.

Potato Curry with Yogurt

Variations of this simple Indian curry are popular in Singapore, where fusion dishes like this one cater for a community that includes people from all over Asia, as well as from Europe and the Americas.

Ingredients

6 garlic cloves, chopped
25g/1oz fresh root ginger, peeled and chopped
30ml/2 tbsp ghee, or 15ml/1 tbsp oil and 15g/½oz/1 tbsp butter
6 shallots, halved lengthways and sliced along the grain
2 fresh green chillies, seeded and finely sliced
10ml/2 tsp sugar
a handful of fresh or dried curry leaves
2 cinnamon sticks
5–10ml/1–2 tsp ground turmeric
15ml/1 tbsp garam masala
500g/1¼lb waxy potatoes, cut into bitesize pieces
2 tomatoes, peeled, seeded and quartered
250ml/8fl oz/1 cup Greek (US strained plain) yogurt
salt and ground black pepper
5ml/1 tsp red chilli powder, and fresh coriander (cilantro) and mint leaves, finely chopped, to garnish
1 lemon, quartered, to serve

Serves 4

1 Using a mortar and pestle or a food processor, grind the garlic and ginger to a coarse paste. Heat the ghee in a heavy pan and stir in the shallots and chillies, until fragrant. Add the garlic and ginger paste with the sugar, and stir until the mixture begins to colour. Stir in the curry leaves, cinnamon sticks, turmeric and garam masala, and toss in the potatoes, making sure they are coated in the spice mixture.

2 Pour in just enough cold water to cover the potatoes. Bring to the boil, then reduce the heat and simmer until the potatoes are just cooked – they should still have a bite to them.

3 Season with salt and pepper to taste. Gently toss in the tomatoes to heat them through. Fold in the yogurt so that it is streaky. Sprinkle with the chilli powder, coriander and mint. Serve immediately from the pan, with lemon to squeeze over.

veg. & coconut curry Energy 198kcal/827kJ; Protein 3.4g; Carbohydrate 19.2g, of which sugars 18.7g; Fat 12.6g, of which saturates 1.8g; Cholesterol 0mg; Calcium 191mg; Fibre 6.4g; Sodium 312mg.
potato curry w. yogurt Energy 231kcal/967kJ; Protein 6.7g; Carbohydrate 26.2g, of which sugars 7.4g; Fat 12.4g, of which saturates 4.1g; Cholesterol 0mg; Calcium 110mg; Fibre 2g; Sodium 63mg.

Mooli, Beetroot & Carrot Stir-fry

This is a dazzlingly colourful dish with a crunchy texture and fragrant taste. It is low in saturated fat and is cholesterol-free and would be ideal for a summer lunch.

Ingredients

25g/1oz/⅓ cup pine nuts
115g/4oz mooli (daikon), peeled
115g/4oz raw beetroot (beet), peeled
115g/4oz carrots, peeled
15ml/1 tbsp vegetable oil
1 orange
30ml/2 tbsp chopped fresh coriander (cilantro)
salt and ground black pepper

Serves 4

1 Heat a non-stick wok or frying pan. Add the pine nuts and toss over medium heat until golden brown. Remove the nuts and spread them on a plate. Set aside.

2 Using a sharp knife, cut the mooli, beetroot and carrots into long, thin strips. Keep them separate on a chopping board.

3 Reheat the wok or frying pan, then add the oil. When the oil is hot, add the mooli, beetroot and carrots and stir-fry for 2–3 minutes over medium to high heat.

4 Remove the vegetables from the wok, put them in a bowl and keep hot.

5 Cut the orange in half. Squeeze the juice, using a citrus juicer or a reamer, and pour the juice into a bowl.

6 Arrange the vegetables on a warmed platter, sprinkle over the coriander and season twith salt and pepper.

7 Reheat the wok or frying pan, then pour in the orange juice and simmer for 2 minutes.

8 Drizzle the reduced orange juice over the top of the stir-fried vegetables, sprinkle the top with the pine nuts, and serve immediately.

Mixed Stir-fry with Peanut Sauce

Wherever you go in Asia, stir-fried vegetables will be on the menu.

Ingredients

6 Chinese black mushrooms (dried shiitake), soaked in lukewarm water for 20 minutes
20 tiger lily buds, soaked in lukewarm water for 20 minutes
60ml/4 tbsp sesame oil
225g/8oz tofu, sliced
1 large onion, finely sliced
1 large carrot, finely sliced
300g/11oz pak choi (bok choy), leaves separated from stems
225g/8oz can bamboo shoots, drained and rinsed
50ml/2fl oz/¼ cup soy sauce
10ml/2 tsp sugar

For the peanut sauce

15ml/1 tbsp sesame oil
2 garlic cloves, finely chopped
2 fresh red chillies, seeded and finely chopped
90g/3½oz/scant 1 cup unsalted roasted peanuts, finely chopped
150ml/5fl oz/⅔ cup coconut milk
30ml/2 tbsp hoisin sauce
15ml/1 tbsp soy sauce
15ml/1 tbsp sugar

Serves 4–6

1 To make the sauce, heat the oil in a wok and stir-fry the garlic and chillies until they begin to colour, then add almost all of the peanuts. Stir-fry for 2–3 minutes, then add the remaining ingredients. Boil, then simmer until thickened. Keep warm.

2 Drain the mushrooms and lily buds and squeeze out any excess water. Cut the mushroom caps into strips and discard the stalks. Trim off the hard ends of the lily buds and tie a knot in the centre of each one.

3 Heat 30ml/2 tbsp of the oil in a wok and brown the tofu on both sides. Drain and cut it into strips.

4 Heat the remaining oil in the wok and stir-fry the onion, carrot and pak choi stems for 2 minutes. Add the mushrooms, lily buds, tofu and bamboo shoots and stir-fry for 1 minute more. Toss in the pak choi leaves, soy sauce and sugar. Stir-fry until heated through. Garnish with the remaining peanuts and serve with the peanut sauce.

mooli, beetroot & carrot Energy 103kcal/427kJ; Protein 2.1g; Carbohydrate 7.8g, of which sugars 7.5g; Fat 7.2g, of which saturates 0.7g; Cholesterol 0mg; Calcium 33mg; Fibre 2.1g; Sodium 31mg.
stir-fry w. peanut sauce Energy 157kcal/656kJ; Protein 5.5g; Carbohydrate 13g, of which sugars 11.4g; Fat 9.6g, of which saturates 2.1g; Cholesterol 0mg; Calcium 110mg; Fibre 5.5g; Sodium 65mg.

Stir-fried Seeds & Vegetables

The contrast between the crunchy seeds and vegetables and the rich, savoury sauce is what makes this dish so delicious. Serve it on its own, or with rice or noodles.

Ingredients

30ml/2 tbsp vegetable oil
30ml/2 tbsp sesame seeds
30ml/2 tbsp sunflower seeds
30ml/2 tbsp pumpkin seeds
2 garlic cloves, finely chopped
2.5cm/1in piece fresh root ginger, peeled and finely chopped
2 large carrots, cut into batons
2 large courgettes (zucchini), cut into batons
90g/3½oz/1½ cups oyster mushrooms, torn in pieces
150g/5oz watercress or spinach leaves, coarsely chopped
small bunch fresh mint or coriander (cilantro), leaves and stems chopped
60ml/4 tbsp black bean sauce
30ml/2 tbsp light soy sauce
15ml/1 tbsp palm sugar (jaggery) or light muscovado (brown) sugar
30ml/2 tbsp rice vinegar

Serves 4

1 Heat the oil in a wok. Add the seeds. Toss over a medium heat for 1 minute, then add the garlic and ginger and continue to stir-fry until the ginger is aromatic and the garlic is golden. Do not let the garlic burn or it will taste bitter.

2 Add the carrot and courgette batons and the sliced oyster mushrooms to the wok and stir-fry over a medium heat for a further 5 minutes, or until all the vegetables are crisp-tender and are golden at the edges.

3 Add the watercress or spinach with the fresh herbs. Toss over the heat for 1 minute, then stir in the black bean sauce, soy sauce, sugar and vinegar. Stir-fry for 1–2 minutes, until combined and hot. Serve immediately.

Cook's Tip

Oyster mushrooms are delicate, so it is better to tear them into pieces along the lines of the gills, rather than slice them.

Mixed Vegetables Monk-style

Chinese monks eat neither meat nor fish, so "Monk-style" dishes are fine for vegetarians.

Ingredients

50g/2 oz dried tofu sticks
115g/4oz fresh lotus root, peeled and sliced
10g/¼oz dried cloud ear (wood ear) mushrooms
8 dried Chinese mushrooms
15ml/1 tbsp vegetable oil
75g/3oz/¾ cup drained, canned straw mushrooms
115g/4oz/1 cup baby corn cobs, cut in half
30ml/2 tbsp light soy sauce
15ml/1 tbsp sake or dry sherry
10ml/2 tsp sugar
150ml/¼ pint/⅔ cup vegetable stock
75g/3oz/¾ cup mangetouts (snow peas)
5ml/1 tsp cornflour (cornstarch)
15ml/1 tbsp cold water
salt

Serves 4

1 Put the tofu sticks in a bowl. Cover them with hot water and leave to soak for 1 hour. The wood ears and dried Chinese mushrooms should be soaked in separate bowls of hot water for 20 minutes.

2 Drain the wood ears, trim off and discard the hard base from each and cut the rest into bitesize pieces. Drain the mushrooms, trim off and discard the stems and slice the caps.

3 Drain the tofu sticks. Cut them into 5cm/2in long pieces, discarding any hard pieces.

4 Heat the oil in a wok and stir-fry the wood ears, Chinese mushrooms and lotus root for about 30 seconds. Add the tofu, straw mushrooms, baby corn cobs, soy sauce, sherry, sugar and stock. Boil, then simmer, covered for 20 minutes.

5 Trim the mangetouts and cut them in half. Add to the vegetable mixture, with salt to taste, and cook, uncovered, for 2 minutes more. Mix the cornflour to a paste with the water and add to the wok. Cook, stirring, until the sauce thickens. Serve immediately.

stir-fried seeds & veg. Energy 205kcal/849kJ; Protein 6.9g; Carbohydrate 9.7g, of which sugars 7.7g; Fat 15.6g, of which saturates 2g; Cholesterol 0mg; Calcium 159mg; Fibre 3.4g; Sodium 294mg.
mixed veg. monk-style Energy 95kcal/399kJ; Protein 3.3g; Carbohydrate 12g, of which sugars 4.6g; Fat 3.6g, of which saturates 0.4g; Cholesterol 0mg; Calcium 91mg; Fibre 1.4g; Sodium 885mg.

Stir-fried Vegetables & Rice

The ginger gives this mixed rice and vegetable dish a wonderful flavour.

Ingredients

115g/4oz/generous ½ cup brown basmati rice, rinsed and drained
350ml/12fl oz/1½ cups vegetable stock
2.5cm/1in piece fresh root ginger
1 garlic clove, halved
5cm/2in piece pared lemon rind
115g/4oz/1½ cups shiitake mushrooms
15ml/1 tbsp vegetable oil
175g/6oz baby carrots, trimmed
225g/8oz baby courgettes (zucchini), halved
175–225g/6–8oz/about 1½ cups broccoli, broken into florets
6 spring onions (scallions), diagonally sliced
15ml/1 tbsp light soy sauce
10ml/2 tsp toasted sesame oil

Serves 2–4

1 Put the rice in a pan and pour in the vegetable stock. Thinly slice the ginger and add it to the pan with the garlic and lemon rind. Slowly bring to the boil, then cover and simmer for 20–25 minutes until the rice is tender. Discard the flavourings and keep the rice hot.

2 Slice the mushrooms, discarding the stems. Heat the oil in a wok and stir-fry the carrots for 4–5 minutes, the add the mushrooms and courgettes and stir-fry for 2–3 minutes. Add the broccoli and spring onions and cook for 3 minutes more, by which time all the vegetables should be tender but should still retain a bit of "bite".

3 Add the cooked rice to the vegetables, and toss briefly over the heat to mix and heat through. Toss with the soy sauce and sesame oil. Spoon into a bowl and serve immediately.

Cook's Tip
Keep fresh root ginger in the freezer. It can be sliced or grated and thaws very quickly.

Coconut Noodles & Vegetables

When everyday vegetables are livened up with Thai spices and flavours, the result is a delectable dish that everyone will enjoy.

Ingredients

30ml/2 tbsp sunflower oil
1 lemon grass stalk, finely chopped
15ml/1 tbsp red curry paste
1 onion, thickly sliced
3 courgettes (zucchini), thickly sliced
115g/4oz Savoy cabbage, thickly sliced
2 carrots, thickly sliced
150g/5oz broccoli, stem thickly sliced and florets separated
2 x 400ml/14fl oz cans coconut milk
475ml/16fl oz/2 cups vegetable stock
150g/5oz dried egg noodles
30ml/2 tbsp soy sauce
60ml/4 tbsp chopped fresh coriander (cilantro)

For the garnish

2 lemon grass stalks, split
1 bunch fresh coriander (cilantro)
8–10 small fresh red chillies

Serves 4–6

1 Heat the oil in a wok. Add the lemon grass and red curry paste and stir-fry for 2–3 seconds. Add the onion and cook over medium heat, stirring occasionally, until softened.

2 Add the courgettes, cabbage, carrots and slices of broccoli stem. Toss the vegetables with the onion mixture. Cook over low heat, stirring occasionally, for a further 5 minutes.

3 Increase the heat, stir in the coconut milk and vegetable stock and bring to the boil. Add the broccoli florets and the noodles, lower the heat and simmer gently for 20 minutes.

4 To make the garnish, gather the coriander into a small bouquet and lay it on a platter. Tuck the lemon grass halves into the coriander bouquet and add the chillies to resemble flowers.

5 Stir the soy sauce and chopped coriander into the noodle mixture. Spoon on to the platter, taking care not to disturb the herb bouquet, and serve immediately.

vegetables & rice Energy 430kcal/1788kJ; Protein 12.5g; Carbohydrate 58.2g, of which sugars 11.2g; Fat 16.2g, of which saturates 2.2g; Cholesterol 0mg; Calcium 127mg; Fibre 6.5g; Sodium 569mg.
coconut noodles & veg. Energy 192kcal/808kJ; Protein 5.6g; Carbohydrate 29.4g, of which sugars 11.5g; Fat 6.6g, of which saturates 1.4g; Cholesterol 8mg; Calcium 83mg; Fibre 2.4g; Sodium 554mg.

Tung Tong

Popularly called "gold bags", these crisp pastry purses have a coriander-flavoured filling based on water chestnuts and corn. They are the perfect vegetarian snack and look very impressive.

Ingredients

18 spring roll wrappers, about 8cm/3¼in square, thawed if frozen
oil, for deep-frying
plum sauce, to serve

For the filling

4 baby corn cobs
130g/4½oz can water chestnuts, drained and chopped
1 shallot, coarsely chopped
1 egg, separated
30ml/2 tbsp cornflour (cornstarch)
60ml/4 tbsp water
small bunch fresh coriander (cilantro), chopped
salt and ground black pepper

Makes 18

1 Make the filling. Place the baby corn, water chestnuts, shallot and egg yolk in a food processor or blender. Process to a coarse paste. Place the egg white in a cup and whisk it lightly with a fork.

2 Put the cornflour in a small pan and stir in the water until smooth. Add the corn mixture and chopped coriander and season with salt and pepper to taste. Cook over a low heat, stirring constantly, until thickened.

3 Leave the filling to cool slightly, then place 5ml/1 tsp in the centre of a spring roll wrapper. Brush the edges with the beaten egg white, then gather up the points and press them firmly together to make a pouch or bag.

4 Repeat with remaining wrappers and filling, keeping the finished bags and the wrappers covered until needed so they do not dry out.

5 Heat the oil in a deep-fryer or wok until a cube of bread, added to the oil, browns in about 45 seconds. Fry the bags, in batches, for about 5 minutes, until golden brown. Drain on kitchen paper and serve hot, with the plum sauce.

Vegetable Tempura

These deep-fried fritters are perfect for parties.

Ingredients

2 medium courgettes (zucchini)
½ medium aubergine (eggplant)
1 large carrot
½ small Spanish onion
1 egg
120ml/4fl oz/½ cup iced water
115g/4oz/1 cup plain (all-purpose) flour
salt and ground black pepper
vegetable oil, for deep-frying
sea salt flakes, lemon slices and Japanese soy sauce (shoyu), to serve

Serves 4

1 Using a potato peeler, pare strips of peel from the courgettes and aubergine to give a striped effect.

2 Cut the courgettes, aubergine and carrot into strips about 7.5–10cm/3–4in long and 3mm/⅛in wide.

3 Put the courgettes, aubergine and carrot into a colander and sprinkle liberally with salt. Leave for about 30 minutes, then rinse thoroughly under cold running water. Drain well.

4 Thinly slice the onion from top to base, discarding the plump pieces in the middle. Separate the layers so that there are lots of fine, long strips. Mix all the vegetables together and season with salt and pepper.

5 Make the batter immediately before frying. Mix the egg and iced water in a bowl, then sift in the flour. Mix briefly with a fork or chopsticks. Do not overmix; the batter should remain lumpy. Add the vegetables to the batter and mix to combine.

6 Half-fill a wok with oil and heat to 180°C/350°F. Scoop up one heaped tablespoon of the mixture at a time and carefully lower it into the oil. Deep-fry in batches for approximately 3 minutes, until golden brown and crisp. Drain on kitchen paper. Serve each portion with salt, slices of lemon and a tiny bowl of Japanese soy sauce for dipping.

tung tong Energy 55kcal/229kJ; Protein 1.2g; Carbohydrate 6.3g, of which sugars 0.4g; Fat 2.9g, of which saturates 0.4g; Cholesterol 12mg; Calcium 19mg; Fibre 0.5g; Sodium 42mg.
vegetable tempura Energy 313kcal/1305kJ; Protein 7.1g; Carbohydrate 30.6g, of which sugars 7.3g; Fat 18.9g, of which saturates 2.5g; Cholesterol 48mg; Calcium 94mg; Fibre 3.6g; Sodium 28mg.

Stir-fried Prawns with Mangetouts

Mangetout means "eat all" and you'll want to do just that when a recipe is as good as this one is. The prawns remain beautifully succulent and the sauce is delicious.

Ingredients

300ml/½ pint/1¼ cups fish stock
350g/12oz raw tiger prawns (jumbo shrimp), peeled and deveined
15ml/1 tbsp vegetable oil
1 garlic clove, finely chopped
225g/8oz/2 cups mangetouts (snow peas)
1.5ml/¼ tsp salt
15ml/1 tbsp mirin (sweet rice wine) or dry sherry
15ml/1 tbsp oyster sauce
5ml/1 tsp cornflour (cornstarch)
5ml/1 tsp caster (superfine) sugar
15ml/1 tbsp cold water
1.5ml/¼ tsp sesame oil

Serves 4

1 Bring the fish stock to the boil in a frying pan. Add the prawns. Cook gently for 2 minutes until the prawns have turned pink, then lift them out on a slotted spoon and set aside.

2 Heat the vegetable oil in a non-stick frying pan or wok. When the oil is very hot, add the chopped garlic and cook for a few seconds, then add the mangetouts. Sprinkle with the salt. Stir-fry for 1 minute.

3 Add the prawns and mirin or sherry to the pan or wok. Toss the ingredients together over the heat for a few seconds, then add the oyster sauce and toss again.

4 Mix the cornflour and sugar to a paste with the water. Add to the pan and cook, stirring constantly, until the sauce thickens slightly. Drizzle with sesame oil.

Cook's Tip

Mirin is a sweet rice wine from Japan. It has quite a delicate flavour and is used for cooking. Rice wine for drinking is called sake. Both are available from Asian food stores. If you cannot locate mirin, dry sherry can be used instead.

Salt & Pepper Prawns

These succulent shellfish beg to be eaten with the fingers, so provide finger bowls or hot cloths for all your guests.

Ingredients

15–18 large raw prawns (shrimp), in the shell, about 450g/1lb
vegetable oil, for deep-frying
3 shallots or 1 small onion, very finely chopped
2 garlic cloves, crushed
1cm/½in piece fresh root ginger, peeled and very finely grated
1–2 fresh red chillies, seeded and finely sliced
2.5ml/½ tsp caster (superfine) sugar or to taste
3–4 spring onions (scallions), shredded, to garnish

For the fried salt

10ml/2 tsp salt
5ml/1 tsp Sichuan peppercorns

Serves 3–4

1 Make the fried salt by dry-frying the salt and peppercorns in a heavy frying pan over medium heat until the peppercorns begin to release their aroma. Cool the mixture, then tip into a mortar and crush with a pestle.

2 Carefully remove the heads and legs from the raw prawns and discard. Leave the body shells and the tails in place. Pat the prepared prawns dry with sheets of kitchen paper.

3 Heat the oil for deep frying to 190°C/375°F. Fry the prawns for 1 minute, then lift them out and drain thoroughly on kitchen paper. Spoon 30ml/2 tbsp of the hot oil into a large frying pan, leaving the rest of the oil to one side to cool.

4 Heat the oil in the frying pan. Add the fried salt, with the shallots or onion, garlic, ginger, chillies and sugar. Toss together for 1 minute.

5 Add the prawns and toss them over the heat for about 1 minute more until they are coated and the shells are pleasantly impregnated with the seasonings. Spoon the shellfish mixture into heated serving bowls and garnish with the shredded spring onions.

prawns w. mangetouts Energy 125kcal/524kJ; Protein 17.6g; Carbohydrate 5.2g, of which sugars 3.6g; Fat 3.4g, of which saturates 0.4g; Cholesterol 171mg; Calcium 96mg; Fibre 1.3g; Sodium 436mg.
salt & pepper prawns Energy 122kcal/514kJ; Protein 20.1g; Carbohydrate 2.7g, of which sugars 2.4g; Fat 3.5g, of which saturates 0.5g; Cholesterol 219mg; Calcium 97mg; Fibre 0.3g; Sodium 1197mg.

Gong Boa Prawns

A sweet and sour sauce complements tiger prawns perfectly.

Ingredients

350g/12oz raw tiger prawns (jumbo shrimp)
½ cucumber, about 75g/3oz
300ml/½ pint/1¼ cups fish stock
15ml/1 tbsp vegetable oil
2.5ml/½ tsp crushed dried chillies
½ green (bell) pepper, seeded and cut into 2.5cm/1in strips
1 small carrot, thinly sliced
30ml/2 tbsp tomato ketchup
45ml/3 tbsp rice vinegar
15ml/1 tbsp sugar
150ml/¼ pint/⅔ cup vegetable stock
50g/2oz/½ cup drained canned pineapple chunks
10ml/2 tsp cornflour (cornstarch) mixed with 15ml/1 tbsp cold water
salt

Serves 4

1 Peel and devein the prawns. Rub them with 2.5ml/½ tsp salt; leave them for a few minutes, then wash and pat dry.

2 Using a narrow peeler or cannelle knife, pare strips of skin off the cucumber to give a stripy effect. Cut the cucumber in half lengthways and scoop out the seeds with a teaspoon. Cut the flesh into 5mm/¼in crescents.

3 Bring the fish stock to the boil in a pan. Add the prawns, lower the heat and poach the prawns for 2 minutes until they turn pink, then lift them out using a slotted spoon and set aside.

4 Heat the oil in a non-stick frying pan or wok over a high heat. Fry the chillies for a few seconds, then add the pepper strips and carrot slices and stir-fry for 1 minute more.

5 Stir the tomato ketchup, vinegar, sugar, stock and 1.5ml/¼ tsp salt into the pan and cook for 3 minutes more.

6 Add the prawns, cucumber and pineapple and cook for 2 minutes. Add the cornflour paste and cook, stirring constantly, until the sauce thickens. Serve immediately.

Chilli & Coconut Prawns

Supply plenty of bread or rice when serving these superb prawns. The sauce is so tasty that diners will want to savour every last drop. Be warned, though, the chilli makes these fiery, even though tamarind has a taming influence.

Ingredients

8 shallots, chopped
4 garlic cloves, chopped
8–10 dried red chillies, soaked in warm water until soft, squeezed dry, seeded and chopped
5ml/1 tsp shrimp paste
30ml/2 tbsp vegetable or groundnut (peanut) oil
250ml/8fl oz/1 cup coconut cream
500g/1¼lb fresh prawns (shrimp), peeled and deveined
10ml/2 tsp tamarind paste
15ml/1 tbsp palm sugar (jaggery)
salt and ground black pepper
2 fresh red chillies, seeded and finely chopped, and fresh coriander (cilantro) leaves, finely chopped, to garnish
crusty bread or steamed rice and pickles, to serve

Serves 4

1 Using a mortar and pestle or food processor, grind the shallots, garlic and dried chillies to a coarse paste. Beat in the shrimp paste.

2 Heat the oil in a wok and stir in the paste until fragrant. Add the coconut cream and let it bubble up until it separates. Toss in the prawns, reduce the heat and simmer for 3 minutes.

3 Stir in the tamarind paste and the sugar and cook for a further 2 minutes until the sauce is very thick. Season with salt and pepper and scatter the chopped chillies and coriander over the top. Serve immediately with chunks of fresh, crusty bread to mop up the sauce, or with steamed rice and pickles.

Cook's Tip

Tamarind used to be an exotic ingredient, available only as pods which needed to be processed before use. Fortunately the paste is now a stocked supermarket item.

gong boa prawns Energy 147kcal/617kJ; Protein 16.3g; Carbohydrate 13.2g, of which sugars 10.7g; Fat 3.5g, of which saturates 0.5g; Cholesterol 171mg; Calcium 88mg; Fibre 1.1g; Sodium 296mg.
chilli & prawns Energy 211kcal/886kJ; Protein 23.6g; Carbohydrate 14.8g, of which sugars 13.1g; Fat 6.8g, of which saturates 1g; Cholesterol 244mg; Calcium 152mg; Fibre 1.1g; Sodium 351mg.

Prawns with Jasmine Rice

Strips of omelette are used to garnish this rice dish. Use your wok for frying the omelette – the sloping sides make it easy to spread the beaten egg thinly and then to slide it out.

Ingredients
45ml/3 tbsp vegetable oil
1 egg, beaten
1 onion, chopped
15ml/1 tbsp chopped garlic
15ml/1 tbsp shrimp paste
1kg/2¼lb/4 cups cooked jasmine rice
350g/12oz cooked shelled prawns (shrimp)
50g/2oz thawed frozen peas
oyster sauce, to taste
2 spring onions (scallions), chopped
15–20 Thai basil leaves, roughly snipped, plus a sprig, to garnish

Serves 4–6

1 Heat 15ml/1 tbsp of the oil in a wok or frying pan. Add the beaten egg and swirl it around to set like a thin pancake.

2 Cook the pancake (on one side only) over a gentle heat until golden. Slide the pancake on to a board, roll up and cut into thin strips. Set aside.

3 Heat the remaining oil in the wok or pan, add the onion and garlic and stir-fry for 2–3 minutes. Stir in the shrimp paste and mix well until thoroughly combined.

4 Add the rice, prawns and peas and toss and stir together, until everything is heated through.

5 Season with oyster sauce to taste, taking great care as the shrimp paste is salty. Mix in the spring onions and basil leaves. Transfer to a serving dish and top with the strips of egg pancake. Serve, garnished with a sprig of basil.

Cook's Tip
Leave a few prawns (shrimp) in their shells for an additional garnish, if you like.

Long Beans with Prawns

Popular in many Asian countries, long beans – like many other vegetables – are often stir-fried with garlic. This Cambodian recipe is livened up with prawns, as well as other flavourings, and works well either as a side dish or on its own with rice.

Ingredients
45ml/3 tbsp vegetable oil
2 garlic cloves, finely chopped
25g/1oz galangal or root ginger, finely shredded
450g/1lb fresh prawns (shrimp), shelled and deveined
1 onion, halved and finely sliced
450g/1lb long beans, trimmed and cut into 7.5cm/3in lengths
120ml/4fl oz/½ cup soy sauce

For the marinade
30ml/2 tbsp fish sauce
juice of 2 limes
10ml/2 tsp sugar
2 garlic cloves, crushed
1 lemon grass stalk, trimmed and finely sliced

Serves 4

1 To make the marinade, beat the fish sauce and lime juice in a bowl with the sugar, until it has dissolved. Stir in the garlic and lemon grass. Toss in the prawns, cover, and chill for 1–2 hours.

2 Heat 30ml/2 tbsp of the oil in a wok or heavy pan. Stir in the chopped garlic and galangal or root ginger. Just as they begin to colour, toss in the marinated prawns. Stir-fry for a minute or until the prawns turn pink. Lift the prawns out on to a plate, reserving as much of the oil, garlic and galangal or root ginger as you can.

3 Add the remaining oil to the wok. Add the onion and stir-fry until slightly caramelized. Stir in the beans, then pour in the soy sauce. Cook for 2–3 minutes, until the beans are tender. Add the prawns and stir-fry until heated through. Serve immediately.

Cook's Tip
This recipe uses an unusually large quantity of soy sauce. If you feel it will be too salty for your taste, use less or choose a light variety.

prawns w. rice Energy 354kcal/1494kJ; Protein 17.8g; Carbohydrate 53.4g, of which sugars 0.9g; Fat 9.2g, of which saturates 1.5g; Cholesterol 158mg; Calcium 117mg; Fibre 0.8g; Sodium 233mg.
long beans w. prawns Energy 187kcal/782kJ; Protein 22.6g; Carbohydrate 9.3g, of which sugars 7.9g; Fat 6.9g, of which saturates 0.9g; Cholesterol 219mg; Calcium 156mg; Fibre 3.2g; Sodium 485mg.

Prawns with Tamarind

The sour, tangy flavour that is characteristic of many Asian dishes comes from tamarind. Fresh tamarind pods can sometimes be bought, but preparing them for cooking is a laborious process. It is much easier to use ready-made tamarind paste, which is available in many Asian supermarkets.

Ingredients

6 dried red chillies
30ml/2 tbsp vegetable oil
30ml/2 tbsp chopped onion
30ml/2 tbsp palm sugar (jaggery) or light muscovado (brown) sugar
30ml/2 tbsp chicken stock
15ml/1 tbsp fish sauce
90ml/6 tbsp tamarind juice, made by mixing tamarind paste with warm water
450g/1lb raw prawns (shrimp), peeled
15ml/1 tbsp fried chopped garlic
30ml/2 tbsp fried sliced shallots
2 spring onions (scallions), chopped, to garnish

Serves 4–6

1 Heat a wok or large frying pan, but do not add any oil at this stage. Add the dried chillies and dry-fry them by pressing them against the surface of the wok or pan with a spatula, turning them occasionally.

2 Add the oil to the wok or pan and reheat. Cook the chopped onion over a medium heat, stirring occasionally, for 2–3 minutes, until softened and golden brown.

3 Add the sugar, stock, fish sauce, dry-fried red chillies and the tamarind juice, stirring constantly until the sugar has dissolved. Bring to the boil, then lower the heat slightly.

4 Add the prawns, garlic and shallots. Toss over the heat for 3–4 minutes, until the prawns are cooked. Garnish with the spring onions and serve.

Cook's Tip
Do not let the chillies burn when dry-frying as they will turn bitter.

Sinigang

Many Filipinos would consider this soured soup-like stew to be their national dish. It is always served with noodles or rice. In addition, fish – in the form of either prawns or thin slivers of fish fillet – is often added for good measure.

Ingredients

15ml/1 tbsp tamarind pulp
150ml/¼ pint/⅔ cup warm water
2 tomatoes
115g/4oz spinach or Chinese leaves (Chinese cabbage)
115g/4oz peeled cooked large prawns (shrimp), thawed if frozen
1.2 litres/2 pints/5 cups prepared fish stock
½ mooli (daikon), peeled and diced
115g/4oz green beans, cut into 1cm/½in lengths
225g/8oz piece of cod or haddock fillet, skinned and cut into strips
fish sauce, to taste
squeeze of lemon juice, to taste
salt and ground black pepper
boiled rice or noodles, to serve

Serves 4–6

1 Put the tamarind pulp in a bowl and pour over the warm water. Set aside while you peel and chop the tomatoes, discarding the seeds. Strip the spinach or Chinese leaves from the stems and tear into small pieces.

2 Remove the heads and shells from the prawns, leaving the tails intact.

3 Pour the prepared fish stock into a large pan and add the diced mooli. Cook the mooli for 5 minutes, then add the beans and continue to cook for 3–5 minutes more.

4 Add the fish strips, tomato and spinach to the pan. Strain in the tamarind juice and cook for 2 minutes. Stir in the prawns and cook for 1–2 minutes until pink. Season with salt and pepper and add a little fish sauce and lemon juice to taste. Transfer the sinigang to individual serving bowls and serve immediately, with rice or noodles.

prawns w. tamarind Energy 112kcal/469kJ; Protein 13.4g; Carbohydrate 5.5g, of which sugars 5.2g; Fat 4.1g, of which saturates 0.5g; Cholesterol 146mg; Calcium 65mg; Fibre 0.2g; Sodium 321mg.
sinigang Energy 52kcal/218kJ; Protein 10.6g; Carbohydrate 1.3g, of which sugars 1.3g; Fat 0.5g, of which saturates 0.1g; Cholesterol 55mg; Calcium 31mg; Fibre 0.6g; Sodium 62mg.

Seared Prawn Salad

In this intensely flavoured salad, prawns and mango are partnered with a sweet-sour garlic dressing.

Ingredients

675g/1½lb medium raw prawns (shrimp), shelled and deveined with tails on
finely shredded rind of 1 lime
½ fresh red chilli, seeded and finely chopped
30ml/2 tbsp olive oil, plus extra for brushing
1 ripe mango, cut into strips
2 carrots, cut into long thin shreds
10cm/4in piece cucumber, sliced
1 small red onion, halved and thinly sliced
a few sprigs of fresh coriander (cilantro)
a few sprigs of fresh mint
45ml/3 tbsp roasted peanuts, roughly chopped
salt and ground black pepper

For the dressing

1 large garlic clove, chopped
10–15ml/2–3 tsp sugar
juice of 2 limes
15–30ml/1–2 tbsp fish sauce
1 fresh red chilli, seeded
5–10ml/1–2 tsp light rice vinegar

Serves 6

1 Place the prawns in a bowl and add the lime rind and chilli. Season with salt and pepper and spoon the oil over them. Leave to marinate for 30–40 minutes.

2 For the dressing, pound the garlic with 10ml/2 tsp sugar until smooth. Work in the juice of 1½ limes and 15ml/1 tbsp of the fish sauce. Pour into a bowl and add half the chilli. Taste, then add more sugar, lime juice, fish sauce and vinegar as needed.

3 Toss the mango, carrots, cucumber and onion with half the dressing. Arrange the salad on individual plates or in bowls.

4 Heat a griddle pan until very hot. Brush with a little oil, then sear the prawns for 2–3 minutes on each side, until they turn pink. Arrange the prawns on the salads. Sprinkle with the remaining dressing and scatter the herb sprigs, chilli and peanuts over the top. Serve immediately.

Prawns with Yellow Curry Paste

Fish and shellfish, such as prawns, and coconut milk, were made for each other. This is a very quick recipe if you buy the yellow curry paste ready-made. It keeps well in a screw-top jar in the refrigerator for up to four weeks.

Ingredients

600ml/1 pint/2½ cups coconut milk
30ml/2 tbsp yellow curry paste
15ml/1 tbsp fish sauce
2.5ml/½ tsp salt
5ml/1 tsp sugar
450g/1lb raw king prawns (jumbo shrimp), thawed if frozen, peeled and deveined
225g/8oz cherry tomatoes
juice of ½ lime
red (bell) peppers, seeded and cut into thin strips, and fresh coriander (cilantro) leaves, to garnish

Serves 4–6

1 Put half the coconut milk in a wok or large pan and bring to the boil. Add the yellow curry paste and stir until it disperses. Lower the heat and simmer gently for about 10 minutes.

2 Add the fish sauce, salt, sugar and remaining coconut milk to the sauce. Simmer for 5 minutes more.

3 Add the prawns and cherry tomatoes. Simmer gently for about 5 minutes until the prawns are pink and tender. Spoon into a serving dish, sprinkle with lime juice and garnish with strips of pepper and coriander.

Cook's Tips

- *Unused coconut milk can be stored in the refrigerator for 1–2 days, or poured into a freezer container and frozen.*
- *If making your own coconut milk, instead of discarding the spent coconut, it can be reused to make a second batch of coconut milk. This will be of a poorer quality and should only be used to extend a good quality first quantity of milk.*
- *Leave newly made coconut milk to stand for 10 minutes. The coconut cream will float to the top – skim off with a spoon.*

seared prawn salad Energy 156kcal/656kJ; Protein 20.9g; Carbohydrate 8.9g, of which sugars 8.4g; Fat 4.3g, of which saturates 0.7g; Cholesterol 219mg; Calcium 102mg; Fibre 1.4g; Sodium 397mg.
prawns w. curry paste Energy 94kcal/397kJ; Protein 13.8g; Carbohydrate 7g, of which sugars 6.9g; Fat 1.4g, of which saturates 0.4g; Cholesterol 146mg; Calcium 92mg; Fibre 0.4g; Sodium 434mg.

Prawn & Cauliflower Curry

This is a basic fisherman's curry. Simple to make, it would usually be eaten from a communal bowl.

Ingredients

450g/1lb raw tiger prawns (jumbo shrimp), peeled, deveined and cleaned
juice of 1 lime
15ml/1 tbsp vegetable oil
1 red onion, roughly chopped
2 garlic cloves, roughly chopped
2 Thai chillies, seeded and chopped
1 cauliflower, broken into florets
5ml/1 tsp sugar
2 star anise, dry-fried and ground
10ml/2 tsp fenugreek, dry-fried and ground
450ml/¾ pint/2 cups coconut milk
1 bunch fresh coriander (cilantro), chopped, to garnish
salt and ground black pepper

Serves 4

1 In a bowl, toss the prawns in the lime juice and set aside. Heat a wok or heavy pan and add the oil. Stir in the onion, garlic and chillies. As they brown, add the cauliflower. Stir-fry for 2–3 minutes.

2 Toss in the sugar and spices. Add the coconut milk, stirring to make sure it is thoroughly combined. Reduce the heat and simmer for 10–15 minutes, or until the liquid has reduced and thickened a little. Add the prawns and lime juice and cook for 1–2 minutes, or until the prawns turn opaque. Season to taste, and sprinkle with coriander. Serve hot.

Cook's Tip
To devein prawns, make a shallow cut down the back of the prawn, lift out the thin, black vein, then rinse thoroughly under cold, running water.

Variation
Other popular combinations include prawns (shrimp) with butternut squash or pumpkin.

Mango & Prawn Curry

This sweet, spicy curry is simple to make, and the addition of mango and tamarind produces a very full, rich flavour. If you have time, make the sauce the day before to give the flavours time to develop.

Ingredients

1 green mango
5ml/1 tsp hot chilli powder
15ml/1 tbsp paprika
2.5ml/½ tsp ground turmeric
4 garlic cloves, crushed
10ml/2 tsp finely grated ginger
30ml/2 tbsp ground coriander
10ml/2 tsp ground cumin
15ml/1 tbsp palm sugar (jaggery)
400g/14oz can coconut milk
10ml/2 tsp salt
15ml/1 tbsp tamarind paste
1kg/2¼lb large prawns (shrimp)
chopped coriander (cilantro), to garnish
steamed white rice, chopped tomato, cucumber and onion salad, to serve

Serves 4

1 Wash, stone (pit) and slice the mango and set aside. In a large bowl, combine the chilli powder, paprika, turmeric, garlic, ginger, ground coriander, ground cumin and palm sugar. Add 400ml/14fl oz/1⅔ cups cold water to the bowl and stir to combine the ingredients.

2 Pour the spice mixture into a wok and place over a high heat and bring the mixture to the boil. Cover the wok with a lid, reduce the heat to low and simmer gently for 8–10 minutes.

3 Add the mango, coconut milk, salt and tamarind paste to the wok and stir to combine. Bring to a simmer and then add the whole prawns.

4 Cover the wok and cook gently for 10–12 minutes, or until the prawns have turned pink and are cooked.

5 Serve the curry garnished with chopped coriander, accompanied by steamed white rice and a tomato, cucumber and onion salad.

prawn & cauliflower Energy 157kcal/664kJ; Protein 24.7g; Carbohydrate 10.4g, of which sugars 9.4g; Fat 2.2g, of which saturates 0.6g; Cholesterol 219mg; Calcium 169mg; Fibre 2.7g; Sodium 351mg.
mango & prawn Energy 151kcal/648kJ; Protein 22.1g; Carbohydrate 14.1g, of which sugars 14g; Fat 1.1g, of which saturates 0.5g; Cholesterol 263mg; Calcium 143mg; Fibre 1g; Sodium 2102mg.

Baked Stuffed Crab Shells

This French-inspired dish has been given an Asian twist with a combination of bean thread noodles and cloud ear mushrooms. It is time-consuming to cook the crabs yourself, so use freshly cooked crab meat from your fishmonger or supermarket. You will also need four small, empty crab shells. Cleaned shells can, in fact, be bought in some Asian markets, but many fishmongers will sell dressed crab within the shell so this does ease the preparation two-fold. As a last resort, four small individual ovenproof dishes will do.

Ingredients

25g/1oz dried bean thread (cellophane) noodles
6 dried cloud ear (wood ear) mushrooms
450g/1lb fresh crab meat
15ml/1 tbsp vegetable oil
10ml/2 tsp fish sauce
2 shallots, finely chopped
2 garlic cloves, finely chopped
2.5cm/1in fresh root ginger, peeled and grated
1 small bunch coriander (cilantro), stalks removed, leaves chopped
1 egg, beaten
25g/1oz/2 tbsp butter
salt and ground black pepper
fresh dill fronds, to garnish
chilli sauce, to serve

Serves 4

1 Preheat the oven to 180°C/350°F/Gas 4. Soak the bean thread noodles and cloud ear mushrooms separately in bowls of lukewarm water for 15 minutes. Squeeze dry and chop finely.

2 In a bowl, mix together the noodles and mushrooms with the crab meat. Add the oil, fish sauce, shallots, garlic, ginger and coriander. Season, then stir in the beaten egg.

3 Spoon the mixture into four small crab shells or use individual ovenproof dishes, packing it in tightly, and dot the top of each one with a little butter. Place the shells on a baking tray and cook for about 20 minutes, or until the filling in each shell is nicely browned.

4 Garnish with dill and serve immediately with a little chilli sauce to drizzle over the top.

Crab Meat in Vinegar

A refreshing summer tsumami (a Japanese dish that accompanies alcoholic drinks). For the dressing, use a Japanese or Greek cucumber, if possible – they are about one-third of the size of ordinary salad cucumbers and contain less water.

Ingredients

½ red (bell) pepper, seeded
pinch of salt
275g/10oz cooked white crab meat, or 2 x 165g/5½oz canned white crab meat, drained
about 300g/11oz Japanese, Greek or salad cucumber

For the vinegar mixture

15ml/1 tbsp rice vinegar
10ml/2 tsp caster (superfine) sugar
10ml/2 tsp awakuchi shoyu

Serves 4

1 Slice the red pepper into thin strips lengthways. Sprinkle with a little salt and leave for about 15 minutes. Rinse well and drain.

2 For the vinegar mixture, combine the rice vinegar, sugar and awakuchi shoyu in a small bowl.

3 Loosen the crab meat and mix it with the sliced red pepper in a mixing bowl. Divide among four small bowls.

4 If you use salad cucumber, scoop out the seeds. Finely grate the cucumber with a fine-toothed grater or use a food processor. Drain in a fine-meshed sieve (or strainer).

5 Mix the cucumber with the vinegar mixture, and pour a quarter on to the crab meat mixture in each bowl. Serve cold immediately, before the cucumber loses its colour.

Variation

The vinegar mixture is best made using awakuchi shoyu, but ordinary shoyu can be used instead. It will make a darker dressing, however.

stuffed crab shells Energy 215kcal/897kJ; Protein 23.3g; Carbohydrate 7.3g, of which sugars 1.9g; Fat 10.4g, of which saturates 4g; Cholesterol 132mg; Calcium 174mg; Fibre 1.1g; Sodium 718mg.
crab meat in vinegar Energy 82kcal/345kJ; Protein 13.3g; Carbohydrate 5.6g, of which sugars 5.4g; Fat 0.8g, of which saturates 0.1g; Cholesterol 50mg; Calcium 100mg; Fibre 0.9g; Sodium 560mg.

Mussels with Lemon Grass

Lemon grass and basil give this fragrant dish a subtle flavour. It makes a lovely light appetizer.

Ingredients

1.75kg/4–4½lb fresh mussels in their shells
2 lemon grass stalks
5cm/2in fresh root ginger, peeled
5–6 fresh basil sprigs
2 shallots, finely chopped
150ml/¼ pint/⅔ cup fish stock

Serves 4

1 Scrub the mussels under cold running water, scraping off any barnacles with a small, sharp knife. Pull or cut off the hairy "beards". Discard any mussels with damaged shells and any that remain open when they are sharply tapped.

2 Cut each lemon grass stalk in half and bruise with a rolling pin or a pestle. Cut the ginger into thin slices.

3 Pull the basil leaves off the stems and roughly chop half of them. Reserve the remainder.

4 Put the mussels, lemon grass, chopped basil, ginger, shallots and stock in a wok. Bring to the boil, cover and simmer for 5 minutes.

5 Discard the lemon grass and any mussels that remain closed, scatter over the reserved basil leaves and serve immediately.

Variations

• *Substitute half the total weight of mussels for clams. Clams take slightly longer to cook so add them to the wok with the other ingredients as in Step 4, and cook for 2 minutes before adding the mussels and simmering for a further 5 as directed.*
• *The liquor from the mussels combines with the fish stock to make a delicious sauce. Add a splash of white wine, if you like, but take care not to overwhelm the lemon grass flavour.*

Aromatic Mussels with Chilli

This dish is a version of the French classic, moules marinière, with the mussels being steamed open in a herb-infused stock with lemon grass and chilli instead of wine and parsley. The treatment also works with clams and snails.

Ingredients

600ml/1 pint/2½ cups chicken stock or beer, or a mixture of the two
1 fresh red chilli, seeded and chopped
2 shallots, finely chopped
3 lemon grass stalks, finely chopped
1 bunch ginger or basil leaves
1kg/2¼lb fresh mussels, cleaned and bearded
salt and ground black pepper

Serves 4

1 Pour the stock or beer into a deep pan. Add the chilli, shallots, lemon grass and most of the ginger or basil leaves, retaining a few leaves for the garnish. Bring to the boil. Cover and simmer for 10–15 minutes, then season to taste.

2 Check the mussels and discard any that are tightly closed or which fail to close when tapped on the work surface. Any mussels with damaged shells should also be discarded.

3 Add the remaining mussels to the stock. Stir well, cover and cook for 2 minutes, or until the mussels have opened. Discard any that remain closed. Ladle the mussels and cooking liquid into individual bowls.

Cook's Tips

• *Any mussels that will not close before cooking may be dead, and therefore rotten. Tightly-closed shells tend to signify the same – generally, these are the ones that will not open upon contact with the steam and should therefore also be discarded.*
• *Aromatic ginger leaves are hard to find outside Asia. If you can't find them, basil or coriander (cilantro) will work well.*

mussels w. lemon grass Energy 130kcal/551kJ; Protein 21.5g; Carbohydrate 3g, of which sugars 2.3g; Fat 2.3g, of which saturates 0.5g; Cholesterol 58mg; Calcium 230mg; Fibre 0.5g; Sodium 629mg.
mussels w. chilli Energy 75kcal/318kJ; Protein 13.6g; Carbohydrate 1.5g, of which sugars 1.1g; Fat 1.7g, of which saturates 0.3g; Cholesterol 30mg; Calcium 176mg; Fibre 0.8g; Sodium 162mg.

Pan-steamed Mussels with Herbs

Now that fresh lemon grass is readily available, this dish is very easy to prepare.

Ingredients

1kg/2¼lb fresh mussels
2 lemon grass stalks, finely chopped
4 shallots, chopped
4 kaffir lime leaves, coarsely torn
2 fresh red chillies, sliced
15ml/1 tbsp fish sauce
30ml/2 tbsp fresh lime juice
thinly sliced spring onions (scallions) and coriander (cilantro) leaves, to garnish

Serves 4–6

1 Clean the mussels by pulling off the beards, scrubbing the shells well and removing any barnacles. Discard any mussels that are broken or which do not close when tapped sharply.

2 Place the mussels in a large, heavy pan and add the lemon grass, shallots, kaffir lime leaves, chillies, fish sauce and lime juice. Mix well. Cover the pan tightly and steam the mussels over a high heat, shaking the pan occasionally, for 5–7 minutes, until the shells have opened.

3 Using a slotted spoon, transfer the cooked mussels to a warmed serving dish or individual bowls. Discard any mussels that have failed to open.

4 Garnish the mussels with the thinly sliced spring onions and coriander leaves. Serve immediately.

Cook's Tips

• Most recipes use fresh black mussels, although rather more luxurious options include the New Zealand green-shelled (green-lipped) mussel and the meaty rope-grown variety.
• With their warty, dark green skin, kaffir limes are not the prettiest fruit, but they are an invaluable ingredient in Chinese and South-east Asian cooking. They have little juice, but the rind is intensely aromatic. The leaves add a more subtle flavour.

Steamed Mussels in Coconut Milk

Mussels steamed in coconut milk and fresh aromatic herbs and spices make an ideal dish for informal entertaining. A wok makes short work of the cooking and the dish is great for a relaxed dinner with friends.

Ingredients

15ml/1 tbsp sunflower oil
6 garlic cloves, roughly chopped
15ml/1 tbsp finely chopped fresh root ginger
2 large fresh red chillies, seeded and finely sliced
6 spring onions (scallions), finely chopped
400ml/14fl oz/1⅔ cups coconut milk
45ml/3 tbsp light soy sauce
2 limes
5ml/1 tsp caster (superfine) sugar
1.6kg/3½lb mussels, scrubbed and beards removed
a large handful of chopped coriander (cilantro)
salt and ground black pepper

Serves 4

1 Heat the wok over a high heat and then add the oil. Stir in the garlic, ginger, chillies and spring onions and stir-fry for 30 seconds. Pour in the coconut milk, then add the soy sauce.

2 Grate the zest of the limes into the coconut milk mixture and add the sugar. Stir to mix and bring to the boil. Add the mussels. Return to the boil, cover and cook briskly for about 5–6 minutes, or until all the mussels have opened. Discard any mussels that remain closed.

3 Remove the wok from the heat and stir the chopped coriander into the mussel mixture. Season the mussels well with salt and pepper. Ladle into warmed bowls and serve.

Cook's Tip

For an informal supper with friends, take the wok straight to the table rather than serving in individual bowls. A wok makes a great serving dish, and there's something utterly irresistible about eating the mussels straight from it.

mussels w. herbs Energy 73kcal/310kJ; Protein 13.4g; Carbohydrate 1.5g, of which sugars 1.1g; Fat 1.6g, of which saturates 0.3g; Cholesterol 30mg; Calcium 155mg; Fibre 0.4g; Sodium 159mg.
steamed mussels Energy 165kcal/701kJ; Protein 22.1g; Carbohydrate 7.3g, of which sugars 7.2g; Fat 5.6g, of which saturates 1g; Cholesterol 48mg; Calcium 276mg; Fibre 0.2g; Sodium 1165mg.

Mussels & Clams with Lemon Grass

Wine is seldom used in green curries but in this recipe it adds depth of flavour to the sauce.

Ingredients

1.8kg/4lb fresh mussels
450g/1lb baby clams
120ml/4fl oz/½ cup dry white wine
1 bunch spring onions (scallions), chopped
2 lemon grass stalks, chopped
6 kaffir lime leaves, chopped
10ml/2 tsp green curry paste
200ml/7fl oz/scant 1 cup coconut cream
30ml/2 tbsp chopped fresh coriander (cilantro)
salt and ground black pepper
garlic chives, to garnish

Serves 6

1 Clean the mussels by pulling off the beards, scrubbing the shells well and scraping off any barnacles with the blade of a knife. Scrub the clams. Discard any mussels or clams that are damaged or broken or which do not close immediately when tapped sharply.

2 Put the wine in a large pan with the spring onions, lemon grass and lime leaves. Stir in the curry paste. Simmer until the wine has almost evaporated.

3 Add the mussels and clams to the pan and increase the heat to high. Cover tightly and steam the shellfish for 5–6 minutes, until they open.

4 Using a slotted spoon, transfer the mussels and clams to a heated serving bowl, cover and keep hot. Discard any shellfish that remain closed. Strain the cooking liquid into a clean pan through a sieve (strainer) lined with muslin (cheesecloth) and simmer briefly to reduce to about 250ml/8fl oz/1 cup.

5 Stir the coconut cream and chopped coriander into the sauce and season with salt and pepper to taste. Heat through. Pour the sauce over the mussels and clams, garnish with the garlic chives and serve immediately.

Clams with Miso & Mustard Sauce

Sweet and juicy, clams are excellent with this sweet-and-sour dressing.

Ingredients

900g/2lb carpet shell clams
15ml/1 tbsp sake
8 spring onions (scallions), green and white parts separated, then chopped in half
10g/¼oz dried wakame

For the dressing

60ml/4 tbsp shiro miso
20ml/4 tsp sugar
30ml/2 tbsp sake
15ml/1 tbsp rice vinegar
about 1.5ml/¼ tsp salt
7.5ml/1½ tsp English (hot) mustard

Serves 4

1 Wash the clams under running water. Discard any that remain open when tapped. Pour 1cm/½in water into a small pan. Add the clams and sake, cover, then bring to the boil. Cook for 5 minutes, then remove from the heat and leave to stand for 2 minutes.

2 Drain the clams, discarding any which have failed to open, and keep the liquid in a small bowl. When they have cooled slightly, remove the meat from most of the clam shells.

3 Cook the white part of the spring onions in a pan of boiling water for 2 minutes, then add the remaining green parts and cook for 2 minutes more. Drain well.

4 Mix the shiro miso, sugar, sake, rice vinegar and salt for the dressing, in a small pan. Stir in 45ml/3 tbsp of the reserved clam liquid, and heat gently, stirring until the sugar has dissolved. Add the mustard, check the seasoning, and remove from the heat and leave to cool.

5 Soak the wakame in a bowl of water for about 10 minutes. Drain and squeeze out excess moisture.

6 Mix together the clams, onions, wakame and dressing in a bowl. Heap up in a large bowl or divide among four small bowls and serve cold.

mussels w. lemon grass Energy 237kcal/993kJ; Protein 22.5g; Carbohydrate 2.8g, of which sugars 1.7g; Fat 13.8g, of which saturates 10.3g; Cholesterol 58mg; Calcium 238mg; Fibre 0.9g; Sodium 606mg.
clams w. miso/mustard Energy 114kcal/482kJ; Protein 12.8g; Carbohydrate 13.2g, of which sugars 11.6g; Fat 0.6g, of which saturates 0.2g; Cholesterol 50mg; Calcium 71mg; Fibre 0.3g; Sodium 1764mg.

Steamed Scallops with Ginger

It helps to have two woks when making this dish. Borrow an extra one from a friend, or use a large, heavy pan with a trivet for steaming the second plate of scallops. Take care not to overcook the tender seafood.

Ingredients

24 king scallops in their shells, cleaned
15ml/1 tbsp very finely shredded fresh root ginger
5ml/1 tsp very finely chopped garlic
1 large fresh red chilli, seeded and very finely chopped
15ml/1 tbsp light soy sauce
15ml/1 tbsp Chinese rice wine
a few drops of sesame oil
2–3 spring onions (scallions), very finely shredded
15ml/1 tbsp very finely chopped fresh chives
noodles or rice, to serve

Serves 4

1 Remove the scallops from their shells, then remove the membrane and hard white muscle from each one. Arrange the scallops on two plates. Rinse the shells, dry and set aside.

2 Fill two woks with 5cm/2in water and place a trivet in the base of each one. Bring to the boil.

3 Meanwhile, mix together the ginger, garlic, chilli, soy sauce, rice wine, sesame oil, spring onions and chives.

4 Spoon the flavourings over the scallops. Lower a plate into each of the woks. Turn the heat to low, cover and steam for 10–12 minutes.

5 Divide the scallops among four, or eight, of the reserved shells and serve immediately with noodles or rice.

Cook's Tip
Use the freshest scallops you can find. If you ask your fishmonger to shuck them, remember to ask for the shells.

Scallops & Tiger Prawns

Serve this light, delicate dish for lunch or supper accompanied by aromatic steamed rice or fine rice noodles and stir-fried pak choi or broccoli.

Ingredients

15ml/1 tbsp stir-fry oil or sunflower oil
500g/1¼lb raw tiger prawns (jumbo shrimp), peeled
1 star anise
225g/8oz scallops, halved horizontally if large
2.5cm/1in piece fresh root ginger, peeled and grated
2 garlic cloves, thinly sliced
1 red (bell) pepper, seeded and cut into thin strips
115g/4oz/1¾ cups shiitake or button (white) mushrooms, thinly sliced
juice of 1 lemon
5ml/1 tsp cornflour (cornstarch), mixed to a paste with 30ml/2 tbsp cold water
30ml/2 tbsp light soy sauce
salt and ground black pepper
chopped fresh chives, to garnish

Serves 4

1 Heat the oil in a wok until very hot. Put in the prawns and star anise and stir-fry over a high heat for 2 minutes.

2 Add the scallops, ginger and garlic and stir-fry for 1 minute more, by which time the prawns should have turned pink and the scallops opaque. Season with a little salt and plenty of pepper and then remove from the wok using a slotted spoon. Discard the star anise.

3 Add the red pepper and mushrooms to the wok and stir-fry for 1–2 minutes. Pour in the lemon juice, cornflour paste and soy sauce, bring to the boil and bubble this mixture for 1–2 minutes, stirring all the time, until the sauce is smooth and slightly thickened.

4 Stir the prawns and scallops into the sauce, cook for a few seconds until heated through, then season with salt and ground black pepper. Spoon onto individual plates and serve garnished with the chives.

scallops w. ginger Energy 392kcal/1621kJ; Protein 13.6g; Carbohydrate 4.5g, of which sugars 2.5g; Fat 34.1g, of which saturates 22.4g; Cholesterol 115mg; Calcium 63mg; Fibre 0.4g; Sodium 168mg.
scallops/tiger prawns Energy 212kcal/892kJ; Protein 36.3g; Carbohydrate 6.6g, of which sugars 3.3g; Fat 4.6g, of which saturates 0.8g; Cholesterol 270mg; Calcium 122mg; Fibre 1g; Sodium 877mg.

Spiced Scallops & Sugar Snap Peas

This is a great dish for special-occasion entertaining.

Ingredients

45ml/3 tbsp oyster sauce
10ml/2 tsp soy sauce
5ml/1 tsp sesame oil
5ml/1 tsp golden caster (superfine) sugar
30ml/2 tbsp sunflower oil
2 fresh red chillies, finely sliced
4 garlic cloves, finely chopped
10ml/2 tsp finely chopped fresh root ginger
250g/9oz sugar snap peas, trimmed
500g/1 ¼lb king scallops, cleaned and halved, roes discarded
3 spring onions (scallions), finely shredded

For the noodle cakes

250g/9oz fresh thin egg noodles
10ml/2 tsp sesame oil
120ml/4fl oz/½ cup sunflower oil

Serves 4

1 Cook the noodles in boiling water until tender. Drain, toss with the sesame oil and 15ml/1 tbsp of the sunflower oil and spread out on a large baking sheet. Leave to dry in a warm place for 1 hour.

2 Heat 15ml/1 tbsp of the oil in a wok. Add a quarter of the noodle mixture, flatten it and shape it into a cake.

3 Cook the cake for about 5 minutes on each side until crisp and golden. Drain on kitchen paper and keep hot while you make the remaining three noodle cakes in the same way.

4 Mix the oyster sauce, soy sauce, sesame oil and sugar, stirring until the sugar has dissolved completely.

5 Heat a wok, add the sunflower oil, then stir-fry the chillies, garlic, ginger and sugar snaps for 1–2 minutes. Add the scallops and spring onions and stir-fry for 1 minute, then add the sauce mixture and cook for 1 minute.

6 Place a noodle cake on each plate, top with the scallop mixture and serve immediately.

Lemon Grass Snails

Served straight from the steamer, these taste great.

Ingredients

24 fresh snails in their shells
225g/8oz lean minced (ground) pork, passed through the mincer (grinder) twice
3 lemon grass stalks, trimmed and finely chopped or ground (reserve the outer leaves)
2 spring onions (scallions), finely chopped
25g/1oz fresh root ginger, peeled and finely grated
1 fresh red chilli, seeded and finely chopped
10ml/2 tsp sesame or groundnut (peanut) oil
sea salt and ground black pepper
chilli sauce or other sauce, for dipping

Serves 4

1 Pull the snails out of their shells and place them in a colander. Rinse the snails thoroughly in plenty of cold water and pat dry with kitchen paper. Rinse the shells and leave to drain.

2 Chop the snails finely and put them in a bowl. Add the minced pork, lemon grass, spring onions, ginger, chilli and oil. Season with salt and pepper and mix well.

3 Select the best of the lemon grass leaves and tear each one into thin ribbons, roughly 7.5cm/3in long. Bend each ribbon in half and put it inside a snail shell, so that the ends are poking out. The idea is that each diner pulls the ends of the lemon grass ribbon to gently prize the steamed morsel out of its shell.

4 Using your fingers, stuff each shell with the snail and pork mixture, gently pushing it between the lemon grass ends to the back of the shell so that it fills the shell completely.

5 Fill a pan a third of the way up with water and bring it to the boil. Arrange the snail shells, open side up, in a steamer that fits the pan. Cover and steam for about 10 minutes, until the mixture is cooked. Serve hot with chilli sauce or another strong-flavoured dipping sauce of your choice.

spiced scallops Energy 689kcal/2888kJ; Protein 41.4g; Carbohydrate 59.9g, of which sugars 6.2g; Fat 33.3g, of which saturates 5.4g; Cholesterol 78mg; Calcium 73mg; Fibre 5g; Sodium 700mg.
lemon grass snails Energy 136kcal/573kJ; Protein 24.2g; Carbohydrate 0.2g, of which sugars 0.2g; Fat 4.3g, of which saturates 1.1g; Cholesterol 70mg; Calcium 9mg; Fibre 0.1g; Sodium 70mg.

Stuffed Squid with Shiitake Mushrooms

The smaller the squid, the sweeter the dish will taste. Be very careful not to overcook the flesh as it toughens very quickly.

Ingredients

8 small squid
50g/2oz cellophane noodles
30ml/2 tbsp groundnut (peanut) oil
2 spring onions (scallions), finely chopped
8 shiitake mushrooms, halved if large
250g/9oz minced (ground) pork
1 garlic clove, chopped
30ml/2 tbsp fish sauce
5ml/1 tsp caster (superfine) sugar
15ml/1 tbsp finely chopped fresh coriander (cilantro)
5ml/1 tsp lemon juice
salt and ground black pepper

Serves 4

1 Cut off the tentacles of the squid just below the eye. Remove the transparent "quill" from inside the body and rub off the skin on the outside. Wash the squid thoroughly in cold water and set aside on a plate.

2 Bring a pan of water to the boil and add the noodles. Remove from the heat and set aside to soak for 20 minutes.

3 Preheat the oven to 200°C/400°F/Gas 6. Heat 15ml/1 tbsp of the oil in a preheated wok and stir-fry the spring onions, shiitake mushrooms, pork and garlic for 4 minutes until the meat is golden and the spring onions and mushrooms have softened.

4 Drain the noodles and add to the wok, with the fish sauce, sugar, coriander, lemon juice and salt and pepper to taste.

5 Stuff the squid with the mixture and secure with cocktail sticks (toothpicks). Arrange the squid in an ovenproof dish, drizzle over the remaining oil and prick each squid twice. Bake in the preheated oven for 10 minutes. Serve hot.

Five-spice Squid

Squid is perfect for stir-frying as it should be cooked quickly. The spicy sauce makes the ideal accompaniment.

Ingredients

450g/1lb small squid, cleaned
45ml/3 tbsp oil
2.5cm/1in fresh root ginger, grated
1 garlic clove, crushed
8 spring onions (scallions), cut into 2.5cm/1in lengths
1 red (bell) pepper, seeded and cut into strips
1 fresh green chilli, seeded and thinly sliced
6 mushrooms, sliced
5ml/1 tsp Chinese five-spice powder
30ml/2 tbsp black bean sauce
30ml/2 tbsp soy sauce
5ml/1 tsp sugar
15ml/1 tbsp Chinese rice wine or dry sherry

Serves 6

1 Rinse the squid and pull away the outer skin. Dry on kitchen paper. Slit the squid open and score the inside into diamonds with a sharp knife. Cut the squid into strips.

2 Heat the oil in a preheated wok. Stir-fry the squid quickly. Remove the squid strips from the wok with a slotted spoon and set aside.

3 Add the ginger, garlic, spring onions, red pepper, chilli and mushrooms to the oil remaining in the wok and stir-fry for 2 minutes.

4 Return the squid to the wok and stir in the five-spice powder. Stir in the black bean sauce, soy sauce, sugar and rice wine or dry sherry. Bring to the boil and cook, stirring, for 1 minute. Serve immediately.

Variation

Use button (white) mushrooms for this recipe, or try a mixture of cultivated and wild mushrooms. Dried shiitake mushrooms would also be good but must be first soaked in water.

squid w. mushrooms Energy 356kcal/1486kJ; Protein 21.8g; Carbohydrate 15.2g, of which sugars 3.6g; Fat 23.6g, of which saturates 11.1g; Cholesterol 321mg; Calcium 55mg; Fibre 1.9g; Sodium 352mg.
five-spice squid Energy 134kcal/562kJ; Protein 15.1g; Carbohydrate 4.8g, of which sugars 3.5g; Fat 6.2g, of which saturates 0.9g; Cholesterol 203mg; Calcium 23mg; Fibre 0.9g; Sodium 956mg.

Squid with Broccoli

The slightly chewy squid contrasts beautifully with the crisp crunch of the broccoli to give this dish the perfect combination of textures so beloved by the Chinese.

Ingredients

300ml/½ pint/1¼ cups fish stock
350g/12oz prepared squid, cut into large pieces
225g/8oz broccoli
15ml/1 tbsp vegetable oil
2 garlic cloves, finely chopped
15ml/1 tbsp Chinese rice wine or dry sherry
10ml/2 tsp cornflour (cornstarch)
2.5ml/½ tsp caster (superfine) sugar
45ml/3 tbsp cold water
15ml/1 tbsp oyster sauce
2.5ml/½ tsp sesame oil
noodles, to serve

Serves 4

1 Bring the fish stock to the boil in a wok or pan. Add the squid pieces and cook for 2 minutes over medium heat until they are tender and have curled. Drain the squid pieces and set aside until required.

2 Trim the broccoli and cut it into small florets. Bring a pan of lightly salted water to the boil, add the broccoli and cook for 2 minutes until crisp-tender. Drain thoroughly.

3 Heat the vegetable oil in a wok or non-stick frying pan. When the oil is hot, add the garlic, stir-fry for a few seconds, then add the squid, broccoli and rice wine or sherry. Stir-fry the mixture over medium heat for about 2 minutes.

4 Mix the cornflour and sugar to a paste with the water. Stir the mixture into the wok or pan, with the oyster sauce. Cook, stirring, until the sauce thickens slightly. Just before serving, stir in the sesame oil. Serve with noodles.

Variation
Use pak choi (bok choy) instead of broccoli when it is available.

Squid in Hot Yellow Sauce

Simple fishermen's dishes such as this one are cooked in coastal regions throughout Asia. This one includes enough chillies to set your tongue on fire. To temper the heat, the dish is often served with rice or sago porridge, and finely shredded green mango tossed in lime juice.

Ingredients

500g/1¼lb fresh squid
juice of 2 limes
5ml/1 tsp salt
4 shallots, chopped
4 garlic cloves, chopped
25g/1oz galangal, chopped
25g/1oz fresh turmeric, chopped
6–8 fresh red chillies, seeded and chopped
30ml/2 tbsp vegetable oil
7.5ml/1½ tsp palm sugar (jaggery)
2 lemon grass stalks, crushed
4 lime leaves
400ml/14fl oz/1⅔ cups coconut milk
salt and ground black pepper
crusty bread or steamed rice, to serve

Serves 4

1 First prepare the squid. Hold the body sac in one hand and pull off the head with the other. Sever the tentacles just above the eyes, and discard the rest of the head and innards. Clean the body sac inside and out and remove the skin. Pat the squid dry, cut it into thick slices and put them in a bowl, along with the tentacles. Mix the lime juice with the salt and rub it into the squid. Set aside for 30 minutes.

2 Meanwhile, using a mortar and pestle or food processor, grind the shallots, garlic, galangal, turmeric and chillies to a coarse paste.

3 Heat the oil in a wok or heavy pan, and stir in the coarse paste. Cook the paste until fragrant, then stir in the palm sugar, lemon grass and lime leaves. Drain the squid of any juice and toss it around the wok, coating it in the flavourings.

4 Pour in the coconut milk and bring it to the boil. Reduce the heat and simmer for 5–10 minutes, until the squid is tender. Season and serve with crusty bread or steamed rice.

squid w. broccoli Energy 127kcal/536kJ; Protein 16g; Carbohydrate 4.4g, of which sugars 0.9g; Fat 4.8g, of which saturates 0.8g; Cholesterol 197mg; Calcium 44mg; Fibre 1.5g; Sodium 103mg.
squid in hot sauce Energy 185kcal/780kJ; Protein 19.8g; Carbohydrate 9.4g, of which sugars 7.6g; Fat 8g, of which saturates 1.4g; Cholesterol 281mg; Calcium 50mg; Fibre 0.2g; Sodium 739mg.

Salmon with Shallots & Galangal

This is a thin, soupy curry with wonderfully strong flavours. Serve it in bowls with lots of sticky rice to soak up the delicious juices.

Ingredients
450g/1lb salmon fillet
500ml/17fl oz/2¼ cups vegetable stock
4 shallots, finely chopped
2 garlic cloves, finely chopped
2.5cm/1in piece fresh galangal, finely chopped
tender bulbous portion of 1 lemon grass stalk, finely chopped
2.5ml/½ tsp dried chilli flakes
15ml/1 tbsp fish sauce
5ml/1 tsp palm sugar (jaggery) or light muscovado (brown) sugar
Fresh crusty bread, to serve

Serves 4

1 Wrap the salmon in clear film (plastic wrap) and place in the freezer for 30–40 minutes to firm up the flesh slightly.

2 Remove the fish from the freezer, unwrap it and remove the skin, then use a sharp knife to cut the fish into 2.5cm/1in cubes, removing any stray bones with your fingers or with tweezers as you do so.

3 Pour the stock into a large, heavy pan and bring it to the boil over a medium heat. Add the shallots, garlic, galangal, lemon grass, chilli flakes, fish sauce and sugar. Bring back to the boil, stir well, then reduce the heat and simmer gently for 15 minutes.

4 Add the fish cubes to the stock, bring back to the boil, then turn off the heat. Leave the curry to stand for 10–15 minutes until the fish is cooked through, then serve in heated bowls with plenty of fresh crusty bread to mop up the juices.

Variations
Rosy pink salmon looks particularly pretty, but other types of fish would work equally well in this curry. Try cod, pollack, hoki or haddock. Monkfish is also suitable.

Salmon & Black-eyed Beans

This dish will keep for 4–5 days in a cool place.

Ingredients
150g/5oz salmon fillet, boned and skinned
400g/14oz can black-eyed beans (peas) in brine
50g/2oz fresh shiitake mushrooms, stalks removed
50g/2oz carrot, peeled
50g/2oz mooli (daikon), peeled
5g/⅛oz piece of dashi-konbu about 10cm/4in square
60ml/4 tbsp water
5ml/1 tsp caster (superfine) sugar
15ml/1 tbsp soy sauce
7.5ml/1½ tsp mirin (sweet rice wine)
salt
2.5cm/1in fresh root ginger, peeled

Serves 4

1 Slice the salmon into 1cm/½in thick pieces. Thoroughly salt the fillet and leave for 1 hour, then wash away the salt and cut it into 1cm/½in cubes. Par-boil in rapidly boiling water in a small pan for 30 seconds, then drain. Rinse under running water.

2 Slice the fresh ginger thinly lengthways, then stack the slices and cut into thin threads. Soak in cold water for 30 minutes, then drain well.

3 Drain the can of beans and tip the liquid into a medium pan. Set the beans and pan of liquid aside.

4 Chop all the vegetables into 1cm/½in cubes. Wipe the dried konbu with a damp dish towel or kitchen paper, then snip into shreds with scissors.

5 Add the salmon, vegetables and konbu to the bean liquid with the beans, water, sugar and 1.5ml/¼ tsp salt. Bring to the boil. Reduce the heat to low and cook for 6 minutes or until the carrot is cooked. Add the soy sauce and cook for about 4 minutes. Add the mirin, then remove the pan from the heat, mix well and check the seasoning. Leave for an hour. Serve garnished with the fresh sliced ginger.

salmon w. shallots/galangal Energy 220kcal/915kJ; Protein 23.8g; Carbohydrate 3g, of which sugars 2.6g; Fat 12.6g, of which saturates 2.2g; Cholesterol 56mg; Calcium 36mg; Fibre 0.2g; Sodium 320mg.
salmon & beans Energy 387kcal/1633kJ; Protein 33.7g; Carbohydrate 43.5g, of which sugars 5.6g; Fat 9.9g, of which saturates 1.9g; Cholesterol 38mg; Calcium 70mg; Fibre 8.2g; Sodium 588mg.

Sweet Soy Salmon

Teriyaki sauce forms the marinade for the salmon in this recipe. Served with soft-fried noodles, it makes a stunning dish, which people of all ages will enjoy.

Ingredients

350g/12oz salmon fillet
30ml/2 tbsp soy sauce
30ml/2 tbsp sake
60ml/4 tbsp mirin or sweet sherry
5ml/1 tsp soft light brown sugar
10ml/2 tsp grated fresh root ginger
3 garlic cloves, 1 crushed and 2 sliced into rounds
15ml/1 tbsp vegetable oil
225g/8oz dried egg noodles, cooked and drained
50g/2oz/1 cup alfalfa sprouts
10ml/2 tsp sesame seeds, lightly toasted

Serves 4

1 If you have time, chill the salmon briefly in the freezer to make it easier to slice. Using a sharp chopping knife, cut the salmon into thin slices. Place the slices of fish in a shallow dish.

2 In a measuring jug (pitcher), mix together the soy sauce, sake, mirin or sherry, sugar, ginger and crushed garlic. Pour the mixture over the salmon, cover and leave for 30 minutes in a cool place.

3 Preheat the grill (broiler). Drain the salmon, and scrape off and reserve the marinade. Place the salmon in a single layer on a baking sheet. Grill (broil) for 2–3 minutes without turning.

4 Meanwhile, heat a wok until hot, add the oil and swirl it around. Add the garlic rounds and cook until golden brown but not burnt.

5 Add the cooked noodles and reserved marinade to the wok and stir-fry for 3–4 minutes, until the marinade has reduced slightly to a syrupy glaze and coats the noodles.

6 Toss in the alfalfa sprouts, then remove immediately from the heat. Transfer to warmed serving plates and top with the salmon. Sprinkle with the toasted sesame seeds and serve.

Asian Seared Salmon

Salmon fillets only take a few minutes to cook, but make sure you allow enough time for the fish to soak up all the flavours of the marinade before you start to cook.

Ingredients

grated rind and juice of 1 lime
15ml/1 tbsp soy sauce
2 spring onions (scallions), sliced
1 fresh red chilli, seeded and finely chopped
2.5cm/1in piece fresh root ginger, peeled and grated
1 lemon grass stalk, finely chopped
4 salmon fillets, each about 175g/6oz
30ml/2 tbsp olive oil
salt and ground black pepper
45ml/3 tbsp fresh coriander (cilantro), to garnish
cooked egg noodles and stir-fried carrot, peppers and mangetouts (snow peas), to serve

Serves 4

1 Put the grated lime rind in a jug (pitcher) and pour in the lime juice. Add the soy sauce, spring onions, chilli, ginger and lemon grass. Season with pepper and stir well.

2 Place the salmon in a shallow non-metallic dish and pour the lime mixture over. Cover and marinate in the refrigerator for at least 30 minutes.

3 Brush a griddle pan with 15ml/1 tbsp of the olive oil and heat until hot. Remove the fish from the marinade, pat dry and add to the griddle pan. Cook the salmon fillets for 6 minutes, turning once.

4 When the salmon fillets are almost cooked, pour the remaining marinade into a separate pan and heat it. Add the salmon fillets to the hot marinade and simmer for 1–2 minutes.

5 Serve the salmon on a bed of egg noodles and stir-fried vegetables. Garnish with coriander.

sweet soy salmon Energy 392kcal/1649kJ; Protein 19.3g; Carbohydrate 43.6g, of which sugars 4g; Fat 15.1g, of which saturates 2.9g; Cholesterol 45mg; Calcium 50mg; Fibre 2g; Sodium 664mg.
asian salmon Energy 370kcal/1539kJ; Protein 35.8g; Carbohydrate 0.6g, of which sugars 0.5g; Fat 24.9g, of which saturates 4.1g; Cholesterol 88mg; Calcium 60mg; Fibre 0.6g; Sodium 350mg.

Salmon & Shimeji Parcels

In this recipe, the vegetables and salmon are wrapped and steamed with sake in their own moisture.

Ingredients

450g/1lb salmon fillet, skinned
30ml/2 tbsp sake or dry sherry
15ml/1 tbsp shoyu
about 250g/9oz/3 cups fresh shimeji mushrooms
8 fresh shiitake mushrooms
2.5cm/1in carrot
2 spring onions (scallions)
115g/4oz/1 cup mangetouts (snow peas)
salt

Serves 4

1 Cut the salmon into bitesize pieces. Marinate in the sake and shoyu for about 15 minutes, then drain and reserve the marinade. Preheat the oven to 190°C/375°F/Gas 5.

2 Clean the shimeji mushrooms and chop off the hard root. Remove and discard the stems from the shiitake. Carve a small white cross in the brown top of each shiitake cap.

3 Slice the carrot very thinly, then cut out 8–12 maple-leaf or flower shapes. Carefully slice the spring onions in half lengthways. Trim the mangetouts.

4 Cut four sheets of foil, each about 29 x 21cm/11½ x 8½in wide. Place the long side of one sheet facing towards you. Arrange the salmon and shimeji mushrooms in the centre, then place a spring onion diagonally across them. Put two shiitake on top, three to four mangetouts in a fan shape and then sprinkle with a few carrot leaves.

5 Sprinkle the marinade and a good pinch of salt over the top. Fold the two longer sides of the foil together, then fold the shorter sides to seal. Repeat to make four parcels.

6 Bake the parcels on a baking sheet for 15–20 minutes in the middle of the preheated oven. When the foil has expanded into a balloon, the dish is ready to serve.

Teriyaki Salmon en Papillote

The aromatic smell that wafts out of these fish parcels as you open them is deliciously tempting.

Ingredients

2 carrots
2 courgettes (zucchini)
6 spring onions (scallions)
2.5cm/1in piece fresh root ginger, peeled
1 lime
2 garlic cloves, thinly sliced
30ml/2 tbsp teriyaki marinade or fish sauce
5–10ml/1–2 tsp clear sesame oil
4 salmon fillets, about 200g/7oz each
ground black pepper
rice, to serve

Serves 4

1 Cut the carrots, courgettes and spring onions into matchsticks and set them aside. Cut the ginger into matchsticks and put these in a small bowl. Using a zester, pare the lime thinly. Add the pared rind to the ginger, with the garlic. Squeeze the lime juice.

2 Place the teriyaki marinade or fish sauce into a bowl and stir in the lime juice and sesame oil.

3 Preheat the oven to 220°C/425°F/Gas 7. Cut out four rounds of baking parchment, each with a diameter of 40cm/16in. Season the salmon with pepper. Lay a fillet on one side of each paper round, about 3cm/1¼ in off centre.

4 Sprinkle a quarter of the ginger mixture over each and pile a quarter of the vegetable matchsticks on top. Spoon a quarter of the teriyaki or fish sauce mixture over the top.

5 Fold the bare side of the baking parchment over the salmon and roll the edges of the parchment over to seal each parcel very tightly.

6 Place the salmon parcels on a baking sheet and cook in the oven for about 10–12 minutes, depending on the thickness of the fillets. Put the parcels on plates and serve with rice.

salmon & shimeji parcels Energy 231kcal/964kJ; Protein 25.2g; Carbohydrate 3.9g, of which sugars 3.3g; Fat 12.9g, of which saturates 2.2g; Cholesterol 56mg; Calcium 48mg; Fibre 2g; Sodium 328mg.
salmon en papillote Energy 321kcal/1337kJ; Protein 31.6g; Carbohydrate 5.3g, of which sugars 4.8g; Fat 16.6g, of which saturates 2.9g; Cholesterol 75mg; Calcium 46mg; Fibre 0.6g; Sodium 873mg.

Green Hoki Curry

Any firm-fleshed fish can be used for this curry, which gains its rich colour from a mixture of fresh herbs.

Ingredients

4 garlic cloves, roughly chopped
5cm/2in piece fresh root ginger, peeled and roughly chopped
2 fresh green chillies, seeded and roughly chopped
grated rind and juice of 1 lime
5ml/1 tsp coriander seeds
5ml/1 tsp five-spice powder
75ml/5 tbsp sesame oil
2 red onions, finely chopped
900g/2lb hoki fillets, skinned
400ml/14fl oz/1⅔ cups coconut milk
45ml/3 tbsp fish sauce
50g/2oz fresh coriander (cilantro)
50g/2oz fresh mint leaves
50g/2oz fresh basil leaves
6 spring onions (scallions), chopped
150ml/¼ pint/⅔ cup sunflower or groundnut (peanut) oil
sliced fresh green chilli and chopped fresh coriander (cilantro), to garnish
cooked Basmati or Thai fragrant rice and lime wedges, to serve

Serves 4

1 First make the curry paste. Combine the garlic, fresh root ginger, green chillies and the lime juice in a food processor. Add the coriander seeds and five-spice powder, with half the sesame oil. Whiz to a fine paste, then set aside.

2 Heat a wok and stir-fry the red onions in the remaining sesame oil for 2 minutes. Add the fish and stir-fry for 1–2 minutes to seal on all sides.

3 Lift out the red onions and fish and put them on a plate. Add the curry paste to the wok or pan and fry for 1 minute, stirring. Return the hoki fillets and red onions to the wok, pour in the coconut milk and bring to the boil. Lower the heat, add the fish sauce and simmer for 5–7 minutes until the fish is cooked through.

4 Meanwhile, process the herbs, spring onions, lime rind and oil in a food processor to a coarse paste. Stir into the fish curry. Garnish with chilli and coriander and serve with the cooked rice and lime wedges.

Hoki Stir-fry

Any firm white fish, such as monkfish, hake or cod, can be used for this attractive stir-fry. You can vary the vegetables according to what is available, but try to include at least three different colours.

Ingredients

675g/1½ lb hoki fillet, skinned
pinch of five-spice powder
2 carrots
115g/4oz/1 cup small mangetouts (snow peas)
115g/4oz asparagus spears
4 spring onions (scallions)
45ml/3 tbsp groundnut (peanut) oil
2.5cm/1in piece fresh root ginger, peeled and cut into thin slivers
2 garlic cloves, finely chopped
300g/11oz/scant 1½ cups beansprouts
8–12 small baby corn cobs
15–30ml/1–2 tbsp light soy sauce
salt and ground black pepper

Serves 4–6

1 Cut the hoki into finger-size strips and season with salt, pepper and five-spice powder. Cut the carrots diagonally into slices as thin as the mangetouts.

2 Trim the mangetouts. Trim the asparagus spears and cut in half crossways. Trim the spring onions and cut them diagonally into 2cm/¾ in pieces, keeping the white and green parts separate. Set aside.

3 Heat a wok, then pour in the oil. As soon as it is hot, add the ginger and garlic. Stir-fry for 1 minute, then add the white parts of the spring onions and cook for 1 minute more.

4 Add the hoki strips and stir-fry for 2–3 minutes, until all the pieces of fish are opaque. Add the beansprouts and toss them around to coat them in the oil, then put in the carrots, mangetouts, asparagus and corn. Continue to stir-fry for 3–4 minutes, by which time the fish should be cooked, but all the vegetables will still be crunchy. Add soy sauce to taste, toss everything quickly together, then stir in the green parts of the spring onions. Serve immediately.

green hoki curry Energy 608kcal/2527kJ; Protein 41g; Carbohydrate 13.3g, of which sugars 9.5g; Fat 43.8g, of which saturates 5.9g; Cholesterol 0mg; Calcium 168mg; Fibre 1.3g; Sodium 313mg.
hoki stir-fry Energy 183kcal/764kJ; Protein 22.4g; Carbohydrate 5g, of which sugars 3.8g; Fat 8.2g, of which saturates 1.1g; Cholesterol 0mg; Calcium 49mg; Fibre 2.3g; Sodium 295mg.

Hot & Fragrant Trout

This wickedly hot spice paste could be used as a marinade for any fish or meat. It also makes a wonderful spicy dip for grilled meat.

Ingredients

2 large fresh green chillies, seeded and coarsely chopped
5 shallots, peeled
5 garlic cloves, peeled
30ml/2 tbsp fresh lime juice
30ml/2 tbsp fish sauce
15ml/1 tbsp light muscovado (brown) sugar
4 kaffir lime leaves, rolled into cylinders and thinly sliced
2 trout or similar firm-fleshed fish, about 350g/12oz each, cleaned
fresh garlic chives, to garnish
boiled rice, to serve

Serves 4

1 Wrap the chillies, shallots and garlic in a foil package. Place under a hot grill (broiler) for 10 minutes, until softened.

2 When the package is cool enough to handle, tip the contents into a mortar or food processor and pound with a pestle or process to a paste.

3 Add the lime juice, fish sauce, sugar and lime leaves and mix well. With a teaspoon, stuff this paste inside the fish. Smear a little of the paste on the skin too.

4 Grill (broil) the fish for about 5 minutes on each side, until just cooked through. Lift the fish on to a platter, garnish with garlic chives and serve with rice.

Cook's Tip

It is now possible to buy farmed trout of exceptional quality quite inexpensively, so this dish can be prepared as a regular treat rather than an occasional indulgence. Healthy, farm-reared trout tends to have paler skin, rather than the bright pink pigment we have come to associate with trout flesh.

Trout with Tamarind

Sometimes trout can taste rather bland, but this spicy sauce really gives it a zing.

Ingredients

4 trout, cleaned
6 spring onions (scallions), sliced
60ml/4 tbsp soy sauce
15ml/1 tbsp vegetable oil
30ml/2 tbsp chopped fresh coriander (cilantro) and strips of fresh red chilli, to garnish

For the sauce

50g/2oz tamarind pulp
105ml/7 tbsp boiling water
2 shallots, coarsely chopped
1 fresh red chilli, seeded and chopped
1cm/½in piece fresh root ginger, peeled and chopped
5ml/1 tsp soft light brown sugar
45ml/3 tbsp fish sauce

Serves 4

1 Slash the trout diagonally four or five times on each side. Place them in a shallow dish that is large enough to hold them all in a single layer.

2 Fill the cavity in each trout with spring onions and douse each fish with soy sauce. Carefully turn the fish over to coat both sides with the sauce. Sprinkle any remaining spring onions over the top.

3 To make the sauce, put the tamarind pulp in a small bowl and pour on the boiling water. Mash it well with a fork until it has softened.

4 Tip the tamarind mixture into a food processor or blender, and add the shallots, fresh chilli, ginger, sugar and fish sauce. Process to a coarse pulp. Scrape into a bowl.

5 Heat the oil in a large frying pan or wok and cook the trout, one at a time if necessary, for about 5 minutes on each side, until the skin is crisp and browned and the flesh cooked.

6 If cooking in batches, keep the cooked trout hot until all four fish have been fried. Serve the trout on warmed plates and spoon over some of the sauce. Sprinkle with the coriander and chilli and offer the remaining sauce separately.

hot & fragrant trout Energy 171kcal/719kJ; Protein 27.2g; Carbohydrate 3.9g, of which sugars 3.9g; Fat 5.3g, of which saturates 1.2g; Cholesterol 112mg; Calcium 44mg; Fibre 0g; Sodium 102mg.
trout w. tamarind Energy 329kcal/1384kJ; Protein 47.9g; Carbohydrate 8.1g, of which sugars 6.3g; Fat 11.9g, of which saturates 2.5g; Cholesterol 192mg; Calcium 96mg; Fibre 1.2g; Sodium 978mg.

Trout with Black Rice

Pink trout fillets cooked with ginger make a stunning contrast to black rice.

Ingredients

2.5cm/1in piece fresh root ginger, peeled and grated
1 garlic clove, crushed
1 fresh red chilli, seeded and finely chopped
30ml/2 tbsp soy sauce
2 trout fillets, each about 200g/7oz
oil, for greasing

For the rice

15ml/1 tbsp sesame oil
50g/2oz/¾ cup fresh shiitake mushrooms, stems discarded, caps sliced
8 spring onions (scallions), finely chopped
150g/5oz/¾ cup black rice
4 slices fresh root ginger or galangal
900ml/1½ pints/3¾ cups boiling water or chicken stock

Serves 2

1 Make the rice. Heat the sesame oil in a pan and fry the mushrooms with half the spring onions for 2–3 minutes.

2 Add the rice and sliced ginger to the pan and stir well. Cover with the boiling water or stock and bring to the boil. Reduce the heat, cover and simmer for 25–30 minutes or until the rice is tender. Drain well and cover to keep warm.

3 While the rice is cooking, preheat the oven to 200°C/400°F/Gas 6. In a small bowl mix together the grated ginger, garlic, chilli and soy sauce.

4 Place the fish, skin side up, in a lightly oiled shallow baking dish. Using a sharp knife, make several slits in the skin of the fish, then spread the ginger paste all over the fillets.

5 Cover the dish tightly with foil and cook in the oven for 20–25 minutes or until the trout fillets are cooked through.

6 Divide the rice between two warmed serving plates. Remove the ginger. Lay the fish on top and sprinkle over the reserved spring onions, to garnish.

Marinated Sea Trout

Sea trout has a superb texture and a flavour like that of wild salmon. It is best served with strong but complementary flavours, such as chillies and lime, that cut the richness of its flesh.

Ingredients

6 sea trout cutlets, each about 115g/4oz, or wild or farmed salmon
2 garlic cloves, chopped
1 fresh long red chilli, seeded and chopped
45ml/3 tbsp chopped Thai basil
15ml/1 tbsp sugar or palm sugar (jaggery)
3 limes
400ml/14fl oz/1⅔ cups coconut milk
15ml/1 tbsp fish sauce

Serves 6

1 Place the sea trout cutlets side by side in a shallow dish. Using a pestle, pound the garlic and chilli in a large mortar to break both up roughly. Add 30ml/2 tbsp of the Thai basil with the sugar and continue to pound to a rough paste.

2 Grate the rind from 1 lime and squeeze the juice. Mix the rind and juice into the chilli paste, with the coconut milk. Pour the mixture over the cutlets. Cover and chill for about 1 hour. Cut the remaining limes into wedges.

3 Take the fish out of the refrigerator so that it can return to room temperature. Remove the cutlets from the marinade. Either cook on a barbecue, in an oiled hinged wire fish basket, or under a hot grill (broiler). Cook the fish for 4 minutes on each side, trying not to move them. They may stick to the grill rack if not seared first.

4 Strain the remaining marinade into a pan, reserving the contents of the sieve (strainer). Bring the marinade to the boil, then simmer gently for 5 minutes, stirring. Stir in the contents of the sieve and continue to simmer for 1 minute more. Add the fish sauce and the remaining Thai basil.

5 Lift each fish cutlet on to a plate, pour over the sauce and serve with the lime wedges.

trout w. black rice Energy 560kcal/2362kJ; Protein 45.6g; Carbohydrate 63.5g, of which sugars 3.3g; Fat 15.5g, of which saturates 1.4g; Cholesterol 0mg; Calcium 46mg; Fibre 2.3g; Sodium 1187mg.
marinated sea trout Energy 157kcal/662kJ; Protein 23.1g; Carbohydrate 5.9g, of which sugars 5.9g; Fat 4.7g, of which saturates 0.1g; Cholesterol 0mg; Calcium 46mg; Fibre 0.4g; Sodium 141mg.

Steamed Trout Fillets

This simple dish can be prepared extremely quickly, and is suitable for any fish fillets. Serve it on a bed of noodles accompanied by ribbons of colourful vegetables such as carrots and peppers.

Ingredients

8 pink trout fillets of even thickness, about 115g/4oz each, skinned
50ml/2fl oz coconut cream
grated rind and juice of 2 limes
45ml/3 tbsp chopped fresh coriander (cilantro)
15ml/1 tbsp sunflower or groundnut (peanut) oil
2.5–5ml/½–1 tsp chilli oil
salt and ground black pepper
lime slices and coriander (cilantro) sprigs, to garnish

Serves 4

1 Cut four rectangles of baking parchment, about twice the size of the trout fillets. Place a fillet on each piece and season lightly with salt and pepper.

2 Mix together the coconut, lime rind and chopped coriander and spread a quarter of the mixture over each trout fillet. Sandwich another trout fillet on top.

3 Mix the lime juice with the oils, adjusting the quantity of chilli oil to your own taste, and drizzle the mixture over the trout "sandwiches".

4 Prepare a steamer. Fold up the edges of the paper and pleat them over the trout to make parcels, making sure they are well sealed. Place in the steamer insert and steam over the simmering water for about 10–15 minutes, depending on the thickness of the trout fillets. Serve at once.

Cook's Tip

Chilli oil is widely available, but you can also make your own by adding 15ml/1 tbsp dried chilli flakes to 150ml/¼ pint/⅔ cup hot olive oil. Leave to cool, then bottle and store in a cool place.

Spicy Trout Parcels

Banana leaves make very good wrappers for fish cooked over coals. Sturdy enough to be handled without tearing, they seal in flavours and keep fish moist.

Ingredients

350g/12oz freshwater fish fillets, such as trout, cut into bitesize chunks
6 banana leaves
vegetable oil, for brushing
sticky rice, noodles or salad, to serve

For the marinade

2 shallots
5cm/2in turmeric root, peeled and grated
2 spring onions (scallions), finely sliced
2 garlic cloves, crushed
1–2 fresh green chillies, seeded and finely chopped
15ml/1 tbsp fish sauce
2.5ml/½ tsp raw cane sugar
salt and ground black pepper

Serves 4

1 To make the marinade, grate the shallots into a bowl, then combine with the other marinade ingredients. Season with salt and pepper. Toss the chunks of fish in the marinade, then cover and chill for 6 hours, or overnight.

2 Prepare a barbecue. Place one of the banana leaves on a flat surface and brush it with oil. Place the marinated fish on the banana leaf, spreading it out evenly, then fold over the sides to form an envelope. Place this envelope, fold side down, on top of another leaf and fold that one in the same manner. Repeat with the remaining leaves until they are all used up.

3 Secure the last layer of banana leaf with a piece of bendy wire. Place the banana leaf packet on the barbecue. Cook for about 20 minutes, turning it over from time to time to make sure it is cooked on both sides – the outer leaves will burn, but this is normal.

4 Carefully untie the wire (it will be hot) and unravel the packet. Check that the fish is cooked and serve with sticky rice, noodles or salad.

steamed trout fillets Energy 241kcal/1005kJ; Protein 25g; Carbohydrate 0.9g, of which sugars 0.9g; Fat 15.3g, of which saturates 7g; Cholesterol 0mg; Calcium 21mg; Fibre 0.2g; Sodium 75mg.
spicy trout parcels Energy 126kcal/528kJ; Protein 17.2g; Carbohydrate 0.7g, of which sugars 0.6g; Fat 6.1g, of which saturates 0.3g; Cholesterol 0mg; Calcium 12mg; Fibre 0.2g; Sodium 50mg.

Coconut Baked Snapper

Adding a couple of fresh red chillies to the marinade gives this dish a really spicy flavour. Serve the snapper with plain boiled rice.

Ingredients

1 snapper, about 1kg/2¼lb, scaled and cleaned
400ml/14fl oz/1⅔ cups coconut milk
105ml/7 tbsp dry white wine
juice of 1 lime
45ml/3 tbsp light soy sauce
1–2 fresh red chillies, seeded and finely sliced (optional)
60ml/4 tbsp chopped fresh parsley
45ml/3 tbsp chopped fresh coriander (cilantro)
salt and ground black pepper

Serves 4

1 Lay the snapper in an ovenproof shallow dish and season with a little salt and plenty of pepper.

2 Make the marinade. Mix together the coconut milk, wine, lime juice, soy sauce and chillies, if using. Stir in the herbs and pour over the fish. Cover with clear film (plastic wrap) and marinate in the refrigerator for about 4 hours, turning the fish over halfway through.

3 Preheat the oven to 190°C/375°F/Gas 5. Take the fish out of the marinade and wrap loosely in foil, spooning over the marinade before sealing the parcel.

4 Support the fish parcel in a roasting pan, put the pan in the oven and bake for 30–40 minutes, until the fish is cooked through and the flesh comes away easily from the bone.

Cook's Tips

• *Any type of snapper or trout can be used for this recipe. If you prefer, use one small fish per person, but be aware that small snapper can be very bony.*
• *Use light coconut milk for a less rich version of this dish. The flavour will be just as good.*

Red Snapper in Banana Leaves

Whole snappers infused with coconut cream, herbs and chilli make an impressive main course.

Ingredients

4 small red snapper, gutted and cleaned
4 large squares of banana leaf
50ml/2fl oz/¼ cup coconut cream
90ml/6 tbsp chopped coriander (cilantro)
90ml/6 tbsp chopped mint
juice of 3 limes
3 spring onions (scallions), finely sliced
4 kaffir lime leaves, finely shredded
2 fresh red chillies, seeded and finely sliced
4 lemon grass stalks, split lengthways
salt and ground black pepper
steamed rice and steamed Asian greens, to serve

Serves 4

1 Using a small sharp knife, score the fish diagonally on each side. Half fill a wok with water and bring to the boil.

2 Dip each square of banana leaf into the boiling water in the wok for 15–20 seconds so they become pliable. Lift out carefully, rinse under cold water and dry with kitchen paper.

3 Place the coconut cream, chopped herbs, lime juice, spring onions, lime leaves and chillies in a bowl and stir. Season well.

4 Lay the banana leaves flat and place a fish and a split lemon grass stalk in the centre of each of them. Spread the herb mixture over each fish and fold over each banana leaf to form a neat parcel. Secure each parcel tightly with a bamboo skewer.

5 Place the parcels in a single layer in one or two tiers of a large bamboo steamer and place over a wok of simmering water. Cover tightly and steam for 15–20 minutes, or until the fish is cooked through.

6 Remove the fish from the steamer and serve in their banana-leaf wrappings, with steamed rice and greens.

coconut baked snapper Energy 175kcal/738kJ; Protein 31.6g; Carbohydrate 1g, of which sugars 0.9g; Fat 4.2g, of which saturates 0.8g; Cholesterol 58mg; Calcium 92mg; Fibre 0.5g; Sodium 165mg.
red snapper Energy 185kcal/781kJ; Protein 39.4g; Carbohydrate 0.9g, of which sugars 0.8g; Fat 2.7g, of which saturates 0.6g; Cholesterol 74mg; Calcium 87mg; Fibre 0.1g; Sodium 168mg.

Steamed Sea Bass with Ginger

This is a delicious recipe for any whole white fish, such as sea bass or cod.

Ingredients

200ml/7fl oz/scant 1 cup coconut milk
10ml/2 tsp raw cane or muscovado (molasses) sugar
about 15ml/1 tbsp vegetable oil
2 garlic cloves, finely chopped
1 fresh red chilli, seeded and finely chopped
4cm/1½in fresh root ginger, peeled and grated
750g/1lb 10oz sea bass, gutted and skinned on one side
1 star anise, ground
1 bunch fresh basil, stalks removed
30ml/2 tbsp cashew nuts
sea salt and ground black pepper
rice and salad, to serve

Serves 4

1 Heat the coconut milk with the sugar in a small pan, stirring until the sugar dissolves, then remove from the heat. Heat the oil in a small frying pan and stir in the garlic, chilli and ginger. Cook until they begin to brown, then add the mixture to the coconut milk and mix well to combine.

2 Place the fish, skin side down, on a wide piece of foil and tuck up the sides to form a boat-shaped container. Using a sharp knife, cut several diagonal slashes into the flesh on the top and rub with the ground star anise. Season with salt and pepper and spoon the coconut milk over to coat the fish.

3 Sprinkle half the basil leaves over the top of the fish and pull the foil packet almost closed. Lay the packet in a steamer. Cover the steamer, bring the water to the boil, reduce the heat and simmer for 20–25 minutes, or until just cooked.

4 Roast the cashew nuts in the frying pan, adding extra oil if necessary. Drain the nuts on kitchen paper, then grind them to crumbs. When the fish is cooked, lift it out of the foil and transfer it to a serving dish. Spoon the cooking juices over, sprinkle with the cashew nut crumbs and garnish with the remaining basil leaves. Serve with rice and a salad.

Baked Sea Bass with Lemon Grass

Moist, tender sea bass is finely flavoured with a combination of aromatic ingredients in this simple clay-pot dish.

Ingredients

1 sea bass, about 675g/1½lb, cleaned and scaled
30ml/2 tbsp olive oil
2 lemon grass stalks, finely sliced
1 red onion, finely shredded
1 fresh red chilli, seeded and finely chopped
5cm/2in piece fresh root ginger, finely shredded
45ml/3 tbsp chopped fresh coriander (cilantro)
pared rind and juice of 2 limes
30ml/2 tbsp light soy sauce
salt and ground black pepper

Serves 2–3

1 Soak a fish clay pot in cold water for 20 minutes, then drain. Make four to five diagonal slashes on both sides of the fish. Repeat the slashes on one side in the opposite direction to give an attractive cross-hatched effect. Rub the sea bass inside and out with salt, pepper and 15ml/1 tbsp of the olive oil.

2 Mix the sliced lemon grass, red onion, chilli, ginger, coriander and lime rind in a bowl.

3 Place a little of the lemon grass and red onion mixture in the base of the clay pot, then lay the fish on top. Sprinkle the remaining mixture over the fish, then sprinkle over the lime juice, soy sauce and the remaining olive oil. Cover and place in an unheated oven.

4 Set the oven to 220°C/425°F/Gas 7 and cook the fish for 30–40 minutes, or until the flesh flakes easily when tested with a knife. Serve immediately.

Variation
This recipe will taste equally delicious with red or grey mullet, red snapper, salmon or tilapia. Depending on their weight, you may need to use two smaller fish rather than a single one.

sea bass w. ginger Energy 198kcal/830kJ; Protein 21.8g; Carbohydrate 6.9g, of which sugars 5.9g; Fat 9.5g, of which saturates 1.6g; Cholesterol 80mg; Calcium 177mg; Fibre 0.9g; Sodium 151mg.
sea bass/lemon grass Energy 298kcal/1248kJ; Protein 43.7g; Carbohydrate 1.6g, of which sugars 1.1g; Fat 13g, of which saturates 1.9g; Cholesterol 180mg; Calcium 298mg; Fibre 0.3g; Sodium 156mg.

Fried Sea Bass with Leeks

Sea bass tastes sensational when given this simple treatment.

Ingredients

1 sea bass, about 1.4–1.5kg/3–3½ lb, scaled and cleaned
8 spring onions (scallions)
60ml/4 tbsp teriyaki marinade
30ml/2 tbsp cornflour (cornstarch)
juice of 1 lemon
30ml/2 tbsp rice wine vinegar
5ml/1 tsp ground ginger
60ml/4 tbsp groundnut (peanut) oil
2 leeks, shredded
2.5cm/1in piece fresh root ginger, peeled and grated
105ml/7 tbsp fish stock
30ml/2 tbsp dry sherry
5ml/1 tsp caster (superfine) sugar
salt and ground black pepper

Serves 4

1 Make several diagonal slashes on either side of the sea bass, then season the fish inside and out with salt and ground black pepper. Trim the spring onions, cut them in half lengthways, then slice them diagonally into 2cm/¾ in lengths. Put half of the spring onions in the cavity of the fish and reserve the rest.

2 In a shallow dish, mix together the teriyaki marinade, the cornflour, lemon juice, rice wine vinegar and ground ginger to make a smooth, runny paste. Turn the fish in the marinade to coat it thoroughly, working it into the slashes, then leave it to marinate for 20–30 minutes, turning it several times.

3 Heat a wok or frying pan that is large enough to hold the sea bass comfortably. Add the oil, then the leeks and grated ginger. Fry gently for about 5 minutes, until the leeks are tender. Remove the leeks and ginger and drain on kitchen paper.

4 Lift the sea bass out of the marinade and lower it into the hot oil. Fry over a medium heat for 2–3 minutes on each side. Stir the stock, sherry and sugar into the marinade. Season. Pour the mixture over the fish. Return the leeks, ginger and reserved spring onions to the wok. Cover and simmer for about 15 minutes, until the fish is cooked. Serve immediately.

Steamed Sea Bass with Chilli Sauce

By leaving the fish whole and on the bone, maximum flavour is retained.

Ingredients

1 large or 2 medium firm fish such as sea bass or grouper, scaled and cleaned
30ml/2 tbsp rice wine
3 fresh red chillies, seeded and thinly sliced
2 garlic cloves, finely chopped
2cm/¾ in piece fresh root ginger, peeled and finely shredded
2 lemon grass stalks, crushed and finely chopped
2 spring onions (scallions), chopped
30ml/2 tbsp fish sauce
juice of 1 lime
1 fresh banana leaf or baking parchment

For the chilli sauce

10 fresh red chillies, seeded and chopped
4 garlic cloves, chopped
60ml/4 tbsp fish sauce
15ml/1 tbsp sugar
75ml/5 tbsp fresh lime juice

Serves 4

1 Thoroughly rinse the fish under cold running water. Pat it dry with kitchen paper. With a sharp knife, slash the skin of the fish a few times on both sides.

2 Mix together the rice wine, chillies, garlic, shredded ginger, lemon grass and spring onions in a non-metallic bowl. Add the fish sauce and lime juice and mix to a paste. Place the fish on the banana leaf or parchment and spread the spice paste evenly over it, rubbing it into the slashes.

3 Put a rack or a small upturned plate in the base of a wok. Pour in boiling water to a depth of 5cm/2in. Lift the banana leaf or parchment and fish, and place on the rack or plate. Cover and steam for 10–15 minutes, or until the fish is cooked.

4 Meanwhile, make the sauce. Place all the ingredients in a food processor and process until smooth. If the mixture seems to be too thick, add a little cold water. Scrape into a serving bowl.

5 Serve the fish hot, on the banana leaf if you like, with the sweet chilli sauce to spoon over the top.

sea bass w. leeks Energy 300kcal/1253kJ; Protein 31.1g; Carbohydrate 7.5g, of which sugars 6.7g; Fat 15.4g, of which saturates 2g; Cholesterol 120mg; Calcium 229mg; Fibre 2.6g; Sodium 271mg.
sea bass w. chilli Energy 216kcal/910kJ; Protein 36.3g; Carbohydrate 7.5g, of which sugars 5.5g; Fat 4.7g, of which saturates 0.7g; Cholesterol 140mg; Calcium 246mg; Fibre 0.5g; Sodium 1192mg.

Mackerel with Black Beans

Shiitake mushrooms, ginger and salted black beans are perfect partners for robustly flavoured mackerel fillets.

Ingredients

20 dried shiitake mushrooms
15ml/1 tbsp finely julienned fresh root ginger
3 star anise
8 x 115g/4oz mackerel fillets
45ml/3 tbsp dark soy sauce
15ml/1 tbsp Chinese rice wine
15ml/1 tbsp salted black beans
6 spring onions (scallions), finely shredded
30ml/2 tbsp sunflower oil
5ml/1 tsp sesame oil
4 garlic cloves, very thinly sliced
sliced cucumber and steamed basmati rice, to serve

Serves 4

1 Place the dried mushrooms in a large bowl and cover with boiling water. Soak for 20 minutes. Drain, reserving the soaking liquid, discard the stems and slice the caps thinly.

2 Place a trivet or a steamer rack in a large wok and pour in 5cm/2in of the mushroom liquid (top up with water if necessary). Add half the ginger and the star anise.

3 Divide the mackerel between two lightly oiled heatproof plates, skin side up. Cut three diagonal slits in each one. Insert the remaining ginger strips and sprinkle over the mushrooms. Bring the liquid to the boil and put one of the plates on the trivet.

4 Cover the wok, reduce the heat and steam for about 10–12 minutes, or until the mackerel is cooked. Repeat with the second plate of fish. Put all the fish on a platter and keep warm.

5 Ladle 105ml/7 tbsp of the steaming liquid from the wok into a pan with the soy sauce, wine and black beans. Place over a gentle heat and bring to a simmer. Spoon over the fish and sprinkle over the spring onions.

6 Heat the oils and stir-fry garlic for a few minutes until lightly golden. Pour over the fish and serve with sliced cucumber and steamed basmati rice.

Grilled Mackerel with Tamarind

Oily fish like mackerel are cheap and nutritious. They go very well with a tart or sour accompaniment, like these tamarind-flavoured lentils. Serve with chopped fresh tomatoes, onion salad and flat bread, or new potatoes and green beans.

Ingredients

250g/9oz/1 cup red lentils, or yellow split peas (soaked overnight in water)
1 litre/1¾ pints/4 cups water
30ml/2 tbsp sunflower oil
2.5ml/½ tsp each mustard seeds, cumin seeds, fennel seeds, and fenugreek or cardamom seeds
5ml/1 tsp ground turmeric
3–4 dried red chillies, crumbled
30ml/2 tbsp tamarind paste
5ml/1 tsp soft brown sugar
30ml/2 tbsp chopped fresh coriander (cilantro)
4 mackerel or 8 large sardines
salt and ground black pepper
fresh red chilli slices and chopped coriander (cilantro), to garnish
flat bread and tomatoes, to serve

Serves 4

1 Rinse the lentils or split peas, drain them and put them in a pan. Pour in the water and bring to the boil. Lower the heat, partially cover the pan and simmer the pulses for 30–40 minutes, stirring occasionally, until they are tender and mushy.

2 Heat the oil in a wok or shallow pan. Add the mustard seeds, then cover and cook for a few seconds, until they pop. Remove the lid, add the rest of the seeds, with the turmeric and chillies and fry for a few more seconds.

3 Stir in the pulses, with salt to taste. Mix well; stir in the tamarind paste and sugar. Bring to the boil, then simmer for 10 minutes, until thick. Stir in the chopped fresh coriander.

4 Meanwhile, clean the fish then heat a ridged grilling pan until very hot. Make six diagonal slashes on either side of each fish and remove the head from each one if you wish. Season inside and out, then cook for 5–7 minutes on each side, until the skin is crisp. Serve with the dhal, flat bread and tomatoes, garnished with red chilli and chopped coriander.

mackerel w. beans Energy 693kcal/2872kJ; Protein 45.5g; Carbohydrate 1.9g, of which sugars 0.5g; Fat 55.9g, of which saturates 10.4g; Cholesterol 128mg; Calcium 35mg; Fibre 0.6g; Sodium 152mg.
mackerel w. tamarind Energy 578kcal/2420kJ; Protein 43.5g; Carbohydrate 35.2g, of which sugars 1.5g; Fat 30.2g, of which saturates 5.7g; Cholesterol 80mg; Calcium 48mg; Fibre 3.1g; Sodium 110mg.

Sour Carp Wraps

Carp is popular in China and South-east Asia. For a slightly simpler version of this dish, toss the cooked fish in the herbs and serve it with noodles or rice and a salad.

Ingredients

500g/1¼lb carp fillets, each cut into 3 or 4 pieces
30ml/2 tbsp sesame oil or vegetable oil
10ml/2 tsp ground turmeric
1 small bunch each fresh coriander (cilantro) and basil, stalks removed
20 lettuce leaves or rice wrappers
fish sauce or other dipping sauce, to serve

For the marinade

30ml/2 tbsp tamarind paste
15ml/1 tbsp soy sauce
juice of 1 lime
1 fresh green or red chilli, finely chopped
2.5cm/1in galangal root, peeled and grated
a few sprigs of fresh coriander (cilantro) leaves, finely chopped

Serves 4

1 Prepare the marinade by mixing together all the marinade ingredients in a bowl. Toss the fish pieces in the marinade, cover with clear film (plastic wrap) and chill in the refrigerator for at least 6 hours, or overnight.

2 Lift the pieces of fish out of the marinade and lay them on a plate. Heat a wok or heavy pan, add the oil and stir in the turmeric. Working quickly, so that the turmeric doesn't burn, add the fish pieces, gently moving them around the wok for 2–3 minutes.

3 Add any remaining marinade to the pan and cook for a further 2–3 minutes, or until the pieces of fish are cooked.

4 To serve, divide the fish among four plates, sprinkle with the coriander and basil, and add some of the lettuce leaves or rice wrappers and a small bowl of dipping sauce to each serving. To eat, tear off a bitesize piece of fish, place it on a wrapper with a few herb leaves, fold it up into a roll, then dip it into the sauce.

Clay Pot Catfish

Wonderfully easy and tasty, this is a classic clay pot dish. Clay pots are regularly used for cooking and they enhance both the look and taste of this traditional favourite. However, you can use any heavy pot or pan. Serve with chunks of bread to mop up the caramelized, smoky sauce at the bottom of the pot.

Ingredients

30ml/2 tbsp sugar
15ml/1 tbsp sesame oil or vegetable oil
2 garlic cloves, crushed
45ml/3 tbsp fish sauce
350g/12oz catfish fillets, cut diagonally into 2 or 3 pieces
4 spring onions (scallions), cut into bitesize pieces
ground black pepper
chopped fresh coriander (cilantro), to garnish
fresh bread, to serve

Serves 4

1 Place the sugar in a clay pot or heavy pan, and add 15ml/1 tbsp water to wet it. Heat the sugar until it begins to turn golden brown, then add the oil and crushed garlic.

2 Stir the fish sauce into the caramel mixture and add 120ml/4fl oz/½ cup boiling water, then toss in the catfish pieces, making sure they are well coated with the sauce. Cover the pot, reduce the heat and simmer for about 5 minutes.

3 Remove the lid, season with ground black pepper and gently stir in the spring onions. Simmer for a further 3–4 minutes to thicken the sauce, garnish with fresh coriander, and serve straight from the pot with chunks of fresh bread.

Cook's Tip

When using a traditional clay pot, always use a low to medium heat and heat the pot slowly, otherwise there is a risk of cracking it. They are designed to be used over a low flame, so if using an electric stove, use a heat diffuser.

sour carp wraps Energy 205kcal/856kJ; Protein 23.1g; Carbohydrate 1.6g, of which sugars 1.5g; Fat 11.9g, of which saturates 1.8g; Cholesterol 84mg; Calcium 102mg; Fibre 1.1g; Sodium 327mg.
clay pot catfish Energy 128kcal/537kJ; Protein 16.4g; Carbohydrate 8.3g, of which sugars 8.3g; Fat 3.4g, of which saturates 0.4g; Cholesterol 40mg; Calcium 18mg; Fibre 0.2g; Sodium 54mg.

Grey Mullet with Pork

This unusual combination of fish and meat makes a spectacular main dish.

Ingredients

1 grey mullet or snapper, about 900g/2lb, gutted and cleaned
50g/2oz lean pork
3 dried Chinese mushrooms, soaked in hot water until soft
2.5ml/½ tsp cornflour (cornstarch)
30ml/2 tbsp light soy sauce
15ml/1 tbsp vegetable oil
15ml/1 tbsp finely shredded fresh root ginger
15ml/1 tbsp shredded spring onion (scallion)
salt and ground black pepper
sliced spring onion (scallion), to garnish
rice, to serve

Serves 4

1 Make four diagonal cuts on either side of the fish and rub with a little salt; place the fish on a heatproof serving dish.

2 Cut the pork into thin strips. Place in a bowl. Drain the soaked mushrooms, remove and discard the stalks and slice the caps thinly. Add the mushrooms to the pork, with the cornflour and half the soy sauce. Stir in 5ml/1 tsp of the oil and a little black pepper. Arrange the pork mixture along the length of the fish. Sprinkle the ginger shreds over the top.

3 Cover the fish loosely with foil. Have ready a large pan or roasting pan, which is big enough to fit the heatproof dish inside it on a metal trivet. Pour in boiling water to a depth of 5cm/2in. Place the dish in the pan or roasting pan, cover and steam over a high heat for 15 minutes.

4 Test the fish by pressing the flesh gently. If it comes away from the bone with a slight resistance, the fish is cooked. Carefully pour away any excess liquid from the dish.

5 Heat the remaining oil in a small pan. When it is hot, fry the spring onion for a few seconds, then pour it over the fish, taking great care as it will splatter. Drizzle with the remaining soy sauce, garnish with sliced spring onion and serve with rice.

Skate Wings with Wasabi

Whole skate wings dipped in a tempura batter and deep-fried until crisp and golden look stunning.

Ingredients

4 x 250g/9oz skate wings
65g/2½oz/9 tbsp cornflour (cornstarch)
65g/2½oz/9 tbsp plain (all-purpose) flour
5ml/1 tsp salt
5ml/1 tsp Chinese five-spice powder
15ml/1 tbsp sesame seeds
200ml/7fl oz/scant 1 cup ice-cold soda water (club soda)
sunflower oil, for frying

For the mayonnaise

200ml/7fl oz/scant 1 cup mayonnaise
15ml/1 tbsp light soy sauce
finely grated rind and juice of 1 lime
5ml/1 tsp wasabi
15ml/1 tbsp finely chopped spring onion (scallion)

Serves 4

1 Using kitchen scissors, trim away the frill from the edges of the skate wings and discard. Set the fish aside.

2 In a large mixing bowl combine the cornflour, plain flour, salt, five-spice powder and sesame seeds. Gradually pour in the soda water and stir to mix. (It will be quite lumpy.)

3 Heat the oil for deep-frying. One at a time, dip the skate wings in the batter, then lower them carefully into the hot oil and deep-fry for 4–5 minutes, until the skate is fully cooked and crispy. Drain on kitchen paper. Set aside and keep warm.

4 Meanwhile, mix together all the mayonnaise ingredients and divide among four small bowls. Serve immediately with the skate wings.

Cook's Tip

Look for packets of tempura batter mix at health food shops and Asian markets. It doesn't take long to make your own batter, but sometimes seconds count.

grey mullet w. pork Energy 228kcal/960kJ; Protein 34.7g; Carbohydrate 0.7g, of which sugars 0.6g; Fat 9.8g, of which saturates 2.3g; Cholesterol 62mg; Calcium 46mg; Fibre 0.1g; Sodium 647mg.
skate wings Energy 705kcal/2921kJ; Protein 31.9g; Carbohydrate 11.7g, of which sugars 1.2g; Fat 59.3g, of which saturates 11g; Cholesterol 38mg; Calcium 112mg; Fibre 0.5g; Sodium 792mg.

Grilled Swordfish Steaks

Crisp grilled asparagus with a shoyu and sake coating is an excellent accompaniment for marinated game fish.

Ingredients

4 x 175g/6oz swordfish steaks
2.5ml/½ tsp salt
300g/11oz shiro miso
45ml/3 tbsp sake

For the asparagus

25ml/1½ tbsp shoyu
25ml/1½ tbsp sake
8 asparagus spears, the hard ends discarded, each spear cut into three

Serves 4

1 Place the swordfish in a shallow container. Sprinkle with the salt on both sides and leave for 2 hours. Drain and wipe the fish with kitchen paper.

2 Mix the miso and sake, then spread half across the bottom of the cleaned container. Cover with a sheet of muslin (cheesecloth) the size of a dish towel, folded in half, then open the fold.

3 Place the swordfish, side by side, on top, and cover with the muslin. Spread the rest of the miso mixture on the muslin. Make sure the muslin is touching the fish. Marinate for 2 days in the coolest part of the refrigerator.

4 Preheat the grill (broiler) to medium. Oil the wire rack and grill (broil) the fish slowly for about 8 minutes on each side, turning every 2 minutes. If the steaks are thin, check every time you turn the fish to see if they are ready.

5 Mix the shoyu and sake in a small bowl. Grill the asparagus for 2 minutes on each side, then dip into the bowl. Return to the grill for 2 minutes more on each side. Dip into the sauce again and set aside.

6 Serve the steak hot on four individual serving plates. Garnish with the drained, grilled asparagus.

Spicy Pan-seared Tuna

This popular dish can be made with many types of thick-fleshed fish. Tuna is particularly suitable because it is delicious pan-seared and served a little rare.

Ingredients

1 small cucumber
10ml/2 tsp sesame oil
2 garlic cloves, crushed
4 tuna steaks

For the dressing

4cm/1½in fresh root ginger, peeled and roughly chopped
1 garlic clove, roughly chopped
2 fresh green chillies, seeded and roughly chopped
45ml/3 tbsp raw cane sugar
45ml/3 tbsp fish sauce
juice of 1 lime
60ml/4 tbsp water

Serves 4

1 To make the dressing, grind the ginger, garlic and chillies to a pulp with the sugar, using a mortar and pestle. Stir in the fish sauce, lime juice and water, and mix well. Leave the dressing to stand for 15 minutes.

2 Cut the cucumber in half lengthways and remove the seeds. Cut the flesh into long, thin strips. Toss the cucumber in the dressing and leave to soak for at least 15 minutes.

3 Wipe a heavy pan with the oil and rub the garlic around it. Heat the pan and add the tuna steaks. Sear for a few minutes on both sides, so that the outside is slightly charred but the inside is still rare. Lift the steaks on to a warm serving dish.

4 Using tongs or chopsticks, lift the cucumber strips out of the dressing and arrange them around the steaks. Drizzle the dressing over the tuna, and serve immediately.

Cook's Tip

Fresh root ginger is a wonderful ingredient. Thin slices can be added to boiling water to make a refreshing tea, and grated ginger makes a great addition to curries and stir-fries. Ginger freezes successfully and can be shaved or grated from frozen.

grilled swordfish Energy 240kcal/1009kJ; Protein 37g; Carbohydrate 2.8g, of which sugars 2.5g; Fat 8.2g, of which saturates 1.8g; Cholesterol 81mg; Calcium 18mg; Fibre 0.3g; Sodium 2269mg.
spicy pan-seared tuna Energy 176kcal/731kJ; Protein 12.3g; Carbohydrate 1.6g, of which sugars 1.6g; Fat 13.4g, of which saturates 2.2g; Cholesterol 14mg; Calcium 18mg; Fibre 0.3g; Sodium 25mg.

Sweet & Sour Fish

When fish such as red mullet or snapper is cooked in this way the skin becomes crisp, while the flesh stays moist and juicy.

Ingredients

1 large or 2 medium fish, such as snapper or mullet, heads removed
20ml/4 tsp cornflour (cornstarch)
120ml/4fl oz/½ cup vegetable oil
15ml/1 tbsp chopped garlic
15ml/1 tbsp chopped fresh root ginger
30ml/2 tbsp chopped shallots
225g/8oz cherry tomatoes
30ml/2 tbsp red wine vinegar
30ml/2 tbsp sugar
30ml/2 tbsp tomato ketchup
15ml/1 tbsp fish sauce
45ml/3 tbsp water
salt and ground black pepper
coriander (cilantro) leaves and shredded spring onions (scallions), to garnish

Serves 4–6

1 Rinse and dry the fish. Score the skin diagonally on both sides, then coat the fish lightly all over with 15ml/3 tsp of the cornflour. Shake off any excess.

2 Heat the oil in a wok or large frying pan. Add the fish and cook over a medium heat for 6–7 minutes. Turn the fish over and cook for 6–7 minutes more, until it is crisp and brown.

3 Remove the fish and place on a large platter. Pour off all but 30ml/2 tbsp of the oil from the wok or pan and reheat. Add the garlic, ginger and shallots and cook over a medium heat, stirring occasionally, for about 4 minutes, until golden.

4 Add the cherry tomatoes and cook until they burst open. Stir in the vinegar, sugar, tomato ketchup and fish sauce. Lower the heat and simmer gently for 1–2 minutes, then taste and adjust the seasoning.

5 In a cup, mix the remaining 5ml/1 tsp cornflour to a paste with the water. Stir into the sauce. Heat, stirring, until it thickens. Pour the sauce over the fish, garnish with coriander leaves and shredded spring onions and serve.

Aromatic Fish Stew

Lemon grass and ginger give this delicate stew of fish, prawns, new potatoes and broccoli an appetizing aromatic flavour.

Ingredients

25g/1oz/2 tbsp butter
1 large onion, chopped
20ml/4 tsp plain (all-purpose) flour
400ml/14fl oz/1⅔ cups light fish stock
150ml/¼ pint/⅔ cup white wine
2.5cm/1in piece fresh root ginger, peeled and finely chopped
2 lemon grass stalks, trimmed and finely chopped
450g/1lb new potatoes, scrubbed and halved if necessary
450g/1lb white fish fillets
275g/10oz small broccoli florets
150ml/¼ pint/⅔ cup double (heavy) cream
175g/6oz large, cooked, peeled prawns (shrimp)
60ml/4 tbsp chopped fresh garlic chives
salt and ground black pepper
crusty bread, to serve

Serves 4

1 Melt the butter in a large pan. Add the onions and cook for 3–4 minutes. Stir in the flour and cook for 1 minute.

2 Stir in the fish stock, white wine, ginger, lemon grass and new potatoes. Season with salt and pepper and bring to the boil. Cover and cook for 15 minutes, or until the potatoes are almost tender.

3 Remove the skin from the fish fillets and cut the fillets into large chunks. Add the chunks of fish to the pan with the broccoli and cream. Stir gently.

4 Simmer gently for 4 minutes, taking care not to break up the fish, then add the prawns and heat through in the sauce. Adjust the seasoning and sprinkle in the chives. Serve in heated bowls with plenty of crusty bread.

Cook's Tip
Don't overcook the prawns, or they will toughen.

sweet & sour fish Energy 233kcal/969kJ; Protein 21.9g; Carbohydrate 6.3g, of which sugars 3g; Fat 13.5g, of which saturates 1.6g; Cholesterol 54mg; Calcium 16mg; Fibre 0.5g; Sodium 335mg.
aromatic fish Energy 515kcal/2148kJ; Protein 34.9g; Carbohydrate 27.6g, of which sugars 5.9g; Fat 27.4g, of which saturates 16.2g; Cholesterol 202mg; Calcium 131mg; Fibre 3.7g; Sodium 218mg.

Fish Moolie

This is a very popular South-east Asian fish curry in a coconut sauce, which is truly delicious. Choose a firm-textured fish so that the pieces stay intact during the brief cooking process. Halibut and cod work equally well.

Ingredients

500g/1¼lb monkfish or other firm-textured fish fillets, skinned and cut into 2.5cm/1in cubes
2.5ml/½ tsp salt
50g/2oz/⅔ cup desiccated (dry unsweetened) coconut
6 shallots, chopped
6 blanched almonds
2–3 garlic cloves, roughly chopped
2.5cm/1in piece fresh root ginger, peeled and sliced
2 lemon grass stalks, trimmed
10ml/2 tsp ground turmeric
45ml/3 tbsp vegetable oil
2 × 400ml/14fl oz cans coconut milk
1–3 fresh chillies, seeded and sliced
salt and ground black pepper
fresh chives, to garnish
boiled rice, to serve

Serves 4

1 Put the fish cubes in a shallow dish and sprinkle with the salt. Dry fry the coconut in a wok, turning all the time until it is crisp and golden, then tip into a food processor and process to an oily paste. Scrape into a bowl and reserve.

2 Add the shallots, almonds, garlic and ginger to the food processor. Chop the bulbous part of each lemon grass stalk and add to the processor with the turmeric. Process the mixture to a paste. Bruise the remaining lemon grass stalks.

3 Heat the oil in a wok. Cook the onion mixture for 2–3 minutes. Stir in the coconut milk and bring to the boil, stirring. Add the fish, most of the chilli and the lemon grass stalks. Cook for 3–4 minutes. Stir in the coconut paste and cook for a further 2–3 minutes only. Adjust the seasoning.

4 Remove the lemon grass. Transfer the moolie to a hot serving dish and sprinkle with the remaining slices of chilli. Garnish with chopped and whole chives and serve with rice.

Seafood Laksa

A laksa is a Malaysian stew of fish, poultry, meat or vegetables with noodles.

Ingredients

3 medium-hot fresh red chillies, seeded
4–5 garlic cloves
5ml/1 tsp mild paprika
10ml/2 tsp shrimp paste
25ml/1½ tbsp chopped fresh root ginger
250g/9oz small red shallots
25g/1oz fresh coriander (cilantro)
45ml/3 tbsp groundnut (peanut) oil
5ml/1 tsp fennel seeds, crushed
2 fennel bulbs, cut into thin wedges
600ml/1 pint/2½ cups fish stock
450ml/¾ pint/scant 2 cups coconut milk
juice of 1–2 limes
30–45ml/2–3 tbsp fish sauce
450g/1lb firm white fish fillet, cut into chunks
20 large raw prawns (shrimp), shelled and deveined
small bunch of basil
300g/11oz thin vermicelli rice noodles, cooked
2 spring onions (scallions), sliced

Serves 4–5

1 Process the chillies, garlic, paprika, shrimp paste, ginger and two shallots to a paste in a food processor. Set aside the coriander leaves. Add the stems to the paste with 15ml/1 tbsp oil and process again until fairly smooth.

2 Cook the remaining shallots, the fennel seeds and fennel wedges in the remaining oil in a large pan. When lightly browned, add 45ml/3 tbsp of the paste and stir-fry for about 2 minutes. Pour in the fish stock and simmer for 8–10 minutes.

3 Add the coconut milk, the juice of 1 lime and 30ml/2 tbsp of the fish sauce. Bring to a simmer and adjust the flavouring.

4 Add the fish into chunks. Cook for 2–3 minutes, then add the prawns and cook until they turn pink. Chop most of the basil and add to the pan with chopped coriander leaves.

5 Divide the noodles among 4–5 wide bowls, then ladle in the stew. Sprinkle with spring onions and whole basil leaves. Serve.

fish moolie Energy 319kcal/1335kJ; Protein 22.4g; Carbohydrate 16.7g, of which sugars 14.9g; Fat 18.6g, of which saturates 8.3g; Cholesterol 18mg; Calcium 96mg; Fibre 3g; Sodium 249mg.
seafood laksa Energy 524kcal/2199kJ; Protein 43.1g; Carbohydrate 65.1g, of which sugars 6.3g; Fat 10.1g, of which saturates 2g; Cholesterol 233mg; Calcium 162mg; Fibre 1.9g; Sodium 356mg.

Chicken with Lemon Sauce

Succulent chicken with a refreshing lemony sauce and just a hint of lime is a sure winner as a family meal that is quick and easy to prepare.

Ingredients

4 small skinless chicken breast fillets
5ml/1 tsp sesame oil
15ml/1 tbsp dry sherry
1 egg white, lightly beaten
30ml/2 tbsp cornflour (cornstarch)
15ml/1 tbsp vegetable oil
salt and ground white pepper
chopped coriander (cilantro) leaves and spring onions (scallions) and lemon wedges, to garnish

For the sauce

45ml/3 tbsp fresh lemon juice
30ml/2 tbsp sweetened lime juice
45ml/3 tbsp caster (superfine) sugar
10ml/2 tsp cornflour (cornstarch)
90ml/6 tbsp cold water

Serves 4

1 Arrange the chicken fillets in a single layer in a bowl. Mix the sesame oil with the sherry and add 2.5ml/½ tsp salt and 1.5ml/¼ tsp pepper. Pour over the chicken, cover and marinate for 15 minutes at room temperature.

2 Mix together the egg white and cornflour. Add the mixture to the chicken and turn the chicken with tongs until thoroughly coated.

3 Heat the vegetable oil in a non-stick frying pan or wok and fry the chicken fillets for about 15 minutes until they are golden brown on both sides.

4 Meanwhile, make the sauce. Combine the lemon juice, lime juice, sugar, cornflour and water in a small pan. Add 1.5ml/¼ tsp salt. Bring to the boil over a low heat, stirring constantly until the sauce is smooth and has thickened.

5 Cut the chicken into pieces and place on a warm serving plate. Pour the sauce over, garnish with the coriander leaves, spring onions and lemon wedges.

Chicken Rendang

This makes a marvellous dish for a buffet. Serve it with prawn crackers.

Ingredients

1 chicken, about 1.4kg/3lb
5ml/1 tsp sugar
75g/3oz/1 cup desiccated (dry unsweetened) coconut
4 small onions, chopped
2 garlic cloves, chopped
2.5cm/1in piece fresh root ginger, peeled and sliced
1–2 lemon grass stalks, root trimmed
2.5cm/1in piece fresh galangal, peeled and sliced
75ml/5 tbsp vegetable oil
10–15ml/2–3 tsp chilli powder
400ml/14fl oz can coconut milk
10ml/2 tsp salt
fresh chives and deep-fried anchovies, to garnish

Serves 4

1 Joint the chicken into eight pieces and remove the skin, sprinkle with the sugar and leave to stand for 1 hour. Meanwhile, dry-roast the coconut in a wok, turning all the time until it is crisp and golden. Tip into a food processor and process to an oily paste. Set aside.

2 Add the onions, garlic and ginger to the processor. Cut off the lower 5cm/2in of the lemon grass, chop and add to the processor with the galangal. Process to a fine paste.

3 Heat the oil in a wok or large pan and fry the onion mixture for a few minutes. Reduce the heat, stir in the chilli powder and cook for 2–3 minutes, stirring constantly. Spoon in 120ml/4fl oz/½ cup of the coconut milk and add salt to taste.

4 As soon as the mixture bubbles, add the chicken pieces, turning them until they are well coated with the spices. Pour in the coconut milk, stirring constantly to prevent curdling. Bruise the top of the lemon grass stalks and add to the wok or pan. Cover and cook for 45 minutes until the chicken is tender.

5 Just before serving stir in the coconut paste. Bring to just below boiling point, then simmer for 5 minutes. Garnish with fresh chives and deep-fried anchovies and serve.

chicken w. lemon Energy 235kcal/995kJ; Protein 30.9g; Carbohydrate 23.3g, of which sugars 14.1g; Fat 2.2g, of which saturates 0.5g; Cholesterol 88mg; Calcium 15mg; Fibre 0g; Sodium 97mg.
chicken rendang Energy 501kcal/2098kJ; Protein 55.4g; Carbohydrate 7.2g, of which sugars 7.2g; Fat 28.1g, of which saturates 12.5g; Cholesterol 158mg; Calcium 45mg; Fibre 2.6g; Sodium 1233mg.

Salt "Baked" Chicken

This is a wonderful way of cooking chicken. All the delicious, succulent juices are sealed inside the salt crust – yet the flavour isn't too salty.

Ingredients

1.5kg/3–3½lb corn-fed chicken
1.5ml/¼ tsp fine sea salt
2.25kg/5lb coarse rock salt
15ml/1 tbsp vegetable oil
2.5cm/1in piece fresh root ginger, finely chopped
4 spring onions (scallions), cut into fine rings
boiled rice, garnished with shredded spring onions (scallions), to serve

Serves 8

1 Rinse the chicken. Pat it dry, both inside and out, with kitchen paper, then rub the inside with the sea salt. Place four pieces of damp kitchen paper on the bottom of a heavy deep pan or wok just large enough to hold the chicken.

2 Sprinkle a layer of rock salt over the kitchen paper, about 1cm/½in thick. Place the chicken on top of the layer of salt.

3 Pour the remaining salt over the chicken until it is completely covered. Dampen six more pieces of kitchen paper and place these around the rim of the pan or wok. Cover with a tight-fitting lid. Put the pan or wok over a high heat for 10 minutes or until it gives off a slightly smoky smell.

4 Immediately reduce the heat to medium and continue to cook the chicken for 30 minutes without lifting the lid. After 30 minutes, turn off the heat and leave for a further 10 minutes before carefully lifting the chicken out of the salt. Brush off any salt still clinging to the chicken and allow the bird to cool for 20 minutes before cutting it into serving-size pieces.

5 Heat the oil in a small pan until very hot. Add the ginger and spring onions and fry for a few seconds, then pour into a heatproof bowl and use as a dipping sauce for the chicken. Serve the chicken with rice, garnished with spring onions.

Spicy Fried Chicken

You cannot visit Malaysia or Singapore without trying the famous fried chicken. Indonesian in origin, ayam goreng puts Western fried chicken to shame. First the chicken is cooked in spices and flavourings to ensure a depth of taste, then it is simply deep-fried to form a crisp, golden skin.

Ingredients

2 shallots, chopped
4 garlic cloves, chopped
50g/2oz fresh root ginger or galangal, peeled and chopped
25g/1oz fresh turmeric, chopped
2 lemon grass stalks, chopped
6 whole chicken legs, separated into drumsticks and thighs
30ml/2 tbsp kecap manis
salt and ground black pepper
vegetable oil, for deep-frying

Serves 4

1 Using a mortar and pestle or food processor, grind the shallots, garlic, ginger or galangal, turmeric and lemon grass to a paste. Scrape into a bowl and set aside.

2 Place the chicken pieces in a heavy pan or flameproof pot and smear with the spice paste. Add the kecap manis and 150ml/¼ pint/⅔ cup water. Bring to the boil, reduce the heat and cook the chicken for about 25 minutes, turning it from time to time, until the liquid has evaporated. The chicken should be dry before deep-frying, but the spices should be sticking to it. Season with salt and pepper.

3 Heat enough oil for deep-frying in a wok. Fry the chicken pieces in batches until golden brown and crisp. Drain them on kitchen paper and serve hot.

4 Served with a sambal, or pickle, this makes a delicious snack, but for a main course, serve with yellow or fragrant coconut rice and a salad. If you cannot find kecap manis, use soy sauce sweetened with palm sugar (jaggery). This is sold in Chinese and Asian markets, or substitute the same quantity of dark soy sauce and 15ml/1 tbsp sugar.

salt "baked" chicken Energy 133kcal/561kJ; Protein 30g; Carbohydrate 0g, of which sugars 0g; Fat 1.4g, of which saturates 0.4g; Cholesterol 88mg; Calcium 6mg; Fibre 0g; Sodium 75mg.
spicy fried chicken Energy 300kcal/1250kJ; Protein 31.9g; Carbohydrate 2.1g, of which sugars 0.9g; Fat 18.3g, of which saturates 2.9g; Cholesterol 158mg; Calcium 19mg; Fibre 0.2g; Sodium 136mg.

Caramelized Chicken Wings

Eaten with the fingers, these caramelized chicken wings are irresistible.

Ingredients
75ml/5 tbsp sugar
30ml/2 tbsp vegetable oil
25g/1oz fresh root ginger, grated
12 chicken wings, split in two
chilli oil, for drizzling
mixed pickled vegetables, to serve

Serves 2–4

1 Heat the sugar with 60ml/4 tbsp water in a heavy pan until it forms a golden syrup. Heat the oil in a wok and stir-fry the ginger until fragrant. Add the chicken wings, brown them, then pour in the syrup and coat the chicken. Cover and cook for 30 minutes, until the chicken is tender. Drizzle chilli oil over and serve with pickles.

Barbecue Chicken

Perfect for a summer party.

Ingredients
1 chicken, cut into 8 pieces
lime wedges and fresh red chillies, to garnish

For the marinade
bulbs from 2 lemon grass stalks, chopped
2.5cm/1in piece fresh root ginger, peeled and thinly sliced
6 garlic cloves, coarsely chopped
4 shallots, coarsely chopped
½ bunch coriander (cilantro) roots, chopped
15ml/1 tbsp soft light brown sugar
120ml/4fl oz/½ cup coconut milk
30ml/2 tbsp fish sauce
30ml/2 tbsp light soy sauce

Serves 4–6

1 Make the marinade by processing all the ingredients in a food processor until smooth. Put the chicken pieces in a dish, pour over the marinade, cover and marinate for at least 4 hours.

2 Drain the chicken, reserving the marinade and cook over moderately hot coals for 20–30 minutes, turning and brushing with the marinade once or twice. Garnish and serve immediately.

Star Anise Chicken

The pungent flavour of star anise penetrates the chicken fillets and adds a wonderful aniseedy kick to the smoky flavour contributed by the barbecue. Serve the chicken with a refreshing salad.

Ingredients
4 skinless chicken breast fillets
2 whole star anise
30ml/2 tbsp soy sauce
30ml/2 tbsp vegetable oil
ground black pepper

Serves 4

1 Lay the skinless chicken breast fillets side by side in a shallow, non-metallic dish and add both pieces of star anise, keeping them whole.

2 Place the soy sauce in a small bowl. Add the oil and whisk together with a fork until the mixture emulsifies. Season to taste with black pepper to make a simple marinade.

3 Pour the marinade over the chicken and stir to coat each breast fillet all over. Cover the dish with clear film (plastic wrap) and chill in the refrigerator for up to 8 hours.

4 Prepare a barbecue. Cook the chicken fillets over medium hot coals for 8–10 minutes on each side, spooning over the marinade from time to time, until the chicken is cooked through. Transfer to a platter and serve immediately.

Variation
In wetter weather, this dish can be prepared indoors. Simply place the marinaded chicken fillets under a grill (broiler) and cook, turning once, for the same amount of time.

Cook's Tip
With its aroma of liquorice, star anise is the chief component in Chinese five-spice powder. In China, the points of the star are sometimes snapped off and sucked as a breath freshener.

chicken wings Energy 393kcal/1641kJ; Protein 30.5g; Carbohydrate 14.4g, of which sugars 14.4g; Fat 24.1g, of which saturates 6.3g; Cholesterol 134mg; Calcium 16mg; Fibre 0g; Sodium 91mg.
barbeque chicken Energy 374kcal/1553kJ; Protein 30.4g; Carbohydrate 6.1g, of which sugars 5.4g; Fat 25.4g, of which saturates 7.4g; Cholesterol 157mg; Calcium 28mg; Fibre 0.5g; Sodium 145mg.
star anise chicken Energy 210kcal/884kJ; Protein 36.1g; Carbohydrate 0.3g, of which sugars 0.3g; Fat 7.2g, of which saturates 1.2g; Cholesterol 105mg; Calcium 8mg; Fibre 0g; Sodium 357mg.

Crispy Five-spice Chicken

Tender strips of chicken fillet, with a delicately spiced rice flour coating, become deliciously crisp and golden when shallow-fried.

Ingredients

200g/7oz thin egg noodles
30ml/2 tbsp sunflower oil
2 garlic cloves, very thinly sliced
1 fresh red chilli, seeded and sliced
½ red (bell) pepper, seeded and very thinly sliced
300g/11oz carrots, peeled and cut into thin strips
300g/11oz Chinese broccoli or Chinese greens, roughly sliced
45ml/3 tbsp hoisin sauce
45ml/3 tbsp soy sauce
15ml/1 tbsp caster (superfine) sugar
4 skinless chicken breast fillets, cut into strips
2 egg whites, lightly beaten
115g/4oz/1 cup rice flour
15ml/1 tbsp five-spice powder
salt and ground black pepper
vegetable oil, for frying

Serves 4

1 Cook the noodles in boiling water for 2–4 minutes, or according to the packet instructions, drain and set aside.

2 Heat a wok, add the sunflower oil, and when it is hot add the garlic, chilli, red pepper, carrots and the broccoli or greens. Stir-fry over a high heat for 2–3 minutes.

3 Add the sauces and sugar to the wok and cook for a further 2–3 minutes. Add the drained noodles, toss to combine, then remove from the heat, cover and keep warm.

4 Dip the chicken strips into the egg white. Combine the rice flour and five-spice powder in a shallow dish and season. Add the chicken strips to the flour mixture and toss to coat.

5 Heat about 2.5cm/1in oil in a clean wok. When hot, shallow-fry the chicken for 3–4 minutes until crisp and golden.

6 To serve, divide the noodle mixture among warmed plates or bowls and top each serving with the chicken.

Bang Bang Chicken

Toasted sesame paste gives this dish an authentic flavour, although crunchy peanut butter can be used instead.

Ingredients

3 chicken breast fillets
1 garlic clove, crushed
2.5ml/½ tsp black peppercorns
1 small onion, halved
1 large cucumber, peeled, seeded and cut into thin strips
salt and ground black pepper

For the sauce

45ml/3 tbsp toasted sesame paste
15ml/1 tbsp light soy sauce
15ml/1 tbsp wine vinegar
2 spring onions (scallions), chopped
2 garlic cloves, crushed
5 × 1cm/2 × ½in piece fresh root ginger, peeled and cut into matchsticks
15ml/1 tbsp Sichuan peppercorns, dry-fried and crushed
5ml/1 tsp soft light brown sugar

For the chilli oil

60ml/4 tbsp groundnut (peanut) oil
5ml/1 tsp chilli powder

Serves 4

1 Place the chicken in a pan. Just cover with water, add the garlic, peppercorns and onion and bring to the boil. Skim the surface, season to taste, then cover. Cook for 25 minutes or until the chicken is just tender. Drain, reserving the stock.

2 Make the sauce by mixing the toasted sesame paste with 45ml/3 tbsp of the chicken stock, saving the rest for soup. Add the soy sauce, vinegar, spring onions, garlic, ginger and crushed peppercorns to the sesame mixture. Stir in sugar to taste.

3 Make the chilli oil by gently heating the oil and chilli powder together until foaming. Simmer for 2 minutes, cool, then strain off the red-coloured oil and discard the sediment.

4 Spread out the cucumber batons on a platter. Cut the chicken into pieces the same size as the batons and arrange on top. Pour over the sauce, drizzle on the chilli oil and serve.

five-spice chicken Energy 679kcal/2849kJ; Protein 43.9g; Carbohydrate 75.8g, of which sugars 17g; Fat 23.2g, of which saturates 3.7g; Cholesterol 103mg; Calcium 96mg; Fibre 6.3g; Sodium 1207mg.
bang bang chicken Energy 200kcal/838kJ; Protein 29.5g; Carbohydrate 2.8g, of which sugars 2.4g; Fat 7.9g, of which saturates 1.3g; Cholesterol 79mg; Calcium 89mg; Fibre 1.2g; Sodium 338mg.

Chicken with Hijiki Seaweed

The taste of hijiki – a type of seaweed – is somewhere between rice and vegetable. It goes well with meat or tofu products, especially when stir-fried in the wok first with a little oil.

Ingredients

90g/3½oz dried hijiki seaweed
150g/5oz chicken breast fillet
½ small carrot, about 5cm/2in
15ml/1 tbsp vegetable oil
100ml/3fl oz/scant ½ cup instant dashi powder plus 1.5ml/¼ tsp dashi-no-moto
30ml/2 tbsp sake
30ml/2 tbsp caster (superfine) sugar
45ml/3 tbsp shoyu
a pinch of cayenne pepper

Serves 2

1 Soak the hijiki in cold water for about 30 minutes. It will be ready to cook when it can be easily crushed between the fingers. Pour into a sieve (strainer) and wash under running water. Drain.

2 Peel the skin from the chicken and par-boil the skin in rapidly boiling water for 1 minute, then drain. With a sharp knife, shave off all the yellow fat from the skin. Discard the clear membrane between the fat and the skin as well. Cut the skin into thin strips about 5mm/¼in wide and 2.5cm/1in long. Cut the meat into small, bitesize chunks.

3 Peel and chop the carrot into long, narrow matchsticks.

4 Heat the oil in a wok or frying pan and stir-fry the strips of chicken skin for 5 minutes, or until golden and curled up. Add the chicken meat and keep stirring until the colour changes.

5 Add the hijiki and carrot, then stir-fry for a further minute. Add the remaining ingredients. Lower the heat and toss over the heat for 5 minutes more.

6 Remove the wok from the heat and stand for 10 minutes. Season and serve in small individual bowls.

Stir-fried Chicken with Chillies

This is good home cooking. There are variations of this dish, using pork or seafood, throughout South-east Asia so, for a smooth and easy introduction to the cooking of the region, this is a good place to start. Serve with a salad, rice wrappers and a dipping sauce.

Ingredients

15ml/1 tbsp sugar
30ml/2 tbsp sesame or groundnut (peanut) oil
2 garlic cloves, finely chopped
2–3 fresh green or red chillies, seeded and finely chopped
2 lemon grass stalks, finely sliced
1 onion, finely sliced
350g/12oz skinless chicken breast fillets, cut into bitesize strips
30ml/2 tbsp soy sauce
15ml/1 tbsp fish sauce
1 bunch fresh coriander (cilantro), stalks removed, leaves chopped
salt and ground black pepper
chilli sambal, to serve

Serves 4

1 Put the sugar into a pan with 5ml/1 tsp water. Heat gently until the sugar has dissolved and formed a caramel syrup. Set aside.

2 Heat a large wok or heavy pan and add the sesame or groundnut oil. Stir in the chopped garlic, chillies and lemon grass, and stir-fry until they become fragrant and golden. Add the onion and stir-fry for 1 minute, then add the chicken strips.

3 When the chicken is cooked through, add the soy sauce, fish sauce and caramel syrup. Stir to mix and heat through, then season with a little salt and pepper. Stir in the coriander into the chicken and serve with chilli sambal.

Cook's Tip

When adding the oil to the hot wok, drizzle it around the inner rim like a necklace. The oil will run down to coat the entire surface of the wok. Swirl the wok several times to make sure the coating is even.

chicken w. hijiki Energy 154kcal/644kJ; Protein 10g; Carbohydrate 10.4g, of which sugars 10.2g; Fat 8.4g, of which saturates 2g; Cholesterol 39mg; Calcium 76mg; Fibre 1.1g; Sodium 884mg.
stir-fried chicken Energy 196kcal/819kJ; Protein 27.2g; Carbohydrate 0.4g, of which sugars 0.4g; Fat 9.5g, of which saturates 1.3g; Cholesterol 79mg; Calcium 7mg; Fibre 0g; Sodium 424mg.

Chicken with Mixed Vegetables

Far East Asian cooks are experts in making delicious dishes from a relatively small amount of meat and a lot of vegetables. Good news for anyone trying to eat less fat.

Ingredients

350g/12oz skinless chicken breast fillets
20ml/4 tsp vegetable oil
300ml/½ pint/1¼ cups chicken stock
75g/3oz/¾ cup drained, canned straw mushrooms
50g/2oz/½ cup sliced, drained, canned bamboo shoots
50g/2oz/⅓ cup drained, canned water chestnuts, sliced
1 small carrot, sliced
50g/2oz/½ cup mangetouts (snow peas)
15ml/1 tbsp dry sherry
15ml/1 tbsp oyster sauce
5ml/1 tsp caster (superfine) sugar
5ml/1 tsp cornflour (cornstarch)
15ml/1 tbsp cold water
salt and ground white pepper

Serves 4

1 Put the chicken in a shallow bowl. Add 5ml/1 tsp of the oil, 1.5ml/¼ tsp salt and a pinch of pepper. Cover and set aside for 10 minutes in a cool place.

2 Bring the stock to the boil in a pan. Add the chicken fillets and cook for 12 minutes, or until tender. Drain and slice, reserving 75ml/5 tbsp of the chicken stock.

3 Heat the remaining oil in a non-stick frying pan or wok, add all the vegetables and stir-fry for 2 minutes. Stir in the sherry, oyster sauce, caster sugar and reserved stock. Add the chicken to the pan and cook for 2 minutes more.

4 Mix the cornflour to a paste with the water. Add the mixture to the pan and cook, stirring, until the sauce thickens slightly. Season to taste with salt and pepper and serve immediately.

Cook's Tip
Water chestnuts give a dish great texture as they remain crunchy, no matter how long you cook them for.

Chicken with Young Ginger

Ginger plays a big role in Far East Asian cooking, particularly in the stir-fried dishes. Whenever possible, the juicier and more pungent young ginger is used. This is a simple and delicious way to cook chicken, pork or beef.

Ingredients

30ml/2 tbsp groundnut (peanut) oil
3 garlic cloves, finely sliced in strips
50g/2oz fresh young root ginger, finely sliced in strips
2 fresh red chillies, seeded and finely sliced in strips
4 chicken breast fillets or 4 boned chicken legs, skinned and cut into bitesize chunks
30ml/2 tbsp fish sauce
10ml/2 tsp sugar
1 small bunch coriander (cilantro) stalks removed, roughly chopped
ground black pepper
jasmine rice and crunchy salad or baguette, to serve

Serves 4

1 Heat a wok or heavy pan and add the oil. Add the garlic, ginger and chillies, and stir-fry until fragrant and golden. Add the chicken and toss it around the wok for 1–2 minutes.

2 Stir in the fish sauce and sugar, and stir-fry for a further 4–5 minutes until cooked. Season with pepper and add some of the fresh coriander.

3 Transfer the chicken to a serving dish and garnish with the remaining coriander. Serve hot with jasmine rice and a crunchy salad with fresh herbs, or with chunks of baguette.

Cook's Tip
Young ginger is generally available in Chinese and South-east Asian markets. It has smooth, thin skin, which clings to the flesh, whereas older ginger has thicker skin and is easier to peel. The flavour of young ginger has citric tones and the flesh is really juicy.

chicken w. vegetables Energy 154kcal/646kJ; Protein 22.2g; Carbohydrate 4.9g, of which sugars 3.4g; Fat 4.3g, of which saturates 0.7g; Cholesterol 61mg; Calcium 17mg; Fibre 1g; Sodium 61mg.
chicken w. ginger Energy 222kcal/935kJ; Protein 36.4g; Carbohydrate 3g, of which sugars 2.9g; Fat 7.3g, of which saturates 1.1g; Cholesterol 105mg; Calcium 32mg; Fibre 0.6g; Sodium 101mg.

Kung Po Chicken

This recipe, which hails from the Sichuan region of western China, has become one of the classic recipes in the Chinese repertoire. The combination of yellow salted beans and hoisin, spiked with chilli and softened with cashews, makes for a very tasty and spicy sauce.

Ingredients

1 egg white
10ml/2 tsp cornflour (cornstarch)
2.5ml/½ tsp salt
2–3 skinless chicken breast fillets, cut into neat pieces
30ml/2 tbsp yellow salted beans
15ml/1 tbsp hoisin sauce
5ml/1 tsp soft light brown sugar
15ml/1 tbsp dry sherry
15ml/1 tbsp wine vinegar
4 garlic cloves, crushed
150ml/¼ pint/⅔ cup chicken stock
45ml/3 tbsp sunflower oil
2–3 dried chillies, broken into small pieces
115g/4oz/1 cup roasted cashew nuts
fresh coriander (cilantro), to garnish

Serves 3

1 Lightly whisk the egg white in a dish, whisk in the cornflour and salt, then add the chicken and stir until coated.

2 In a separate bowl, mash the salted beans with a spoon. Stir in the hoisin sauce, brown sugar, dry sherry, vinegar, garlic and chicken stock.

3 Heat a wok, add the oil and then stir-fry the chicken, turning constantly, for about 2 minutes until tender. Either drain the chicken over a bowl to collect excess oil, or lift out each piece with a slotted spoon, leaving the oil in the wok.

4 Heat the reserved oil and fry the chilli pieces for 1 minute. Return the chicken to the wok and pour in the bean sauce mixture. Bring to the boil and stir in the cashew nuts. Spoon into a heated serving dish, garnish with coriander leaves and serve immediately.

Stir-fried Chicken with Basil

Thai basil, which is sometimes known as holy basil, has a unique, pungent flavour that is both spicy and sharp. Deep-frying the leaves adds another dimension to this quick and easy chicken dish.

Ingredients

45ml/3 tbsp vegetable oil
4 garlic cloves, thinly sliced
2–4 fresh red chillies, seeded and finely chopped
450g/1lb skinless chicken breast fillets, cut into bitesize pieces
45ml/3 tbsp fish sauce
10ml/2 tsp dark soy sauce
5ml/1 tsp sugar
10–12 fresh Thai basil leaves
2 fresh red chillies, seeded and finely chopped, and about 20 deep-fried Thai basil leaves, to garnish

Serves 4–6

1 Heat the oil in a wok or large, heavy frying pan. Add the garlic and chillies and stir-fry over a medium heat for about 1–2 minutes until the garlic is golden. Take care not to let the garlic burn, otherwise it will taste bitter.

2 Add the pieces of chicken to the wok or pan, in batches if necessary, and stir-fry until the chicken changes colour.

3 Stir in the fish sauce, soy sauce and sugar. Continue to stir-fry the mixture for 3–4 minutes, or until the chicken is fully cooked and golden brown.

4 Stir in the fresh Thai basil leaves. Spoon the mixture on to a warm platter, or into individual dishes. Garnish with the chopped chillies and deep-fried Thai basil and serve.

Cook's Tip

To deep-fry Thai basil leaves, heat groundnut (peanut) oil to 190°C/375°F. Add the leaves, which must be completely dry, and deep-fry them for about 30 seconds until they are crisp and translucent. Lift out the leaves and drain on kitchen paper.

kung po chicken Energy 490kcal/2040kJ; Protein 37.7g; Carbohydrate 12.4g, of which sugars 2.6g; Fat 31.9g, of which saturates 5.6g; Cholesterol 82mg; Calcium 24mg; Fibre 1.9g; Sodium 204mg.
stir-fried chicken/basil Energy 135kcal/566kJ; Protein 18.3g; Carbohydrate 1.1g, of which sugars 1g; Fat 6.4g, of which saturates 1g; Cholesterol 53mg; Calcium 21mg; Fibre 0.4g; Sodium 167mg.

Cashew Chicken

One of the most popular items on any Chinese restaurant menu, Cashew Chicken is easy to recreate at home.

Ingredients

450g/1lb skinless chicken breast fillets
1 red (bell) pepper
2 garlic cloves
4 dried red chillies
30ml/2 tbsp vegetable oil
30ml/2 tbsp oyster sauce
15ml/1 tbsp soy sauce
pinch of sugar
1 bunch spring onions (scallions), cut into 5cm/2in lengths
175g/6oz/1½ cups cashew nuts, roasted
coriander (cilantro) leaves, to garnish

Serves 4–6

1 Remove and discard the skin from the chicken breast fillets and trim off any excess fat. With a sharp knife, cut the chicken into bitesize pieces and set aside.

2 Halve the red pepper, scrape out the seeds and membranes and discard, then cut the flesh into 2cm/¾ in dice. Peel and thinly slice the garlic and chop the dried red chillies.

3 Preheat a wok and then heat the oil. The best way to do this is to drizzle a "necklace" of oil around the inner rim of the wok, so that it drops down to coat the entire inner surface. Make sure the coating is even by swirling the wok.

4 Add the garlic and dried chillies to the wok and stir-fry over a medium heat until golden. Do not let the garlic burn, otherwise it will taste bitter.

5 Add the chicken to the wok and stir-fry until it is cooked through, then add the red pepper. If the mixture is very dry, add a little water.

6 Stir in the oyster sauce, soy sauce and sugar. Add the spring onions and cashew nuts. Stir-fry for 1–2 minutes more, until heated through. Spoon into a warm dish and serve immediately, garnished with the coriander leaves.

Lemon & Sesame Chicken

These delicate strips of chicken are at their best if you leave them to marinate overnight.

Ingredients

4 large chicken breast fillets, skinned and cut into strips
15ml/1 tbsp light soy sauce
15ml/1 tbsp Chinese rice wine
2 garlic cloves, crushed
10ml/2 tsp finely grated fresh root ginger
1 egg, lightly beaten
150g/5oz cornflour (cornstarch)
sunflower oil, for deep-frying
toasted sesame seeds, to sprinkle
rice or noodles, to serve

For the sauce

15ml/1 tbsp sunflower oil
2 spring onions (scallions), finely sliced
1 garlic clove, crushed
10ml/2 tsp cornflour (cornstarch)
90ml/6 tbsp chicken stock
10ml/2 tsp finely grated lemon rind
30ml/2 tbsp lemon juice
10ml/2 tsp sugar
2.5ml/½ tsp sesame oil
salt

Serves 4

1 Mix the chicken strips with the soy sauce, wine, garlic and ginger in a bowl. Toss together to combine, then cover and marinate in the refrigerator for 8–10 hours.

2 When ready to cook, add the beaten egg to the chicken and mix well, then drain off any excess liquid. Put the cornflour in a plastic bag, add the chicken pieces and shake to coat the strips.

3 Deep-fry the chicken in hot oil for 3–4 minutes for each batch. As each batch cooks, lift it out and drain on kitchen paper. Reheat the oil and deep-fry all the chicken in batches for a second time, for 2–3 minutes. Remove and drain well.

4 To make the sauce, add the oil to a hot wok and stir-fry the spring onions and garlic for 1–2 minutes. Add the remaining ingredients and cook for 2–3 minutes until thickened. Return the chicken to the wok, toss lightly to coat with sauce, and sprinkle over the sesame seeds. Serve with rice or noodles.

cashew chicken Energy 314kcal/1307kJ; Protein 24.7g; Carbohydrate 10.2g, of which sugars 6.2g; Fat 19.6g, of which saturates 3.7g; Cholesterol 53mg; Calcium 24mg; Fibre 1.7g; Sodium 268mg.
lemon & sesame Energy 450kcal/1892kJ; Protein 38.2g; Carbohydrate 37.1g, of which sugars 2.5g; Fat 17.6g, of which saturates 2.6g; Cholesterol 157mg; Calcium 25mg; Fibre 0.1g; Sodium 397mg.

Stir-fried Giblets with Garlic

Throughout China and the neighbouring countries, there is a keen appreciation of offal or variety meats. Giblets are popular and are used in various ways. Apart from being tossed into the stockpot, they are often stir-fried with garlic and ginger and served with rice. This dish, featuring fish sauce, is typical of Southern China.

Ingredients

30ml/2 tbsp groundnut (peanut) oil
2 shallots, halved and finely sliced
2 garlic cloves, finely chopped
1 fresh red chilli, seeded and finely sliced
25g/1oz fresh root ginger, peeled and shredded
225g/8oz chicken livers, trimmed and finely sliced
115g/4oz mixed giblets, finely sliced
15–30ml/1–2 tbsp fish sauce
1 small bunch coriander (cilantro), finely chopped
ground black pepper
steamed rice, to serve

Serves 2–4

1 Heat the oil in a wok or heavy pan. Stir in the shallots, garlic, chilli and ginger, and stir-fry until golden. Add the chicken livers and mixed giblets and stir-fry for a few minutes more, until browned on all sides.

2 Stir in the fish sauce, adjusting the quantity according to taste, and half the chopped coriander. Season with ground black pepper and garnish with the rest of the coriander. Serve hot, with steamed fragrant rice.

Variations

- *If you are not keen on giblets, simply increase the quantity of chicken livers to 275g/12oz.*
- *Alternatively, try this recipe with thinly-sliced lamb's liver.*
- *A red onion can be substituted for the shallots, and a red (bell) pepper used instead of chilli for a milder taste.*
- *Use Worcestershire sauce instead of fish sauce for a fusion version of this dish.*

Fragrant Grilled Chicken

If you have time, prepare the chicken in advance and leave it to marinate in the refrigerator for several hours – or even overnight – until ready to cook.

Ingredients

450g/1lb chicken breast fillets, with the skin on
30ml/2 tbsp sesame oil
2 garlic cloves, crushed
2 coriander (cilantro) roots, finely chopped
2 small fresh red chillies, seeded and finely chopped
30ml/2 tbsp fish sauce
5ml/1 tsp sugar
lime wedges, to garnish
cooked rice, to serve

For the sauce

90ml/6 tbsp rice vinegar
60ml/4 tbsp sugar
2.5ml/½ tsp salt
2 garlic cloves, crushed
1 small fresh red chilli, seeded and finely chopped
115g/4oz/4 cups fresh coriander (cilantro), finely chopped

Serves 4

1 Lay the chicken breast fillets between two sheets of clear film (plastic wrap), baking parchment or foil and beat with the side of a rolling pin or the flat side of a meat tenderizer until the meat is about half its original thickness. Place in a large, shallow dish or bowl.

2 Mix together the sesame oil, garlic, coriander roots, red chillies, fish sauce and sugar in a jug (pitcher), stirring until the sugar has dissolved. Pour the mixture over the chicken and turn to coat. Cover with clear film and set aside to marinate in a cool place for at least 20 minutes. Meanwhile, make the sauce.

3 Heat the vinegar in a small pan, add the sugar and stir until dissolved. Add the salt and stir until the mixture begins to thicken. Add the remaining sauce ingredients, stir well, then spoon the sauce into a serving bowl.

4 Preheat the grill (broiler) and cook the chicken for 5 minutes. Turn and baste with the marinade, then cook for 5 minutes more, or until cooked through and golden. Serve with rice and the sauce, garnished with lime wedges.

stir-fried giblets Energy 134kcal/556kJ; Protein 15.2g; Carbohydrate 1.5g, of which sugars 1.1g; Fat 7.4g, of which saturates 1.3g; Cholesterol 290mg; Calcium 12mg; Fibre 0.2g; Sodium 359mg.
grilled chicken Energy 284kcal/1195kJ; Protein 36.8g; Carbohydrate 16.4g, of which sugars 16.3g; Fat 8.3g, of which saturates 1.5g; Cholesterol 106mg; Calcium 65mg; Fibre 1.3g; Sodium 71mg.

Roast Lime Chicken

Sweet potatoes are an inspired addition in this spicy chicked dish.

Ingredients

4 garlic cloves, 2 finely chopped and 2 bruised but left whole
small bunch coriander (cilantro), with roots, coarsely chopped
5ml/1 tsp ground turmeric
5cm/2in piece fresh turmeric
1 roasting chicken, about 1.5kg/3¼lb
1 lime, cut in half
4 medium/large sweet potatoes, peeled and cut into thick wedges
300ml/½ pint/1¼ cups chicken or vegetable stock
30ml/2 tbsp soy sauce
salt and ground black pepper

Serves 4

1 Preheat the oven to 190°C/375°F/Gas 5. Calculate the cooking time for the chicken, allowing 20 minutes per 500g/1¼lb, plus 20 minutes. Using a food processor, grind the garlic, coriander, 10ml/2 tsp salt and turmeric to a paste.

2 Place the chicken in a roasting pan and smear it with the paste. Squeeze the lime juice over; place the lime halves and garlic cloves in the cavity. Cover with foil and roast in the oven.

3 Meanwhile, par-boil the sweet potatoes for 10 minutes, drain and place around the chicken. Baste and sprinkle with salt and pepper. Replace the foil and return the chicken to the oven.

4 About 20 minutes before the end of cooking, remove the foil and baste the chicken. Turn the sweet potatoes over.

5 When the chicken is cooked, drain the juices into the pan, lift it on to a carving board, tent with foil and leave it to rest.

6 Put the sweet potatoes in a serving dish and keep them hot. Pour away the fat from the roasting pan, but keep the juices. Heat on top of the stove until bubbling. Pour in the stock. Bring to the boil, stirring constantly, then stir in the soy sauce. Strain into a gravy boat. Serve with the chicken and sweet potatoes.

Orange Glazed Poussins

Succulent poussins coated in a spiced citrus glaze make a great alternative to a traditional roast.

Ingredients

4 poussins, 300–350g/11–12oz each
juice and finely grated rind of 2 oranges
2 garlic cloves, crushed
15ml/1 tbsp grated fresh root ginger
90ml/6 tbsp soy sauce
75ml/5 tbsp clear honey
2–3 star anise
30ml/2 tbsp Chinese rice wine
about 20 kaffir lime leaves
a large bunch of spring onions (scallions), shredded
60ml/4 tbsp butter
1 large orange, segmented, to garnish

Serves 4

1 Place the poussins in a deep, non-metallic dish. Combine the orange rind and juice, garlic, ginger, half the soy sauce, half the honey, star anise and rice wine, then coat the poussins with the mixture. Cover and marinate in the refrigerator for at least 6 hours.

2 Line a large, heatproof plate with the kaffir lime leaves and spring onions. Lift the poussins out of the marinade and place on the leaves. Reserve the marinade.

3 Place a trivet or steamer rack in the base of a large wok and pour in 5cm/2in water. Bring to the boil and carefully lower the plate of poussins on to the trivet. Cover, reduce the heat to low and steam for 45 minutes–1 hour, or until the poussins are cooked through and tender. (Check the water level regularly and add more as needed.)

4 Remove the poussins from the wok and keep hot while you make the glaze. Wipe out the wok and pour in the reserved marinade, butter and the remaining soy sauce and honey. Bring to the boil, then reduce the heat and cook gently for 10–15 minutes, or until thick. Spoon the glaze over the poussins and serve immediately, garnished with the orange segments.

roast lime chicken Energy 620kcal/2581kJ; Protein 47g; Carbohydrate 21.3g, of which sugars 5.7g; Fat 38.9g, of which saturates 11.4g; Cholesterol 240mg; Calcium 43mg; Fibre 2.4g; Sodium 228mg.
glazed poussins Energy 544kcal/2264kJ; Protein 36.2g; Carbohydrate 5.8g, of which sugars 5.8g; Fat 42.1g, of which saturates 14.5g; Cholesterol 215mg; Calcium 16mg; Fibre 0g; Sodium 207mg.

Chicken & Coconut Milk Curry

A mild coconut curry flavoured with turmeric, coriander and cumin seeds that demonstrates the influence of Malaysian cooking on Asian cuisine.

Ingredients

60ml/4 tbsp vegetable oil
1 large garlic clove, crushed
1 chicken, weighing about 1.5kg/3–3½lb, chopped into 12 large pieces
400ml/14fl oz/1⅔ cups coconut cream
250ml/8fl oz/1 cup chicken stock
30ml/2 tbsp fish sauce
30ml/2 tbsp sugar
juice of 2 limes

To garnish

2 small fresh red chillies, seeded and finely chopped
1 bunch spring onions (scallions), thinly sliced

For the curry paste

5ml/1 tsp dried chilli flakes
2.5ml/½ tsp salt
5cm/2in piece fresh turmeric or 5ml/1 tsp ground turmeric
2.5ml/½ tsp coriander seeds
2.5ml/½ tsp cumin seeds
5ml/1 tsp dried shrimp paste

Serves 4

1 First make the curry paste. Put all the ingredients in a mortar, food processor or spice grinder and pound, process or grind to a smooth paste.

2 Heat the oil in a wok or frying pan and cook the garlic until golden. Add the chicken and brown on all sides. Remove the chicken and set aside.

3 Reheat the oil and add the curry paste and then half the coconut cream. Cook for a few minutes until fragrant.

4 Return the chicken to the wok or pan, add the stock, mixing well, then add the remaining coconut cream, the fish sauce, sugar and lime juice. Stir well and bring to the boil, then lower the heat and simmer for 15 minutes.

5 Spoon the curry into four warm serving bowls, garnish with the chillies and spring onions and serve immediately.

Thai Chicken Curry

This flavourful and fragrant, creamy curry is quite easy to make.

Ingredients

400ml/14oz can unsweetened coconut milk
6 skinless, chicken breast fillets, finely sliced
225g/8oz can bamboo shoots, drained and sliced
30ml/2 tbsp fish sauce
15ml/1 tbsp soft light brown sugar
cooked jasmine rice, to serve

For the green curry paste

4 fresh green chillies, seeded
1 lemon grass stalk, sliced
1 small onion, sliced
3 garlic cloves
1cm/½in piece galangal or fresh root ginger, peeled
grated rind of ½ lime
5ml/1 tsp coriander seeds
5ml/1 tsp cumin seeds
2.5ml/½ tsp fish sauce

To garnish

1 fresh red chilli, seeded and cut into fine strips
finely pared rind of ½ lime, finely shredded
fresh Thai purple basil or coriander (cilantro), chopped

Serves 6

1 First make the green curry paste: put all the ingredients in a food processor and process to a thick paste. Set aside.

2 Bring half the coconut milk to the boil in a large frying pan, then reduce the heat and simmer for about 5 minutes, or until reduced by half. Stir in the green curry paste and simmer for a further 5 minutes.

3 Add the finely sliced chicken breasts to the pan with the remaining coconut milk, bamboo shoots, fish sauce and sugar. Stir well to combine all the ingredients and bring the curry back to simmering point, then simmer gently for about 10 minutes, or until the chicken slices are cooked through. The mixture will look grainy or curdled during cooking; this is quite normal.

4 Spoon the curry and rice into warmed bowls, garnish with the chilli, lime rind, and basil or coriander, and serve.

chicken/coconut Energy 706kcal/2935kJ; Protein 48.1g; Carbohydrate 15.8g, of which sugars 15.6g; Fat 50.4g, of which saturates 12.8g; Cholesterol 240mg; Calcium 91mg; Fibre 1.5g; Sodium 305mg.
thai chicken curry Energy 236kcal/991kJ; Protein 33.8g; Carbohydrate 7.2g, of which sugars 5.9g; Fat 8.3g, of which saturates 1.6g; Cholesterol 165mg; Calcium 149mg; Fibre 3.1g; Sodium 253mg.

Chicken & Tofu Curry

This very spice curry has great textures and flavours.

Ingredients

30ml/2 tbsp groundnut (peanut) or soya oil
2 garlic cloves, crushed
2 onions, chopped
2.5cm/1in piece fresh root ginger, finely chopped
4 skinless chicken fillets, cut into bitesize pieces
15–30ml/1–2 tbsp Thai green or red curry paste
45ml/3 tbsp soy sauce
150g/5oz marinated deep-fried tofu
grated rind and juice of 1 lime
120ml/4fl oz/½ cup chicken stock
pinch of sugar
90g/3½oz watercress
20g/¾oz fresh coriander (cilantro), chopped
400ml/14fl oz/1⅔ cups coconut milk
30ml/2 tbsp peanuts, toasted and chopped, to garnish

Serves 4

1 Heat the oil in a non-stick wok or large frying pan, then stir-fry the garlic, onion and ginger for 4–5 minutes, until golden brown and softened. Add the chicken pieces and stir-fry for 2–3 minutes, until browned all over. Add the curry paste and stir to coat the chicken. Add the soy sauce, tofu, grated lime rind and juice, the stock and sugar, and stir-fry for 2 minutes.

2 Add the watercress and coriander, reserving a little for the garnish, and stir-fry for a further 2 minutes. Add the coconut milk and heat through gently, stirring occasionally, but do not allow to come to the boil.

3 Season to taste then serve garnished with the peanuts and reserved coriander.

Variation
Vary the vegetable accompaniments used to suit the season – mangetouts (snow peas), baby corn, courgettes (zucchini), carrots, broccoli florets and green beans all work well.

Yellow Chicken Curry

The pairing of slightly sweet coconut milk and fruit with savoury chicken and spices is at once a comforting and exotic combination.

Ingredients

300ml/½ pint/1¼ cups chicken stock
30ml/2 tbsp tamarind paste mixed with a little warm water
15ml/1 tbsp sugar
200ml/7fl oz/scant 1 cup coconut milk
1 green papaya, peeled, seeded and thinly sliced
250g/9oz skinless chicken breast fillets, diced
juice of 1 lime
lime slices, to garnish

For the curry paste

1 fresh red chilli, seeded and coarsely chopped
4 garlic cloves, coarsely chopped
3 shallots, coarsely chopped
2 lemon grass stalks, sliced
5cm/2in piece fresh turmeric, coarsely chopped, or 5ml/1 tsp ground turmeric
5ml/1 tsp shrimp paste
5ml/1 tsp salt

Serves 4

1 Make the yellow curry paste. Put the red chilli, garlic, shallots, lemon grass, turmeric, shrimp paste and salt in a food processor. Process to a paste, adding a little water if needed.

2 Pour the stock into a wok or medium pan and bring it to the boil. Stir in the curry paste. Bring back to the boil and add the tamarind juice, sugar and coconut milk. Add the papaya and chicken and cook over a medium to high heat for about 15 minutes, stirring frequently, until the chicken is cooked.

3 Stir in the lime juice, transfer to a warm dish and serve immediately, garnished with lime slices.

Cook's Tip
Fresh turmeric resembles root ginger in appearance and is a member of the same family. When preparing it, wear gloves to protect your hands from staining.

chicken & tofu Energy 444kcal/1851kJ; Protein 37.3g; Carbohydrate 14.6g, of which sugars 10g; Fat 26.7g, of which saturates 3.2g; Cholesterol 70mg; Calcium 699mg; Fibre 3.6g; Sodium 222mg.
yellow chicken curry Energy 149kcal/633kJ; Protein 17.2g; Carbohydrate 18.9g, of which sugars 17.2g; Fat 1.1g, of which saturates 0.3g; Cholesterol 50mg; Calcium 70mg; Fibre 2.8g; Sodium 153mg.

Chicken & Lemon Grass Curry

A tasty curry in less than 20 minutes – what more can anyone ask?

Ingredients

45ml/3 tbsp vegetable oil
2 garlic cloves, crushed
500g/1¼lb skinless, boneless chicken thighs, diced
45ml/3 tbsp fish sauce
120ml/4fl oz/½ cup chicken stock
5ml/1 tsp sugar
1 lemon grass stalk, chopped into 4 sticks and lightly crushed
5 kaffir lime leaves, rolled into cylinders and thinly sliced across, plus extra to garnish

For the curry paste

1 lemon grass stalk, coarsely chopped
2.5cm/1in piece fresh galangal, peeled and coarsely chopped
2 kaffir lime leaves, chopped
3 shallots, coarsely chopped
6 coriander (cilantro) roots, coarsely chopped
2 garlic cloves
2 fresh green chillies, seeded and coarsely chopped
5ml/1 tsp shrimp paste
5ml/1 tsp ground turmeric

chopped roasted peanuts and chopped fresh coriander (cilantro), to garnish

Serves 4

1 Make the curry paste. Place all the ingredients in a large mortar or food processor and pound with a pestle or process to a smooth paste.

2 Heat the vegetable oil in a wok, add the garlic and cook over a low heat, stirring frequently, until golden brown. Be careful not to let the garlic burn or it will taste bitter. Add the curry paste and stir-fry for 30 seconds more.

3 Add the chicken pieces to the pan and stir until thoroughly coated with the curry paste. Stir in the fish sauce and chicken stock, then add the sugar, and cook, stirring constantly, for 2 minutes more.

4 Add the lemon grass and lime leaves, reduce the heat and simmer for 10 minutes. Spoon the curry into four warmed dishes, garnish and serve immediately.

Red Chicken Curry

Bamboo shoots give this a lovely crunchy texture.

Ingredients

1 litre/1¾ pints/4 cups coconut milk
30ml/2 tbsp red curry paste
450g/1lb skinless chicken breast fillets, cut into bitesize pieces
30ml/2 tbsp fish sauce
15ml/1 tbsp sugar
225g/8oz drained canned bamboo shoots, rinsed and sliced
5 kaffir lime leaves, torn
salt and ground black pepper
chopped fresh red chillies and kaffir lime leaves, to garnish

Serves 4–6

1 Pour half of the coconut milk into a wok or large heavy pan. Bring to the boil, stirring constantly until it has separated.

2 Stir in the red curry paste and cook the mixture for about 2–3 minutes, stirring constantly.

3 Add the chicken pieces, fish sauce and sugar to the wok or pan. Stir well, then cook for 5–6 minutes until the chicken changes colour and is cooked through, stirring constantly to prevent the mixture from sticking to the bottom of the pan.

4 Pour the remaining coconut milk into the pan, then add the sliced bamboo shoots and torn kaffir lime leaves. Bring back to the boil over a medium heat, stirring constantly to prevent the mixture sticking, then taste and season if necessary.

5 To serve, spoon the curry into a warmed serving dish and garnish with chopped chillies and kaffir lime leaves.

Cook's Tip

It is essential to use chicken breast fillets, rather than any other cut, for this curry, as it is cooked very quickly. Look out for diced chicken or strips of chicken (which are often labelled "stir-fry chicken") in the supermarket.

chicken & lemon grass Energy 122kcal/512kJ; Protein 17.4g; Carbohydrate 3.7g, of which sugars 3g; Fat 4.3g, of which saturates 0.8g; Cholesterol 85mg; Calcium 77mg; Fibre 1.6g; Sodium 131mg.
red chicken curry Energy 261kcal/1105kJ; Protein 29.6g; Carbohydrate 19.6g, of which sugars 18.3g; Fat 7.8g, of which saturates 1.5g; Cholesterol 79mg; Calcium 95mg; Fibre 1.1g; Sodium 837mg.

Green Chicken Curry

Use more or fewer chillies in this dish, depending on how hot you like your curry.

Ingredients

4 spring onions (scallions), trimmed and coarsely chopped
1–2 fresh green chillies, seeded and coarsely chopped
2cm/¾ in piece fresh root ginger, peeled
2 garlic cloves
5ml/1 tsp fish sauce
large bunch fresh coriander (cilantro)
small handful of fresh parsley
30–45ml/2–3 tbsp water
30ml/2 tbsp sunflower oil
4 skinless, chicken breast fillets, diced
1 green (bell) pepper, seeded and thinly sliced
600ml/1 pint/2½ cups coconut milk
salt and ground black pepper
hot coconut rice, to serve

Serves 3–4

1 Put the spring onions, chillies, ginger, garlic, fish sauce and herbs in a food processor. Pour in 30ml/2 tbsp of the water and process to a smooth paste, adding more water if required.

2 Heat half the oil in a large frying pan. Cook the diced chicken until evenly browned. Transfer to a plate. Heat the remaining oil in the pan. Add the green pepper and stir-fry for 3–4 minutes, then add the chilli and ginger paste. Stir-fry for a further 3–4 minutes, until the mixture becomes fairly thick.

3 Return the chicken to the pan and add the coconut liquid. Season with salt and pepper and bring to the boil, then reduce the heat, half cover the pan and simmer for 8–10 minutes.

4 When the chicken is cooked, transfer it, with the green pepper, to a plate. Boil the cooking liquid remaining in the pan for 10–12 minutes, until it is well reduced and fairly thick.

5 Return the chicken and pepper to the green curry sauce, stir well and cook gently for 2–3 minutes to heat through. Spoon the curry over the coconut rice, and serve immediately.

Chicken & Sweet Potato Curry

Ho Chi Minh City is home to many stalls specializing in curries like this one. They all use Indian curry powder and coconut milk.

Ingredients

45ml/3 tbsp Indian curry powder
15ml/1 tbsp ground turmeric
500g/1¼lb skinless boneless chicken thighs or chicken breast fillets
25ml/1½ tbsp raw cane sugar
30ml/2 tbsp sesame oil
2 shallots, chopped
2 garlic cloves, chopped
4cm/1½in galangal, peeled and chopped
2 lemon grass stalks, chopped
10ml/2 tsp chilli paste or dried chilli flakes
2 medium sweet potatoes, peeled and cubed
45ml/3 tbsp chilli sambal
600ml/1 pint/2½ cups coconut milk
1 small bunch each fresh basil and coriander (cilantro), stalks removed
salt and ground black pepper

Serves 4

1 In a small bowl, mix together the curry powder and turmeric. Put the chicken in a bowl and coat with half of the spice. Set aside.

2 Heat the sugar in a small pan with 7.5ml/1½ tsp water, until the sugar dissolves and the syrup turns golden. Remove from the heat and set aside.

3 Heat a wok or heavy pan and add the oil. Stir-fry the shallots, garlic, galangal and lemon grass. Stir in the rest of the turmeric and curry powder with the chilli paste or flakes, followed by the chicken, and stir-fry for 2–3 minutes.

4 Add the sweet potatoes, then the chilli sambal, syrup, coconut milk and 150ml/¼ pint/⅔ cup water, mixing thoroughly to combine the flavours.

5 Bring to the boil, reduce the heat and cook for about 15 minutes until the chicken is cooked through. Season and stir in half the basil and coriander. Spoon into warmed bowls, garnish with the remaining herbs and serve immediately.

green chicken curry Energy 208kcal/877kJ; Protein 28g; Carbohydrate 8g, of which sugars 7.9g; Fat 7.4g, of which saturates 1.3g; Cholesterol 79mg; Calcium 76mg; Fibre 0.7g; Sodium 237mg.
chicken & potato Energy 384kcal/1621kJ; Protein 29.5g; Carbohydrate 39.7g, of which sugars 20.7g; Fat 13.1g, of which saturates 2.5g; Cholesterol 131mg; Calcium 181mg; Fibre 5.8g; Sodium 373mg.

Curry with Coconut & Chilli Relish

Fresh and roasted coconut gives this chicken curry its unique flavour.

Ingredients

15–30ml/1–2 tbsp tamarind pulp
1 fresh coconut, grated (shredded)
30–45ml/2–3 tbsp vegetable oil
1–2 cinnamon sticks
12 chicken thighs, boned and cut into bitesize strips lengthways
600ml/1 pint/2½ cups coconut milk
15ml/1 tbsp brown sugar
1 fresh green and 1 red chilli, seeded and sliced
fresh coriander (cilantro) leaves, finely chopped (reserve a few leaves for garnishing)
2 limes
salt and ground black pepper
steamed rice, to serve

For the rempah spice paste

6–8 dried red chillies, soaked in warm water until soft, seeded and squeezed dry
6–8 shallots, chopped
4–6 garlic cloves, chopped
25g/1oz fresh root ginger, chopped
5ml/1 tsp shrimp paste
10ml/2 tsp ground turmeric
10ml/2 tsp five-spice powder

Serves 4

1 First make the rempah. Using a mortar and pestle or food processor, grind the chillies, shallots, garlic and ginger to a paste. Beat in the shrimp paste and stir in the dried spices.

2 Soak the tamarind pulp in 150ml/¼ pint/⅔ cup warm water until soft. Squeeze to extract the juice, then strain. In a heavy pan, roast half the grated coconut until brown, then grind it in a food processor until it resembles sugar grains.

3 Heat the oil in a heavy pan and stir in the rempah and cinnamon sticks until fragrant. Add the chicken, coconut milk, tamarind water and sugar. Cook gently for 10 minutes. Thicken by stirring in half the ground roasted coconut, and season.

4 Make a relish by mixing the remaining grated coconut with the chillies, coriander and juice of 1 lime. Cut the other lime into wedges. Spoon the curry into a serving dish and garnish with coriander. Serve with the rice, relish and lime wedges.

Jungle Curry of Guinea Fowl

A traditional wild food country curry, this dish can be made using any game, fish or chicken.

Ingredients

1 guinea fowl or similar game bird
15ml/1 tbsp vegetable oil
10ml/2 tsp green curry paste
15ml/1 tbsp fish sauce
2.5cm/1in piece fresh galangal, peeled and finely chopped
15ml/1 tbsp fresh green peppercorns
3 kaffir lime leaves, torn
15ml/1 tbsp whisky
300ml/½ pint/1¼ cups chicken stock
50g/2oz snake beans or yard-long beans, cut into 2.5cm/1in lengths (about ½ cup)
225g/8oz/3¼ cups chestnut mushrooms, sliced
1 piece drained canned bamboo shoot, about 50g/2oz, shredded

Serves 4

1 Cut up the guinea fowl, remove and discard the skin, then take all the meat off the bones. Chop the meat into bitesize pieces and set aside on a plate.

2 Heat the oil in a wok or frying pan and add the curry paste. Stir-fry over a medium heat for 30 seconds, until the paste gives off its aroma. Add the fish sauce and the guinea fowl meat and stir-fry until the meat is browned all over. Add the galangal, peppercorns, lime leaves and whisky, then pour in the stock.

3 Bring to the boil. Add the vegetables, return to a simmer and cook gently for 2–3 minutes, until they are just cooked. Spoon into a dish, and serve.

Cook's Tip

Fresh green peppercorns are simply unripe berries. They are sold on the stem and look rather like miniature Brussels sprout stalks. Look for them at Thai supermarkets. If unavailable, substitute bottled green peppercorns, but rinse well and drain them before adding them to the curry.

curry w. coconut Energy 706kcal/2935kJ; Protein 48.1g; Carbohydrate 15.8g, of which sugars 15.6g; Fat 50.4g, of which saturates 12.8g; Cholesterol 240mg; Calcium 91mg; Fibre 1.5g; Sodium 305mg.
curry of guinea fowl Energy 321kcal/1345kJ; Protein 42.2g; Carbohydrate 1.1g, of which sugars 0.7g; Fat 15g, of which saturates 4.4g; Cholesterol 0mg; Calcium 72mg; Fibre 1.1g; Sodium 136mg.

Chinese Duck Curry

The duck used in this dish is best marinated for as long as possible – preferably overnight – although it tastes good even if you only marinate it briefly.

Ingredients

4 duck breast portions, skin and bones removed
30ml/2 tbsp five-spice powder
30ml/2 tbsp sesame oil
grated rind and juice of 1 orange
1 medium butternut squash, peeled and cubed
10ml/2 tsp red curry paste
30ml/2 tbsp fish sauce
15ml/1 tbsp palm sugar (jaggery) or soft light brown sugar
300ml/½ pint/1¼ cups coconut milk
2 fresh red chillies, seeded
4 kaffir lime leaves, torn
small bunch coriander (cilantro), chopped, to garnish

Serves 4

1 Cut the duck meat into bitesize pieces and place in a bowl with the five-spice powder, sesame oil, and orange rind and juice. Stir well to mix all the ingredients and coat the duck in the marinade. Cover the bowl with clear film (plastic wrap) and set aside in a cool place to marinate for at least 15 minutes.

2 Meanwhile, bring a pan of water to the boil. Add the squash and cook for 10–15 minutes, until just tender. Drain well and set aside in a bowl.

3 Pour the marinade from the duck into a wok and heat until boiling. Stir in the curry paste and cook for 2–3 minutes, until well blended and fragrant. Add the duck and cook for 3–4 minutes, stirring constantly, until browned on all sides.

4 Add the fish sauce and sugar and cook for 2 minutes more. Stir in the coconut milk until the mixture is smooth, then add the cooked squash, with the chillies and lime leaves.

5 Simmer gently, stirring frequently, for 5 minutes, then spoon into a dish, sprinkle with the coriander and serve.

Red Duck Curry

Slow simmering is the secret of this wonderful duck curry.

Ingredients

4 skinless duck breast fillets
400ml/14fl oz can coconut milk
200ml/7fl oz/scant 1 cup chicken stock
30ml/2 tbsp red curry paste
8 spring onions (scallions), finely sliced
10ml/2 tsp grated fresh root ginger
30ml/2 tbsp Chinese rice wine
15ml/1 tbsp fish sauce
15ml/1 tbsp soy sauce
2 lemon grass stalks, halved lengthways
3–4 kaffir lime leaves
300g/11oz pea aubergines (eggplants)
10ml/2 tsp sugar
salt and ground black pepper
10–12 fresh basil and mint leaves, to garnish
steamed jasmine rice, to serve

Serves 4

1 Using a sharp knife, cut the duck breast portions into neat bitesize pieces and set aside on a plate.

2 Place a wok over a low heat and add the coconut milk, stock, curry paste, spring onions, ginger, rice wine, fish and soy sauces, lemon grass and lime leaves. Stir well to mix, then bring to the boil over a medium heat.

3 Add the duck, aubergines and sugar to the wok and simmer for 25–30 minutes, stirring occasionally.

4 Remove the wok from the heat and leave to stand, covered, for about 15 minutes. Season to taste.

5 Ladle the duck curry into shallow bowls, garnish with fresh mint and basil leaves, and serve with steamed jasmine rice.

Cook's Tip
Tiny pea aubergines (eggplants) are sold in Asian stores. If you can't find them, use regular aubergines, cut into neat chunks.

chinese duck Energy 295kcal/1241kJ; Protein 31.4g; Carbohydrate 13.3g, of which sugars 12.3g; Fat 15.9g, of which saturates 3.1g; Cholesterol 165mg; Calcium 102mg; Fibre 2g; Sodium 427mg.
red duck curry Energy 241kcal/1017kJ; Protein 31.1g; Carbohydrate 10.2g, of which sugars 10g; Fat 10.5g, of which saturates 2.3g; Cholesterol 165mg; Calcium 65mg; Fibre 1.8g; Sodium 546mg.

Duck with Pineapple

Duck and pineapple is a favourite combination, but the fruit must not be allowed to dominate as you will upset the delicate balance in sweet-sour flavour.

Ingredients

15ml/1 tbsp dry sherry
15ml/1 tbsp dark soy sauce
2 small skinless duck breast fillets
15ml/1 tbsp vegetable oil
2 garlic cloves, finely chopped
1 small onion, sliced
1 red (bell) pepper, seeded and cut into 2.5cm/1in squares
75g/3oz/½ cup drained, canned pineapple chunks
90ml/6 tbsp pineapple juice
15ml/1 tbsp rice vinegar
5ml/1 tsp cornflour (cornstarch)
15ml/1 tbsp cold water
5ml/1 tsp sesame oil
salt and ground white pepper
1 spring onion (scallion), shredded, to garnish

Serves 4

1 Mix together the sherry and soy sauce. Stir in 2.5ml/½ tsp salt and 1.5ml/¼ tsp white pepper. Put the duck fillets in a bowl and add the marinade. Cover with clear film (plastic wrap) and leave in a cool place for 1 hour.

2 Drain the duck fillets and place them on a rack in a grill (broiler) pan, or on a preheated griddle pan. Cook using medium to high heat, for 10 minutes on each side. Leave to cool for 10 minutes, then cut the duck into bitesize pieces.

3 Heat the vegetable oil in a non-stick frying pan or wok and stir-fry the garlic and onion for 1 minute. Add the red pepper, pineapple chunks, duck, pineapple juice and vinegar and toss over the heat for 2 minutes.

4 Mix the cornflour to a paste with the water. Add the mixture to the pan with 1.5ml/¼ tsp salt. Cook, stirring, until the sauce thickens. Stir in the sesame oil. Spoon the duck and pineapple mixture into four warmed bowls, garnish with the spring onion shreds, and serve.

Duck with Pineapple & Ginger

Save time and effort by using the boneless duck breast fillets that are widely available.

Ingredients

2 duck breast fillets
4 spring onions (scallions), chopped
15ml/1 tbsp light soy sauce
225g/8oz can pineapple rings
75ml/5 tbsp water
4 pieces drained Chinese stem ginger in syrup, plus 45ml/3 tbsp syrup from the jar
30ml/2 tbsp cornflour (cornstarch) mixed to a paste with a little water
¼ each red and green (bell) pepper, seeded and cut into thin strips
salt and ground black pepper
cooked thin egg noodles, baby spinach and green beans, blanched, to serve

Serves 2–3

1 Strip the skin from the duck. Select a shallow bowl that will fit into your steamer and that will accommodate the duck fillets side by side. Spread out the spring onions in the bowl, arrange the duck on top and cover with baking parchment. Set the steamer over boiling water. Cook the duck for about 1 hour until tender. Remove the duck and leave to cool slightly.

2 Cut the duck fillets into thin slices. Place on a plate and moisten them with a little of the cooking juices from the steaming bowl. Strain the remaining juices into a small pan and set aside. Cover the duck slices and keep hot.

3 Drain the canned pineapple rings, reserving 75ml/5 tbsp of the juice. Add this to the reserved cooking juices in the pan, together with the measured water. Stir in the ginger syrup, then stir in the cornflour paste and cook, stirring until thickened. Season to taste.

4 Cut the pineapple and ginger into attractive shapes. Put the cooked noodles, baby spinach and green beans on a plate, add slices of duck and top with the pineapple, ginger and pepper strips. Pour over the sauce and serve.

duck w. pineapple Energy 682kcal/2861kJ; Protein 62.6g; Carbohydrate 40.3g, of which sugars 33.7g; Fat 34.4g, of which saturates 5.8g; Cholesterol 330mg; Calcium 83mg; Fibre 4g; Sodium 1419mg.
duck w. pine. & ginger Energy 253kcal/1071kJ; Protein 20.8g; Carbohydrate 33.1g, of which sugars 23.8g; Fat 6.8g, of which saturates 1.4g; Cholesterol 110mg; Calcium 31mg; Fibre 1.1g; Sodium 515mg.

Duck with Pineapple & Coriander

Marinating the duck really boosts the flavour, so remember to allow enough time for this.

Ingredients

1 small duck, skinned, trimmed and jointed
1 pineapple, skinned, cored and cut in half crossways
45ml/3 tbsp sesame or vegetable oil
4cm/1½in fresh root ginger, peeled and finely sliced
1 onion, sliced
salt and ground black pepper
1 bunch fresh coriander (cilantro), stalks removed, to garnish

For the marinade

3 shallots, grated
45ml/3 tbsp soy sauce
30ml/2 tbsp fish sauce
10ml/2 tsp five-spice powder
15ml/1 tbsp sugar
3 garlic cloves, crushed
1 bunch fresh basil, stalks removed, leaves finely chopped

Serves 4–6

1 To make the marinade, mix all the ingredients in a bowl and beat together until the sugar has dissolved. Place the duck joints in a wide dish and rub with the marinade. Cover and chill for 6 hours or overnight.

2 Take one of the pineapple halves and cut into 4–6 slices, and then again into half-moons, and set aside. Take the other pineapple half and chop it to a pulp. Using your hands, squeeze all the juice from the pulp into a bowl. Discard the pulp and reserve the juice.

3 Heat 30ml/2 tbsp of the oil in a wide pan. Stir in the ginger and the onion. When they begin to soften, add the duck to the pan and brown on both sides. Pour in the pineapple juice and any remaining marinade, then add water so that the duck is just covered. Bring to the boil, then simmer for about 25 minutes.

4 Meanwhile, heat the remaining oil in a heavy pan and sear the pineapple slices on both sides. Add to the duck, season to taste, and cook for a further 5 minutes, or until the duck is tender. Arrange on a serving dish, garnish with coriander and serve.

Duck in Spicy Orange Sauce

Although this dish has something in common with duck à l'orange, the use of spices, lemon grass and chillies makes it quite different. Serve with steamed rice and a vegetable dish. This satisfying meal is bound to go down well with family and guests.

Ingredients

4 duck legs
4 garlic cloves, crushed
50g/2oz fresh root ginger, peeled and finely sliced
2 lemon grass stalks, trimmed, cut into 3 pieces and crushed
2 dried whole red chillies
15ml/1 tbsp palm sugar (jaggery)
5ml/1 tsp five-spice powder
30ml/2 tbsp chilli sambal
900ml/1½ pints/3¾ cups fresh orange juice
sea salt and ground black pepper
1 lime, cut into quarters, to serve

Serves 4

1 Place the duck legs, skin side down, in a large heavy pan or flameproof clay pot. Cook them on both sides over a medium heat for about 10 minutes, until browned and crispy. Transfer them to a plate and set aside.

2 Stir the garlic, ginger, lemon grass and chillies into the fat left in the pan, and cook until golden. Add the sugar, five-spice powder and chilli sambal, and mix well.

3 Stir in the orange juice and return the duck legs to the pan. Cover the pan and gently cook the duck for 1–2 hours, until the meat is tender and the sauce has reduced.

4 Skim any fat from the top of the sauce, then taste and adjust the flavouring if necessary. Serve in heated bowls, with lime wedges for squeezing over the duck.

Variation
You could substitute the duck for chicken thigh portions.

duck w. pine. & coriander Energy 303kcal/1285kJ; Protein 18.9g; Carbohydrate 46g, of which sugars 15g; Fat 7.3g, of which saturates 0.9g; Cholesterol 73mg; Calcium 54mg; Fibre 3.8g; Sodium 95mg.
duck in orange sauce Energy 280kcal/1181kJ; Protein 30.8g; Carbohydrate 23.8g, of which sugars 23.8g; Fat 10g, of which saturates 2g; Cholesterol 165mg; Calcium 48mg; Fibre 0.4g; Sodium 195mg.

Duck & Sesame Stir-fry

This recipe is intended for game birds, as farmed duck would usually have too much fat. If you do use farmed duck, you should remove the skin and fat layer, before cooking.

Ingredients

250g/9oz skinless wild duck breast fillets
15ml/1 tbsp sesame oil
15ml/1 tbsp vegetable oil
4 garlic cloves, finely sliced
2.5ml/½ tsp dried chilli flakes
15ml/1 tbsp fish sauce
15ml/1 tbsp light soy sauce
1 head broccoli, cut into small florets
coriander (cilantro) sprigs and 15ml/1 tbsp toasted sesame seeds, to garnish

Serves 4

1 Cut the duck into bitesize pieces. Heat the oils in a wok or large frying pan and stir-fry the garlic over medium heat until it is golden brown – do not let it burn.

2 Add the duck pieces to the pan and stir-fry for a further 2 minutes, until the meat begins to brown.

3 Stir in the chilli flakes, fish sauce, soy sauce and 120ml/4fl oz/½ cup water.

4 Add the broccoli florets and continue to stir-fry the mixture over a medium heat for about 2 minutes, until the duck pieces are just cooked through.

5 Serve immediately on warmed plates, garnished with sprigs of coriander and sesame seeds.

Cook's Tip

Large wok lids are cumbersome and can be difficult to store in a small kitchen. If you need to cover a wok it may be easier to just place a circle of baking parchment against the food surface to keep cooking juices in.

Fruity Duck Chop Suey

Skinning the duck reduces the fat, but this is still an indulgent recipe. If this worries you, use less duck and more noodles. Pineapple gives the dish a lovely fresh flavour.

Ingredients

250g/9oz fresh sesame noodles
2 skinless duck breast fillets
3 spring onions (scallions), cut into strips
2 celery sticks, cut into strips
1 fresh pineapple, peeled, cored and cut into strips
300g/11oz mixed vegetables, such as carrots, peppers, beansprouts and cabbage, shredded or cut into strips
90ml/6 tbsp plum sauce

Serves 4

1 Cook the noodles in a large pan of boiling water for 3 minutes. Drain. Slice the duck breast fillets into strips.

2 Meanwhile, heat a wok. Add the strips of duck and stir-fry for 2–3 minutes, Drain off all but 30ml/2 tbsp of the fat. Add the spring onions and celery to the wok and stir-fry for 2 minutes more.

3 Use a slotted spoon to remove the ingredients from the wok and set them aside in a bowl. Add the pineapple strips and mixed vegetables, and stir-fry for 2 minutes more.

4 Add the cooked noodles and plum sauce to the wok, then replace the duck, spring onion and celery mixture.

5 Stir-fry the duck mixture for about 2 minutes more, or until the noodles and vegetables are hot and the duck is cooked through. Serve immediately.

Cook's Tip

Fresh sesame noodles can be bought from large supermarkets – they are usually found in the chiller cabinets by fresh pasta.

duck & sesame stir fry Energy 172kcal/718kJ; Protein 17.3g; Carbohydrate 2g, of which sugars 1.7g; Fat 10.6g, of which saturates 2.2g; Cholesterol 69mg; Calcium 71mg; Fibre 2.9g; Sodium 78mg.
fruity duck chop suey Energy 603kcal/2553kJ; Protein 36.3g; Carbohydrate 93g, of which sugars 28.1g; Fat 14.2g, of which saturates 1.7g; Cholesterol 138mg; Calcium 96mg; Fibre 6.9g; Sodium 167mg.

Braised Duck in Soy Sauce

The Chinese communities at home and abroad often braise duck, goose, chicken or pork in soy sauce and warm flavourings, such as star anise and cinnamon. Such dishes are found at Chinese hawker stalls and coffee shops, and there are many variations on the theme. Turmeric and lemon grass are sometimes added to the flavourings and, to achieve their desired fiery kick, chillies are always included.

Ingredients

1 duck (about 2kg/4½lb), washed and trimmed
15–30ml/1–2 tbsp Chinese five-spice powder
25g/1oz fresh turmeric, chopped
25g/1oz galangal, chopped
4 garlic cloves, chopped
30ml/2 tbsp sesame oil
12 shallots, peeled and left whole
2–3 lemon grass stalks, halved and lightly crushed
4 cinnamon sticks
8 star anise
12 cloves
600ml/1 pint/2½ cups light soy sauce
120ml/4fl oz/½ cup dark soy sauce
30–45ml/2–3 tbsp palm sugar (jaggery)
steamed jasmine rice and salad, to serve

Serves 4–6

1 Rub the duck, inside and out, with the five-spice powder and place in the refrigerator, uncovered, for 6–8 hours.

2 Using a mortar and pestle or food processor, grind the turmeric, galangal and garlic to a smooth paste. Heat the oil in a heavy pan and stir in the spice paste until it becomes fragrant. Stir in the shallots, lemon grass, cinnamon sticks, star anise and cloves. Pour in the soy sauces and stir in the sugar.

3 Place the duck in the pan, baste with the sauce, and add 550ml/18fl oz/2½ cups water. Bring to the boil, reduce the heat and cover the pan. Simmer gently for 4–6 hours, basting from time to time, until the duck is very tender. Garnish with the leftover spices, if you like, and serve with rice and salad.

Marmalade & Soy Roast Duck

Sweet-and-sour flavours, such as marmalade and soy sauce, complement the rich, fatty taste of duck beautifully. Serve these robustly flavoured duck breast fillets with simple accompaniments such as steamed sticky rice and pak choi (bok choy).

Ingredients

6 duck breast fillets
45ml/3 tbsp fine-cut marmalade
45ml/3 tbsp light soy sauce
salt and ground black pepper

Serves 6

1 Preheat the oven to 190°C/375°F/Gas 5. Place the duck breasts skin side up on a grill (broiler) rack and place in the sink. Pour boiling water all over the duck. This shrinks the skin and helps it crisp during cooking. Pat the duck dry with kitchen paper and transfer to a roasting pan.

2 Combine the marmalade and soy sauce, and brush over the duck. Season with a little salt and some black pepper and roast for 20–25 minutes, basting occasionally with the marmalade mixture in the pan.

3 Remove the duck breast fillets from the oven and leave to rest for 5 minutes. Slice the duck breast fillets and serve drizzled with any juices left in the pan.

Variation

- *Marmalade gives the duck a lovely citrus flavour but this recipe also works well if you substitute black cherry jam. Use a little plum sauce instead of the light soy sauce if you like, but not too much as the flavour of the cherries will be swamped.*
- *If the occasion calls for a little ceremony, roast a whole duck. You will need to prick the skin of the bird all over before roasting, so that the fat, which is trapped in a layer beneath the skin, will be released during cooking. This excess oily matter can then be drained off during cooking.*

duck in soy sauce Energy 119kcal/498kJ; Protein 10.2g; Carbohydrate 4.6g, of which sugars 3.4g; Fat 6.9g, of which saturates 1.5g; Cholesterol 50mg; Calcium 35mg; Fibre 1.1g; Sodium 412mg.
marmalade & soy duck Energy 160kcal/672kJ; Protein 19.9g; Carbohydrate 5.8g, of which sugars 5.8g; Fat 6.5g, of which saturates 2g; Cholesterol 110mg; Calcium 16mg; Fibre 0.1g; Sodium 645mg.

Stir-fried Crispy Duck

This stir-fry is delicious wrapped in steamed mandarin pancakes, with a little extra plum sauce.

Ingredients

350g/12oz duck breast fillets
30ml/2 tbsp plain (all-purpose) flour
60ml/4 tbsp oil
1 bunch spring onions (scallions), cut in strips, plus extra to garnish
275g/10oz/2½ cups finely shredded green cabbage
225g/8oz can water chestnuts, drained and sliced
50g/2oz/½ cup unsalted cashew nuts
cucumber, cut in strips
45ml/3 tbsp plum sauce
15ml/1 tbsp soy sauce
salt and ground black pepper

Serves 2

1 Remove any skin from the duck breast, then trim off a little of the fat. Thinly slice the meat. Season the flour with plenty of salt and pepper and use it to coat the pieces of duck all over.

2 Heat the oil in a wok and cook the duck slices in batches over a high heat until golden and crisp. Keep stirring to prevent the duck from sticking. As each batch cooks, remove the duck with a slotted spoon and drain on kitchen paper.

3 Add the spring onions to the wok and cook for 2 minutes, then stir in the cabbage and cook for 5 minutes, or until it has softened.

4 Return the duck to the pan with the water chestnuts, cashews and cucumber. Stir-fry for 2 minutes. Add the plum sauce and soy sauce, season with salt and black pepper to taste, then heat for 2 minutes. Serve in individual bowls, garnished with the sliced spring onions.

Cook's Tip

Water chestnuts are the perfect foil for the rich duck in this stir-fry, remaining crisp and crunchy after cooking.

Anita Wong's Duck

To the Chinese, duck is a symbol of marital harmony.

Ingredients

1 duck with giblets, about 2.25kg/5lb
60ml/4 tbsp vegetable oil
2 garlic cloves, chopped
2.5cm/1in piece fresh root ginger, peeled and thinly sliced
45ml/3 tbsp bean paste
30ml/2 tbsp light soy sauce
15ml/1 tbsp dark soy sauce
15ml/1 tbsp sugar
2.5ml/½ tsp five-spice powder
3 star anise points
450ml/¾ pint/scant 2 cups duck stock (see Cook's Tip)
salt
shredded spring onions (scallions), to garnish

Serves 4–6

1 Make the stock (see Cook's Tip), strain into a bowl and blot the surface with kitchen paper to remove excess fat. Measure 450ml/¾ pint/scant 2 cups into a jug (pitcher).

2 Heat the oil in a large pan. Fry the garlic without browning, then add the duck. Turn frequently until the outside is slightly brown. Transfer to a plate.

3 Add the ginger to the pan, then stir in the bean paste. Cook for 1 minute, then add both soy sauces, the sugar and the five-spice powder. Return the duck to the pan and fry until the outside is coated. Add the star anise and stock, and season to taste. Cover tightly; simmer gently for 2–2½ hours or until tender. Skim off the excess fat. Leave to cool completely.

4 Cut the duck into serving portions and pour over the sauce. Garnish with spring onion curls and serve cold.

Cook's Tip

To make the stock, put the duck giblets in a heavy pan with a small onion and a piece of bruised fresh root ginger. Cover with 600ml/1 pint/2½ cups water, bring to the boil and then simmer, covered, for 20 minutes.

stir-fried duck Energy 682kcal/2846kJ; Protein 36.9g; Carbohydrate 41.3g, of which sugars 26.3g; Fat 44.4g, of which saturates 7.5g; Cholesterol 151mg; Calcium 174mg; Fibre 5.8g; Sodium 844mg.
anita wong's duck Energy 233kcal/977kJ; Protein 22.7g; Carbohydrate 4.2g, of which sugars 1g; Fat 14.2g, of which saturates 3.1g; Cholesterol 113mg; Calcium 23mg; Fibre 1.3g; Sodium 652mg.

Peking Duck

As the Chinese discovered centuries ago, this is quite the best way to eat duck.

Ingredients
1 duck, about 2.25kg/5lb
45ml/3 tbsp clear honey
5ml/1 tsp salt
1 bunch spring onions (scallions), cut into strips
½ cucumber, seeded and cut into matchsticks
24–32 mandarin pancakes

For the dipping sauces
120ml/4fl oz/½ cup hoisin sauce
120ml/4fl oz/½ cup plum sauce

Serves 8

1 Place the duck on a trivet in the sink and scald with boiling water to firm up the skin. Drain thoroughly. Tie kitchen string (twine) firmly around the legs of the bird and hang it in a cool place, with a bowl underneath to catch the drips. Leave the duck overnight.

2 Next day, blend the honey, 30ml/2 tbsp water and salt and brush half the mixture over the duck skin. Hang up again for 2–3 hours. Repeat and leave to dry completely for a further 3–4 hours.

3 Preheat the oven to 230°C/450°F/Gas 8. Stand the duck on a rack in a roasting pan, place in the oven and reduce the temperature to 180°C/350°F/Gas 4. Roast for 1¾ hours without basting. Check the skin is crisp; if not, increase the oven temperature to the maximum. Roast for 15 minutes more.

4 Pat the cucumber pieces dry on kitchen paper. Heat the pancakes by steaming them in a foil parcel for 5–10 minutes over boiling water. Pour the dipping sauces into small dishes to share between the guests.

5 Carve the duck into 4cm/1½in pieces. At the table, each guest smears a little sauce on a pancake, tops it with a small amount of crisp duck skin and meat and adds cucumber and spring onion strips before rolling the pancake up and eating it.

Garlic-roasted Quails with Honey

This is a great Indo-Chinese favourite made with quails or other small poultry such as poussins. Crispy, tender and juicy, they are simple to prepare and delicious to eat. Once skewered, the quail can be roasted in the oven or cooked over a barbecue. Serve with fragrant steamed rice and keep the skewers in place as it will make them easier to dip.

Ingredients
150ml/¼ pint/⅔ cup mushroom soy sauce
45ml/3 tbsp honey
15ml/1 tbsp sugar
8 garlic cloves, crushed
15ml/1 tbsp black peppercorns, crushed
30ml/2 tbsp sesame oil
8 quails or poussins
hot chilli sauce, to serve

Serves 4

1 In a bowl, beat the mushroom soy sauce with the honey and sugar until the sugar has dissolved. Stir in the garlic, crushed peppercorns and sesame oil.

2 Open out and skewer the quails or poussins, put them in a dish and rub the marinade over them. Cover and chill for at least 4 hours.

3 Preheat the oven to 230°C/450°F/ Gas 8. Place the quails breast side down in a roasting pan or on a wire rack set over a baking tray, then put them in the oven for 10 minutes.

4 Take the quails or poussin out and turn them over so they are breast side up, baste well with the juices and return them to the oven for a further 15–20 minutes until cooked through. Serve immediately with chilli sauce for dipping or drizzling.

Cook's Tip
The quails can be roasted whole, or split down the backbone, opened out and secured with skewers. For the New Year, Tet, whole chickens are marinated in similar garlicky flavourings and cooked over charcoal or in the oven.

peking duck Energy 174kcal/734kJ; Protein 16.9g; Carbohydrate 14.9g, of which sugars 4.7g; Fat 5.3g, of which saturates 1.7g; Cholesterol 85mg; Calcium 21mg; Fibre 0.7g; Sodium 334mg.
quails w. honey Energy 488kcal/2033kJ; Protein 41.6g; Carbohydrate 0g, of which sugars 0g; Fat 35.9g, of which saturates 9.1g; Cholesterol 218mg; Calcium 16mg; Fibre 0g; Sodium 150mg.

Warm Lamb & Noodle Salad

Here, thin slices of wok-fried lamb, fresh vegetables and rice noodles are tossed in an aromatic dressing.

Ingredients

30ml/2 tbsp red curry paste
60ml/4 tbsp sunflower oil
750g/1lb 11oz lamb neck (US shoulder or breast) fillets, thinly sliced
250g/9oz sugar snap peas
500g/1¼lb fresh rice noodles
1 red (bell) pepper, seeded and very thinly sliced
1 cucumber, sliced paper thin
6–7 spring onions (scallions), sliced diagonally
a large handful of fresh mint leaves

For the dressing

15ml/1 tbsp sunflower oil
juice of 2 limes
1 garlic clove, crushed
15ml/1 tbsp sugar
15ml/1 tbsp fish sauce
30ml/2 tbsp soy sauce

Serves 4

1 In a shallow dish, mix together the red curry paste and half the oil. Add the lamb slices and toss to coat. Cover and leave to marinate in the refrigerator for up to 24 hours.

2 Blanch the sugar snap peas in a pan of lightly salted boiling water for 1–2 minutes. Drain, refresh under cold water, drain again thoroughly and transfer to a large bowl.

3 Put the noodles in a separate bowl and pour over boiling water to cover. Leave to soak for 5–10 minutes, until tender, then drain well and separate into strands with your fingers.

4 Add the noodles to the sugar snap peas, then add the sliced red pepper, cucumber and spring onions. Toss lightly to mix.

5 Heat a wok over a high heat and add the remaining sunflower oil. Stir-fry the lamb, in two batches, for 3–4 minutes, or until cooked through, then add to the bowl of salad.

6 Place all the dressing ingredients in a jar, screw on the lid and shake well. Pour the dressing over the warm salad, sprinkle over the mint leaves and toss well to combine. Serve immediately.

Birthday Noodles with Hoisin Lamb

This sumptuous dish gets its name from the inclusion of boiled eggs in the recipe. Eggs symbolize continuity and fertility in China, so it is considered a fitting dish for birthday celebrations.

Ingredients

350g/12oz thick egg noodles
1kg/2¼ lb lean neck fillets of lamb
30ml/2 tbsp vegetable oil
115g/4oz fine green beans, trimmed and blanched
salt and ground black pepper
2 hard-boiled eggs, halved, and 2 spring onions (scallions), finely chopped, to garnish

For the marinade

2 garlic cloves, crushed
10ml/2 tsp grated fresh root ginger
30ml/2 tbsp soy sauce
30ml/2 tbsp rice wine
1–2 dried red chillies
30ml/2 tbsp vegetable oil

For the sauce

15ml/1 tbsp cornflour (cornstarch)
30ml/2 tbsp soy sauce
30ml/2 tbsp rice wine
grated rind and juice of ½ orange
15ml/1 tbsp hoisin sauce
15ml/1 tbsp wine vinegar
5ml/1 tsp soft light brown sugar

Serves 4

1 Bring a large pan of water to the boil and cook the noodles for 2 minutes. Drain, rinse and drain again. Set aside.

2 Cut the lamb into 5cm/2in thick medallions. Mix the ingredients for the marinade in a large shallow dish. Add the lamb and leave to marinate for at least 4 hours or overnight.

3 Heat the oil in a heavy pan. Fry the lamb for 5 minutes until browned. Add just enough water to cover. Bring to the boil, skim, then simmer for 40 minutes or until the meat is tender.

4 Make the sauce. Blend the cornflour with the remaining ingredients in a bowl. Stir into the lamb and mix well. Add the noodles and beans and simmer until cooked. Add salt and pepper to taste. Divide among four large bowls, garnish with hard-boiled egg halves and spring onions and serve.

lamb & noodle salad Energy 820kcal/3418kJ; Protein 46g; Carbohydrate 76.4g, of which sugars 9.4g; Fat 36g, of which saturates 11.7g; Cholesterol 143mg; Calcium 55mg; Fibre 4.1g; Sodium 709mg.
noodles w. hoisin lamb Energy 605kcal/2545kJ; Protein 35.8g; Carbohydrate 62.8g, of which sugars 1.7g; Fat 25.3g, of which saturates 9g; Cholesterol 207mg; Calcium 48mg; Fibre 2.5g; Sodium 289mg.

Aromatic Pork with Basil

The combination of moist, juicy pork and mushrooms, crisp green mangetouts and fragrant basil in this ginger- and garlic-infused stir-fry is absolutely delicious.

Ingredients

40g/1½oz cornflour (cornstarch)
500g/1¼lb pork fillet (tenderloin), thinly sliced
15ml/1 tbsp sunflower oil
10ml/2 tsp sesame oil
15ml/1 tbsp very finely shredded fresh root ginger
3 garlic cloves, thinly sliced
200g/7oz/scant 2 cups mangetouts (snow peas), halved
300g/11oz/generous 4 cups mixed mushrooms, sliced if large
120ml/4fl oz/½ cup Chinese cooking wine
45ml/3 tbsp soy sauce
a small handful of sweet basil leaves
salt and ground black pepper
steamed jasmine rice, to serve

Serves 4

1 Place the cornflour in a strong plastic bag. Season well and add the sliced pork. Shake the bag to coat the pork in flour and then remove the pork and shake off any excess flour. Set aside.

2 Preheat the wok over a high heat and add the oils. When very hot, stir in the ginger and garlic and cook for 30 seconds. Add the pork and cook over a high heat for about 5 minutes, stirring often, until sealed.

3 Add the mangetouts and mushrooms to the wok and stir-fry for 2–3 minutes. Add the Chinese cooking wine and soy sauce, stir-fry for 2–3 minutes and remove from the heat.

4 Just before serving, stir the sweet basil leaves into the pork. Serve with steamed jasmine rice.

Cook's Tip
For the mushroom medley, try to include fresh shiitake and oyster mushrooms as well as cultivated button (white) ones.

Lemon Grass Pork

Chillies and lemon grass flavour this simple stir-fry, while peanuts add an interesting contrast in texture. Look for jars of chopped lemon grass, which are handy when the fresh vegetable isn't available.

Ingredients

675g/1½lb boneless pork loin
2 lemon grass stalks, finely chopped
4 spring onions (scallions), thinly sliced
5ml/1 tsp salt
12 black peppercorns, coarsely crushed
30ml/2 tbsp groundnut (peanut) oil
2 garlic cloves, chopped
2 fresh red chillies, seeded and chopped
5ml/1 tsp soft light brown sugar
30ml/2 tbsp fish sauce
25g/1oz/¼ cup roasted unsalted peanuts, chopped
ground black pepper
coarsely torn coriander (cilantro) leaves, to garnish
cooked rice noodles, to serve

Serves 4

1 Trim any excess fat from the pork. Cut the meat across into 5mm/¼in thick slices, then cut each slice into 5mm/¼in strips. Put the pork into a bowl with the lemon grass, spring onions, salt and crushed peppercorns; mix well. Cover with clear film (plastic wrap) and marinate in a cool place for 30 minutes.

2 Preheat a wok, add the oil and swirl it around. Add the pork mixture and stir-fry over a medium heat for about 3 minutes, until browned all over.

3 Add the garlic and red chillies and stir-fry for a further 5–8 minutes over a medium heat, until the pork is cooked through and tender.

4 Add the sugar, fish sauce and chopped peanuts and toss to mix, then season to taste with black pepper. Serve immediately on a bed of rice noodles, garnished with the coarsely torn coriander leaves.

aromatic pork Energy 298kcal/1248kJ; Protein 30.4g; Carbohydrate 14.6g, of which sugars 4.8g; Fat 9.8g, of which saturates 2.4g; Cholesterol 79mg; Calcium 41mg; Fibre 2g; Sodium 903mg.
lemon grass pork Energy 297kcal/1240kJ; Protein 37.9g; Carbohydrate 2.1g, of which sugars 1.7g; Fat 15.2g, of which saturates 3.6g; Cholesterol 106mg; Calcium 20mg; Fibre 0.6g; Sodium 119mg.

Pork Chops with Field Mushrooms

Barbecued pork chops are delicious with noodles.

Ingredients

4 pork chops
4 large field (portabello) mushrooms
45ml/3 tbsp vegetable oil
4 fresh red chillies, seeded and thinly sliced
45ml/3 tbsp fish sauce
90ml/6 tbsp fresh lime juice
4 shallots, chopped
5ml/1 tsp roasted ground rice
60ml/4 tbsp spring onions (scallions), shredded
coriander (cilantro) leaves, to garnish

For the marinade

2 garlic cloves, chopped
15ml/1 tbsp sugar
15ml/1 tbsp fish sauce
30ml/2 tbsp soy sauce
15ml/1 tbsp sesame oil
15ml/1 tbsp whisky or dry sherry
2 lemon grass stalks, finely chopped
2 spring onions (scallions), chopped

Serves 4

1 Make the marinade. Combine the garlic, sugar, sauces, oil and whisky or sherry in a large, shallow dish. Stir in the lemon grass and the chopped spring onions.

2 Add the pork chops, turning to coat them in the marinade. Cover and leave to marinate for 1–2 hours.

3 Lift the chops out of the marinade and place them on a barbecue grid over hot coals or on a grill (broiler) rack. Add the mushrooms and brush them with 15ml/1 tbsp of the oil. Cook the pork chops for 5–7 minutes on each side and the mushrooms for about 2 minutes. Brush both with the marinade while cooking.

4 Heat the remaining oil in a wok or small frying pan, then remove the pan from the heat and stir in the chillies, fish sauce, lime juice, shallots, ground rice and half the shredded spring onions. Put the pork chops and mushrooms on a large serving plate and spoon over the sauce. Garnish with the coriander leaves and remaining shredded spring onion.

Chinese Spiced Pork Chops

Finger-licking pork chops are family favourites.

Ingredients

4 large pork chops, about 200g/7oz each
15ml/1 tbsp five-spice powder
30ml/2 tbsp soy sauce
30ml/2 tbsp garlic-infused oil

Serves 4

1 Arrange the pork chops in a single layer in a baking dish. Sprinkle with the five-spice powder, then drizzle over the soy sauce and garlic-infused oil. Rub the mixture into the meat. Cover the dish and chill for 2 hours.

2 Preheat the oven to 160°C/325°F/Gas 3. Uncover the dish and bake for 30–40 minutes, or until the pork is cooked through and tender. Serve immediately.

Sweet & Sour Pork Strips

This makes a marvellous warm salad.

Ingredients

30ml/2 tbsp dark soy sauce
15ml/1 tbsp clear honey
400g/14oz pork fillet (tenderloin)
6 shallots, very thinly sliced lengthways
1 lemon grass stalk, thinly sliced
5 kaffir lime leaves, thinly sliced
5cm/2in piece fresh root ginger, peeled and finely sliced
½ red chilli, seeded and shredded
small bunch fresh coriander (cilantro), chopped

For the dressing

30ml/2 tbsp soft light brown sugar
30ml/2 tbsp fish sauce
juice of 2 limes
20ml/4 tsp thick tamarind juice, made by mixing tamarind paste with warm water

Serves 4

1 Preheat the grill (broiler). Stir the soy sauce and honey together. Cut the pork lengthways into four fat strips. Place in a grill pan, coat with the soy sauce mixture, then grill (broil) for about 10–15 minutes, turning and basting the strips frequently, until the meat is cooked through.

2 Slice the cooked pork across the grain, then shred. Place in a large bowl and add the remaining ingredients. Toss with the dressing, made by whisking all the ingredients together.

chops w. mushrooms Energy 342kcal/1423kJ; Protein 34g; Carbohydrate 1.7g, of which sugars 1.2g; Fat 22.1g, of which saturates 5.3g; Cholesterol 110mg; Calcium 21mg; Fibre 1.2g; Sodium 89mg.
sweet & sour pork Energy 194kcal/812kJ; Protein 19.4g; Carbohydrate 5.2g, of which sugars 0.5g; Fat 6.3g, of which saturates 1.6g; Cholesterol 55mg; Calcium 21mg; Fibre 0.2g; Sodium 64mg.
chinese spiced pork Energy 722kcal/2986kJ; Protein 32.6g; Carbohydrate 1.9g, of which sugars 0.6g; Fat 65g, of which saturates 22.5g; Cholesterol 144mg; Calcium 24mg; Fibre 0g; Sodium 647mg.

Stir-fried Pork with Dried Shrimp

You might expect the dried shrimp to give this dish a fishy flavour, but instead it simply imparts a delicious savoury taste.

Ingredients
250g/9oz pork fillet (tenderloin), sliced
30ml/2 tbsp vegetable oil
2 garlic cloves, finely chopped
45ml/3 tbsp dried shrimp
10ml/2 tsp dried shrimp paste
30ml/2 tbsp soy sauce
juice of 1 lime
15ml/1 tbsp light muscovado (brown) sugar
1 small fresh red or green chilli, seeded and finely chopped
4 pak choi (bok choy) or 450g/1lb spring greens (collards), shredded

Serves 4

1 Place the pork in the freezer for about 30 minutes, until firm. Using a sharp knife, cut it into thin, even slices.

2 Heat the oil in a preheated wok or large frying pan and cook the garlic until golden brown. Add the pork and stir-fry for about 4 minutes, until just cooked through.

3 Add the dried shrimp, then stir in the shrimp paste, with the soy sauce, lime juice and sugar.

4 Add the chilli and pak choi or spring greens and toss over the heat until the vegetables are just wilted.

5 Transfer the stir-fry to warmed individual bowls and serve immediately, making each portion includes some of the salty citrus sauce that will have collected in the bottom of the wok.

Cook's Tip
Shrimp paste is made from tiny crustaceans, which have been salted, dried, pounded and then left to ferment before being shaped into a solid block or packed into a tub or jar. The extremely pungent odour vanishes when the paste is cooked.

Sweet & Sour Pork

This is a modern Chinese classic. The delicate flavour of pork combines beautifully with the tangy flavour of this easy-to-make sweet and sour sauce. Serve this dish very simply, accompanied by plain boiled rice and steamed Asian greens.

Ingredients
45ml/3 tbsp light soy sauce
15ml/1 tbsp Chinese rice wine
15ml/1 tbsp sesame oil
5ml/1 tsp ground black pepper
500g/1¼lb pork loin, cut into 1cm/½in cubes
65g/2½oz/9 tbsp cornflour (cornstarch)
1 carrot
1 red (bell) pepper
4 spring onions (scallions)
65g/2½oz/9 tbsp plain (all-purpose) flour
5ml/1 tsp bicarbonate of soda (baking soda)
sunflower oil, for deep-frying
10ml/2 tsp finely grated garlic
5ml/1 tsp finely grated fresh root ginger
60ml/4 tbsp tomato ketchup
30ml/2 tbsp sugar
15ml/1 tbsp rice vinegar
15ml/1 tbsp cornflour (cornstarch) blended with 120ml/4fl oz/½ cup water

Serves 4

1 In a large mixing bowl, combine 15ml/1 tbsp of the soy sauce with the rice wine, sesame oil and pepper. Add the pork and toss to mix. Cover and chill for 3–4 hours. Meanwhile, cut the carrots, pepper and spring onions in shreds, and set aside.

2 Combine the cornflour, plain flour and bicarbonate of soda in a bowl. Add a pinch of salt and mix in 150ml/¼ pint/⅔ cup cold water to make a thick batter. Add the pork and mix well.

3 Separate the pork cubes and deep-fry them, in batches in hot oil, for 1–2 minutes, or until golden. Drain on kitchen paper.

4 Mix the garlic, ginger, tomato ketchup, sugar, the remaining soy sauce, rice vinegar and cornflour mixture in a small pan. Stir over a medium heat for 2–3 minutes, until thickened. Add the carrot, red pepper and spring onions, stir and remove from the heat.

5 Reheat the deep-frying oil and then re-fry the pork pieces in batches for 1–2 minutes, until golden and crisp. Drain and add to the sauce and toss to mix well. Serve solo or with egg-fried rice or noodles.

pork w. dried shrimp Energy 169kcal/702kJ; Protein 16.6g; Carbohydrate 5.7g, of which sugars 5.6g; Fat 8.9g, of which saturates 1.6g; Cholesterol 39mg; Calcium 198mg; Fibre 2.4g; Sodium 202mg.
sweet & sour pork Energy 727kcal/3035kJ; Protein 32.7g; Carbohydrate 76.5g, of which sugars 39.4g; Fat 32.8g, of which saturates 5.8g; Cholesterol 272mg; Calcium 85mg; Fibre 2.7g; Sodium 1048mg.

Pork Belly with Five Spices

This recipe originated in China, but travelled to Thailand when colonists from southern China settled in the country. Over the centuries, the dish has evolved and Thai cooks have provided their own unique imprint.

Ingredients

1 large bunch fresh coriander (cilantro) with roots
30ml/2 tbsp vegetable oil
1 garlic clove, crushed
30ml/2 tbsp five-spice powder
500g/1¼lb pork belly, cut into 2.5cm/1in pieces
400g/14oz can chopped tomatoes
150ml/¼ pint/⅔ cup hot water
30ml/2 tbsp dark soy sauce
45ml/3 tbsp fish sauce
30ml/2 tbsp sugar
1 lime, halved

Serves 4

1 Cut off the coriander roots. Chop five of them finely and freeze the remainder for another occasion. Chop the coriander stalks and leaves and set them aside. Keep the roots separate.

2 Heat the oil in a large pan and cook the garlic until golden brown. Stirring constantly, add the chopped coriander roots and then the five-spice powder.

3 Add the pork and stir-fry until the meat is thoroughly coated in spices and has browned. Stir in the tomatoes and hot water. Bring to the boil, then stir in the soy sauce, fish sauce and sugar.

4 Reduce the heat, cover the pan and simmer for 30 minutes. Stir in the chopped coriander stalks and leaves, squeeze over the lime juice and ladle into bowls. Serve.

Cook's Tip

Make sure that you buy Chinese five-spice powder, as the Indian variety is made up from quite different spices.

Braised Pork Belly with Greens

Pork belly becomes meltingly tender in this slow-braised dish flavoured with orange, cinnamon, star anise and ginger. The flavours meld and mellow during cooking to produce a rich, complex, rounded taste. Serve simply with rice and steamed greens.

Ingredients

800g/1¾lb pork belly, trimmed and cut into 12 pieces
400ml/14fl oz/1⅔ cups beef stock
75ml/5 tbsp soy sauce
finely grated rind and juice of 1 large orange
15ml/1 tbsp finely shredded fresh root ginger
2 garlic cloves, sliced
15ml/1 tbsp hot chilli powder
15ml/1 tbsp muscovado (molasses) sugar
3 cinnamon sticks
3 cloves
10 black peppercorns
2–3 star anise
steamed greens and rice, to serve

Serves 4

1 Place the pork in a wok and pour over water to cover. Bring the water to the boil. Cover, reduce the heat and cook gently for 30 minutes.

2 Drain the pork and return to the wok with the stock, soy sauce, orange rind and juice, ginger, garlic, chilli powder, muscovado sugar, cinnamon sticks, cloves, peppercorns and star anise.

3 Pour over water to just cover the pork belly pieces and cook on a high heat until the mixture comes to a boil.

4 Cover the wok tightly with a lid, then reduce the heat to low and cook gently for 1½ hours, stirring occasionally to prevent the pork from sticking to the base of the wok.

5 Taste the sauce and season to taste. You are unlikely to need pepper, with peppercorns a prime ingredient, but may wish to add a little salt. Serve in warmed bowls.

pork belly Energy 581kcal/2405kJ; Protein 20.6g; Carbohydrate 11.6g, of which sugars 11.5g; Fat 50.5g, of which saturates 17.1g; Cholesterol 90mg; Calcium 71mg; Fibre 2.3g; Sodium 109mg.
pork belly w. greens Energy 543kcal/2260kJ; Protein 38.9g; Carbohydrate 6.6g, of which sugars 6.4g; Fat 40.4g, of which saturates 14.6g; Cholesterol 142mg; Calcium 19mg; Fibre 0g; Sodium 1475mg.

Stir-fried Pork Ribs

Sweet-and-sour spare ribs, a Chinese classic adopted by culinary cultures the world over, has given rise to some interesting variations. This version includes basil leaves and fish sauce. This is finger food at its finest, requiring finger bowls and plenty of napkins, and is perfect served with sticky rice and a salad.

Ingredients

45ml/3 tbsp hoisin sauce
45ml/3 tbsp fish sauce
10ml/2 tsp five-spice powder
45ml/3 tbsp vegetable or sesame oil
900g/2lb pork ribs
3 garlic cloves, crushed
4cm/1½in fresh root ginger, peeled and grated
1 bunch fresh basil, stalks removed, leaves shredded

Serves 4–6

1 In a bowl, mix together the hoisin sauce, fish sauce and five-spice powder with 15ml/1 tbsp of the oil.

2 Bring a large wok or pan of water to the boil, then add the pork ribs, bring back to the boil and blanch for 10 minutes. Lift the pork ribs out with a slotted spoon and drain well, then set them aside. Discard the liquid.

3 Heat the remaining oil in a clean wok. Add the crushed garlic and grated ginger and cook, stirring, until fragrant, then add the blanched pork ribs.

4 Stir-fry for about 5 minutes, or until the pork ribs are well browned, then add the hoisin sauce mixture, turning the ribs so that each one is thoroughly coated. Continue stir-frying for 10–15 minutes, or until there is almost no liquid in the wok and the ribs are caramelized and slightly blackened.

5 Add the shredded basil leaves and stir. Serve the ribs straight from the pan or in individual warmed dishes. Offer dinner guests finger bowls containing water and slices of lemon or lime, and plenty of napkins to wipe sticky fingers.

Sticky Pork Ribs

Many people assume pork ribs to be high in fat, but these fall well within acceptable limits. Take the time to marinate the meat as this allows all the flavours to permeate.

Ingredients

30ml/2 tbsp caster (superfine) sugar
2.5ml/½ tsp five-spice powder
45ml/3 tbsp hoisin sauce
30ml/2 tbsp yellow bean sauce
3 garlic cloves, finely chopped
15ml/1 tbsp cornflour (cornstarch)
2.5ml/½ tsp salt
16 meaty pork ribs
chives and sliced spring onion (scallion), to garnish
salad or rice, to serve

Serves 4

1 Combine the caster sugar, five-spice powder, hoisin sauce, bean sauce, garlic, cornflour and salt in a bowl. Mix well.

2 Place the pork ribs in an ovenproof dish and pour the marinade over. Mix thoroughly, cover with clear film (plastic wrap) and leave in a cool place for 1 hour.

3 Preheat the oven to 180°C/350°F/Gas 4. Unwrap the ovenproof dish, replace the plastic wrap with foil and bake the pork ribs for 40 minutes. Baste the ribs from time to time with the cooking juices.

4 Remove the foil, baste the ribs and continue to cook for 20 minutes until glossy and brown. Garnish with chives and sliced spring onion and serve with a salad or rice.

Cook's Tips

- *The ribs barbecue very well. Par-cook them in the oven for 40 minutes as described in the main recipe, then transfer them to the barbecue for 15 minutes to finish cooking. The sauce coating makes the ribs liable to burn, so watch them closely.*
- *Don't forget finger bowls when serving these. They are not called sticky ribs for nothing.*

stir-fried ribs Energy 633kcal/2638kJ; Protein 42.9g; Carbohydrate 11.5g, of which sugars 11.2g; Fat 45.2g, of which saturates 14.1g; Cholesterol 149mg; Calcium 43mg; Fibre 0.5g; Sodium 250mg.
sticky pork ribs Energy 239kcal/1006kJ; Protein 32.4g; Carbohydrate 14.5g, of which sugars 10.9g; Fat 6g, of which saturates 2.1g; Cholesterol 95mg; Calcium 17mg; Fibre 0.1g; Sodium 291mg.

Cha Shao

This dish is often known as barbecue pork and is very popular in southern China. The marinade can be heated and served as a sauce.

Ingredients

900g/2lb pork fillet (tenderloin), trimmed
15ml/1 tbsp clear honey
45ml/3 tbsp rice wine
spring onion (scallion) curls, to garnish

For the marinade

150ml/¼ pint/⅔ cup dark soy sauce
90ml/6 tbsp rice wine
150ml/¼ pint/⅔ cup well-flavoured chicken stock
15ml/1 tbsp soft light brown sugar
1cm/½in piece fresh root ginger, peeled and finely sliced
40ml/2½ tbsp chopped onion

Serves 6

1 Mix all the marinade ingredients in a pan and bring to the boil, stirring. Simmer gently for 15 minutes. Leave to cool.

2 Put the pork fillets side by side in a shallow dish. Pour over 250ml/8fl oz/1 cup of the marinade, cover and chill for at least 8 hours, turning the meat over several times.

3 Preheat the oven to 200°C/400°F/Gas 6. Drain the pork fillets, reserving the marinade in the dish. Place the meat on a rack over a roasting pan and pour water into the pan to a depth of 1cm/½ in. Place the pan in the oven and roast for 20 minutes.

4 Stir the honey and rice wine or sherry into the marinade. Remove the meat from the oven and place in the marinade, turning to coat. Put back on the rack and roast for 20–30 minutes or until cooked. Serve hot or cold, in slices, garnished with spring onion curls.

Cook's Tip
You will have extra marinade when making this dish. Chill or freeze this and use to baste other grilled (broiled) dishes.

Roasted & Marinated Pork

Japanese cooks often use a soy sauce and citrus marinade to flavour meat, adding it before or after cooking. If possible, leave the meat to marinate overnight.

Ingredients

600g/1⅓lb pork fillet (tenderloin)
1 garlic clove, crushed
generous pinch of salt
4 spring onions (scallions), trimmed, white part only, shredded finely
10g/¼oz dried wakame seaweed, soaked in water for 20 minutes and drained
10cm/4in celery stick, trimmed and cut in thin shreds
1 carton mustard and cress (fine curled cress)

For the marinade

105ml/7 tbsp shoyu
45ml/3 tbsp sake
60ml/4 tbsp mirin (sweet rice wine)
1 lime, sliced into thin rings

Serves 4

1 Preheat the oven to 200°C/400°F/Gas 6. Rub the pork with crushed garlic and salt, and leave for 15 minutes. Meanwhile, mix the marinade ingredients in a container that is big enough to hold the pork. Set the marinade aside.

2 Roast the pork for 20 minutes, then turn the meat over and reduce the oven temperature to 180°C/350°F/Gas 4. Roast for a further 20 minutes, until the pork is cooked.

3 Add the hot pork to the marinade, cover and set aside for at least 2 hours.

4 Soak the shreds of spring onion and celery in iced water until curled. Drain well. Cut the drained wakame seaweed into narrow strips.

5 Lift the pork from the marinade, blot it with kitchen paper, then slice and arrange on a large platter. Surround with the vegetables and seaweed.

6 Strain the marinade into a gravy boat and serve with the pork and accompaniments.

cha shao Energy 211kcal/886kJ; Protein 32.5g; Carbohydrate 4.8g, of which sugars 4.7g; Fat 6g, of which saturates 2.1g; Cholesterol 95mg; Calcium 14mg; Fibre 0g; Sodium 996mg.
roasted/marinated pork Energy 198kcal/830kJ; Protein 32.6g; Carbohydrate 0.9g, of which sugars 0.9g; Fat 6.2g, of which saturates 2.1g; Cholesterol 95mg; Calcium 24mg; Fibre 0.4g; Sodium 114mg.

Curried Pork with Pickled Garlic

This very rich curry is best accompanied by lots of plain rice and perhaps a light vegetable dish. It could serve four with a vegetable curry on the side, and perhaps some steamed greeens, such as pak choi (bok choy) or curly kale.

Ingredients

130g/4½oz lean pork steaks
30ml/2 tbsp vegetable oil
1 garlic clove, crushed
15ml/1 tbsp red curry paste
130ml/4½fl oz/generous ½ cup coconut cream
2.5cm/1in piece fresh root ginger, finely chopped
30ml/2 tbsp vegetable or chicken stock
30ml/2 tbsp fish sauce
5ml/1 tsp sugar
2.5ml/½ tsp ground turmeric
10ml/2 tsp lemon juice
4 pickled garlic cloves, finely chopped
strips of lemon and lime rind, to garnish

Serves 2

1 Place the pork steaks in the freezer for 30–40 minutes, until firm, then, using a sharp knife, cut the meat into fine slivers, trimming off any excess fat.

2 Heat the oil in a wok or large, heavy frying pan and cook the garlic over a low to medium heat until golden brown. Do not let it burn. Add the curry paste and stir it in well.

3 Add the coconut cream and stir until the liquid begins to reduce and thicken. Stir in the pork. Cook for 2 minutes more, until the pork is cooked through.

4 Add the ginger, stock, fish sauce, sugar and turmeric, stirring constantly, then add the lemon juice and pickled garlic and heat through. Serve in warmed bowls, garnished with strips of rind.

Cook's Tip
Asian stores sell pickled garlic. It is well worth investing in, as the taste is sweet and delicious.

Pork & Butternut Curry

This curry can be made with butternut squash, pumpkin or winter melon. It is delicious served with rice and a fruit-based salad, or even just with chunks of fresh crusty bread to mop up the tasty sauce.

Ingredients

30ml/2 tbsp groundnut (peanut) oil
25g/1oz galangal, finely sliced
2 fresh red chillies, peeled, seeded and finely sliced
3 shallots, halved and finely sliced
30ml/2 tbsp kroeung or magic paste
10ml/2 tsp ground turmeric
5ml/1 tsp ground fenugreek
10ml/2 tsp palm sugar (jaggery)
450g/1lb pork loin, cut into bitesize chunks
30ml/2 tbsp fish sauce
900ml/1½ pints/3¾ cups coconut milk
1 butternut squash, peeled, seeded and cut into bitesize chunks
4 kaffir lime leaves
sea salt and ground black pepper
1 small bunch fresh coriander (cilantro), coarsely chopped and 1 small bunch fresh mint, stalks removed, to garnish
rice or noodles and salad, to serve

Serves 4–6

1 Heat the oil in a large wok or heavy pan. Stir in the galangal, chillies and shallots and stir-fry until fragrant. Add the kroeung or magic paste and stir-fry until it begins to colour. Add the turmeric, fenugreek and sugar and stir to combine.

2 Stir in the chunks of pork loin and stir-fry until golden brown on all sides. Stir in the fish sauce and pour in the coconut milk.

3 Bring to the boil, add the squash and the lime leaves, and reduce the heat. Cook gently, uncovered, for 15–20 minutes, until the squash and pork are tender and the sauce has reduced. Season to taste. Garnish the curry with the coriander and mint, and serve with rice or noodles and salad.

Cook's Tip
Increase the number of chillies if you want a really hot curry.

curried pork w. garlic Energy 227kcal/947kJ; Protein 16.3g; Carbohydrate 9.8g, of which sugars 6.1g; Fat 14g, of which saturates 2.4g; Cholesterol 41mg; Calcium 30mg; Fibre 1g; Sodium 474mg.
pork & butternut Energy 149kcal/628kJ; Protein 17g; Carbohydrate 10.6g, of which sugars 10.2g; Fat 4.6g, of which saturates 1.5g; Cholesterol 47mg; Calcium 71mg; Fibre 0.7g; Sodium 221mg.

Pork & Pineapple Curry

The heat of this curry balances out its sweetness to make a smooth and fragrant dish. It takes very little time to cook.

Ingredients

400ml/14fl oz can or carton coconut milk
10ml/2 tsp red curry paste
400g/14oz pork loin steaks, trimmed and thinly sliced
15ml/1 tbsp fish sauce
5ml/1 tsp soft light brown sugar
15ml/1 tbsp tamarind juice, made by mixing tamarind paste with warm water
2 kaffir lime leaves, torn
½ medium pineapple, peeled and chopped
1 fresh red chilli, seeded and finely chopped, to garnish

Serves 4

1 Pour the coconut milk into a bowl and let it settle, so that the cream rises to the surface. Scoop the cream into a measuring jug (cup). You should have about 250ml/8fl oz/1 cup. If necessary, add a little of the coconut milk to obtain the precise measure.

2 Pour the coconut cream into a large pan and bring it to the boil. Cook for about 10 minutes, until the cream separates, stirring frequently to prevent it from sticking to the base of the pan and scorching.

3 Add the red curry paste and stir it in until well mixed. Cook, stirring occasionally, for about 4 minutes, until the paste is fragrant.

4 Add the sliced pork and stir in the fish sauce, sugar and tamarind juice. Cook, stirring constantly, for 1–2 minutes, until the sugar has dissolved and the pork is no longer pink.

5 Add the remaining coconut milk and the lime leaves. Bring to the boil, then stir in the pineapple. Reduce the heat and simmer gently for 3 minutes, or until the pork is fully cooked. Spoon into warmed bowls and sprinkle over the chilli to act as a colourful garnish. Serve immediately.

Black Pepper Pork

Thanks to the ginger and black pepper, this dish is beautifully warming. Fairly simple preparation, and mild spicing, make it a perfect, and healthy, alternative to the family takeaway on Friday night.

Ingredients

1 litre/1¾ pints/4 cups pork stock or water
45ml/3 tbsp fish sauce
30ml/2 tbsp soy sauce
15ml/1 tbsp sugar
4 garlic cloves, crushed
40g/1½oz fresh root ginger, peeled and finely shredded
15ml/1 tbsp ground black pepper
675g/1½lb pork shoulder or rump, cut into bitesize cubes
steamed jasmine rice, crunchy salad and pickles or stir-fried greens, such as water spinach or long beans, to serve

Serves 4–6

1 In a large heavy pan, bring the stock or water, fish sauce and soy sauce to the boil.

2 Reduce the heat and stir in the sugar, garlic, ginger, black pepper and pork. Cover the pan and simmer for about 1½ hours, until the pork is very tender and the liquid has reduced significantly.

3 Serve the pork with steamed jasmine rice, drizzling the braised juices over it, and accompany it with a fresh crunchy salad, pickles or stir-fried greens, such as the stir-fried water spinach with fish sauce, or long beans.

Cook's Tip

If you have time, make this dish a day ahead so that all the flavours blend. Complete the dish to the end of Step 1, cool it quickly, cover and place in a refrigerator overnight. Next day, lift off any fat that has solidified on the surface, and reheat until piping hot. An electric wok is ideal for this.

pork & pineapple Energy 187kcal/790kJ; Protein 22.2g; Carbohydrate 15.3g, of which sugars 15.3g; Fat 4.5g, of which saturates 1.6g; Cholesterol 63mg; Calcium 55mg; Fibre 1.2g; Sodium 449mg.
black pepper pork Energy 154kcal/647kJ; Protein 24.4g; Carbohydrate 4g, of which sugars 3.7g; Fat 4.5g, of which saturates 1.6g; Cholesterol 71mg; Calcium 13mg; Fibre 0.1g; Sodium 613mg.

Cinnamon Meat Loaf

Similar to the Vietnamese steamed pâtés, this type of meat loaf is usually served as a snack or light lunch, with a crusty baguette. Accompanied with either tart pickles or a crunchy salad, and splashed with piquant sauce, it is light and very tasty.

Ingredients

30ml/2 tbsp fish sauce
25ml/1½ tbsp ground cinnamon
10ml/2 tsp sugar
5ml/1 tsp ground black pepper
15ml/1 tbsp potato starch
450g/1lb lean minced (ground) pork
25g/1oz pork fat, very finely chopped
4 shallots, very finely chopped
oil, for greasing
chilli oil or hot chilli sauce, for drizzling
red chilli strips, to garnish
bread or noodles, to serve

Serves 4–6

1 In a large bowl, mix together the fish sauce, ground cinnamon, sugar and black pepper. Beat in the potato starch.

2 Add the minced pork, the chopped pork fat, and the shallots to the bowl and mix thoroughly. Cover and put in the refrigerator for 3–4 hours.

3 Preheat the oven to 180°C/350°F/Gas 4. Lightly oil a baking tin pan and spread the pork mixture in it – it should feel springy. This is due to the potato starch.

4 Cover with foil and bake in the oven for 35–40 minutes, removing the foil for the last 10 minutes.

5 Slice the meat loaf into strips. Drizzle the strips with chilli oil or hot chilli sauce, and serve them hot with bread or noodles.

Cook's Tip
Serve the meat loaf as a nibble with drinks by cutting it into bitesize squares or fingers.

Pork & Spring Onion Pancakes

Unusually, these pancakes are made from a batter based on mung beans.

Ingredients

225g/8oz/1¼ cups skinned, split mung beans
50g/2oz/⅓ cup glutinous rice
15ml/1 tbsp light soy sauce
15ml/1 tbsp roasted sesame seeds, crushed
2.5ml/½ tsp bicarbonate of soda
115g/4oz/½ cup beansprouts, blanched and dried
1 garlic clove, crushed
4 spring onions (scallions), chopped
115g/4oz cooked lean pork, shredded
30ml/2 tbsp sesame oil, plus extra for drizzling
salt and ground black pepper
fresh chives, to garnish
light soy sauce, to serve

Serves 4–6

1 Pick over the mung beans and put them in a bowl. Add the glutinous rice and pour in water to cover. Leave to soak for at least 8 hours.

2 Tip the beans and rice into a sieve (strainer), rinse under cold water, then drain. Put the mixture into a food processor and process to a batter with the consistency of thick cream.

3 Add the soy sauce, sesame seeds and bicarbonate of soda and process briefly to mix. When ready to cook, tip the batter into a bowl and add the beansprouts, garlic, spring onions and pork. Season to taste.

4 Heat about 10ml/2 tsp of the sesame oil in a large frying pan. Spoon in half the batter and spread it into a thick pancake.

5 Drizzle a little more sesame oil over the surface of the pancake, cover and cook over a medium heat until the underside is cooked. Invert the pancake on to a plate. Slide it back into the pan and cook on the other side for 3–4 minutes. Keep hot while cooking a second pancake. Cut the pancakes into wedges, garnish with chives, and serve with soy sauce.

cinnamon meat loaf Energy 158kcal/661kJ; Protein 16.8g; Carbohydrate 7.7g, of which sugars 4.5g; Fat 6.8g, of which saturates 1.5g; Cholesterol 47mg; Calcium 19mg; Fibre 0.8g; Sodium 54mg.
pork & spring onion pancakes Energy 90kcal/376kJ; Protein 6.7g; Carbohydrate 8.9g, of which sugars 1.6g; Fat 3.1g, of which saturates 0.6g; Cholesterol 12mg; Calcium 17mg; Fibre 1g; Sodium 195mg.

Beef & Shiitake Salad

Rare steak, spicy mushrooms and crisp lettuce make a superb salad.

Ingredients

675g/1½lb beef fillet (tenderloin) or rump (round) steak
30ml/2 tbsp olive oil
2 small mild fresh red chillies, seeded and sliced
225g/8oz/3¼ cups shiitake mushrooms, sliced

For the dressing

3 spring onions (scallions), finely chopped
2 garlic cloves, finely chopped
juice of 1 lime
15–30ml/1–2 tbsp fish or oyster sauce, to taste
5ml/1 tsp soft light brown sugar
30ml/2 tbsp chopped fresh coriander (cilantro)

To serve

1 cos or romaine lettuce, torn into strips
175g/6oz cherry tomatoes, halved
5cm/2in piece cucumber, peeled, halved and thinly sliced
45ml/3 tbsp toasted sesame seeds

Serves 4

1 Preheat the grill (broiler) until hot, then cook the steak for 2–4 minutes on each side depending on how well done it is preferred. (In Thailand, the beef is traditionally served quite rare.) Leave to cool for at least 15 minutes.

2 Use a very sharp knife to slice the meat as thinly as possible and place the slices in a bowl.

3 Heat the olive oil in a small frying pan. Add the seeded and sliced red chillies and the sliced mushrooms and cook for 5 minutes, stirring occasionally. Turn off the heat and add the grilled steak slices to the pan, then stir well to coat the beef slices in the chilli and mushroom mixture.

4 Stir all the ingredients for the dressing together, then pour it over the meat mixture and toss gently.

5 Arrange the salad ingredients on a serving plate. Spoon the warm steak mixture in the centre and sprinkle the sesame seeds over. Serve immediately.

Seared Garlic Beef

Flavoured with lots of garlic, the tender chunks of beef are wrapped in lettuce leaves and dipped in a piquant lime sauce. Beef is well suited to searing, and this can be done in a pan, but can also be chargrilled if you prefer.

Ingredients

350g/12oz beef fillet (tenderloin) or sirloin, cut into bitesize chunks
15ml/1 tbsp sugar
juice of 3 limes
2 garlic cloves, crushed
7.5ml/1½ tsp ground black pepper
30ml/2 tbsp unsalted roasted peanuts, finely chopped
12 lettuce leaves

For the marinade

15ml/1 tbsp groundnut (peanut) oil
45ml/3 tbsp mushroom soy sauce
10ml/2 tsp soy sauce
15ml/1 tbsp sugar
2 garlic cloves, crushed
7.5ml/1½ tsp ground black pepper

Serves 4

1 To make the marinade, beat together the oil, the two soy sauces and the sugar in a bowl, until the sugar has dissolved. Add the garlic and pepper and mix well. Add the beef and coat in the marinade. Leave for 1–2 hours.

2 In a small bowl, stir the sugar into the lime juice, until it has dissolved. Add the garlic and black pepper and beat well. Stir in the peanuts and put aside.

3 Heat a wok or heavy pan and sear the meat on all sides. Serve immediately with lettuce leaves for wrapping and the lime sauce for dipping.

Variation
This delicious dish can also be made with quail or even ostrich. The marinade ensures that the meat remains juicy. If using poultry, ensure it is fully cooked and not simply seared.

beef & shiitake Energy 441kcal/1834kJ; Protein 42.3g; Carbohydrate 3.9g, of which sugars 3.8g; Fat 28.5g, of which saturates 8.3g; Cholesterol 98mg; Calcium 110mg; Fibre 2.6g; Sodium 119mg.
seared garlic beef Energy 237kcal/986kJ; Protein 21.9g; Carbohydrate 5.2g, of which sugars 4.7g; Fat 14.3g, of which saturates 4.3g; Cholesterol 51mg; Calcium 12mg; Fibre 0.5g; Sodium 324mg.

Sizzling Steak

If you order this in a restaurant, it will probably be brought to the table on an individual hot metal platter set on a thick wooden board. This is a simpler version, which can easily be made at home.

Ingredients

2 rump (round) or sirloin steaks, total weight about 450g/1lb
15–30ml/1–2 tbsp vegetable oil
shredded spring onion (scallion), to garnish

For the marinade and sauce

15ml/1 tbsp brandy
15ml/1 tbsp rich brown sauce
30ml/2 tbsp sunflower oil
a few drops of sesame oil
2 garlic cloves, halved or crushed
150ml/¼ pint/⅔ cup beef stock
30ml/2 tbsp tomato ketchup
15ml/1 tbsp oyster sauce
15ml/1 tbsp Worcestershire sauce
salt and sugar

Serves 2

1 Put the steaks side by side in a bowl. Mix the brandy, brown sauce, sunflower oil, sesame oil and garlic and pour this marinade over the steaks. Cover and leave for 1 hour, turning once. Drain the meat well, reserving the marinade.

2 Heat the oil in a heavy, ridged frying pan and fry the steaks for 3–5 minutes on each side, depending on how well done you like them. Transfer to a plate and keep warm.

3 Pour the marinade into the frying pan. Stir in the beef stock, ketchup, oyster sauce and Worcestershire sauce, with salt and sugar to taste. Bring to the boil, boil rapidly to reduce by half, then taste again and adjust the seasoning if necessary.

4 Serve each steak on a very hot plate, pouring the sauce over each portion just before serving. Garnish with the spring onion.

Cook's Tip
If you don't have a ridged frying pan, simply use a large, heavy based frying pan instead.

Seared Beef Rolls

Marinated in a mixture of vinegar, sake and shoyu, seared beef is a Japanese speciality.

Ingredients

500g/1¼lb chunk of beef thigh (a long, thin chunk looks better than a thick, round chunk)
generous pinch of salt
10ml/2 tsp vegetable oil
½ cucumber, cut into matchsticks
½ lemon, thinly sliced

For the marinade

200ml/7fl oz/scant 1 cup rice vinegar
70ml/4½ tbsp sake
135ml/4½fl oz/scant ⅔ cup shoyu
15ml/1 tbsp caster (superfine) sugar
1 garlic clove, thinly sliced
1 small onion, thinly sliced
sansho

Serves 4

1 Mix the marinade ingredients in a small pan and warm through until the sugar has dissolved. Remove from the heat and leave to cool.

2 Generously sprinkle the beef with the salt and rub well into the meat. Leave for 2–3 minutes, then rub the oil in evenly with your fingers. Fill a bowl with cold water.

3 Heat a griddle. When it is very hot, sear the beef, turning frequently until about 5mm/¼in of its depth is cooked. Immediately plunge the beef into the bowl of cold water for a few seconds to stop it from cooking further.

4 Drain and dry the meat with kitchen paper, and lay it in a shallow dish. Pour the marinade over, cover and place in the refrigerator for 1 day.

5 Drain the beef, reserving the marinade, and slice it thinly. Top each slice with a little onion and garlic from the marinade, and add some cucumber matchsticks. Roll up and secure with a cocktail stick (toothpick).

6 Serve the seared beef rolls with the lemon slices and the strained marinade, for dipping.

sizzling beef Energy 469kcal/1956kJ; Protein 53.1g; Carbohydrate 4.1g, of which sugars 3.8g; Fat 26.7g, of which saturates 7.4g; Cholesterol 115mg; Calcium 20mg; Fibre 0.1g; Sodium 409mg.
seared beef rolls Energy 258kcal/1079kJ; Protein 28.7g; Carbohydrate 9.8g, of which sugars 9.8g; Fat 11.7g, of which saturates 4.8g; Cholesterol 73mg; Calcium 20mg; Fibre 0.3g; Sodium 82mg.

Chargrilled Beef & Shrimp Sauce

For these kebabs, thin strips of beef are marinated, chargrilled and served with shrimp sauce – a tasty combination. A teaspoon of shrimp paste is sometimes added to the marinade, but you may find the pungency of the accompanying shrimp sauce is sufficient.

Ingredients

450g/1lb beef rump (round), or fillet (tenderloin), cut across the grain into thin strips
lettuce leaves
1 small bunch fresh coriander (cilantro), to garnish
Vietnamese shrimp sauce, for dipping

For the marinade

2 lemon grass stalks, trimmed and chopped
2 shallots, chopped
2 garlic cloves, peeled and chopped
1 fresh red chilli, seeded and chopped
10ml/2 tsp sugar
30ml/2 tbsp fish sauce
15ml/1 tbsp soy sauce
15ml/1 tbsp groundnut (peanut) oil

Serves 4

1 For the marinade, pound the lemon grass, shallots, garlic and chilli with the sugar using a mortar and pestle, until it forms a paste. Beat in the fish sauce, soy sauce and groundnut oil. Toss the beef in the marinade, cover, and marinate for 1–2 hours.

2 Soak bamboo or wooden skewers in water for 20 minutes so they don't burn over the charcoal.

3 Prepare a barbecue, or preheat a conventional grill (broiler). Drain the skewers, thread them with the beef and place them over the coals. Cook for not much more than a minute on each side.

4 Wrap the beef in the lettuce leaves, garnish with the fresh coriander and serve with the pungent Vietnamese shrimp sauce for dipping.

Chilli Beef & Butternut

Stir-fried beef and sweet, orange-fleshed squash flavoured with warm spices, oyster sauce and fresh herbs makes a robust main course when served with rice or egg noodles. The addition of chilli and fresh root ginger gives the dish a wonderful vigorous bite.

Ingredients

30ml/2 tbsp sunflower oil
2 onions, cut into thick slices
500g/1¼lb butternut squash, peeled, seeded and cut into thin strips
675g/1½lb fillet steak (beef tenderloin)
60ml/4 tbsp soy sauce
90g/3½oz/½ cup golden caster (superfine) sugar
1 fresh bird's eye chilli or a milder red chilli, seeded and chopped
15ml/1 tbsp finely shredded fresh root ginger
30ml/2 tbsp fish sauce
5ml/1 tsp ground star anise
5ml/1 tsp five-spice powder
15ml/1 tbsp oyster sauce
4 spring onions (scallions), shredded
a small handful of sweet basil leaves
a small handful of mint leaves

Serves 4

1 Heat a wok over a medium-high heat and add the oil. When hot, stir in the onions and squash. Stir-fry for 2–3 minutes, then reduce the heat, cover and cook gently for 5–6 minutes, or until the vegetables are just tender.

2 Place the beef between two sheets of clear film (plastic wrap) and beat, with a mallet or rolling pin, until thin. Using a sharp knife, cut into thin strips.

3 In a separate wok, mix the soy sauce, sugar, chilli, ginger, fish sauce, star anise, five-spice powder and oyster sauce. Cook for 3–4 minutes, stirring frequently.

4 Add the beef to the soy sauce mixture in the wok and cook over a high heat for 3–4 minutes. Remove from the heat. Add the onion and squash slices to the beef and toss well with the spring onions and herbs. Serve immediately.

beef & shrimp sauce Energy 229kcal/952kJ; Protein 25.8g; Carbohydrate 1.5g, of which sugars 1.1g; Fat 13.3g, of which saturates 4.6g; Cholesterol 65mg; Calcium 10mg; Fibre 0.2g; Sodium 340mg.
chilli beef Energy 500kcal/2093kJ; Protein 41.3g; Carbohydrate 36.9g, of which sugars 33.8g; Fat 21.7g, of which saturates 7.2g; Cholesterol 98mg; Calcium 91mg; Fibre 2.9g; Sodium 1243mg.

Beef with Black Bean Sauce

The black bean sauce gives this low-fat dish a lovely rich flavour. The beef is first simmered in stock and then stir-fried with garlic, ginger, chilli and green pepper.

Ingredients

350g/12oz rump (round) steak, trimmed and thinly sliced
15ml/1 tbsp vegetable oil
300ml/½ pint/1¼ cups beef stock
2 garlic cloves, finely chopped
5ml/1 tsp grated fresh root ginger
1 fresh red chilli, seeded and finely chopped
15ml/1 tbsp black bean sauce
1 green (bell) pepper, seeded and cut into 2.5cm/1in squares
15ml/1 tbsp dry sherry
5ml/1 tsp cornflour (cornstarch)
5ml/1 tsp caster (superfine) sugar
45ml/3 tbsp cold water
salt
rice noodles, to serve

Serves 4

1 Place the sliced steak in a bowl. Add 5ml/1 tsp of the oil and stir to coat.

2 Bring the stock to the boil in a large pan. Add the sliced steak and cook for 2 minutes, stirring constantly to prevent the slices from sticking together. Lift out the beef and set aside.

3 Heat the remaining oil in a wok. Stir-fry the garlic, ginger and chilli with the black bean sauce for a few seconds.

4 Add the pepper and a little water. Cook for about 2 minutes more, then stir in the sherry. Add the beef slices to the pan and spoon the sauce over to coat them.

5 Mix the cornflour and sugar to a paste with the water. Pour the mixture into the pan. Cook, stirring, until the sauce has thickened. Season and serve immediately, with rice noodles.

Cook's Tip

For extra colour, use half each of a green and red pepper.

Spicy Shredded Beef

The essence of this recipe is that the beef is cut into very fine strips. This is easier to achieve if the piece of beef is placed in the freezer for 30 minutes until it is very firm before being sliced with a sharp knife.

Ingredients

225g/8oz rump (round) or fillet (tenderloin) beef steak
15ml/1 tbsp each light and dark soy sauce
15ml/1 tbsp medium-dry sherry
5ml/1 tsp soft dark brown sugar or golden sugar
90ml/6 tbsp vegetable oil
1 large onion, thinly sliced
2.5cm/1in piece fresh root ginger, peeled and grated
1–2 carrots, cut into matchsticks
2–3 fresh or dried chillies, halved, seeded (optional) and chopped
salt and ground black pepper
fresh chives, to garnish

Serves 2

1 With a sharp knife, slice the beef very thinly, then cut each slice into fine strips or shreds.

2 Mix together the light and dark soy sauces with the sherry and sugar in a bowl. Add the strips of beef and stir well to ensure they are evenly coated with the marinade.

3 Heat a wok and add half the oil. When it is hot, stir-fry the onion and ginger for 3–4 minutes, then transfer to a plate. Add the carrots, stir-fry for 3–4 minutes until slightly softened, then transfer to a plate and keep warm.

4 Heat the remaining oil in the wok, then quickly add the beef, with the marinade, followed by the chillies. Cook over high heat for 2 minutes, stirring all the time.

5 Return the fried onion and ginger to the wok and stir-fry for 1 minute more. Season with salt and pepper to taste, cover and cook for 30 seconds. Spoon the meat into two warmed bowls and add strips of the carrot. Garnish with fresh chives and serve immediately.

beef w. black bean Energy 219kcal/912kJ; Protein 19.5g; Carbohydrate 8.4g, of which sugars 5.8g; Fat 12g, of which saturates 3.1g; Cholesterol 33mg; Calcium 69mg; Fibre 4.5g; Sodium 907mg.
spicy shredded beef Energy 532kcal/2207kJ; Protein 27.3g; Carbohydrate 19.3g, of which sugars 15.4g; Fat 38.1g, of which saturates 5.8g; Cholesterol 66mg; Calcium 59mg; Fibre 3.3g; Sodium 1154mg.

Beef with Tomatoes

This colourful and fresh-tasting mixture is the perfect way of serving sun-ripened tomatoes from the garden or farmers' market.

Ingredients

350g/12oz lean rump (round) steak, trimmed of fat
15ml/1 tbsp vegetable oil
300ml/½ pint/1¼ cups beef stock
1 garlic clove, finely chopped
1 small onion, sliced into rings
5 tomatoes, quartered
15ml/1 tbsp tomato purée (paste)
5ml/1 tsp caster (superfine) sugar
15ml/1 tbsp dry sherry
salt and ground white pepper
noodles, to serve

Serves 4

1 Slice the rump steak thinly. Place the steak slices in a bowl, add 5ml/1 tsp of the vegetable oil and stir to coat.

2 Bring the stock to the boil in a large pan. Add the beef and cook for 2 minutes, stirring constantly. Lift out the beef and set it aside on a plate.

3 Heat the remaining oil in a non-stick frying pan or wok until very hot. Stir-fry the garlic and onion for a few seconds.

4 Add the beef to the pan or wok, then tip in the tomatoes. Stir-fry for 1 minute more over high heat.

5 Mix the tomato purée, sugar, sherry and 15ml/1 tbsp cold water in a cup or small bowl. Stir into the beef and tomato mixture in the pan or wok, add salt and pepper to taste and mix thoroughly. Cook for 1 minute until the sauce is hot. Serve in heated bowls, with noodles.

Variation
Add 5–10ml/1–2 tsp soy sauce to the tomato purée (paste). You will not need to add any extra salt.

Stir-fried Beef & Mushrooms

Garlic and salted black beans is a classic Cantonese seasoning for beef.

Ingredients

30ml/2 tbsp soy sauce
30ml/2 tbsp Chinese rice wine
10ml/2 tsp cornflour (cornstarch)
10ml/2 tsp sesame oil
450g/1lb beef fillet (tenderloin), trimmed of fat
12 dried shiitake mushrooms
25ml/1½ tbsp salted black beans
5ml/1 tsp sugar
45ml/3 tbsp groundnut (peanut) oil
4 garlic cloves, thinly sliced
2.5cm/1in piece fresh root ginger, cut into fine strips
200g/7oz open cap mushrooms, sliced
1 bunch spring onions (scallions), sliced diagonally
1 fresh red chilli, seeded and finely shredded
salt and ground black pepper

Serves 4

1 In a large bowl, mix half the soy sauce, half the rice wine, half the cornflour and all the sesame oil with 15ml/1 tbsp cold water until smooth. Add a good pinch of salt and pepper. Slice the beef very thinly and add to the cornflour mixture. Rub the mixture into the beef. Set aside for 30 minutes.

2 Pour boiling water over the dried mushrooms and soak for 25 minutes. Drain, reserving 45ml/3 tbsp of the soaking water. Remove and discard the hard stalks and cut the caps in half. Mash the black beans with the sugar in a small bowl. Stir the remaining cornflour, soy sauce and rice wine together in another bowl.

3 Heat the oil in a wok and stir-fry the beef for 30–45 seconds, until just brown. Transfer it to a plate, then stir-fry the garlic, ginger, dried and fresh mushrooms for 2 minutes. Add half the spring onions with the mashed black beans and stir-fry for another 1–2 minutes.

4 Stir the beef back into the mixture in the wok, then add the reserved shiitake soaking water. Add the cornflour mixture and simmer, stirring until the sauce thickens. Sprinkle the chilli and reserved spring onions over the beef and serve.

beef w. tomatoes Energy 172kcal/723kJ; Protein 20.5g; Carbohydrate 6.7g, of which sugars 6.4g; Fat 6.8g, of which saturates 1.9g; Cholesterol 52mg; Calcium 18mg; Fibre 1.6g; Sodium 74mg.
beef & mushrooms Energy 208kcal/873kJ; Protein 25.9g; Carbohydrate 4.7g, of which sugars 1.5g; Fat 8.8g, of which saturates 3.5g; Cholesterol 69mg; Calcium 20mg; Fibre 1.1g; Sodium 590mg.

Sichuan Beef with Tofu

China's western province is famous for its spicy cuisine, full of strong flavours. Sichuan peppercorns, which feature in this meat dish are not, in fact, peppercorns, but the dried berries of a type of ash tree. But, they do have a very peppery flavour.

Ingredients

200g/7oz/1 cup fragrant jasmine or basmati rice
30ml/2 tbsp groundnut (peanut) or soya oil
4 garlic cloves, finely chopped
600g/1lb 6oz beef rump (round) steak or fillet (tenderloin), cut into thin strips
500g/1¼lb firm tofu, drained and diced
1 head broccoli, coarsely chopped
90ml/6 tbsp soy sauce
pinch of sugar
juice of 1 lime
ground Sichuan peppercorns
sweet chilli sauce or another dipping sauce, to serve

Serves 4

1 Cook the rice in a large pan of salted boiling water until tender, following the instructions on the packet, then put it into a bowl and keep it hot.

2 Heat the oil in a large non-stick wok or frying pan, then add the garlic and stir-fry for a few seconds, until golden. Increase the heat to high, add the strips of steak and stir-fry for 1–2 minutes to seal.

3 Add the tofu cubes and broccoli and stir-fry for a few seconds. Stir in the soy sauce, sugar, lime juice and ground Sichuan peppercorns, then stir-fry for about 2 minutes. Transfer to warm serving plates or bowls and serve immediately with the rice and chilli sauce or other sauce.

Cook's Tip
Tofu, also known as bean curd, is a form of vegetable protein based on soya beans. There are two basic types: soft or silken tofu, which has a very light texture, and firm tofu, which is the type used in the recipe above.

Stir-fried Beef with Sesame Sauce

Similar to stir-fried beef with saté, the spicy peanut sauce, this recipe has a deliciously rich, spicy and nutty flavour.

Ingredients

450g/1lb beef sirloin or fillet (tenderloin), cut into thin strips
15ml/1 tbsp groundnut (peanut) or sesame oil
2 garlic cloves, finely chopped
2 fresh red chillies, seeded and finely chopped
7.5ml/1½ tsp sugar
30ml/2 tbsp sesame paste
30–45ml/2–3 tbsp beef stock or water
sea salt and ground black pepper
red chilli strips, to garnish
1 lemon, cut into quarters, to serve

For the marinade

15ml/1 tbsp groundnut (peanut) oil
30ml/2 tbsp fish sauce
30ml/2 tbsp soy sauce

Serves 4

1 In a bowl, mix together the ingredients for the marinade. Toss in the beef, making sure it is well coated. Leave to marinate for 30 minutes.

2 Heat the groundnut or sesame oil in a wok. Add the garlic and chillies and cook until golden and fragrant. Stir in the sugar. Add the beef, tossing it around the wok to sear it.

3 Stir in the sesame paste and enough stock or water to thin it down. Cook for 1–2 minutes, making sure the beef is coated with the sauce.

4 Season the sauce with salt and pepper. Spoon into warmed bowls, garnish with chilli strips and serve with lemon wedges.

Variations
Chicken breast fillet or pork fillet can be used instead of beef, but extend the cooking time to ensure that the poultry or pork is fully coated. Serve chicken or pork with orange wedges instead of lemon.

sichuan beef Energy 646kcal/2694kJ; Protein 55g; Carbohydrate 46.9g, of which sugars 4.1g; Fat 26.2g, of which saturates 7.6g; Cholesterol 87mg; Calcium 731mg; Fibre 3.8g; Sodium 1714mg.
beef w. sesame sauce Energy 269kcal/1119kJ; Protein 26.2g; Carbohydrate 0g, of which sugars 0g; Fat 18.2g, of which saturates 5.2g; Cholesterol 65mg; Calcium 31mg; Fibre 0.3g; Sodium 73mg.

Stir-fried Beef with Oyster Sauce

Another simple but very tasty recipe. It is often made with just straw mushrooms, when these are available fresh, but oyster mushrooms make a good substitute and using a mixture makes the dish extra interesting.

Ingredients
450g/1lb rump (round) steak
30ml/2 tbsp soy sauce
15ml/1 tbsp cornflour (cornstarch)
45ml/3 tbsp vegetable oil
15ml/1 tbsp chopped garlic
15ml/1 tbsp chopped fresh root ginger
225g/8oz/3¼ cups mixed mushrooms such as shiitake, oyster and straw
30ml/2 tbsp oyster sauce
5ml/1 tsp sugar
4 spring onions (scallions), cut into short lengths
ground black pepper
2 fresh red chillies, seeded and cut into strips, to garnish

Serves 4–6

1 Place the steak in the freezer for 30–40 minutes, until firm, then slice it on the diagonal into long thin strips. Mix together the soy sauce and cornflour in a large bowl. Add the steak, turning to coat well, cover with clear film (plastic wrap) and marinate at room temperature for 1–2 hours.

2 Heat half the oil in a wok. Add the garlic and ginger and cook for 1–2 minutes, until fragrant. Drain the steak, add it to the wok and stir-fry for a further 1–2 minutes, until the steak is tender. Remove from the wok and set aside.

3 Heat the remaining oil in the wok and stir-fry the mushrooms until golden brown. Return the steak to the wok and mix it with the mushrooms.

4 Spoon the oyster sauce and sugar into the wok, mix well, then add ground black pepper to taste. Toss over the heat until all the ingredients are thoroughly combined, then stir in the spring onions.

5 Tip the mixture on to a heated serving platter, garnish with the strips of red chilli and serve.

Simmered Beef Slices & Vegetables

This one-pot dish is a family favourite in Japan. It is a good example of how a small amount of meat can be stretched with vegetables to make a tasty and nutritious low-fat meal.

Ingredients
250g/9oz lean fillet (beef tenderloin) or rump (round) steak, trimmed of fat and very thinly sliced
1 large onion
15ml/1 tbsp vegetable oil
450g/1lb small potatoes, halved then soaked in water
1 carrot, cut into 5mm/¼in rounds
45ml/3 tbsp frozen peas, thawed and blanched for 1 minute

For the seasonings
30ml/2 tbsp caster (superfine) sugar
75ml/5 tbsp shoyu
15ml/1 tbsp mirin (sweet rice wine)
15ml/1 tbsp sake or dry sherry

Serves 4

1 Cut the thinly sliced beef slices into 2cm/¾in wide strips, and slice the onion lengthways into 5mm/¼n pieces.

2 Heat the vegetable oil in a pan and lightly fry the beef and onion slices. When the colour of the meat changes, drain the potatoes and add to the pan.

3 Once the potatoes are coated with the oil in the pan, add the carrot. Pour in just enough water to cover, then bring to the boil, skimming a few times.

4 Boil vigorously for 2 minutes, then rearrange the ingredients so that the potatoes are underneath the beef and vegetables.

5 Reduce the heat to medium-low and add all the seasonings. Simmer for 20 minutes, partially covered, or until most of the liquid has evaporated.

6 Check if the potatoes are cooked. Add the peas and cook to heat through, then remove the pan from the heat. Serve the beef and vegetables immediately in four small serving bowls.

beef w. oyster sauce Energy 205kcal/852kJ; Protein 18.4g; Carbohydrate 3.5g, of which sugars 1g; Fat 13.1g, of which saturates 3.7g; Cholesterol 45mg; Calcium 10mg; Fibre 0.5g; Sodium 53mg.
beef slices & veg. Energy 276kcal/1160kJ; Protein 17.8g; Carbohydrate 31.5g, of which sugars 13.2g; Fat 9.2g, of which saturates 2.9g; Cholesterol 36mg; Calcium 28mg; Fibre 2.3g; Sodium 1394mg.

Braised Beef in Peanut Sauce

This slow-cooked stew was originally Spanish. It retains much of its original charm, but has acquired a uniquely oriental flavour. Rice and peanuts are used to thicken the juices, yielding a rich, glossy sauce.

Ingredients

900g/2lb braising steak
30ml/2 tbsp vegetable oil
15ml/1 tbsp annatto seeds
2 medium onions, chopped
2 garlic cloves, crushed
275g/10oz celeriac or swede, roughly chopped
475ml/16fl oz/2 cups beef stock
375g/12oz new potatoes, peeled and cut into large dice
15ml/1 tbsp fish sauce
30ml/2 tbsp tamarind sauce
10ml/2 tsp sugar
1 bay leaf
1 fresh thyme sprig
45ml/3 tbsp long-grain rice
30ml/2 tbsp peanut butter
15ml/1 tbsp white wine vinegar
salt and ground black pepper

Serves 4–6

1 Cut the beef into 2.5cm/1in cubes and set aside. Heat the oil in a flameproof casserole, add the annatto seeds and stir until the oil is dark red in colour. Remove the seeds with a slotted spoon and discard.

2 Add the onions, garlic and celeriac or swede to the casserole and fry for 3–5 minutes, until softened but not coloured. Add the beef and fry until lightly and evenly browned. Add the stock, potatoes, fish sauce, tamarind sauce, sugar, bay leaf and thyme. Bring to a simmer, cover and cook for 2 hours.

3 Meanwhile, soak the rice in cold water for 30 minutes. Drain the rice and grind with the peanut butter in a mortar with a pestle or in a food processor.

4 When the beef is tender, add 60ml/4 tbsp of the cooking liquid to the rice and nut mixture. Blend until smooth, then stir into the casserole. Simmer gently, uncovered, for about 15–20 minutes, until thickened. Stir in the wine vinegar, and spoon into warmed bowls. Serve.

Beef Stew with Star Anise

This stew is prized as a breakfast dish, and on chilly mornings people often queue up for a bowl of it on their way to work. Traditionally, it has an orange hue from the oil in which annatto seeds have been fried, but here the colour comes from turmeric.

Ingredients

500g/1¼lb lean beef, cut into bitesize cubes
15ml/1 tbsp ground turmeric
30ml/2 tbsp sesame or vegetable oil
3 shallots, chopped
3 garlic cloves, chopped
2 fresh red chillies, seeded and chopped
2 lemon grass stalks, cut into several pieces and bruised
15ml/1 tbsp curry powder
4 star anise, roasted and ground to a powder
700ml/scant 1¼ pints hot beef or chicken stock, or boiling water
45ml/3 tbsp fish sauce
30ml/2 tbsp soy sauce
15ml/1 tbsp raw cane sugar
1 bunch fresh basil, stalks removed
salt and ground black pepper
1 onion, halved and finely sliced, and chopped fresh coriander (cilantro) leaves, to garnish
steamed fragrant rice, or chunks of baguette, to serve

Serves 4–6

1 Toss the beef in the ground turmeric and set aside. Heat a wok or heavy pan and add the oil. Stir in the shallots, garlic, chillies and lemon grass, and cook until they become fragrant.

2 Add the curry powder, all but 10ml/2 tsp of the roasted star anise, and the beef. Brown the beef, then pour in the stock or water, fish sauce, soy sauce and sugar. Stir and bring to the boil. Reduce the heat and cook gently for about 40 minutes, or until the meat is tender and the liquid has reduced.

3 Season to taste with salt and pepper, stir in the reserved roasted star anise, and add the basil. Transfer the stew to a serving dish and garnish with the sliced onion and coriander. Serve with steamed rice, or chunks of baguette.

beef in peanut sauce Energy 365kcal/1529kJ; Protein 30.8g; Carbohydrate 17.5g, of which sugars 16.4g; Fat 19.6g, of which saturates 6.2g; Cholesterol 65mg; Calcium 64mg; Fibre 1.2g; Sodium 238mg.
beef stew w. star anise Energy 147kcal/615kJ; Protein 18.2g; Carbohydrate 2.7g, of which sugars 1.6g; Fat 7.1g, of which saturates 2.9g; Cholesterol 44mg; Calcium 10mg; Fibre 0.5g; Sodium 405mg.

Spicy Meat Balls

Serve these spicy little beef and chilli patties with egg noodles and chilli sambal.

Ingredients

1cm/½in cube shrimp paste
1 large onion, roughly chopped
1–2 fresh red chillies, seeded and chopped
2 garlic cloves, crushed
15ml/1 tbsp coriander seeds
5ml/1 tsp cumin seeds
450g/1lb lean minced (ground) beef
10ml/2 tsp dark soy sauce
5ml/1 tsp soft dark brown sugar
juice of 1½ lemons
a little beaten egg
vegetable oil, for shallow frying
salt and ground black pepper
1 green and 2 fresh red chillies, to garnish
chilli sambal, to serve

Serves 4–6

1 Wrap the shrimp paste in a piece of foil and warm in a frying pan for 5 minutes, turning a few times. Unwrap and put in a food processor.

2 Add the onion, chillies and garlic to the food processor and process until finely chopped. Set aside. Dry-fry the coriander and cumin seeds in a hot frying pan for 1 minute, to release the aroma. Tip the seeds into a mortar and grind with a pestle.

3 Put the meat in a large bowl. Stir in the onion mixture, ground spices, soy sauce, brown sugar, lemon juice and beaten egg. Season to taste.

4 Heat the oil in a wok or large frying pan and fry the meat balls for 4–5 minutes, turning often, until cooked through and browned. You may have to do this in batches.

5 Drain the meat balls on kitchen paper, and then pile them on to a warm serving platter or into a large serving bowl. Finely slice the green chilli and one of the red chillies and sprinkle over the meat balls. Garnish with the remaining red chilli, if you like. Serve with the chilli sambal.

Beef with Charred Aubergines

To obtain the unique, smoky flavour that is integral to this dish, aubergines are charred over a flame, or charcoal grill, then skinned, chopped to a pulp and added to a minced meat mixture. Although popular in parts of South-east Asia, the method is more associated with the cooking of India, the Middle East, and North Africa.

Ingredients

2 aubergines (eggplant)
15ml/1 tbsp vegetable or groundnut (peanut) oil
2 shallots, finely chopped
4 garlic cloves, peeled and finely chopped
1 fresh red chilli, finely chopped
350g/12oz minced (ground) beef
30ml/2 tbsp fish sauce
sea salt and ground black pepper
crusty bread or rice and salad, to serve

Serves 4

1 Place the aubergines directly over an open flame. Turn them over from time to time, until the skin is charred all over. Put the aubergines into a plastic bag to sweat for a few minutes.

2 Hold each aubergine by its stalk under running cold water, while you peel off the skin. Squeeze out the excess water and chop the aubergines roughly on a board.

3 Heat the oil in a large, heavy pan. Stir in the shallots, garlic and chilli and fry until golden. Add the minced beef and stir-fry for about 5 minutes.

4 Stir in the fish sauce and the aubergine and cook gently, stirring frequently, for about 20 minutes, until the meat is tender. Season with salt and pepper and serve with crusty bread or rice and a salad.

Variation
This dish can also be made with beef or pork – either way it is delicious served with chunks of fresh, crusty bread.

spicy meat balls Energy 213kcal/881kJ; Protein 13.2g; Carbohydrate 3.4g, of which sugars 2.6g; Fat 16.3g, of which saturates 5.1g; Cholesterol 41mg; Calcium 23mg; Fibre 0.5g; Sodium 180mg.
beef w. aubergines Energy 251kcal/1050kJ; Protein 27.2g; Carbohydrate 7.2g, of which sugars 6.2g; Fat 12.8g, of which saturates 2.9g; Cholesterol 75mg; Calcium 29mg; Fibre 3g; Sodium 87mg.

Citrus Beef Curry

This superbly aromatic curry is not too hot but nonetheless full of flavour. For a special meal, it goes perfectly with fried noodles.

Ingredients

450g/1lb rump (round) steak
30ml/2 tbsp sunflower oil
30ml/2 tbsp medium curry paste
2 bay leaves
400ml/14fl oz/1⅔ cups coconut milk
300ml/½ pint/1¼ cups beef stock
30ml/2 tbsp lemon juice
45ml/3 tbsp fish sauce
15ml/1 tbsp sugar
115g/4oz baby (pearl) onions, peeled but left whole
225g/8oz new potatoes, halved
115g/4oz/1 cup unsalted roasted peanuts, roughly chopped
115g/4oz fine green beans, halved
1 red (bell) pepper, seeded and thinly sliced
unsalted roasted peanuts, to garnish

Serves 4

1 Trim any fat off the beef and use a sharp knife to cut it into 5cm/2in strips.

2 Heat the oil in a large, heavy pan, add the curry paste and cook over a medium heat for 30 seconds, stirring constantly.

3 Add the beef and cook, stirring, for 2 minutes until it is beginning to brown and is thoroughly coated with the spices.

4 Stir in the bay leaves, coconut milk, stock, lemon juice, fish sauce and sugar, and bring to the boil, stirring.

5 Add the onions and potatoes, then bring back to the boil, reduce the heat and simmer, uncovered, for 5 minutes.

6 Stir in the peanuts, beans and pepper and simmer for a further 10 minutes, or until the beef and potatoes are tender. Serve in warmed shallow bowls, with a spoon and fork, to enjoy all the rich and creamy juices. Sprinkle with extra unsalted roasted peanuts, to garnish.

Beef Rendang

Marinating beef cubes in an aromatic spice paste gives this dish a great flavour.

Ingredients

1kg/2¼lb beef topside (pot roast) or rump (round) steak, cubed
115g/4oz fresh coconut, grated, or desiccated (dry unsweetened)
15ml/1 tbsp tamarind pulp, soaked in 90ml/6 tbsp water until soft
45ml/3 tbsp vegetable or groundnut (peanut) oil
2 onions, halved and sliced
3 lemon grass stalks, trimmed, halved and bruised
2 cinnamon sticks
1.2 litres/2 pints/5 cups coconut milk
15ml/1 tbsp sugar
salt and ground black pepper
bread and salad, to serve

For the spice paste

8–10 dried red chillies, soaked in warm water until soft, seeded and squeezed dry
8 shallots, chopped
4–6 garlic cloves, chopped
50g/2oz fresh galangal, chopped
25g/1oz fresh turmeric, chopped
15ml/1 tbsp coriander seeds
10ml/2 tsp cumin seeds
5ml/1 tsp black peppercorns

Serves 6

1 For the spice paste, grind the soaked chillies, shallots, garlic, galangal and turmeric until smooth. In a small pan, dry-roast the seeds with the peppercorns, then grind to a powder and stir into the spice paste. Use to coat the beef. Marinate for 1 hour.

2 Next, dry-roast the grated coconut in a heavy pan. Tip into a food processor, grind until it resembles brown sugar and set aside. Squeeze the tamarind, then strain it to extract the juice.

3 Heat the oil in a wok and fry the onions, lemon grass and cinnamon sticks for 3–4 minutes. Add the beef with all the spice paste and stir-fry until lightly browned. Pour in the coconut milk and tamarind juice. Bring to the boil, stirring, then simmer until the sauce begins to thicken.

4 Stir in the sugar and the ground coconut, and simmer, stirring occasionally, until the meat is tender (this may take 2–4 hours, depending on the cut). Season and serve with bread and salad.

citrus beef curry Energy 476kcal/1990kJ; Protein 33.8g; Carbohydrate 27.5g, of which sugars 16.3g; Fat 26.4g, of which saturates 6.6g; Cholesterol 69mg; Calcium 77mg; Fibre 4.1g; Sodium 169mg.
beef rendang Energy 289kcal/1210kJ; Protein 30.2g; Carbohydrate 15.4g, of which sugars 8.6g; Fat 12.2g, of which saturates 5g; Cholesterol 73mg; Calcium 63mg; Fibre 1.4g; Sodium 465mg.

Beef Curry in Sweet Peanut Sauce

This curry is deliciously rich and thick. It is usually served with rice, but would also make a good filling for pitta breads.

Ingredients

600ml/1 pint/2½ cups coconut milk
45ml/3 tbsp red curry paste
45ml/3 tbsp fish sauce
30ml/2 tbsp light muscovado (brown) sugar
2 lemon grass stalks, bruised
450g/1lb rump (round) steak, cut into thin strips
75g/3oz/¾ cup roasted peanuts, ground
2 fresh red chillies, sliced
5 kaffir lime leaves, torn
salt and ground black pepper
2 salted eggs, cut in wedges, and 10–15 Thai basil leaves, to garnish (optional)

Serves 4–6

1 Pour half the coconut milk into a large, heavy pan. Place over a medium heat and bring to the boil, stirring constantly until the milk separates.

2 Stir in the red curry paste and cook for 2–3 minutes until the mixture is fragrant and thoroughly blended. Add the fish sauce, sugar and bruised lemon grass stalks. Mix well.

3 Continue to cook until the colour deepens. Gradually add the remaining coconut milk, stirring constantly. Bring back to the boil, stirring constantly.

4 Add the beef and peanuts. Cook, stirring constantly, for 8–10 minutes, or until most of the liquid has evaporated. Add the chillies and lime leaves. Season to taste and serve, garnished with wedges of salted eggs and Thai basil leaves.

Cook's Tip
If you don't have the time to make your own red curry paste, you can buy a ready-made Thai curry paste. There is a wide range available in most Asian stores and large supermarkets.

Dry Beef & Peanut Butter Curry

Although this is called a dry curry, the method of cooking keeps the beef succulent.

Ingredients

400g/14oz can coconut milk
900g/2lb stewing beef, finely chopped
300ml/½ pint/1¼ cups beef stock
30–40ml/2–3 tbsp red curry paste
30ml/2 tbsp crunchy peanut butter
juice of 2 limes
lime slices, shredded coriander (cilantro) and fresh red chilli slices, to garnish

Serves 4–6

1 Strain the coconut milk into a bowl, retaining the thicker coconut milk in the strainer or sieve.

2 Pour the thin coconut milk from the bowl into a large, heavy pan, then scrape in half the residue from the sieve. Reserve the remaining thick coconut milk. Add the chopped beef. Pour in the beef stock and bring to the boil. Reduce the heat, cover the pan and simmer gently for 50 minutes.

3 Strain the beef, reserving the cooking liquid, and place a cupful of liquid in a wok. Stir in 30–45ml/2–3 tbsp of the curry paste, according to taste. Boil rapidly until all the liquid has evaporated. Stir in the reserved thick coconut milk, the peanut butter and the beef. Simmer, uncovered, for 15–20 minutes, adding a little more cooking liquid if the mixture starts to stick to the pan, but keep the curry dry.

4 Just before serving, stir in the lime juice. Serve in warmed bowls, garnished with the lime slices, shredded coriander and sliced red chillies.

Variation
The curry is equally delicious made with lean leg or shoulder of lamb, or with pork fillet (tenderloin).

beef curry/peanut sauce Energy 227kcal/953kJ; Protein 21g; Carbohydrate 14.3g, of which sugars 11.5g; Fat 9.9g, of which saturates 2.6g; Cholesterol 44mg; Calcium 92mg; Fibre 2.5g; Sodium 723mg.
beef & peanut butter Energy 296kcal/1238kJ; Protein 35.2g; Carbohydrate 4.9g, of which sugars 4.5g; Fat 15.2g, of which saturates 4.8g; Cholesterol 103mg; Calcium 66mg; Fibre 0.7g; Sodium 262mg.

Green Beef Curry

Use good-quality meat for this quick-cook curry. Sirloin steak is recommended, but tender rump steak could be used instead. If you buy the curry paste, there's very little additional preparation.

Ingredients

450g/1lb sirloin steak
15ml/1 tbsp vegetable oil
45ml/3 tbsp green curry paste
600ml/1 pint/2½ cups coconut milk
4 kaffir lime leaves, torn
15–30ml/1–2 tbsp fish sauce
5ml/1 tsp palm sugar (jaggery) or light muscovado (brown) sugar
150g/5oz small Thai aubergines (eggplants), halved
small handful of fresh Thai basil leaves
2 fresh green chillies, finely shredded, to garnish

Serves 4–6

1 Trim off any excess fat from the beef. Using a sharp knife, cut it into long, thin strips. Set the beef strips aside on a plate.

2 Heat the oil in a wok. Add the curry paste and cook for 1–2 minutes, until it you can smell the fragrances.

3 Stir in half the coconut milk, a little at a time. Cook, stirring frequently, for about 5–6 minutes, until an oily sheen appears on the surface of the liquid.

4 Add the beef to the pan with the kaffir lime leaves, fish sauce, sugar and aubergine halves. Cook for 2–3 minutes, then stir in the remaining coconut milk.

5 Bring back to a simmer and cook until the meat and aubergines are tender. Stir in the Thai basil just before serving. Garnish with the shredded green chillies.

Cook's Tip
It's easiest to slice the beef if if you place it in the freezer for about 20 minutes to firm up first.

Oxtail in Hot Tangy Sauce

Considered a delicacy in some parts of South-east Asia, oxtail and the tails of water buffalo are generally cooked for special feasts. In Malaysia and Singapore, oxtail is cooked in European-style stews by the Eurasians and Hainanese but the Malays and Indonesians prefer to cook it slowly in a hot, tangy sauce.

Ingredients

8 shallots, chopped
8 garlic cloves, chopped
4–6 fresh red chillies, seeded and chopped
25g/1oz fresh galangal, chopped
30ml/2 tbsp rice flour or plain (all-purpose) flour
15ml/1 tbsp ground turmeric
8–12 oxtail joints, cut roughly the same size and trimmed of fat
45ml/3 tbsp vegetable oil
400g/14oz can plum tomatoes, drained
2 lemon grass stalks, halved and bruised
a handful of fresh kaffir lime leaves
225g/8oz tamarind pulp, soaked in 600ml/1 pint/2½ cups water, squeezed and strained
30–45ml/2–3 tbsp sugar
salt and ground black pepper
fresh coriander (cilantro) leaves, roughly chopped

Serves 4–6

1 Using a mortar and pestle or food processor, grind the shallots, garlic, chillies and galangal to a coarse paste. Mix the flour with the ground turmeric and spread it on a flat surface. Roll the oxtail in the flour and set aside.

2 Heat the oil in a heavy pan or earthenware pot. Stir in the spice paste and cook until fragrant and golden. Add the oxtail joints and brown on all sides. Add the tomatoes, lemon grass stalks, lime leaves and tamarind juice. Add enough water to cover the oxtail, and bring it to the boil. Skim off any fat from the surface. Reduce the heat, put the lid on the pan and simmer the oxtail for 2 hours.

3 Stir in the sugar, season and continue to cook, uncovered, for a further 30–40 minutes, until the meat is very tender. Sprinkle with the coriander and serve straight from the pan.

green beef curry Energy 176kcal/738kJ; Protein 17.6g; Carbohydrate 6.2g, of which sugars 6.1g; Fat 9.2g, of which saturates 3.3g; Cholesterol 44mg; Calcium 36mg; Fibre 0.5g; Sodium 159mg.
oxtail in sauce Energy 386kcal/1611kJ; Protein 34.5g; Carbohydrate 11.3g, of which sugars 6.6g; Fat 22.6g, of which saturates 7.7g; Cholesterol 125mg; Calcium 31mg; Fibre 1.2g; Sodium 191mg.

Steamed Rice

Rice is such a staple food in China, that "have you had rice?" is a synonym for "have you eaten?" Stick to the amounts given in this recipe for fail-safe results.

Ingredients

225g/8oz/generous 1 cup long grain rice, rinsed and drained
a pinch of salt

Serves 4

1 Put the rice into a heavy pan or clay pot. Add 600ml/1 pint/2½ cups water to cover the rice by 2.5cm/1in. Add the salt, and then bring the water to the boil. Reduce the heat, cover the pan and cook gently for about 20 minutes, or until all the water has been absorbed.

2 Remove the pan from the heat and leave to steam, covered, for a further 5–10 minutes. Fluff up with a fork, and serve.

Fragrant Coconut Rice

Originally from India and Thailand, coconut rice is popular throughout Asia. Rich and nourishing, it is often served with a tangy fruit and vegetable salad, and complements some of the spicier curries from the continent. The pandanus provides the fragrance.

Ingredients

1 litre/1¾ pints/4 cups coconut milk
450g/1lb/2¼ cups short grain rice, washed and drained
1 pandanus (screwpine) leaf, tied in a loose knot
salt

Serves 4

1 Heat the coconut milk in a heavy pan and stir in the rice with a little salt. Add the pandanus leaf and bring the liquid to the boil. Simmer until the liquid has been absorbed.

2 Turn off the heat and cover with a clean dish towel and the lid. Steam for a further 15–20 minutes. Fluff it up and serve.

Steamed Sticky Rice

Sticky rice requires a long soak in water before being cooked in a bamboo steamer. It is used for savoury and sweet dishes, especially rice cakes, and is available in Chinese and Asian stores, as well as some supermarkets.

Ingredients

350g/12oz/1¾ cups sticky rice

Serves 4

1 Put the rice into a large bowl and fill the bowl with cold water. Leave the rice to soak for at least 6 hours, then drain, rinse thoroughly, and drain again.

2 Fill a wok or heavy pan one-third full with water. Place a bamboo steamer, with the lid on, over the wok or pan and bring the water to the boil.

3 Uncover the steamer and place a dampened piece of muslin (cheesecloth) over the rack. Tip the rice into the middle and spread it out. Fold the muslin over the rice, cover and steam for 25 minutes until the rice is tender but firm. The measured quantity of rice grains doubles when cooked.

Cook's Tip

The measured quantity of rice grains doubles when cooked, which is a useful point to remember when planning to cook sticky rice for a meal. The grains clump together when cooked, making this type of rice ideal for moulding. It is fairly bulky, so is often served with a dipping sauce.

Variation

Sticky rice can be enjoyed as a sweet, filling snack with sugar and coconut milk.

steamed rice Energy 202kcal/845kJ; Protein 4.2g; Carbohydrate 44.9g, of which sugars 0g; Fat 0.3g, of which saturates 0g; Cholesterol 0mg; Calcium 11mg; Fibre 0g; Sodium 0mg.
fragrant coconut rice Energy 459kcal/1927kJ; Protein 9.1g; Carbohydrate 102g, of which sugars 12.3g; Fat 1.3g, of which saturates 0.5g; Cholesterol 0mg; Calcium 94mg; Fibre 0g; Sodium 275mg.
steamed sticky rice Energy 314kcal/1314kJ; Protein 6.5g; Carbohydrate 69.8g, of which sugars 0g; Fat 0.5g, of which saturates 0g; Cholesterol 0mg; Calcium 17mg; Fibre 0g; Sodium 0mg.

Chicken & Basil Coconut Rice

For this dish, the rice is partially boiled before being simmered with coconut so that it fully absorbs the additional flavours.

Ingredients

350g/12oz/1¾ cups jasmine rice, rinsed
30–45ml/2–3 tbsp groundnut (peanut) oil
1 large onion, finely sliced into rings
1 garlic clove, crushed
1 fresh red chilli, seeded and finely sliced
1 fresh green chilli, seeded and finely sliced
generous handful of basil leaves
3 skinless chicken breast fillets, about 350g/12oz, finely sliced
5mm/¼in piece of lemon grass, pounded or finely chopped
600ml/1 pint/2½ cups coconut cream
salt and ground black pepper

Serves 4

1 Bring a pan of lightly salted water to the boil. Add the rice to the pan and boil for about 6 minutes, until partially cooked. Drain and set aside.

2 Heat the oil in a frying pan and fry the onion rings for 5–10 minutes until golden and crisp. Lift out, drain on kitchen paper and set aside.

3 Fry the garlic and chillies in the same oil for 2–3 minutes, then add the basil leaves and fry briefly until they begin to wilt.

4 Remove a few basil leaves and set them aside for the garnish, then add the chicken slices to the pan with the lemon grass and fry for 2–3 minutes until golden.

5 Add the rice and stir-fry for a few minutes to coat the grains, then pour in the coconut cream. Cook for 4–5 minutes or until the rice is tender, adding a little more water if necessary. Adjust the seasoning.

6 Pile the rice into a warmed serving dish, sprinkle with the fried onion rings and basil leaves, and serve immediately.

Savoury Fried Rice

The title makes this sound like rather an ordinary dish, but it is nothing of the kind. Chilli, nuts and toasted coconut give the mixture of rice and beans and wilted greens plenty of flavour, and the egg that is stirred in provides the protein. For a tangy contrast, lime juice is poured over.

Ingredients

30ml/2 tbsp vegetable oil
2 garlic cloves, finely chopped
1 small fresh red chilli, seeded and finely chopped
50g/2oz/½ cup cashew nuts, toasted
50g/2oz/⅔ cup desiccated (dry unsweetened) coconut, toasted
2.5ml/½ tsp palm sugar (jaggery) or light muscovado (brown) sugar
30ml/2 tbsp light soy sauce
15ml/1 tbsp rice vinegar
1 egg
115g/4oz/1 cup green beans, sliced
½ spring cabbage or 115g/4oz spring greens (collards) or pak choi (bok choy), shredded
90g/3½oz/½ cup jasmine rice, cooked
lime wedges, to serve

Serves 2

1 Heat the oil in a wok or large, heavy frying pan. Add the garlic and cook over a medium to high heat until golden. Do not let it burn or it will taste bitter.

2 Add the red chilli, cashew nuts and toasted coconut to the wok or pan and stir-fry briefly, taking care to prevent the coconut from scorching. Stir in the sugar, soy sauce and rice vinegar. Toss over the heat for 1–2 minutes.

3 Push the stir-fry to one side of the wok or pan and break the egg into the empty side. When the egg is almost set, stir it into the garlic and chilli mixture with a wooden spatula or spoon.

4 Add the green beans, greens and cooked rice. Stir over the heat until the greens have just wilted, then spoon into a dish to serve. Offer the lime wedges separately, for squeezing over the rice.

chicken & basil rice Energy 492kcal/2064kJ; Protein 28.8g; Carbohydrate 83.1g, of which sugars 11.6g; Fat 4.8g, of which saturates 0.9g; Cholesterol 61mg; Calcium 83mg; Fibre 1.1g; Sodium 220mg.
savoury fried rice Energy 571kcal/2368kJ; Protein 16.1g; Carbohydrate 30.5g, of which sugars 8.7g; Fat 43.7g, of which saturates 18.2g; Cholesterol 95mg; Calcium 187mg; Fibre 8.5g; Sodium 1197mg.

Fried Rice with Mushrooms

A tasty rice and mushroom dish that is very low in saturated fat, yet sufficiently filling to be almost a meal in itself.

Ingredients

225g/8oz/1 1/4 cups long grain rice
15ml/1 tbsp vegetable oil
1 egg, lightly beaten
2 garlic cloves, crushed
175g/6oz/2 1/4 cups button (white) mushrooms or mixed wild and cultivated mushrooms, sliced
15ml/1 tbsp light soy sauce
1.5ml/1/4 tsp salt
2.5ml/1/2 tsp sesame oil
cucumber matchsticks, to garnish

Serves 4

1 Rinse the rice until the water runs clear, then drain well. Place in a pan. Measure the depth of the rice against your index finger, then cover with cold water to the same depth.

2 Bring the water to the boil. Stir the rice, boil for a few minutes, then cover the pan. Lower the heat to a simmer and cook for 5–8 minutes until all of the water has been absorbed.

3 Remove the pan from the heat and, without lifting the lid, leave for another 10 minutes before forking up the rice.

4 Heat 5ml/1 tsp of the vegetable oil in a non-stick frying pan or wok. Add the egg and cook, stirring with a chopstick or wooden spoon until scrambled. Immediately remove the egg and set aside in a bowl.

5 Add the remaining vegetable oil in the pan or wok. When it is hot, stir-fry the garlic for a few seconds, then add the mushrooms and stir-fry for 2 minutes, adding a little water, if needed, to prevent burning. Stir in the cooked rice and cook for 4 minutes more.

6 Add the scrambled egg, soy sauce, salt and sesame oil. Mix together and cook for 1 minute to heat through. Serve the rice immediately, garnished with cucumber matchsticks.

Stir-fried Rice with Vegetables

The ginger gives this rice dish a wonderful flavour. Serve it as a vegetarian main course or as an unusual vegetable accompaniment.

Ingredients

115g/4oz/generous 1/2 cup brown basmati rice, rinsed and drained
350ml/12fl oz/1 1/2 cups vegetable stock
2.5cm/1in piece of fresh root ginger, finely sliced
1 garlic clove, halved
5cm/2in piece of pared lemon rind
115g/4oz/1 1/2 cups shiitake mushrooms
15ml/1 tbsp groundnut (peanut) oil
15ml/1 tbsp ghee or butter
175g/6oz baby carrots, trimmed
225g/8oz baby courgettes (zucchini), halved
175–225g/6–8oz/about 1 1/2 cups broccoli, broken into florets
6 spring onions (scallions), sliced
15ml/1 tbsp light soy sauce
10ml/2 tsp toasted sesame oil

Serves 2–4

1 Put the rice in a pan and pour in the stock. Add the ginger, garlic and lemon rind. Slowly bring to the boil, then cover and cook very gently for 20–25 minutes until the rice is tender. Remove the pan from the heat. Discard the flavourings and keep the pan covered with a clean dish towel and the lid so that the rice stays warm.

2 Slice the mushrooms, discarding the stems. Heat the oil and ghee or butter in a wok and stir-fry the carrots for 4–5 minutes until partially tender.

3 Add the mushrooms and courgettes, stir-fry for 2–3 minutes, then add the broccoli and spring onions and cook for a further 3 minutes, by which time all the vegetables should be tender but should still retain a bit of "bite".

4 Add the cooked rice to the vegetables, and toss briefly over the heat to mix and heat through. Toss with the soy sauce and sesame oil. Spoon into a bowl and serve immediately.

rice w. mushrooms Energy 245kcal/1023kJ; Protein 6.6g; Carbohydrate 45.4g, of which sugars 0.4g; Fat 3.8g, of which saturates 0.7g; Cholesterol 48mg; Calcium 21mg; Fibre 0.5g; Sodium 287mg.
stir-fried rice Energy 430kcal/1788kJ; Protein 12.5g; Carbohydrate 58.2g, of which sugars 11.2g; Fat 16.2g, of which saturates 2.2g; Cholesterol 0mg; Calcium 127mg; Fibre 6.5g; Sodium 569mg.

Special Fried Rice

More colourful and elaborate than other fried rice dishes, special fried rice is a meal in itself.

Ingredients

50g/2oz/1⅓ cup cooked peeled prawns (shrimp)
3 eggs
5ml/1 tsp salt
2 spring onions (scallions), finely chopped
60ml/4 tbsp vegetable oil
115g/4oz lean pork, finely diced
15ml/1 tbsp light soy sauce
15ml/1 tbsp Chinese rice wine
450g/1lb/6 cups cooked rice
115g/4oz green peas

Serves 4

1 Pat the prawns dry with kitchen paper. Put the eggs in a bowl with a pinch of the salt and a few pieces of spring onion. Whisk lightly.

2 Heat half the oil in a wok, add the pork and stir-fry until golden. Add the prawns and cook for 1 minute, then add the soy sauce and rice wine. Spoon the pork and prawn mixture into a bowl and keep hot.

3 Heat the remaining oil in the wok and lightly scramble the eggs. Add the rice and stir well with chopsticks.

4 Add the remaining salt and spring onions, the stir-fried prawns, pork and peas. Toss well over the heat to combine and serve either hot or cold.

Variation
If you don't have any Chinese rice wine, substitute dry sherry.

Cook's Tip
The weight of rice increases about two and a half times after cooking. When a recipe calls for cooked rice, use just under half the weight in uncooked rice.

Fragrant Harbour Fried Rice

This tasty rice dish celebrates the Chinese name for Hong Kong, which is Fragrant Harbour.

Ingredients

about 90ml/6 tbsp vegetable oil
2 eggs, beaten
8 shallots, sliced
115g/4oz peeled cooked prawns (shrimp)
3 garlic cloves, crushed
115g/4oz cooked pork, cut into thin strips
4 Chinese dried mushrooms, soaked, stems removed and sliced
115g/4oz Chinese sausage, cooked and sliced at an angle
225g/8oz/generous 1 cup long grain rice, cooked, cooled quickly and chilled
30ml/2 tbsp light soy sauce
115g/4oz/1 cup frozen peas, thawed
2 spring onions (scallions), shredded
salt and ground black pepper
coriander (cilantro) leaves, to garnish

Serves 4

1 Heat about 15ml/1 tbsp of the oil in a frying pan, add the eggs and make an omelette. Slide the omelette out, roll it up and cut into strips. Set aside.

2 Heat a wok, add 15ml/1 tbsp of the remaining oil and stir-fry the shallots until crisp and golden. Remove and set aside. Add the prawns and garlic to the wok, with a little more oil if needed, fry for 1 minute, then remove.

3 Heat 15ml/1 tbsp more oil in the wok and stir-fry the pork and mushrooms for 2 minutes; add the cooked Chinese sausage slices and heat for a further 2 minutes. Lift the ingredients out of the wok and keep warm.

4 Reheat the wok with the remaining oil and stir-fry the rice until it glistens. Stir in the soy sauce, salt and pepper, plus half the cooked ingredients. Add the peas and half the spring onions and toss over the heat until the peas are cooked. Pile the fried rice on a heated platter, top with the remaining cooked ingredients and garnish with the coriander leaves.

special fried rice Energy 343kcal/1434kJ; Protein 20.2g; Carbohydrate 40.5g, of which sugars 4.2g; Fat 11.2g, of which saturates 1.6g; Cholesterol 124mg; Calcium 91mg; Fibre 2.4g; Sodium 632mg.
fragrant fried rice Energy 450kcal/1872kJ; Protein 14.5g; Carbohydrate 51g, of which sugars 4.4g; Fat 20.9g, of which saturates 3.1g; Cholesterol 113mg; Calcium 48mg; Fibre 1.1g; Sodium 58mg.

Pineapple Rice

This way of presenting rice not only looks spectacular, it also tastes so good that it can easily be served solo.

Ingredients

75g/3oz/¾ cup unsalted peanuts
1 large pineapple
45ml/3 tbsp groundnut (peanut) or sunflower oil
1 onion, chopped
1 garlic clove, crushed
2 chicken breast fillets, about 225g/8oz, cut into strips
225g/8oz/generous 1 cup jasmine rice, rinsed
600ml/1 pint/2½ cups chicken stock
1 lemon grass stalk, bruised
2 thick slices of ham, cut into julienne strips
1 fresh red chilli, seeded and very finely sliced
salt

Serves 4

1 Dry-fry the peanuts in a non-stick frying pan until golden. When cool, grind one-sixth of them in a coffee or herb mill and chop the remainder.

2 Cut a lengthways slice of pineapple, slicing through the leaves, then cut out the flesh to leave a neat shell. Chop 115g/4oz of the pineapple into cubes. Save the remainder for another dish.

3 Heat the oil in a large pan and fry the onion and garlic for 3–4 minutes until soft. Add the chicken strips and stir-fry over a medium heat for a few minutes until evenly brown.

4 Add the rice to the pan. Toss with the chicken mixture for a few minutes, then pour in the stock, with the lemon grass and a little salt. Bring to just below boiling point, then lower the heat, cover the pan and simmer gently for 10–12 minutes until both the rice and the chicken pieces are tender.

5 Stir the chopped peanuts, the pineapple cubes and the strips of ham into the rice, then spoon the mixture into the pineapple shell. Sprinkle the ground peanuts and the sliced chilli over the top and serve.

Fried Jasmine Rice with Prawns

When you only have a short time for lunch, this simple stir-fry will fill the gap.

Ingredients

45ml/3 tbsp vegetable oil
1 egg, beaten
1 onion, chopped
15ml/1 tbsp chopped garlic
15ml/1 tbsp shrimp paste
1kg/2¼lb/4 cups cooked jasmine rice
350g/12oz cooked peeled prawns (shrimp)
50g/2oz thawed frozen peas
oyster sauce, to taste
2 spring onions (scallions), chopped
15–20 Thai basil leaves, roughly snipped, plus an extra sprig, to garnish

Serves 4–6

1 Heat 15ml/1 tbsp of the oil in a wok or frying pan. Add the beaten egg and swirl it around to set like a thin pancake.

2 Cook the pancake (on one side only) over a gentle heat until golden. Slide the pancake on to a board, roll up and cut into thin strips. Set aside.

3 Heat the remaining oil in the wok or pan, add the onion and garlic and stir-fry for 2–3 minutes. Stir in the shrimp paste and mix well until thoroughly combined.

4 Add the rice, prawns and peas and toss and stir together, until everything is heated through.

5 Season with oyster sauce to taste, taking great care as the shrimp paste is salty. Mix in the spring onions and basil leaves. Transfer to a serving dish and top with the strips of egg pancake. Serve, garnished with a sprig of basil.

Cook's Tip
Thai basil, also known as holy basil, has a unique, pungent flavour that is both spicy and sharp. It can be found in most Asian food stores.

pineapple rice Energy 563kcal/2356kJ; Protein 28.9g; Carbohydrate 66.2g, of which sugars 19.8g; Fat 20.5g, of which saturates 2.8g; Cholesterol 56mg; Calcium 62mg; Fibre 3.5g; Sodium 189mg.
jasmine rice w. prawns Energy 354kcal/1494kJ; Protein 17.8g; Carbohydrate 53.4g, of which sugars 0.9g; Fat 9.2g, of which saturates 1.5g; Cholesterol 158mg; Calcium 117mg; Fibre 0.8g; Sodium 233mg.

Chinese Jewelled Rice

Another fried rice medley, this time with crab meat and water chestnuts, providing contrasting textures and flavours.

Ingredients

350g/12oz/1¾ cups white long grain rice
45ml/3 tbsp vegetable oil
1 onion, roughly chopped
4 dried black Chinese mushrooms, soaked for 10 minutes in warm water to cover
115g/4oz cooked ham, diced
175g/6oz drained canned white crab meat
75g/3oz/½ cup drained canned water chestnuts
115g/4oz/1 cup peas, thawed if frozen
30ml/2 tbsp oyster sauce
5ml/1 tsp granulated sugar
salt

Serves 4

1 Rinse the rice in cold water, drain well, then add to a pan of lightly salted boiling water. Cook for 10–12 minutes. Drain, refresh under cold water, drain again and cool quickly.

2 Heat half the oil in a wok. When very hot, stir-fry the rice for 3 minutes. Transfer the cooked rice to a bowl and set aside.

3 Heat the remaining oil in the wok and cook the onion until softened but not coloured. Drain the mushrooms, cut off and discard the stems, then chop the caps.

4 Add the chopped mushrooms to the wok, with all the remaining ingredients except the rice. Stir-fry for 2 minutes, then add the rice and stir-fry for about 3 minutes more. Spoon into heated bowls and serve.

Cook's Tip
Always preheat a wok before stir-frying. When you add the oil, drizzle it in a "necklace" just below the rim of the hot wok. As the oil runs down, it will coat the inner surface evenly as it heats through.

Jewelled Rice with Fried Eggs

This vibrant, colourful stir-fry makes a tasty light meal, or can be served as an accompaniment to simply grilled meat or fish.

Ingredients

2 fresh corn on the cob
60ml/4 tbsp sunflower oil
2 garlic cloves, finely chopped
4 red Asian shallots, thinly sliced
1 small fresh red chilli, finely sliced
90g/3½oz carrots, cut into thin matchsticks
90g/3½oz fine green beans, cut into 2cm/¾in lengths
1 red (bell) pepper, seeded and cut into 1cm/½in dice
90g/3½oz/1¼ cups baby button (white) mushrooms
500g/1¼lb/5 cups cooked long grain rice, completely cooled
45ml/3 tbsp light soy sauce
10ml/2 tsp green curry paste
4 eggs
crisp green salad leaves and lime wedges, to serve

Serves 4

1 First shuck the corn cobs. Remove all the papery leaves, and the silky threads, then with a sharp knife cut at the base of the kernels right down the length of the cob.

2 Heat 30ml/2 tbsp of the sunflower oil in a wok over a high heat. When hot, add the garlic, shallots and chilli. Stir-fry for about 2 minutes.

3 Add the carrots, green beans, corn, red pepper and mushrooms to the wok and stir-fry for 3–4 minutes. Add the cooked, cooled rice and stir-fry for a further 4–5 minutes.

4 Mix together the light soy sauce and curry paste and add to the wok. Toss to mix well and stir-fry for 2–3 minutes.

5 Meanwhile, fry the eggs one at a time in the remaining oil in a frying pan. As each egg is cooked, remove it from the pan and place on a plate. Keep the cooked eggs hot.

6 Ladle the rice into four bowls or plates and top each portion with a fried egg. Serve with crisp green salad leaves and wedges of lime to squeeze over.

chinese jewelled rice Energy 474kcal/1979kJ; Protein 22.5g; Carbohydrate 77.5g, of which sugars 4.3g; Fat 7.8g, of which saturates 1.1g; Cholesterol 48mg; Calcium 86mg; Fibre 1.9g; Sodium 710mg.
jewelled rice w. eggs Energy 392kcal/1648kJ; Protein 13.6g; Carbohydrate 51.4g, of which sugars 8.2g; Fat 16.1g, of which saturates 3.6g; Cholesterol 261mg; Calcium 79mg; Fibre 2.2g; Sodium 968mg.

Festive Rice

This pretty rice dish is traditionally shaped into a cone and surrounded by a variety of accompaniments before being served.

Ingredients

450g/1lb/2⅔ cups jasmine rice
60ml/4 tbsp oil
2 garlic cloves, crushed
2 onions, thinly sliced
2.5ml/½ tsp ground turmeric
750ml/1¼ pints/3 cups water
400ml/14fl oz can coconut milk
1–2 lemon grass stalks, bruised

For the accompaniments

omelette strips
2 fresh red chillies, seeded and shredded
cucumber chunks
tomato wedges
deep-fried onions
prawn (shrimp) crackers

Serves 8

1 Put the jasmine rice in a large strainer and rinse it thoroughly under cold water. Drain well.

2 Heat the oil in a frying pan with a lid. Cook the garlic, onions and turmeric over a low heat for 2–3 minutes, until the onions have softened. Add the rice and stir well to coat in oil.

3 Pour in the water and coconut milk and add the lemon grass. Bring to the boil, stirring. Cover the pan and cook gently for 12 minutes, or until all the liquid has been absorbed by the rice.

4 Remove the pan from the heat and lift the lid. Cover with a clean dish towel, replace the lid and leave to stand in a warm place for 15 minutes.

5 Remove the lemon grass, mound the rice mixture in a cone on a platter and garnish with the accompaniments, then serve.

Cook's Tip

Jasmine rice is widely available in most supermarkets and Asian stores. It is also known as Thai fragrant rice. It has a delicately scented, almost milky, aroma.

Garlic & Ginger Rice

Throughout China and South-east Asia, when rice is served on the side, it is usually steamed and plain, or fragrant with the flavours of ginger and herbs. The combination of garlic and ginger is popular in both countries and compliments almost any vegetable, fish or meat dish.

Ingredients

15ml/1 tbsp vegetable or groundnut (peanut) oil
2–3 garlic cloves, finely chopped
25g/1oz fresh root ginger, finely chopped
225g/8oz/generous 1 cup long grain rice, rinsed in several bowls of water and drained
900ml/1½ pints/3¾ cups chicken stock
a bunch of fresh coriander (cilantro) leaves, finely chopped
a bunch of fresh basil and mint, (optional), finely chopped

Serves 4–6

1 Heat the oil in a clay pot or heavy pan. Stir in the garlic and ginger and fry until golden. Stir in the rice and allow it to absorb the flavours for 1–2 minutes.

2 Pour in the stock and stir to make sure the rice doesn't stick. Bring the stock to the boil, then reduce the heat. Sprinkle the coriander over the surface of the stock with the finely chopped basil and mint, if using. Cover the pan, and leave to cook gently for 20–25 minutes, until the rice has absorbed all the liquid.

3 Turn off the heat and gently fluff up the rice to mix in the herbs. Cover and leave to infuse for 10 minutes before serving.

Cook's Tip

Use homemade chicken stock if possible. It has a superior flavour to stock made using cubes and you can control the level of salt. Whenever you have a chicken carcass – after a roast chicken dinner, for instance – make and freeze the stock.

festive rice Energy 303kcal/1263kJ; Protein 6.4g; Carbohydrate 49.5g, of which sugars 4.2g; Fat 8.6g, of which saturates 2g; Cholesterol 53mg; Calcium 41mg; Fibre 0.5g; Sodium 212mg.
garlic & ginger rice Energy 165kcal/658kJ; Protein 3.9g; Carbohydrate 31.7g, of which sugars 0.5g; Fat 2.3g, of which saturates 0.2g; Cholesterol 0mg; Calcium 40mg; Fibre 1.1g; Sodium 8mg.

Fried Rice with Chicken

This substantial and tasty supper dish is based on jasmine rice cooked in coconut milk. Diced chicken, red pepper and corn kernels add colour and extra flavour.

Ingredients

475ml/16fl oz/2 cups water
50g/2oz/½ cup coconut milk powder
350g/12oz/1¾ cups jasmine rice, rinsed
30ml/2 tbsp groundnut (peanut) oil
2 garlic cloves, chopped
1 small onion, finely chopped
2.5cm/1in piece fresh root ginger, peeled and grated
225g/8oz skinned chicken breast fillets, cut into 1cm/½in pieces
1 red (bell) pepper, seeded and sliced
115g/4oz/1 cup drained canned whole kernel corn
5ml/1 tsp chilli oil
5ml/1 tsp hot curry powder
2 eggs, beaten
salt
spring onion (scallion) shreds, to garnish

Serves 4

1 Pour the water into a pan and whisk in the coconut milk powder. Add the rice and bring to the boil. Reduce the heat, cover and cook for 12 minutes, or until the rice is tender and the liquid has been absorbed. Spread the rice on a baking sheet and cool down as quickly as possible.

2 Heat the oil in a wok, add the garlic, onion and ginger and stir-fry over a medium heat for 2 minutes.

3 Push the onion mixture to the sides of the wok, add the chicken to the centre and stir-fry for 2 minutes. Add the rice and toss well. Stir-fry over a high heat for about 3 minutes more, until the chicken is cooked through.

4 Stir in the sliced red pepper, corn, chilli oil and curry powder, with salt to taste. Toss over the heat for 1 minute. Stir in the beaten eggs and cook for 1 minute more. Garnish with the spring onion shreds and serve.

Fragrant Rice with Chicken & Mint

Serve this refreshing dish simply drizzled with fish sauce, or as part of a celebratory meal.

Ingredients

350g/12oz/1¾ cups long grain rice, rinsed and drained
2–3 shallots, halved and finely sliced
1 bunch of fresh mint, stalks removed, leaves finely shredded
2 spring onions (scallions), finely sliced, to garnish
chilli sambal, to serve

For the stock

2 meaty chicken legs
1 onion, peeled and quartered
4cm/1½in fresh root ginger, peeled and coarsely chopped
15ml/1 tbsp fish sauce
3 black peppercorns
1 bunch of fresh mint
sea salt

Serves 4

1 To make the stock, put the chicken legs into a deep pan. Add all the other ingredients, except the salt, and pour in 1 litre/1¾ pints/4 cups water. Bring the water to the boil, skim, then cover and simmer for 1 hour.

2 Remove the lid, increase the heat and cook for a further 30 minutes to reduce the stock. Skim, strain and season with salt. Measure 750ml/1¼ pints/3 cups stock. Remove the chicken meat from the bone and shred.

3 Put the rice in a heavy pan and stir in the stock, which should be roughly 2.5cm/1in above the rice; if not, top it up. Bring the liquid to the boil, cover the pan and cook for about 25 minutes, or until all the water has been absorbed.

4 Remove the pan from the heat and fork in the shredded chicken, shallots and most of the mint. Cover the pan again and leave the flavours to mingle for 10 minutes. Tip the rice into bowls, or on to a serving dish, garnish with the remaining mint and the spring onions, and serve with chilli sambal.

fried rice w. chicken Energy 489kcal/2044kJ; Protein 16.3g; Carbohydrate 82.9g, of which sugars 7.5g; Fat 10.1g, of which saturates 1.7g; Cholesterol 95mg; Calcium 50mg; Fibre 1.4g; Sodium 249mg.
fragrant rice Energy 426kcal/1784kJ; Protein 25.6g; Carbohydrate 72.9g, of which sugars 1.8g; Fat 3.1g, of which saturates 0.7g; Cholesterol 92mg; Calcium 53mg; Fibre 0.5g; Sodium 82mg.

Stir-fried Rice with Sausage

This traditional stir-fried rice recipe includes Chinese pork sausage, or strips of pork combined with prawns or crab. Prepared this way, the dish can be eaten as a snack, or as part of a meal with grilled and roasted meats accompanied by a vegetable dish or salad.

Ingredients

25g/1oz dried cloud ear (wood ear) mushrooms, soaked in water for 20 minutes
15ml/1 tbsp vegetable or sesame oil
1 onion, sliced
2 fresh green or red chillies, seeded and finely chopped
2 Chinese sausages (15cm/6in long), each sliced into 10 pieces
175g/6oz prawns (shrimp), shelled and deveined
30ml/2 tbsp fish sauce, plus extra for drizzling
10ml/2 tsp five-spice powder
1 bunch of fresh coriander (cilantro), stalks removed, leaves finely chopped
450g/1lb/4 cups cold steamed rice
ground black pepper

Serves 4

1 Drain the soaked cloud ear mushrooms, put them on a board and cut them into strips, discarding any very tough bits.

2 Heat a wok or heavy pan and add the oil. Add the onion and chillies. Fry until they begin to colour, then stir in the mushrooms.

3 Add the sausage slices, moving them around the wok or pan until they begin to brown. Add the prawns and move them around until they turn opaque. Stir in the fish sauce, the five-spice powder and 30ml/2 tbsp of the coriander.

4 Season well with pepper, then quickly add the rice, making sure it doesn't stick to the pan. As soon as the rice is heated through, sprinkle with the remainder of the coriander and serve with fish sauce to drizzle over it.

Fried Rice with Pork

This is great for using up last night's leftover rice, but for safety's sake, it must have been cooled quickly and kept in the refrigerator, then fried until heated all the way through.

Ingredients

45ml/3 tbsp vegetable oil
1 onion, chopped
15ml/1 tbsp chopped garlic
115g/4oz tender pork, cut into small cubes
2 eggs, beaten
500g/2¼lb/5 cups cooked rice
30ml/2 tbsp fish sauce
15ml/1 tbsp dark soy sauce
2.5ml/½ tsp caster (superfine) sugar

To serve

4 spring onions (scallions), finely sliced
2 fresh red chillies, sliced
1 lime, cut into wedges

Serves 4–6

1 Heat the oil in a wok or large frying pan. Add the onion and garlic and cook for about 2 minutes until softened.

2 Add the pork to the softened onion and garlic. Stir-fry until the pork changes colour and is fully cooked.

3 Tip in the beaten eggs and stir-fry over the heat until scrambled into small lumps.

4 Add the rice and continue to stir and toss, to coat it with the oil and prevent it from sticking.

5 Add the fish sauce, soy sauce and sugar and mix well. Continue to fry until the rice is hot. Spoon into warmed bowls and serve, with sliced spring onions, chillies and lime wedges.

Cook's Tips

- *The rice used in this and similar stir-fries is usually made the day before and added cold to the dish.*
- *If you like, you can drizzle sweet, sour or hot chilli dipping sauce over the stir-fries when serving.*

rice w. sausage Energy 388kcal/1632kJ; Protein 16.3g; Carbohydrate 45.8g, of which sugars 1.9g; Fat 16.8g, of which saturates 5.8g; Cholesterol 105mg; Calcium 91mg; Fibre 0.7g; Sodium 491mg.
fried rice w. pork Energy 229kcal/965kJ; Protein 7.5g; Carbohydrate 36.2g, of which sugars 1.5g; Fat 7g, of which saturates 1.3g; Cholesterol 55mg; Calcium 34mg; Fibre 0.4g; Sodium 147mg.

Fried Rice with Beef

One of the joys of cooking Chinese food is the ease and speed with which a really good meal can be prepared. This delectable beef and rice stir-fry can be on the table in 15 minutes.

Ingredients
200g/7oz beef steak, chilled
15ml/1 tbsp vegetable oil
2 garlic cloves, finely chopped
1 egg
250g/9oz/2¼ cups cooked jasmine rice
½ medium head broccoli, coarsely chopped
30ml/2 tbsp dark soy sauce
15ml/1 tbsp light soy sauce
5ml/1 tsp light muscovado (brown) sugar
15ml/1 tbsp fish sauce
ground black pepper
chilli sauce, to serve

Serves 4

1 Trim the steak and cut into very thin strips with a sharp knife.

2 Heat the oil in a wok or frying pan and cook the garlic over a low to medium heat until golden. Do not let it burn. Increase the heat to high, add the steak and stir-fry for 2 minutes.

3 Move the pieces of beef to the edges of the wok or pan and break the egg into the centre. When the egg starts to set, break it up with chopsticks and then stir-fry it with the meat.

4 Add the rice and toss all the contents of the wok together, scraping up any residue on the base, then add the broccoli, soy sauces, sugar and fish sauce and stir-fry for 2 minutes more. Season to taste with pepper, spoon into heated bowls and serve immediately with chilli sauce.

Cook's Tip
Soy sauce is made from fermented soya beans. The first extraction is sold as light soy sauce and has a delicate, "beany" fragrance. Dark soy sauce is more intensely flavoured and has been allowed to mature for longer. The darker kind is also traditionally used to intensify the colour of a dish.

Five Ingredients Rice

The Japanese love rice so much they invented many ways to enjoy it. Here, chicken and vegetables are cooked with short grain rice making a healthy light lunch.

Ingredients
275g/10oz/1¼ cups Japanese short grain rice
90g/3½oz carrot, peeled
2.5ml/½ tsp lemon juice
90g/3½oz canned bamboo shoots, drained
225g/8oz/3 cups oyster mushrooms
8 fresh parsley sprigs
350ml/12fl oz/1½ cups water and 7.5ml/1½ tsp instant dashi powder
150g/5oz skinless chicken breast fillet, cut into 2cm/¾in chunks
30ml/2 tbsp shoyu
30ml/2 tbsp sake
25ml/1½ tbsp mirin (sweet rice wine)
pinch of salt

Serves 4

1 Put the rice in a large bowl and wash under cold water until the water remains clear. Drain and set aside for 30 minutes.

2 Using a sharp knife, cut the carrot into 5mm/¼in rounds, then cut the discs into flowers. Slice the canned bamboo shoots into thin matchsticks.

3 Tear the oyster mushrooms into thin strips. Chop the parsley. Put it in a sieve (strainer) and pour over hot water from the kettle to wilt the leaves. Allow to drain and then set aside.

4 Heat the dashi stock in a large pan and add the carrots and bamboo shoots. Bring to the boil and add the chicken. Remove any scum that forms on the surface, then add the shoyu, sake, mirin and salt.

5 Add the rice and mushrooms and cover with a tight-fitting lid. Bring back to the boil, wait 5 minutes, then reduce the heat and simmer for 10 minutes. Remove from the heat without lifting the lid and leave to stand for 15 minutes. Add the wilted herbs and serve.

fried rice w. beef Energy 385kcal/1606kJ; Protein 20.7g; Carbohydrate 52.7g, of which sugars 2.5g; Fat 9.8g, of which saturates 2.8g; Cholesterol 81mg; Calcium 59mg; Fibre 1.6g; Sodium 590mg.
five ingredients rice Energy 331kcal/1386kJ; Protein 16.2g; Carbohydrate 61.1g, of which sugars 5.5g; Fat 1.2g, of which saturates 0.2g; Cholesterol 26mg; Calcium 32mg; Fibre 1.5g; Sodium 567mg.

Brown Rice with Lime

It is unusual to find brown rice in Chinese recipes, but the nutty flavour of the grains is enhanced by the fragrance of limes and lemon grass in this delicious dish.

Ingredients

2 limes
1 lemon grass stalk
225g/8oz/generous 1 cup brown long grain rice
15ml/1 tbsp olive oil
1 onion, chopped
2.5cm/1in piece fresh root ginger, peeled and finely chopped
7.5ml/1½ tsp coriander seeds
7.5ml/1½ tsp cumin seeds
750ml/1¼ pints/3 cups vegetable stock
60ml/4 tbsp chopped fresh coriander (cilantro)
spring onion (scallion) green and toasted coconut strips, to garnish
1 lime cut into 4 wedges, to serve

Serves 4

1 Pare the limes, using a cannelle knife (zester) or fine grater, taking care to avoid cutting the bitter pith. Set the rind aside. Finely chop the lower bulbous portion of the lemon grass stalk and set it aside.

2 Rinse the rice in plenty of cold water until the water runs clear. Tip it into a sieve (strainer) and drain thoroughly.

3 Heat the oil in a large pan. Add the onion, ginger, coriander and cumin seeds, lemon grass and lime rind and cook over a low heat for 2–3 minutes.

4 Add the rice to the pan and cook, stirring it constantly, for 1 minute, then pour in the stock and bring to the boil. Reduce the heat to very low and cover the pan. Cook gently for 30 minutes, then check the rice. If it is still crunchy, cover the pan and cook for 3–5 minutes more. Remove from the heat.

5 Stir in the fresh coriander, fluff up the rice grains with a fork, cover the pan and leave to stand for 10 minutes. Transfer to a warmed dish, garnish with spring onion green and toasted coconut strips, and serve with lime wedges.

Chinese Leaves & Black Rice

The slightly nutty, chewy black glutinous rice contrasts beautifully with the Chinese leaves in this tasty stir-fry, which looks very dramatic. It is a good dish for dieters as it is low in saturated fat.

Ingredients

225g/8oz/1⅓ cups black glutinous rice or brown rice
900ml/1½ pints/3¾ cups vegetable stock
15ml/1 tbsp vegetable oil
225g/8oz Chinese leaves (Chinese cabbage), cut into 1cm/½in strips
4 spring onions (scallions), thinly sliced
salt and ground white pepper
2.5ml/½ tsp sesame oil

Serves 4

1 Rinse the rice until the water runs clear, then drain and tip into a pan. Add the stock and bring to the boil. Lower the heat, cover the pan and cook gently for 30 minutes.

2 Remove the pan from the heat and leave it to stand for 15 minutes without lifting the lid.

3 Heat the vegetable oil in a non-stick frying pan or wok. Stir-fry the Chinese leaves over medium heat for 2 minutes, adding a little water to prevent them from burning.

4 Drain the rice, stir it into the pan and cook for 4 minutes, using two spatulas or spoons to toss it with the Chinese leaves over the heat.

5 Add the spring onions, with salt and white pepper to taste. Drizzle over the sesame oil. Cook for 1 minute more, stirring constantly. Serve immediately.

Variation

This works well with any type of cabbage. It's particularly good with thinly-sliced Brussels sprouts, and you can add some chopped Chinese or purple-sprouting broccoli for good measure.

brown rice w. lime Energy 235kcal/996kJ; Protein 4.3g; Carbohydrate 47.3g, of which sugars 1.9g; Fat 4.5g, of which saturates 0.8g; Cholesterol 0mg; Calcium 35mg; Fibre 1.9g; Sodium 6mg.
Chinese leaves & black rice Energy 243kcal/1029kJ; Protein 4.8g; Carbohydrate 48.9g, of which sugars 3.8g; Fat 4.5g, of which saturates 0.7g; Cholesterol 0mg; Calcium 37mg; Fibre 2.4g; Sodium 6mg.

Red Rice and Aduki Beans

This is a savoury version of a popular Japanese sweetmeat.

Ingredients

65g/2½oz/⅓ cup dried aduki beans
5ml/1 tsp salt
300g/11oz/1½ cups glutinous rice, washed and drained
50g/2oz/¼ cup Japanese short grain rice, washed and drained
45ml/3 tbsp roasted sesame seeds mixed with 5ml/1 tsp sea salt

Serves 4

1 Put the aduki beans in a heavy pan and pour in 450ml/¾ pint/ scant 2 cups water. Bring to the boil, then simmer, covered, for 20–30 minutes, or until the beans look swollen but are still firm. Drain, reserving the liquid in a large bowl. Add the salt. Return the beans to the pan.

2 Bring another 450ml/¾ pint/ scant 2 cups water to the boil. Add to the beans and boil, then simmer for 30 minutes, until the beans' skins start to crack. Drain and add the liquid to the bowl of salted liquid you saved earlier. Cover the beans and leave to cool.

3 Add the rice to the bean liquid. Leave to soak for 4–5 hours. Drain the rice and reserve the liquid. Mix the rice and beans.

4 Bring a steamer of water to the boil. Turn off the heat. Place a tall glass in the centre of the steaming compartment. Pour the rice and beans into the steamer and gently pull the glass out. The hole in the middle will allow even distribution of the steam. Steam on high for 10 minutes.

5 Using your fingers, sprinkle the rice mixture with the reserved liquid from the bowl. Cover again and repeat the process twice more at 10 minute intervals, then leave to steam for 15 minutes more. Remove from the heat. Leave to stand for 10 minutes, then spoon into a large bowl, sprinkle with the sesame seed mixture and serve.

Sticky Rice Parcels

It is a pleasure to cut these parcels open and discover the delicious filling inside.

Ingredients

450g/1lb/2⅔ cups glutinous rice
20ml/4 tsp vegetable oil
15ml/1 tbsp dark soy sauce
1.5ml/¼ tsp five-spice powder
15ml/1 tbsp dry sherry
4 skinless, boneless chicken thighs, each cut into 4 pieces
8 dried Chinese mushrooms, soaked, stems removed and caps diced
25g/1oz dried shrimps, soaked and drained
50g/2oz/½ cup canned bamboo shoots, drained and sliced
300ml/½ pint/1¼ cups chicken stock
10ml/2 tsp cornflour (cornstarch), mixed with 15ml/1 tbsp cold water
4 lotus leaves, soaked in warm water until soft
salt and ground white pepper

Serves 4

1 Rinse the rice in a colander until the water runs clear, then soak in a bowl of water for 2 hours. Drain the rice and tip it into a bowl. Stir in 5ml/1 tsp of the oil and 2.5ml/½ tsp salt.

2 Line a large steamer with muslin or cheesecloth. Add the soaked rice, cover and steam for 45 minutes, stirring occasionally. Leave to cool.

3 Mix the soy sauce, five-spice powder and sherry in a bowl, stir in the chicken pieces, cover and marinate for 20 minutes.

4 Heat the remaining oil in a wok, stir-fry the chicken for 2 minutes, then add the mushrooms, shrimps, bamboo shoots and stock. Mix well, bring to the boil, then simmer for 10 minutes. Add the cornflour paste and cook, stirring, until the sauce has thickened. Season to taste.

5 Spread one-eighth of the rice to a round in the centre of each lotus leaf. Divide the chicken mixture among the leaves, putting it on top of the rice, and then top with more rice. Fold the leaves around the filling to make four neat parcels. Steam, seam side down, for 30 minutes over a high heat. Serve.

red rice Energy 432kcal/1807kJ; Protein 12.4g; Carbohydrate 78.7g, of which sugars 0.5g; Fat 7.2g, of which saturates 1g; Cholesterol 0mg; Calcium 105mg; Fibre 2.2g; Sodium 496mg.
sticky rice parcels Energy 565kcal/2369kJ; Protein 37.3g; Carbohydrate 87.1g, of which sugars 0.3g; Fat 6.1g, of which saturates 0.7g; Cholesterol 102mg; Calcium 101mg; Fibre 0.2g; Sodium 336mg.

Rice Cakes with Dipping Sauce

Easy to make, these rice cakes will keep almost indefinitely in an airtight container. Start making them at least a day before you plan to serve them, so the rice can dry out overnight.

Ingredients

175g/6oz/1 cup Thai jasmine rice
oil, for deep-frying and greasing
dipping sauce, for serving

Serves 4–6

1 Preheat the oven to the lowest setting. Grease a baking sheet. Wash the rice in several changes of water. Put it in a pan, add 350ml/12fl oz/1½ cups water and cover tightly. Bring to the boil, reduce the heat and simmer gently for about 15 minutes.

2 Remove the lid and fluff up the rice. Spoon it on to the baking sheet and press it down with the back of a spoon. Leave in the oven to dry out overnight.

3 Break the rice into bitesize pieces. Heat the oil in a wok or deep-fryer to 190°C/375°F or until a cube of bread, added to oil, browns in 40 seconds. Deep-fry the rice cakes, in batches, for about 1 minute, until they puff up but are not browned. Remove and drain well. Serve with the dipping sauce.

Cook's Tip

For a spicy meat-based dipping sauce to serve with the rice cakes, soak 6 dried red chillies in warm water, drain, then grind to a paste with 2 chopped shallots, 2.5ml/½ tsp salt, 2 chopped garlic cloves, 4 chopped coriander (cilantro) roots and 10 white peppercorns. Heat 250ml/8fl oz/1 cup coconut milk. When it starts to separate, stir in the chilli paste and cook for 3 minutes. Add 15ml/1 tbsp shrimp paste and 115g/4oz minced (ground) pork. Cook, stirring, for 10 minutes, then stir in 4 chopped cherry tomatoes, 15ml/1 tbsp each fish sauce and brown sugar, 30ml/2tbsp each tamarind juice and chopped roasted peanuts, and 2 chopped spring onions (scallions). Cook until thick, then pour into a bowl and cool.

Sticky Rice Cakes Filled with Pork

These rice cakes are substantial enough to serve for supper, with a salad and dipping sauce.

Ingredients

15ml/1 tbsp vegetable oil
2 garlic cloves, chopped
225g/8oz lean pork, cut into bitesize chunks
30ml/2 tbsp fish sauce
2.5ml/½ tsp sugar
10ml/2 tsp ground black pepper
115g/4oz lotus seeds, soaked for 6 hours and drained
2 lotus or banana leaves, trimmed and cut into 25cm/10in squares
500g/1¼lb/5 cups cooked sticky rice
salt

Makes 2 cakes

1 Heat the oil in a heavy pan. Stir in the garlic, until it begins to colour, then add the pork, fish sauce, sugar and pepper. Cover and cook over a low heat for about 45 minutes, or until the pork is tender. Leave to cool, then shred the pork.

2 Meanwhile, cook the lotus seeds in boiling water for about 10 minutes. When soft, drain, pat dry and leave to cool.

3 Place a quarter of the cooked sticky rice in the middle of each lotus or banana leaf. Place half the shredded pork and half the lotus seeds on the rice.

4 Drizzle some of the cooking juices from the pork over the top. Place another quarter of the rice on top, moulding and patting it with your fingers to make sure the pork and lotus seeds are enclosed like a cake. Fold the leaf edge nearest to you over the rice, tuck in the sides, and fold the whole packet over to form a tight, square bundle. Tie it with string. Repeat with the second leaf and the remaining ingredients.

5 Fill a wok one-third full of water. Place a double-tiered bamboo steamer, with its lid on, on top. Bring the water to the boil, lift the bamboo lid and place a rice cake on the rack in each tier. Cover and steam for about 45 minutes. Carefully open up the parcels and serve.

rice cakes Energy 180kcal/750kJ; Protein 2.3g; Carbohydrate 25.7g, of which sugars 2.3g; Fat 7.5g, of which saturates 0.9g; Cholesterol 0mg; Calcium 7mg; Fibre 0.1g; Sodium 136mg.
sticky rice cakes w. pork Energy 555kcal/2343kJ; Protein 32.3g; Carbohydrate 80.9g, of which sugars 2.6g; Fat 13.6g, of which saturates 3g; Cholesterol 71mg; Calcium 65mg; Fibre 1.1g; Sodium 84mg.

Chinese Clay Pot Rice with Chicken

This Cantonese dish is a great family one-pot meal. It can also be found on Chinese stalls and in some coffee shops. The traditional clay pot ensures that the ingredients remain moist, while allowing the flavours to mingle, but any earthenware pot such as a Spanish or Portuguese one will do. This recipe also works well with prawns or strips of pork fillet.

Ingredients

500g/1 ¼lb chicken breast fillets, cut into thin strips
5 dried shiitake mushrooms, soaked in hot water for 30 minutes, until soft
1 Chinese sausage, sliced
750ml/1 ¼pints/3 cups chicken stock
225g/8oz/generous 1 cup long grain rice, washed and drained
fresh coriander (cilantro) leaves, finely chopped, to garnish

For the marinade

30ml/2 tbsp sesame oil
45ml/3 tbsp oyster sauce
30ml/2 tbsp soy sauce
25g/1oz fresh root ginger, finely grated (shredded)
2 spring onions (scallions), trimmed and finely sliced
1 fresh red chilli, seeded and finely sliced
5ml/1 tsp sugar

Serves 4

1 In a bowl, mix together the ingredients for the marinade. Toss in the chicken, making sure it is well coated. Set aside.

2 Drain the shiitake mushrooms and squeeze out excess water. Remove any hard stems and halve the caps. Add the mushroom caps and the Chinese sausage to the chicken.

3 Bring the stock to the boil in the clay pot. Stir in the rice and bring it back to the boil. Reduce the heat, cover the pot, and simmer on a low heat for 15–20 minutes, until almost all the liquid has been absorbed.

4 Spread the marinated mixture over the top of the rice and cover the pot. Leave to steam for about 10–15 minutes, until all the liquid is absorbed and the chicken is cooked. Garnish with coriander and serve.

Nasi Goreng

One of the most popular and best-known dishes from Indonesia, this is a marvellous way to use up left-over rice and meats.

Ingredients

350g/12oz/1¾ cups basmati rice (dry weight), cooked and cooled
2 eggs
30ml/2 tbsp water
105ml/7 tbsp sunflower oil
10ml/2 tsp shrimp paste
2–3 fresh red chillies
2 garlic cloves, crushed
1 onion, sliced
225g/8oz fillet (tenderloin) of pork or beef, cut into strips
115g/4oz cooked, peeled prawns
225g/8oz cooked chicken, chopped
30ml/2 tbsp dark soy sauce
salt and ground black pepper
deep-fried onions, to serve

Serves 4–6

1 Separate the grains of the cooked rice with a fork. Cover and set aside. Beat the eggs with the water and seasoning.

2 Heat 15ml/1 tbsp of the oil in a frying pan or wok, pour in about half the egg mixture and cook until set, without stirring. Roll up the omelette, slide it on to a plate, cut into strips and set aside. Make another omelette in the same way.

3 Put the shrimp paste and half the shredded chillies into a food processor. Add the garlic and onion. Process to a paste.

4 Heat the remaining oil in a wok. Fry the paste, without browning, until it gives off a spicy aroma.

5 Add the strips of pork or beef and toss the meat over the heat, to seal in the juices. Cook the meat in the wok for about 2 minutes, stirring constantly.

6 Add the prawns, cook for 2 minutes, then add the chicken, rice, and soy sauce, with salt and pepper to taste, stirring constantly. Serve in individual bowls, garnished with omelette strips, shredded chilli and deep-fried onions.

clay pot rice Energy 371kcal/1560kJ; Protein 36.2g; Carbohydrate 46.8g, of which sugars 1g; Fat 4g, of which saturates 1.2g; Cholesterol 93mg; Calcium 54mg; Fibre 0.7g; Sodium 721mg.
nasi goreng Energy 463kcal/1929kJ; Protein 27.3g; Carbohydrate 49.4g, of which sugars 2.1g; Fat 17.1g, of which saturates 2.7g; Cholesterol 151mg; Calcium 49mg; Fibre 0.5g; Sodium 288mg.

Fresh Rice Noodles

Dried rice noodles are generally available in Asian supermarkets, but fresh ones are quite different and not that difficult to make. The freshly made noodle sheets can be served as a snack, drenched in sugar or honey, or dipped into a savoury sauce.

Ingredients

225g/8oz/2 cups rice flour
600ml/1 pint/2½ cups water
a pinch of salt
15ml/1 tbsp vegetable oil, plus extra for brushing
slivers of fresh red chilli and fresh ginger, and coriander (cilantro) leaves, to garnish (optional)

Serves 4

1 Place the flour in a bowl and stir in some of the water to form a paste. Pour in the rest of the water, beating it to make a lump-free batter. Add the salt and oil and leave to stand for 15 minutes.

2 Meanwhile, fill a wide pan with water. Cut a piece of smooth cotton cloth a little larger than the diameter of the pan. Stretch it over the top of the pan, pulling the edges tautly down over the sides, then wind a piece of string around the edge, to secure.

3 Using a sharp knife, make three small slits, about 2.5cm/1in from the edge of the cloth, at regular intervals. Bring the water to the boil.

4 Stir the batter and ladle 30–45ml/2–3 tbsp on to the cloth, swirling it to form a 13–15cm/5–6in wide circle. Cover with a domed lid, such as a wok lid, and steam for 1 minute, or until the noodle sheet is translucent.

5 Carefully insert a spatula or knife under the noodle sheet and prise it off the cloth. (If it doesn't peel off easily, you may need to steam it a little longer.) Transfer the noodle sheet to a lightly oiled baking tray, brush lightly with oil, and cook the remaining batter in the same way. Garnish with slivers of fresh chillies and the corinader leaves, if you like.

Plain Noodles with Four Flavours

A wonderfully simple way of serving noodles, this dish allows each individual diner to season their own, sprinkling over the four flavours as they like. Flavourings are always put out in little bowls whenever noodles are served.

Ingredients

4 small fresh red or green chillies
60ml/4 tbsp fish sauce
60ml/4 tbsp rice vinegar
sugar
mild or hot chilli powder
350g/12oz fresh or dried noodles

Serves 4

1 Finely chop the chillies, and mix half of them with the fish sauce in a bowl. Mix the remaining chillies with the rice vinegar in another small bowl. Put the sugar and chilli powder in separate small bowls. Cook the noodles until tender, following the instructions on the packet. Drain well, tip into a large bowl, and serve with the four flavours handed separately.

Soft Fried Noodles

This is a great dish for times when you are feeling a little peckish and fancy something simple but satisfying. Drain the cooked noodles and ladle them into the wok a few at a time, swirling them with the onions, so they don't all clump together on contact with the hot oil.

Ingredients

30ml/2 tbsp vegetable oil
30ml/2 tbsp finely chopped spring onions (scallions)
350g/12oz dried egg noodles, cooked and drained
soy sauce, to taste
salt and ground black pepper

Serves 4–6

1 Heat the oil in a wok and fry the spring onions for about 30 seconds. Add the noodles and separate the strands. Fry the noodles until they are heated through, lightly browned and crisp on the outside, but still soft inside. Season with soy sauce, salt and pepper. Serve immediately.

fresh rice noodles Energy 217kcal/908kJ; Protein 6.4g; Carbohydrate 46.1g, of which sugars 1.5g; Fat 0.6g, of which saturates 0.1g; Cholesterol 0mg; Calcium 51mg; Fibre 1.3g; Sodium 11mg.
noodles w. four flavours Energy 321kcal/1341kJ; Protein 4.5g; Carbohydrate 72.4g, of which sugars 1g; Fat 0.2g, of which saturates 0g; Cholesterol 0mg; Calcium 12mg; Fibre 0.2g; Sodium 278mg.
soft fried noodles Energy 262kcal/1107kJ; Protein 7.2g; Carbohydrate 42g, of which sugars 1.3g; Fat 8.5g, of which saturates 1.8g; Cholesterol 18mg; Calcium 18mg; Fibre 1.8g; Sodium 105mg.

Egg Fried Noodles

Yellow bean sauce gives these noodles a lovely savoury flavour.

Ingredients

350g/12oz medium-thick egg noodles
60ml/4 tbsp vegetable oil
4 spring onions (scallions), cut into 1cm/½in rounds
juice of 1 lime
15ml/1 tbsp soy sauce
2 garlic cloves, finely chopped
175g/6oz skinless, boneless chicken breast, sliced
175g/6oz raw prawns (shrimp), peeled and deveined
175g/6oz squid, cleaned and cut into rings
15ml/1 tbsp yellow bean sauce
15ml/1 tbsp fish sauce
15ml/1 tbsp soft light brown sugar
2 eggs
coriander (cilantro) leaves, to garnish

Serves 4–6

1 Cook the noodles in a pan of boiling water until just tender, then drain well and set aside.

2 Heat half the oil in a wok or large frying pan. Add the spring onions, stir-fry for 2 minutes, then add the noodles, lime juice and soy sauce and stir-fry for 2–3 minutes. Transfer the mixture to a bowl and keep warm.

3 Heat the remaining oil in the wok or pan. Add the garlic, chicken, prawns and squid. Stir-fry over a high heat until cooked. Stir in the yellow bean paste, fish sauce and sugar, then break the eggs into the mixture, stirring gently until they set.

4 Add the noodles, toss lightly to mix, and heat through. Serve garnished with coriander leaves.

Cook's Tip
Be careful not to overcook the prawns (shrimp). If they turn pink before the chicken and squid are cooked, remove them from the wok or pan.

Fried Noodles with Ginger

Here is a simple noodle dish that is low in saturated fat and would go well with most Oriental dishes. It can also be served as a light meal for 2 or 3 people.

Ingredients

handful of fresh coriander (cilantro)
225g/8oz dried egg noodles
10ml/2 tsp sesame oil
15ml/1 tbsp groundnut (peanut) oil or vegetable oil
5cm/2in piece fresh root ginger, cut into fine shreds
6–8 spring onions (scallions), cut into shreds
30ml/2 tbsp light soy sauce
salt and ground black pepper

Serves 4

1 Strip the leaves from the coriander stalks. Pile them on to a chopping board and coarsely chop them using a cleaver or large, sharp knife.

2 Bring a large pan of lightly salted water to the boil and cook the noodles according to the instructions on the packet.

3 Drain the noodles, rinse under cold water, drain again and tip into a bowl. Add the sesame oil and toss to coat.

4 Heat a wok until hot, add the groundnut or vegetable oil and swirl it around. Add the ginger and stir-fry for a few seconds, then add the noodles and spring onions. Stir-fry for 3–4 minutes, until the noodles are hot.

5 Drizzle over the soy sauce, then sprinkle the chopped coriander on top of the noodles.

6 Add salt and ground black pepper to taste. Toss and serve in heated bowls.

Variation
If you don't like the flavour of coriander (cilantro), use flat leaf parsley or even some chopped rocket (arugula).

egg fried noodles Energy 410kcal/1728kJ; Protein 26.2g; Carbohydrate 45.6g, of which sugars 4.2g; Fat 15g, of which saturates 3g; Cholesterol 224mg; Calcium 60mg; Fibre 2g; Sodium 422mg.
fried noodles w. ginger Energy 253kcal/1067kJ; Protein 7.4g; Carbohydrate 41.6g, of which sugars 2.2g; Fat 7.5g, of which saturates 1.6g; Cholesterol 17mg; Calcium 25mg; Fibre 1.9g; Sodium 637mg.

Spicy Fried Noodles

This is a wonderfully versatile dish as you can adapt it to include your favourite ingredients.

Ingredients

225g/8oz egg thread noodles
60ml/4 tbsp vegetable oil
2 garlic cloves, finely chopped
175g/6oz pork fillet (tenderloin), sliced into thin strips
1 skinless, boneless chicken breast portion (about 175g/6oz), sliced into thin strips
115g/4oz/1 cup cooked peeled prawns (shelled shrimp), rinsed if canned
45ml/3 tbsp fresh lemon juice
45ml/3 tbsp fish sauce
30ml/2 tbsp soft light brown sugar
2 eggs, beaten
½ fresh red chilli, seeded and finely chopped
50g/2oz/¼ cup beansprouts
60ml/4 tbsp roasted peanuts, chopped
3 spring onions (scallions), cut into 5cm/2in lengths and shredded
45ml/3 tbsp chopped fresh coriander (cilantro)

Serves 4

1 Bring a large pan of water to the boil. Add the noodles, remove the pan from the heat and leave for 5 minutes.

2 Heat 45ml/3 tbsp of the oil in a wok and cook the garlic for 30 seconds. Add the pork and chicken and stir-fry until lightly browned, then add the prawns; stir-fry for 2 minutes. Stir in the lemon juice, then add the fish sauce and sugar.

3 Drain the noodles and add to the wok or pan with the remaining 15ml/1 tbsp oil. Toss all the ingredients together, then pour the beaten eggs over the noodles. Stir-fry until almost set, then add the chilli and beansprouts.

4 Divide the roasted peanuts, spring onions and coriander leaves into two equal portions, add one portion to the pan and stir-fry for about 2 minutes.

5 Tip the noodles on to a serving platter. Sprinkle on the remaining peanuts, spring onions and chopped coriander; serve.

Chinese Stir-fried Noodles

This Chinese dish of stir-fried rice noodles and seafood is one of the most popular items on the hawker stalls. Breakfast, lunch, supper, mid-morning, mid-afternoon or late evening, there's always a bowl of these noodles to be had. Variations include red snapper, clams and pork.

Ingredients

45ml/3 tbsp vegetable oil
2 garlic cloves, finely chopped
2 fresh red chillies, seeded and finely sliced
1 Chinese sausage, finely sliced
12 fresh prawns (shrimp), peeled
2 small squid, trimmed, cleaned, skinned and sliced
500g/1¼lb cooked rice noodles
30ml/2 tbsp light soy sauce
45ml/3 tbsp kecap manis
2–3 mustard green leaves, chopped
a handful of beansprouts
2 eggs, lightly beaten
ground black pepper
fresh coriander (cilantro) leaves, finely chopped, to garnish

Serves 3–4

1 Heat a wok and add the oil. Stir in the garlic and chillies and fry until fragrant. Add the Chinese sausage, followed by the prawns and squid, tossing them to mix thoroughly. Stir-fry for 3–4 minutes, until the prawns and squid are cooked.

2 Toss in the noodles and mix well. Add the soy sauce and kecap manis, and toss in the mustard leaves and beansprouts. Stir-fry for 1–2 minutes, until the leaves begin to wilt.

3 Quickly stir in the eggs for a few seconds until set. Season with black pepper, and spoon into heated bowls. Garnish with coriander and serve immediately.

Variations

- *You can replace kecap manis with the same quantity of dark soy sauce mixed with a little sugar.*
- *If you are unable to locate Chinese sausage (available from Asian stores), substitute pepperoni or use thinly sliced pork fillet.*

spicy fried noodles Energy 597kcal/2504kJ; Protein 39.3g; Carbohydrate 50.8g, of which sugars 10.3g; Fat 27.8g, of which saturates 5.5g; Cholesterol 226mg; Calcium 76mg; Fibre 2.9g; Sodium 250mg.
stir-fried noodles Energy 618kcal/2582kJ; Protein 24.8g; Carbohydrate 100g, of which sugars 1.1g; Fat 12.9g, of which saturates 2.1g; Cholesterol 217mg; Calcium 96mg; Fibre 0.5g; Sodium 716mg.

Noodles with Yellow Bean Sauce

Served solo, steamed leeks, courgettes and peas might be bland, but add a punchy bean sauce and they acquire an attitude that even the addition of noodles can't assuage.

Ingredients

150g/5oz thin egg noodles
200g/7oz baby leeks, sliced lengthways
200g/7oz baby courgettes (zucchini), halved lengthways
200g/7oz sugar snap peas, trimmed
200g/7oz/1¾ cups fresh or frozen peas
15ml/1 tbsp vegetable oil
5 garlic cloves, sliced
45ml/3 tbsp yellow bean sauce
45ml/3 tbsp sweet chilli sauce
30ml/2 tbsp sweet soy sauce
50g/2oz/½ cup cashew nuts, to garnish

Serves 4

1 Cook the noodles according to the packet instructions, drain and set aside.

2 Line a large bamboo steamer with some perforated baking parchment and add the leeks, courgettes, sugar snaps and peas. Cover and stand over a wok of simmering water. Steam the vegetables for about 5 minutes, then remove and set aside. Drain and dry the wok.

3 Heat the vegetable oil in the wok and stir-fry the sliced garlic for 1–2 minutes.

4 In a separate bowl, mix together the yellow bean, sweet chilli and soy sauces, then pour into the wok. Stir to mix with the garlic, then add the steamed vegetables and the noodles and toss together to combine.

5 Cook the vegetables and noodles for 2–3 minutes, stirring frequently, until heated through.

6 Divide the vegetable noodles among four warmed serving bowls and sprinkle over the cashew nuts to garnish.

Egg Noodles with Asparagus

This dish is simplicity itself with a wonderful contrast of textures and flavours. Use young asparagus, which is beautifully tender and cooks in minutes. If you have a large wok, you can easily double the quantities of noodles and vegetables to serve four. Don't double the soy sauce, though – just add enough to taste.

Ingredients

115g/4oz dried egg noodles
15ml/1 tbsp vegetable oil
1 small onion, chopped
2.5/1in piece fresh root ginger, grated
2 garlic cloves, crushed
175g/6oz young asparagus spears, trimmed
115g/4oz/½ cup beansprouts
4 spring onions (scallions), sliced
45ml/3 tbsp light soy sauce
salt and ground black pepper

Serves 2

1 Bring a large pan of salted water to the boil. Add the noodles and cook until just tender. Drain, rinse under cold running water, drain again and set aside.

2 Heat a wok and add the oil. When the oil is very hot, stir-fry the onion, ginger and garlic for 2–3 minutes.

3 Add the asparagus and stir-fry for a further 2-3 minutes, then add the noodles and beansprouts and toss over fairly high heat for 2 minutes, until the noodles are hot.

4 Stir in the spring onions and soy sauce and mix well to combine. Season to taste, adding salt sparingly as the sauce will add quite a salty flavour. Stir-fry for 1 minute more before serving in a large bowl or in individual bowls.

Variation

For a contrast in textures, stir-fry half the asparagus spears and cook the rest under a hot grill (broiler) or on a hot griddle pan until lightly charred.

noodles/yellow bean Energy 296kcal/1241kJ; Protein 14.2g; Carbohydrate 44.9g, of which sugars 7.4g; Fat 7.8g, of which saturates 1.6g; Cholesterol 11mg; Calcium 61mg; Fibre 8.2g; Sodium 209mg.
noodles w. asparagus Energy 339kcal/1427kJ; Protein 12.6g; Carbohydrate 50.1g, of which sugars 7.9g; Fat 11.2g, of which saturates 2.2g; Cholesterol 17mg; Calcium 71mg; Fibre 4.8g; Sodium 1712mg.

Sesame Noodles with Spring Onions

This simple but very tasty warm salad can be prepared and cooked in just a few minutes.

Ingredients

2 garlic cloves, roughly chopped
30ml/2 tbsp Chinese sesame paste
15ml/1 tbsp dark sesame oil
30ml/2 tbsp soy sauce
30ml/2 tbsp rice wine
15ml/1 tbsp honey
pinch of five-spice powder
350g/12oz soba or buckwheat noodles
4 spring onions (scallions), finely sliced diagonally
salt and ground black pepper
50g/2oz beansprouts
7.5cm/3in piece of cucumber, cut into matchsticks
toasted sesame seeds

Serves 4

1 Process the garlic, sesame paste, oil, soy sauce, rice wine, honey and five-spice powder with a pinch each of salt and pepper in a blender or food processor until smooth.

2 Cook the noodles in a pan of boiling water until just tender, following the directions on the packet. Drain the noodles immediately and tip them into a bowl.

3 Toss the hot noodles with the dressing and the spring onions. Top with the beansprouts, cucumber and sesame seeds and serve in individual bowls.

Cook's Tips

- *If you can't find Chinese sesame paste, then use either tahini paste or smooth peanut butter instead.*
- *Five-spice powder is a fantastic ingredient for perking up dishes and adding a good depth of flavour. The five different spices – Sichuan pepper, cinnamon, cloves, fennel seeds and star anise – complement each ther. The aniseed flavour of star anise predominates.*

Sesame Noodle Salad

Toasted sesame oil adds a nutty flavour to this warm Asian-style salad.

Ingredients

250g/9oz medium egg noodles
200g/7oz/1¾ cup sugar snap peas or mangetouts (snow peas)
2 tomatoes
3 spring onions (scallions)
2 carrots, cut into julienne
30ml/2 tbsp chopped fresh coriander (cilantro)
15ml/1 tbsp sesame seeds
fresh coriander (cilantro), to garnish

For the dressing

10ml/2 tsp light soy sauce
15ml/1 tbsp toasted sesame seed oil
15ml/1 tbsp vegetable oil
4cm/1½in piece fresh root ginger, finely grated
1 garlic clove, crushed

Serves 4

1 Bring a large pan of lightly salted water to the boil. Add the egg noodles, and bring back to the boil. Cook for 2 minutes.

2 Slice the sugar snap peas or mangetouts diagonally, add to the pan and cook for a further 2 minutes. Drain and rinse under cold running water.

3 Meanwhile, make the dressing. Whisk together the soy sauce, sesame and sunflower oils, grated fresh root ginger and crushed garlic in a small bowl.

4 Cut the tomatoes in half and scoop out the seeds with a teaspoon, then chop roughly. Using a sharp knife, cut the spring onions into fine shreds.

5 Tip the noodles and the peas or mangetouts into a large bowl and add the carrots, tomatoes and coriander.

6 Pour the dressing over the top of the noodle mixture, and toss with your hands to combine. Serve in a large salad bowl or platter, or on individual salad plates. Sprinkle with the sesame seeds and top with the spring onions and coriander.

noodles/spring onions Energy 410kcal/1735kJ; Protein 12.4g; Carbohydrate 71g, of which sugars 6.2g; Fat 10g, of which saturates 0.7g; Cholesterol 0mg; Calcium 80mg; Fibre 3.5g; Sodium 539mg.
sesame noodle salad Energy 386kcal/1622kJ; Protein 10.9g; Carbohydrate 52.9g, of which sugars 8.6g; Fat 16g, of which saturates 3g; Cholesterol 19mg; Calcium 85mg; Fibre 5.1g; Sodium 310mg.

Rice Noodles with Fresh Herbs

Raid the kitchen garden (or your favourite stall at the farmers' market) for the best combination of fresh herbs to make this stunning yet very simple salad. Sharp flavourings – lime juice and fish sauce – provide the dressing, and the textures of crisp vegetables and soft chillies contrast beautifully with the rice vermicelli.

Ingredients

½ small cucumber
225g/8oz dried rice vermicelli
4–6 lettuce leaves, shredded
115g/4oz/½ cup beansprouts
1 bunch mixed basil, coriander (cilantro), mint and oregano, stalks removed, leaves shredded
juice of ½ lime
fish sauce, to drizzle

Serves 4

1 Peel the cucumber and cut it in half lengthways. Remove and discard the seeds using a teaspoon, then cut the flesh into matchsticks.

2 Add the rice sticks to a pan of boiling water, loosening them gently, and cook for 3–4 minutes, or until just tender – they should retain a bit of bite or firmness in the centre. Drain, rinse under cold water, and drain again.

3 In a bowl, toss the shredded lettuce, beansprouts, cucumber and herbs together. Add the noodles and lime juice and toss together to mix.

4 Drizzle with a little fish sauce for seasoning, and serve immediately on its own, or with stir-fried seafood or chicken as a complete meal.

Cook's Tip

If possible, really go to town on the herb selection, using different varieties of mint, ginger leaves, oregano and thyme to provide the leafy bedding for this dish and give it a really distinctive, fragrant flavour.

Sweet & Hot Vegetable Noodles

This noodle dish has the colour of fire, but only the mildest suggestion of heat. Ginger and plum sauce give it its fruity flavour, while lime adds a delicious tang.

Ingredients

130g/4½oz dried rice noodles
30ml/2 tbsp groundnut (peanut) oil
2.5cm/1in piece fresh root ginger, sliced into thin batons
1 garlic clove, crushed
130g/4½oz canned bamboo shoots, drained, sliced into thin batons
2 medium carrots, sliced into batons
130g/4½oz/generous ⅔ cup beansprouts
1 small white cabbage, shredded
30ml/2 tbsp fish sauce
30ml/2 tbsp soy sauce
30ml/2 tbsp plum sauce
10ml/2 tsp sesame oil
15ml/1 tbsp palm sugar (jaggery) or light muscovado (brown) sugar
juice of ½ lime
90g/3½oz mooli (daikon), sliced into thin batons
small bunch fresh coriander (cilantro), chopped
60ml/4 tbsp sesame seeds, toasted

Serves 4

1 Cook the noodles in a large pan of boiling water, following the instructions on the packet. Meanwhile, heat the oil in a wok or large frying pan and stir-fry the ginger and garlic for about 3 minutes over a medium heat, until golden.

2 Drain the noodles and set them aside. Add the bamboo shoots to the wok, increase the heat to high and stir-fry for 5 minutes.

3 Add the carrots, beansprouts and cabbage and stir-fry for a further 5 minutes, until they are beginning to char on the edges.

4 Stir in the sauces, sesame oil, sugar and lime juice. Add the mooli and coriander, toss to mix, then spoon into a warmed bowl, sprinkle with toasted sesame seeds and serve.

rice noodles w. herbs Energy 217kcal/908kJ; Protein 6.4g; Carbohydrate 46.1g, of which sugars 1.5g; Fat 0.6g, of which saturates 0.1g; Cholesterol 0mg; Calcium 51mg; Fibre 1.3g; Sodium 11mg.
sweet/hot noodles Energy 368kcal/1530kJ; Protein 8.8g; Carbohydrate 45.8g, of which sugars 17.6g; Fat 16.5g, of which saturates 2.3g; Cholesterol 0mg; Calcium 200mg; Fibre 6.2g; Sodium 650mg.

Thai Noodles with Chinese Chives

This recipe requires a little time for preparation, but the cooking time is very fast.

Ingredients

350g/12oz dried rice noodles
1cm/½in piece fresh root ginger, peeled and grated
30ml/2 tbsp light soy sauce
45ml/3 tbsp vegetable oil
225g/8oz Quorn (mycoprotein), cut into small cubes
2 garlic cloves, crushed
1 large onion, cut into thin wedges
115g/4oz fried tofu, thinly sliced
1 fresh green chilli, seeded and thinly sliced
175g/6oz/¾ cup beansprouts
2 large bunches garlic chives, total weight about 115g/4oz, cut into 5cm/2in lengths
50g/2oz/½ cup roasted peanuts, ground
30ml/2 tbsp dark soy sauce
30ml/2 tbsp chopped fresh coriander (cilantro), and 1 lemon, cut into wedges, to garnish

Serves 4

1 Place the noodles in a bowl, cover with warm water and leave to soak for 30 minutes. Drain and set aside.

2 Mix the ginger, light soy sauce and 15ml/1 tbsp of the oil in a bowl. Add the Quorn, then set aside for 10 minutes. Drain, reserving the marinade.

3 Heat 15ml/1 tbsp of the remaining oil in a frying pan and cook the garlic for a few seconds. Add the Quorn and stir-fry for 3–4 minutes. Using a slotted spoon, transfer to a plate.

4 Heat the remaining oil in the pan and stir-fry the onion for 3–4 minutes, until softened and tinged with brown. Add the tofu and chilli, stir-fry briefly and then add the noodles. Stir-fry over a medium heat for 4–5 minutes.

5 Stir in the beansprouts, garlic chives and most of the ground peanuts, reserving a little for the garnish. Stir well, then add the Quorn, the dark soy sauce and the reserved marinade.

6 When hot, spoon on to serving plates and garnish with the remaining ground peanuts, the coriander and lemon.

Stir-fried Noodles with Beansprouts

Beansprouts are highly nutritious and make a valuable contribution to this low-fat dish, which combines egg noodles with peppers and soy sauce.

Ingredients

175g/6oz dried egg noodles
15ml/1 tbsp vegetable oil
1 garlic clove, finely chopped
1 small onion, halved and sliced
225g/8oz/1 cup beansprouts
1 small red (bell) pepper, seeded and cut into strips
1 small green (bell) pepper, seeded and cut into strips
2.5ml/½ tsp salt
1.5ml/¼ tsp ground white pepper
30ml/2 tbsp light soy sauce

Serves 4

1 Bring a pan of water to the boil. Cook the noodles for 4 minutes until just tender, or according to the instructions on the packet. Drain, refresh under cold water and drain again.

2 Heat the oil in a non-stick frying pan or wok. When the oil is very hot, add the garlic, stir briefly, then add the onion slices. Cook, stirring, for 1 minute, then add the beansprouts and peppers. Stir-fry for 2–3 minutes.

3 Stir in the cooked noodles and toss over the heat, using two spatulas or wooden spoons, for 2–3 minutes or until the ingredients are well mixed and have heated through.

4 Season to taste with salt and ground white pepper. Add the soy sauce and stir thoroughly before serving the noodle mixture in heated bowls.

Cook's Tip

Store beansprouts in the refrigerator and use within a day of purchase, as they tend to lose their crispness and become slimy and unpleasant quite quickly. The most commonly used beansprouts are sprouted mung beans, but you could use other types of beansprouts instead.

noodles w. chinese leaves Energy 444kcal/1857kJ; Protein 16g; Carbohydrate 77.6g, of which sugars 4.3g; Fat 6.5g, of which saturates 0.9g; Cholesterol 0mg; Calcium 230mg; Fibre 5g; Sodium 1227mg.
noodles w. beansprouts Energy 244kcal/1030kJ; Protein 8g; Carbohydrate 39.9g, of which sugars 7.8g; Fat 7g, of which saturates 1.5g; Cholesterol 13mg; Calcium 34mg; Fibre 3.5g; Sodium 352mg.

Crispy Fried Rice Vermicelli

This crisp tangle of fried rice vermicelli is tossed in a piquant sauce.

Ingredients

vegetable oil, for deep and shallow frying
175g/6oz rice vermicelli
15ml/1 tbsp chopped garlic
4–6 small dried red chillies
30ml/2 tbsp chopped shallots
15ml/1 tbsp dried shrimps, rinsed
115g/4oz minced (ground) pork
115g/4oz raw peeled prawns, (shrimp), chopped
30ml/2 tbsp brown bean sauce
30ml/2 tbsp rice wine vinegar
45ml/3 tbsp fish sauce
75g/3oz soft light brown sugar
30ml/2 tbsp lime juice
115g/4oz/½ cup beansprouts

For the garnish

2 spring onions, shredded
30ml/2 tbsp fresh coriander (cilantro) leaves
2-egg omelette, rolled and sliced
2 fresh red chillies, seeded and cut into thin strips

Serves 4–6

1 Heat oil for deep-frying. Break the vermicelli into 7.5cm/3in lengths and deep-fry in handfuls until they puff up. Lift out with a slotted spoon and drain on kitchen paper.

2 Heat 30ml/2 tbsp oil in a wok and fry the garlic, chillies, shallots and shrimps for about 1 minute. Add the pork and stir-fry for 3–4 minutes, until no longer pink. Add the prawns and fry for 2 minutes. Spoon into a bowl and set aside.

3 Add the brown bean sauce, vinegar, fish sauce and sugar. Bring to a gentle boil, stir to dissolve the sugar and cook until thick and syrupy.

4 Add the lime juice and adjust the seasoning. The sauce should be sweet, sour and salty. Add the pork and prawn mixture with the beansprouts and stir them into the sauce.

5 Add the fried rice noodles to the wok and toss gently to coat them in the sauce. Serve in warmed bowls, garnished with the spring onions, coriander leaves, omelette strips and chillies.

Toasted Noodles with Vegetables

Slightly crisp noodle cakes topped with vegetables make a superb dish.

Ingredients

15ml/1 tbsp vegetable oil
175g/6oz dried egg vermicelli, cooked and drained
2 garlic cloves, finely chopped
115g/4oz/1 cup baby corn cobs, halved lengthways
115g/4oz/1½ cups fresh shiitake mushrooms, halved
3 celery sticks, sliced
1 carrot, diagonally sliced
115g/4oz/½ cup mangetouts (snow peas)
75g/3oz/¾ cup sliced, drained, canned bamboo shoots
15ml/1 tbsp cornflour (cornstarch) mixed with 15ml/1 tbsp water
15ml/1 tbsp dark soy sauce
5ml/1 tsp sugar
300ml/½ pint/1¼ cups vegetable stock
salt and ground white pepper
spring onion (scallion) curls, to garnish

Serves 4

1 Heat 2.5ml/½ tsp oil in a non-stick frying pan or wok. When it starts to smoke, spread half the noodles over the base. Fry for 2–3 minutes until lightly toasted. Carefully turn the noodles over (they stick together like a cake), fry the other side, then slide on to a heated serving plate. Repeat with the remaining noodles to make two cakes. Keep hot.

2 Heat the remaining oil in the clean pan, then fry the garlic for a few seconds. Add the corn cobs and the mushrooms and stir-fry for 3 minutes. Add the remaining vegetables and stir-fry for 2 minutes or until the vegetables are crisp-tender.

3 Add the cornflour paste, soy sauce, sugar and stock. Cook, stirring, until the sauce thickens. Season, divide between the noodle cakes, garnish and serve.

Variation
Sliced fennel tastes good in this stir-fry, either as an addition or instead of the sliced bamboo shoots.

fried rice vermicelli Energy 204kcal/854kJ; Protein 10.6g; Carbohydrate 33.9g, of which sugars 4.3g; Fat 2.9g, of which saturates 0.6g; Cholesterol 76mg; Calcium 38mg; Fibre 1.2g; Sodium 206mg.
toasted noodles w. veg. Energy 230kcal/964kJ; Protein 7.9g; Carbohydrate 44.6g, of which sugars 5.4g; Fat 2.4g, of which saturates 0.3g; Cholesterol 0mg; Calcium 52mg; Fibre 2.8g; Sodium 623mg.

Prawn Noodle Salad

Light and refreshing, this salad has all the tangy flavour of the sea.

Ingredients

115g/4oz cellophane noodles, soaked in hot water until soft
16 cooked peeled prawns (shrimp)
1 small green (bell) pepper, seeded and cut into strips
½ cucumber, cut into strips
1 tomato, cut into strips
2 shallots, finely sliced
salt and ground black pepper
coriander (cilantro) leaves, to garnish

For the dressing

15ml/1 tbsp rice vinegar
30ml/2 tbsp fish sauce
30ml/2 tbsp fresh lime juice
pinch of salt
2.5ml/½ tsp fresh root ginger, grated
1 lemon grass stalk, finely chopped
1 fresh red chilli, seeded and finely sliced
30ml/2 tbsp mint, roughly chopped
few sprigs tarragon, roughly chopped
15ml/1 tbsp chopped chives

Serves 4

1 Make the dressing by combining all the ingredients in a small bowl or jug (pitcher); whisk well.

2 Drain the noodles, then plunge them in a saucepan of boiling water for 1 minute. Drain, rinse under cold running water and drain again well.

3 In a large bowl, combine the noodles with the prawns, pepper, cucumber, tomato and shallots. Lightly season with salt and pepper, then toss with the dressing.

4 Spoon the noodles on to individual plates, arranging the prawns on top. Garnish with a few of the coriander leaves and serve immediately.

Variation
Instead of prawns, try squid, scallops, mussels or crab.

Stir-fried Prawns with Noodles

One of the most appealing aspects of Asian food is its appearance. Ingredients are carefully chosen so that each dish, even a simple stir-fry like this one, is balanced in terms of colour, texture and flavour.

Ingredients

130g/4½oz rice noodles
30ml/2 tbsp groundnut (peanut) oil
1 large garlic clove, crushed
150g/5oz large prawns (shrimp), peeled and deveined
15g/½oz dried shrimp
1 piece mooli (daikon), about 75g/3oz, grated
15ml/1 tbsp fish sauce
30ml/2 tbsp soy sauce
30ml/2 tbsp light muscovado (brown) sugar
30ml/2 tbsp lime juice
90g/3½oz/⅓ cup beansprouts
40g/1½oz/⅓ cup peanuts, chopped
15ml/1 tbsp sesame oil
chopped coriander (cilantro), 5ml/1 tsp dried chilli flakes and 2 shallots, finely chopped, to garnish

Serves 4

1 Soak the noodles in a bowl of boiling water for 5 minutes, or according to the packet instructions. Heat the oil in a wok or large frying pan. Add the garlic, and stir-fry over a medium heat for 2–3 minutes, until golden brown.

2 Add the prawns, dried shrimp and grated mooli and stir-fry for a further 2 minutes. Stir in the fish sauce, soy sauce, sugar and lime juice.

3 Drain the noodles thoroughly, then snip them into smaller lengths with scissors. Add to the wok or pan with the beansprouts, peanuts and sesame oil. Toss to mix, then stir-fry for 2 minutes. Serve immediately, garnished with the coriander, chilli flakes and shallots.

Cook's Tip
Some cooks salt the mooli and leave it to drain, then rinse and dry before use.

prawn noodle salad Energy 156kcal/653kJ; Protein 7.4g; Carbohydrate 29.4g, of which sugars 5.4g; Fat 0.7g, of which saturates 0.1g; Cholesterol 49mg; Calcium 68mg; Fibre 2.1g; Sodium 417mg.
prawns w. noodles Energy 397kcal/1675kJ; Protein 21.3g; Carbohydrate 56.5g, of which sugars 3.2g; Fat 11.1g, of which saturates 2.4g; Cholesterol 89mg; Calcium 72mg; Fibre 3.3g; Sodium 567mg.

Singapore Noodles

Dried Chinese mushrooms add an intense flavour to this lightly curried dish.

Ingredients

20g/¾oz dried shiitake mushrooms
225g/8oz fine egg noodles
10ml/2 tsp sesame oil
45ml/3 tbsp groundnut (peanut) oil
2 garlic cloves, crushed
1 small onion, chopped
1 fresh green chilli, seeded and thinly sliced
10ml/2 tsp curry powder
115g/4oz green beans, halved
115g/4oz Chinese leaves (Chinese cabbage), thinly shredded
4 spring onions (scallions), sliced
30ml/2 tbsp soy sauce
115g/4oz cooked prawns (shrimp), peeled and deveined
salt

Serves 4

1 Soak the mushrooms for 30 minutes. Drain, reserving 30ml/2 tbsp of the water. Discard the stems and slice the caps.

2 Bring a pan of lightly salted water to the boil and cook the noodles according to the directions on the packet. Drain, tip into a bowl and toss with the sesame oil.

3 Heat the groundnut oil in a preheated wok and stir-fry the garlic, onion and chilli for 3 minutes. Stir in the curry powder and cook for 1 minute. Add the mushrooms, green beans, Chinese leaves and spring onions. Stir-fry for 3–4 minutes until the vegetables are tender, but still crisp.

4 Add the noodles, soy sauce, reserved mushroom soaking water and prawns. Toss over the heat for 2–3 minutes until the noodles and prawns are heated through.

Cook's Tip
Ring the changes with the vegetables used in this dish. Try mangetouts (snow peas), broccoli, sweet peppers or baby corn cobs. The prawns (shrimp) can be omitted.

Stir-fried Noodles in Seafood Sauce

Recent discoveries along the Yellow River suggest that the Chinese were enjoying noodles made from millet some 4000 years ago! If it was indeed the Chinese who invented pasta, it seems appropriate to include a Chinese-style pasta dish.

Ingredients

225g/8oz Chinese egg noodles
8 spring onions (scallions), trimmed
8 asparagus spears, plus extra steamed asparagus spears, to serve
5cm/2in piece fresh root ginger, peeled
30ml/2 tbsp stir-fry oil
3 garlic cloves, chopped
60ml/4 tbsp oyster sauce
450g/1lb cooked crab meat (all white, or two-thirds white and one-third brown)
30ml/2 tbsp rice wine vinegar
15–30ml/1–2 tbsp light soy sauce

Serves 4

1 Put the noodles in a large pan, cover with lightly salted boiling water, cover and leave for 3–4 minutes, or for the time suggested on the packet. Drain, tip into a bowl and set aside.

2 Cut off the green spring onion tops and slice them thinly. Set aside. Cut the white parts into 2cm/¾ in lengths and quarter them lengthways. Cut the asparagus spears on the diagonal into 2cm/¾ in pieces, and slice the ginger into very fine matchsticks.

3 Heat the stir-fry oil in a pan or wok until very hot, then add the ginger, garlic and white spring onion batons. Stir-fry over a high heat for 1 minute.

4 Add the oyster sauce, crab meat, rice wine vinegar and soy sauce to taste. Stir-fry for about 2 minutes, until the crab and sauce are hot. Add the noodles and toss until heated through.

5 At the last moment, toss in the spring onion tops and serve with a few extra asparagus spears.

singapore noodles Energy 314kcal/1316kJ; Protein 19.2g; Carbohydrate 50.3g, of which sugars 5.9g; Fat 4g, of which saturates 0.6g; Cholesterol 70mg; Calcium 74mg; Fibre 1.6g; Sodium 81mg.
noodles in sauce Energy 385kcal/1622kJ; Protein 28.5g; Carbohydrate 45.9g, of which sugars 6.4g; Fat 10.9g, of which saturates 2.2g; Cholesterol 98mg; Calcium 167mg; Fibre 2.4g; Sodium 1233mg.

Noodles with Crab & Mushrooms

This is a dish of contrasting flavours, textures and colours, and requires some skill and dexterity from the cook. While one hand gently turns the noodles in the pan, the other takes chunks of fresh crab meat and drops them into the steaming wok. Here the crab meat is cooked separately to make it easier.

Ingredients

25g/1oz dried cloud ear (wood ear) mushrooms, soaked in warm water for 20 minutes
115g/4oz dried cellophane noodles, soaked in warm water for 20 minutes
30ml/2 tbsp vegetable or sesame oil
3 shallots, halved and thinly sliced
2 garlic cloves, crushed
2 fresh green or red chillies, seeded and sliced
1 carrot, peeled and cut into thin diagonal rounds
5ml/1 tsp sugar
45ml/3 tbsp oyster sauce
15ml/1 tbsp soy sauce
225g/8oz fresh, raw crab meat, cut into bitesize chunks
ground black pepper
fresh coriander (cilantro) leaves, to garnish

Serves 4

1 Remove the centres from the soaked cloud ear mushrooms and cut the mushrooms in half. Drain the soaked noodles and cut them into 30cm/12in pieces and put aside.

2 Heat a wok and add 15ml/1 tbsp of the oil. Stir in the shallots, garlic and chillies, and cook until fragrant. Add the carrots and cook for 1 minute, then add the mushrooms and cook for 1 minute more. Stir in the sugar with the oyster and soy sauces, followed by the noodles. Pour in 400ml/14fl oz/1⅔ cups water or chicken stock, cover the wok and cook for about 5 minutes, or until the noodles are soft and have absorbed most of the sauce.

3 Meanwhile, heat the remaining oil in a heavy pan. Add the crab meat and cook until it is nicely pink and tender. Season well with black pepper. Arrange the noodles and crab meat on a serving dish and garnish with coriander.

Buckwheat Noodles with Salmon

Young pea sprouts are only available for a short time. You can substitute watercress, mustard cress, young leeks or your favourite green vegetable or herb in this dish.

Ingredients

225g/8oz buckwheat or soba noodles
15ml/1 tbsp oyster sauce
juice of ½ lemon
30–45ml/2–3 tbsp olive oil, preferably light oil
115g/4oz smoked salmon, cut into fine strips
115g/4oz young pea sprouts
2 ripe tomatoes, peeled, seeded and cut into strips
15ml/1 tbsp chopped chives
salt and ground black pepper

Serves 4

1 Cook the buckwheat or soba noodles in a large pan of boiling water, following the directions on the packet. Drain, then rinse under cold running water and drain well.

2 Tip the noodles into a large bowl. Add the oyster sauce and lemon juice and season with pepper to taste. Moisten with the olive oil and toss to coat the strands.

3 Add the smoked salmon, pea sprouts, tomatoes and chives. Mix well and serve at once, either straight from the bowl or on individual salad plates.

Cook's Tips

- *A light olive oil is recommended for this salad so that the delicate flavour of the pea sprouts is not overwhelmed. An alternative would be to use another light, flavourless oil, such as sunflower or safflower oil.*
- *Buckwheat noodles are pale in colour and pliable. They are often eaten with a thick, gravy-like sauce in China. They come in different shapes depending on how the dough is rolled. You might encounter round and long noodles, flat noodles, or thin noodle sheets where the dough has been pared with a knife.*

noodles w. crab Energy 252kcal/1051kJ; Protein 12.9g; Carbohydrate 35.7g, of which sugars 10.3g; Fat 6.3g, of which saturates 0.7g; Cholesterol 41mg; Calcium 97mg; Fibre 1.6g; Sodium 770mg.
noodles w. salmon Energy 343kcal/1443kJ; Protein 16.3g; Carbohydrate 47.9g, of which sugars 3.8g; Fat 10.9g, of which saturates 1.2g; Cholesterol 10mg; Calcium 29mg; Fibre 3.5g; Sodium 814mg.

Noodles with Prawns & Ham

This recipe combines prawns with ham and chicken, which may seem unconventional until you remember that the Spanish do something very similar in their paella.

Ingredients

30ml/2 tbsp vegetable oil
2 garlic cloves, sliced
5ml/1 tsp fresh root ginger, peeled and chopped
2 fresh red chillies, seeded and chopped
75g/3oz lean ham, thinly sliced
1 skinless chicken breast fillet, thinly sliced
16 uncooked tiger prawns (jumbo shrimp), peeled, tails left intact and deveined
115g/4oz green beans, trimmed
225g/8oz/1 cup beansprouts
50g/2oz Chinese chives
450g/1lb egg noodles, cooked in boiling water until tender, then drained
30ml/2 tbsp dark soy sauce
15ml/1 tbsp oyster sauce
salt and ground black pepper
5ml/1 tsp sesame oil
2 spring onions (scallions), cut into strips, and fresh coriander (cilantro) leaves, to garnish

Serves 4–6

1 Heat 15ml/1 tbsp of the oil in a wok or large frying pan. When the oil is hot, fry the garlic, ginger and chillies for 2 minutes, until aromatic.

2 Add the prepared ham, chicken, prawns and green beans to the wok or frying pan.

3 Stir-fry the meat for about 2 minutes over high heat or until the chicken and prawns are thoroughly cooked. Transfer the mixture to a bowl and set aside.

4 Heat the remaining oil in the wok or frying pan. When the oil is hot, add the beansprouts and Chinese chives. Stir-fry for 1–2 minutes.

5 Add the noodles and toss to mix. Season with soy sauce, oyster sauce, salt and pepper. Drizzle with sesame oil and serve in individual bowls, garnished with spring onions and coriander.

Curried Noodles with Chicken

Chicken or pork can be used in this tasty dish. It is so quick and easy to prepare and cooks in next to no time, making it the perfect snack for busy people.

Ingredients

30ml/2 tbsp vegetable oil
10ml/2 tsp magic paste
1 lemon grass stalk, finely chopped
5ml/1 tsp red curry paste
90g/3½oz skinless chicken breast fillets or pork fillet (tenderloin), sliced into thin strips
30ml/2 tbsp light soy sauce
400ml/14fl oz/1⅔ cups coconut milk
2 kaffir lime leaves, rolled into cylinders and thinly sliced
250g/9oz dried medium egg noodles
90g/3½oz Chinese leaves (Chinese cabbage), shredded
90g/3½oz spinach or watercress, shredded
juice of 1 lime
small bunch fresh coriander (cilantro) or flat leaf parsley, chopped

Serves 2

1 Heat the oil in a wok or large, heavy frying pan. Add the magic paste and lemon grass and stir-fry over a low to medium heat for 4–5 seconds, until they give off their aroma.

2 Stir in the curry paste, then add the strips of chicken or pork to the wok or pan. Stir-fry over a medium to high heat for 2 minutes, until the chicken or pork is coated in the paste and seared on all sides.

3 Add the soy sauce, coconut milk and sliced lime leaves. Bring the coconut milk to a simmer, then add the noodles. Simmer gently for about 4 minutes, tossing the mixture occasionally to make sure that the noodles cook evenly and do not clump together.

4 Add the Chinese leaves and the shredded spinach or watercress. Stir well. Add the lime juice. Spoon into a serving bowl or two individual bowls, sprinkle with the chopped fresh coriander or parsley, and serve.

noodles w. prawns/ham Energy 302kcal/1277kJ; Protein 25.9g; Carbohydrate 35.5g, of which sugars 2.6g; Fat 7.3g, of which saturates 1.7g; Cholesterol 122mg; Calcium 56mg; Fibre 2.4g; Sodium 1031mg.
noodles w. chicken Energy 702kcal/2965kJ; Protein 28.7g; Carbohydrate 101.6g, of which sugars 14.2g; Fat 23g, of which saturates 4.9g; Cholesterol 69mg; Calcium 187mg; Fibre 4.7g; Sodium 1564mg.

Sesame Duck & Noodle Salad

This salad is complete in itself and makes a lovely summer lunch.

Ingredients
2 skinless duck breast fillets
1 tbsp oil
150g/5oz sugar snap peas
2 carrots, cut into 7.5cm/3in batons
225g/8oz medium egg noodles
6 spring onions (scallions), sliced
salt
30ml/2 tbsp coriander (cilantro) leaves, to garnish

For the marinade
15ml/1 tbsp sesame oil
5ml/1 tsp ground coriander
5ml/1 tsp five-spice powder

For the dressing
15ml/1 tbsp garlic vinegar or white wine vinegar
5ml/1 tsp soft light brown sugar
5ml/1 tsp soy sauce
15ml/1 tbsp toasted sesame seeds
45ml/3 tbsp sunflower oil
30ml/2 tbsp sesame oil
ground black pepper

Serves 4

1 Slice the duck breast fillets thinly across and put them in a shallow dish. Mix the ingredients for the marinade, pour over the duck and coat thoroughly. Cover and leave to marinate in a cool place for 30 minutes.

2 Heat the oil in a frying pan, add the slices of duck breast and stir-fry for 3-4 minutes until cooked. Set aside.

3 Bring a pan of lightly salted water to the boil. Place the sugar snap peas and carrots in a steamer that will fit on top of the pan. When the water boils, add the noodles. Place the steamer on top and steam the vegetables, while cooking the noodles for the time suggested on the packet. Set the steamed vegetables aside. Drain the noodles, refresh them under cold running water and drain again. Place them in a serving bowl.

4 Make the dressing by whisking all the ingredients in a bowl. Pour over the noodles and mix well. Add the sugar snap peas, carrots, spring onions and duck slices and toss to mix. Garnish with the coriander leaves and serve.

Shredded Duck & Noodle Salad

This piquant marinated duck salad makes a mouthwatering first course or a delicious light meal. If you like, toss the salad in a quick and easy dressing made by whisking together soy sauce, mirin, sugar, garlic and chilli oil.

Ingredients
4 skinless duck breast fillets, sliced
30ml/2 tbsp Chinese rice wine
10ml/2 tsp finely grated fresh root ginger
60ml/4 tbsp soy sauce
15ml/1 tbsp sesame oil
15ml/1 tbsp clear honey
10ml/2 tsp five-spice powder
toasted sesame seeds, to sprinkle

For the noodles
150g/5oz cellophane noodles, cooked
large handful of fresh mint and coriander (cilantro) leaves
1 red (bell) pepper, seeded and finely sliced
4 spring onions (scallions), finely shredded and sliced
50g/2oz mixed salad leaves

Serves 4

1 Place the duck breast slices in a non-metallic bowl. Mix together the rice wine, ginger, soy sauce, sesame oil, clear honey and five-spice powder. Toss to coat, cover and marinate in the refrigerator for 3–4 hours.

2 Heat the oil in a frying pan, add the slices of duck breast and stir-fry for 3-4 minutes until cooked. Set aside.

3 Double over a large sheet of heavy foil. Place the foil on a heatproof plate. Place the duck breast portions on it and spoon the marinade over. Fold the foil to enclose the duck and juices and scrunch the edges to seal. Steam on a rack over simmering water for 50–60 minutes, then leave to rest for 15 minutes.

4 Mix the noodles, herbs, red pepper, spring onions and salad leaves in a bowl. Remove the skin from the duck and shred the flesh. Divide the noodle salad among four plates and top with the duck. Sprinkle with the sesame seeds and serve immediately.

sesame duck & noodle Energy 550kcal/2301kJ; Protein 25.3g; Carbohydrate 47g, of which sugars 4.2g; Fat 31.6g, of which saturates 5.2g; Cholesterol 99mg; Calcium 70mg; Fibre 4.5g; Sodium 192mg.
shredded duck salad Energy 398kcal/1671kJ; Protein 32.8g; Carbohydrate 41.7g, of which sugars 10.8g; Fat 11.6g, of which saturates 2.2g; Cholesterol 165mg; Calcium 40mg; Fibre 1g; Sodium 1688mg.

Lamb & Ginger Noodle Stir-fry

Fresh root ginger adds a bright tang to this lamb and noodle dish, giving it a simultaneously hot and yet refreshing taste.

Ingredients

45ml/3 tbsp sesame oil
3 spring onions (scallions), sliced
2 garlic cloves, crushed
2.5cm/1in piece fresh root ginger, peeled and finely sliced
1 fresh red chilli, seeded and finely sliced
1 red (bell) pepper, seeded and sliced
450g/1lb lean boneless lamb, cut into fine strips
115g/4oz/1½ cups fresh shiitake mushrooms, sliced
2 carrots, cut into matchstick strips
300g/11oz fresh Chinese egg noodles
300g/11oz pak choi (bok choy), shredded
soy sauce, to serve

Serves 4

1 Heat half the oil in a wok. Stir-fry the spring onions and garlic for about 5 minutes, or until golden. Add the ginger, chilli and red pepper and fry for 5 minutes more, until the chilli and pepper start to soften. Remove the vegetables and set aside.

2 Add the remaining oil and stir-fry the lamb in batches until golden. Add the mushrooms and carrots and stir-fry for 2–3 minutes.

3 Remove the lamb mixture from the wok and set aside with the red pepper mixture. Add the noodles and pak choi to the wok and stir-fry for 5 minutes.

4 Finally, replace all the cooked ingredients and stir-fry for a couple more minutes. Serve in heated bowls, with soy sauce.

Cook's Tip
If fresh egg noodles are not available, use the dried type. Cook them according to the packet instructions, drain and rinse under cold water, then drain well.

Wheat Noodles with Stir-fried Pork

Dried wheat noodles, sold in straight bundles like sticks, are versatile and robust. They keep well, so are handy items to have in the storecupboard, ready for quick and easy recipes like this one.

Ingredients

225g/8oz pork loin, cut into thin strips
225g/8oz dried wheat noodles, soaked in lukewarm water for 20 minutes
15ml/1 tbsp groundnut (peanut) oil
2 garlic cloves, finely chopped
2–3 spring onions (scallions), trimmed and chopped
45ml/3 tbsp kroeung or magic paste
15ml/1 tbsp fish sauce
30ml/2 tbsp unsalted roasted peanuts, finely chopped
chilli oil, for drizzling

For the marinade

30ml/2 tbsp fish sauce
30ml/2 tbsp soy sauce
15ml/1 tbsp peanut oil
10ml/2 tsp sugar

Serves 4

1 In a bowl, combine the ingredients for the marinade, stirring constantly until the all the sugar dissolves. Toss in the strips of pork, making sure that they are well coated in the marinade. Put aside for 30 minutes.

2 Drain the wheat noodles. Bring a large pan of water to the boil. Drop in the noodles, untangling them with chopsticks, if necessary. Cook for 4–5 minutes, until tender.

3 Drain the noodles thoroughly, then divide them among individual serving bowls. Keep the noodles warm until the dish is ready to serve.

4 Meanwhile, heat a wok. Add the oil and stir-fry the garlic and spring onions, until fragrant. Add the pork, tossing it around the wok for 2 minutes. Stir in the kroeung or magic paste and fish sauce for 2 minutes – add a splash of water if the wok gets too dry – and tip the pork on top of the noodles. Sprinkle the peanuts over the top and drizzle with chilli oil to serve.

lamb & ginger Energy 820kcal/3418kJ; Protein 46g; Carbohydrate 76.4g, of which sugars 9.4g; Fat 36g, of which saturates 11.7g; Cholesterol 143mg; Calcium 55mg; Fibre 4.1g; Sodium 709mg.
noodles w. pork Energy 340kcal/1435kJ; Protein 19.6g; Carbohydrate 46g, of which sugars 4.4g; Fat 9.9g, of which saturates 1.4g; Cholesterol 35mg; Calcium 23mg; Fibre 1.9g; Sodium 41mg.

Cellophane Noodles with Pork

Simple, speedy and very satisfying, this is an excellent way of using mung bean noodles. It scores high on presentation too, thanks to the contrast between the translucent, thread-like noodles and the vibrant colour of the vegetables.

Ingredients

200g/7oz cellophane noodles
30ml/2 tbsp vegetable oil
15ml/1 tbsp magic paste
200g/7oz minced (ground) pork
1 fresh green or red chilli, seeded and finely chopped
300g/11oz/scant 1½ cups beansprouts
bunch spring onions (scallions), finely chopped
30ml/2 tbsp soy sauce
30ml/2 tbspfish sauce
30ml/2 tbsp sweet chilli sauce
15ml/1 tbsp light brown sugar
30ml/2 tbsp rice vinegar
30ml/2 tbsp roasted peanuts, chopped, to garnish
small bunch fresh coriander (cilantro), chopped, to garnish

Serves 2

1 Place the noodles in a large bowl, cover with boiling water and soak for 10 minutes. Drain the noodles and set aside until ready to use.

2 Heat the oil in a wok or large, heavy frying pan. Add the magic paste and stir-fry for 2–3 seconds, then add the pork. Stir-fry the meat, breaking it up with a wooden spatula, for 2–3 minutes, until browned all over.

3 Add the chopped chilli to the meat and stir-fry for 3–4 seconds, then add the beansprouts and chopped spring onions, stir-frying for a few seconds after each addition.

4 Snip the noodles into 5cm/2in lengths and add to the wok or pan, with the soy sauce, fish sauce, sweet chilli sauce, sugar and rice vinegar.

5 Toss the ingredients together over the heat until the noodles have warmed through. Pile on to a platter or into a large bowl. Sprinkle the peanuts and coriander over the top and serve.

Rice Rolls Stuffed with Pork

Steamed rice sheets are very tasty when filled with pork, rolled up, drizzled in herb oil, and then dipped in a hot chilli sauce. Generally, they are eaten as a snack, or served as a starter.

Ingredients

25g/1oz dried cloud ear (wood ear) mushrooms, soaked in warm water for 30 minutes
350g/12oz minced (ground) pork
30nl/2 tbsp fish sauce
10ml/2 tsp sugar
15ml/1 tbsp vegetable or groundnut (peanut) oil
2 garlic cloves, finely chopped
2 shallots, finely chopped
2 spring onions (scallions), trimmed and finely chopped
24 fresh rice sheets, 7.5cm/3in square
ground black pepper
herb oil, for drizzling
hot chilli sauce, for dipping

Serves 6

1 Drain the mushrooms and squeeze out any excess water. Cut off and discard the hard stems. Finely chop the rest of the mushrooms and put them in a bowl. Add the minced pork, fish sauce, and sugar and mix well.

2 Heat the oil in a wok or heavy pan. Add the garlic, shallots and onions. Stir-fry until golden. Add the pork mixture and stir-fry for 5–6 minutes, until the pork is cooked. Season with pepper.

3 Place the rice sheets on a flat surface. Spoon a tablespoon of the pork mixture onto the middle of each sheet. Fold one side over the filling, tuck in the sides, and roll to enclose the filling, so that it resembles a short spring roll.

4 Place the filled rice rolls on a serving plate, drizzle with herb oil, and serve with chilli sauce.

Cook's Tip

To make life easy, prepared, fresh rice sheets are available in Asian markets and grocery stores.

noodles w. pork Energy 593kcal/2504kJ; Protein 47.8g; Carbohydrate 72.1g, of which sugars 4.7g; Fat 14.6g, of which saturates 2.8g; Cholesterol 106mg; Calcium 53mg; Fibre 3.2g; Sodium 1461mg.
rice rolls stuffed w. pork Energy 160kcal/670kJ; Protein 13.8g; Carbohydrate 16g, of which sugars 2.4g; Fat 4.4g, of which saturates 1.1g; Cholesterol 37mg; Calcium 13mg; Fibre 0.6g; Sodium 43mg.

Crispy Noodles with Beef

Rice vermicelli is deep-fried before being added to this multi-textured dish.

Ingredients

450g/1lb rump (round) steak
teriyaki sauce, for brushing
175g/6oz rice vermicelli
groundnut (peanut) oil, for deep-frying and stir-frying
8 spring onions (scallions), diagonally sliced
2 garlic cloves, crushed
4–5 carrots, cut into julienne strips
1–2 fresh red chillies, seeded and finely sliced
2 small courgettes (zucchini), diagonally sliced
5ml/1 tsp grated fresh root ginger
60ml/4 tbsp rice vinegar
90ml/6 tbsp light soy sauce
about 475ml/16fl oz/2 cups spicy stock

Serves 4

1 Beat the steak to about 2.5cm/1in thick. Place in a shallow dish, brush with teriyaki sauce and marinate for 2–4 hours.

2 Separate the rice vermicelli into manageable loops. Pour oil into a large wok to a depth of about 5cm/2in, and heat until a strand of vermicelli cooks as soon as it is lowered into the oil.

3 Carefully add a loop of vermicelli to the oil. Almost immediately, turn to cook on the other side, then remove and drain on kitchen paper. Repeat with the remaining loops. Transfer the cooked noodles to a bowl and keep them warm.

4 Clean out the wok and heat 15ml/1 tbsp groundnut oil. Fry the steak for about 30 seconds on each side, then remove and cut into thick slices.

5 Add a little extra oil to the wok, and stir-fry the spring onions, garlic and carrots for 5–6 minutes. Add the chillies, courgettes and ginger and stir-fry for 1–2 minutes.

6 Stir in the rice vinegar, soy sauce and stock. Cook for 4 minutes until the sauce has thickened slightly. Return the steak to the wok and cook for a further 1–2 minutes. Spoon the steak, vegetables and sauce over the noodles and toss lightly.

Chap Chae

A Korean stir-fry of beef, mixed vegetables and noodles.

Ingredients

225g/8oz rump (round) steak
marinade (see Cook's Tip)
115g/4oz cellophane noodles, soaked for 20 minutes in hot water to cover, then drained
4 Chinese dried mushrooms, soaked, stems removed, caps sliced
oil, for stir-frying
2 eggs, separated
1 carrot, cut into matchsticks
1 onion, sliced
2 courgettes (zucchini) and ½ red (bell) pepper, cut into strips
4 button mushrooms, sliced
75g/3oz/⅓ cup beansprouts
15ml/1 tbsp light soy sauce
salt and ground black pepper
sliced spring onions (scallions) and sesame seeds, to garnish

Serves 4

1 Put the steak in the freezer until it is firm enough to cut into 5cm/2in strips, and mix with the marinade in a shallow dish. Cook the noodles in boiling water for 5 minutes. Drain and snip into short lengths.

2 For the garnish, first fry the beaten egg yolks and then the whites in oil in a small frying pan. When set, remove, cut into diamond shapes and set aside.

3 Heat the oil in a wok. Drain the beef and stir-fry it until it changes colour. Add the vegetables; cook until crisp and tender.

4 Add the noodles and season with soy sauce, salt and pepper. Cook for 1 minute. Spoon into a serving dish and garnish with egg diamonds, spring onions and sesame seeds.

Cook's Tip

To make the marinade, blend together 15ml/1 tbsp sugar, 30ml/2 tbsp light soy sauce, 45ml/3 tbsp sesame oil, 4 finely chopped spring onions (scallions), 1 crushed garlic clove and 10ml/2 tsp crushed toasted sesame seeds.

crispy noodles w. beef Energy 410kcal/1712kJ; Protein 30.7g; Carbohydrate 41.4g, of which sugars 6.6g; Fat 13.5g, of which saturates 3g; Cholesterol 66mg; Calcium 49mg; Fibre 1.9g; Sodium 1687mg.
chap chae Energy 321kcal/1337kJ; Protein 19.6g; Carbohydrate 28.5g, of which sugars 4.2g; Fat 14g, of which saturates 3.7g; Cholesterol 128mg; Calcium 52mg; Fibre 1.6g; Sodium 348mg.

Chow Mein

This is a hugely popular way of dealing with leftovers.

Ingredients
225g/8oz lean beef steak
225g/8oz can bamboo shoots, drained
1 leek, trimmed
25g/1oz dried shiitake mushrooms, soaked until soft
150g/5oz Chinese leaves (Chinese cabbage)
450g/1lb cooked egg noodles, drained
90ml/6 tbsp vegetable oil
30ml/2 tbsp dark soy sauce
15ml/1 tbsp cornflour (cornstarch)
15ml/1 tbsp dry sherry
5ml/1 tsp sesame oil
5ml/1 tsp caster (superfine) sugar
salt and ground black pepper

Serves 2–3

1 Slice the beef, bamboo shoots and leek into matchsticks. Drain the mushrooms, reserving 90ml/6 tbsp of the soaking water. Cut off and discard the stems, then slice the caps. Chop the Chinese leaves and sprinkle with salt. Pat the noodles dry.

2 Heat a third of the oil in a large frying pan and sauté the noodles. After turning them over once, use a wooden spatula to press against the bottom of the pan until they form a flat, even cake. Cook for about 4 minutes or until crisp at the bottom. Turn over, cook for 3 minutes more, then slide on to a heated plate and keep warm.

3 Heat 30ml/2 tbsp of the remaining oil in a wok. Add the leek and meat strips and stir-fry for 10–15 seconds. Sprinkle over half the soy sauce and then add the bamboo shoots and mushrooms. Toss for 1 minute, then push to one side.

4 Heat the remaining oil in the centre of the wok and sauté the Chinese leaves for 1 minute. Mix with the meat and vegetables and toss together for 30 seconds.

5 Mix the cornflour with the reserved mushroom water. Stir into the wok with the sherry, sesame oil, sugar and remaining soy sauce. Cook for 15 seconds to thicken, then serve with the noodle cake.

Special Chow Mein

A more elaborate chow mein, this shows how extra ingredients can be incorporated. Chinese sausages are available from most Chinese supermarkets.

Ingredients
450g/1lb egg noodles
45ml/3 tbsp vegetable oil
2 garlic cloves, sliced
5ml/1 tsp chopped fresh root ginger
2 fresh red chillies, seeded and chopped
2 Chinese sausages, total weight about 75g/3oz, rinsed and sliced (optional)
1 skinless, boneless chicken breast portion, thinly sliced
16 uncooked tiger prawns (jumbo shrimp), peeled, tails left intact, and deveined
115g/4oz/scant 1 cup green beans
225g/8oz/1 cup beansprouts
small bunch garlic chives
30ml/2 tbsp soy sauce
15ml/1 tbsp oyster sauce
15ml/1 tbsp sesame oil
salt and ground black pepper
2 shredded spring onions (scallions) and fresh coriander (cilantro) leaves, to garnish

Serves 4–6

1 Cook the noodles in a large pan of boiling water, according to the instructions on the packet. Drain well.

2 Heat 15ml/1 tbsp of the oil in a wok and stir-fry the garlic, ginger and chillies for 2 minutes. Add the sausage slices, if using, with the chicken, prawns and beans. Stir-fry over a high heat for 2 minutes, or until the chicken and prawns are cooked. Transfer the mixture to a bowl and set aside.

3 Heat the rest of the oil in the wok. Add the beansprouts and garlic chives and stir-fry for 1–2 minutes. Add the drained noodles and toss over the heat to mix. Season with the soy sauce, oyster sauce and salt and pepper to taste. Return the prawn mixture to the wok. Mix well with the noodles and toss until heated through.

4 Stir in the sesame oil. Spoon into a warmed bowl and serve, garnished with the spring onions and coriander leaves.

chow mein Energy 604kcal/2541kJ; Protein 41.1g; Carbohydrate 71.5g, of which sugars 15.1g; Fat 18.9g, of which saturates 4.5g; Cholesterol 100mg; Calcium 115mg; Fibre 7.4g; Sodium 1194mg.
special chow mein Energy 359kcal/1516kJ; Protein 19.6g; Carbohydrate 47.6g, of which sugars 2.9g; Fat 11.4g, of which saturates 2.3g; Cholesterol 106mg; Calcium 53mg; Fibre 2.3g; Sodium 1102mg.

Fried Noodles with Beef & Saté

If you relish chillies and peanuts, this delicious dish makes the perfect choice, but remember – it's fiery.

Ingredients

15–30ml/1–2 tbsp vegetable oil
300g/11oz beef sirloin, cut against the grain into thin slices
225g/8oz dried rice sticks (vermicelli), soaked in warm water for 20 minutes
225g/8oz/1 cup beansprouts
5–10ml/1–2 tsp fish sauce
1 small bunch each of fresh basil and mint, stalks removed, leaves shredded, to garnish
pickles, to serve

For the saté

4 dried Serrano chillies, seeded
60ml/4 tbsp groundnut (peanut) oil
4–5 garlic cloves, crushed
5–10ml/1–2 tsp curry powder
40g/1½oz/⅓ cup roasted peanuts, finely ground

Serves 4

1 To make the saté, grind the Serrano chillies in a mortar with a pestle. Heat the oil in a heavy pan and stir in the garlic until it begins to colour. Add the chillies, curry powder and the peanuts and stir over a low heat, until the mixture forms a paste. Remove the pan from the heat and leave the mixture to cool.

2 Heat a wok or heavy pan, and pour in 15ml/1 tbsp of the oil. Add the sliced beef and cook for 1–2 minutes, and stir in 7.5ml/1½ tsp of the spicy peanut saté. Tip the beef on to a clean plate and set aside. Drain the rice sticks.

3 Add 7.5ml/1½ tsp oil to the wok and add the rice sticks and 15ml/1 tbsp saté. Toss the noodles until coated and cook for 4–5 minutes. Toss in the beef for 1 minute, then add the beansprouts with the fish sauce. Tip the noodles on to a serving dish and sprinkle with the basil and mint. Serve with pickles.

Variation
Prawns (shrimp), pork or chicken can be used instead of beef, and the fresh herbs can be varied accordingly.

Bamie Goreng

This fried noodle dish is wonderfully accommodating. You can add other vegetables, such as mushrooms, tiny pieces of chayote, broccoli, leeks or beansprouts. Use whatever is to hand, balancing textures, colours and flavours.

Ingredients

450g/1lb dried egg noodles
2 eggs
25g/1oz/2 tbsp butter
90ml/6 tbsp vegetable oil
1 chicken breast fillet, sliced
115g/4oz pork fillet (tenderloin), sliced
115g/4oz calf's liver, sliced (optional)
2 garlic cloves, crushed
115g/4oz peeled cooked prawns (shrimp)
115g/4oz pak choi (bok choy)
2 celery sticks, finely sliced
4 spring onions (scallions), shredded
about 60ml/4 tbsp chicken stock
dark soy sauce and light soy sauce
salt and ground black pepper
deep-fried onions and shredded spring onions (scallions), to garnish

Serves 6–8

1 Cook the noodles in a pan of lightly salted water for about 3–4 minutes. Drain, rinse and drain again. Set aside.

2 Put the eggs in a bowl, beat and season to taste. Heat the butter with 5ml/1 tsp oil in a small pan, add the eggs and stir over a low heat until scrambled but still moist. Set aside.

3 Heat the remaining oil in a wok and fry the chicken, pork and liver, if using, with the garlic for 2–3 minutes, until the meat has changed colour. Add the prawns, pak choi, sliced celery and shredded spring onions and toss to mix.

4 Add the noodles and toss over the heat until the prawns and noodles are heated through and the greens are lightly cooked. Add enough stock to moisten, and season with dark and light soy sauce to taste. Add the scrambled eggs and toss to mix. Spoon on to a serving platter and serve, garnished with onions.

noodles w. beef & saté Energy 566kcal/2353kJ; Protein 24.4g; Carbohydrate 50.5g, of which sugars 2.1g; Fat 28.8g, of which saturates 5.7g; Cholesterol 44mg; Calcium 52mg; Fibre 2.3g; Sodium 253mg.
bamie goreng Energy 478kcal/2010kJ; Protein 16.8g; Carbohydrate 64.2g, of which sugars 5.1g; Fat 18.9g, of which saturates 3.2g; Cholesterol 86mg; Calcium 323mg; Fibre 2.9g; Sodium 466mg.

Stir-fried Chinese Leaves

This simple way of cooking Chinese leaves preserves their delicate flavour and is very quick to prepare.

Ingredients

675g/1½lb Chinese leaves (Chinese cabbage)
15ml/1 tbsp vegetable oil
2 garlic cloves, finely chopped
2.5 m/1in piece of fresh root ginger, finely chopped
2.5ml/½ tsp salt
15ml/1 tbsp oyster sauce
4 spring onions (scallions), cut into 2.5cm/1in lengths

Serves 4

1 Stack the Chinese leaves together and cut them into 2.5cm/1in slices.

2 Heat the oil in a wok or large deep pan. Stir-fry the garlic and ginger for 1 minute.

3 Add the Chinese leaves to the wok or pan and stir-fry for 2 minutes. Sprinkle the salt over and drizzle with the oyster sauce. Toss the leaves over the heat for 2 minutes more.

4 Stir in the spring onions. Toss the mixture well, transfer it to a heated serving plate and serve.

Variation

Use the same treatment for shredded cabbage and leeks. If you want to cut down on preparation time, you can often find this combination of vegetables, ready-prepared, in bags at the supermarket.

Cook's Tip

For guests who are vegetarian, substitute 15 ml/1 tbsp light soy sauce and 5ml/1 tsp of caster (superfine) sugar for the oyster sauce. This rule can be applied to many dishes.

Stir-fried Beansprouts

This fresh and crunchy vegetable, which is synonymous with Chinese restaurants, tastes even better when stir-fried at home.

Ingredients

15ml/1 tbsp vegetable oil
1 garlic clove, finely chopped
5ml/1 tsp grated fresh root ginger
1 small carrot, cut into matchsticks
50g/2oz/½ cup canned bamboo shoots, drained and cut into matchsticks
450g/1lb/2 cups beansprouts
2.5ml/½ tsp salt
large pinch of ground white pepper
15ml/1 tbsp Chinese rice wine or dry sherry
15ml/1 tbsp light soy sauce
2.5ml/½ tsp sesame oil

Serves 4

1 Heat the vegetable oil in a non-stick frying pan or wok. Add the chopped garlic and grated ginger and stir-fry for a few minutes, over a high heat.

2 Add the carrot and bamboo shoot matchsticks to the pan or wok and stir-fry for a few minutes.

3 Add the beansprouts to the pan or wok with the salt and pepper. Drizzle over the rice wine or sherry and toss the beansprouts over the heat for 3 minutes until hot.

4 Sprinkle over the soy sauce and sesame oil, toss to mix thoroughly, then spoon into a bowl and serve immediately.

Variation

Add a handful of almond slices, grilled (broiled) until golden.

Cook's Tip

Beansprouts keep best when stored in the refrigerator or other cool place in a bowl of cold water, but you must remember to change the water daily.

stir-fried chinese leaves Energy 77kcal/321kJ; Protein 2.6g; Carbohydrate 9.8g, of which sugars 9.6g; Fat 3.2g, of which saturates 0.3g; Cholesterol 0mg; Calcium 87mg; Fibre 3.7g; Sodium 74mg.
stir-fried beansprouts Energy 76kcal/318kJ; Protein 3.9g; Carbohydrate 6.9g, of which sugars 4.5g; Fat 3.4g, of which saturates 0.5g; Cholesterol 0mg; Calcium 31mg; Fibre 2.3g; Sodium 278mg.

Spinach with Spicy Chickpeas

This richly flavoured dish makes an excellent accompaniment to a dry curry, or with a rice-based stir fry. It is particularly good served drizzled with a little plain yogurt – the sharp, creamy flavour complements the complex spices perfectly.

Ingredients

200g/7oz dried chickpeas
30ml/2 tbsp sunflower oil
2 onions, halved and thinly sliced
10ml/2 tsp ground coriander
10ml/2 tsp ground cumin
5ml/1 tsp hot chilli powder
2.5ml/½ tsp ground turmeric
15ml/1 tbsp medium curry powder
400g/14oz can chopped tomatoes
5ml/1 tsp caster (superfine) sugar
salt and ground black pepper
30ml/2 tbsp chopped mint leaves
115g/4oz baby leaf spinach
steamed rice or bread, to serve

Serves 4

1 Soak the chickpeas in cold water overnight. Drain, rinse and place in a large pan. Cover with water and bring to the boil. Reduce the heat and simmer for 45 minutes to 1¼ hours, or until just tender. Drain and set aside.

2 Heat the oil in a wok, add the onions and cook over a low heat for 15 minutes, until lightly golden.

3 Add the ground coriander and cumin, chilli powder, turmeric and curry powder to the onions in the wok and stir-fry for 1–2 minutes.

4 Add the tomatoes, sugar and 105ml/7 tbsp water to the wok and bring to the boil. Cover, reduce the heat and simmer gently for 15 minutes, stirring occasionally.

5 Add the chickpeas to the wok, season well and cook gently for 8–10 minutes. Stir in the chopped mint.

6 Divide the spinach leaves between shallow bowls, top with the chickpea mixture and serve with some steamed rice or chunks of bread.

Cabbage in Coconut Milk

The idea of cooking cabbage in coconut milk comes from Melaka and Johor, where the culinary culture is influenced by the Chinese, Malay, and Peranakans. With good agricultural ground, there is an abundance of vegetables which, in this part of Malaysia, are often cooked in coconut milk. For this dish, you could use green beans, curly kale, or any type of cabbage, all of which are delicious served with steamed, braised or grilled fish dishes.

Ingredients

4 shallots, chopped
2 garlic cloves, chopped
1 lemon grass stalk, trimmed and chopped
25g/1oz fresh root ginger, peeled and chopped
2 red chillies, seeded and chopped
5ml/1 tsp shrimp paste
5ml/1 tsp turmeric powder
5ml/1 tsp palm sugar (jaggery)
15ml/1 tbsp sesame or groundnut (peanut) oil
400ml/14fl oz/1⅔ cups coconut milk
450g/1lb Chinese leaves (Chinese cabbage) or kale, cut into thick ribbons, or pak choi (bok choy), separated into leaves, or a mixture of the two
salt and ground black pepper

Serves 4

1 Using a mortar and pestle or food processor, grind the shallots, garlic, lemon grass, ginger and chillies to a paste. Scrape into a bowl and add the shrimp paste, turmeric and sugar. Beat well to combine the ingredients.

2 Heat the oil in a wok or heavy pan, and stir in the spice paste. Cook until fragrant and beginning to colour.

3 Pour in the coconut milk, mix well, and let it bubble it up to thicken.

4 Drop in the cabbage leaves, coating them in the coconut milk, and cook for a minute or two until wilted. Season with salt and pepper to taste, spoon into a warmed serving dish and serve immediately.

spinach w. chickpeas Energy 267kcal/1122kJ; Protein 13.3g; Carbohydrate 35.5g, of which sugars 10.2g; Fat 9g, of which saturates 1.1g; Cholesterol 0mg; Calcium 170mg; Fibre 8.2g; Sodium 83mg.
cabbage/coconut Energy 112kcal/469kJ; Protein 2.1g; Carbohydrate 13g, of which sugars 12.6g; Fat 6.1g, of which saturates 1g; Cholesterol 0mg; Calcium 89mg; Fibre 2.6g; Sodium 119mg.

Morning Glory with Fried Shallots

This recipe isn't a novel way of using the pretty creeper that twines along your fence, but rather relates to its Asian cousin. This leafy annual vine requires a good deal of moisture to grow and favours boggy ground, hence the synonym "swamp cabbage". It is widely cultivated in China and South-east Asia.

Ingredients

2 bunches morning glory, total weight about 250g/9oz, trimmed and coarsely chopped into 2.5cm/1in lengths
30ml/2 tbsp vegetable oil
4 shallots, thinly sliced
6 large garlic cloves, thinly sliced
sea salt
1.5ml/¼ tsp dried chilli flakes

Serves 4

1 Place the morning glory in a steamer and steam over a pan of boiling water for 30 seconds, until just wilted. If necessary, cook it in batches. Place the leaves in a bowl or spread them out on a large serving plate.

2 Heat the oil in a wok and stir-fry the shallots and garlic over a medium to high heat until golden. Spoon the mixture over the morning glory, sprinkle with a little sea salt and the chilli flakes and serve immediately.

Cook's Tip

Other names for morning glory include water spinach, water convolvulus and swamp cabbage. It is a green leafy vegetable with long jointed stems and arrow-shaped leaves. The stems remain crunchy while the leaves wilt like spinach when cooked. It is a staple stir-fry ingredient of many South-east Asian cultures, and works best when prepared simply, as here.

Variation

Use spinach instead of morning glory, or substitute young spring greens (collards), sprouting broccoli or Swiss chard. The texture may be tougher, so blanch leaves before using if necessary.

Asian-style Courgette Fritters

This is an excellent cultural fusion: a twist on Japanese tempura, using Indian spices and gram flour in the batter. Also known as besan, gram flour is more commonly used in Indian cooking and gives a wonderfully crisp texture, while the courgette baton inside becomes meltingly tender. If you're feeling adventurous, vary the vegetable content by dipping some thinly sliced squash or pumpkin batons with the courgettes. This is an ideal treat for kids.

Ingredients

90g/3½oz/¾ cup gram flour
5ml/1 tsp baking powder
2.5ml/½ tsp ground turmeric
10ml/2 tsp ground coriander
5ml/1 tsp ground cumin
5ml/1 tsp chilli powder
250ml/8fl oz/1 cup beer
600g/1lb 6oz courgettes (zucchini), cut into batons
sunflower oil, for deep-frying
salt
steamed basmati rice, natural (plain) yogurt and pickles, to serve

Serves 4

1 Sift the gram flour, baking powder, turmeric, coriander, cumin and chilli powder into a large bowl. Stir lightly to mix through.

2 Season the mixture with salt and make a hollow in the centre. Pour in a little of the beer, and gradually mix in the surrounding dry ingredients. Add more beer, continuing to mix gently, to make a thick batter. Be careful not to overmix.

3 Fill a large wok, one-third full with sunflower oil and heat to 180°C/350°F or until a cube of bread, dropped into the oil, browns in 45 seconds.

4 Working in batches, dip the courgette batons in the spiced batter and then deep-fry for 1–2 minutes, or until crisp and golden. Lift out of the wok using a slotted spoon. Drain on kitchen paper and keep warm.

5 Serve the courgette fritters on heated plates, or on banana leaves if these are available, with steamed basmati rice, yogurt and pickles.

morning glory w. shallots Energy 58kcal/240kJ; Protein 2.9g; Carbohydrate 4.2g, of which sugars 2g; Fat 3.4g, of which saturates 0.4g; Cholesterol 0mg; Calcium 112mg; Fibre 2g; Sodium 89mg.
asian-style fritters Energy 241kcal/999kJ; Protein 7.3g; Carbohydrate 15.3g, of which sugars 4.6g; Fat 15.6g, of which saturates 1.9g; Cholesterol 0mg; Calcium 83mg; Fibre 3.8g; Sodium 15mg.

Broccoli with Soy Sauce

A wonderfully simple dish that you will want to make again and again. The broccoli cooks in next to no time, so don't start cooking until you are almost ready to eat.

Ingredients
450g/1lb broccoli
15ml/1 tbsp vegetable oil
2 garlic cloves, crushed
30ml/2 tbsp light soy sauce
salt
fried garlic slices, to garnish

Serves 4

1 Cut the thick stems from the broccoli; cut off any particularly woody bits, then cut the stems lengthways into thin slices. Separate the head of the broccoli into large florets.

2 Bring a pan of lightly salted water to the boil. Add the broccoli and cook for 3–4 minutes until tender but still crisp.

3 Tip the broccoli into a colander, drain thoroughly and arrange in a heated serving dish.

4 Heat the oil in a small pan. Fry the garlic for 2 minutes to release the flavour, then remove it with a slotted spoon. Pour the oil carefully over the broccoli, taking care as it will splatter. Drizzle the soy sauce over the broccoli, sprinkle over the fried garlic and serve.

Cook's Tip
Fried garlic slices make a good garnish but take care that the oil used does not get too hot; if the garlic burns, it will taste unpleasantly bitter.

Variation
Most leafy vegetables taste delicious prepared this way. Try blanched cos or romaine lettuce and you may be surprised at how crisp and clean the taste is.

Broccoli with Sesame Seeds

This simple treatment is ideal for broccoli and other brassicas, including Brussels sprouts. Adding a sprinkling of toasted sesame seeds to give extra crunch is an inspired touch, and there are a number of other easy ways to vary the recipe according to taste.

Ingredients
225g/8oz purple-sprouting broccoli
15ml/1 tbsp vegetable oil
15ml/1 tbsp soy sauce
15ml/1 tbsp toasted sesame seeds
salt and ground black pepper

Serves 2

1 Using a sharp knife, cut off and discard any thick stems from the broccoli and cut the broccoli into long, thin florets. Stems that are young and tender can be sliced into rounds.

2 Remove any bruised or discoloured portions of the stem along with any florets that are no longer firm and tightly curled.

3 Heat the vegetable oil in a wok or large frying pan and add the broccoli. Stir-fry for 3–4 minutes, or until tender, adding a splash of water if the pan becomes too dry.

4 Mix the soy sauce with the sesame seeds, then season with salt and ground black pepper. Add to the broccoli, toss to combine and serve immediately.

Variations
- *Sprouting broccoli has been used for this recipe, but when it is not available an ordinary variety of broccoli, such as calabrese, will also work very well.*
- *An even better choice would be Chinese broccoli, which is often available in Asian markets under the name gailan.*
- *Try this recipe with some pickled ginger. The flavour goes spectacularly well with broccoli or calabrese, and the resulting pale pink colour contrasts beautifully with the dark green. Pickled ginger is a little less potent than its fresh counterpart.*

broccoli w. soy sauce Energy 65kcal/271kJ; Protein 5.2g; Carbohydrate 2.7g, of which sugars 2.2g; Fat 3.8g, of which saturates 0.6g; Cholesterol 0mg; Calcium 64mg; Fibre 2.9g; Sodium 543mg.
broccoli w. sesame Energy 270kcal/1115kJ; Protein 13.1g; Carbohydrate 5.4g, of which sugars 4.6g; Fat 21.7g, of which saturates 3.3g; Cholesterol 0mg; Calcium 229mg; Fibre 7.1g; Sodium 1089mg.

Sautéed Green Beans

The smoky flavour of the dried shrimps used in this recipe adds an extra dimension to green beans cooked in this way.

Ingredients

450g/1lb green beans
15ml/1 tbsp vegetable oil
3 garlic cloves, finely chopped
5 spring onions (scallions), cut into 2.5cm/1in lengths
25g/1oz dried shrimps, soaked in warm water and drained
15ml/1 tbsp light soy sauce
salt

Serves 4

1 Trim the green beans. Cut each green bean in half.

2 Bring a pan of lightly salted water to the boil and cook the beans for 3–4 minutes until tender but still crisp. Drain, refresh under cold water and drain again.

3 Heat the oil in a non-stick frying pan or wok until very hot. Stir-fry the garlic and spring onions for 30 seconds, then add the shrimps. Mix lightly.

4 Add the green beans and soy sauce. Toss the mixture over the heat until the beans are hot. Serve immediately.

Variation
For more colour and a contrast in texture, stir-fry sliced red, yellow or orange (bell) peppers in the wok and cook for a few minutes until just tender but still crunch. Add the garlic and spring onions and proceed as above.

Cook's Tip
Don't be tempted to use too many dried shrimps. Their flavour is very strong and could overwhelm the more delicate taste of the green beans.

Green Beans with Ginger

This is a simple and delicious way of enlivening green beans. The dish can be served hot or cold and, accompanied by an omelette and some crusty bread, makes a perfect light lunch or supper.

Ingredients

450g/1lb/3 cups green beans
15ml/1 tbsp olive oil
5ml/1 tsp sesame oil
2 garlic cloves, crushed
2.5cm/1in piece fresh root ginger, finely chopped
30ml/2 tbsp dark soy sauce

Serves 4

1 Steam the beans over a pan of boiling salted water, or in an electric steamer, for 4 minutes or until just tender.

2 Meanwhile, heat the olive oil and sesame oil in a heavy pan. Add the crushed garlic and sauté for 2 minutes.

3 Stir in the ginger and soy sauce and cook, stirring constantly, for a further 2–3 minutes until the liquid has reduced, then pour this mixture over the warm beans.

4 Leave for a few minutes to allow all the flavours to mingle, then toss the beans several times before tipping into a bowl.

Variation
Substitute other green beans, if you wish. Runner beans and other flat varieties should be cut diagonally into thick slices before steaming.

Cook's Tip
Sesame oil has a delicious, nutty taste and is valued more for its flavour than as a cooking medium. It burns easily, so if you do use it for frying, mix it with other more durable oils such as the olive oil used in this recipe.

sautéed green beans Energy 62kcal/254kJ; Protein 2.4g; Carbohydrate 4.2g, of which sugars 3.1g; Fat 4.1g, of which saturates 0.6g; Cholesterol 0mg; Calcium 42mg; Fibre 2.5g; Sodium 534mg.
green beans w. ginger Energy 64kcal/265kJ; Protein 2.6g; Carbohydrate 4.6g, of which sugars 3.2g; Fat 4.1g, of which saturates 0.6g; Cholesterol 0mg; Calcium 42mg; Fibre 2.6g; Sodium 534mg.

Dry-cooked Green Beans

A particular style of Sichuan cooking is to "dry cook", which basically means that no stock or water is involved. The slim green beans available all the year round from supermarkets are ideal for use in this quick and tasty recipe, but, as with all of these versatile vegetable dishes, there are worthy substitutes.

Ingredients
175ml/6fl oz/¾ cup sunflower oil
450/1lb fresh green beans, topped, tailed and cut in half
5 x 1cm/2 x ½in piece fresh root ginger, peeled and cut into matchsticks
5ml/1 tsp sugar
10ml/2 tsp light soy sauce
salt and ground black pepper

Serves 6

1 Heat the oil in a wok. When the oil is just beginning to smoke, carefully add the beans and stir-fry them for 1–2 minutes until just tender.

2 Lift out the green beans on to a plate lined with kitchen paper. Using a ladle carefully remove all but 30ml/2 tbsp oil from the wok. The excess oil will play no further part in this recipe, so should be allowed to cool completely before being strained and bottled for future use.

3 Reheat the remaining oil in the wok, add the ginger and stir-fry for a minute or two to flavour the oil.

4 Return the green beans to the wok, stir in the sugar, soy sauce and salt and pepper, and toss together quickly to ensure the beans are well coated. Tip the beans into a heated bowl and serve immediately.

Variation
Fresh green beans are available for most of the year now, but this simple recipe works just as well with other more seasonal vegetables such as baby asparagus spears or okra.

Carrots in Sweet Vinegar

This fascinating side dish is a Japanese invention, whereby carrot strips are made tender and sweet thanks to several hours' marinating in rice vinegar, shoyu and mirin. They make an excellent accompaniment for and contrast to rich dishes such as fried aubergine with miso sauce.

Ingredients
2 large carrots, peeled
5ml/1 tsp salt
30ml/2 tbsp sesame seeds

For the marinade
75ml/5 tbsp rice vinegar
30ml/2 tbsp shoyu
45ml/3 tbsp mirin (sweet rice wine)

Serves 4

1 Cut the carrots into thin matchsticks, 5cm/2in long. Put the carrots and salt into a mixing bowl, and mix well with your hands. After 25 minutes, rinse the wilted carrot in cold water, then drain.

2 In another bowl, mix together the marinade ingredients. Add the carrots, and leave to marinate for 3 hours.

3 Put a wok on a high heat, add the sesame seeds and toss constantly until the seeds start to pop. Remove from the heat and cool.

4 Chop the sesame seeds with a large, sharp knife on a large chopping board. Place the carrots in a bowl, sprinkle with the sesame seeds and serve cold.

Cook's Tip
This marinade is called san bai zu, and is one of the essential basic sauces in Japanese cooking. Shoyu is an essential ingredient and you should use the pale awakuchi soy sauce if available. Dilute the marinade with 15ml/1 tbsp second dashi stock, then add sesame seeds and a few dashes of sesame oil for a very tasty and healthy salad dressing.

dry-cooked beans Energy 223kcal/917kJ; Protein 1.4g; Carbohydrate 3.1g, of which sugars 2.4g; Fat 22.9g, of which saturates 2.8g; Cholesterol 0mg; Calcium 27mg; Fibre 1.7g; Sodium 0mg.
carrots in sweet vinegar Energy 110kcal/461kJ; Protein 2g; Carbohydrate 16.4g, of which sugars 16g; Fat 4.5g, of which saturates 0.7g; Cholesterol 0mg; Calcium 70mg; Fibre 1.8g; Sodium 1040mg.

Stir-fried Asparagus with Chillies

Asparagus is one of those vegetables that is still at its best when in season. It tastes best when freshly lifted and cut and is so delicious that it is inevitably snapped up during the brief period when it is available. This is a particularly delightful way of cooking it.

Ingredients

30ml/2 tbsp groundnut (peanut) oil
2 garlic cloves, finely chopped
2 fresh red chillies, seeded and finely chopped
25g/1oz fresh galangal or root ginger, finely shredded
1 lemon grass stalk, trimmed and finely sliced
350g/12oz fresh asparagus spears, trimmed
30ml/2 tbsp fish sauce
30ml/2 tbsp soy sauce
5ml/1 tsp sugar
30ml/2 tbsp unsalted roasted peanuts, finely chopped
1 small bunch fresh coriander (cilantro), finely chopped

Serves 2–4

1 Heat a large wok and add the oil. Stir in the garlic, chillies, galangal or ginger and lemon grass and stir-fry until the ingredients become fragrant and begin to turn golden.

2 Add the asparagus and stir-fry for a further 1–2 minutes, until it is just tender but not too soft.

3 Stir in the fish sauce, soy sauce and sugar. Spoon on to a serving plates, sprinkle with the peanuts and coriander and serve immediately.

Variations

- *This recipe also works well with broccoli, green beans, baby leeks or courgettes (zucchini), cut into strips when the asparagus is not at its best. You may lose a little in bulk if using smaller vegetables, so a medley of all four would work well.*
- *For a touch of sweetness, add a little sweet chilli sauce with the fish sauce when making the dressing for the asparagus.*

Asparagus with Crispy Noodles

An easily prepared dish of tender asparagus spears tossed with sesame seeds and served on a bed of crispy, deep-fried noodles is just as perfect for casual entertaining as for a light mid-week supper. The lightly cooked asparagus retains all its fresh flavour and bite and contrasts wonderfully with the noodles.

Ingredients

15ml/1 tbsp sunflower oil
350g/12oz thin asparagus spears
5ml/1 tsp salt
5ml/1 tsp ground black pepper
5ml/1 tsp golden caster (superfine) sugar
30ml/2 tbsp Chinese cooking wine
45ml/3 tbsp light soy sauce
60ml/4 tbsp oyster sauce
10ml/2 tsp sesame oil
60ml/4 tbsp toasted sesame seeds

For the noodles

50g/2oz dried cellophane noodles or thin rice vermicelli
sunflower oil, for deep-frying

Serves 4

1 First make the crispy noodles. Fill a wok one-third full of oil and heat to 180°C/350°F or until a cube of bread, dropped into the oil, browns in 45 seconds. Add a small bunch of noodles to the oil; they will crisp and puff up in seconds.

2 Using a slotted spoon, remove from the wok and drain on kitchen paper. Set aside. Cook the remaining noodles in the same way.

3 Heat a clean wok over a high heat and add the sunflower oil. Add the asparagus and stir-fry for 3 minutes.

4 Add the salt, pepper, sugar, wine and both sauces to the wok and stir-fry for 2–3 minutes. Add the sesame oil, toss to combine and remove from the heat.

5 To serve, divide the crispy noodles between 4 warmed plates or bowls and top with the asparagus and juices. Scatter over the toasted sesame seeds and serve immediately.

stir-fried asparagus Energy 79kcal/327kJ; Protein 4g; Carbohydrate 4.9g, of which sugars 4.5g; Fat 4.9g, of which saturates 0.7g; Cholesterol 0mg; Calcium 53mg; Fibre 2.5g; Sodium 540mg.
asparagus w. crispy noodles Energy 131kcal/547kJ; Protein 4.6g; Carbohydrate 16.5g, of which sugars 6.9g; Fat 5.6g, of which saturates 0.6g; Cholesterol 0mg; Calcium 31mg; Fibre 2g; Sodium 1047mg.

Aubergines with Sesame Sauce

Steaming is a wonderful way of cooking aubergines as it is the perfect foil to their tendency to soak up oil.

Ingredients

2 large aubergines (eggplants)
400ml/14fl oz/1⅔ cups second dashi stock made using water and instant dashi powder
25ml/1½ tbsp sugar
15ml/1 tbsp shoyu
15ml/1 tbsp sesame seeds, ground
15ml/1 tbsp sake
15ml/1 tbsp cornflour (cornstarch)
salt

For the vegetables

130g/4½oz shimeji mushrooms
115g/4oz/¾ cup fine green beans
100ml/3fl oz/scant ½ cup second dashi stock
25ml/1½ tbsp sugar
15ml/1 tbsp sake
1.5ml/¼ tsp salt
dash of shoyu

Serves 4

1 Peel the aubergines and cut them in quarters lengthways. Prick all over then soak in salted water for 30 minutes. Drain and steam in a covered bamboo basket for 20 minutes.

2 Mix the stock, sugar, shoyu and 1.5ml/¼ tsp salt in a large pan. Add the aubergines, cover and simmer for a further 15 minutes. Mix a few tablespoonfuls of stock from the pan with the ground sesame seeds. Add this mixture to the pan and stir well to combine.

3 Mix the sake and the cornflour, add to the pan with the aubergines and stock and shiver the pan over the heat until the sauce becomes quite thick. Remove the pan from the heat.

4 Prepare the vegetables. Cut off the hard base part of the mushrooms and separate the large block into smaller chunks. Trim the beans and cut them in half.

5 Mix the remaining ingredients with the beans and mushrooms in a pan and cook for 7 minutes until just tender. Serve the aubergines and their sauce in individual bowls with the vegetables on the top.

Braised Aubergine & Courgettes

Black bean sauce is the key to this simple, spicy and sensational accompaniment.

Ingredients

1 large aubergine (eggplant), havled and sliced
2 small courgettes (zucchini)
2 fresh red chillies
2 garlic cloves
15ml/1 tbsp vegetable oil
1 small onion, diced
15ml/1 tbsp black bean sauce
15ml/1 tbsp dark soy sauce
45ml/3 tbsp cold water
salt

Serves 4

1 Layer all the slices of aubergine in a colander, sprinkling each layer with salt. Leave the aubergine in the sink to stand for about 20 minutes. Cut the courgettes into wedges.

2 Remove the stalks from the chillies, cut them in half lengthways and scrape out and discard the pith and seeds. Chop the chillies finely.

3 Cut the garlic cloves in half. Place them cut side down and chop them finely by slicing first in one direction and then in the other.

4 Rinse the aubergine slices under cold running water to remove the salt. Drain and dry thoroughly on kitchen paper.

5 Heat the oil in a wok or non-stick frying pan. Quickly stir-fry the garlic, chillies and onion with the black bean sauce.

6 Add the aubergine and stir-fry for 2 minutes, sprinkling over a little water to prevent them from burning. Stir in the courgettes, soy sauce and water. Cook, stirring often, for 5 minutes. Spoon into a heated dish and serve.

Variation
For a fiery result, retain the chilli seeds and add to the mixture.

aubergines w. sesame sauce Energy 79kcal/333kJ; Protein 2.9g; Carbohydrate 10.2g, of which sugars 9.6g; Fat 2.9g, of which saturates 0.5g; Cholesterol 0mg; Calcium 52mg; Fibre 3.3g; Sodium 272mg.
braised aubergine Energy 66kcal/276kJ; Protein 3g; Carbohydrate 6.1g, of which sugars 4.2g; Fat 3.5g, of which saturates 0.5g; Cholesterol 0mg; Calcium 34mg; Fibre 2.9g; Sodium 270mg.

Charred Aubergine with Chillies

One of the wonderful things about aubergines is that they can be placed in the flames of a fire, or over hot charcoal, or directly over a gas flame of a stove, and still taste great.

Ingredients

2 aubergines (eggplants)
30ml/2 tbsp groundnut (peanut) or vegetable oil
2 spring onions (scallions), finely sliced
2 red Serrano chillies, seeded and finely sliced
15ml/1 tbsp fish sauce
25g/1oz/½ cup fresh basil leaves
salt
15ml/1 tbsp roasted peanuts, crushed
hot chilli sauce, to serve

Serves 4

1 Place the aubergines over a barbecue or under a hot grill (broiler), or directly over a gas flame, and, turning them, cook until charred all over and soft when pressed. Put them into a plastic bag to sweat for 1 minute.

2 Holding the aubergines by the stalks, carefully peel off the skin under cold running water. Squeeze the excess water from the peeled flesh, remove the stalk and pull the flesh apart in long strips. Place these strips in a serving dish.

3 Heat the oil in a small pan and quickly stir in the spring onions. Remove the pan from the heat and stir in the chillies, fish sauce, basil leaves and a little salt to taste. Pour this dressing over the aubergines, toss gently and scatter the peanuts over the top. Serve at room temperature and, for those who like a little extra fire, splash on some hot chilli sauce.

Cook's Tip
If you cook the aubergines outside over a barbecue, the flesh is even easier to remove. Simply slit the tough, blackened skins and scoop out the flesh using a spoon, then pull the flesh apart into strips and continue as before.

Seven-spice Aubergines

Seven spice powder is the key ingredient that gives these aubergines a lovely warm flavour, and so well with the light, curry batter.

Ingredients

2 egg whites
90ml/6 tbsp cornflour (cornstarch)
5ml/1 tsp salt
15ml/1 tbsp Thai or Chinese seven-spice powder
15ml/1 tbsp mild chilli powder
500g/1¼lb aubergines (eggplant), thinly sliced
sunflower oil, for deep-frying
fresh mint leaves, to garnish
steamed rice or noodles and hot chilli sauce, to serve

Serves 4

1 Put the egg whites in a large greasefree bowl and beat with an electric whisk until light and foamy, but not dry.

2 Combine the cornflour, salt, seven-spice powder and chilli powder and spread evenly on to a large plate.

3 Fill a wok one-third full of oil and heat to 180°C/350°F or until a cube of day-old bread, dropped into the oil, browns in 40 seconds.

4 Dip the aubergine slices in the egg white and then into the spiced flour mixture to coat. Deep-fry in batches for 3–4 minutes, or until crisp and golden. Drain on kitchen paper and transfer to a platter to keep hot.

5 Serve the aubergine garnished with mint leaves and with hot chilli sauce on the side for dipping.

Cook's Tip
Seven-spice powder is a commercial blend of spices, usually comprising coriander, cumin, cinnamon, star anise, chillli, cloves and lemon peel.

aubergine w. chillies Energy 100kcal/419kJ; Protein 2.1g; Carbohydrate 9.4g, of which sugars 8.8g; Fat 6.4g, of which saturates 0.9g; Cholesterol 0mg; Calcium 42mg; Fibre 3.7g; Sodium 15mg.
seven-spice aubergines Energy 203kcal/850kJ; Protein 2.7g; Carbohydrate 23.5g, of which sugars 2.5g; Fat 11.7g, of which saturates 1.4g; Cholesterol 0mg; Calcium 17mg; Fibre 2.5g; Sodium 45mg.

Chinese Potatoes with Chilli Beans

East meets West in this American-style dish with a Chinese flavour – the sauce is particularly tasty.

Ingredients

4 medium firm or waxy potatoes, cut into thick chunks
30ml/2 tbsp sunflower or groundnut (peanut) oil
3 spring onions, (scallions) sliced
1 large fresh chilli, seeded and sliced
2 garlic cloves, crushed
400g/14oz can red kidney beans, drained
30ml/2 tbsp soy sauce
15ml/1 tbsp sesame oil
15ml/1 tbsp sesame seeds, to garnish
chopped fresh coriander (cilantro) or parsley, to garnish
salt and ground black pepper

Serves 4

1 Cook the potatoes in a large pan of boiling water for 20–30 minutes or until they are just tender. Take care not to overcook. Drain, return to the clean pan and cover to keep warm.

2 Heat the oil in a large frying pan or wok over a medium-high heat. Add the spring onions and chilli and stir-fry for about 1 minute, then add the garlic and stir-fry for a few seconds longer.

3 Add the potatoes, stirring well, then the beans and finally the soy sauce and sesame oil.

4 Season to taste and continue to cook the vegetables until they are well heated through. Shake the pan occasionally, but do not stir or you risk breaking up the potatotes.

5 Spoon the mixture on to a heated platter, sprinkle with the sesame seeds and the coriander or parsley and serve hot.

Cook's Tip
When returning the cooked potatoes to the clean pan in step 1, cover them with a few sheets of kitchen paper before replacing the pan lid. This will stop them turning soggy.

New Potatoes in Dashi Stock

As the stock evaporates in this delicious dish, the onion becomes meltingly soft and caramelized, making a wonderful sauce that coats the potatoes.

Ingredients

15ml/1 tbsp vegetable oil
15ml/1 tbsp toasted sesame oil
1 small onion, thinly sliced
1kg/2¼lb baby new potatoes, unpeeled
200ml/7fl oz/scant 1 cup water with 5ml/1 tsp instant dashi powder
45ml/3 tbsp shoyu, dark soy sauce or kecap manis

Serves 4

1 Heat the vegetable and sesame oils in a wok or large pan. Add the onion slices and stir-fry for 30 seconds, then add the potatoes. Stir constantly, until all the potatoes are well coated in sesame oil, and have begun to sizzle.

2 Pour on the dashi stock and shoyu, dark soy sauce or kecap manis and reduce the heat to the lowest setting. Cover the wok or pan and cook for 15 minutes, using a slotted spoon to turn the potatoes every 5 minutes so that they cook evenly.

3 Uncover the wok or pan for a further 5 minutes to reduce the liquid. If there is already very little liquid remaining, remove the wok or pan from the heat, cover and leave to stand for 5 minutes. Check that the potatoes are cooked, then remove from the heat.

4 Transfer the potatoes and onions to a deep serving bowl. Pour the sauce over the top and serve immediately.

Cook's Tip
Toasted sesame oil is recommended because of its distinctive aroma, but mixing it with vegetable oil not only moderates the flavour, it also lessens the likelihood of the oil burning when heated in the pan.

potatoes/chilli beans Energy 272kcal/1141kJ; Protein 9.7g; Carbohydrate 34.8g, of which sugars 5.7g; Fat 11.4g, of which saturates 1.6g; Cholesterol 0mg; Calcium 107mg; Fibre 7.6g; Sodium 936mg.
potatoes in dashi stock Energy 210kcal/890kJ; Protein 4.8g; Carbohydrate 42.4g, of which sugars 4.9g; Fat 3.5g, of which saturates 0.7g; Cholesterol 0mg; Calcium 21mg; Fibre 2.7g; Sodium 829mg.

Slow-cooked Shiitake with Shoyu

Shiitake mushrooms cooked slowly are so rich and filling, that some people call them "vegetarian steak". This is a useful side dish which also makes a flavoursome addition to other dishes.

Ingredients

20 dried shiitake mushrooms
30ml/2 tbsp vegetable oil
30ml/2 tbsp shoyu
5ml/1 tsp toasted sesame oil

Serves 4

1 Start soaking the dried shiitake the day before. Put them in a large bowl almost full of water. Cover the shiitake with a plate or lid to stop them floating to the surface of the water. Leave to soak overnight.

2 Remove the shiitake from the soaking water and gently squeeze out the water with your fingers.

3 Measure 120ml/4fl oz/½ cup of the liquid in the bowl, and set aside.

4 Heat the oil in a wok or a large frying pan. Stir-fry the shiitake over a high heat for 5 minutes, stirring continuously.

5 Reduce the heat to the lowest setting, then stir in the reserved soaking liquid and the shoyu.

6 Cook the mushrooms until there is almost no moisture left, stirring frequently. Sprinkle with the toasted sesame oil and remove from the heat.

7 Leave to cool, then slice and arrange the shiitake on a large plate and serve.

Variation
Cut the slow-cooked shiitake into thin strips. Mix with 600g/1⅓lb/5¼ cups cooked brown rice and 15ml/1 tbsp finely chopped chives. Sprinkle with toasted sesame seeds.

Fragrant Mushrooms in Lettuce Leaf Saucers

This quick and easy vegetable dish looks great served on lettuce leaves, and it means the mushrooms can be scooped up and eaten with the fingers. It's a lovely treat for children.

Ingredients

30ml/2 tbsp vegetable oil
2 garlic cloves, finely chopped
2 baby cos or romaine lettuces, or 2 Little Gem (Bibb) lettuces
1 lemon grass stalk, chopped
2 kaffir lime leaves, rolled in cylinders and thinly sliced
200g/7oz/3 cups oyster or chestnut mushrooms, or a mixture of the two, sliced
1 small fresh red chilli, seeded and finely chopped
juice of ½ lemon
30ml/2 tbsp light soy sauce
5ml/1 tsp palm sugar (jaggery) or light muscovado (brown) sugar
small bunch fresh mint, leaves removed from the stalks

Serves 2

1 Heat the oil in a wok or frying pan. Add the garlic and cook over a medium heat, stirring occasionally, until golden. Do not let it burn or it will taste bitter.

2 Meanwhile, separate the individual lettuce leaves. Rinse them well, dry in a salad spinner or blot with kitchen paper, and set aside.

3 Increase the heat under the wok or pan and add the chopped lemon grass, sliced lime leaves and sliced mushrooms. Stir-fry for about 2 minutes.

4 Add the chilli, lemon juice, soy sauce and sugar to the wok or pan. Toss the mixture over the heat to combine the ingredients together, then stir-fry for a further 2 minutes.

5 Arrange the lettuce leaves on one large or two individual salad plates. Spoon a small amount of the mushroom mixture on to each leaf, top with a mint leaf and serve.

slow cooked shiitake w. shoyu Energy 16kcal/69kJ; Protein 2g; Carbohydrate 1g, of which sugars 0.8g; Fat 0.5g, of which saturates 0.1g; Cholesterol 0mg; Calcium 7mg; Fibre 1.1g; Sodium 539mg.
mushrooms in lettuce saucers Energy 145kcal/600kJ; Protein 3.6g; Carbohydrate 5.5g, of which sugars 4g; Fat 12.2g, of which saturates 1.5g; Cholesterol 0mg; Calcium 87mg; Fibre 2g; Sodium 12mg.

Mushroom & Choi Sum Stir-fry

Use the mushrooms recommended for this dish – wild oyster and shiitake mushrooms have particularly distinctive, delicate flavours that work well when stir-fried.

Ingredients

4 dried black Chinese mushrooms
150ml/¼ pint/⅔ cup hot water
450g/1lb pak choi (bok choy) or choi sum
50g/2oz/¾ cup oyster mushrooms, preferably wild
50g/2oz/¾ cup fresh shiitake mushrooms
15ml/1 tbsp vegetable oil
1 garlic clove, crushed
30ml/2 tbsp oyster sauce

Serves 4

1 Soak the dried Chinese mushrooms in the hot water for 15 minutes to soften.

2 Tear the pak choi or choi sum into bitesize pieces with your fingers. Place in a bowl and set aside.

3 If any of the oyster or shiitake mushrooms are particularly large, use a sharp knife to halve them.

4 Strain the Chinese mushrooms and cut off the stems. Heat a wok, then add the oil. When the oil is hot, stir-fry the garlic until it has softened but not coloured.

5 Add the greens to the wok and stir-fry for 1 minute. Toss in the oyster and shiitake mushrooms with the Chinese mushroom caps, and stir-fry for 1 minute.

6 Add the oyster sauce, toss well and serve immediately.

Cook's Tip
Pak choi, also called bok choy, and its cousin, choi sum, are both attractive members of the cabbage family, with long, smooth white stems and dark green leaves. Choi sum is also known as flowering cabbage and is distinguished by its yellow flowers.

Fried Vegetables with Chilli Sauce

A wok makes the ideal pan for frying slices of aubergine, butternut squash and courgette because they become beautifully tender and succulent. The beaten egg in this recipe gives a satisfyingly substantial batter.

Ingredients

3 large (US extra large) eggs
1 aubergine (eggplant), halved lengthways and cut into long, thin slices
½ small butternut squash, peeled, seeded and cut into long, thin slices
2 courgettes (zucchini), trimmed and cut into long, thin slices
105ml/7 tbsp vegetable or sunflower oil
salt and ground black pepper
sweet chilli sauce, or a dip of your own choice, to serve (see below for suggestion)

Serves 4

1 Beat the eggs in a large bowl. Season the egg mixture with salt and pepper. Add the slices of aubergine, butternut squash and courgette. Toss the vegetables slices until they are coated all over in the egg.

2 Have a warmed dish ready lined with kitchen paper. Heat the oil in a wok. When it is hot, add the vegetables, one strip at a time, making sure that each strip has plenty of egg clinging to it.

3 Do not cook more than eight strips of vegetable at a time or the oil will cool down too much.

4 As each strip turns golden and is cooked, lift it out, using a wire basket or slotted spoon, and transfer to the plate. Keep hot while cooking the remaining vegetables. Serve with the sweet chilli sauce as a dip.

Variation
Instead of sweet chilli sauce, try a simple mix of mango chutney and chilli dip. The spicy fruity flavour goes particularly well with the butternut squash.

mushroom & choi sum Energy 57kcal/237kJ; Protein 3.7g; Carbohydrate 2.1g, of which sugars 1.8g; Fat 3.8g, of which saturates 0.5g; Cholesterol 0mg; Calcium 193mg; Fibre 2.7g; Sodium 159mg.
vegetables w. chilli sauce Energy 113kcal/468kJ; Protein 5.2g; Carbohydrate 3.6g, of which sugars 3.1g; Fat 8.8g, of which saturates 1.6g; Cholesterol 95mg; Calcium 56mg; Fibre 2g; Sodium 36mg.

Steamed Vegetables with Chilli Dip

An inexpensive bamboo steamer is a great wok accessory, making it possible to cook vegetables quickly and easily so that they retain maximum nutrients and keep their colour. Mix in fresh vegetables, add a spicy dip and you have a healthy and tasty dish.

Ingredients

1 head broccoli, divided into florets
130g/4½oz/scant 1 cup green beans, trimmed
130g/4½oz asparagus, trimmed
½ head cauliflower, divided into florets
8 baby corn cobs
130g/4½oz/1 cup mangetouts (snow peas) or sugar snap peas
salt

For the dip

1 fresh green chilli, seeded
4 garlic cloves, peeled
4 shallots, peeled
2 tomatoes, halved
5 pea aubergines (eggplants)
30ml/2 tbsp lemon juice
30ml/2 tbsp soy sauce
2.5ml/½ tsp salt
5ml/1 tsp sugar

Serves 4

1 Place the broccoli, green beans, asparagus and cauliflower in a bamboo steamer and steam over boiling water in a wok for about 4 minutes, until just tender but still with a "bite". Transfer to a bowl and add the corn cobs and mangetouts or sugar snap peas. Season to taste with a little salt. Toss to mix.

2 Make the dip. Preheat the grill (broiler). Wrap the chilli, garlic cloves, shallots, tomatoes and aubergines in a foil package. Grill (broil) for 10 minutes, until the vegetables have softened, turning the package over once or twice.

3 Unwrap the foil and tip its contents into a mortar or food processor. Add the lemon juice, soy sauce, salt and sugar. Pound with a pestle or process to a fairly liquid paste.

4 Scrape the dip into a serving bowl or four individual bowls. Serve, surrounded by the steamed and raw vegetables.

Roasties with Peanut Sauce

Whether a side dish or a main course, these roasted vegetables served with a dipping sauce are a real treat.

Ingredients

1 long, slender aubergine (eggplant), partially peeled and cut into long strips
2 courgettes (zucchini), partially peeled and cut into long strips
1 thick, long sweet potato, cut into long strips
2 leeks, trimmed, halved widthways and lengthways
2 garlic cloves, chopped
25g/1oz fresh root ginger, peeled and chopped
60ml/4 tbsp vegetable or groundnut (peanut) oil
salt
30ml/3 tbsp roasted peanuts, ground
fresh crusty bread, to serve

For the sauce

4 garlic cloves, chopped
2–3 fresh red chillies, seeded and chopped
5ml/1 tsp shrimp paste
115g/4oz/1 cup roasted peanuts, crushed
15ml/1 tbsp dark soy sauce
juice of 1 lime
5ml/1 tsp Chinese rice vinegar
10ml/2 tsp clear honey
salt and ground black pepper

Serves 4

1 Preheat the oven to 200°C/400°F/Gas 6. Arrange the vegetables in a shallow oven dish. Using a food processor, grind the garlic and ginger to a paste, and smear it over the vegetables. Sprinkle with a little salt and pour over the oil. Roast for about 45 minutes, until the vegetables are tender and slightly browned – toss them in the oil halfway through cooking.

2 Meanwhile, make the sauce. Using a food processor, grind the garlic and chillies to a paste. Beat in the shrimp paste and peanuts. Stir in the soy sauce, lime juice, vinegar and honey, and blend with a little water so that the sauce is the consistency of pouring cream. Season with salt and pepper and adjust the sweet and sour balance to taste.

3 Arrange the roasted vegetables on a plate. Drizzle the sauce over them, or serve it separately in a bowl. Sprinkle the ground peanuts over the top and serve warm with fresh crusty bread.

vegetables w. chilli dip Energy 108kcal/454kJ; Protein 11.5g; Carbohydrate 10.7g, of which sugars 9.2g; Fat 2.3g, of which saturates 0.5g; Cholesterol 0mg; Calcium 119mg; Fibre 7.6g; Sodium 590mg.
roasties w. peanut sauce Energy 361kcal/1502kJ; Protein 11.9g; Carbohydrate 22.7g, of which sugars 11.1g; Fat 25.4g, of which saturates 4.1g; Cholesterol 0mg; Calcium 76mg; Fibre 6.9g; Sodium 292mg.

Sweet-and-Sour Vegetables with Tofu

Big, bold and beautiful, this is a hearty stir-fry that will satisfy the hungriest guests.

Ingredients

4 shallots
3 garlic cloves
30ml/2 tbsp groundnut (peanut) oil
250g/9oz Chinese leaves (Chinese cabbage), shredded
8 baby corn cobs, sliced diagonally
2 red (bell) peppers, seeded and thinly sliced
200g/7oz/1¾ cups mangetouts (snow peas), trimmed and sliced
250g/9oz firm tofu, rinsed, drained and cut in 1cm/½in cubes
60ml/4 tbsp vegetable stock
30ml/2 tbsp light soy sauce
15ml/1 tbsp sugar
30ml/2 tbsp rice vinegar
2.5ml/½ tsp dried chilli flakes
small bunch of fresh coriander (cilantro), chopped

Serves 4

1 Slice the shallots thinly using a sharp knife. Finely chop the garlic cloves.

2 Heat the oil in a wok or large frying pan and cook the shallots and garlic for 2–3 minutes over a medium heat, until golden. Do not let the garlic burn or it will taste bitter.

3 Add the shredded Chinese leaves, toss over the heat for 30 seconds, then add the sliced baby-corn cobs and repeat the process.

4 Add the red peppers, mangetouts and tofu in the same way as the leaves and baby-corn, each time adding a single ingredient and tossing it over the heat for about 30 seconds before adding the next ingredient.

5 Pour in the stock and soy sauce. Mix together the sugar and vinegar in a small bowl, stirring until the sugar has dissolved, then add to the wok or pan. Tip the mixture into a warmed bowl, sprinkle over the chilli flakes and coriander, toss to mix well and serve.

Spring Vegetable Stir-fry

Fast, fresh and packed with healthy vegetables, this stir-fry is delicious served with marinated tofu and rice or noodles. This recipe contains very little saturated fat, so scores highly with slimmers, but has sufficient bulk to ward off hunger. Ideal as a quick supper on the go.

Ingredients

2 spring onions (scallions)
175g/6oz spring greens or collard greens
15ml/1 tbsp vegetable oil
5ml/1 tsp toasted sesame oil
1 garlic clove, chopped
2.5cm/1in piece fresh root ginger, finely chopped
225g/8oz baby carrots
350g/12oz broccoli florets
175g/6oz asparagus tips
30ml/2 tbsp light soy sauce
15ml/1 tbsp apple juice
15ml/1 tbsp sesame seeds, toasted

Serves 4

1 Trim the spring onions and cut them diagonally into thin slices, using a sharp knife.

2 Wash the spring greens or collard greens and drain in a colander, then blot with kitchen paper and shred finely.

3 Heat a frying pan or wok over high heat. Add the vegetable oil and the sesame oil, and reduce the heat. Add the garlic and sauté for 2 minutes. Do not let the garlic burn or it will gain a bitter taste.

4 Add the chopped ginger, carrots, broccoli and asparagus tips to the pan and stir-fry for 4 minutes.

5 Add the spring onions and spring greens or collard greens and stir-fry for a further 2 minutes.

6 Add the soy sauce and apple juice and cook for 1–2 minutes until the vegetables are tender. If they appear too dry, simply add a little water to soften them up.

7 Tip the mixture into warmed serviing bowls or four individual dishes, sprinkle the sesame seeds on top and serve.

sweet-&-sour veg. Energy 144kcal/604kJ; Protein 5.2g; Carbohydrate 23.7g, of which sugars 18.2g; Fat 3.7g, of which saturates 0.5g; Cholesterol 0mg; Calcium 73mg; Fibre 4.7g; Sodium 611mg.
spring vegetable stir-fry Energy 134kcal/554kJ; Protein 7.8g; Carbohydrate 9.4g, of which sugars 8.6g; Fat 7.4g, of which saturates 1.1g; Cholesterol 0mg; Calcium 195mg; Fibre 6.2g; Sodium 566mg.

Cucumber & Shallot Salad

In Malaysia and Singapore, this light, refreshing salad is served with Indian food almost as often as the cooling mint-flavoured cucumber raita. The Malays also enjoy this salad with many of their spicy fish and grilled meat dishes. It can be made ahead of time and keeps well in the refrigerator. Serve it as a salad, or a relish.

Ingredients

1 cucumber, peeled, halved lengthways and seeded
4 shallots, halved lengthways and sliced finely along the grain
1–2 fresh green chillies, seeded and sliced finely lengthways
60ml/4 tbsp coconut milk
5–10ml/1–2 tsp cumin seeds, dry-roasted and ground to a powder
salt
1 lime, quartered, to serve

Serves 4

1 Slice the cucumber halves finely and sprinkle with salt. Set aside for about 15 minutes. Rinse well and drain off any excess water.

2 Put the cucumber, shallots and chillies in a bowl. Pour in the coconut milk and toss well. Sprinkle most of the roasted cumin over the top.

3 Just before serving, toss the salad again, season with salt, and sprinkle over the rest of the roasted cumin. Serve with lime wedges to squeeze over the salad.

Cook's Tip
You can buy Thai red shallots at Asian markets and food stores.

Variations
Use mild red onions instead of shallots and add some fresh pineapple, chopped into small pieces. Omit the chillies.

Sweet-and-Sour Cucumber Salad

This salad is a great addition to a summer barbecue or the salad table, and is a delightful accompaniment to any meat, poultry and seafood dishes. The best cucumbers to use here are the short, fat Asian ones.

Ingredients

2 cucumbers
30ml/2 tbsp sugar
100ml/3½fl oz/½ cup rice vinegar
juice of half a lime
2 green Thai chillies, seeded and finely sliced
2 shallots, halved and finely sliced
1 small bunch each fresh coriander (cilantro) and mint, stalks removed, leaves finely chopped
salt
fresh coriander leaves, to garnish

Serves 4–6

1 Use a vegetable peeler to remove strips of the cucumber peel. Halve the cucumbers lengthways and cut into slices. Place the slices on a plate and sprinkle with a little salt. Leave them to stand for 15 minutes. Put the cucumber slices in a colander, rinse off the salt under cold running water, drain and pat dry with kitchen paper.

2 In a bowl, mix the sugar with the vinegar until it has dissolved, then stir in the lime juice and a little salt to taste.

3 Add the chillies, shallots, herbs and cucumber to the dressing and leave to stand for 15–20 minutes. Garnish with coriander leaves and a flower, if you like.

Cook's Tips
• *To add a dash of exotic colour to this flavoursome salad, decorate the dish with edible flowers, such as nasturtiums, or blue borage blossoms.*
• *If you can only find an English salad cucumber, opt for a single, medium-sized one.*

cucumber & shallot salad Energy 17kcal/68kJ; Protein 0.7g; Carbohydrate 3.3g, of which sugars 2.7g; Fat 0.1g, of which saturates 0g; Cholesterol 0mg; Calcium 19mg; Fibre 0.7g; Sodium 15mg.
sweet-&-sour cucumber Energy 60kcal/250kJ; Protein 1.3g; Carbohydrate 13.8g, of which sugars 12.2g; Fat 0.3g, of which saturates 0g; Cholesterol 0mg; Calcium 42mg; Fibre 1.5g; Sodium 6mg.

Cucumber Jewel Salad

With its clean taste and bright, jewel-like colours, this salad makes a perfect accompaniment to a variety of spicy dishes and curries. Pomegranate seeds, though not traditional, make a beautiful garnish.

Ingredients

1 small cucumber
1 onion, thinly sliced
1 small, ripe pineapple or 425g/15oz can pineapple rings
1 green (bell) pepper, seeded and thinly sliced
3 firm tomatoes, chopped
30ml/2 tbsp sugar
45–60ml/3–4 tbsp white wine vinegar
120ml/4fl oz/½ cup water
salt
seeds of 1–2 pomegranates, to garnish

Serves 8

1 Halve the cucumber lengthways, remove the seeds, slice and spread on a plate with the onion. Sprinkle with salt. After about 10 minutes, rinse off the salt thoroughly and pat dry.

2 If using a fresh pineapple, peel and core it, removing all the eyes, then cut it into bitesize pieces. If using canned pineapple, drain the rings and cut them into small wedges. Place the pineapple in a bowl with the cucumber, onion, green pepper and tomatoes.

3 Heat the sugar, vinegar and measured water in a pan, stirring until the sugar has dissolved. Remove the pan from the heat and leave to cool. When cold, add a little salt to taste and pour over the fruit and vegetables. Cover and chill until required. Serve in small bowls, garnished with pomegranate seeds.

Variation
To make this Indonesian-style, salt a salad cucumber as described in the recipe. Make half the dressing and pour it over the cucumber. Add a few chopped spring onions. Cover and chill. Serve scattered with toasted sesame seeds.

Mixed Salad with Lettuce Wraps

Traditionally, an Asian-style table salad is served to accompany spring rolls and pork or shrimp balls, where pieces of the salad might be wrapped around a meaty morsel. When served on its own, as here, the vegetables and fruit in this dish are usually folded into little packets using lettuce leaves or rice wrappers, and then dipped in a sauce, or added bit by bit to bowls of rice or noodles. The salad itself can vary from a bowl of fresh, leafy herbs to a more tropical combination of beansprouts, water chestnuts, mangoes, bananas, star fruit, peanuts and rice noodles.

Ingredients

1 crunchy lettuce, leaves separated
½ cucumber, peeled and thinly sliced
2 carrots, finely sliced
200g/7oz/1 cup beansprouts
2 unripe star fruit, finely sliced
2 green bananas, finely sliced
1 firm papaya, cut in half, seeds removed, peeled and finely sliced
Leaves from 1 bunch fresh mint and leaves from 1 bunch fresh basil
juice of 1 lime
dipping sauce, to serve

Serves 4–6

1 Arrange the salad ingredients attractively on a large plate, with the lettuce leaves placed on one side so that they can be used as wrappers.

2 Squeeze the lime juice over the sliced fruits, particularly the bananas to help them retain their colour, and place the salad in the middle of the table. Serve with a dipping sauce.

Cook's Tip
As this salad is meant to be eaten in the hand, supply guests with some napkins, plus finger bowls filled with warm water. Add some lime and lemon slices to the water so that everyone can freshen up afterwards.

cucumber jewel salad Energy 53kcal/224kJ; Protein 0.9g; Carbohydrate 12.3g, of which sugars 12.1g; Fat 0.3g, of which saturates 0.1g; Cholesterol 0mg; Calcium 20mg; Fibre 1.5g; Sodium 6mg.
salad w. lettuce wraps Energy 107kcal/453kJ; Protein 3.1g; Carbohydrate 23g, of which sugars 20.6g; Fat 0.9g, of which saturates 0.2g; Cholesterol 0mg; Calcium 72mg; Fibre 3.8g; Sodium 14mg.

Bamboo Shoot Salad

This hot, sharp-flavoured salad is the perfect foil for rich roast duck or pork.

Ingredients
400g/14oz canned bamboo shoots, in large pieces
25g/1oz/about 3 tbsp glutinous rice
30ml/2 tbsp shallots, chopped
15ml/1 tbsp garlic, chopped
45ml/3 tbsp spring onions (scallions), chopped
30ml/2 tbsp fish sauce
30ml/2 tbsp fresh lime juice
5ml/1 tsp sugar
2.5ml/½ tsp dried chilli flakes
20–25 small fresh mint leaves
15ml/1 tbsp toasted sesame seeds

Serves 4

1 Drain the bamboo shoots, rinse them under cold running water, then drain again and pat thoroughly dry with kitchen paper. Set aside.

2 Dry-roast the rice in a frying pan until it is golden brown. Leave to cool slightly, then tip into a mortar and grind to fine crumbs with a pestle.

3 Transfer the rice to a serving bowl and add the shallots, garlic, spring onions, fish sauce, lime juice, sugar, chillies and half the mint leaves. Mix well.

4 Add the bamboo shoots to the bowl and toss to mix. Serve sprinkled with the toasted sesame seeds and the remaining mint leaves.

Variation
Use canned whole bamboo shoots, if you can get hold of them – they have more flavour than sliced ones.

Cook's Tip
Despite the name, glutinous rice does not, in fact, contain any gluten – it's just sticky.

Soya Beansprout Salad

High in protein and fat, soya beansprouts are nutritious as well as being good to eat. favoured in Cambodia. Unlike mung beansprouts, they are slightly poisonous when raw and need to be parboiled before use, though this only takes a minute. This salad is often eaten with noodles and rice.

Ingredients
450g/1lb/2 cups fresh soya beansprouts
2 spring onions (scallions), finely sliced
1 small bunch fresh coriander (cilantro), stalks removed

For the dressing
30ml/2 tbsp fish sauce
15ml/1 tbsp white rice vinegar
10ml/2 tsp palm sugar (jaggery) or soft dark brown sugar.
15ml/1 tbsp sesame oil
1 red chilli, seeded and finely sliced
15g/½oz fresh young root ginger, finely shredded

Serves 4

1 First make the dressing. In a bowl, beat the oil, tuk trey and rice vinegar with the sugar, until it dissolves. Stir in the chilli and ginger and leave to stand for 30 minutes to allow the flavours to develop.

2 Bring a large pan of salted water to the boil. Drop in the beansprouts and blanch for 1 minute only. Tip into a colander, drain, then refresh under running cold water until cool. Drain again and put them into a clean dishtowel. Shake out the excess water.

3 Put the beansprouts into a bowl and add the spring onions. Pour over the dressing and toss well. Garnish with coriander leaves and serve.

Variation
Any other edible sprouted bean or pea can be used instead of the beansprouts.

bamboo shoot salad Energy 72kcal/305kJ; Protein 3.9g; Carbohydrate 13g, of which sugars 6.2g; Fat 0.7g, of which saturates 0.1g; Cholesterol 0mg; Calcium 31mg; Fibre 1.9g; Sodium 185mg.
soya beansprout salad Energy 95kcal/396kJ; Protein 4.5g; Carbohydrate 8.4g, of which sugars 5.6g; Fat 5.6g, of which saturates 0.5g; Cholesterol 3mg; Calcium 54mg; Fibre 2.4g; Sodium 79mg.

Mixed Seaweed Salad

Seaweed is a nutritious, alkaline food which is rich in fibre. Its unusual flavours are a great complement to fish and tofu dishes. This salad is extremely low in fat.

Ingredients

5g/1/8oz each dried wakame, dried arame and dried hijiki seaweeds
about 130g/4½oz fresh enokitake mushrooms
15ml/1 tbsp rice vinegar
6.5ml/1¼ tsp salt
2 spring onions (scallions)
a few ice cubes
½ cucumber, cut lengthways
250g/9oz mixed salad leaves

For the dressing

60ml/4 tbsp rice vinegar
7.5ml/1½ tsp toasted sesame oil
15ml/1 tbsp shoyu
15ml/1 tbsp water with a pinch of instant dashi powder
2.5cm/1in piece fresh root ginger, finely grated

Serves 4

1 Soak the dried wakame seaweed for 10 minutes in one bowl of water and, in a separate bowl of water, soak the dried arame and hijiki seaweeds together for 30 minutes.

2 Trim the hard end of the enokitake mushroom stalks, then cut the bunch in half and separate the stems.

3 Cook the wakame and enokitake in boiling water for 2 minutes, then add the arame and hijiki for a few seconds. Immediately remove from the heat.

4 Drain in a sieve (strainer) and sprinkle over the vinegar and salt while still warm. Chill until needed.

5 Slice the spring onions into long, thin, strips, then soak in a bowl of cold water with a few ice cubes added to make them curl up. Drain. Slice the cucumber into thin, half-moon shapes.

6 Mix the dressing ingredients in a bowl. Arrange the mixed salad leaves in a large bowl with the cucumber on top, then add the seaweed and enokitake mixture. Decorate the salad with spring onion curls and serve with the dressing.

Hijiki & Radish Salad

Hijiki is a mild-tasting seaweed and combined with radishes, cucumber and beansprouts, it makes a refreshing salad that is the perfect accompaniment to a rich main dish.

Ingredients

15g/½oz/½ cup hijiki seaweed
250g/9oz/1¼ cups radishes, sliced into very thin rounds
1 small cucumber, finely sliced
75g/3oz/⅔ cup beansprouts

For the dressing

15ml/1 tbsp sunflower oil
15ml/1 tbsp toasted sesame oil
5ml/1 tsp light soy sauce
30ml/2 tbsp rice vinegar or 15ml/1 tbsp wine vinegar
15ml/1 tbsp mirin (sweet rice wine)

Serves 4

1 Soak the hijiki in a bowl of cold water for 10–15 minutes until it is rehydrated, then drain, rinse under cold running water and drain again. It should almost triple in volume.

2 Place the hijiki in a pan of water. Bring the water to the boil, then reduce the heat and simmer the hijiki for about 30 minutes or until tender.

3 Meanwhile, make the dressing. Whisk the oils with the vinegar and mirin in a bowl until combined, add the soy sauce, and whisk again to mix well.

4 Drain the cooked hijiki in a sieve (strainer) and arrange it in a shallow bowl or platter or on individual salad plates with the prepared radishes, cucumber and beansprouts. Pour over the dressing and toss lightly to combine.

Cook's Tip
Hijiki is a type of seaweed that is popular in Japan. It resembles wakame and is generally sold dried and finely shredded. It is available in airtight packages in many supermarkets and Asian stores. It keeps very well in the storecupboard.

mixed seaweed salad Energy 26kcal/107kJ; Protein 1.5g; Carbohydrate 2.1g, of which sugars 2g; Fat 1.3g, of which saturates 0.2g; Cholesterol 0mg; Calcium 28mg; Fibre 1.2g; Sodium 272mg.
hijiki & radish salad Energy 70kcal/289kJ; Protein 1.2g; Carbohydrate 2.5g, of which sugars 2.1g; Fat 5.7g, of which saturates 0.8g; Cholesterol 0mg; Calcium 21mg; Fibre 1g; Sodium 98mg.

Cabbage Salad

This is a simple and delicious way of serving a somewhat mundane vegetable. A wok comes in handy for stir-frying the aromatic vegetables.

Ingredients

30ml/2 tbsp vegetable oil
2 large fresh red chillies, seeded and cut into thin strips
6 garlic cloves, thinly sliced
6 shallots, thinly sliced
1 small cabbage, shredded
30ml/2 tbsp coarsely chopped roasted peanuts, to garnish

For the dressing

30ml/2 tbsp fish sauce
grated rind of 1 lime
30ml/2 tbsp fresh lime juice
120ml/4fl oz/½ cup coconut milk

Serves 4–6

1 Make the dressing by mixing the fish sauce, lime rind, lime juice and coconut milk in a bowl. Whisk until thoroughly combined, then set aside.

2 Heat the oil in a wok. Stir-fry the chillies, garlic and shallots over a medium heat for 3–4 minutes, until the shallots are brown and crisp. Remove with a slotted spoon and set aside.

3 Bring a large pan of lightly salted water to the boil. Add the shredded cabbage and blanch for 2–3 minutes. Tip it into a colander, drain well and put into a bowl.

4 Whisk the dressing again, add it to the warm cabbage and toss to combine. Transfer the salad to a serving dish. Just before serving, sprinkle with the fried shallot mixture and garnish with the chopped peanuts.

Variations

- *Other vegetables, such as cauliflower, broccoli and Chinese leaves (Chinese cabbage), can be cooked in this way.*
- *As a healthier option, use low-fat or light coconut milk if you prefer. You can create your own lighter version by using equal parts full-cream coconut milk and distilled water.*

Pak Choi with Lime Dressing

The lime dressing in this dish is usually made using fish sauce, but vegetarians could use mushroom sauce instead. This is a wok recipe that packs a fiery punch so be aware of delicate palates if you are entertaining guests. You can simply use fewer chillies if you prefer, or discard the seeds before you begin stir-frying. Alternatively, simply replace the chillies with red (bell) pepper strips, which will add just as much colour, with a milder impact.

Ingredients

30ml/2 tbsp oil
3 fresh red chillies, cut into thin strips
4 garlic cloves, thinly sliced
6 spring onions (scallions), sliced diagonally
2 pak choi (bok choy), shredded
15ml/1 tbsp crushed peanuts

For the dressing

30ml/2 tbsp fresh lime juice
15–30ml/1–2 tbsp fish sauce
250ml/8fl oz/1 cup whole or low-fat coconut milk

Serves 4

1 Make the dressing. Put the lime juice and fish sauce in a bowl and mix well together, then gradually whisk in the coconut milk until combined.

2 Heat the oil in a wok and stir-fry the chillies for 2–3 minutes, until crisp. Transfer to a plate using a slotted spoon. Add the garlic to the wok and stir-fry for 30–60 seconds, until golden brown. Transfer to the plate.

3 Stir-fry the white parts of the spring onions for about 2–3 minutes, then add the green parts and stir-fry for 1 minute more. Transfer to the plate.

4 Bring a large pan of lightly salted water to the boil and add the pak choi. Stir twice, then drain immediately.

5 Place the pak choi in a large bowl, add the dressing and toss to mix. Spoon into a large serving bowl, sprinkle with the crushed peanuts and the stir-fried ingredients and serve.

cabbage salad Energy 96kcal/400kJ; Protein 2.7g; Carbohydrate 7.7g, of which sugars 6.6g; Fat 6.2g, of which saturates 0.9g; Cholesterol 0mg; Calcium 50mg; Fibre 2.2g; Sodium 147mg.
pak choi w. lime Energy 93kcal/384kJ; Protein 2.9g; Carbohydrate 6.2g, of which sugars 5.7g; Fat 6.4g, of which saturates 0.9g; Cholesterol 0mg; Calcium 157mg; Fibre 2.1g; Sodium 354mg.

Pickled Broccoli in Miso

Broccoli stem is usually wasted because of the fibrous texture, but you will be surprised how tasty it is when marinated or pickled. In this recipe, miso and garlic give a kick to its subtle flavour. The pickle, which will keep for a few days, also makes a good accompaniment to drinks.

Ingredients

3 broccoli stems (use the florets in another dish, if you wish)
2 Japanese or salad cucumbers, ends trimmed
200ml/7fl oz/scant 1 cup miso (any kind)
15ml/1 tbsp sake
1 garlic clove, crushed

Serves 4

1 Peel the broccoli stems and quarter them lengthways. With a vegetable peeler, peel the cucumber every 5mm/¼in to make green-and-white stripes. Cut in half lengthways. Scoop out the centre with a teaspoon. Cut into 7.5cm/3in lengths.

2 Mix the miso, sake and crushed garlic in a deep, plastic or metal container with a lid. Remove half the miso mix.

3 Lay some of the broccoli stems and cucumber flat in the container and push into the miso mix. Spread a little of the reserved miso over the top of the broccoli and cucumber.

4 Repeat this process to make a few layers of vegetables and miso, filling up the container. Cover with the lid and leave in the refrigerator for 1–5 days.

5 Take out the vegetables, wash off the miso under running water, then wipe with kitchen paper. Cut the broccoli stem pieces in half then slice into thin strips lengthways. Cut the cucumber into 5mm/¼in thick half-moon slices. Serve cold.

Variation
Carrot, turnip, kohlrabi, celery, radish or thinly sliced cabbage stems can be used in this way.

Tofu & Broccoli Salad

This bold-flavoured salad could be served with buckwheat to make a delicious meal.

Ingredients

250g/9oz firm tofu, drained and cubed, or 250g/9oz smoked tofu, cubed
250g/9oz broccoli, cut into large florets
15ml/1 tbsp olive oil
1 garlic clove, finely chopped
350g/12oz/4½ cups chestnut mushrooms, sliced
4 spring onions (scallions), thinly sliced
75g/3oz/¾ cup pine nuts, toasted

For the marinade

1 garlic clove, crushed
2.5cm/1in piece fresh root ginger, finely grated
45ml/3 tbsp soy sauce
45ml/3 tbsp tamari soy sauce
45ml/3 tbsp Chinese rice wine or dry sherry
1.5ml/¼ tsp cumin seeds, toasted and coarsely crushed
1.5ml/¼ tsp caster (superfine) sugar
ground black pepper

Serves 4

1 Prepare the marinade by stirring all the ingredients together in a jug (pitcher). Place the tofu cubes in a bowl, pour in the marinade, toss to coat and leave to marinate for at least 1 hour.

2 Meanwhile steam the broccoli for 4–5 minutes, until just tender, then refresh under cold running water. Drain well then place in a large bowl.

3 Heat the oil in a large, heavy frying pan or wok. Add the garlic and stir-fry over a low heat for 1 minute, until golden. Do not allow the garlic to burn.

4 Add the mushrooms to the pan and fry over a high heat for 4–5 minutes, until cooked through. Add to the broccoli and season with ground black pepper.

5 Once marinated, toss the tofu and its marinade with the broccoli, mushrooms and spring onions. Sprinkle with the pine nuts and serve immediately.

pickled broccoli in miso Energy 54kcal/227kJ; Protein 5.6g; Carbohydrate 4.9g, of which sugars 3.8g; Fat 1g, of which saturates 0.2g; Cholesterol 0mg; Calcium 66mg; Fibre 2.9g; Sodium 1789mg.
tofu & broccoli Energy 235kcal/975kJ; Protein 12.3g; Carbohydrate 3.3g, of which sugars 2.6g; Fat 19.3g, of which saturates 1.8g; Cholesterol 0mg; Calcium 366mg; Fibre 3.1g; Sodium 280mg.

Noodle, Tofu & Beansprout Salad

Bean thread noodles look like spun glass on this stunning salad, which owes its goodness to fresh beansprouts, diced tomato and cucumber in a sweet-sour dressing.

Ingredients

25g/1oz cellophane noodles
500g/1¼lb mixed sprouted beans and pulses (aduki, chickpea, mung, red lentil)
4 spring onions (scallions), finely shredded
115g/4oz firm tofu, diced
1 ripe plum tomato, seeded and diced
½ cucumber, peeled, seeded and diced
60ml/4 tbsp chopped fresh coriander (cilantro)
45ml/3 tbsp chopped fresh mint
60ml/4 tbsp rice vinegar
10ml/2 tsp caster sugar
10ml/2 tsp sesame oil
5ml/1 tsp chilli oil
salt and ground black pepper

Serves 4

1 Place the cellophane noodles in a bowl and pour over enough boiling water to cover. Cover and leave to soak for 12–15 minutes.

2 Drain the noodles and then refresh them under cold, running water and drain again. Using a pair of scissors, cut the noodles into roughly 7.5cm/3in lengths and transfer to a bowl.

3 Fill a wok one-third full of boiling water and place over high heat. Add the sprouted beans and pulses and blanch the mixture for 1 minute. Drain, transfer to the noodle bowl and add the spring onions, tofu, tomato, cucumber and herbs.

4 Combine the rice vinegar, sugar, sesame oil and chilli oil and toss into the noodle mixture. Transfer to a serving dish and chill for 30 minutes before serving.

Cook's Tip
If you leave the salad to stand for half an hour to an hour, the flavours will improve as they develop and fuse together.

Fried Tofu Salad with Tangy Sauce

The sweet-sour sauce makes this traditional street snack the perfect foil to grilled meats and stir-fried noodles. If you cannot find kecap manis, simply use dark soy sauce with a little more tomato ketchup to achieve the same balance of flavour.

Ingredients

vegetable oil, for deep-frying
450g/1lb firm rectangular tofu, rinsed, patted dry and cut into blocks
1 small cucumber, partially peeled in strips, seeded and shredded
2 spring onions (scallions), trimmed, halved and shredded
2 handfuls of fresh beansprouts rinsed and drained
fresh coriander (cilantro) leaves, to garnish

For the sauce

30ml/2 tbsp tamarind pulp, soaked in water until soft
15ml/1 tbsp sesame or groundnut (peanut) oil
4 shallots, finely chopped
4 garlic cloves, finely chopped
2 fresh red chillies, seeded
2.5ml/½ tsp shrimp paste
115g/4oz/1 cup roasted peanuts, crushed
30–45ml/2–3 tbsp kecap manis
15ml/1 tbsp tomato ketchup

Serves 4

1 First make the sauce. Squeeze the tamarind pulp to soften it in the water, and then strain through a sieve (strainer). Measure out 120ml/4fl oz/½ cup tamarind pulp.

2 Heat the oil in a wok or heavy pan, and stir in the shallots, garlic and chillies, until fragrant. Stir in the shrimp paste and the peanuts, until they emit a nutty aroma. Add the kecap manis, tomato ketchup and tamarind pulp and blend to form a thick sauce. Set aside and leave to cool.

3 Deep-fry the blocks of tofu in oil until golden brown all over. Pat dry on kitchen paper and cut each block into slices. Arrange the fried tofu slices on a plate with the cucumber, spring onions and beansprouts. Drizzle a little of the sauce over the top and serve the remainder separately in a bowl, garnished with the fresh coriander leaves.

noodle, tofu etc. Energy 126kcal/528kJ; Protein 7.2g; Carbohydrate 14.8g, of which sugars 7.2g; Fat 4.4g, of which saturates 0.6g; Cholesterol 0mg; Calcium 209mg; Fibre 3.1g; Sodium 17mg.
tofu salad Energy 423kcal/1749kJ; Protein 17.9g; Carbohydrate 7.8g, of which sugars 4.5g; Fat 35.8g, of which saturates 5.3g; Cholesterol 0mg; Calcium 607mg; Fibre 2.8g; Sodium 296mg.

Fried Egg Salad

Chillies and eggs may seem unlikely partners, but actually work very well together. The peppery flavour of the watercress makes it the perfect foundation for this tasty and unusual salad.

Ingredients

15ml/1 tbsp groundnut (peanut) oil
1 garlic clove, thinly sliced
4 eggs
2 shallots, thinly sliced
2 small fresh red chillies, seeded and thinly sliced
½ small cucumber, finely diced
1cm/½in piece fresh root ginger, peeled and grated
juice of 2 limes
30ml/2 tbsp soy sauce
5ml/1 tsp caster (superfine) sugar
small bunch coriander (cilantro)
1 bunch watercress, coarsely chopped

Serves 2

1 Heat the oil in a frying pan. Add the garlic and cook over a low heat until it starts to turn golden. Crack in the eggs. Break the yolks with a wooden spatula, then fry until the eggs are almost firm. Remove from the pan and set aside.

2 Mix the shallots, chillies, cucumber and ginger in a bowl. In a separate bowl, whisk the lime juice with the soy sauce and sugar. Pour this dressing over the vegetables and toss lightly.

3 Set aside a few coriander sprigs for the garnish. Chop the rest and add them to the salad. Toss it again.

4 Reserve a few watercress sprigs and arrange the remainder on two serving plates. Cut the fried eggs into slices and divide them between the watercress mounds. Spoon the shallot mixture over them and serve, garnished with the reserved coriander and watercress.

Variation

Chinese sausages, which taste a bit like pepperoni, would make a good addition to the salad if thinly sliced.

Mooli, Broad Beans & Salmon Roe

This unusual combination of muted colours, flavours and textures makes it ideal company for a refreshing glass of cold sake.

Ingredients

200g/7oz mooli (daikon), peeled
1 nori sheet
1kg/2¼lb broad (fava) beans in their pods, shelled
1.5ml/¼ tsp wasabi paste from tube or 2.5ml/½ tsp wasabi powder mixed with 1.5ml/¼ tsp water
20ml/4 tsp shoyu
60ml/4 tbsp ikura
salt

Serves 4

1 Grate the mooli finely with a mooli grater, or use a food processor to chop it into fine shreds. Place the mooli in a sieve and let the juices drain. Meanwhile, tear the nori with your hands into flakes about 1cm/½in square.

2 In a small pan, cook the broad beans in plenty of rapidly boiling salted water for about 4 minutes. Drain and immediately cool under running water. Remove the skins.

3 Mix the wasabi paste with the shoyu in a small mixing bowl. Add the nori flakes, toasted if you wish, and skinned beans, and mix well.

4 Divide the beans among four individual small bowls, heap on the grated mooli, then spoon the ikura on top. Serve cold. Ask your guests to mix everything well just before eating.

Cook's Tips

- *The bright inner green part of broad beans makes a delicious snack when cooked. Simply boil shelled, unskinned beans in very salty water then drain. To eat, snap off the top part of the skin and squeeze the contents into your mouth.*
- *Toast the nori sheet before tearing into small pieces. Do this by waving the edges over a medium gas flame a few times.*

fried egg salad Energy 235kcal/977kJ; Protein 14.8g; Carbohydrate 6.4g, of which sugars 5.6g; Fat 17.2g, of which saturates 3.9g; Cholesterol 381mg; Calcium 154mg; Fibre 1.2g; Sodium 1234mg.
mooli, broad beans etc. Energy 79kcal/335kJ; Protein 7.4g; Carbohydrate 11.6g, of which sugars 2.5g; Fat 0.6g, of which saturates 0.1g; Cholesterol 0mg; Calcium 59mg; Fibre 6.1g; Sodium 369mg.

Aubergine Salad

Roasting aubergines really brings out their flavour.

Ingredients

2 aubergines (eggplants)
15ml/1 tbsp vegetable oil
30ml/2 tbsp dried shrimp, soaked in warm water for 10 minutes
15ml/1 tbsp coarsely chopped garlic
1 hard-boiled egg, chopped
4 shallots, thinly sliced into rings
fresh coriander (cilantro) leaves and 2 fresh red chillies, seeded and sliced, to garnish

For the dressing

30ml/2 tbsp fresh lime juice
5ml/1 tsp soft light brown sugar
30ml/2 tbsp fish sauce

Serves 4–6

1 Preheat the grill (broiler) to medium. Prick the aubergines several times with a skewer, then arrange on a baking sheet. Cook them under the grill for 30–40 minutes, or until they are charred and tender. Remove and set aside until they are cool enough to handle.

2 Meanwhile, make the dressing. Put the lime juice, sugar and fish sauce into a small bowl. Whisk well with a fork or balloon whisk. Cover with clear film (plastic wrap) and set aside.

3 When the aubergines are cool enough to handle, peel off the skin and cut the flesh into medium slices.

4 Heat the oil in a small frying pan. Drain the dried shrimp thoroughly and add them to the pan with the garlic. Cook over a medium heat for about 3 minutes, until golden. Remove from the pan and set aside.

5 Arrange the aubergine slices on a serving dish. Top with the hard-boiled egg, shallots and dried shrimp mixture. Drizzle over the dressing and garnish with the coriander and red chillies.

Variation

For a special occasion, use salted duck's or quail's eggs instead.

Mixed Salad with Coconut

Tender young vegetables, dry roasted coconut and dried prawns make a salad that is a feast of flavours and textures. In towns close to the Thai-Malaysian border, where influences from both cuisines are at work, this salad is known as kerabu, and often served with some of the spicier dishes of the region.

Ingredients

115g/4oz fresh coconut, grated
30ml/2 tbsp dried prawns (shrimp), soaked in warm water until soft
225g/8oz/1 cup beansprouts, rinsed and drained
1 small cucumber, peeled, seeded and cut into julienne strips
2–3 spring onions (scallions), trimmed, cut into 2.5cm/1in pieces and halved lengthways
a handful of young, tender mangetouts (snow peas), halved diagonally
a handful of green beans, halved lengthways
a handful of fresh chives, chopped into 2.5cm/1in pieces
a handful of fresh mint leaves, finely chopped
2–3 fresh red chillies, seeded and sliced finely lengthways
juice of 2 limes
10ml/2 tsp sugar
salt and ground black pepper

Serves 4

1 Dry-roast the coconut in a heavy pan until it is lightly browned and emits a nutty aroma. Using a mortar and pestle or a food processor, grind the roasted coconut to a coarse powder. Tip the powder into a bowl and set aside.

2 Drain the soaked dried prawns, add them to the mortar or food processor and grind them coarsely too.

3 Put the vegetables, herbs and chillies into a bowl. Mix the lime juice with the sugar and pour it over the salad. Season with salt and pepper. Add the ground coconut and dried prawns to the salad, and toss well until thoroughly mixed.

4 To serve, divide the salad among four individual salad plates, mounding it up in the centre.

aubergine salad Energy 61kcal/254kJ; Protein 4.8g; Carbohydrate 3.6g, of which sugars 2.8g; Fat 3.2g, of which saturates 0.6g; Cholesterol 57mg; Calcium 75mg; Fibre 1.6g; Sodium 408mg.
mixed salad w. coconut Energy 141kcal/585kJ; Protein 4.5g; Carbohydrate 6.4g, of which sugars 5.1g; Fat 11g, of which saturates 9.1g; Cholesterol 8mg; Calcium 54mg; Fibre 4.6g; Sodium 86mg.

Lotus Stem Salad

You may be lucky enough to find fresh lotus stems in an Asian market, or, as here, you can use the ones preserved in brine.

Ingredients
½ cucumber
225g/8oz jar preserved lotus stems, drained and cut into 5cm/2in strips
2 shallots, finely sliced
25g/1oz/½ cup fresh basil leaves, shredded
salt
fresh coriander (cilantro) leaves, to garnish

For the dressing
juice of 1 lime
30ml/2 tbsp fish sauce
1 fresh red chilli, seeded and chopped
1 garlic clove, crushed
15ml/1 tbsp sugar

Serves 4

1 To make the dressing, mix together the dressing ingredients in a bowl, whisk well and set aside.

2 Peel the cucumber and cut it into 5cm/2in batons. Soak the batons in cold salted water for 20 minutes. Put the lotus stems into a bowl of water. Using a pair of chopsticks, stir the water so that the loose fibres of the stems wrap around the sticks.

3 Drain the stems and put them in a clean bowl. Drain the cucumber batons and add to the bowl, then add the shallots, shredded basil leaves and the prepared dressing. Toss to mix and then leave the salad to marinate for 20 minutes before serving. Garnish with fresh coriander leaves.

Variation
If you cannot find the lotus stems, lotus roots make a good substitute and are readily available in Asian markets. When buying fresh, choose roots that feel heavy for their size, as this is an indication that they are full of liquid. They should be peeled and soaked in water with a little lemon juice before being added to the salad, to retain their pale colour.

Rice Salad

The sky's the limit with this recipe. Use whichever fruits and vegetables, and even leftover cooked shellfish or roasted meats, are at your disposal, then simply mix with cooked rice and pour over the fragrant dressing. Canned tuna also works well in this salad.

Ingredients
350g/12oz/3 cups cooked rice
1 Asian pear, cored and diced
50g/2oz dried shrimp, chopped
1 avocado, peeled, stoned (pitted) and diced
½ medium cucumber, finely diced
2 lemon grass stalks, finely chopped
30ml/2 tbsp sweet chilli sauce
1 fresh green or red chilli, seeded and finely sliced
115g/4oz/1 cup flaked (sliced) almonds, toasted
small bunch fresh coriander (cilantro), chopped
fresh Thai sweet basil leaves, to garnish

For the dressing
10ml/2 tsp shrimp paste
15ml/1 tbsp palm sugar (jaggery) or light muscovado (brown) sugar
2 kaffir lime leaves, torn into small pieces
½ lemon grass stalk, sliced

Serves 4–6

1 To make the dressing, put 300ml/½ pint/1¼ cups water in a small pan with the shrimp paste, sugar, kaffir lime leaves and lemon grass. Heat gently, stirring, until the sugar dissolves, then bring to boiling point and simmer for 5 minutes. Strain into a bowl and set aside until cold.

2 Put the cooked rice in a large salad bowl and fluff up the grains with a fork. Add the Asian pear, dried shrimp, avocado, cucumber, lemon grass and sweet chilli sauce. Mix well.

3 Add the diced chilli, flaked almonds and chopped coriander to the bowl of rice salad and toss well to combine.

4 Divide the salad among four to six individual bowls, garnish with Thai basil leaves and serve with the bowl of dressing to spoon over the top.

lotus stem salad Energy 40kcal/168kJ; Protein 1.4g; Carbohydrate 8.3g, of which sugars 7.5g; Fat 0.3g, of which saturates 0g; Cholesterol 0mg; Calcium 55mg; Fibre 1.7g; Sodium 573mg.
rice salad Energy 398kcal/1664kJ; Protein 16.2g; Carbohydrate 34.9g, of which sugars 6.7g; Fat 22.4g, of which saturates 2.6g; Cholesterol 63mg; Calcium 249mg; Fibre 4.1g; Sodium 550mg.

Fruit & Vegetable Salad

This colourful fruit salad is traditionally presented with the main course and serves as a cooler to counteract hot, spicy dishes.

Ingredients

1 small pineapple
1 small mango, peeled and sliced
1 green apple, cored and sliced
6 rambutans or lychees, peeled and stoned (pitted)
115g/4oz/1 cup green beans, trimmed and halved
1 red onion, sliced
1 small cucumber, cut into short sticks
115g/4oz/½ cup beansprouts
2 spring onions (scallions), sliced
1 ripe tomato, quartered
225g/8oz cos, romaine or iceberg lettuce leaves

For the coconut dipping sauce

30ml/2 tbsp coconut cream
30ml/2 tbsp sugar
75ml/5 tbsp boiling water
1.5ml/¼ tsp chilli sauce
15ml/1 tbsp fish sauce
juice of 1 lime

Serves 4–6

1 Make the coconut dipping sauce. Spoon the coconut cream, sugar and boiling water into a screw-top jar. Add the chilli and fish sauces and lime juice, close tightly and shake to mix.

2 Trim both ends of the pineapple with a serrated knife, then cut away the outer skin. Remove the central core with an apple corer. Alternatively, quarter the pineapple lengthways and remove the portion of core from each wedge with a knife. Chop the pineapple and set aside with the other fruits.

3 Bring a small pan of lightly salted water to the boil over a medium heat. Add the green beans to the pan and cook for 3–4 minutes, until just tender but still retaining some "bite". Tip into a colander. Drain, refresh under cold running water, drain well again and set aside.

4 To serve, arrange all the fruits and vegetables in small heaps on a platter or in a shallow bowl. Pour the coconut sauce into a small serving bowl and serve separately as a dip.

Green Mango Salad

This simple salad has a refreshingly tangy, sweet flavour and a lovely texture, and is delicious served with steamed or stir-fried prawns, and with barbecued or seared beef.

Ingredients

450g/1lb green mangoes
grated rind and juice of 2 limes
30ml/2 tbsp sugar
30ml/2 tbsp fish sauce
2 fresh green chillies, seeded and finely sliced
1 small bunch fresh coriander (cilantro), stalks removed, finely chopped
salt

Serves 4

1 Peel, halve and stone (pit) the green mangoes, and slice them into thin strips.

2 In a bowl, mix together the lime rind and juice, sugar and fish sauce. Add the mango strips with the chillies and about three quarters of the coriander. Add salt to taste and leave to stand for 20 minutes to allow the flavours to mingle.

3 Serve on individual salad plates, garnished with the remaining chopped coriander.

Variation

Top the salad with crayfish tails. You can usually buy these preserved in brine, in a 320g/11½oz can. Simply drain and arrange on the salad as you wish.

Cook's Tip

Although the sweet and juicy orange and yellow mangoes and papayas are devoured in vast quantities when ripe, they are also popular for cooking when green. Their rather different, tart flavour and crunchy texture make them ideal for salads and stews. Green mangoes have a dark green skin and can be found at many Chinese and Asian markets.

fruit & vegetable salad Energy 151kcal/645kJ; Protein 3.4g; Carbohydrate 34.3g, of which sugars 33g; Fat 1.1g, of which saturates 0.2g; Cholesterol 0mg; Calcium 78mg; Fibre 4.8g; Sodium 35mg.
green mango salad Energy 69kcal/293kJ; Protein 1.2g; Carbohydrate 16.2g, of which sugars 15.8g; Fat 0.4g, of which saturates 0.1g; Cholesterol 0mg; Calcium 39mg; Fibre 3.6g; Sodium 7mg.

Green Papaya Salad

This salad appears in many guises throughout Asia. If green papaya is not easy to find, try using finely grated carrots, or thinly sliced cucumber, green apple, white cabbage or fennel. For extra colour and crunch, mix in a handful of sliced radishes just before seasoning the salad.

Ingredients

1 green papaya
4 garlic cloves, roughly chopped
15ml/1 tbsp chopped shallots, or onion
3–4 fresh red chillies, seeded and sliced
2.5ml/½ tsp salt
2–3 snake beans or 6 green beans
2 tomatoes, seeded and cut into very thin wedges
45ml/3 tbsp fish sauce
15ml/1 tbsp sugar
juice of 1 lime
30ml/2 tbsp coarsely crushed roasted peanuts
1 fresh red chilli, seeded and sliced, to garnish

Serves 4

1 Cut the papaya in half lengthwise. Scrape out the seeds with a spoon, then peel using a vegetable peeler or a small sharp knife. Shred the flesh finely the grater attachment of a food processor, or a microplane grater.

2 Put the garlic, shallots, chillies and salt in a large mortar and grind to a rough paste with a pestle. Add the shredded papaya, a little at a time, pounding until, after each new addition, it becomes slightly limp and soft.

3 Cut the snake beans or green beans into 2cm/¾in lengths. Add the sliced beans and the wedges of tomato to the mortar and crush them very lightly with the pestle.

4 Season the mixture with the fish sauce, sugar and lime juice. Transfer the salad to a large serving dish or four individual salad plates and sprinkle with the crushed peanuts. Garnish with slices of red chilli and serve.

Gado Gado

This Indonesian salad packs a punch combining lightly steamed vegetables and hard-boiled eggs with a richly flavoured peanut and soy sauce dressing.

Ingredients

225g/8oz new potatoes, halved
2 carrots, cut into sticks
115g/4oz green beans
½ small cauliflower, broken into florets
¼ firm white cabbage, shredded
200g/7oz/¾ cup bean or lentil sprouts
4 eggs, hard-boiled and quartered
bunch of watercress

For the sauce

90ml/6 tbsp crunchy peanut butter
1 garlic clove, crushed
30ml/2 tbsp dark soy sauce
15ml/1 tbsp dry sherry or Chinese rice wine
10ml/2 tsp caster (superfine) sugar
15ml/1 tbsp fresh lemon juice
5ml/1 tsp anchovy essence

Serves 6

1 Place the halved potatoes in a metal colander or steamer and set over a pan of gently boiling water. Cover the pan or steamer with a lid and cook the potatoes for 10 minutes.

2 Add the rest of the vegetables to the steamer and steam for a further 10 minutes until tender. Cool and arrange on a platter with the egg quarters and the watercress, if using.

3 Beat together all the sauce ingredients with 300ml/½ pint/1¼ cups cold water in a large mixing bowl until smooth. Drizzle a little over the salad then pour the rest into a small bowl and serve separately.

Variations

There are a whole range of nut butters, such as hazelnut, almong or cashew, available in larger supermarkets. Alternatively, make your own peanut butter by blending 225g/8oz peanuts with 120ml/4fl oz/½ cup oil in a food processor.

green papaya salad Energy 109kcal/461kJ; Protein 3.4g; Carbohydrate 16.5g, of which sugars 15.9g; Fat 3.8g, of which saturates 0.7g; Cholesterol 0mg; Calcium 40mg; Fibre 3.5g; Sodium 811mg.
gado gado Energy 235kcal/979kJ; Protein 12.7g; Carbohydrate 18.3g, of which sugars 10.6g; Fat 12.5g, of which saturates 3.2g; Cholesterol 127mg; Calcium 91mg; Fibre 4.8g; Sodium 494mg.

Pickled Ginger

The Chinese love cooking with ginger. Warming, good for the heart, and believed to aid digestion, it finds its way into salads, soups, stir-fries and puddings. Pickled ginger is an immensely useful condiment, easy to prepare and often served with noodles and rice.

Ingredients

225g/8oz fresh young ginger, peeled
10ml/2 tsp salt
200ml/7fl oz/1 cup white rice vinegar
50g/2oz/¼ cup sugar

Serves 4–6

1 Place the ginger in a bowl and sprinkle with salt. Cover and place in the refrigerator for 24 hours.

2 Drain off any excess liquid and pat the ginger dry with a clean dish towel.

3 Slice each knob of ginger very finely along the grain, like thin rose petals, and place them in a clean bowl or a sterilized jar suitable for storing.

4 In a small bowl beat the vinegar and 50ml/2fl oz/¼ cup water with the sugar, until it has dissolved. Pour the pickling liquid over the ginger and cover or seal. Store in the refrigerator or a cool place for about a week.

Cook's Tips

- *Juicy and tender with a pinkish-yellow skin, young ginger is less fibrous than the mature rhizome. When pickled in vinegar, the flesh turns pale pink.*
- *Aside from its obvious application in Chinese cookery, pickled ginger is also served with sushi. It can also enliven less exotic dishes such as a pear and walnut salad, a few slices of cold roast duck, or even something as simple as a ham sandwich. It is valued for the way in which it cuts through oily flavours so this pickle also tastes good with smoked mackerel.*

Pickled Vegetables

Popular pickles includes the trio of cucumber, mooli and carrot – green, white and orange in colour. These tend to be served as snacks for nibbling, or as part of a table salad. They are also used as accompaniments to grilled meats and shellfish.

Ingredients

300ml/½ pint/1¼ cups white rice vinegar
90g/3½oz/scant ½ cup sugar
450g/1lb carrots, cut into 5cm/2in matchsticks
450g/1lb mooli (daikon), halved lengthways, and cut into thin crescents
600g/1lb 6oz cucumbers, partially peeled in strips and cut into 5cm/2in matchsticks
15ml/1 tbsp salt

Serves 4–6

1 Put the vinegar and sugar in a large bowl and whisk with a fork or balloon whisk until all the sugar has dissolved.

2 Add the carrots and mooli to the vinegar mixture and toss well to coat. Cover the bowl with clear film (plastic wrap) and place in the refrigerator for 24 hours.

3 Spread out the cucumber strips on several plates and sprinkle with the salt. Leave for 30 minutes, then tip into a colander, rinse under cold water and drain well.

4 Add the cucumber slices to the carrot and mooli and toss well in the pickling liquid. Cover and refrigerate as before.

5 Lift the vegetables out of the pickling liquid to serve immediately, or spoon them into a jar. Seal with clear film and a tight-fitting lid and store in the refrigerator.

Cook's Tip

To sterilize pickling jars, place them in a deep pan and pour in enough hot water to cover them. Allow the water to boil for ten minutes, then remove the jars, drain and allow to air-dry.

pickled ginger Energy 36kcal/151kJ; Protein 0.2g; Carbohydrate 9.1g, of which sugars 9.1g; Fat 0.1g, of which saturates 0g; Cholesterol 0mg; Calcium 20mg; Fibre 0.4g; Sodium 678mg.
pickled vegetables Energy 104kcal/438kJ; Protein 1.8g; Carbohydrate 24.5g, of which sugars 24.1g; Fat 0.5g, of which saturates 0.2g; Cholesterol 0mg; Calcium 59mg; Fibre 3.1g; Sodium 1013mg.

Kimchi

This Korean speciality is now enjoyed all over Asia, thanks to the immigrants who couldn't live without the favourite food of the home country. In the past, large stone pots were filled with this pickled cabbage, and buried in the ground for the winter.

Ingredients

675g/1½lb Chinese leaves (Chinese cabbage), shredded
1 large or 2 medium yam beans, total weight about 675g/1½lb or 2 hard pears, peeled and thinly sliced
60ml/4 tbsp salt
200ml/7fl oz/scant 1 cup water
4 spring onions (scallions), chopped
4 garlic cloves, crushed
2.5cm/1in piece fresh root ginger, peeled and finely chopped
10–15ml/2–3 tsp chilli powder

Serves 6–8

1 Place the Chinese leaves and yam beans or pears in a bowl and sprinkle evenly with salt. Mix well, then press the vegetable mixture down into the bowl.

2 Pour the water over the vegetables, if necessary putting a plate over them so that they remain submerged, then cover the bowl and leave overnight in a cool place.

3 The following day, drain off the brine from the vegetables and set it aside. Mix the brined vegetables with the spring onions, garlic, ginger and chilli powder. Pack the mixture into a 900g/2lb jar or two smaller ones. Pour over the reserved brine.

4 Cover with clear film (plastic wrap) and place on a sunny windowsill or in a warm place for 2–3 days.

Cook's Tip

Today, it is recommended that the mixture is stored in the refrigerator after its initial spell in the sunshine. It will keep for several weeks in a tightly lidded jar.

Pickled Shallots

Pickling shallots in this way demands some patience while the vinegar and spices work their magic, but the results are definitely worth the wait. Thinly sliced, the shallots are often used as a condiment with South-east Asian meals.

Ingredients

5–6 small fresh red or green bird's eye chillies
500g/1¼lb Thai pink shallots, peeled
2 large garlic cloves, peeled and halved and green shoots removed

For the vinegar

40g/1½oz/3 tbsp sugar
10ml/2 tsp salt
5cm/2in piece fresh root ginger, peeled and sliced
15ml/1 tbsp coriander seeds
2 lemon grass stalks, cut in half lengthways
4 kaffir lime leaves or pared strips of lime rind
600ml/1 pint/2½ cups cider vinegar
15ml/1 tbsp chopped fresh coriander (cilantro)

Makes 2–3 jars

1 The chillies can be left whole or halved and seeded. If leaving the chillies whole, prick them several times. Bring a large pan of water to the boil. Add the chillies, shallots and garlic. Blanch for 1–2 minutes, then drain. Rinse all the vegetables under cold water, then drain again.

2 Prepare the vinegar. Put the sugar, salt, ginger, coriander seeds, lemon grass and lime leaves or lime rind in a pan, pour in the vinegar and bring to the boil. Reduce the heat to low and simmer for 3–4 minutes. Leave to cool.

3 Remove and discard the ginger, then bring the vinegar back to the boil. Add the fresh coriander, garlic and chillies and cook for 1 minute.

4 Pack the shallots into sterilized jars, with the lemon grass, lime leaves, chillies and garlic among them. Pour over the hot vinegar. Cool, then seal and store in a cool, dark place for 2 months before eating.

kimchi Energy 45kcal/190kJ; Protein 2.3g; Carbohydrate 8.5g, of which sugars 8g; Fat 0.4g, of which saturates 0g; Cholesterol 0mg; Calcium 76mg; Fibre 3.2g; Sodium 240mg.
pickled shallots Energy 92kcal/391kJ; Protein 3.1g; Carbohydrate 19.9g, of which sugars 19.8g; Fat 0.6g, of which saturates 0g; Cholesterol 0mg; Calcium 80mg; Fibre 3.2g; Sodium 23mg.

Fried Pineapple

This is a very simple and quick dessert to make. The slightly sharp flavour of the fruit makes this a very refreshing treat, ideal for serving at the end of a rich or spicy meal.

Ingredients

1 pineapple
40g/1½oz/3 tbsp butter
15ml/1 tbsp desiccated (dry unsweetened) coconut
60ml/4 tbsp soft light brown sugar
60ml/4 tbsp fresh lime juice
lime slices, to decorate
thick and creamy natural (plain) yogurt, to serve

Serves 4

1 Using a sharp knife, cut the top off the pineapple and peel off the skin, taking care to remove the eyes. Cut the pineapple in half and remove and discard the woody core. Cut the flesh lengthways into 1cm/½in wedges.

2 Heat the butter in a large, heavy frying pan or wok. When it has melted, add the pineapple wedges and cook over a medium heat for 1–2 minutes on each side, or until they have turned pale golden in colour.

3 Meanwhile, dry-fry the coconut in a small frying pan until lightly browned. Remove from the heat and set aside.

4 Sprinkle the sugar into the pan with the pineapple, add the lime juice and cook, stirring constantly, until the sugar has dissolved to make a syrupy sauce.

5 Divide the pineapple wedges among four bowls, sprinkle with the coconut, decorate with the lime slices and serve with the yogurt.

Variation
A generous splash of rum, added with the lime juice, turns this dessert into an adult treat, perfect with after-dinner drinks.

Pineapple with Papaya Sauce

Pineapple cooked this way takes on a superb flavour and is sensational when served with the sweet papaya sauce. This sauce can also be served with savoury dishes, particularly grilled chicken and game birds as well as pork and lamb.

Ingredients

1 sweet pineapple
melted butter, for greasing and brushing
2 pieces drained stem ginger in syrup, cut into fine matchsticks, plus 30ml/2 tbsp stem ginger syrup from the jar
30ml/2 tbsp demerara (raw) sugar
pinch of ground cinnamon
fresh mint sprigs, to decorate

For the sauce

1 ripe papaya, peeled and seeded
175ml/6fl oz/¾ cup apple juice

Serves 6

1 Peel the pineapple and take spiral slices off the outside to remove the eyes. Cut it crossways into six slices, each 2.5cm/1in thick. Line a baking sheet with a sheet of foil, rolling up the sides to make a rim. Grease the foil with melted butter. Preheat the grill (broiler).

2 Arrange the pineapple slices on the lined baking sheet. Brush with butter, then top with the ginger matchsticks, sugar and cinnamon. Drizzle over the stem ginger syrup. Grill (broil) for 5–7 minutes or until the slices are golden and lightly charred on the surface.

3 Meanwhile, make the sauce. Cut a few slices from the papaya and set aside, then purée the rest with the apple juice in a blender or food processor.

4 Press the purée through a sieve (strainer) placed over a bowl, then stir in any juices from cooking the pineapple.

5 Serve the pineapple slices with a little sauce drizzled around each plate. Decorate with the reserved papaya slices and the mint sprigs.

fried pineapple Energy 238kcal/1004kJ; Protein 1.2g; Carbohydrate 36.2g, of which sugars 36.2g; Fat 11g, of which saturates 7.2g; Cholesterol 21mg; Calcium 47mg; Fibre 2.9g; Sodium 67mg.
pineapple w. papaya sauce Energy 97kcal/415kJ; Protein 0.7g; Carbohydrate 24.7g, of which sugars 24.7g; Fat 0.2g, of which saturates 0g; Cholesterol 0mg; Calcium 33mg; Fibre 2.3g; Sodium 19mg.

Banana Fritters

These delicious deep-fried bananas are quick to cook, but easy to get wrong! They should be cooked at the last minute, so that the batter is crisp and the banana inside is soft and warm. It's also important that the oil for deep-frying has reached the correct temperature, so that the batter cooks on contact. If it isn't hot enough, the batter will slide off the bananas and may turn into a pappy mess.

Ingredients

115g/4oz/1 cup self-raising (self-rising) flour
40g/1½ oz/¼ cup rice flour
2.5ml/½ tsp salt
200ml/7fl oz/scant 1 cup water
finely grated lime rind (optional)
8 baby bananas
vegetable oil, for deep frying
strips of lime rind, to garnish
caster (superfine) sugar, for dredginug
lime wedges, to serve

Serves 8

1 Sift together the self-raising flour, rice flour and salt into a bowl. Add just enough water to make a smooth, coating batter. Mix well, then add the lime rind, if using.

2 Heat the oil in a deep fryer or wok to 190°C/375°F. Meanwhile, peel the bananas. Dip them into the batter several times until well coated, then deep-fry until crisp and golden.

3 Drain on kitchen paper. Serve hot, dredged with caster sugar and garnished with strips of lime. Offer the lime wedges for squeezing over the bananas.

Cook's Tip

Tiny bananas are available from some Asian stores and many larger supermarkets, alternatively use small bananas and cut in half lengthways and then in half again.

Variation

Instead of lime, add finely grated orange rind to the batter.

Deep-fried Bananas

These deliciously sweet and crunchy treats are a favourite with children and adults alike.

Ingredients

115g/4oz/1 cup plain (all-purpose) flour
2.5ml/½ tsp bicarbonate of soda (baking soda)
pinch of salt
30ml/2 tbsp sugar
1 egg, beaten
90ml/6 tbsp water
30ml/2 tbsp shredded coconut or 15ml/1 tbsp sesame seeds
4 firm bananas
vegetable oil, for deep-frying
fresh mint sprigs, to decorate
30ml/2 tbsp clear honey, to serve (optional)

Serves 4

1 Sift the flour, bicarbonate of soda and salt into a large bowl. Stir in the sugar and the egg, and whisk in just enough of the water to make quite a thin batter. Whisk in the shredded coconut or sesame seeds so that they are evenly distributed.

2 Peel the bananas. Carefully cut each one in half lengthways, then in half crossways to make 16 pieces of about the same size. Don't do this until you are ready to cook them because, once peeled, bananas quickly discolour.

3 Heat the oil in a wok or deep-fryer to a temperature of 190°C/375°F or until a cube of bread, dropped in the oil, browns in about 45 seconds. Dip the banana pieces in the batter, then gently drop a few into the oil. Deep-fry until golden brown, then lift out and drain well on kitchen paper.

4 Cook the remaining banana pieces in the same way. Serve immediately with honey, if using, and decorated with sprigs of fresh mint.

Variations

This recipe works just as well with many other types of fruit, such as pineapple rings or apple wedges.

banana fritters Energy 204kcal/855kJ; Protein 3.9g; Carbohydrate 26.6g, of which sugars 14.8g; Fat 9.8g, of which saturates 4.4g; Cholesterol 48mg; Calcium 47mg; Fibre 1.7g; Sodium 75mg.
deep-fried bananas Energy 377kcal/1571kJ; Protein 5g; Carbohydrate 39.6g, of which sugars 22.7g; Fat 22.5g, of which saturates 9.9g; Cholesterol 63mg; Calcium 26mg; Fibre 3.2g; Sodium 30mg.

Toffee Plums with Coconut Rice

Red, juicy plums seared in a wok with sugar acquire a rich caramel coating.

Ingredients

6 or 8 firm, ripe plums
90g/3½oz/½ cup caster (superfine) sugar

For the rice

115g/4oz sticky glutinous rice
150ml/¼ pint/⅔ cup coconut cream
45ml/3 tbsp caster (superfine) sugar
a pinch of salt

Serves 4

1 First prepare the rice. Rinse it in several changes of water, then leave to soak overnight in a bowl of cold water.

2 Line a large bamboo steamer that will fit in your wok with muslin (cheesecloth). Drain the rice and transfer to the steamer.

3 Cover the rice and steam over simmering water for 25–30 minutes, until the rice is tender. (Check the water level and add more if necessary.) Transfer the steamed rice to a wide bowl and set aside.

4 Combine the coconut cream with the sugar and salt and pour into a clean wok. Heat gently and bring to the boil, then remove from the heat and pour over the rice. Stir to mix well.

5 Using a sharp knife, cut the plums in half and remove their stones (pits). Sprinkle the sugar over the cut sides.

6 Heat a non-stick wok over a medium-high flame. Working in batches, place the plums in the wok, cut side down, and cook for 1–2 minutes, or until the sugar caramelizes. You may need to wipe out the wok with kitchen paper in between batches.

7 Mould the rice into rounds and place on warmed plates, then spoon over the caramelized plums. Alternatively, simply spoon the rice into four warmed bowls and top with the plums. Drizzle any syrup remaining in the wok over and around the fruit.

Papaya Baked with Ginger

Ginger is responsible for enhancing the flavour of papaya in this recipe, which takes no more than ten minutes to prepare. Take care not to overcook the papaya or its flesh will become very watery.

Ingredients

2 ripe papayas
2 pieces stem ginger in syrup, drained, plus 15ml/1 tbsp syrup from the jar
8 amaretti or other dessert biscuits (cookies), coarsely crushed
45ml/3 tbsp raisins
shredded, finely pared rind and juice of 1 lime
25g/1oz/¼ cup pistachio nuts, chopped
15ml/1 tbsp light brown muscovado sugar
60ml/4 tbsp double (heavy) cream, plus extra to serve

Serves 4

1 Preheat the oven to 200°C/400°F/Gas 6. Cut the papayas in half and scoop out their seeds.

2 Place the halves in a baking dish and set aside. Cut the stem ginger into fine matchsticks.

3 Make the filling. Combine the crushed amaretti biscuits, stem ginger matchsticks and raisins in a bowl.

4 Stir in the lime rind and juice, two thirds of the nuts, then add the sugar and cream. Mix well.

5 Fill the papaya halves and drizzle with the ginger syrup. Sprinkle with the remaining nuts. Bake for about 25 minutes or until tender.

6 Serve each papaya half with a generous helping of cream.

Variation
For a slightly different serving suggestion, try Greek (US strained plain) yogurt and almonds instead of cream and pistachios.

toffee plums w. rice Energy 271kcal/1148kJ; Protein 2.8g; Carbohydrate 66.3g, of which sugars 43.4g; Fat 0.4g, of which saturates 0.2g; Cholesterol 0mg; Calcium 52mg; Fibre 0.8g; Sodium 86mg.
papaya w. ginger Energy 292kcal/1228kJ; Protein 3.6g; Carbohydrate 44.6g, of which sugars 35.7g; Fat 12.3g, of which saturates 5.7g; Cholesterol 17mg; Calcium 84mg; Fibre 4.2g; Sodium 127mg.

Chinese-style Toffee Apples

Crunchy apple wedges fried until crisp in a light batter, then dipped in caramel, makes a sweet, gloriously sticky dessert.

Ingredients

115g/4oz/1 cup plain (all-purpose) flour
10ml/2 tsp baking powder
60ml/4 tbsp cornflour (cornstarch)
4 firm apples
sunflower oil, for deep-frying
200g/7oz/1 cup caster (superfine) sugar

Serves 4

1 In a large mixing bowl, combine the flour, baking powder, cornflour and 175ml/6fl oz/¾ cup water. Stir to make a smooth batter and set aside.

2 Peel and core the apples, then cut each one into 8 thick wedges. Fill a large bowl with ice cubes and chilled water.

3 Fill a wok one-third full of sunflower oil and heat to 180°C/350°F or until a cube of bread, dropped into the oil, browns in 45 seconds.

4 Working quickly, in batches, dip the apple wedges in the batter, drain off any excess and deep-fry for 2 minutes, or until golden brown. Remove with a slotted spoon and place on kitchen paper to drain.

5 Reheat the oil to 180°C/350°F and fry the wedges for a second time, again giving them about 2 minutes. Drain well on kitchen paper and set aside.

6 Very carefully, pour off all but 30ml/2 tbsp of the oil from the wok and stir in the sugar. Heat gently until the sugar melts and starts to caramelize. When the mixture is light brown, add a few pieces of apple at a time and toss to coat evenly.

7 Plunge the coated pieces briefly into the iced water to set the caramel, then remove with a slotted spoon and serve.

Pumpkin Purée in Banana Leaves

This is a traditional pudding that can be made with small, sweet pumpkins, butternut squash or sweet cassava. If opting for the traditional pumpkin, find a lighter-coloured one as it is likely have a softer texture. This is a very moreish dessert, or snack, which can be eaten hot or cold.

Ingredients

1 small pumpkin, about 1.3kg/3lb peeled, seeded and cubed
250ml/8fl oz/1 cup coconut milk
45ml/3 tbsp palm sugar (jaggery)
15ml/1 tbsp tapioca starch
12 banana leaves, cut into 15cm/6in squares
salt

Serves 6

1 Bring a pan of salted water to the boil. Add the pumpkin flesh and cook for 15 minutes, or until tender. Drain and mash with a fork or purée in a blender.

2 In a pan, heat the coconut milk with the sugar and a pinch of salt. Blend the tapioca starch with 15ml/1 tbsp water and 15ml/1 tbsp of the hot coconut milk. Add it to the coconut milk and beat well. Beat the mashed pumpkin into the coconut milk or, if using a blender, add the coconut milk to the pumpkin and purée together.

3 Spoon equal amounts of the pumpkin purée into the centre of each banana leaf square. Fold in the sides and thread a cocktail stick (toothpick) through the open ends to enclose the purée completely.

4 Fill the bottom third of a wok with water. Place a bamboo steamer on top. Place as many stuffed banana leaves as you can into the steamer, folded side up – you may have to cook them in batches. Cover the steamer and steam parcels for 15 minutes. Unwrap them and serve hot or cold.

Cook's Tip
'Sweet' squashes are essentially the smaller variety of squash.

chinese toffee apples Energy 457kcal/1940kJ; Protein 3.4g; Carbohydrate 97.3g, of which sugars 61.6g; Fat 8.8g, of which saturates 1.1g; Cholesterol 0mg; Calcium 73mg; Fibre 2.5g; Sodium 14mg.
pumpkin purée Energy 76kcal/323kJ; Protein 1.7g; Carbohydrate 17g, of which sugars 13.6g; Fat 0.6g, of which saturates 0.3g; Cholesterol 0mg; Calcium 79mg; Fibre 2.2g; Sodium 46mg.

Pumpkin with Coconut Custard

Sweet and fragrant, this dessert is sheer indulgence. The hot coconut sauce is the perfect topping for the custard-filled pumpkin.

Ingredients

1 small pumpkin, about 1.3kg/3lb, halved, seeded and fibres removed
400ml/14fl oz/1⅔ cups coconut milk
3 large (US extra large) eggs
45ml/3 tbsp palm sugar (jaggery), plus a little extra for sprinkling
salt

For the sauce

250ml/8fl oz/1 cup coconut cream
30ml/2 tbsp palm sugar

Serves 4–8

1 Preheat the oven to 180°C/350°F/Gas 4. Place the pumpkin halves, skin side down, in a baking dish.

2 In a large bowl, whisk the coconut milk with a pinch of salt, the eggs and sugar, until the mixture is thick and smooth. Pour the custard into each pumpkin half and sprinkle a little extra sugar over the top of the custard and the rim of the pumpkin.

3 Bake in the oven for 35–40 minutes. The pumpkin should feel tender when a skewer is inserted in it, and the custard should feel firm when lightly touched. If you like, you can brown the top further under the grill (broiler).

4 Just before serving, heat the coconut cream in a pan with a pinch of salt and the sugar. Scoop out servings of pumpkin flesh with the custard and place it in bowls. Pour a little sweetened coconut cream over the top to serve.

Variation

Baked mangoes or butternut squash are the obvious substitutes for pumpkin, but – surprisingly – baked avocadoes also combine wonderfully well with sweet ingredients. Sweetened avocado is also immensely popular in Brazil. If using, you may need to adjust the quantity of custard, and the cooking time.

Pumpkin & Sweet Potato Pudding

A favourite among many Malays and Indonesians this dish can be served as a sweet snack, or as a nourishing and warming breakfast.

Ingredients

900ml/1½ pints/3¾ cups coconut milk
½ small pumpkin, seeded and cut into bitesize cubes
2 sweet potatoes, cut into bitesize pieces
1 pandanus (screwpine) leaf
150g/5oz/¾ cup palm sugar (jaggery)
2.5ml/½ tsp salt
3 bananas, cut into thick diagonal slices

Serves 4–6

1 Pour the coconut milk into a heavy pan and bring it to the boil. Stir in the pumpkin, sweet potatoes and pandanus leaf.

2 Continue to boil for 1 minute more, then reduce the heat and simmer for about 15 minutes, until the pumpkin and sweet potato are tender but not too soft.

3 Using a slotted spoon, lift the pumpkin and sweet potato pieces out of the coconut milk and put them on a plate.

4 Add the sugar and salt to the coconut milk and stir until the sugar has dissolved. Bring the sweetened coconut milk to the boil, then reduce the heat and simmer for 5 minutes.

5 Add the bananas to the sweetened coconut milk and simmer for 4 minutes. Put the pumpkin and sweet potato back into the pan and gently mix all the ingredients together. Remove the pandanus leaf and serve warm on individual salad plates.

Variation

Orange and pumpkin go well together. Toss the mixture with orange segments, instead of banana, just before serving, if you like.

pumpkin w. custard Energy 217kcal/906kJ; Protein 4.5g; Carbohydrate 16.3g, of which sugars 15.7g; Fat 15.4g, of which saturates 11.9g; Cholesterol 71mg; Calcium 71mg; Fibre 1.3g; Sodium 87mg.
pumpkin/sweet potato Energy 230kcal/980kJ; Protein 2.7g; Carbohydrate 55.8g, of which sugars 48.7g; Fat 1g, of which saturates 0.6g; Cholesterol 0mg; Calcium 116mg; Fibre 3g; Sodium 180mg.

Coconut Custard Pots

This traditional dessert can be baked or steamed, and the pots are popularly served as a topping for sweet sticky rice. The coconut custard also works well with a selection of fresh fruit, where it can be spooned over the top as desired. In terms of flavour, mangoes and tamarillos go particularly well with the custard and rice.

Ingredients

4 eggs
75g/3oz/6 tbsp soft light brown sugar
250ml/8fl oz/1 cup coconut milk
5ml/1 tsp vanilla, rose or jasmine extract
fresh mint leaves and icing (confectioners') sugar, to decorate
sliced fruit, to serve

Serves 4

1 Preheat the oven to 150°C/300°F/Gas 2. Whisk the eggs and sugar in a bowl until smooth. Add the coconut milk and extract and whisk well.

2 Strain the mixture into a jug (pitcher), then pour it into four individual heatproof glasses, ramekins or an ovenproof dish.

3 Stand the glasses, ramekins or dish in a roasting pan. Fill the pan with hot water to reach halfway up the sides of the ramekins or dish.

4 Bake for about 35–40 minutes, or until the custards are set. Test with a fine skewer or cocktail stick (toothpick).

5 Remove the roasting pan from the oven, lift out the ramekins or dish and leave to cool before decorate with the mint leaves and a dusting of icing sugar. Serve with sliced fruit.

Cook's Tip
If you bake this in one large dish, you may need to extend the cooking time. Simply check the mixture has set before serving.

Coconut & Mandarin Custards

These scented custards with a fabulous melt-in-the-mouth texture are best served warm. However, they are also delicious served chilled, making them perfect for easy entertaining. If you prefer, make the praline the day before.

Ingredients

200ml/7fl oz/scant 1 cup coconut cream
200ml/7fl oz/scant 1 cup double (heavy) cream
2.5ml/½ tsp finely ground star anise
75ml/5 tbsp golden caster (superfine) sugar
15ml/1 tbsp very finely grated mandarin or orange rind
4 egg yolks

For the praline

175g/6oz/scant 1 cup caster (superfine) sugar
50g/2oz/½ cup roughly chopped mixed nuts, to serve

Serves 4

1 Make the praline. Place the sugar in a non-stick wok with 15–30ml/1–2 tbsp water. Cook over a medium heat until the sugar dissolves and turns light gold.

2 Remove the syrup from the heat and pour on to a baking sheet lined with baking parchment. Spread it out using the back of a spoon, then sprinkle the chopped nuts evenly over the top and leave to harden.

3 Meanwhile place the coconut cream, double cream, star anise, sugar, mandarin or orange rind and egg yolks in a large bowl. Whisk to combine and pour the mixture into four lightly greased ramekins or small, heatproof bowls.

4 Place the ramekins or cups in a large steamer, cover and place in a wok and steam over gently simmering water for 12–15 minutes, or until the custards are just set.

5 Carefully lift the custards from the steamer and leave to cool slightly for about 10 minutes. Meanwhile, break the hardened praline into rough pieces and serve it on top of, or alongside, the custards once the latter have cooled.

coconut custard Energy 433kcal/1792kJ; Protein 10.2g; Carbohydrate 7.8g, of which sugars 7.8g; Fat 40.5g, of which saturates 29g; Cholesterol 170mg; Calcium 168mg; Fibre 4.6g; Sodium 108mg.
coconut & mandarin Energy 643kcal/2688kJ; Protein 6.7g; Carbohydrate 71g, of which sugars 69.3g; Fat 38.9g, of which saturates 19.6g; Cholesterol 270mg; Calcium 100mg; Fibre 0.4g; Sodium 115mg.

Steamed Ginger Custards

Delicate and warming, ginger custard is a favourite among the Chinese. These individual custards are often served warm, straight from the steamer, and enjoyed as a mid-afternoon snack. They work just as well served as a chilled dessert, however.

Ingredients

115g/4oz fresh root ginger, chopped
400ml/14fl oz/1⅔ cups coconut milk
60ml/4 tbsp sugar
2 egg whites

Serves 4

1 Using a mortar and pestle or food processor, grind the ginger to a fine paste. Press the ginger paste through a fine sieve (strainer) set over a bowl, or twist it in a piece of muslin (cheesecloth), to extract the juice.

2 Fill a wok one-third of the way up with water. Place a bamboo steamer in the wok, bring the water to the boil and reduce the heat to low.

3 In a bowl, whisk the coconut milk, sugar and egg whites with the ginger juice until the mixture is smooth and the sugar has dissolved.

4 Pour the mixture into four individual heatproof bowls and place them in the steamer. Cover and steam for 15–20 minutes, until the mixture sets.

5 Remove the bowls from the steamer and leave to cool. Cover them with clear film (plastic wrap) and place in the refrigerator overnight. Serve the custards chilled or at room temperature as desired.

Variation
Slice about 6 pieces of preserved (stem) ginger and add them to the coconut mixture before pouring into bowls for steaming. It will intensify the flavour of this sweet custard dessert.

Coconut Rice Pudding

This rice pudding is often accompanied by fruits in syrup, or sautéed bananas or pineapple.

Ingredients

90g/3½oz/½ cup pudding rice
600ml/1 pint/2½ cups coconut milk
300ml/½ pint/1¼ cups full-fat (whole) milk
75g/2¾oz/scant ½ cup caster (superfine) sugar
25g/1oz/2 tbsp butter, plus extra for greasing
45ml/3 tbsp grated fresh or desiccated (dry unsweetened) coconut, toasted
1 small, ripe pineapple
30ml/2 tbsp sesame oil
5cm/2in piece of fresh root ginger, peeled and grated
shavings of toasted coconut, to decorate

Serves 4–6

1 Preheat the oven to 150°C/300°F/Gas 2. Grease an ovenproof dish. In a bowl, mix the rice with the coconut milk, milk and 50g/2oz/¼ cup of the sugar and pour it into the ovenproof dish. Dot pieces of butter over the top and place the dish in the oven.

2 After 30 minutes, take the dish out and gently stir in the toasted coconut. Return it to the oven for a further 1½ hours, or until almost all the milk is absorbed and a golden skin has formed on top of the pudding.

3 Using a sharp knife, peel the pineapple and remove the core, then cut the flesh into bitesize cubes.

4 Towards the end of the cooking time, heat the oil in a large wok or heavy pan. Stir in the ginger, stir-fry until it becomes aromatic, then add the pineapple cubes, turning them over to sear on both sides. Sprinkle the ingredients with the remaining sugar and continue to cook until the pineapple is slightly caramelized in texture.

5 Serve the pudding spooned into bowls and topped with the hot, caramelized pineapple and toasted coconut.

ginger custards Energy 89kcal/380kJ; Protein 2g; Carbohydrate 20.8g, of which sugars 20.8g; Fat 0.4g, of which saturates 0.2g; Cholesterol 0mg; Calcium 50mg; Fibre 0.3g; Sodium 159mg.
coconut rice pudding Energy 259kcal/1087kJ; Protein 5.8g; Carbohydrate 34g, of which sugars 19.9g; Fat 11.5g, of which saturates 8.2g; Cholesterol 19mg; Calcium 152mg; Fibre 1g; Sodium 153mg.

Sago Pudding with Palm Syrup

Palm, also known as jaggery, makes a sweet syrup to pour over this delicious sago and coconut pudding.

Ingredients

1 pandanus (screwpine) leaf, tied in a knot
250g/9oz pearl sago, picked over, washed and drained
400ml/14fl oz/1⅔ cups coconut milk, lightly beaten
salt

For the syrup

250ml/8fl oz/1 cup water
175g/6oz/¾ cup palm sugar (jaggery)

Serves 4

1 Bring a deep pan of water to the boil. Drop in the pandanus leaf and let the sago pour into the water through the fingertips of one hand, while you stir with a wooden spoon with the other, to prevent the pearls from sticking.

2 Boil for 5 minutes, then remove from the heat, cover the pan and leave the sago to steam for about 10 minutes – the pearls should be swollen and translucent. Drain the sago through a sieve (strainer) and rinse under running cold water.

3 Reserve the pandanus leaf and put the sago into a bowl. Stir in 15–30ml/1–2 tbsp of the coconut milk – enough to bind it together –with a pinch of salt. Spoon the sago into a lightly greased mould, or four separate moulds, packing it down gently, and leave it to set at room temperature.

4 Meanwhile, make the syrup. Put the water and palm sugar into a heavy pan and stir over a high heat until the sugar has dissolved. Bring to the boil and boil for 2 minutes. Drop in the reserved pandanus leaf, then simmer for 10 minutes.

5 Beat the rest of the coconut milk with a pinch of salt. Turn the mould, or individual moulds, upside down in a shallow bowl and slip them off the pudding. Spoon the coconut milk over the top, allowing it to flow down the sides and form a pool in the dish, and pour over the hot syrup. Serve immediately, while the syrup is still hot.

Tapioca with Banana & Coconut

This is the type of dessert that everybody's mother or grandmother makes. Sweet and nourishing, the tapioca pearls are cooked in coconut milk and sweetened with bananas and sugar.

Ingredients

550ml/18fl oz/2½ cups water
40g/1½oz tapioca pearls
550ml/18fl oz/2½ cups coconut milk
90g/3½oz/½ cup sugar
3 ripe bananas, diced
salt

Serves 4

1 Pour the water into a pan and bring it to the boil. Stir in the tapioca pearls, reduce the heat and simmer for about 20 minutes, until translucent.

2 Pour in the coconut milk, then add the sugar and a pinch of salt. Cook gently for 30 minutes.

3 Stir in the diced bananas and cook them for 5–10 minutes until soft. Spoon into individual warmed bowls and serve immediately while still hot.

Variations

Instead of adding the diced bananas to the warm tapioca mixture, try one of the following, adjusting the cooking time as needed so that the fruit is fully cooked:

- *sliced rhubarb*
- *small apple or pear, cut into wedges*
- *nectarine or mango slices*

Cook's Tip

A pinch of salt added to this recipe enhances the flavour of the coconut milk and counterbalances the sweetness. You can try the recipe with sweet potato, taro root, yellow corn or rice.

sago pudding Energy 416kcal/1777kJ; Protein 0.7g; Carbohydrate 109.4g, of which sugars 50.6g; Fat 0.4g, of which saturates 0.2g; Cholesterol 0mg; Calcium 59mg; Fibre 0.3g; Sodium 115mg.
tapioca w. banana Energy 226kcal/964kJ; Protein 1.5g; Carbohydrate 57.2g, of which sugars 45.9g; Fat 0.7g, of which saturates 0.4g; Cholesterol 0mg; Calcium 57mg; Fibre 0.9g; Sodium 154mg.

Tapioca Pudding

This pudding, made from large pearl tapioca and coconut milk and served warm, is much lighter than its well-known Western-style counterpart. You can adjust the sweetness to your taste. Serve with lychees or the smaller, similar-tasting longans – a fruit also known as "dragon's eyes".

Ingredients
115g/4oz/⅔ cup tapioca
475ml/16fl oz/2 cups water
175g/6oz/¾ cup sugar
pinch of salt
250ml/8fl oz/1 cup coconut milk
250g/9oz prepared tropical fruits
finely shredded lime rind and shaved fresh coconut (optional), to decorate

Serves 4

1 Put the tapioca in a bowl and pour over warm water to cover. Leave to soak for 1 hour so the grains swell. Drain.

2 Pour the measured water in a large pan and bring to the boil over a medium heat. Add the sugar and salt and stir until dissolved.

3 Add the tapioca and coconut milk, reduce the heat to low and simmer gently for 10 minutes, or until the tapioca becomes transparent.

4 Spoon into one large or four individual bowls and serve warm with the tropical fruits. Decorate with the lime rind and coconut shavings, if using.

Cook's Tips
• *The fruit of the longan tree* (Euphoria longana), *longanas are still little known outside Asia, at least in comparison with the more popular lychee. Longanas are indigenous to India and Burma, but are also cultivated in China, and can be eaten raw, dried or preserved in syrup. The fruit is also popular in sweet and sour dishes, and may be used to make a liqueur.*
• *Any unused coconut milk can be transferred to a plastic tub and stored in the refrigerator for a day or two, or poured into a freezer container and frozen for use on another occasion.*
• *You can use a vegetable peeler to shave the fresh coconut for the decoration.*

Black Rice Pudding

This baked pudding has a distinct character and flavour all of its own. Black glutinous rice, also known as black sticky rice, has long dark grains and a nutty taste reminiscent of wild rice. Its intriguing appearance is rather likely to arouse curiosity among guests who have never eaten black rice before.

Ingredients
175g/6oz/1 cup black or white glutinous rice
30ml/2 tbsp soft light brown sugar
475ml/16fl oz/2 cups coconut milk
3 eggs
30ml/2 tbsp sugar

Serves 4–6

1 Combine the glutinous rice and brown sugar in a pan. Pour in half the coconut milk and 250ml/8fl oz/1 cup water.

2 Bring to the boil, reduce the heat to low and simmer, stirring occasionally, for 15–20 minutes, or until the rice has absorbed most of the liquid. Preheat the oven to 150°C/300°F/Gas 2.

3 Spoon the rice mixture into a single large ovenproof dish or divide it among individual ramekins. Beat the eggs with the remaining coconut milk and sugar in a bowl.

4 Strain the egg mixture into a jug (pitcher), then pour it evenly over the par-cooked rice in the dish or ramekins.

5 Place the dish or ramekins in a roasting pan. Carefully pour in enough hot water to come halfway up the sides of the dish or ramekins, then cover with foil and bake for about 35–60 minutes, or until the custard has set. Serve warm or cold.

Cook's Tip
White glutinous rice will suit this recipe if you'd prefer to use it, but traditionally it is more often used in savoury recipes.

tapioca pudding Energy 324kcal/1384kJ; Protein 1g; Carbohydrate 84.7g, of which sugars 57.2g; Fat 0.4g, of which saturates 0.2g; Cholesterol 0mg; Calcium 51mg; Fibre 1.8g; Sodium 74mg.
black rice pudding Energy 249kcal/1044kJ; Protein 4g; Carbohydrate 42.5g, of which sugars 14.4g; Fat 7g, of which saturates 5.5g; Cholesterol 0mg; Calcium 33mg; Fibre 1.4g; Sodium 78mg.

Sweet Rice Dumplings

These rice dumplings are filled with mung bean paste and then simmered in a ginger-infused syrup.

Ingredients

For the syrup
25g/1oz fresh root ginger, peeled and finely shredded
115g/4oz/generous ½ cup sugar

For the filling
40g/1½oz dried split mung beans, soaked for 6 hours and drained
25g/1oz/2 tbsp sugar

For the dough
225g/8oz/2 cups sticky glutinous rice flour
175ml/6fl oz/¾ cup boiling water

Serves 4–6

1 To make the syrup, stir the ginger and sugar in a heavy pan over a low heat, until the sugar begins to brown. Take the pan off the heat and stir in 400ml/14fl oz/1⅔ cups water – it will bubble and spit. Return the pan to the heat and bring to the boil, stirring. Reduce the heat and simmer for 5 minutes.

2 To make the filling, put the soaked mung beans in a pan with the sugar and add the water to cover. Bring to the boil, stirring all the time, until the sugar has dissolved. Simmer for 15–20 minutes until the mung beans are soft. When all the water has been absorbed, pound to a smooth paste and leave until cool. Roll the filling into 16–20 small balls.

3 To make the dough, put the flour in a bowl. Make a well in the centre and gradually pour in the water, drawing in the flour to form a dough. When cool enough to handle, knead the dough for a few minutes, until soft, smooth and springy.

4 Divide the dough in half and roll each half into a sausage, about 25cm/10in long. Divide each sausage into 8–10 pieces, and roll each piece into a ball. Take a ball of dough and flatten it in the palm of your hand. Place a ball of the mung bean filling in the centre of the dough and seal it by pinching and rolling the dough. Repeat with the remaining balls.

5 Cook the filled dumplings in a pan of boiling water for 2–3 minutes, until they rise to the surface. Heat the syrup in a heavy pan, drop in the cooked dumplings, and simmer for a further 2–3 minutes. Serve at room temperature, or chilled.

Mung Bean Dumplings

These sweet and savoury rice dumplings are often served with jasmine tea.

Ingredients
100g/3½oz/scant ½ cup split mung beans, soaked for 6 hours and drained
115g/4oz/generous ½ cup caster (superfine) sugar
300g/10½oz/scant 3 cups glutinous rice flour
50g/2oz/½ cup rice flour
1 medium potato, boiled in its skin, peeled and mashed
75g/3oz/6 tbsp sesame seeds
vegetable oil, for deep-frying

Serves 6

1 Put the mung beans in a large pan with half the caster sugar and pour in 450ml/¾ pint/scant 2 cups water. Bring to the boil, stirring constantly until all the sugar has dissolved. Reduce the heat and simmer gently for 15–20 minutes until the mung beans are soft. You may need to add more water if the beans are becoming dry, otherwise they may burn.

2 Once the mung beans are soft and all the water has been absorbed, reduce the beans to a smooth paste in a mortar and pestle or food processor and leave to cool.

3 In a large bowl, beat the flours and remaining sugar into the mashed potato. Add about 200ml/7fl oz/scant 1 cup water to bind the mixture into a moist dough. Divide the dough into 24 pieces, roll each one into a small ball, then flatten with the heel of your hand to make a disc and lay out on a lightly floured board.

4 Divide the mung bean paste into 24 small portions. Place one portion of mung bean paste in the centre of a dough disc. Fold over the edges of the dough and then shape into a ball. Repeat for the remaining dumplings.

5 Spread the sesame seeds on a plate and roll the dumplings in them until evenly coated. Heat enough oil for deep-frying in a wok or heavy pan. Fry the balls in batches until golden. Drain on kitchen paper and serve warm.

sweet rice dumplings Energy 231kcal/975kJ; Protein 2.7g; Carbohydrate 54.7g, of which sugars 24.5g; Fat 0.3g, of which saturates 0g; Cholesterol 0mg; Calcium 23mg; Fibre 0.9g; Sodium 4mg.
mung bean dumplings Energy 514kcal/2151kJ; Protein 10.4g; Carbohydrate 79.6g, of which sugars 20.9g; Fat 17.2g, of which saturates 2.2g; Cholesterol 0mg; Calcium 127mg; Fibre 5.1g; Sodium 13mg.

Sweet & Spicy Rice Fritters

These delicious little golden balls of rice are scented with sweet, warm spices and will fill the kitchen with wonderful aromas while you're cooking. To enjoy them at their best, serve piping hot, as soon as you've dusted them with sugar.

Ingredients

175g/6oz cooked basmati rice
2 eggs, lightly beaten
60ml/4 tbsp caster (superfine) sugar
a pinch of nutmeg
2.5ml/½ tsp ground cinnamon
a pinch of ground cloves
10ml/2 tsp vanilla extract
50g/2oz/½ cup plain (all-purpose) flour
10ml/2 tsp baking powder
a pinch of salt
25g/1oz desiccated (dry unsweetened shredded) coconut
sunflower oil, for deep-frying
icing (confectioners') sugar, to dust

Serves 4

1 Place the cooked rice, eggs, sugar, nutmeg, cinnamon, cloves and vanilla extract in a large bowl and whisk together by hand, or with an electric whisk, to combine.

2 Sift in the flour, baking powder and salt and add the coconut. Mix well until thoroughly combined.

3 Fill a wok one-third full of the oil and heat to 180°C/350°F or until a cube of bread, dropped into the oil, browns in 45 seconds. Alternatively, use a deep-fryer and follow the manufacturer's directions.

4 Very gently, drop tablespoonfuls of the mixture into the oil, one at a time, and fry for 2–3 minutes, or until golden. Carefully remove the fritters from the wok using a slotted spoon and drain well on kitchen paper.

5 Divide the fritters into four portions and serve them in dessert bowls or one plates, or simply pile them up on a single large platter. Dust the fritters generously with some sifted icing sugar and serve immediately.

Coconut Rice Fritters

These delicious rice fritters can be served at any time and go especially well with a mug of steaming milky coffee or hot chocolate.

Ingredients

150g/5oz/⅔ cup long grain rice, cooked
30ml/2 tbsp coconut milk powder
45ml/3 tbsp sugar
2 egg yolks
juice of ½ lemon
75g/3oz desiccated (dry unsweetened shredded) coconut
oil, for deep-frying
icing sugar, for dusting

Makes 28

1 Place 75g/3oz of the cooked rice in a mortar and pound with a pestle until smooth and sticky. Alternatively, process in a food processor.

2 Pour the pounded rice into a bowl and mix in the remaining rice, the coconut milk powder, sugar, egg yolks and lemon juice.

3 Spread out the desiccated coconut on a tray or plate. With wet hands, divide the rice mixture into thumb-sized pieces and roll them in the coconut to make neat balls.

4 Heat the oil in a wok or deep-fryer to 180°C/350°F. Fry the coconut rice balls, three or four at a time, for 1–2 minutes, until the coconut is evenly browned.

5 As each fritter browns, lift it out, drain on kitchen paper and transfer to a plate. Dust the fritters with icing sugar. Place a wooden skewer in each one and serve.

Cook's Tip
To make a hot chocolate for two, prepare a syrup with 30ml/2 tbsp sugar and 120ml/4fl oz/½ cup water and melt 115g/4oz good-quality plain (semisweet) chocolate in it. Finally, whisk in 200ml/7fl oz/scant 1 cup evaporated milk over a low heat.

sweet & spicy fritters Energy 316kcal/1321kJ; Protein 6.6g; Carbohydrate 45.7g, of which sugars 16.3g; Fat 12.4g, of which saturates 4.8g; Cholesterol 95mg; Calcium 46mg; Fibre 1.3g; Sodium 38mg.
coconut rice fritters Energy 61kcal/254kJ; Protein 0.5g; Carbohydrate 3.5g, of which sugars 1.9g; Fat 5.1g, of which saturates 2.1g; Cholesterol 14mg; Calcium 4mg; Fibre 0.4g; Sodium 2mg.

Coconut Pancakes

These pancakes are as light as they are sweet, and make a delicious dessert. Serve them with honey.

Ingredients
75g/3oz/¾ cup plain (all-purpose) flour, sifted
60ml/4 tbsp rice flour
45ml/3 tbsp caster (superfine) sugar
50g/2oz/⅔ cup desiccated (dry unsweetened shredded) coconut
1 egg
275ml/9fl oz/generous 1 cup coconut milk
vegetable oil, for frying
lime wedges and maple syrup, to serve

Makes 8

1 Place the plain flour, rice flour, sugar and coconut in a bowl, stir to mix and then make a small well in the centre. Break the egg into the well and pour in the coconut milk.

2 With a whisk or fork, beat the egg into the coconut milk and then gradually incorporate the surrounding dry ingredients, whisking constantly until the mixture forms a batter. The mixture will not be entirely smooth, because of the coconut, but there shouldn't be any large lumps.

3 Heat a little oil in a 13cm/5in non-stick frying pan. Pour in about 45ml/3 tbsp of the mixture and quickly spread to a thin layer with the back of a spoon.

4 Cook over a high heat for about 30–60 seconds, until bubbles appear on the surface of the pancake, then turn it over with a spatula and cook the other side until golden.

5 Slide the pancake on to a plate and keep it warm in a very low oven. Make more pancakes in the same way. Serve warm with lime wedges for squeezing and maple syrup for drizzling.

Variation
Serve with maple syrup instead of honey, if you like.

Pancakes with Red Bean Paste

In China, sweetened red beans are often used in desserts and sweetmeats because the rich colour is associated with good luck.

Ingredients
175g/6oz/1 scant cup aduki beans, soaked overnight in cold water to cover
115g/4oz/1 cup plain (all-purpose) flour
1 large (US extra large) egg, lightly beaten
300ml/½ pint/1¼ cups semi-skimmed (low-fat) milk
5ml/1 tsp vegetable oil
75g/3oz/6 tbsp caster (superfine) sugar
2.5ml/½ tsp vanilla extract
fromage frais or natural (plain) yogurt, to serve (optional)

Serves 4

1 Bring 600ml/1 pint/2½ cups water to the boil in a pan. Drain the beans in a sieve (strainer), add them to the pan and boil rapidly for 10 minutes.

2 Skim the surface, lower the heat, cover the pan and simmer, stirring occasionally, for 40 minutes or until the beans are soft.

3 Sift the flour into a bowl, make a well in the centre and add the egg and half the milk, drawing in the flour. Whisk in the remaining milk to make a smooth batter. Set aside.

4 Heat a 20cm/8in non-stick omelette pan and brush lightly with the vegetable oil. When hot, add the batter to make 8 thin pancakes, regreasing the pan as necessary. Cover with foil.

5 When the beans are soft and all the water has been absorbed, process them in a food processor until a smooth paste is produced. Add the sugar and vanilla extract and blitz until the sugar has dissolved.

6 Preheat the grill (broiler). Spread a little of the bean paste on the centre of each pancake and fold them into parcels, pressing down lightly with your fingers to flatten. Place on a baking sheet and grill (broil) for a few minutes until crisp and lightly toasted on each side. Serve with fromage frais or yogurt.

coconut pancakes Energy 200kcal/837kJ; Protein 2.6g; Carbohydrate 21.9g, of which sugars 8.8g; Fat 11.7g, of which saturates 4.4g; Cholesterol 24mg; Calcium 33mg; Fibre 1.3g; Sodium 49mg.
pancakes w. bean paste Energy 368kcal/1562kJ; Protein 17.2g; Carbohydrate 69.1g, of which sugars 24.8g; Fat 4.5g, of which saturates 1.6g; Cholesterol 52mg; Calcium 183mg; Fibre 4.5g; Sodium 59mg.

Celebration Rice Cake

Not a dry snack from the health food store, but a sumptuous celebration gateau, made from Thai fragrant rice, tangy cream and with a fresh fruit topping.

Ingredients

225g/8oz/generous 1 cup fragrant rice, rinsed
1 litre/1¾ pints/4 cups milk
115g/4oz/scant ½ cup caster (superfine) sugar
6 green cardamom pods, crushed
2 bay leaves
300ml/½ pint/1¼ cups whipping cream
6 eggs, separated
red and white currants, sliced star (carambola) fruit and kiwi fruit, to decorate

For the topping

250ml/8fl oz/1 cup double (heavy) cream
150g/5oz/⅔ cup low-fat soft cheese
5ml/1 tsp vanilla extract
grated rind of 1 lemon
40g/1½oz/3 tbsp caster sugar

1 Grease and line a 25cm/10in round, deep cake tin (pan). Cook the rice in a pan of boiling unsalted water for 3 minutes, then drain, return to the pan and pour in the milk. Stir in the caster sugar, cardamoms and bay leaves. Bring to the boil, then lower the heat and simmer for 20 minutes, stirring occasionally. Cool, then remove the bay leaves and cardamom husks.

2 Preheat the oven to 180°C/350°F/Gas 4. Spoon the rice mixture into a bowl. Beat in the cream and then the egg yolks. Whisk the egg whites until they form soft peaks, then fold them into the rice mixture.

3 Spoon into the prepared tin and bake for 45–50 minutes until risen and golden brown. Chill overnight in the tin. Turn the cake out on to a large serving plate.

4 Whip the cream until stiff, then gently fold in the soft cheese, vanilla extract, lemon rind and sugar. Cover the top of the cake with the cream mixture, swirling it attractively. Decorate with red and white currants, sliced star fruit and kiwi fruit.

Golden Steamed Sponge Cake

Cakes are not traditionally served for dessert in China, but this light sponge is very popular and is often served on the dim sum trolley at lunchtime.

Ingredients

175g/6oz/1½ cups plain (all-purpose) flour
5ml/1 tsp baking powder
1.5ml/¼ tsp bicarbonate of soda (baking soda)
3 large (US extra large) eggs
115g/4oz/⅔ cup soft light brown sugar
45ml/3 tbsp walnut oil
30ml/2 tbsp golden (light corn) syrup
5ml/1 tsp vanilla extract

Serves 8

1 Sift the flour, baking powder and bicarbonate of soda into a bowl. Line an 18cm/7in diameter bamboo steamer or cake tin (pan) with baking parchment.

2 In a mixing bowl, whisk the eggs with the sugar until thick and frothy. Beat in the walnut oil and syrup, then set the mixture aside for about 30 minutes.

3 Add the sifted flour, baking powder and bicarbonate of soda to the egg mixture with the vanilla extract, and beat rapidly by hand or with an electric whisk to form a thick batter that is free from lumps.

4 Pour the batter into the paper-lined steamer or tin. Cover and steam over boiling water for 30 minutes or until the sponge springs back when gently pressed with a finger. Leave to cool for a few minutes before serving.

Variation

This cake is usually served on its own, cut into slabs or wedges. To dress it up a bit, add a scoop each of apricot compote and thick, creamy yogurt to each dessert plate. Alternatively, top it with icing – a simple combination of mascarpone and cream cheese with some vanilla essence will work – and walnut halves.

celebration rice cake Energy 492kcal/2047kJ; Protein 12.1g; Carbohydrate 41g, of which sugars 23.1g; Fat 31.9g, of which saturates 18.7g; Cholesterol 189mg; Calcium 197mg; Fibre 0g; Sodium 165mg.
golden steamed sponge cake Energy 150kcal/632kJ; Protein 4.4g; Carbohydrate 20g, of which sugars 3.3g; Fat 6.5g, of which saturates 1g; Cholesterol 71mg; Calcium 42mg; Fibre 0.7g; Sodium 37mg.

Grilled Fruit with Lime Cheese

Grilled fruits make a fine finale to an *al fresco* party, whether they are cooked over hot coals or under a hot grill. The lemon grass skewers give the fruit a subtle lemon tang.

Ingredients

4 long fresh lemon grass stalks
1 mango, peeled, stoned (pitted) and sliced
1 papaya, peeled, seeded and diced
1 star fruit, cut into slices and halved
8 fresh bay leaves
nutmeg
60ml/4 tbsp maple syrup
50g/2oz/⅓ cup demerara (raw) sugar

For the lime cheese

150g/5oz/⅔ cup curd cheese or low-fat soft cheese
120ml/4fl oz/½ cup double (heavy) cream
grated rind and juice of ½ lime
30ml/2 tbsp icing (confectioner's) sugar

Serves 4

1 Prepare the barbecue or preheat the grill (broiler). Cut the top of each lemon grass stalk into a point with a sharp knife. Discard the outer leaves, then use the back of the knife to bruise the length of each stalk to release the oils. Thread each stalk, skewer-style, with the fruit pieces and bay leaves.

2 Support a piece of foil on a baking sheet and roll up the edges to make a rim. Grease the foil, lay the kebabs on top and grate a little nutmeg over each. Drizzle the maple syrup over, dust liberally with the sugar and grill (broil) for 5 minutes.

3 Make the lime cheese by combining the cheese, cream, grated lime rind, juice and icing sugar in a bowl. Serve immediately with the lightly charred fruit kebabs.

Cook's Tip

Only fresh lemon grass will work as skewers for this recipe. The preserved kind is a useful store-cupboard (pantry) item for making curries, but too soft to stay on skewers.

Fruits in Lemon Grass Syrup

This exotic and refreshing fruit salad can be made with any combination of tropical fruits, so don't feel you have to stick to those suggested here. Just go for a balance of colour, flavour and texture.

Ingredients

1 firm papaya
1 small pineapple
2 small star fruit, sliced into stars
12 fresh lychees, peeled and stoned (pitted) or 14oz/400g can lychees
2 firm yellow or green bananas, peeled and cut diagonally into slices
mint leaves, to decorate

For the syrup

115g/4oz/generous ½ cup caster (superfine) sugar
2 lemon grass stalks, bruised and halved lengthways

Serves 6

1 To make the syrup, put 225ml/7½ fl oz/1 cup water into a heavy pan with the sugar and lemon grass stalks. Bring to the boil, stirring constantly until the sugar has dissolved, then reduce the heat and simmer for 15 minutes. Leave to cool.

2 Peel and halve the papaya, remove the seeds and slice the flesh crossways. Peel the pineapple and slice it into rounds. Remove the core and cut each round in half. (Keep the core and slice it for a stir-fry.)

3 Put all the fruit into a bowl. Pour the syrup, including the lemon grass stalks, over the top and toss to combine. Cover and chill for 6 hours, or overnight. Before serving in dessert bowls, remove the lemon grass stalks and decorate each portion with mint leaves.

Variation

You can flavour the syrup with ginger rather than lemon grass if you prefer. Either use fresh or preserved (stem) ginger, cut into thick slices, and add to the pan with the water and sugar.

fruit/lime cheese Energy 360kcal/1508kJ; Protein 7.1g; Carbohydrate 43.4g, of which sugars 43.3g; Fat 19.3g, of which saturates 12g; Cholesterol 50mg; Calcium 98mg; Fibre 3.7g; Sodium 219mg.
fruits/lemon grass Energy 174kcal/742kJ; Protein 1.3g; Carbohydrate 44.2g, of which sugars 43.4g; Fat 0.3g, of which saturates 0g; Cholesterol 0mg; Calcium 38mg; Fibre 2.7g; Sodium 6mg.

Clementines in Spiced Syrup

The unusual fruit of a small evergreen tree, harvested just before ripening, star anise is a useful spice. Not only does it add a delicate flavour, but it also makes an attractive decoration, especially with citrus fruits.

Ingredients

350ml/12fl oz/1½ cups sweet dessert wine
75g/3oz/6 tbsp caster (superfine) sugar
6 star anise
1 cinnamon stick
1 vanilla pod (bean)
30ml/2 tbsp Cointreau or another orange liqueur (see Variations)
1 strip of thinly pared lime rind
12 clementines

Serves 6

1 Put the wine, sugar, star anise and cinnamon in a large pan. Split the vanilla pod and add it to the pan with the lime rind.

2 Bring to the boil, lower the heat and simmer for 10 minutes, stirring frequently to ensure that all the sugar is dissolved.

3 Pour the spiced vanilla syrup into a bowl and set aside to cool. When it is completely cold, stir in the Cointreau.

4 Peel the clementines. Leave some clementines whole and cut the rest in half. Arrange them in a shallow dish. Pour over the spicy syrup and chill overnight.

5 Serve chilled, spooning the clementines into a glass serving bowl, or six individual dessert dishes.

Variations

- *Tangerines or oranges can be used instead of clementines, if you prefer.*
- *As an alternative to the Cointreau, you can use Grand Marnier or Mandarine Napoléon. The latter is made by blending a distillate of fresh tangerine peels with cognac.*

Papayas in Jasmine Flower Syrup

The fragrant syrup can be prepared in advance, using fresh jasmine flowers from a house plant or the garden. It tastes fabulous with papayas, but it is also good with all sorts of desserts. Try it with ice cream or spooned over lychees or mangoes.

Ingredients

105ml/7 tbsp water
45ml/3 tbsp soft light brown sugar
20–30 jasmine flowers, plus a few extra, to decorate (optional)
2 ripe papayas
juice of 1 lime

Serves 2

1 Place the water and sugar in a small pan. Heat gently, stirring occasionally, until the sugar has dissolved, then simmer, without stirring, over a low heat for 4 minutes.

2 Pour into a bowl, leave to cool slightly, then add the jasmine flowers. Leave to steep for at least 20 minutes.

3 Peel the papayas and slice in half lengthways. Scoop out and discard the seeds. Place the papayas on serving plates and squeeze over the lime.

4 Strain the syrup into a clean bowl, discarding the flowers. Spoon the syrup over the papayas. If you like, decorate with a few fresh jasmine flowers.

Variation

If you don't have access to jasmine flowers, flavour the syrup with ginger, vanilla (steep a vanilla pod or bean in the syrup), or use star anise.

Cook's Tip

Although scented white jasmine flowers are perfectly safe to eat, it is important to be sure that they have not been sprayed with pesticides or other harmful chemicals. Washing them may not remove all the residue.

clementines/syrup Energy 4027kcal/17183kJ; Protein 16.2g; Carbohydrate 1053.6g, of which sugars 1053.6g; Fat 1.3g, of which saturates 0g; Cholesterol 0mg; Calcium 880mg; Fibre 15.6g; Sodium 106mg.
papayas in flower syrup Energy 197kcal/837kJ; Protein 1.6g; Carbohydrate 49.9g, of which sugars 49.9g; Fat 0.3g, of which saturates 0g; Cholesterol 0mg; Calcium 81mg; Fibre 6.6g; Sodium 17mg.

Zingy Papaya, Lime & Ginger Salad

This refreshing, fruity salad makes a lovely light breakfast, perfect for the summer months. Choose really ripe, fragrant papayas for the best flavour. Mangoes also work well.

Ingredients

2 large ripe papayas
juice of 1 fresh lime
2 pieces preserved stem ginger, finely sliced

Serves 2

1 Cut the papaya in half lengthways and scoop out the seeds, using a teaspoon. Using a sharp knife, cut the flesh into thin slices and arrange on a platter.

2 Squeeze the lime juice over the papaya and sprinkle with the sliced stem ginger. Serve immediately.

Fruit with Granadilla Dressing

Granadillas or passionfruit make a delectable dressing for an exotic fruit salad. Granadilla flesh has a slight scent of lime.

Ingredients

1 mango
1 papaya
2 kiwi fruit
coconut ice cream, to serve

For the dressing

2 granadillas or 3 passion fruit
thinly pared juice and rind of 1 lime
5ml/1 tsp hazelnut oil
15ml/1 tbsp clear honey

Serves 6

1 Peel the mango and cut it into chunks. Peel and halve the papaya, scoop out the seeds, chop the flesh and add it to the bowl. Peel and slice the kiwi fruit. Mix all the fruit in a bowl.

2 Make the dressing. Halve the granadillas or passion fruit and scoop the seeds into a sieve (strainer) over a small bowl. Press to extract all the juices. Whisk in the remaining ingredients and pour over the fruit. Chill, then seve with the ice cream.

Blush fruit in Rose Pouchong

This delightfully fragrant and quick-to-prepare Asian dessert couples the subtle flavours of apples and raspberries with an infusion of rose-scented tea.

Ingredients

5ml/1 tsp rose pouchong tea
5ml/1 tsp rose water (optional)
50g/2oz/¼ cup sugar
5ml/1 tsp lemon juice
5 dessert apples
175g/6oz/1½ cups fresh raspberries

Serves 4

1 Warm a large teapot. Add the rose pouchong tea and 900ml/1½ pints/3¾ cups of boiling water together with the rose water, if using. Allow to stand and infuse for 4 minutes.

2 Spoon the sugar and the lemon juice into a stainless-steel pan. Pour the tea through a small sieve (strainer) into the pan, and stir to dissolve the sugar.

3 Peel the apples, then cut into quarters and core. Add the apples to the pan of syrup. Return the pan to the heat and bring the syrup to simmering point. Cook the apples for about 5 minutes, until just tender.

4 Transfer the apples and syrup to a large metal tray and leave to cool to room temperature.

5 Pour the cooled apples and syrup into a bowl, add the raspberries and mix to combine. Spoon into individual dishes or bowls and serve immediately.

Variation

A fruit tea such as rosehip and hibiscus could be used instead of the rose pouchong, or try cranberry and raspberry to highlight the flavour of the berries.

papaya, lime & ginger Energy 118kcal/503kJ; Protein 1.7g; Carbohydrate 28.9g, of which sugars 28.9g; Fat 0.3g, of which saturates 0g; Cholesterol 0mg; Calcium 76mg; Fibre 7.2g; Sodium 17mg.
fruit w. granadilla Energy 66kcal/278kJ; Protein 1g; Carbohydrate 14.6g, of which sugars 14.5g; Fat 0.8g, of which saturates 0.1g; Cholesterol 0mg; Calcium 26mg; Fibre 2.9g; Sodium 7mg.
blush fruit Energy 95kcal/409kJ; Protein 1g; Carbohydrate 24g, of which sugars 24g; Fat 0.2g, of which saturates 0.1g; Cholesterol 0mg; Calcium 22mg; Fibre 2.7g; Sodium 4mg.

Jellied Mango Puddings

Light and sophisticated, these jellied mango puddings make delightful desserts. Served with a selection of tropical fruits, they add a refreshing touch to the end of a spicy meal.

Ingredients

750ml/1 ¼ pints/3 cups coconut milk
150g/5oz/¾ cup sugar
15ml/1 tbsp powdered gelatine (gelatin)
1 egg yolk
1 large, ripe mango, stoned (pitted) and puréed
4 slices ripe jackfruit or pineapple, quartered
1 banana, cut into diagonal slices
1 kiwi fruit, sliced
4 lychees, peeled
2 passion fruit, split open, to decorate

Serves 4

1 In a heavy pan, heat the coconut milk with the sugar, stirring all the time, until it has dissolved.

2 Add the gelatine and keep stirring until it has dissolved. Remove from the heat.

3 Put the egg yolk in a bowl and beat together with the mango purée. Add the mixture to the coconut milk and stir until smooth. Spoon the mixture into individual, lightly oiled moulds and leave to cool. Refrigerate for 2–3 hours until set.

4 To serve, arrange the fruit on individual plates, leaving enough room for the jellies. Dip the base of each mould briefly into hot water, and then invert the puddings on to the plates. Lift off the moulds and decorate with passion fruit pulp.

Variation
The tangy fruitiness of mango is particularly delicious in these jellied puddings, and this is the version you are most likely to encounter in its homelands of Malaysia and Singapore. However, papaya, banana, durian or avocado work well also.

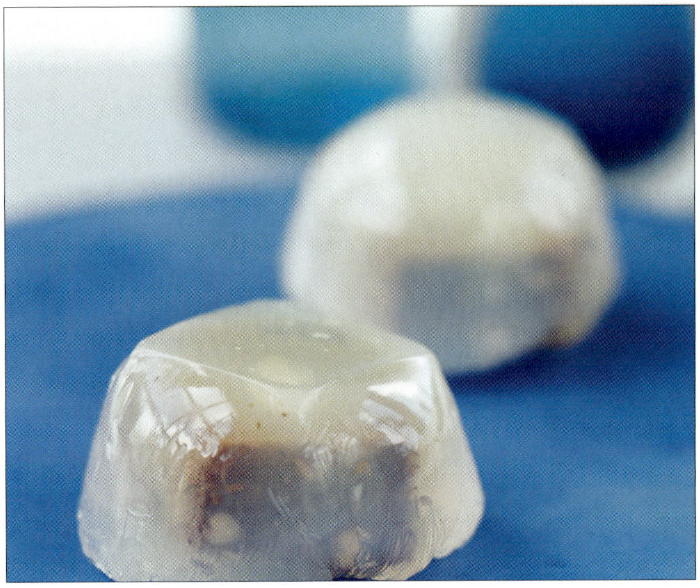

Sweet Aduki Bean Paste Jellies

These jellies look like blocks of ice in which semi-precious jewels have been set.

Ingredients

200g/7oz can aduki beans
40g/1 ½oz/3 tbsp caster (superfine) sugar

For the agar-agar jelly

2 x 5g/⅛oz sachets powdered agar-agar
900ml/1 ½ pints/3¾ cups water
100g/3¾oz/½ cup caster sugar
rind of ¼ orange in one piece

Serves 12

1 Drain the beans and heat them in a pan. When steam begins to rise, reduce the heat and stir in the sugar, one-third at a time, until dissolved. Remove the pan from the heat.

2 To make the jelly, dissolve one agar-agar sachet in half the water in a pan. Add 3 tablespoons of the sugar and the orange rind. Bring to the boil and cook for 2 minutes, stirring constantly. Remove the orange rind the pour half the liquid into a 16 x 10cm/6 x 4in shallow dish. Leave at room temperature to set.

3 Mix the bean paste with the agar-agar liquid in the pan. Move the pan on to a wet dishtowel and stir for 8 minutes. Pour into an 18 x 7.5 x 2cm/7 x 3 x ¾in container and leave to set for 1 hour at room temperature, followed by another hour in the refrigerator. Turn upside down on to a chopping board covered with kitchen paper, leave for 1 minute, then cut into 12 cubes.

4 Line 12 ramekins with clear film (plastic wrap). Cut the jelly block into 12 squares and put one in each ramekin. Place a bean paste cube on top of each one.

5 Using the remaining water and agar-agar, make up another batch of jelly as in Step 2. Stir in the remaining sugar. Boil for 2 minutes then place the pan on a wet dishtowel and stir for 5 minutes. When the mixture starts to thicken, pour it over the cubes in the ramekins. Twist the clear film at the top to seal tightly. Leave to set in the refrigerator for at least 1 hour, then remove the jellies from the ramekins and serve.

jellied mango puddings Energy 305kcal/1300kJ; Protein 2.9g; Carbohydrate 72.6g, of which sugars 72g; Fat 2.4g, of which saturates 0.8g; Cholesterol 50mg; Calcium 109mg; Fibre 3g; Sodium 216mg.
sweet aduki bean paste jellies Energy 94kcal/401kJ; Protein 4.1g; Carbohydrate 20.5g, of which sugars 12.4g; Fat 0.1g, of which saturates 0g; Cholesterol 0mg; Calcium 20mg; Fibre 1.9g; Sodium 2mg.

Coconut Rice Puddings

Sticky rice pudding is a rich and creamy speciality of many Asian countries.

Ingredients
175g/6oz/scant 1 cup jasmine rice
400ml/14fl oz/1⅔ cup coconut milk
2.5ml/½ tsp grated nutmeg, plus extra for sprinkling
large pinch of salt
60ml/4 tbsp golden caster (superfine) sugar
oil, for greasing
2 oranges, skin and pith removed and cut into thin rounds
orange peel twists, to decorate

Serves 4

1 Rinse and drain the rice. Place in a saucepan, cover with water, and bring to the boil. Cook for 5 minutes until the grains are just beginning to soften. Drain well.

2 Place the rice in a muslin-lined steamer, then make a few holes in the muslin to allow the steam to get through. Steam the rice for 15 minutes or until tender.

3 Put the steamed rice in a heavy-based saucepan with the coconut milk, nutmeg, salt and sugar, and cook over a gentle heat until the mixture begins to simmer. Simmer for about 5 minutes until the mixture is thick and creamy, stirring frequently to prevent the rice sticking.

4 Spoon the rice mixture into four lightly oiled 175ml/6fl oz/¾ cup moulds or ramekins and leave to cool.

5 When ready to serve, heat the grill to high. Line a baking tray or the grill rack with foil and place the orange slices on top. Sprinkle the oranges with a little grated nutmeg, then grill for 6 minutes until lightly golden, turning the slices halfway through cooking.

6 When the rice mixture is cold, run a knife around the edge of the moulds or ramekins and turn out the rice. Decorate with the orange peel twists and serve with orange slices.

Coconut Cream Diamonds

Desserts like these are served all over the Far East.

Ingredients
75g/3oz/scant ½ cup jasmine rice, soaked overnight in 175ml/6fl oz/¾ cup water
350ml/12fl oz/1½ cups coconut milk
150ml/¼ pint/⅔ cup single (light) cream
50g/2oz/¼ cup caster (superfine) sugar
raspberries and fresh mint leaves, to decorate

For the coulis
75g/3oz/¾ cup blackcurrants, stalks removed
30ml/2 tbsp caster (superfine) sugar
75g/3oz/½ cup fresh or frozen raspberries

Serves 4–6

1 Put the rice and its soaking water into a food processor and process for a few minutes until the mixture is soupy.

2 Heat the coconut milk and cream in a non-stick pan. When the mixture is on the point of boiling, stir in the rice mixture. Cook over a very gentle heat for 10 minutes, stirring constantly, then add the sugar and cook for a further 10–15 minutes until thick and creamy.

3 Line a rectangular pan with non-stick baking parchment. Pour the coconut rice mixture into the pan, cool, then chill in the refrigerator until the dessert is set and firm.

4 Meanwhile, make the coulis. Put the blackcurrants in a bowl and sprinkle with the sugar. Set aside for about 30 minutes. Tip the blackcurrants and raspberries into a wire sieve (strainer) set over a bowl. Using a spoon, press the fruit against the sides of the sieve so that the juices collect in the bowl. Taste the coulis and add more sugar if necessary.

5 Carefully cut the coconut cream into diamonds. Spoon a little of the coulis on to each dessert plate, arrange the coconut cream diamonds on top and decorate with the fresh raspberries and mint leaves. Serve immediately.

coconut rice puddings Energy 261kcal/1103kJ; Protein 4.3g; Carbohydrate 60.8g, of which sugars 25.9g; Fat 0.6g, of which saturates 0.2g; Cholesterol 0mg; Calcium 75mg; Fibre 1.1g; Sodium 114mg.
coconut diamonds Energy 165kcal/696kJ; Protein 2.4g; Carbohydrate 28.1g, of which sugars 18.8g; Fat 5.2g, of which saturates 3.2g; Cholesterol 14mg; Calcium 59mg; Fibre 0.8g; Sodium 73mg.

Avocado Fool

This sweet avocado dessert can also be served as a thick purée or blended with coconut milk until it is the consistency of thick pouring cream. This makes a delicious drink when a couple of ice cubes are stirred in.

Ingredients
1 avocado, stoned (pitted)
juice of ½ lime
30ml/2 tbsp sweetened condensed milk
30ml/2 tbsp coconut cream
a pinch of salt
fresh mint leaves, to decorate
½ lime, halved, to serve

Serves 2

1 Put the avocado flesh into a food processor or blender and purée it with the lime juice until well mixed.

2 Add the condensed milk, coconut cream and salt and process until the mixture is smooth and creamy.

3 Spoon the mixture into individual bowls or glasses and chill over ice. Decorate with a few mint leaves and serve with lime wedges to squeeze over.

Cook's Tip
Avocadoes discolour quickly when cut and exposed to the air, so prepare them immediately before they are to be used. If you have used only half an avocado and don't want to throw away the other half, you can preserve the rest for a short while by leaving the stone (pit) in place and wrapping it very tightly in clear film (plastic wrap). Store in the refrigerator but use as soon as possible.

Variation
This recipe works equally well with other soft-fleshed fruit, such as bananas, mango and papaya.

Mango & Lime Fool

Canned mangoes are used here for convenience, but the dish tastes even better if made with fresh ones. Choose a variety like the voluptuous Alphonso mango, often prized as the king of its kind in Asia due to its wonderful fragrance and indescribably luscious taste. Simpy peel and slice then process as for the canned.

Ingredients
400g/14oz can sliced mango
grated rind of 1 lime
juice of ½ lime
150ml/¼ pint/⅔ cup double (heavy) cream
90ml/6 tbsp Greek (US strained plain) yogurt
fresh mango slices, to decorate (optional)

Serves 4

1 Drain the canned mango slices and put them in the bowl of a food processor. Add the grated lime rind and the lime juice. Process until the mixture forms a smooth purée. Alternatively, mash the mango slices with a potato masher, then press through a sieve into a bowl with the back of a wooden spoon. Stir in the lime rind and juice.

2 Pour the mango mixture into a jug (pitcher). Set aside while pouring the cream into a bowl and add the yogurt. Whisk until the mixture is thick and then quickly whisk in the mango mixture.

3 Spoon into four tall cups or glasses and chill for 1–2 hours. Just before serving, decorate each glass with fresh mango slices, if you like.

Cook's Tip
When mixing the cream and yogurt mixture with the mango purée, whisk just enough to combine, so as not to lose the lightness of the whipped cream mixture. If you prefer, fold the mixtures together lightly, so that the fool is rippled. The best way to do this is to combine the mixtures in a bowl and use a skewer to stir them and create the rippled effect.

avocado fool Energy 152kcal/632kJ; Protein 2.3g; Carbohydrate 10.8g, of which sugars 10.1g; Fat 11.3g, of which saturates 3.1g; Cholesterol 5mg; Calcium 58mg; Fibre 1.7g; Sodium 57mg.
mango & lime Energy 269kcal/1118kJ; Protein 2.8g; Carbohydrate 15.2g, of which sugars 14.9g; Fat 22.6g, of which saturates 13.8g; Cholesterol 51mg; Calcium 64mg; Fibre 2.6g; Sodium 26mg.

Watermelon Ice

After a hot and spicy meal, the only thing more refreshing than ice-cold watermelon is this watermelon ice.

Ingredients
90ml/6 tbsp caster (superfine) sugar
105ml/7 tbsp water
4 kaffir lime leaves, torn into small pieces
500g/1¼lb watermelon

Serves 4–6

1 Put the sugar, water and lime leaves in a pan. Heat gently, stirring once or twice, until the sugar has dissolved. Pour into a large bowl and set aside to cool.

2 Put the watermelon on a board and cut into wedges with a large knife. Slice the flesh from the rind, remove the seeds with a spoon and chop into cubes.

3 Spoon the watermelon cubes into a food processor. Do this in batches if necessary. Process the watermelon to a slush, then combine with the sugar syrup in the bowl. Mix well then chill in the refrigerator for 3–4 hours.

4 Strain the mixture into a freezerproof container. Freeze for 2 hours, then remove from the freezer and beat with a fork to break up the ice crystals. Return the mixture to the freezer and freeze for 3 hours more, beating the mixture at half-hourly intervals. Freeze until firm.

5 Alternatively, use an ice-cream maker. Pour the chilled mixture into the machine and churn until it is firm enough to scoop. Serve immediately, or scrape into a freezerproof container and store in the freezer as above.

6 About 30 minutes before serving, transfer the frozen watermelon mixture to the refrigerator so that it softens slightly. This allows the full flavour of the watermelon to be enjoyed and makes it easier to scoop.

Coconut Sorbet

Deliciously refreshing and cooling, this tropical sorbet can be found in different versions all over South-east Asia. Other classic Asian sorbets include recipes made with lychees, pineapple, watermelon, and even a delicately-spiced version with lemon grass.

Ingredients
175g/6oz/scant 1 cup caster (superfine) sugar
120ml/4fl oz/½ cup coconut milk
50g/2oz/⅔ cup grated or desiccated (dry unsweetened) coconut
a squeeze of lime juice

Serves 6

1 Place the sugar in a heavy pan and add 200ml/7fl oz/scant 1 cup water. Bring to the boil, stirring constantly, until the sugar has dissolved completely. Reduce the heat and simmer for 5 minutes to make a light syrup.

2 Stir the coconut milk into the sugar syrup, along with most of the coconut and the lime juice. Pour the mixture into a bowl or freezer container and freeze for 1 hour.

3 Take the sorbet out of the freezer and beat it with a fork, or blend it in a food processor, until it is smooth and creamy, then return it to the freezer and leave until frozen.

4 Before serving, remove the sorbet from the freezer and allow to stand at room temperature for 10–15 minutes to soften slightly.

5 Serve the sorbet in small bowls and decorate with the remaining grated coconut.

Cook's Tip
Light and refreshing, this sorbet is very welcome on a hot day, or as a palate refresher during a spicy meal. You could serve it in coconut shells, garnished with sprigs of fresh mint.

watermelon ice Energy 62kcal/263kJ; Protein 0.1g; Carbohydrate 16.3g, of which sugars 16.3g; Fat 0g, of which saturates 0g; Cholesterol 0mg; Calcium 9mg; Fibre 0g; Sodium 1mg.
coconut sorbet Energy 170kcal/717kJ; Protein 0.7g; Carbohydrate 32g, of which sugars 32g; Fat 5.2g, of which saturates 4.5g; Cholesterol 0mg; Calcium 23mg; Fibre 1.2g; Sodium 26mg.

Star Anise Ice Cream

This syrup-based ice cream is flavoured with the clean, warming taste of star anise and is the perfect exotic treat to cleanse the palate.

Ingredients

500ml/17fl oz/2¼ cups double (heavy) cream
8 whole star anise
90g/3½oz/½ cup caster (superfine) sugar
4 large (US extra large) egg yolks
ground star anise, to decorate

Serves 6–8

1 In a heavy pan, heat the cream with the star anise to just below boiling point, then remove from the heat and leave to infuse until cool.

2 In another pan, dissolve the sugar in 150ml/¼ pint/⅔ cup water, stirring constantly. Bring to the boil for a few minutes to form a light syrup, then leave to cool for 1 minute.

3 Whisk the egg yolks in a bowl. Trickle in the hot syrup, whisking constantly, until the mixture becomes mousse-like. Pour in the infused cream through a sieve (strainer), and continue to whisk until well mixed.

4 Pour the mixture into a freezerproof container and freeze for 4 hours, beating twice with a fork or whisking with an electric mixer to break up the ice crystals. To serve, dust with a little ground star anise.

Cook's Tips

- *You can use an ice-cream maker with this recipe, if you have one. Simply pour in the mixture at the beginning of Step 5 and churn until smooth.*
- *Spices play an important role in many traditional Asian ice creams, with their lively tastes of cinnamon, clove, star anise and pandanus (screwpine) leaf also proving popular.*

Green Tea Ice Cream

In the past, the Japanese did not follow a meal with dessert, apart from some fruit. This custom is slowly changing and now many Japanese restaurants offer light desserts such as sorbet or ice cream. Here, ice cream is flavoured with matcha – the finest green powdered tea available.

Ingredients

500ml/17fl oz carton good-quality vanilla ice cream
15ml/1 tbsp matcha (powdered green tea)
15ml/1 tbsp lukewarm water from the kettle
seeds from ¼ pomegranate (optional)

Serves 4

1 Soften the ice cream by transferring it to the refrigerator for 20–30 minutes. Do not allow it to melt.

2 Mix the matcha powder and lukewarm water in a cup and stir well to make a smooth paste.

3 Put half the ice cream into a mixing bowl. Add the matcha liquid and mix thoroughly with a rubber spatula, then add the rest of the ice cream. You can stop mixing at the stage when the ice cream looks a marbled dark green and white, or continue mixing until the ice cream is a uniform pale green. Put the bowl into the freezer.

4 After 1 hour, the ice cream will be ready to serve. Scoop into individual glass cups. If you like, top with pomegranate seeds.

Cook's Tips

- *Matcha is the tea used in the Tea Ceremony, a special tea-making ritual integral to Japanese culture.*
- *Sweet azuki beans and French sweet chestnut purée can be used to make other Japanese-style ice creams. Use 30ml/2 tbsp soft cooked sweet azuki beans or 20ml/4 tsp chestnut purée per 100ml/3fl oz/scant ½ cup good-quality vanilla ice cream.*

star anise ice cream Energy 380kcal/1570kJ; Protein 2.3g; Carbohydrate 12.8g, of which sugars 12.8g; Fat 35.9g, of which saturates 21.5g; Cholesterol 170mg; Calcium 46mg; Fibre 0g; Sodium 18mg.
green tea ice cream Energy 269kcal/1120kJ; Protein 4.9g; Carbohydrate 21.1g, of which sugars 21g; Fat 18.9g, of which saturates 11.3g; Cholesterol 0mg; Calcium 126mg; Fibre 0g; Sodium 75mg.

Coconut & Lemon Grass Ice Cream

The combination of cream and coconut milk makes for a wonderfully rich ice cream. The lemon grass flavouring is very subtle, but quite delicious.

Ingredients

2 lemon grass stalks
475ml/16fl oz/2 cups double (heavy) cream
120ml/4fl oz/½ cup coconut milk
4 large (US extra large) eggs
105ml/7 tbsp caster (superfine) sugar
5ml/1 tsp vanilla extract

Serves 4

1 Cut the lemon grass stalks in half lengthways. Use a mallet or rolling pin to mash the pieces, breaking up the fibres so that all the flavour is released. Retain a few fibres for the decoration.

2 Pour the cream and coconut milk into a pan. Add the lemon grass stalks and heat gently, stirring until the mixture simmers.

3 Put the eggs, sugar and vanilla essence in a large bowl. Using an electric whisk, whisk until the mixture is very light and fluffy.

4 Strain the cream mixture into a heatproof bowl that will fit over a pan of simmering water. Whisk in the egg mixture, then place the bowl over the pan and continue to whisk until the mixture thickens. Remove it from the heat and leave to cool. Chill the coconut custard in the refrigerator for 3–4 hours.

5 Pour the mixture into a plastic tub or similar freezerproof container. Freeze for 4 hours, beating two or three times at hourly intervals with a fork to break up the ice crystals.

6 Alternatively, use an ice-cream maker. Pour the chilled mixture into the machine and churn until it is firm enough to scoop. Serve immediately, or scrape into a freezerproof container and place in the freezer. Allow to soften slightly before serving and decorate with the strands of lemon grass if you wish.

Coconut Ice with Ginger Syrup

This ice cream is delectable and very easy to make in an ice-cream maker, especially if you use the type with a bowl that is placed in the freezer to chill before the ice-cream mixture is added.

Ingredients

400ml/14fl oz can coconut milk
400ml/14fl oz can condensed milk
2.5ml/½ tsp salt

For the gula melaka sauce

150g/5oz/¾ cup palm sugar (jaggery) or muscovado (molasses) sugar
1cm/½in slice fresh root ginger, bruised
1 pandan leaf (if available)
coconut shells (optional) and thinly pared strips of coconut, to serve

Serves 6

1 Chill the cans of coconut and condensed milk very thoroughly. In a bowl, mix the coconut milk with the condensed milk. Gently whisk together with the salt.

2 Pour the mixture into the frozen freezer bowl of an ice-cream maker (or follow the appliance instructions) and churn till the mixture has thickened. (This will take 30–40 minutes.)

3 Transfer the mixture to a lidded plastic tub, cover and freeze until the consistency is right for scooping. If you do not have an ice-cream maker, pour the mixture into a shallow container and freeze on the coldest setting.

4 When ice crystals form around the sides of the ice cream, beat the mixture, then return it to the freezer. Do this at least twice. The more you do it, the creamier the mixture will be.

5 Make the sauce. Dissolve the sugar in 150ml/¼ pint/⅔ cup water in a pan. Add the ginger and bring to the boil. Add the pandan leaf, if using, and simmer for 3–4 minutes. Set aside.

6 Serve the ice cream in coconut shells or in a bowl. Sprinkle with the strips of coconut. Remove the pandan leaf and ginger from the sauce and serve on the side.

coconut/lemon grass Energy 773kcal/3200kJ; Protein 8.4g; Carbohydrate 30.9g, of which sugars 30.9g; Fat 69.4g, of which saturates 41.3g; Cholesterol 353mg; Calcium 109mg; Fibre 0g; Sodium 131mg.
coconut ice w. ginger syrup Energy 276kcal/1168kJ; Protein 6.9g; Carbohydrate 47g, of which sugars 47g; Fat 8.1g, of which saturates 5.1g; Cholesterol 28mg; Calcium 248mg; Fibre 0g; Sodium 347mg.

Mango & Coconut Tofu Whip

This smooth dessert has a truly tropical taste. Few fruits are quite so luscious and sweet as mangoes and their slightly resinous flavour is superbly complemented by coconut cream. Add the magical texture of silken tofu and you will achieve perfection in a glass.

Ingredients
2 large ripe mangoes
200ml/7fl oz/scant 1 cup coconut cream
200g/7oz silken tofu
45ml/3 tbsp maple syrup
mint sprigs or grated lime rind, to decorate

Serves 6

1 Using a sharp knife, peel and stone (pit) the mangoes and coarsely chop the flesh. Place the flesh in a blender or food processor with the coconut cream and silken tofu.

2 Add the maple syrup and process to a smooth, rich cream. Pour into serving glasses or bowls and chill for at least 1 hour before serving. Decorate with mint sprigs or some grated lime rind.

Cook's Tip
Make sure that you buy pure maple syrup for the best flavour.

Variations
- *Silken tofu can also be used to make a berry fruit fool. Tip a 200g/7oz packet of silken tofu into the bowl of a food processor and add 175g/6oz hulled strawberries, raspberries or blackberries. Process the mixture to a smooth purée, then scrape into a bowl and sweeten with a little honey, maple syrup or maize malt syrup.*
- *For a delectable tofu smoothie, blend 2 bananas with 400g/14oz silken tofu, sweeten with honey, and flavour with almond extract. For best results, cut up and freeze the tofu first.*

Pistachio Lassi

This delicate flavour of pistachio nuts combines beautifully with the yogurt to create light dessert that needs very little sweetening. Don't forget to allow a few pistachios for decoration.

Ingredients
8–12 pistachio nuts
300ml/½ pint/1¼ cups natural (plain) yogurt
5ml/1 tsp sugar, to taste

Serves 4

1 Chop four pistachio nuts roughly and set them aside for the decoration. Grind the remaining nuts as finely as you can. Pour the yogurt into a tall jug (pitcher) and add the sugar.

2 Whisk until frothy, then whisk in 300ml/½ pint/1¼ cups water and the finely ground nuts. Whisk for 2 minutes, then pour into chilled glasses. Top with the chopped nuts and serve very cold.

Rose-flavoured Lassi

Sweet and savoury lassi is always in demand at Indian and Malay coffee shops, restaurants and hawker stalls. Soothing and cooling, this Indian yogurt-based drink is an ideal partner to spicy food. Savoury lassi is often salty and flavoured with mint, whereas the sweet drink is fragrant with the traditional essences of rose or pandanus.

Ingredients
300ml/½ pint/1¼ cups natural (plain) yogurt
5–10ml/1–2 tsp rose essence
10ml/2 tsp sugar
6 ice cubes, to serve
rose petals, to decorate

Serves 2

1 In a jug (pitcher), beat the yogurt with 150ml/¼ pint/⅔ cup water, until smooth. Add the rose essence and sugar, adjusting the sweetness to taste, and mix well.

2 Divide the ice cubes between two glasses and pour in the lassi. Decorate with a few rose petals and serve.

mango & coconut Energy 90kcal/382kJ; Protein 3.3g; Carbohydrate 16.5g, of which sugars 16.2g; Fat 1.7g, of which saturates 0.4g; Cholesterol 0mg; Calcium 197mg; Fibre 1.3g; Sodium 96mg.
pistachio lassi Energy 106kcal/442kJ; Protein 5.6g; Carbohydrate 7.5g, of which sugars 7.3g; Fat 6.3g, of which saturates 1.1g; Cholesterol 1mg; Calcium 154mg; Fibre 0.6g; Sodium 115mg.
rose flavoured lassi Energy 104kcal/438kJ; Protein 7.7g; Carbohydrate 16.5g, of which sugars 16.5g; Fat 1.5g, of which saturates 0.8g; Cholesterol 2mg; Calcium 288mg; Fibre 0g; Sodium 125mg.

Sweet Soya Milk with Pandanus

In the streets and markets of many Asian cities, freshly made soya milk is sold daily. Often infused with pandanus leaves, or ginger, and served hot or chilled, it is a sweet and nourishing drink, enjoyed by children and adults. If you can't find pandanus leaves, which are available in some Asian markets, substitute them with a vanilla pod.

Ingredients

225g/8oz/1¼ cups soya beans, soaked overnight and drained
1.5 litres/2½ pints/6 cups water
2 pandanus (screwpine) leaves, slightly bruised
15ml/2 tbsp sugar

Makes 1.2 litres/2 pints/ 5 cups

1 Put a third of the soya beans into a blender with a third of the water. Blend until thick and smooth. Pour the purée into a bowl and repeat with the rest of the beans.

2 Strain the purée through a fine sieve (strainer) set over a bowl to extract the milk. Discard the solids remaining in the sieve. Line the sieve with a piece of muslin (cheesecloth), then strain the milk again.

3 Pour the milk into a pan and bring it to the boil. Stir in the pandanus leaves with the sugar, until it has dissolved. Return the milk to the boil, reduce the heat and simmer for 10 minutes.

4 Remove the pandanus leaves, then ladle the hot milk into cups and serve, You can also leave it to cool, then pour it into a tall jug (pitcher) and chill in the refrigerator.

Variation

To make ginger-flavoured soya milk, stir in 25g/1oz grated fresh root ginger with the sugar. Bring the liquid to the boil and simmer for 10 minutes, then turn off the heat and leave to infuse for 20 minutes more.

Rainbow Drink

Thirst-quenching and appetizing, rainbow drinks are a delightful South-east Asian speciality.

Ingredients

50g/2oz dried split mung beans, soaked for 4 hours and drained
50g/2oz red azuki beans, soaked for 4 hours and drained
25g/1oz/2 tbsp sugar

For the syrup

300ml/½ pint/1¼ cups coconut milk
50g/2oz/¼ cup sugar
25g/1oz tapioca pearls
crushed ice, to serve
15g/½oz jellied agar-agar, soaked in warm water for 30 minutes and shredded into long strands, to decorate

Serves 4

1 Put the mung beans and azuki beans into two separate pans and add 1 tablespoon of sugar each. Pour in enough water to cover and, stirring all the time, bring it to the boil. Reduce the heat and leave both pans to simmer for about 15 minutes, stirring from time to time, until the beans are tender but not mushy – you may have to add more water. Drain the beans, leave to cool and chill separately in the refrigerator.

2 In a heavy pan, bring the coconut milk to the boil. Reduce the heat and stir in the sugar, until it dissolves. Add the tapioca pearls and simmer for about 10 minutes, until they become transparent. Leave to cool and chill in the refrigerator.

3 Divide the mung beans among four tall glasses, add some crushed ice, then the azuki beans and more ice. Pour the coconut syrup over the top and decorate with strands of agar agar. Serve immediately with straws and long spoons.

Cook's Tip

Many variations of rainbow drinks are served throughout South-east Asia in tall clear glasses in markets, restaurants and bars. They usually combine ingredients such as lotus seeds, taro, sweet potato, and tapioca pearls with exotic fruits. Tapioca pearls are also used in the iced drink known as bubble tea, which has become popular on the US West Coast.

soya milk/pandanus Energy 384kcal/1584kJ; Protein 34.8g; Carbohydrate 9.6g, of which sugars 9.6g; Fat 19.2g, of which saturates 3.6g; Cholesterol 0mg; Calcium 156mg; Fibre 0g; Sodium 384mg.
rainbow drink Energy 188kcal/800kJ; Protein 6.3g; Carbohydrate 42.1g, of which sugars 25g; Fat 0.5g, of which saturates 0.2g; Cholesterol 0mg; Calcium 55mg; Fibre 2.5g; Sodium 87mg.

Index

福
瑞兆
さしみ
しょうゆ